FOURTH CANADIAN EDITION

BUSINESS COMMUNICATION

Building Critical Skills

Kitty O. Locker

The Ohio State University

Stephen Kyo Kaczmarek

Columbus State Community College

Kathryn Braun

Sheridan Institute of Technology and Advanced Learning

McGraw-Hill Ryerson
Connect. Learn. Succeed.

Business Communication: Building Critical Skills
Fourth Canadian Edition

ISBN-13: 978-0-07-096983-4
ISBN-10: 0-07-096983-3

1 2 3 4 5 6 7 8 9 10 WCP 1 9 8 7 6 5 4 3 2 1 0

Printed and bound in the United States of America

Care has been taken to trace ownership of copyright material contained in this text; however, the publisher will welcome any information that enables them to rectify any reference or credit for subsequent editions.

Vice President, Editor-in-Chief: Joanna Cotton
Publisher: Cara Yarzab
Marketing Manager: Michele Peach
Developmental Editor: Jennifer Oliver
Editorial Associate: Marina Seguin
Photo/Permissions Researcher: Robyn Craig
Supervising Editor: Graeme Powell
Copy Editor: Rodney Rawlings
Production Coordinator: Lena Keating
Cover and Interior Design: Valid Design & Layout/Dave Murphy
Cover Image: Veer/Corbis Photography
Page Layout: S R Nova Pvt Ltd., Bangalore, India
Printer: Worldcolor Press, Inc.

Library and Archives Canada Cataloguing in Publication

Locker, Kitty O.
   Business communication: building critical skills/Kitty O. Locker,
Stephen Kyo Kaczmarek, Kathryn Braun.—4th Canadian ed.

Includes index.

ISBN 978-0-07-096983-4

1. Business communication—Textbooks. 2. Business writing—Textbooks. 3. Communication in organizations—Textbooks. I. Kaczmarek, Stephen Kyo II. Hughes, Kathryn, 1945– III. Title.

HF5718.L63 2009   658.4'5   C2009-905405-1

Brief Contents

Contents

Unit Two

Influencing Your Audience Positively   105

Unit Four

Building Emotional Intelligence: Interpersonal Communication 259

About the Authors

Kitty O. Locker was an Associate Professor of English at Ohio State University, where she taught courses in workplace discourse and research methods. She had taught as Assistant Professor at Texas A&M University and the University of Illinois at Urbana. She received her B.A. from DePauw University and her M.A. and Ph.D. from the University of Illinois at Urbana. Her consulting clients included Abbott Laboratories, AT&T, and the American Medical Association. She developed a complete writing improvement program for Joseph T. Ryerson, the largest steel materials service centre in the USA. In 1994–95, she served as President of the Association for Business Communication (ABC). From 1997–2000, she edited ABC's Journal of Business Communication. She received ABC's Outstanding Researcher Award in 1992 and ABC's Media Gibbs Outstanding Teacher Award in 1998. Kitty Locker passed away in 2005.

Stephen Kyo Kaczmarek is an Associate Professor at Columbus State Community College and a Lecturer at Ohio State University. He teaches courses in business communication, composition, creative writing, freshman experience, film and literature, globalization and culture, and public relations. He has also taught public relations at Ohio Dominican University. Steve received an M.A. in English and B.A.s in journalism and English from Ohio State. He has presented papers at conferences of the Association for Business Communication (ABC), College English Association of Ohio (CEAO), and Conference on College Composition and Communication. His consulting clients include Nationwide Insurance, Red Capital Mortgage Group, and United Energy Systems. He also advises individual clients on job search and interviewing techniques.

Kathryn Braun is a professional writer, editor, and training facilitator specializing in business communications and interpersonal leadership skills. Kathryn is a member of the International Association of Business Communicators, the Plain Language Association INternational, (PLAIN), and the Halton/Peel Communications Association. Kathryn taught rhetoric and composition at Sheridan Institute of Technology for 31 years. Currently she trains adults in business and technical report writing, proposal writing, Web writing, revising and editing techniques, active listening strategies, influencing others, interpersonal skills, negotiating and reducing conflict, communicating nonverbally, power reading strategies, and designing and delivering persuasive presentations. Kathryn also coaches adults in English pronunciation and interpersonal leadership skills. She has a Masters in English and is Myers-Briggs-certified.

Preface

Whatever students' career choices, communicating effectively is essential for their success. *Business Communication: Building Critical Skills* provides a practical approach for building communication competencies.

The fourth Canadian edition builds on the outstanding features of the previous three editions:

- The **PAIBOC** ("payback") **model** emphasizes the rhetorical analysis that informs all successful communication. PAIBOC prompts students to consider **P**urpose, **A**udiences, **I**nformation, **B**enefits, **O**bjections, and **C**ontext to create audience-centred messages. Effective communicators use PAIBOC analysis to think, listen, read, speak, and write for intended results.
- Each module states the specific **Conference Board of Canada's *Employability Skills 2000+*** that relate to text material and examples.
- **Current examples of Canadians' experiences** demonstrate communication theory in action.
- The **modular format** offers total flexibility. Easily tailored to any course length or organization, the modules can be taught in any order.

Our Audience

Context creates meaning: people learn best when the context is familiar and relevant. Therefore, this edition provides contemporary Canadian illustrations, references, examples, and stories. The young Canadians whose profiles begin each Unit represent the working-life realities of their communities.

Responding to Reviewer Needs

This fourth Canadian edition of *Business Communication: Building Critical Skills* has been extensively revised with the help of teachers across Canada. I am indebted to those reviewers whose constructive comments improved both the form and the content of the text.

You will find many changes as a result of this excellent feedback. For example, the new design improves readability; the modules listed on Unit page openers increase accessibility; the end-of-model summaries highlight key ideas; and the many new examples provide easy reference.

The new **Revising and Editing Resources** section emphasizes the revising and editing stages of the writing process. This section describes specific strategies writers use to review, rewrite, edit, and proofread their work.

As reviewers requested, Unit 5's modules on **researching and reporting** have been expanded. Module 19 describes how to take great notes, why it's important to document sources correctly and ethically, and how to do so. Unit 5 also offers many more examples of typical business reports.

The fourth Canadian edition's revised end-of-model questions and exercises challenge students to think critically about contemporary business communications, and about their own potential contribution to their communities. Moreover, this edition offers increased coverage of the business applications and social repercussions of communication technology.

What's New in the Fourth Canadian Edition

Module 1: Introducing Business Communications

- Introduces the skills valued in our "conceptual age"
- Proves the interdependence of communication competencies and workplace success
- Introduces the concept of literacy as a powerful tool for transformation
- Challenges students to apply their knowledge and understanding by comparing academic to business writing

Module 2: Adapting Your Message to Your Audience

- Offers in-depth analysis and relevant examples of the impact of discourse communities and corporate culture on meaning-making
- Provides a variety of strategies for audience analysis

Module 3: Communicating Across Cultures

- Expands intercultural communication to include generational differences
- Introduces the concept of emotional intelligence, and its importance in communication efficacy

Module 4: Planning, Writing, and Revising

- Expands information on proven revising and editing strategies
- Expands information on overcoming writer's block
- Challenges students to use both right- and left-brain techniques in creating notes

Module 5: Designing Documents, Slides, and Screens

- Further explains the rhetorical purposes of design choices
- Provides new, relevant examples of how design shapes meaning
- Challenges students to develop their own design criteria, and to analyze both hardcopy and electronic design choices

Module 6: Influencing Your Audience Positively

- Reinforces the primacy of audience focus with updated examples

Module 7: Communicating with Positive Emphasis

- Emphasizes the psychological, physiological, and economic benefits of positive communication
- Asks students to apply their learning by analyzing the dynamics of tone, courtesy, and power in discourse communities

Module 8: Communicating Reader Benefits

- Demonstrates how to turn product or service features into benefits
- Uses examples of contemporary technology to prove the psychological allure of intrinsic benefits
- Challenges students to apply their learning by researching, analyzing, and solving a relevant environmental and social problem

Module 9: Formatting Hardcopy Letters and Memos

- Provides nine document models, including hardcopy and electronic letters, memos, and short reports

- Asks students to analyze the advantages and disadvantages of word-processing templates
- Challenges students to apply PAIBOC analysis to their electronic communications

Module 10: Writing Email and Electronic Messages

- Uses current examples to demonstrate that the medium is the message
- Provides experts' advice on professional blogging

Module 11: Composing Informative and Positive Messages

- Details the techniques and rhetorical purposes of the direct pattern of organization

Module 12: Composing Negative Messages

- Connects Maslow's needs theory to the rhetorical purposes of the indirect pattern of organization
- Focuses on ethical considerations in organizing negative messages

Module 13: Composing Persuasive Messages

- Explores the elements of persuasion
- Describes the importance of providing readers with psychological freedom
- Challenges students to research and analyze business and ethical considerations of online citizen encyclopedias

Module 14: Listening Actively

- Describes how to develop active listening skills as a key emotional intelligence

Module 15: Working and Writing in Teams

- Describes task-focused group outcome
- Provides a primer on negotiation and conflict resolution strategies
- Details the social and intellectual skills necessary for successful teamwork
- Asks students to analyze their own negotiating skills through an online self-assessment

Module 16: Planning, Managing, and Recording Meetings

- Updates information on virtual meetings
- Provides examples of a meeting agenda and minutes

Module 17: Making Oral Presentations

- Describes how to deal with stage fright
- Demonstrates how to use slides effectively
- Challenges students to create presentations supported by alternative media

Module 18: Researching Information

- Chronicles a recent graduate's real-world researching and reporting experiences
- Explains how and why writers draft a working thesis
- Explains how to research effectively using electronic and print resources
- Describes numerous Internet resources, including research tutorials and alternative search engines

- Details the process of preparing to take notes
- Asks students to analyze and evaluate Web resources

NEW! Module 19: Synthesizing and Documenting Information

- Differentiates between paraphrasing, summarizing, and précis writing
- Presents a systematic approach to summarizing information and creating great notes
- Explains the legal and ethical reasons for accurate documentation
- Describes how to document sources fully
- Models APA in-text citations throughout

Module 20: Writing Information Reports

- Defines and describes types of reports in the context of PAIBOC analysis
- Describes how to create purpose statements, with examples
- Presents the most common information reports
- Showcases seven models of information reports
- Explains revising and editing techniques

Module 21: Writing Proposals and Analytical Reports

- Defines feasibility, yardstick, and justification reports
- Explores business plans, proposals, and RFPs
- Presents model proposals
- Describes communication organizational patterns, with specific examples of each
- Explains how to increase readability through the use of white space, bullets, blueprints, talking heads, and transitions

Module 22: Writing Formal Reports

- Describes the components of formal reports
- Offers a step-by-step approach to project management
- Provides a real-world formal report sample
- Discusses the importance of report medium and style

Module 23: Using Visuals

- Describes how to use a variety of visuals to create compelling stories
- Discusses the ethics of using visual representations, with relevant examples
- Provides a systematic approach to integrating visuals and text

Module 24: Researching Jobs

- Describes a variety of networking strategies and opportunities
- Asks students to apply their knowledge by gathering industry, organization, and career information

Module 25: Creating Persuasive Résumés

- Explains and models contemporary résumé formats
- Describes how to prepare online résumés
- Asks students to apply their learning by analyzing their accomplishments, and reframing these as achievement statements
- Details proofreading strategies

Module 26: Creating Persuasive Application Letters

- Models contemporary application letters
- Explains how to tailor job application materials to a specific organization
- Describes how to write an email application
- Asks students to apply their learning by creating application materials that differentiate them from the competition

Module 27: Managing the Interview Process

- Explains how to prepare an interview strategy
- Describes the communication behaviours of successful interviewees
- Outlines sample questions that interviewees can ask
- Describes how to prepare for behavioural, situational, phone, and video interviews
- Shows how to follow up the interview successfully

Revising and Editing Resources

- Provides specifics on how to create clear, concise, comprehensive, and correct prose
- Identifies the common errors of adult writers, and describes how to correct them
- Offers numerous exercises which allow students to apply their learning

Student Resources

McGraw-Hill Connect™ www.mcgrawhillconnect.ca

Developed in partnership with Youthography, a Canadian youth research company, and hundreds of students from across Canada, *Connect* embraces diverse study behaviours and preferences to maximize active learning and engagement.

With *Connect*, students complete pre- and post-diagnostic assessments that identify knowledge gaps and point them to concepts they need to learn. *Connect* provides students the option to work through recommended learning exercises and create their own personalized study plan using multiple sources of content, including a searchable e-book, multiple-choice and true/false quizzes, interactivities, personal notes, videos, and more. Using the copy, paste, highlight, and sticky note features, students collect, organize, and customize their study plan content to optimize learning outcomes.

Instructor Resources

McGraw-Hill Connect™ www.mcgrawhillconnect.ca

Connect assessment activities don't stop with students! There is material for instructors to leverage as well, including a personalized teaching plan where instructors can choose from a variety of quizzes to use in class, assign as homework, or add to exams. Instructors can edit existing questions and add new ones; track individual student performance—by question, assignment, or in relation to the class overall—with detailed grade reports; integrate grade reports easily with Learning Management Systems such as WebCT and Blackboard; and much more. Instructors can also browse or search teaching resources and text-specific supplements, and organize them into customizable categories. With *Connect*, all teaching resources are located in one convenient place.

- The **Instructor's Manual** includes overviews of each module, key lecture points supported by teaching tips, in-class exercises, answers to textbook assignments, and answers to even-numbered Polishing Your Prose exercises.

- The **Computerized Test Bank** is available through EZ Test Online—a flexible and easy-to-use electronic testing program—that allows instructors to create tests from book-specific items. EZ Test accommodates a wide range of question types and allows instructors to add their own questions. Test items are also available in Word format (Rich Text Format). For secure online testing, exams created in EZ Test can be exported to WebCT and Blackboard. EZ Test Online is supported at www.mhhe.com/eztest where users can download a Quick Start Guide, access FAQs, or log a ticket for help with specific issues.
- **PowerPoint® slides** present key points for each module.
- The **Video Guide** features 27 scenes from films and television shows that illustrate business communication skills in or outside of the workplace. The guide provides a description of the scene as well as scene location, and explains how each scene relates to a business communication concept. Questions for class discussion follow each scene.

Superior Service

Your Integrated *i*Learning Sales Specialist is a McGraw-Hill Ryerson representative who has the experience, product knowledge, training, and support to help you assess and integrate all of the above-noted products, technology, and services into your course for optimum teaching and learning performance. Whether it's using our test bank software, helping your students improve their grades, or putting your entire course online, your *i*Learning Sales Specialist is there to help you do it. Contact your local *i*Learning Sales Specialist today to learn how to maximize all of McGraw-Hill Ryerson's resources!

Teaching, Technology & Learning Conference Series

The educational environment has changed tremendously in recent years, and McGraw-Hill Ryerson continues to be committed to helping you acquire the skills you need to succeed in this new milieu. Our innovative Teaching, Technology & Learning Conference Series brings faculty together from across Canada with 3M Teaching Excellence award winners to share teaching and learning best practices in a collaborative and stimulating environment. Pre-conference workshops on general topics, such as teaching large class sizes and technology integration, are also offered. We will also work with you at your own institution to customize workshops that best suit the needs of your faculty at your institution.

CourseSmart

CourseSmart brings together thousands of textbooks across hundreds of courses in an eTextbook format providing unique benefits to students and faculty. By purchasing an eTextbook, students can save up to 50 percent off the cost of a print textbook, reduce their impact on the environment, and gain access to powerful Web tools for learning including full text search, notes and highlighting, and e-mail tools for sharing notes between classmates. For faculty, CourseSmart provides instant access to review and compare textbooks and course materials in their discipline area without the time, cost, and environmental impact of mailing print examination copies. For further details, contact your *i*Learning Sales Specialist or go to www.coursesmart.com.

Acknowledgments

This fourth Canadian edition is the result of my ongoing collaboration with the McGraw-Hill Ryerson team: Lisa Rahn, Sponsoring Editor; Robyn Craig, Permissions Editor; and Jennifer Oliver, most patient and supportive Developmental Editor.

Reviewers' comments and suggestions also contributed to creating this edition. Thank you so much for your generous ideas and expertise:

Anita Agar, *Sheridan Institute of Technology*
Marc Alcock, *Conestoga College*
Jen Blackwood, *SAIT*
Denise Blay, *Fanshawe College*
Kathryn Brillinger, *Conestoga College*
Paul Burkhart, *University of the Fraser Valley*
Leslie Butler, *Sheridan Institute of Technology*
Kathy Cocchio, *NAIT*
Paula Crooks, *Conestoga College*
Carol Evans, *SIAST*
Janet Fear, *Sheridan Institute of Technology*
Amanda Goldrick-Jones, *University of British Columbia*
Donald E. Holmes, *Humber College*
Christine Hoppenrath, *Capilano University*
Christine Horgan, *SAIT*
Michael Keith Johnson, *University of the Fraser Valley*
Kim Lambrecht, *SAIT*
Peter J. MacDonald, *McMaster University*
Jill Manderson, *Dalhousie University*
Sherine Mansour, *Sheridan Institute of Technology*
Peter C. Miller, *Seneca College*
Tricia Morgan, *Humber College*
Norma-Jean Nielsen, *Canadore College*
Paula Pedwell, *Georgian College*
Judith Pond, *SAIT*
Gwen Roberts, *Sheridan Institute of Technology*
J. Barbara Rose, *University of Toronto*
Rhonda Sandberg, *George Brown College*
Francine Schlosser, *University of Windsor*
Linda Schofield, *Ryerson University*
Kerri Shields, *Centennial College*
Bette Tetreault, *Dalhousie University*
Panteli Tritchew, *Kwantlen Polytechnic University*
Joan Vinall-Cox, *JN the Web*
Kathy Voltan, *Ryerson University*
Bruce Watson, *SAIT*
Doreen Whalen, *Memorial University*
Katherine Anne Woodward, *Grant MacEwan College*

I am particularly indebted to the interviewees, writers, students, and colleagues who continue to teach me so much.

Kathryn Braun

Features of the Fourth Canadian Edition

Unit-Opening Vignettes

Six vignettes profile Canadians and describe how they use business communication skills in their jobs. These vignettes reinforce the relevance of effective communication to students' future careers.

Composing Letters, Memos, and Emails

UNIT 3

- **Module 9:** Formatting Hard Copy Letters and Memos
- **Module 10:** Writing Email and Electronic Messages
- **Module 11:** Composing Informative and Positive Messages
- **Module 12:** Composing Negative Messages
- **Module 13:** Composing Persuasive Messages

Arezoo Ghobadpour writes business messages all day, every day. Although her official title is Office Manager, Arezoo functions as human resources manager, recruiter, researcher, executive assistant to the company president, and as editor and proofreader for her company's electronic and hardcopy documents.

Arezoo works for ACS Incorporated, an international company specializing in carrier management services, including freight audit and payment. Her audiences include both internal and external customers: Arezoo uses email to write letters to other companies, including recruiting agencies, and to memo staff with policy and procedure updates, and responses to queries.

Most of her time is spent performing her HR duties, for which Arezoo feels a true affinity. "Because my position relates to every department and responsibility, I get a lot of variety, every day. I like the challenge of keeping on top of it all, and I like being busy and feeling useful. I am involved in everything and anything: from recruiting, interviewing and maintaining personnel records, to managing group benefits and ensuring legislation compliance.

"Working in the HR field requires me to create and update job descriptions, and write letters of promotion and discipline. I also write human resource policies and standard operating procedures for jobs within my department. I use the job descriptions to create job postings, and to announce openings in the company."

Perhaps because she has had so much practice, Arezoo also likes researching and every part of the writing process: "I like the challenge of solving problems. I love the Internet for allowing me to research anything, instantly! I often research HR topics, such as new legislation, legal requirements, or answers to employees' questions.

"I enjoy everything about writing. I like the creativity when composing my first line, and I love the flow that follows that. Writing is very freeing for me.

"I am a bit of a perfectionist, so I edit and proof documents before they go to anyone outside the company. When we updated our Web site, I proofread all the text before it was posted. I even helped edit our sales and marketing initiative."

Arezoo is also committed to furthering her formal education: "I learned the basics of my job through experience, working as a legal administrative assistant. Now I'm completing a Human Resources Management Certificate program for my CHRP designation. Then I am going to pursue a degree in communications or human resource management. My interest in researching and writing offers infinite possibilities."

PAIBOC ANALYSIS

1. For what purposes does Arezoo write?
2. Identify four different audiences Arezoo writes to.
3. Which of Arezoo's messages would you consider informative and positive? Why?
4. Which of Arezoo's messages would you consider negative? Why?
5. Which of Arezoo's messages would you consider persuasive? Why?

Conference Board of Canada's *Employability Skills 2000+*

Module 1 introduces students to the Conference Board of Canada's *Employability Skills 2000+*, a grouping of critical skills and aptitudes needed for success in the workplace. Each subsequent module begins with an *Employability Skills 2000+ Checklist*, which students can use to focus their learning.

Employability Skills 2000+ Checklist

In this module, the key skills from the Conference Board of Canada's Employability Skills 2000+ are

Communicate
- read and understand information presented in a variety of forms (e.g., words, graphs, charts, diagrams)
- write and speak so others pay attention and understand
- share information using a range of information and communications technologies (e.g., voice, email, computers)
- use relevant scientific, technological, and mathematical knowledge and skills to explain or clarify ideas

Manage Information
- locate, gather, and organize information using appropriate technology and information systems
- access, analyze, and apply knowledge and skills from a variety of disciplines (e.g., the arts, languages, science, technology, mathematics, social sciences, and the humanities)

Think & Solve Problems
- assess situations and identify problems
- recognize the human, interpersonal, technical, scientific, and mathematical dimensions of a problem
- readily use science, technology, and mathematics as ways to think, gain and share knowledge, solve problems, and make decisions
- check to see if a solution works, and act on opportunities for improvement

Participate in Projects & Tasks
- plan, design, or carry out a project or task from start to finish with well-defined objectives and outcomes
- work to agreed quality standards and specifications
- adapt to changing requirements and information
- continuously monitor the success of a project or task and identify ways to improve

Employability Skills 2000+ Icons

These icons indicate which material is directly relevant to the workplace. Highlighting employability skills ensures that students understand how text content is important for achieving their employment goals.

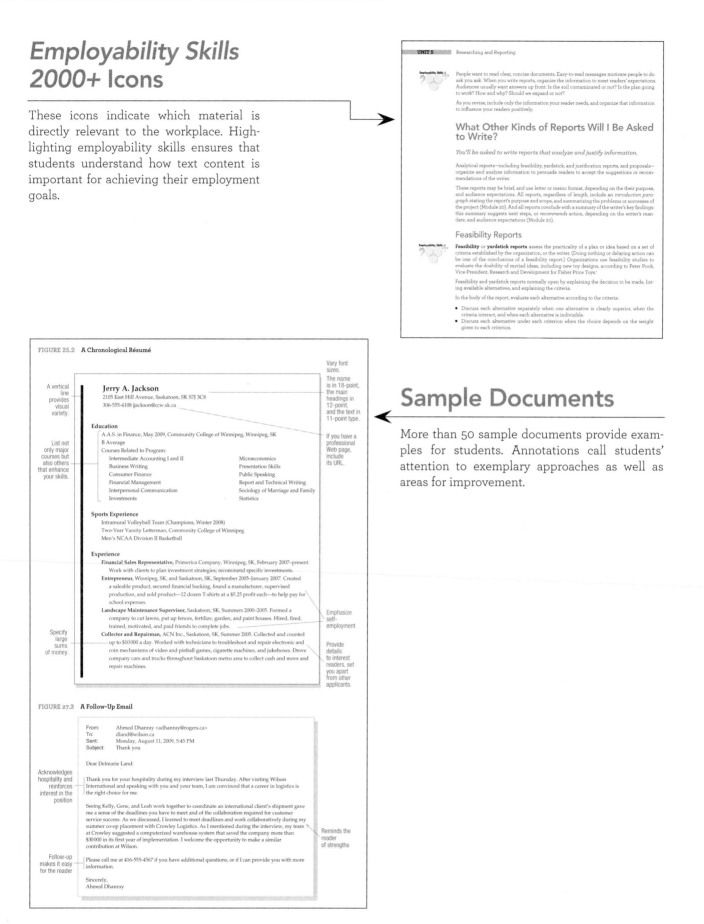

UNIT 5 · Researching and Reporting

People want to read clear, concise documents. Easy-to-read messages motivate people to do ask you ask. When you write reports, organize the information to meet readers' expectations. Audiences usually want answers up front: Is the soil contaminated or not? Is the plan going to work? How and why? Should we expand or not?

As you revise, include only the information your reader needs, and organize that information to influence your readers positively.

What Other Kinds of Reports Will I Be Asked to Write?

You'll be asked to write reports that analyze and justify information.

Analytical reports—including feasibility, yardstick, and justification reports, and proposals—organize and analyze information to persuade readers to accept the suggestions or recommendations of the writer.

These reports may be brief, and use letter or memo format, depending on the their purpose, and audience expectations. All reports, regardless of length, include an *introduction paragraph* stating the report's purpose and scope, and summarizing the problems or successes of the project (Module 20). And all reports *conclude* with a summary of the writer's key findings: this summary suggests next steps, or *recommends* action, depending on the writer's mandate, and audience expectations (Module 20).

Feasibility Reports

Feasibility or **yardstick reports** assess the practicality of a plan or idea based on a set of criteria established by the organization, or the writer. (Doing nothing or delaying action can be one of the conclusions of a feasibility report.) Organizations use feasibility studies to evaluate the doability of myriad ideas, including new toy designs, according to Peter Pook, Vice-President, Research and Development for Fisher Price Toys.[1]

Feasibility and yardstick reports normally open by explaining the decision to be made, listing available alternatives, and explaining the criteria.

In the body of the report, evaluate each alternative according to the criteria:

• Discuss each alternative separately when one alternative is clearly superior, when the criteria interact, and when each alternative is indivisible.
• Discuss each alternative under each criterion when the choice depends on the weight given to each criterion.

Sample Documents

More than 50 sample documents provide examples for students. Annotations call students' attention to exemplary approaches as well as areas for improvement.

FIGURE 25.2   **A Chronological Résumé**

Vary font sizes.
The name is in 18-point, the main headings in 12-point, and the text in 11-point type.

Jerry A. Jackson
2105 East Hill Avenue, Saskatoon, SK S7J 3C8
306-555-4108 jjackson@ccw.sk.ca

A vertical line provides visual variety.

Education
A.A.S. in Finance, May 2009, Community College of Winnipeg, Winnipeg, SK
B Average
Courses Related to Program:

List not only major courses but also others that enhance your skills.

Intermediate Accounting I and II · Microeconomics
Business Writing · Presentation Skills
Consumer Finance · Public Speaking
Financial Management · Report and Technical Writing
Interpersonal Communication · Sociology of Marriage and Family
Investments · Statistics

If you have a professional Web page, include its URL.

Sports Experience
Intramural Volleyball Team (Champions, Winter 2008)
Two-Year Varsity Letterman, Community College of Winnipeg
Men's NCAA Division II Basketball

Experience
Financial Sales Representative, Primerica Company, Winnipeg, SK, February 2007–present. Work with clients to plan investment strategies; recommend specific investments.
Entrepreneur, Winnipeg, SK, and Saskatoon, SK, September 2005–January 2007. Created a saleable product, secured financial backing, found a manufacturer, supervised production, and sold product—12 dozen T-shirts at a $5.25 profit each—to help pay for school expenses.
Landscape Maintenance Supervisor, Saskatoon, SK, Summers 2000–2005. Formed a company to cut lawns, put up fences, fertilize, garden, and paint houses. Hired, fired, trained, motivated, and paid friends to complete jobs.
Collector and Repairman, ACN Inc., Saskatoon, SK, Summer 2005. Collected and counted up to $10000 a day. Worked with technicians to troubleshoot and repair electronic and coin mechanisms of video and pinball games, cigarette machines, and jukeboxes. Drove company cars and trucks throughout Saskatoon metro area to collect cash and move and repair machines.

Specify large sums of money.

Emphasize self-employment

Provide details to interest readers, set you apart from other applicants.

FIGURE 27.3   **A Follow-Up Email**

From: Ahmed Dhanray <adhanray@rogers.ca>
To: dland@wilson.ca
Sent: Monday, August 11, 2009, 5:45 PM
Subject: Thank you

Dear Delmarie Land:

Acknowledges hospitality and reinforces interest in the position

Thank you for your hospitality during my interview last Thursday. After visiting Wilson International and speaking with you and your team, I am convinced that a career in logistics is the right choice for me.

Seeing Kelly, Gene, and Leah work together to coordinate an international client's shipment gave me a sense of the deadlines you have to meet and of the collaboration required for customer service success. As we discussed, I learned to meet deadlines and work collaboratively during my summer co-op placement with Crowley Logistics. As I mentioned during the interview, my team at Crowley suggested a computerized warehouse system that saved the company more than $30000 in its first year of implementation. I welcome the opportunity to make a similar contribution at Wilson.

Reminds the reader of strengths

Follow-up makes it easy for the reader

Please call me at 416-555-4567 if you have additional questions, or if I can provide you with more information.

Sincerely,
Ahmed Dhanray

Expanding a Critical Skill Boxes

Expanding a Critical Skill boxes focus on how a particular skill works in the workplace, and suggest ways students can develop these skills.

EXPANDING A CRITICAL SKILL

Building an Online Community

People spend more time meeting virtually than on any other Internet activity. Social media sites are now "the number one platform for creating and sharing content";[6] and as blogs and Wikis morph into ever-more-sophisticated digital applications, users' demand for participation in online communities will increase. And for employee communication, that's a good thing.

Organizations can use digital media to build on online community of interdependent teams. As is true of all team-building, however, success depends on careful planning. The project managers must consider their purposes, and prospective audiences, content and culture. When they have decided why they want to encourage virtual networking, companies have to consider how to encourage

employees to engage, what content will keep people coming back, what guidelines will communicate appropriate behaviours, who will manage the technological and staffing logistics, and how they will measure success.

Online communities can truly democratize the workplace, facilitate interdisciplinary knowledge sharing, and foster team-building. But the community can only be as good as its blueprint and its members.

Sources: Jason Falls, "Seven Questions to Ask Before Starting an Online Community"; Dave Wilkins and Drew Dambrough, "Developing an Online Community"; Michael Wilson, "Best Practices for Building Successful Online Communities," *IABC CW Bulletin* 7(4) (April 2009), retrieved September 18, 2009, from http://www.iabc.com/cwb/archive/2009/0409/#feature1.

Language Focus Boxes

Language Focus boxes explain the finer points of the English language, and help native English speakers and ESL learners troubleshoot tricky grammar areas.

Language FOCUS

When taking notes, it is best to record them in the language they are given in. If the lecturer is using English, record your notes in English. Do not try to translate into your own language while taking notes, as this might lead to mistakes later when you are studying or writing a report. For example, if you have incorrectly translated a word during a lecture or in a meeting, it will affect the accuracy of your report when you are writing it later and not able to double-check on your translation accuracy.

Cultural Focus Boxes

Cultural Focus boxes explore North Americans' approach to communication, often in juxtaposition with how other regions in the world communicate in business.

Cultural FOCUS

In some cultures, perhaps your own, repeating word for word what a scholar has said is considered the best way to show you have understood and agree with certain points. It is also considered the best way to show respect for that scholar. However, for documents to be acceptable in North America (and many other Western cultures), you have to cite the source and also integrate the points into your own writing. This is how respect for the original writer or thinker is shown; it also demonstrates your own understanding of the ideas. By following the expected rules here, you are showing respect for and understanding of the cultural norms, just as you would expect others to show the same respect while working in your culture.

Checkpoint Boxes

Checkpoint boxes reinforce key concepts presented the module.

Checkpoint

Use the **direct request pattern** in these instances:

- The audience will do as you ask without any resistance.
- You need a response only from the people who are willing to act.
- The audience is busy and may not read all the messages received.
- Your organization's culture prefers direct requests.

Use the **problem-solving pattern** in these cases:

- The audience is likely to object to doing as you ask.
- You need action from everyone.
- You trust the audience to read the entire message.
- You expect logic to be more important than emotion in the decision.

Module Summary

Module Summaries provide a concise recap of the key concepts presented in each module.

MODULE SUMMARY

- Long formal reports can include any of a Transmittal, Executive Summary, Table of Contents with List of Illustrations, the Body itself, and Conclusions and Recommendations.
- Writing a long report takes time and organization:
  - Create a timeline for parts of the report.
  - Write the report in sections, starting with the body, where you present facts that prove your position.
  - Jot down potential headings, both for the whole report, and for the sections in the Body ("The Problem," "The Results," "The Solution," "The Benefits").
  - When you revise the report, reshape the headings into **talking heads**, to preview the subsequent content for the reader, and contribute to clarity and understanding.
  - As you research and analyze your information, prepare an appendix summarizing your sources: responses to questionnaires, your figures and tables, and a complete list of references.
- All reports should include an overview, to preview the report's contents for the reader. In a formal report, this overview is called a **Summary**, or **Executive Summary**. The Summary
  - Sums up the whole report, and includes conclusions and recommendations
  - Goes first, on a separate page

- Is about one-tenth the length of the whole report
- The **Introduction** of the report contains a statement of Purpose and Scope. The **Purpose** statement includes the situation the report addresses, the investigations it summarizes, and the rhetorical purposes (to explain, to describe, to recommend). The **Scope** statement identifies the topics the report covers. The Introduction may also include **Limitations**, factors or problems that limit the scope of the report, or the validity of the recommendations; **Assumptions**, statements whose truth you assume, and which you use to prove your ideas; and **Methods**, explaining how you gathered your data.
- A **Background** or **History** section is for audiences that may need to read the report years later.
- **Conclusions** summarize the main ideas you make in the report body. All reports offer Conclusions. **Recommendations** are action items that would solve, or partially solve the problem.
- Include any supporting material your reader will need in the appendix of the report. The report ends with your sources. Business uses APA, and academia uses MLA (Module 19).
- Your choice of report format, style, and method of submission are as important as your content. Pay attention to the rules and norms of your discourse community. If you are unsure, ask someone who knows.

Assignments

Each module contains a variety of problems and exercises for in-class activities or homework.

ASSIGNMENTS FOR MODULE 15

Questions for Critical Thinking

15.1 Why are so many people so afraid of conflict in groups? Why is it better for groups to deal with conflicts, rather than just trying to ignore them?

15.2 How can teams successfully manage cultural differences among members?

15.3 What do you find most difficult about collaborative writing? What strategies have you developed to make your contributions more effective?

POLISHING YOUR PROSE

Delivering Criticism

No one likes to be told that his or her work isn't good. But criticism is necessary if people and documents are to improve.

Depending on the situation, you may be able to use one of these strategies:

1. Notice what's good as well as what needs work.

   The charts are great. We need to make the text as good as they are.

   I really like the ideas you've used in the slides. We need to edit the bulleted points so they're parallel.

2. Ask questions.

   Were you able to find any books and articles, in addition to sources on the Internet?

   What do you see as the most important revisions to make for the next draft?

3. Refer to the textbook or another authority.

   The module on design says that italic type is hard to read.

   Our instructor told us that presentations should have just three main points.

4. Make statements about your own reaction.

   I'm not sure what you're getting at in this section.

   I wouldn't be convinced by the arguments here.

5. Criticize what's wrong, without making global attacks on the whole document or on the writer as a person.

   There are a lot of typos in this draft.

   You begin almost every sentence with um.

Exercises

Rewrite each criticism to make it less hurtful. You may add or omit information as needed.

1. This is the worst report I've ever seen.
2. My 10-year-old can spell better than you do.
3. I can't believe that you didn't go to the library to get any sources.
4. You've used four different fonts in this report. Didn't you read the book? Don't you know that we're not supposed to use more than two?
5. This design is really lame. It looks like every other brochure I've ever seen.
6. There's no way we'll get a passing grade if we turn this in.
7. Were you asleep? Didn't you hear our instructor say that we had to use at least five sources?
8. This is really creative. You've written the perfect illustration for "How to Fail This Course."
9. This proposal makes no sense.
10. This clip art is sexist. There's no way we should use it.

Check your answers to the odd-numbered exercises on page 550.

Polishing Your Prose Exercises

Concluding each module, Polishing Your Prose exercises provide a review of grammar, style, and usage. Answers to odd-numbered exercises are found at the back of the book to help students check their progress. Answers to even-numbered exercises, which can be assigned for homework or used for quizzes, are included in the Instructor's Manual.

Cases for Communicators

Six Unit-ending cases provide both individual and team activities to solve communication challenges faced by real-life companies and organizations.

CASES FOR COMMUNICATORS

You work for HaberNat, a not-for-profit organization committed to environmental protection. HaberNat's mandate: to generate public and corporate support (opinion and revenue) to influence businesses and governments to act more quickly and firmly on environmental concerns.

HaberNat needs inexpensive ways to communicate its message, and recruit support. The organization wants to explore the feasibility of using community and social networking sites to (1) establish and expand its presence, (2) raise Canadians' awareness of environmental issues, and (3) influence people to act individually and collectively to agitate for change.

Your manager has asked you and your colleagues to research and report on the feasibility of the idea, recommending two free sites that would attract and build grassroots supporters.

Individual Activity

As you begin your research, consider your audience and purposes. Your manager may be the originator, and one of the readers of the report. Your findings, however, must identify and analyze two sites that will appeal to a widely diverse audience: the young demographic that frequents such sites; an older, affluent audience who may visit these sites; political and environmental activists; people who know little or nothing about the environment; HaberNat employees who would be comfortable using these sites to encourage public participation.

You need to know who uses community/social networking sites, when, how and why. What age? What gender? Where do they live? What are their occupations? What, if any, social role do they play in their communities? What sites would environmentally aware people visit?

Who doesn't use these sites? Why not? What have they in common? What would encourage them to frequent such sites?

How useful are these sites? How are they beneficial? How and to whom are they detrimental? How can a potential user assess their value? What criteria exist to evaluate a site's reliability, validity or benefit? And are such criteria necessary?

What municipal/provincial legislation currently shapes users' environmentally conscious attitudes and behaviours? How would people benefit from laws passed to protect the environment? What objections would people have to such legislation?

Where will you get the most current data? Whom will you interview/survey to get the information you need?

Group Activity

Form a group with two or three colleagues. Draft a plan outlining your research, analysis, and writing. Create a timeline for your primary and secondary research, and for analyzing, composing, revising, and editing the report.

Before you draft your survey and interview questions, consider:

- Whom can we interview? Who are the experts?
- Who is the population for a survey?
- Is our sample random, convenience, or judgment?
- What types of questions should we ask—open, closed, probes?
- How does the sample type affect our ability to generalize our findings?

As you write your questions, ask yourself

- Are the questions clear and neutral?
- Do the questions cover the information we need to know to research, analyze, and identify two appropriate sites for HaberNat's purposes?
- What assumptions do my questions make? Are these appropriate assumptions?
- Are we using branching questions where appropriate?
- Are the questions sequenced so that easier ones precede more difficult ones?

Decide on subjects for your interview(s) and your survey, and on the questions you will use. Gather and analyze your results.

Conduct your secondary research. Find relevant information on the most popular sites. Who uses these? Why? When? How often? What benefits to these sites offer? What are the drawbacks? How might HaberNat use them?

Analyze and synthesize your findings. Draw conclusions from your data. Is the idea feasible? If so, recommend two sites. If not, explain why. Brainstorm the stories your data should tell, and create visuals that best tell those stories.

Write the report, with visuals.

Building Effective Messages

- **Module 1:**
  Introducing Business Communications

- **Module 2:**
  Adapting Your Message to Your Audience

- **Module 3:**
  Communicating Across Cultures

- **Module 4:**
  Planning, Writing, and Revising

- **Module 5:**
  Designing Documents, Slides, and Screens

Teenager Skawenniio Barnes wrote the letter that built a library.

The 13-year-old couldn't research her high school assignment because there was no library in the Mohawk community of Kahnawake, Quebec. Her letter to the community chief and the Mohawk council, asking for a library on the reserve, emphasized the many benefits of access to a variety of current reading materials. Barnes wrote passionately about the rewards of reading, such as increased knowledge and vocabulary, and enhanced imagination. She also mentioned that the parents of children in the Mohawk immersion schools, who helped teach their children to read and write in English, needed contemporary resources.

When her words got no immediate action, Barnes sent her letter on to the *Eastern Door*, a community newspaper. People responded positively. Then the Montreal media and Global Television focused on the story. Momentum grew, and Barnes became a member of the new library committee.

Meanwhile, Barnes had entered and won the CosmoGirl! of the Year contest.

In her essay to *CosmoGirl!* magazine, Barnes told her story of trying to establish a community library. The resulting increased media attention garnered national awareness, and boxes of donated books arrived from across the country and around the world.

Retired McGill professor Ian McLachlin heard a CBC interview with Barnes and decided to help. When he discovered that the library needed a feasibility plan, he offered his MBA students the project for an independent study credit. Four students—Erika Rodrigues, Laird McLean, Juan Quiceno, and Rozel Gonzales—took on the project during spring break. McLachlin believed the students were motivated by "the opportunity to work with First Nations people, and … the chance to … do something meaningful with their skills, in an unconventional way."

Through discussions and collaboration with the entire Mohawk community, the MBA student consultants created a detailed feasibility plan. In 2003, two years after Barnes wrote her letter, the Skawenniio Tsi Iewennahnotahkhwa Kahnawake Library was built and filled with books from enthusiastic donors. Nominated by the people in her community, Barnes received the Peter Gzowski Literacy Award for her accomplishment.

Barnes will graduate from Yale University with a Political Science and International Studies degree in 2010. Then she hopes to study law, and return "to the Mohawk nation of the Haudenosaunee Confederacy" to contribute to others' futures.

Skawenniio means "one beautiful word." Barnes' words continue to prove the power of one, and of one's beautiful words.

PAIBOC ANALYSIS

1. Why would a community need a library when the Internet exists?
2. How did Barnes try to persuade her immediate audience?
3. What benefits persuaded other people to get involved?
4. What economic, technological, social, political, and environmental factors helped or hindered Barnes and others in building the library?

Introducing Business Communications

Learning Objectives

After reading and applying the information in Module 1, you'll be able to demonstrate

Knowledge of

- Why we communicate
- What business communication accomplishes
- What communication and interpersonal skills employers seek
- How to begin to analyze communication situations

Skills to

- Identify the characteristics of effective business messages
- Begin to analyze communication situations

Employability Skills 2000+ Checklist

You will need these skills to enter, stay in, and progress in the world of work—whether you work on your own or as a part of a team. These skills can also be applied and used beyond the workplace in a variety of daily activities.

Fundamental Skills

The skills needed as a base for further development. You will be better prepared to progress in the world of work when you can

Communicate

- ○ Read and understand information presented in a variety of forms (e.g., words, graphs, charts, diagrams)
- ○ Write and speak so others pay attention and understand
- ○ Listen and ask questions to understand and appreciate the points of view of others

- ○ Share information using a range of information and communications technologies (e.g., voice, email, computers)
- ○ Use relevant scientific, technological, and mathematical knowledge and skills to explain or clarify ideas

Manage Information

- ○ Locate, gather, and organize information using appropriate technology and information systems
- ○ Access, analyze, and apply knowledge and skills from various disciplines (e.g., the arts, languages, science,

technology, mathematics, social sciences, the humanities)

Use Numbers

- ○ Decide what needs to be measured or calculated
- ○ Observe and record data using appropriate methods, tools, and technology

- ○ Make estimates and verify calculations

Think & Solve Problems

- ○ Assess situations and identify problems
- ○ Seek different points of view and evaluate them based on facts.
- ○ Recognize the human, interpersonal, technical, scientific, and mathematical dimensions of a problem
- ○ Identify the root cause of a problem
- ○ Be creative and innovative in exploring possible solutions

- ○ Readily use science, technology, and mathematics as ways to think, gain and share knowledge, solve problems, and make decisions
- ○ Evaluate solutions to make recommendations or decisions
- ○ Implement solutions
- ○ Check to see if a solution works, and act on opportunities for improvement

Personal Management Skills

The personal skills, attitudes, and behaviours that drive one's potential for growth. You will be able to offer yourself greater possibilities for achievement when you can

Demonstrate Positive Attitudes & Behaviours

- ○ Feel good about yourself and be confident
- ○ Deal with people, problems, and situations with honesty, integrity, and personal ethics

- ○ Recognize your own and other people's good efforts
- ○ Take care of your personal health
- ○ Show interest, initiative, and effort

Be Responsible

- ○ Set goals and priorities balancing work and personal life
- ○ Plan and manage time, money, and other resources to achieve goals
- ○ Assess, weigh, and manage risk
- ○ Be accountable for your actions and the actions of your group
- ○ Be socially responsible and contribute to your community

Be Adaptable

- ○ Work independently or as a part of a team
- ○ Carry out multiple tasks or projects
- ○ Be innovative and resourceful: identify and suggest alternative ways to achieve goals and get the job done
- ○ Be open and respond constructively to change
- ○ Learn from your mistakes and accept feedback
- ○ Cope with uncertainty

Learn Continuously

- ○ Be willing to continuously learn and grow
- ○ Assess personal strengths and areas for development
- ○ Set your own learning goals
- ○ Identify and access learning sources and opportunities
- ○ Plan for and achieve your learning goals

Work Safely

- ○ Be aware of, and act in accordance with personal and group health and safety practices and procedures

Teamwork Skills

These are skills and attributes needed to contribute productively. You will be better prepared to add value to the outcomes of a task, project, or team when you can

Work with Others

- ○ Understand and work within the dynamics of a group
- ○ Ensure that a team's purpose and objectives are clear
- ○ Be flexible: respect, be open to, and be supportive of the thoughts, opinions, and contributions of others in a group
- ○ Recognize and respect people's diversity, individual differences, and perspectives
- ○ Accept and provide feedback in a constructive and considerate manner
- ○ Contribute to a team by sharing information and expertise
- ○ Lead or support when appropriate, motivating a group for high performance
- ○ Understand the role of conflict in a group to reach solutions
- ○ Manage and resolve conflict when appropriate

Participate in Projects & Tasks

- ○ Plan, design, or carry out a project or task from start to finish with well-defined objectives and outcomes
- ○ Develop a plan, seek feedback, test, revise, and implement
- ○ Work to agreed quality standards and specifications
- ○ Select and use appropriate tools and technology for a task or project
- ○ Adapt to changing requirements and information
- ○ Continuously monitor the success of a project or task and identify ways to improve

Why Do We Communicate?

We communicate to connect.

Technology has transformed our expectations about *where*, *when*, and *how* we communicate. *Why* we communicate, however, remains constant: we communicate because of our innate need to make meaning. We communicate to identify and express ourselves, to get work done, to gain recognition, and to make our lives meaningful.

We communicate most successfully when we (1) take the time to consider consciously what results we want and (2) adapt our message content, tone, and style to meet the needs of our audience, so we can achieve those results. Successful communication usually includes elements of persuasion: we cannot get what we want, unless and until we identify and satisfy the other person's wants.

How Is Business Communication Different?

Business communication uses specific formatting and style conventions to get the job done.

Because in business "Time is money," your audience's primary need is to get the message, clearly and completely, the first time. The best business communication meets your audience's expectations—of medium, format, style, and tone—and achieves your purpose(s), as efficiently as possible.

In our global marketplace effective business communication has become more complicated than ever. Most of our messages have multiple purposes, and our audiences a variety of needs. And technology has trained us to expect easy, immediate message transfer while increasing the complexity of our communication methods.

As a result, workers today have to communicate more often, using more media, and with more intelligence and finesse than ever before.

 Cultural FOCUS

In North America, and in northern Europe, people feel that time can be measured and is valuable, and all activities are scheduled accordingly. (Even children's play time is scheduled.) Not only do we believe time is money, but also we believe we can "spend time," "waste time," and "save time." Because of this, North Americans believe business communication needs to be clear and concise—to avoid the waste of valuable time.

FIGURE 1.1   Example of Typical Business Communication

Date: September 28, 2009

To: Lindsay Marshall

From: Brandon Schraff

Subject: Health and Safety Seminar & Future Sessions

Thank you for arranging last week's health and safety seminar for plant personnel. You did a great job; the feedback was positive and I've noticed that staff are applying what they learned.

Lunch and Learn Ideas

For next month's lunch and learn, people suggested the following topics:

- Tips for time management
- Best management practices
- Email etiquette
- Negotiating strategies

Let me know your ideas, and let's talk after the management meeting next Thursday to choose a topic.

Regards,

Brandon

Both the Conference Board of Canada and the U.S. Secretary's Commission on Achieving Necessary Skills (SCANS) identify sophisticated communications skills as one of the keys to careers in the 21st century. (See the complete text of the Conference Board of Canada's Employability Skills 2000+ on page 3. The skills pertinent to each module of this book are listed at the beginning of the module.)

In his study *Education and Technological Revolution: The Role of the Social Sciences and the Humanities in the Knowledge-Based Economy*, University of British Columbia economics professor Robert Allen finds that communications skills are the most sought after in today's economy. "Demand is increasing for those workers who can understand the information generated by computer systems, apply models to problems, deal effectively with customers and other members of a team, speak and write clearly, and make informed and independent judgments."[1]

Author Daniel Pink (*A Whole New Mind*) concurs. Pink claims that the global economy has moved us from the Information Age to the "Conceptual Age," wherein high-level communications skills such as conceptualizing, big-picture thinking, and synthesizing are most valued.[2] And, in fact, today's university and college graduates are discovering that abilities like speaking persuasively with clients, working productively in teams, and managing projects are critical for finding employment.[3]

What Does Business Communication Accomplish?

Communication makes everything happen.

Business communications—oral, nonverbal, and written—go to both internal and external audiences. Internal audiences (Figure 1.2) are other people in the same organization: subordinates, superiors, and peers. External audiences (Figure 1.3) are people outside the

FIGURE 1.2   The Internal Audiences of the Sales Manager, West

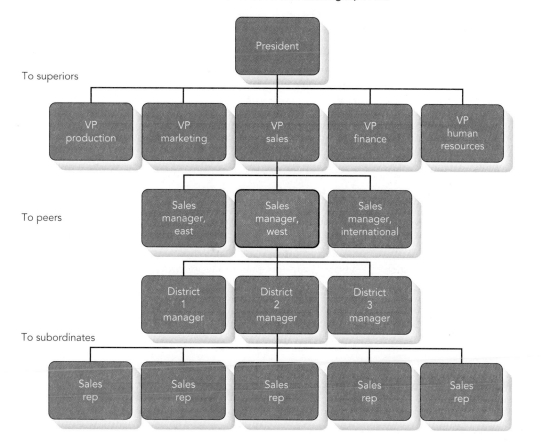

FIGURE 1.3   The Organization's External Audiences

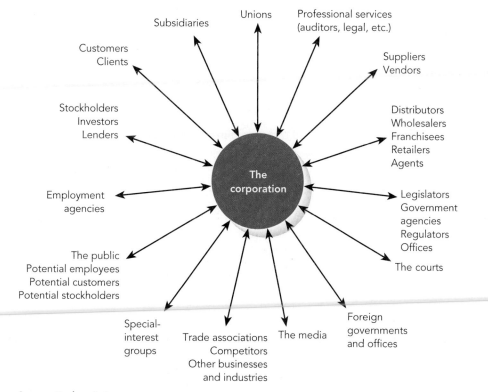

Source: Daphne A. Jameson.

organization: customers, suppliers, unions, stockholders, potential employees, government agencies, the press, and the public.

Today's workers have to be able to use a wide variety of media and strategies to communicate effectively with internal and external audiences. Employers expect graduates—even those in entry-level positions—to know how to interpret comments from informal channels such as the company grapevine, to speak effectively to customers and colleagues, to work well in small groups, and to write well.

Indeed, job postings consistently list "excellent communication skills, verbal and written, strong analytical and decision-making abilities, ability to work well with others" at the top of their position requirements.[4]

Language FOCUS

To **hear something through the grapevine** means you have heard news informally from another person. Other, similar idioms you may hear are "the office scuttlebutt" or "news from around the water cooler." Many idioms and buzzwords are used in everyday business conversation. It is important to remember that not everyone understands these expressions, and when you are working with non–English speakers you may need to modify your language to be clearly understood.

Checkpoint

Business documents have three purposes: to inform, to request or persuade, and to build goodwill. Most documents serve more than one purpose.

What Communications Skills Are Integral to Business Success?

Workers rely on their listening, reading, speaking, interpersonal, and writing skills to get the job done.

Listening, reading, speaking, writing, and working in groups are integral to doing business successfully. In every job, you need to listen to others to find out what you are supposed to do, to learn about the organization's culture and values, and to establish and maintain work relationships. You need to read a variety of informal and formal documents, including text messages, emails, blogs, industry journals, newspapers, magazines, instructions, and reports in order to keep current and keep learning. Your interpersonal communications skills connect you to the grapevine, an informal source of organizational information. Moreover, networking and working with others—inside and outside your workplace—are crucial to developing positive relationships, and to your personal and professional growth.

Business, government, and not-for-profit organizations—in fact, all organizations—also depend on written messages. People in organizations produce written documents for the record, to inform, request, or persuade. When you write to inform, you tell or explain something to your readers; when you write to request or persuade, you want your readers to do something. However, the primary purpose of business messages is to build goodwill with the reader: to create a positive image of yourself, and of your organization, so readers will want to do business with you.

How Much Will I Really Have to Write?

You will have to write a lot.

Technological innovation has created work that requires increasingly sophisticated critical and creative thinking, and writing skills.

Claim 1: Assistants will do all my writing.

Reality: Technology has transformed organizational structures and reduced the need for support staff. Of the assistants who remain, 71 percent are executive assistants whose duties are managerial, not clerical.[5] Most managers today do their own writing.

Businesses today expect their junior engineers to manage projects and write reports. In response to industry complaints about graduates' poor communications skills, universities across Canada now emphasize writing and leadership courses in their undergraduate engineering faculties. According to Gabriel Desjardins, a Queen's University computer engineering graduate working in California's Silicon Valley, "Engineers with excellent writing skills are often promoted over people with superior technical skills."[6]

International literacy surveys consistently find a "clear link" between literacy and employment, with "document literacy" proficiency (the ability to read and write well) corresponding most strongly to higher employment rates and higher salaries.[7] To remain competitive in the global market, according to employers, Canadian professionals need business basics that include "communications, team building, report writing and preparing presentations."[8]

Perhaps you plan to hire someone to write for you. If so, start saving: professional writers get paid $1 to $5 a word for business writing, $1 000 to $10 000 for speech writing, and $500 to $20 000 for editing work.[9]

Claim 2: I'll use form letters or templates when I need to write.

Reality: A **form letter** is a prewritten fill-in-the-blanks letter designed to fit only routine situations. The greater your professional responsibilities, the more frequently you'll face situations that demand creative thinking and writing solutions.

Claim 3: I'm being hired as an accountant, not as a writer.

Reality: Almost every entry-level professional or managerial job requires you to write memos and email messages, and to work productively in small groups. Trades people and technicians also have to write incident reports and instructions. People who do these things well are more likely to be promoted beyond the entry level.

Furthermore, advances in technology have transformed workers' roles and responsibilities. Because of Simply Accounting software, for example, people can do their own low-level accounting tasks. Today, accountants earning between $40 000 and $45 000 annually have to have more specialized knowledge, and "be analytical with good communication and interpersonal skills."[10] Finally, since writing is such a high-level cognitive skill, people who have developed good writing abilities also tend to demonstrate superior reading and thinking

People communicate to plan products and services, to hire, train, and motivate workers, to coordinate manufacturing and delivery, to persuade customers to buy, and to bill for the sale.

skills. And they tend to make higher salaries. Superior communicators achieve more recognition and make more money.

Claim 4: I'll just pick up the phone.

Reality: "If it isn't in writing," says a manager at one company, "it didn't happen." Phone calls often require follow-up letters, memos, or email messages. People in organizations put things in writing to create a record, to make themselves visible, to convey complex data, to make things convenient for the reader, to save money, and to convey their own ideas more effectively. Writing well is an essential way to make yourself visible and convey a favourable impression of you and your organization.

How Much Does Correspondence Cost?

Business correspondence is very expensive, and even more costly when it doesn't work.

Writing costs money. Canadian communications expert and professional speaker Helen Wilkie maintains that written correspondence—emails, letters, reports, memos—is an "integral part of doing business. If a $40,000-a-year employee spends just two hours a day reading, writing and managing email, that's a $9,000 annual cost." Moreover, as Wilkie and other experts point out, two hours a day is a very conservative estimate of the amount of time employees spend composing, revising, and reading written documents.[11]

In many organizations, all external documents have to be approved before they go out. A document might cycle from writer to superior to writer to another superior to writer again three, four, or even eleven times before it is finally approved. The cycling process increases the cost of correspondence.

Poor correspondence costs even more. When writing isn't clear, complete, and correct, you and your organization pay in wasted time, wasted effort, and lost customers.

Poor Writing Is Costly

- Poor writing takes more time to read and interpret.
- It requires more time for revisions.
- It confuses and irritates the reader.
- It delays action while the reader requests more information, or tries to figure out the meaning.

Quite simply, ineffective messages get negative results. A reader who has to guess what the writer means may guess wrongly. A reader who finds a letter or memo unconvincing or insulting won't do what the writer asks.

Whatever the literal content of the words, every letter, memo, and report serves either to enhance or to damage the image the reader has of the writer. Poor messages damage business relationships. Good communication is worth every minute it takes and every penny it costs. In a survey conducted by the International Association of Business Communicators, CEOs said that communication yielded a 235 percent return on investment.[12] Consulting firm Watson Wyatt Worldwide's research corroborates these results. Their most recent study confirmed that organizations that communicate effectively profit dramatically over those that do not. Effective communication translated into a 19.4 percent higher market premium, over 57 percent higher shareholder returns, and reports of higher morale and higher employee retention.[13]

Bottom line: Good communication means good business.

What Makes a Message Effective?

Successful business correspondence builds goodwill by focusing on the reader.

An effective, reader-centred business message meets five criteria:

1. The message is **clear**: the writer chooses the facts—and the organization and language to convey those facts—that enable the reader to get the meaning that the writer intended.
2. The message is **concise**: the writer conveys maximum meaning using as few words as possible.
3. The message is **comprehensive**: the style, organization, and visual impact of the message help the reader to read, understand, and act.
4. The message is **complete**: the reader has enough information to evaluate the message and act on it.
5. The message is **correct**: the information in the message is accurate and is free of errors in punctuation, spelling, grammar, word order, and sentence structure.

An effective message initiates or builds a positive relationship between the writer and the reader (see Modules 6–8).

The Benefits of Becoming a Better Writer

Good business writers are more productive and make more money!

- **Good writing saves time**, because well-written correspondence is easy to read and respond to.
- **It saves money**, because effective writing increases the number of requests that are answered positively and promptly the first time, and presents your point of view—to other people in your organization, to clients, customers, and suppliers, to government agencies, and to the public—more persuasively.
- **Good writing saves energy**, because effective messages reduce the misunderstandings that occur when the reader has to supply missing or unclear information, and because good writing clarifies the issues so that disagreements can surface and be resolved more quickly.
- **It builds goodwill**, because it projects a positive image of your organization and an image of the writer as a knowledgeable, intelligent, capable person.

Checkpoint

Effective business and administrative writing is **clear**, **concise**, **comprehensive**, **complete**, and **correct**. The best messages save the reader time and build goodwill. Whether a message meets these criteria depends on the *interactions among the writer, the audience, the purposes of the message*, and *the situation*. No single set of words will work in all situations.

How Do Effective Communicators Begin to Analyze Business Communication Situations?

They consider the context!

Before you write—or listen, speak, or read—you need to analyze and understand the situation. What do you really want to happen as a result of your communication? How can you get the results you want?

Communication has consequences. To get the results you want, consider these questions:

- **What's the point?** What information am I reading, imparting, or listening to, and why is it relevant?
- **What's my purpose?** What is the intended result? What do I want to happen as a result of this communication? How can I make a favourable impression? Do I want to inform or to confirm plans? Do I want to change attitudes and behaviours? What do I really want as a result?
- **Who's my audience?** What do they already know? What do they need to know to make a decision? What are their wants and needs? What do they value? What's in it for them?
- **Where will the communication happen?** Do I have best possible environment for maximum meaning transfer? If I am trying to resolve a conflict, am I speaking face-to-face with my audience? When reading complicated material, have I found a quiet space? If my message is confidential, have I ensured maximum privacy?

EXPANDING A CRITICAL SKILL

Thinking Creatively

We all have creative potential. However, effective communicators like Barack Obama and Maude Barlow appear to be able to tap into both their critical and their creative faculties to offer insights and innovative solutions.

Solving problems and making decisions require both logical and lateral thinking: we use logic to analyze and identify problems before we apply lateral thinking to brainstorm solutions. Often, however, we are so locked into our own perceptions that we identify the wrong problem; then the solution isn't much use. Thinking creatively means approaching problems with a fresh perspective. We can all learn to think more creatively, to reframe situations, identify the problem correctly, and find workable solutions.

Moreover, since change is the only constant in today's workplace, the ability to bring a fresh perspective to situations is essential for career success. More and more companies are relying on innovative interviewing and hiring practices, such as behavioural and speed interviewing, to find suitable employees. Some recruiters ask prospects to submit taped presentations; young, entrepreneurial companies such as 1-800-Got-Junk interview several candidates altogether and choose the most impressive people for further interviews.

Innovative solutions come out of preparedness: you generate insights best by immersing yourself in the situation. But, like any skill, creative, right-brain, or lateral thinking can be learned with practice. Improve your flexible thinking by approaching even mundane tasks in new ways: brush your teeth with your non-dominant hand, for example. In writing, assess problems creatively using brainstorming and mind-mapping techniques.

Ex-Torontonian Christian Lander, 29, an Internet copywriter in Los Angeles, originated the blog Stuff White People Like in January 2008. The satiric postings attracted thousands of hits and comments, and proved so popular that two months later Random House paid Landers over $300 000 to write a book based on his blog.

IBM's tips for creativity are even more diverse:

- Have an argument.
- Brainstorm with someone 10 years older and someone 10 years younger.
- Clean your desk.
- Come in early and enjoy the quiet.
- Leave the office. Sit with a pencil and a pad of paper. See what happens.

Sources: Mathew Ingram, *Stuff White People Like, the Book*, retrieved March 26, 2008 from http://www.theglobeandmail.com/servlet/story/RTGAM.20080326.WBmingram20080326111531/WBStory/WBmingram; Mathew Ingram, *Stuff White People in Toronto Like*, retrieved March 14, 2008 from http://torontoist.com/2008/03/stuff_white_peo.php; Allan Salkin, *Why Blog? Reason No. 92: Book Deal*, retrieved April 6, 2008 from http://www.nytimes.com/2008/03/30/fashion/30web.html?ref=style.

- **When will the communication happen?** What time of day and what length of time have I chosen to deliver the message? When will the audience really be able to pay attention to my message? If I am reading difficult material, when am I most alert to absorb it? What is the best time of day for my team to meet for highest productivity?

In every communication situation, your success depends on your thinking strategies. You must think both critically and creatively to get the results you want. Use the PAIBOC (Payback) questions (Figure 1.4) to analyze the communication context, and to consider your message from your audience's point of view. Then get creative: brainstorm solutions that might resolve the situation, and meet the psychological needs of the people involved.

FIGURE 1.4   **PAIBOC Questions for Analysis**

Use the PAIBOC (pronounced "payback") questions to analyze business communication problems:

P   What are your **purposes** in writing?

A   Who is your **audience**? How do members of your audience differ? What audience characteristics are relevant to this particular message?

I   What **information** must your message include?

B   What reasons or reader **benefits** can you use to support your position?

O   What **objections** can you expect your readers to have? What negative elements of your message must you deemphasize or overcome?

C   How will the **context** affect the reader's response? Think about your relationship to the reader, the morale in the organization, the economy, the time of year, and any special circumstances.

P   What are your **purposes** in writing or speaking?

What must this message do to solve the problem? What must it do to meet your own needs? What do you want your audience to do, to think, or to feel? List all your purposes, major and minor. Specify exactly what you want your reader to know or think or do. Specify exactly the images of you and your organization you want to project. Answer, "What do I want to happen as a result of this message?"

Even a simple message might have several related purposes: to announce a new policy, to make readers aware of the policy's provisions and requirements, to convince readers that the policy is a good one, to tell readers that the organization cares about its employees, and to show readers that you are a competent writer.

A   Who is your **audience**? How are readers going to feel about your message? What do they care about? What do they value? What's in the message that will appeal to them?

How much does your audience know about your topic? How will audience members respond to your message? Some characteristics of your readers will be irrelevant; focus on ones that matter for this message. Whenever you write to several people or to a group (like a memo or blog to all employees), try to identify the economic, cultural, or situational differences that may affect how various subgroups respond to what you have to say.

I   What **information** must your message include?

Make a list of the points that must be included; check your draft to make sure you include them all. If you're not sure whether a particular fact must be included, ask your instructor or your boss.

To include information without emphasizing it, put it in the middle of a paragraph or document and present it as briefly as possible.

B   What reasons or reader **benefits** can you use to support your position?

Brainstorm to develop reasons for your decision, the logic behind your argument, and possible benefits to readers if they do as you ask. Reasons and reader benefits do not have to be monetary. Making the reader's job easier or more pleasant is a good reader benefit. In an informative or persuasive message, identify at least five reader benefits. In your message, use those that you can develop most easily and most effectively.

Be sure that the benefits are adapted to your reader. Many people do not identify closely with their companies; the fact that the company benefits from a policy will help the reader only if the saving or profit is passed on directly to the employees. That is rarely the case: savings and profits are often eaten up by returns to stockholders, bonuses to executives, and investments in plants and equipment or in research and development.

O   What **objections** can you expect your reader(s) to have? What negative elements of your message must you deemphasize or overcome?

Some negative elements can only be deemphasized. Others can be overcome. Be creative: Is there any advantage associated with (even though not caused by) the negative? Can you rephrase or redefine the negative to make the reader see it differently?

C   How will the **context** affect the reader's response? Think about your relationship to the reader, the morale in the organization, the economy, the time of year, and any special circumstances.

Readers might like you or resent you. You might be younger or older than the people you're writing to. The organization might be prosperous or going through hard times; it might have just been reorganized or it might be stable. All these different situations will affect what you say and how you say it.

Consider the news, interest rates, the economy, and the weather. Think about the general business and regulatory climates, especially as they affect the organization specified in the problem. Use the real world as much as possible. Is the industry in which the problem is set doing well? Is the government agency in which the problem is set enjoying general support? Think about the time of year. If it's fall when you write, is your business in a seasonal slowdown after a busy summer? gearing up for the holiday shopping rush? or going along at a steady pace unaffected by seasons?

To answer these questions, draw on your experience, your courses, and your research. Talk to other students, read newspapers and magazines, search the Internet, and look at a company's annual report. You may want to phone a local businessperson to get information. For instance, if you need more information on reader benefits for a problem set in a bank, call a local bank representative to research services and loan rates.

The remaining modules in this book will show you how to use the PAIBOC ("payback") analysis to create business messages that meet your needs, the needs of the audience, and the needs of the organization.

Language FOCUS

PAIBOC is an **acronym**—a word formed from the initials of other words. Acronyms help people remember information.

MODULE SUMMARY

- Although technology has transformed our expectations about *where*, *when*, and *how* we communicate, we continue to communicate because of our innate need to make meaning.

- Business communication creates, promotes, sells, and delivers products, services, and information.

- In a business context, people write for the record, and to communicate with global audiences simultaneously and instantly.

- Business communication uses specific conventions of formatting, style and medium.

- The most successful communicators make conscious, informed choices, based on their analysis of purpose and audience: they know that they can only get what they want when they understand and acknowledge what their audience wants.

- PAIBOC analysis enables you to make these same conscious rhetorical choices about *what*, *when*, and *how* you communicate to achieve your purposes, and build positive relationships with your audiences.

ASSIGNMENTS FOR MODULE 1

Questions for Critical Thinking

1.1 Why do you need to understand the purposes, audience, and context for a message to know whether a specific choice of words will work?

1.2 Why do writing and speaking become even more important as people rise in the organization?

1.3 If you're just looking for an entry-level job, why is it still important to be able to write and speak well?

1.4 How is "school" writing different from business writing?

Exercises and Problems

1.5 Business Communications Analysis

How do business messages differ from the communication methods you have learned in school? Together with three of your classmates, analyze a minimum of four business messages (memos, emails, slide shows, advertisements, proposals, flyers, brochures), using the following criteria:

- Purposes
- Audiences
- Information (content, length)
- Organization
- Style (wording, sentence length, paragraph length)
- Layout
- Visuals

Create a table comparing academic writing with the business messages you have chosen. Be prepared to present and explain your results.

1.6 Emails for Discussion—Landscape Plants

Your nursery sells plants, not only in your store but also by mail order. Today you've received an email letter from Pat Sykes, complaining that the plants (in a $572 order) did not arrive in satisfactory condition. "All of them were dry and wilted. One came out by the roots when I took it out of the box. Please send me a replacement shipment immediately."

The following email letters are possible approaches to answering this complaint. How well does each message meet the needs of the reader, the writer, and the organization? Is the message clear, complete, and correct? Does it save the reader time? Does it favourably influence the reader? Will it keep the reader as a customer?

1. Dear Sir:

    I checked to see what could have caused the defective shipment you received. After ruling out problems in transit, I discovered that your order was packed by a new worker who didn't understand the need to water plants thoroughly before they are shipped. We have fired the worker, so you can be assured that this will not happen again.

    Although it will cost our company several hundred dollars, we will send you a replacement shipment.

    Let me know if the new shipment arrives safely. We trust that you will not complain again.

2. Dear Pat:

    Sorry we messed up that order. Sending plants across country is a risky business. Some of them just can't take the strain. (Some days I can't take the strain myself!) We'll credit your account for $572.

3. Dear Mr. Smith:

    I'm sorry you aren't happy with your plants, but it isn't our fault. The box clearly says "Open and water immediately." If you had done that, the plants would have been fine. And anybody who is going to buy plants should know that a little care is needed. If you pull by the leaves, you will pull the roots out. Always lift by the stem! Since you don't know how to handle plants, I'm sending you a copy of our brochure, "How to Care for Your Plants." Please read it carefully so that you will know how to avoid disappointment in the future.

    We look forward to your future orders.

4. Dear Ms. Sikes:

    Your letter of the 5th has come to the attention of the undersigned.

    According to your letter, your invoice #47420 arrived in an unsatisfactory condition. Please be advised that it is our policy to make adjustments as per the Terms and Conditions listed on the reverse side of our Acknowledgment of Order. If you will read that document, you will find the following:

    "... if you intend to assert any claim against us on this account, you shall make an exception on your receipt to the carrier and shall, within 30 days after the receipt of any such goods, furnish us detailed written information as to any damage."

    Your letter of the 5th does not describe the alleged damage in sufficient detail. Furthermore, the delivery receipt contains no indication of any exception. If you expect to receive an adjustment, you must comply with our terms and see that the necessary documents reach the undersigned by the close of the business day on the 20th of the month.

5. Dear Pat Sykes:

    Next week you'll receive a replacement shipment of the perennials you ordered.

    Your plants were watered carefully before shipment and packed in specially designed cardboard containers. But if the weather is unusually warm, or if the truck is delayed, small root balls may dry out.

Perhaps this happened with your plants. Plants with small root balls are easier to transplant, so they do better in your yard.

The violas, digitalis, aquilegias, and hostas you ordered are long-blooming perennials that will get even prettier each year. Enjoy your garden!

1.7 Memos for Discussion—Announcing a Web Page

The Acme Corporation has just posted its first Web page. Ed Zeplin in Management Information Systems (MIS) created the page and wants employees to know about it.

The following memos are possible approaches. How well does each message meet the needs of the reader, the writer, and the organization? Is the message clear, complete, and correct? Does it save the reader time? Does it build goodwill?

1. Subject: It's Ready!

    I am happy to tell you that my work is done. Two months ago the CEO finally agreed to fund a Web page for Acme, and now the work of designing and coding is done.

    I wanted all of you to know about Acme's page. (Actually it's more than 40 pages.) Now maybe the computerphobes out there will realize that you really do need to learn how to use this stuff. Sign up for the next training session! The job you save may be my own.

    If you have questions, please do not hesitate to contact me.

    L. Ed Zeplin, MIS

2. Subject: Web Page

    Check out the company Web page at

    www.server.acme.com/homepage.html

3. Subject: Visit Our Web Page

    Our Web pages are finally operational. The 43 pages take 460 MB on the server and were created using HoTMetaL, a program designed to support HTML creation. Though the graphics are sizable and complex, interlacing and code specifying the pixel size serve to minimize download time. Standard HTML coding is enhanced with forms, Java animation, automatic counters, and tracking packages to ascertain who visits our site.

The site content was determined by conducting a survey of other corporate Web sites to become cognizant of the pages made available by our competitors and other companies. The address of our Web page is www.server.acme.com/homepage.html. It is believed that this site will support and enhance our marketing and advertising efforts, improving our outreach to desirable demographic and psychographic marketing groups.

L. Ed Zeplin, MIS

Voice: 713-555-2879; Fax: 713-555-2880; Email: zeplin.1@acme.com

"Only the wired life is worth living."—Anonymous

4. Subject: Web Page Shows Acme Products to the World, Offers Tips to Consumers, and Tells Prospective Employees About Job Possibilities

Since last Friday, Acme's been on the World Wide Web. Check out the page at www.server.acme.com/homepage.html. You can't view the page if you don't have a computer.

I have included pages on our products, tips for consumers, and job openings at Acme in the hope of making our page useful and interesting. Content is the number one thing that brings people back, but I've included some snazzy graphics, too.

When I asked people for ideas for the company pages, almost nobody responded. But if seeing the page inspires you, let me know what else you'd like. I'll try to fit it into my busy schedule.

So check it out. But don't spend too much time on the Web: you need to get your work done, too!

L. Ed Zeplin, MIS

zeplin.1@acme.com

Today's Joke

Fun Links

5. Subject: How to Access Acme's Web Page

Tell your customers that Acme is now on the Web:

www.server.acme.com/homepage.html

Web pages offer another way for us to bring our story to the public. Our major competitors have Web pages; now we do, too. Our advertisements and packaging will feature our Web address. And

people who check out our Web page can learn even more about our commitment to selling quality products, protecting the environment, and meeting customer needs.

If you'd like to learn more about how to use the Web or how to create Web pages for your unit, sign up for one of our workshops. For details and online registration, see www.server.acme.com/training.

If you have comments on Acme's Web pages or suggestions for making them even better, just let me know.

L. Ed Zeplin

zeplin.1@acme.com

1.8 Discussing Strengths

Introduce yourself to a small group of students. Identify three of your strengths that might interest an employer. These might be experience, knowledge, or personality traits (such as enthusiasm).

1.9 Introducing Yourself to Your Instructor

Write a memo (at least 1.5 pages long) introducing yourself to your instructor. Include the following topics:

- *Background:* Where did you grow up? What have you done in terms of school, extracurricular activities, jobs, and family life?
- *Interests:* What are you interested in? What do you like to do? What do you like to think about and talk about?
- *Achievements:* What achievements have given you the greatest personal satisfaction? List at least five. Include achievements that gave you a real sense of accomplishment and pride, whether or not you'd list them on a résumé.
- *Goals:* What do you hope to accomplish this term? Where would you like to be professionally and personally five years from now?

Use a memo format with appropriate headings. Your teacher will provide you with an overview of the memo format. (See Module 9 for examples of memo format.) Use a conversational writing style; check your draft to polish the style and edit for mechanical and grammatical correctness. A good memo will enable your instructor to see you as an individual. Use specific details to make your memo vivid and interesting. Remember that one of your purposes is to interest your reader!

1.10 Describing Your Experiences in and Goals for Writing

Write a blog (at least three paragraphs) to your classmates and instructor describing the experiences you've had writing and what you'd like to learn about writing during this course. Use any of the following questions to prompt you:

- What would you most like to learn in a writing course? What topics would motivate your interest in writing?
- What memories do you have of writing? What made writing fun or miserable in the past?
- What have you been taught about writing? List the topics, rules, and advice you remember.
- What kinds of writing have you done in school? How long have the papers been?
- How has your school writing been evaluated?
  - Did the instructor mark or comment on mechanics and grammar? style? organization? logic? content? audience analysis and adaptation? Have you received extended comments on your papers? Have instructors in different classes had the same standards, or have you changed aspects of your writing for different classes?

- What voluntary writing have you done—journals, poems, stories, essays? Has this writing been just for you, or has some of it been shared or published?
- Have you ever written on a job or in a student or volunteer organization? Have you ever edited or typed other people's writing? What have these experiences led you to think about business writing?
- What do you see as your current strengths and weaknesses in writing skills? What skills do you think you'll need in the future? What kinds of writing do you expect to do after you graduate?

If you need help setting up your blog, go to www.blogger.com for step-by-step instructions. Then visit Seth's Blog at http://sethgodin.typepad.com/seths_blog/2008/04/write-like-a-bl.html to review tips for writing effectively. Edit your final draft for mechanical and grammatical correctness.

Read and respond to three other students' blogs. Prepare a five-minute presentation summarizing students' most positive writing experiences.

POLISHING YOUR PROSE

Sentence Fragments

Faulty sentence construction is a common grammar error. When speaking, we can use hundreds of nonverbal clues, and instant feedback to clarify our meaning. When writing, however, our words and sentences stand alone. Remember that a sentence has a subject and a verb, and expresses a complete thought. If either the subject or the verb is missing, the result is a sentence fragment.

Going to be in Burnaby April 30.

And buy a hybrid car. Maybe a Saturn.

To fix the fragment, add a subject or a verb to express a complete thought.

When I am in Burnaby April 30, I may buy a Saturn hybrid.

Sentence fragments usually occur when a clause contains both a subject and a verb but does not express a complete thought.

Although I often wait to make client calls until after 4 P.M.

Because she saved her work

When he upgrades his computer

The words *although*, *because*, and *when* begin *dependent clauses*, which means the clause cannot stand alone. It depends on a main, *or independent clause* for completion.

Although I often wait to make client calls until after 4 P.M., I still get voicemail instead of a real person.

Because she had saved her work, Paula was able to restore it after the crash.

When he upgrades his computer, he will be able to use the new software.

Words that make clauses dependent include

after	if
although, though	when, whenever
because, since	while, as
before, until	

Sometimes fragments work. For instance, fragments are used in text messages, résumés, advertisements, and some sales and fundraising letters. However, fragments are inappropriate for most business documents. Because they are incomplete, they can confuse or mislead readers.

The biggest problem with grammatical errors like sentence fragments is that readers sometimes assume that people who make errors are unprofessional or illiterate. Of course, using "incorrect" grammar has nothing to do with intelligence; nevertheless, many people use grammar as a yardstick. People who cannot measure up to that yardstick may be stuck in low-level jobs.

Exercises

Find and complete the sentence fragments in the following paragraphs.

1. Because people are constantly fiddling with their BlackBerrys, even during meetings and training sessions. We need to establish some ground rules about checking and rechecking BlackBerrys. Surfing the Web on their laptops. Leaving meetings to look at email and listen to voicemail messages. I am not convinced that our preoccupation with technology is really saving us time and money. Or contributing to productivity.

2. Since it's only a matter of time before government mandates it, I would appreciate your suggestions for going green in the office. And in the building itself. While many of you have already taken responsibility for turning off lights, unplugging PCs and the like. We can make even greater, cost-effective changes. And the benefits? Thereby improving morale and employees' health. And possibly qualifying for municipal grants.

Check your answers to the odd-numbered exercises on page 551.

MODULE
2

Adapting Your Message to Your Audience

Learning Objectives

After reading and applying the information in Module 2, you'll be able to demonstrate

Knowledge of

- The variables of the communication process
- The audiences who may evaluate your business messages
- The importance of adapting your message to your audience
- Audience analysis

Skills to

- Analyze your audience when composing messages
- Begin to shape the content, organization, and form of your messages to meet audience needs

Employability Skills 2000+ Checklist

In this module, the key skills from the Conference Board of Canada's Employability Skills 2000+ are

Communicate

○ write and speak so others pay attention and understand

○ listen and ask questions to understand and appreciate the points of view of others

Think & Solve Problems

○ assess situations and identify problems

○ seek different points of view and evaluate them based on facts

Demonstrate Positive Attitudes & Behaviours

○ deal with people, problems, and situations with honesty, integrity, and personal ethics

○ show interest, initiative, and effort

Be Adaptable

○ be open and respond constructively to change

○ cope with uncertainty

Learn Continuously

○ be willing to continuously learn and grow
○ assess personal strengths and areas for development

○ identify and access learning sources and opportunities

Work with Others

○ understand and work within the dynamics of a group
○ be flexible: respect, be open to, and be supportive of the thoughts, opinions, and contributions of others in a group

○ recognize and respect people's diversity, individual differences, and perspectives
○ accept and provide feedback in a constructive and considerate manner

Audience analysis is fundamental to the success of any message: to capture and hold an audience's attention and to motivate readers and listeners, you must shape your message to meet the audience's goals, interests, and needs.

Checkpoint

Five Kinds of Audiences

Initial: Is first to receive the message; may assign message.

Primary: Decides whether to accept recommendations; acts on message.

Secondary: Comments on message or implements recommendations.

Gatekeeper: Has the power to stop the message before it gets to primary audience.

Watchdog: Has political, social, or economic power; may base future actions on evaluation of message.

Who Is My Audience?

Your audience may include more people than you think.

In an organizational setting, a message may have five audiences.[1]

1. The **initial audience** receives the message first and routes it to other audiences. Sometimes the initial audience also tells you to write the message.
2. The **primary audience** will make the decision to act on your message.
3. The **secondary audience** may be asked to comment on your message or to implement your ideas after they've been approved. Secondary audiences can also include lawyers who may use your message—perhaps years later—as evidence of your organization's culture and practices.
4. A **gatekeeper** has the power to stop your message before it gets to the primary audience. The executive assistant who decides which personnel get to speak to the boss is a gatekeeper. Sometimes the supervisor who assigns the message is also the gatekeeper; however, sometimes the gatekeeper is higher in the organization. Occasionally, gatekeepers exist outside the organization. For example, regulatory boards are gatekeepers.
5. A **watchdog audience**, though it does not have the power to stop the message and will not act directly on it, has political, social, or economic power. The watchdog pays close attention to the transaction between you and the primary audience and may base future actions on its evaluation of your message. The media, boards of directors, and members of program advisory committees can all be watchdogs.

As Figures 2.1 and 2.2 show, one person or group can be part of two audiences. Frequently, a supervisor is both the initial audience and the gatekeeper. The initial audience can also be the primary audience who will act on the message.

FIGURE 2.1   The Audiences for a Marketing Plan

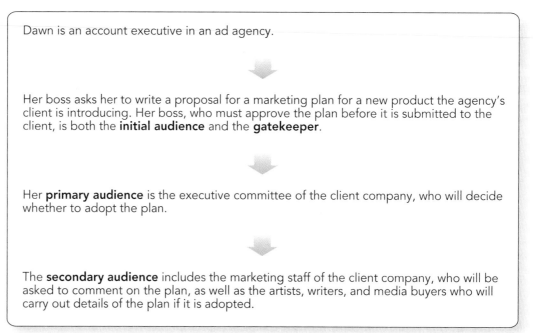

Dawn is an account executive in an ad agency.

Her boss asks her to write a proposal for a marketing plan for a new product the agency's client is introducing. Her boss, who must approve the plan before it is submitted to the client, is both the **initial audience** and the **gatekeeper**.

Her **primary audience** is the executive committee of the client company, who will decide whether to adopt the plan.

The **secondary audience** includes the marketing staff of the client company, who will be asked to comment on the plan, as well as the artists, writers, and media buyers who will carry out details of the plan if it is adopted.

FIGURE 2.2　**The Audiences for a Consulting Report**

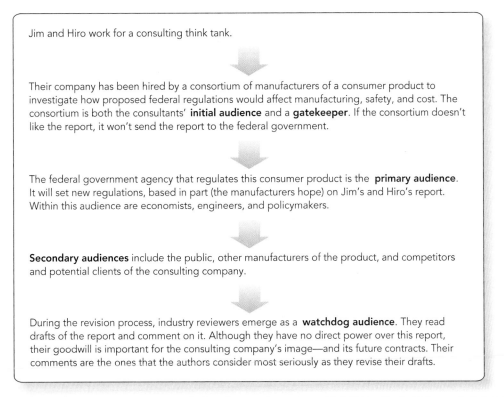

Jim and Hiro work for a consulting think tank.

Their company has been hired by a consortium of manufacturers of a consumer product to investigate how proposed federal regulations would affect manufacturing, safety, and cost. The consortium is both the consultants' **initial audience** and a **gatekeeper**. If the consortium doesn't like the report, it won't send the report to the federal government.

The federal government agency that regulates this consumer product is the **primary audience**. It will set new regulations, based in part (the manufacturers hope) on Jim's and Hiro's report. Within this audience are economists, engineers, and policymakers.

Secondary audiences include the public, other manufacturers of the product, and competitors and potential clients of the consulting company.

During the revision process, industry reviewers emerge as a **watchdog audience**. They read drafts of the report and comment on it. Although they have no direct power over this report, their goodwill is important for the consulting company's image—and its future contracts. Their comments are the ones that the authors consider most seriously as they revise their drafts.

Source: Based on Vincent J. Brown, "Facing Multiple Audiences in Engineering and R&D Writing: The Social Context of a Technical Report," *Journal of Technical Writing and Communication* 24 (1) (1994): 67–75.

Language FOCUS

A **think tank** is a group of people, usually experts in their field, who work together to provide advice. People in the think tank often work for businesses or government to help solve a problem, such as how new laws will affect a company.

Why Is Audience So Important?

People need to know what's in it for them. Successful messages anticipate and meet the audience's needs.

Audience focus is central to both the communication process and message analysis (PAIBOC).

Audience and the Communication Process

Understanding what your audience needs and expects, and adapting your messages accordingly, greatly enhance your chances of communicating successfully.

The communication process is the most complex of human activities, and audience is central to that process. We communicate unceasingly. Our audiences interpret our communication

FIGURE 2.3   **True Communication Is an Exchange of Meaning**

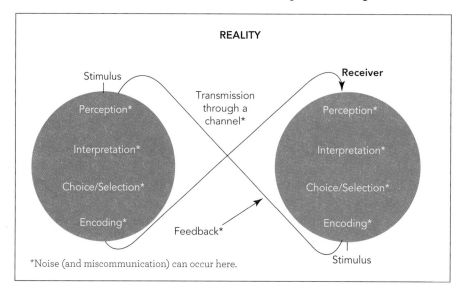

The communication process is complex, because each of us is unique and believes his or her own perceptions of reality (meaning) are true; therefore, misunderstandings can occur during any part of the process.

symbols unceasingly. Our words, tone, volume and rate of speech, posture, stance and gait, height and weight, hairstyle and hair colour, choice of clothing styles, materials, and colours, cell phone, iPod, social media use—all the thousands of symbols we use, intentionally and unintentionally—are perceived and translated according to our audience's perceptions, shaped by age, gender, culture, intelligence, and the experiences unique to every individual.

Employability Skills

Throughout the process, both sender and receiver construct meaning together. Genuine communication occurs when both parties agree on the meaning and significance of the symbols they are exchanging. (See Figure 2.3.)

Suppose you and your friend Mediha are having a cup of coffee together, and you realize you need help studying for the upcoming economics exam. You decide to ask Mediha. You choose to **encode** your request in words. Words, of course, are not the only symbols we use to convey ideas. Thousands and thousands of other messages are embedded in our nonverbal symbols—our surroundings and our own personal style, for example.

Once you have chosen your words, you must **transmit** your **message** to Mediha via a **channel**. Channels include face-to-face, memos, BlackBerrys, iPods, billboards, telephones, television, and radio, to name just a few.

Mediha must **perceive** the message in order to **receive** it. That is, Mediha must have the physical ability to hear your request. Then she **decodes** your words: she makes meaning from your symbols. Then she interprets the message, chooses a response, and encodes it. Her response is **feedback**. Feedback may be direct and immediate, or indirect and delayed; it also consists of both verbal and nonverbal symbols.

Meanwhile, **noise** influences every part of the process. Noise can be physical or psychological. While you're talking to Mediha, the noise in the cafeteria could drown out your words. Or someone could start talking to Mediha just as you make your request. That noise could distort your message to Mediha just as the noise of lawnmowers in spring could interfere with your classroom concentration.

Psychological noise includes emotional, intellectual, or psychological interference: it could include disliking a speaker, being concerned about something other than the message, having preconceived notions about an issue, or harbouring prejudices about the message or the messenger.

For example, Mediha has already studied diligently for the exam, feels that you have not worked hard enough, and resents you asking for help at this stage; she feels overwhelmed by her part-time job; she is worried about her uncle, who is ill; she herself is not feeling well. In any of these possibilities, psychological noise will influence her decision, and her message back to you.

Channel overload occurs when the channel cannot handle all the messages that are being sent. Two people may be speaking to you simultaneously, or a small business may have only two phone lines so no one else can get through when both lines are in use.

Information overload occurs when more messages are transmitted than the human receiver can handle. Because of technology, information overload seems to be a constant modern complaint. Some receivers process information on a "first come, first served" basis. Some may try to select the most important messages and ignore others. A third way is to depend on abstracts or summaries prepared by other people. None of these ways is completely satisfactory.

At every stage, both Mediha and you can misperceive, misinterpret, choose badly, encode poorly, or choose inappropriate channels. Miscommunication also frequently occurs because every individual makes meaning using **different frames of reference**. We always interpret messages in the light of our perceptions, based on personal experiences, our cultures and subcultures, and the time in which we live.

Successful communication depends on identifying and establishing common ground between you and your audience. Choose information that your audience needs and will find interesting. Encode your message in words and other symbols the audience will understand. Transmit the message along channels that your audience pays attention to.

Correctly identifying your audience and then choosing audience-appropriate symbols (words, gestures, illustrations) guarantee a more accurate meaning transfer. Moreover, choosing audience-appropriate symbols and channels means your message will attract and hold your audience's attention.

Walking coach Lee Scott, president of WOW Company, uses newspaper ads, email newsletters, her company Web site, and word of mouth to attract clients from all over Ontario. WOW's walkers—men and women of all cultures, ages, and incomes—have finished first in charity events around the world.

Cultural FOCUS

Not all cultures communicate the same way. Because culture is an unconscious part of who we are, we are not always able to determine whether miscommunication occurs because of what we said or how we said it. Study other cultures and try to determine the most effective way to communicate; however, try to avoid stereotypes. For example, many professional women in North America prefer to be addressed as *Ms.*, not *Mrs.*, even if they are married. But this is not always the case, so it is best to understand the common standards for a culture and also try to determine individual preferences. This understanding will help you learn to communicate effectively in another culture.

Audience and Business Messages

Consider the PAIBOC questions introduced in Module 1. Five of the six questions relate to audience, because successful communication is always audience-focused. You must know and understand your audience to identify the information that will attract and hold their attention, and motivate them to comply with your message. (See Figure 2.4.)

FIGURE 2.4   **PAIBOC Questions for Analysis**

P What are your **purposes** in communicating?

Your purposes come from you and your organization. Your audience determines how you achieve those purposes.

A Who is your **audience**? What audience characteristics are relevant to this particular message?

These questions ask directly about your audience.

I What **information** must your message include?

The information you need to give depends on your audience. You need to add relevant facts when the topic is new to your audience. If your audience has heard something but may have forgotten it, protect readers' egos by saying "As you know," or putting the information in a subordinate clause: "Because we had delivery problems last quarter, …" If your audience is familiar with specific facts, concentrate more on clarifying new information.

B What reasons or reader **benefits** can you use to support your position?

Regardless of your own needs, a good reason or benefit depends on your audience's perception. For some audiences, personal experience counts as a good reason. Other audiences are persuaded more by scientific studies or by experts. For some people, saving money is a good benefit of growing vegetables. Other people may care more about avoiding chemicals, growing varieties that aren't available in grocery stores, or working outside in the fresh air than about costs or convenience.

Module 8 gives more information on developing reader benefits.

O What **objections** can you expect your readers to have? What elements of your message will your audience perceive as negative? How can you arrange the message to overcome audience objections or deemphasize negative elements?

Different audiences have different attitudes. Conventional wisdom holds that GenXers (people born in the 1960s) care much more about work–life balance than they do about company loyalty; supposedly GenYs (children of Boomers—the Echo, or Millennium generation) take for granted their entitlement to company perks and benefits. In an audience made up of Boomers, GenXers, and GenYs, you might find a number of different objections to a new policy mandating increased pension payments.

Module 13 on persuasion gives more information on overcoming objections.

C How will the **context** affect reader response? Consider your relationship to the reader, the reader's values and expectations, recent organizational history and current morale, the economy, the time of year, the place and time of day, and any special circumstances surrounding the message exchange.

People, information, and organizations exist in a context. How well your audience knows you, how they feel about you and your organization, how well the economy is doing, even what's been in the news recently: all influence audience response to your message.

What Do I Need to Know About My Audience?

You need to know everything that's relevant to what you're writing or talking about.

Almost everything about your audience is relevant to some message, but for any particular message, only a few facts about your audience will be relevant. These facts will vary depending on each communication situation (see Table 2.1).

TABLE 2.1   **Identifying Key Audience Characteristics for Messages**

Message or Purpose	Audience	Relevant factors
Memo announcing that the company will reimburse employees for tuition if they take work-related college or university courses	All employees	1. Attitudes toward formal education (some people find courses enjoyable; others might be intimidated) 2. Time available (some might be too busy) 3. Interest in being promoted or in receiving cross-training 4. Attitude toward company (those committed to its success will be more interested in the program)
Letter offering special financing on a new or used car	Postsecondary students	1. Income 2. Expectations of future income (and ability to repay loan) 3. Interest in having a new car 4. Attitude toward cars offered by that dealership 5. Attitude about environmental concerns 6. Knowledge about fuel efficiency and hybrid cars 7. Knowledge of interest rates 8. Access to other kinds of financing
Municipal pamphlet describing new methods of waste sorting and collecting	Municipal homeowners	1. Education 2. Attitudes about home ownership 3. Awareness of environment 4. Feelings about neighbourhood and community

In general, you need to use empathy and critical-thinking tools. **Empathy** is the ability to put yourself in someone else's shoes, to feel with that person. Empathy requires being audience-centred because the audience is *not* just like you.

Critical thinking involves gathering as much information as you can about someone or something, and then making decisions based on that information. You need to use your research and your knowledge about people and about organizations to predict likely responses.

Analyzing Individuals and Members of Groups

When you write or speak to people in your own organization, and in other organizations you work with, you may be able to analyze your audience as individuals. You may already know your audience; it might be easy to get additional information by talking to members of your audience, talking to people who know your audience, and observing your audience.

In other organizational situations, however, you'll analyze your audience as members of a group: "taxpayers who must be notified that they owe more income tax," "customers living in the northeast end of the city," or "employees with small children."

Since audience analysis is central to the success of your message, you'll need to consider the following pertinent information about your audience:

- Their knowledge about your topic
- Their demographic factors, such as age, gender, education, income, class, marital status, number of children, home ownership, location
- Their personality
- Their attitudes, values, and beliefs
- Their past behaviour

Prior Knowledge
Even people in your own organization won't share all your knowledge. Many salespeople in the automotive industry, for example, don't know the technical language of their service mechanics.

Most of the time, you won't know exactly what your audience knows. Moreover, even if you've told readers before, they might not remember the old information when they read the new message. In any case, avoid mind-numbing details. If, however, you want to remind readers of *relevant facts* tactfully,

- Preface statements with "As you know," "As you may know," "As we've discussed," or a similar phrase.
- Always spell out acronyms the first time you use them: "Employee Stock Ownership Plan (ESOP)."
- Provide brief definitions in the text: "the principal (the money you have invested)."
- Put information readers should know in a subordinate clause: "Because the renovation is behind schedule."

EXPANDING A CRITICAL SKILL

Understanding What Your Organization Wants

Michelle wondered whether her boss disliked her. Everyone else who had joined the organization when she did had been promoted. Her boss never seemed to have anything good to say about her or her work.

Michelle and her boss had a communication problem in common: both had made assumptions about the other, and both had failed to check their perceptions. Michelle was proud of her reports; she thought she was the best writer in the office. But her boss valued punctuality, and Michelle's reports were always late. Michelle didn't realize that, in her boss's eyes, she wasn't doing good work. And the boss hadn't clarified that he wanted work done on the due date.

Every workplace has rules about what "counts," and the best communicators ferret these out fast. These rules make up the corporate culture (Module 3), and your awareness of the organizational culture is essential to work life success.

Even in the same industry, different organizations and different supervisors may care about different things. One boss circles misspelled words and posts the offending message on a bulletin board for everyone to see. Other people are more tolerant of errors. One company values original ideas, while another workplace tells employees just to do what they're told. One supervisor likes technology and always buys the latest hardware and software; another is technophobic and has to be persuaded to get needed upgrades. Private-sector clients value short proposals and reports, preferably in PowerPoint™; many governments prefer longer, more detailed paper documents.

To find out what counts in your organization,

- Ask your boss, "What parts of my job are most important? What's the biggest thing I could do to improve my work?"
- Listen to the stories colleagues tell about people who have succeeded and those who have failed. When you see patterns, check for confirmation: "So his real problem was that he didn't socialize with co-workers?" This gives your colleagues a chance to provide feedback: "Well, it was more than never coming to the company picnic. He didn't really seem to care about the company."
- Observe. See who is praised, and who is promoted.

Demographic Factors   **Demographic characteristics** can be objectively quantified, or measured, and include age, gender, religion, education level, income, location, and so on.

Businesses and governments use a variety of demographic data to forecast people's behaviours, and to design their strategies accordingly. For example, in his *Boom, Bust and Echo* books, University of Toronto economics professor David Foot uses his analysis of Canada's changing population demographics to identify economic and social trends. This audience analysis affects decisions about every part of our lives, from social policy and urban design to store lighting and aisle width.

Foot's forecasts proved accurate. Canada's 2006 census results reflect an increasing number of foreign-born and aging workers: immigrants account for over one-fifth, and people 55 years and older for 15 percent of today's' workers. Many Boomers intend to keep on working, and those who leave paid work will do so for self-employment opportunities.[2]

Sometimes demographic information is irrelevant; sometimes it's important. Does age matter? Almost always, since people's perspectives and priorities change as they grow older. For example, if you were explaining a change in your company's pension plan, you would expect older workers to pay much closer attention than younger workers. And you would need to shape your explanation to appeal to both audiences.

Demographic data has certainly determined the sharp increase in small business startups devoted to personal services. For example, the North American concierge industry—providing services from animal care and housesitting to running errands—thrives because it provides time for busy people. And in the hospitality, real estate, accounting, financial, and personal services industries, businesses that cater to specific populations and ethnic groups flourish.

Business and nonprofit organizations get demographic data by surveying their customers, clients, and donors, by using Statistics Canada data, or by purchasing demographic data from marketing companies. For many messages, simply identifying subsets of your audience is enough. For example, a school board trying to win support for a tax increase knows that not everyone living in the district will have children in school. It isn't necessary to know the exact percentages to realize that successful messages need to contain appeals not only to parents but also to voters who won't directly benefit from the improvements that the tax increase will fund.

Personality
Understanding and adapting to your primary audience's personality can also help make your message more effective.

Personality and learning style assessment instruments can provide you with useful insights into your own and others' behaviours. In his bestsellers *Secrets of Powerful Presentations* and *Leadership from Within*, business consultant Peter Urs Bender says that knowing your audience is key to communication success. Bender describes four personality types, and offers a free online assessment for readers to identify their type.[3] Another popular assessment tool, the Myers-Briggs Type Indicator, uses four dimensions (introvert–extrovert, sensing–intuitive, thinking–feeling, judging–perceiving) to identify personality preferences:[4]

1. **Introvert–extrovert**: The source of one's energy. Introverts get their energy from within; extroverts are energized by interacting with other people.
2. **Sensing–intuitive**: How someone gathers information. Sensing types gather information step by step through their senses. Intuitive types see relationships among ideas.
3. **Thinking–feeling**: How someone makes decisions. Thinking types use objective logic to reach decisions. Feeling types make decisions that "feel right."
4. **Judging–perceiving**: The degree of certainty someone needs. Judging types like organization, and prefer to finish one task before starting another. Perceptive types like possibilities, like to keep their options open, and may interrupt their work on one task to start another.

Table 2.2 suggests how you can use this information to adapt a message to your audience.

You'll be most persuasive if you play to your audience's strengths. Indeed, many of the general principles of business communications reflect the types most common among managers. Putting the main point up front satisfies the needs of judging types, and some 75 percent of managers are judging. Giving logical reasons satisfies the needs of the nearly 80 percent of managers who are thinking types.[5]

Cultural FOCUS

North Americans place value in understanding personality "types." Many companies use tests such as the Myers-Briggs to help decide whether an employee will fit in with the corporate culture. Other tests exist, such as the True Colors personality test.

TABLE 2.2   Using Myers-Briggs Types in Persuasive Messages

If Your Audience Is:	Use This Strategy	For This Reason
An introvert	Write a memo and let the reader think about your proposal before responding.	Introverts prefer to think before they speak. Written documents give them the time they need to think through a proposal carefully.
An extrovert	Try out your idea orally, in an informal setting.	Extroverts like to think on their feet. They are energized by people; they'd rather talk than write.
A sensing type	Present your reasoning step by step. Get all your facts exactly right.	Sensing types usually reach conclusions step by step. They want to know why something is important, but they trust their own experience more than someone else's say-so. They're good at facts and expect others to be, too.
An intuitive type	Present the big picture first. Stress the innovative, creative aspects of your proposal.	Intuitive types like solving problems and being creative. They can be impatient with details.
A thinking type	Use logic, not emotion, to persuade. Show that your proposal is fair, even if some people may be hurt by it.	Thinking types make decisions based on logic and abstract principles. They are often uncomfortable with emotion.
A feeling type	Show that your proposal meets the emotional needs of people as well as the dollars-and-cents needs of the organization.	Feeling types are very aware of other people and their feelings. They are sympathetic and like harmony.
A perceiving type	Show that you've considered all the alternatives. Ask for a decision by a specific date.	Perceiving types want to be sure they've considered all the options. They may postpone making a decision, or finishing a project.
A judging type	Present your request quickly.	Judging types are comfortable making quick decisions. They like to come to closure so they can move on to something else.

Source: Based on Isabel Briggs Myers, "Effects of Each Preference in Work Situations," *Introduction to Type* (Palo Alto, CA: Consulting Psychologists Press, 1962, 1980).

Values and Beliefs   **Psychographic characteristics** are qualitative rather than quantitative and include values, beliefs, goals, and lifestyles. Knowing what your audience finds important allows you to organize information in a way that seems natural to your audience, and to choose appeals that audience members will find persuasive.

Looking at values enables a company to identify customer segments. The Canadian-born Tim Hortons chain introduced a more diverse menu (croissants, muffins, soup, and sandwiches) to attract new fast-food clients and to appeal to its original, increasingly weight-conscious customers. Ranked as Canada's "best-managed brand," on the basis of customer service, Tim Hortons continues to expand in Canada and internationally.[6]

Canadian Tire, another national top brand, also remains competitive in a very crowded market through audience analysis. Although still selling automotive and home repair products and services, Canadian Tire has expanded its lines of gardening, landscaping, lighting, and decorating products in response to Canadians' increasing investment (both emotional and financial) in their homes. And the company catalogue—in print since 1928—is now only online, "an environmentally responsible" move that also appeals to an increasing consumer base.[7]

Marketers also use **geodemographic data** to analyze and appeal to audiences according to where they live and what they buy. Postal-code clusters identify current and potential customers on the basis of two assumptions: (1) people are what they buy and (2) birds of a feather flock together: "Our shopping habits are shaped by environment and our desire to belong."

Analyzing Canadians' shopping habits is a $550 million industry, and technological innovation continues to refine research methods. International marketing firms use "global ethnography" to study the impact of culture on consumerism. And researchers increasingly take advantage of the speed and convenience of the Internet to analyze audiences through online surveys and focus groups.[8]

Past Behaviour   Experts in human behaviour believe that we can analyze and predict people's future actions on the basis of their past behaviours: the more recent the behaviour, the more accurate the prediction. On this premise, employers are using "'behavioural-based' interviews" ("Tell me about a situation in which you ran into conflict. What happened and how did you deal with it?") to assess a candidate's potential.[9] (See Module 27 on interviewing skills.)

Analyzing People in Organizations

Audience reaction is also strongly influenced by the perceptions and expectations of the groups to which they belong. These groups are personal, social, religious, political, and class associations, or **discourse communities**. Their members create the affiliation, the rules, and the norms through accepted verbal and nonverbal symbols (discourse). These groups include family, peers, professional associations, clubs, and the workplace—all communities with which your audience identifies. Members communicate through symbols (language, nonverbals) that may or may not be exclusive to their group, but which identify them as members of that group. For example, a sport's team member's uniform symbolizes association, and the team's name reflects the culture and values members hold.

Employability Skills

Checkpoint

A discourse community is a group of people who share assumptions about what channels, formats, and styles to use, what topics to discuss and how to discuss them, and what constitutes evidence.

To get a better idea of what helps create a discourse community or corperate culture, see Exercise 2.12 on page 41.

Discourse communities create meaning and connection through verbal and nonverbal symbols, including uniforms, safety wear, food choices, use of space, observances of religion, time, and levels of courtesy and formality.

Therefore, a discourse community is a group of people who share assumptions about their particular culture and values: what to wear; how to behave; what topics to discuss and how to discuss them; what channels; formats, and styles to use; and what constitutes evidence. Each person is part of several discourse communities, which may or may not overlap.

For example, the Internet hosts thousand and thousands of discourse communities, where the audience might, potentially, be the whole world. Social websites such as BallHype, Facebook, Twitter, LinkedIn, IndianPad, and Free IQ are their own discourse communities with their own set of rules; each reflects the values, norms, and expectations of its users. On Twitter, for example, you may use only 140 characters per message. This limitation defines the kind of discourse, conversation, or meaning members can exchange. And violating the conventions can get you plenty of negative feedback.

Consider your discourse communities: perhaps you wear jeans to signify your membership in the student community; your hairstyle or piercing indicates your membership in a subculture; your iPod holds music that reflects your affiliation to another group. When you go for a job interview, you might cut your hair and put on more formal clothes to reflect the norms of the organization's discourse community that you want to join.

When analyzing an organization's discourse community, consider both nonverbal and verbal clues:

In response to the expectations of established discourse communities, some people create their own. University of Manitoba student Jesse Hamonic did not appreciate the red tape he had to fill out as a requirement of volunteering for a local charity. So he started his own charities. Student Harvest relies on university students across Canada for donations and volunteer work. Hamonic has started two other not-for-profits dependent on student volunteers, and is in the process of establishing his fourth charity organization, one that will use high school volunteers.

- What does the physical environment say about who and what are valued? What departments and services are front and centre? Where is the reception area located? What messages do the decor and furnishings send? How are visitors welcomed? Is the company mission statement prominent? What does the office space layout indicate about the organization's values? Where are the library, training rooms, gymnasium, and cafeteria located? How well are they resourced?
- Where do the managers work? Do bosses dress differently from other employees?
- How are employees treated? How are new hires oriented? How is employee performance recognized? What's featured in the company newsletter? How do people in the organization get important information?
- How do people in the organization communicate? What channels, formats, and styles are preferred for communication? Do they write a paper memo, send an email, or walk down the hall to talk to someone? How formal or informal are people expected to be—in their dress, on the telephone, in meetings?
- What do people talk about? What is not discussed?
- What kind of and how much evidence is needed to be convincing? Is personal evidence convincing? Do people need to supply statistics and formal research to be convincing?

An organization's **culture** is expressed through its values, attitudes, and philosophies. Once established, **organizational** or **corporate** culture can shape members' attitudes and behaviours, and become very difficult to change. Organizational or corporate culture reveals itself verbally in the organization's myths, stories, and heroes, and nonverbally in the allocation of space, money, and power (Module 3).

Checkpoint

An organization's **culture** is its values, attitudes, and philosophies. **Organizational culture** (or *corporate culture*, as it is also called) is revealed verbally in the organization's myths, stories, and heroes, and nonverbally in the allocation of space, money, and power.

The following questions will help you analyze an organization's culture:

- What are the organization's goals? making money? serving customers and clients? advancing knowledge? contributing to the community?
- What does the organization value? diversity or homogeneity? independence or being a team player? creativity or following orders?
- How do people get ahead? Are rewards based on seniority, education, being well liked, making technical discoveries, or serving customers? Are rewards available to only a few top people, or is everyone expected to succeed?
- How formal are behaviour, language, and dress?
- What behavioural expectations predominate? How do employees treat one another? Do employees speak in "I," "we," or "them and us" language? How do employees get organizational information?

Two companies in the same business may express very different cultures. Their company Web sites can offer some clues about what those cultures value, and how they want to project their brand. Royal Bank's standing as Canada's oldest bank is reflected in its corporate Web site colours: conservative dark blue and gold. TD Canada Trust's green and white site—implying a fresh approach—offers photos of young, happy people, apparently delighted by the products and services the bank provides.[10]

Many companies describe their cultures as part of the section on employment. Job candidates who research the corporate culture to identify how their skills match with the company have a significant advantage in an interview. (See Module 27.) Researcher Jennifer Chatman found that new hires who "fit" a company's culture were more likely to stay with the job, be more productive, and be more satisfied than those who did not fit the culture.[11]

Organizations also contain several subcultures. For example, manufacturing and marketing may represent different subcultures in the same organization: workers may dress differently and espouse different values. In a union environment, management and union representatives traditionally employ adversarial language to advance their own subculture's perspective while undermining the other's point of view.

You can learn about organizational culture by paying attention to communication clues and cues. In particular, read the organizational publications (newsletters and blogs), observe people, and listen to their stories. Every discourse community and every culture creates and perpetuates meaning and membership through the stories their members share.

The Sleeman Breweries story, for example, is that the quality of its beer is the result of family recipes handed down through five generations—even though that family no longer owns the company. And McCain Foods continues to present itself as a "family business" culture, despite its founding brothers' feuding, its 20 000 employees, and its multinational, global presence. Meanwhile, Google's cultural story boasts of a "fun and inspiring workspace" where free meals "healthy, yummy, and made with love," casual dress, "shoreline running trails ... and plenty of snacks ... get you through the day."[12]

Your awareness of an organization's spoken and unspoken messages can provide you with important information on its values and norms.

How Do I Use Audience Analysis to Reach My Audience?

Use it to plan strategy, organization, style, document design, and visuals.

Take the time to analyze your audience; then adapt your strategy, style, and organizational pattern to your audience's needs. For paper or electronic documents, you can also adapt the document's design and the photos or illustrations you choose. Always revise your message with your audience in mind.

Employability Skills

Strategy

- Choose appeals and reader benefits that work for the specific audience (Module 8).
- Use details and language that reflect your knowledge of, and respect for the specific audience, the organizational culture, and the discourse community.
- Make it easy for the audience to respond positively.
- Include only necessary information.
- Anticipate and overcome objections (Modules 7, 10, and 12 show you how to emphasize positive aspects, decide how much information to include, and overcome obstacles).

Organization

- Analyze your audience's reaction to the meaning of the message. When your message is positive, you can make your point right away. However, many business messages cause negative reader reaction: messages demanding payment, attempting to sell a product or service, or informing readers of a rate increase or of changes that may inconvenience them. When you must persuade a reluctant reader, and when your audience would see the message negatively, organize the message to break the news gradually (Modules 11 to 13).
- Anticipate and meet the audience's expectations of format: make the organizational pattern clear to the audience. (Modules 9, 20, 21, and 22 show you how to use headings and overviews. Module 17 shows how to use overviews and signposts in oral presentations.)

Style

Many North Americans value "saving" time, and boast of multitasking, and of their busyness. Because we've been trained by technology, we expect immediate gratification. Therefore, most business audiences today expect messages that are short and clear.

Language FOCUS

Multitasking means working on many tasks at the same time. For example, a manager might be overseeing two or three projects, completing a report for a project, and planning an upcoming meeting all at the same time. How often do you study, use the Internet, and listen to music all at once? This is considered multitasking as well.

- Strive for clarity and accessibility: use simple words, a mixture of sentence lengths (average today: 14 words), and short paragraphs with topic sentences (refer to the Revising and Editing Resources at the end of this book).
- Use natural, conversational, personable, tactful language: avoid negative, defensive, arrogant, and "red-flag" words—*unfortunately, fundamentalist, liberal, crazy, incompetent, dishonest*—that may generate a negative reaction.

- Use the language that appeals to your audience. In parts of Canada, including Quebec and some areas of Manitoba and New Brunswick, bilingual messages in English and in French, with French first, are the norm.
- Use natural, conversational language.

Document Design

- Telegraph: use headings, bulleted lists, and a mix of paragraph lengths to create white space.
- Choose the format, footnotes, and visuals expected by the organizational culture or the discourse community. (Module 5 discusses effective document design.)

Photographs and Visuals

- Carefully consider the difference between cartoons and photos of "high art." Photos and visuals can make a document look more informal or more formal.
- Use bias-free photographs. Unintentional cultural, gender, religious, and economic assumptions can offend readers and cost you business.
- Choose photographs and illustrations that project positive cultural meanings for your audience. Middle-Eastern readers, for example, find pictures of barelegged and bare-armed women offensive and may also object to pictures of clean-shaven men.
- Do your research and audience analysis: some cultures (e.g., France and Japan) use evocative photographs that bear little direct relationship to the text. North American audiences expect photos to relate to the text.

What If My Audiences Have Different Needs?

Focus on gatekeepers and decision makers.

When the members of your audience share the same interests and the same level of knowledge, you can use these principles for individual readers or for members of homogenous groups. But sometimes, different members of the audience have different needs.

When you are writing or speaking to pluralistic audiences, meet the needs of gatekeepers and primary audiences first.

Content and Choice of Details

- Always provide an overview—the introductory paragraph or topic sentence—for reader orientation.
- In the body of the document, provide enough evidence to prove your point.

Best Buy and Future Shop have the same parent company and offer similar products. Their customer demographic, however, differs. Future Shop is designed to attract the more upscale customer.

Organization

- Organize your message based on the primary audience's attitudes toward it: give good news up front; provide the explanation before you deliver the bad news. (See Modules 11 to 13.)
- Organize documents to make reading easy: provide a table of contents for documents more than five pages long so that your readers can turn to the portions that interest them.
- Use headings as signposts: use headings to tell readers what they're about to read and to connect ideas throughout your document. This strategy reinforces your credibility through unity and coherence. If the primary audience doesn't need details that other audiences will want, provide those details in attachments or appendices.

Level of Language

- Contemporary business communication uses conversational, semiformal language. Use *I* and *you*, and address your reader by name. Do research, however, to discover if your reader prefers a title: *Mr., Mrs., Ms.* (unmarried or not, some women like this title), *Dr.*
- When both internal and external audiences will read the document, use a slightly more formal style and the third person; avoid *I*.
- Use a more formal style when you write to international audiences.

Technical Terms and Theory

- Know what your reader knows; then provide only the necessary information. Use technical terms only if these will increase reader comprehension (refer to the Revising and Editing Resources at the end of this book).
- Put background information and theory under separate headings. Readers can use the headings to read or skip these sections, as their knowledge dictates.
- If primary audiences will have more knowledge than other audiences, provide a glossary of terms. Early in the document, let readers know that the glossary exists.

How Do I Reach My Audience?

Effective messages make use of multiple channels.

Communication channels include verbal and nonverbal symbols (in-person, electronic, speaking, gesturing, writing, colour, use of space and time). These vary in

- Transmission speed
- Transmission accuracy
- Cost
- Efficiency
- The number of people reached
- Audience impact
- Positive influence

Your purpose, the audience, and the situation—known as the *communication context*—determine which and how many channels you choose (refer to the PAIBOC questions on page 26). However, given the potential for miscommunication, the more channels you use, the better.

The Advantages of Writing

A written message is primarily for the record. Writing makes it easier to do several things:

- Present many specific details of a law, policy, or procedure
- Present extensive or complex financial data
- Minimize undesirable emotions

The Disadvantages of Writing

Writing, however, often requires more time than speaking face to face. Furthermore, once you mail the letter, or hit "Send," your documents, including your email messages, are permanent and potentially available to everyone.

When you do decide to write, use the channel that best meets the expectations and needs of your audience. Text messaging may work for family and friends. Email messages are appropriate for routine business messages to people you already know. Paper is usually better for someone to whom you're writing for the first time.

The Advantages of Oral Communication

Speaking is easier and more efficient when you need to do any of the following:

- Answer questions, resolve conflicts, and build consensus
- Use emotion to help persuade the audience
- Provoke an immediate action or response
- Focus the audience's attention on specific points
- Modify a proposal that may not be acceptable in its original form

Scheduled meetings and oral presentations are more formal than phone calls or stopping someone in the hall. Important messages should use more formal channels, whether they're oral or written.

The Disadvantages of Oral Communication

However, meaning and morale can be jeopardized when people choose efficiency and formality over real communication. For example, some organizations regularly use "town hall meetings"—large-auditorium gatherings—to tell employees about new strategies, policies and procedures, and/or new initiatives. The manager employs only one channel (voice), and even if when the presentation includes slides, the message is often all one-way: top-down. In this "command and control" corporate culture, employees often feel too intimidated or too disaffected to provide feedback. True communication does not occur.

Use Multiple Channels

When ending and receiving both oral and written messages, you maximize success when you

1. Adapt the message to the specific audience
2. Show the audience members how they benefit from the idea, policy, service, or product (Module 8)
3. Anticipate and overcome any objections the audience may have
4. Adopt a good attitude and use positive emphasis (Modules 6 and 7)
5. Use visuals to clarify or emphasize material (Module 23)
6. Specify exactly what the audience should do

Even when everyone in an organization has access to the same channels, different discourse communities often prefer different channels. When a university updated its employee benefits manual, the computer scientists and librarians wanted the information online. Faculty wanted to be able to read the information on paper. Maintenance workers and carpenters wanted to get answers on voicemail.[13]

The bigger your audience, the more complicated channel choice becomes, because few channels reach everyone. When possible, use multiple channels. Always use multiple channels for very important messages. For example, talk to key players about a written document before the meeting where the document will be discussed. Or, in the case of town hall meetings, make sure everyone has a chance to preview the announcements (via email and bulletin boards), and generate feedback through focus groups or team meetings.

MODULE SUMMARY

- Communication is the transfer of meaning: both sender and receiver, using multiple symbols, reach agreement on the meaning intended.

- The communication process includes a **sender**, **receiver**, **message**, **channel(s)**, and **noise**. True communication is transactional: both parties provide **feedback** for meaning clarification. Noise is ever-present; any physical, emotional, or psychological interference interferes with meaning exchange.

- Audience focus is the key to communication success. Empathy and critical thinking are crucial to valid audience analysis. Analyzing your audience's needs and expectations lets you shape messages accordingly, with positive results.

- Business messages may include five audiences: the **initial audience** first receives the message, or tells you to send the message; the decision maker, or **primary audience**, makes the decision or acts on the basis of your message; the **secondary audience** may comment on your message, or implement your ideas after they've been approved; the **gatekeeper** manages your message flow—this person has the power to stop your message before it reaches the primary audience; the **watchdog**

- **audience** has the political, social, or economic power to evaluate your message.

- You need to know everything about your audience that's relevant to your purposes for communicating. Use demographic factors, personality characteristics, values and beliefs, past behaviours, and your own observations and experiences to analyze your audience.

- Audience reaction is also strongly influenced by the perceptions and expectations of the groups to which they belong. These groups, or **discourse communities**, create group norms through verbal and nonverbal symbols. Each of us belongs to a number of very different discourse communities (family, religious affiliation, Facebook, varsity team).

- When you want to understand people in organizations, you need to observe the organizational, or **corporate culture**. People create their corporate culture—values, attitudes and philosophies—and express these through discourse—their stories and behaviours.

- Channel choice is shaped by the organizational culture. However, effective messages use multiple channels, and encourage feedback.

ASSIGNMENTS FOR MODULE 2

Questions for Critical Thinking

2.1 What are your options if your boss's criteria for a document are different from those of the primary audience?

2.2 Emphasizing the importance of audience, salespeople often say, "The customer is king," or "The customer is always right," or "The customer is

in control." To what extent do you feel in control as a customer, a citizen, or a student? What could you do to increase your feelings of control?

2.3 If you are employed, which aspects of your organization's culture match your own values? Describe the culture you would most like to work in.

Exercises and Problems

2.4   Identifying Audiences

In each of the following situations, label the audiences as initial, gatekeeper, primary, secondary, or watchdog.

1. Cheechoo is seeking venture capital so that he can expand his business of offering soccer camps to youngsters. He's met an investment banker whose clients regularly hear presentations from businesspeople seeking capital. The investment banker decides who will get a slot on the program, on the basis of a comprehensive audit of each company's records and business plan.

2. Maria is marketing auto loans. She knows that many car buyers choose one of the financing options presented by the car dealership, so she wants to persuade dealers to include her financial institution in the options they offer.

3. Paul works for the mayor's office in a big city. As part of a citywide cost-cutting measure, a panel has recommended requiring employees who work more than 40 hours in a week to take compensatory time off rather than be paid overtime. The only exceptions will be the police and fire departments. The mayor asks Paul to prepare a proposal for the city council, which will vote on whether to implement the change. Before they vote, council members will hear from (1) citizens, who will have an opportunity to read the proposal and communicate their opinions to the city council; (2) mayors' offices in other cities, who may be asked about their experiences; (3) union representatives, who may be concerned about the reduction in income that will result if the proposal is implemented; (4) department heads, whose ability to schedule work might be limited if the proposal passes; and (5) panel members and government lobbying groups. Council members come up for reelection in six months.

2.5 Choosing a Channel to Reach a Specific Audience

Suppose that your business, government agency, or non-profit group has a product, service, or program targeted for each of the following audiences. What would be the best channel(s) to reach people in that group in your city? Would that channel reach all group members?

1. Renters
2. Small business owners
3. People who use wheelchairs
4. Teenagers who work part-time while attending school
5. Competitive athletes
6. Parents whose children play soccer
7. People willing to work part-time
8. Financial planners
9. Hunters
10. New immigrants

2.6 Introducing a Wellness Program

Assume your organization has decided to implement a wellness program that will give modest rebates to employees who adopt healthful practices (see Module 11, Problem 11.11). As director of human resources, you explain the program and build support for it. Pick a specific organization that you know something about and answer the following questions about it.

1. What percentage of employees currently (a) smoke? (b) drink heavily? (c) are overweight? (d) don't exercise? (e) have high blood pressure? (f) have high cholesterol?
2. Why don't people already follow healthful lifestyles?

3. Do company vending machines, cafeteria, or other facilities make it easy for employees to get low-fat snacks and meals?
4. How much exercise do people get on the job? What work-related injuries are most common?
5. What exactly do people do on the job? Will being healthier help them work more efficiently? deal better with stress? have more confidence interacting with clients and customers?
6. What aspects of health and fitness would employees like to know more about? What topics might seem boring or stale?

2.7 Persuading Your Organization to Adopt Flextime

Flextime is a system that allows employees to set their own starting and stopping times. It is especially appealing to organizations that have a hard time keeping good employees or cannot easily raise salaries, and companies with the philosophy of giving workers as much independence as possible. Most employees prefer flextime. However, in some organizations, the system creates conflict between workers who get the schedules they want and those who have to work traditional hours to cover the phones. Some firms are afraid that the quality of work may suffer if employees and supervisors aren't on the job at the same time. Record keeping may be more complicated.

Identify the major argument that you could use to persuade each of the following organizations to use flextime and the major objection you anticipate. Which of the organizations would be fairly easy to convince? Which would be harder to persuade?

1. A large, successful insurance company
2. A branch bank
3. A small catering service
4. The admissions office on your campus
5. A church, synagogue, temple, or mosque with a staff of two clergy, a director of music, two secretaries, and a custodian
6. A government agency
7. The business where you work part-time

2.8 Analyzing the Other Students in Your College or University

Analyze the students in your college or university. (If your college or university is large, analyze the students in your program of study.) Is there a "typical" student?

If all students are quite different, how are they different? Consider the following kinds of information in your analysis:

- Demographic data
- Age (average; high and low)

- Gender (What proportion are men? What proportion are women?)
- Ethnic background (What groups are represented? How many of each?)
- Languages
- Marital status
- Number of children
- Parents' income/personal or family income
- Going to school full- or part-time
- Outside jobs (What kinds? How many hours a week?)
- Membership in campus organizations
- Religious affiliations
- Political preferences
- Proportion going on for further education after graduation
- Psychographics

What values, beliefs, goals, and lifestyles do students have? Which are common? Which are less common?

What's the relationship between the students' values and their choice of major or program?

What do students hope to gain from the classes they're taking? What motivates them to do their best work in class?

Additional Information

What are students' attitudes toward current campus problems? current political problems?

What is the job market like for students in your school or major? Will students find it easy to get jobs after graduation? How much will they be making? Where will they be working?

After you answer these questions, identify the factors that would be most relevant in each of the following situations:

1. You want to persuade students to participate in an internship program.
2. You want to persuade students to join a not-for-profit charity organization.
3. You want to persuade students to adopt "green habits," including carpooling, taking the bus rather than driving, avoiding products that are packaged or sold in plastic or Styrofoam, and eating locally.
4. You want to know whether the campus placement office is providing adequate services to students.
5. You want to hire students to staff a business that you're starting.

2.9   Analyzing People in Your Organization

1. Analyze your supervisor:
   - Does he or she like short or long explanations?
   - Does he or she want to hear about all the problems in a unit or only the major ones?
   - How important are punctuality and deadlines?
   - How well informed about a project does he or she want to be?
   - Is he or she more approachable in the morning or the afternoon?
   - What are your supervisor's major concerns?
2. Analyze other workers in your organization:
   - Is work "just a job" or do most people really care about the organization's goals?
   - How do workers feel about clients or customers?
   - What are your co-workers' major concerns?
3. Analyze your customers or clients:
   - What attitudes do they have toward the organization and its products or services?
   - How is the way they read affected by education, age, or other factors?
   - What are their major concerns?

As your instructor directs,

a. Write a memo to your instructor summarizing your analysis.
b. Discuss your analysis with a small group of students.
c. Present your analysis orally to the class.
d. Combine your information with classmates' information to present a collaborative report comparing and contrasting your audiences at work.

2.10   Analyzing a Discourse Community

Analyze the way one of your discourse communities uses language. Possible groups are

- Family
- Peers
- YouTube, Facebook, or any social media site to which you belong
- Work teams
- Work blogs
- Wikipedia
- Sports teams
- Associations, organizations, and other service or social groups
- Churches, synagogues, temples, and mosques
- Geographic or ethnic group

Questions to ask include the following:

- What specialized terms might not be known to outsiders?
- What topics do members talk or write about? What topics are considered unimportant or improper?
- What channels do members use to convey messages?
- What forms of language do members use to build goodwill? to demonstrate competence or superiority?

- What strategies or kinds of proof are convincing to members?
- What formats, conventions, or rules do members expect messages to follow?

As your instructor directs,

a. Share your results orally with a small group of students.
b. Present your results in an oral presentation to the class.
c. Present your results in a memo to your instructor.
d. Share your results in an email message to the class.
e. Share your results with a small group of students and write a joint memo reporting the similarities and differences you found.

2.11   Analyzing Corporate Culture on the Web

Use three organizations' Web sites and/or blogs to analyze their corporate cultures.

1. What assumptions can you make about the corporate culture, on the basis of your analysis of these media?
2. What inconsistencies do you find?
3. What aspects of each culture do you like best? What, if anything, do you not like? What questions do you have about the organizations' culture that the Web pages or blogs don't answer?

As your instructor directs,

a. Share your results orally with a small group of students.
b. Present your results in an oral presentation to the class.
c. Present your results in a memo to your instructor.
d. Share your results in an email message to the class.
e. Share your results with a small group of students and write a joint memo reporting the similarities and differences you found.

2.12   Analyzing an Organization's Culture

Interview several people about the culture of their organization. (This exercise provides a great opportunity to get known in a company where you would like to work. See Module 24.)

Possible organizations are

- Work teams
- Sports teams
- Associations, organizations, and other service or social groups
- Churches, synagogues, temples, and mosques
- Geographic or ethnic groups
- Groups of friends

Questions to ask include those in this module and the following:

1. Tell me about someone in this organization you admire. Why is he or she successful?
2. Tell me about someone who failed in this organization. What did he or she do wrong?
3. What ceremonies and rituals does this organization have? Why are they important?
4. Why would someone join this group rather than joining a competitor?

As your instructor directs,

a. Share your results orally with a small group of students.
b. Present your results in an oral presentation to the class.
c. Present your results in a memo to your instructor.
d. Share your results in an email message to the class.
e. Share your results with a small group of students and write a joint memo reporting the similarities and differences you found.

POLISHING YOUR PROSE

Comma Splices

In filmmaking, editors splice, or connect, two segments of film to create one segment. A *comma splice* occurs when writers try to create one sentence by connecting two sentences, or independent clauses, with only a comma.

Incorrect: We shipped the order on Tuesday, it arrived on Wednesday.

Comma splices are almost always inappropriate in business communication. (Poetry and fiction sometimes use comma splices to speed up action or simulate dialect; some sales letters and advertisements use comma splices for the same effect, though not always successfully.)

You can fix a comma splice in four ways:

- If the ideas in the sentences are closely related, use a semicolon: We shipped the order on Tuesday; it arrived on Wednesday.
- Add a coordinating conjunction (*and, yet, but, or, for, nor*): We shipped the order on Tuesday, and it arrived on Wednesday.
- Make the incorrect sentence into two correct ones: We shipped the order on Tuesday. It arrived on Wednesday.
- Make one of the clauses subordinate, or dependent on the other for meaning: Since we shipped the order on Tuesday, it arrived on Wednesday.

Exercises

Fix the comma splices in the following sentences.

1. The conference call came at 1 P.M., we took it immediately.
2. We interviewed two people for the accounting position, we made a job offer to one.
3. Janelle drafted her problem-solving report, she sent a copy to each committee member for review.
4. The director of purchasing went to our Main Street warehouse to inspect the inventory, Chum called him later to ask how things had gone.
5. Katy called the hotel in Montreal for a reservation; the desk staff booked a room for her immediately.
6. Mr. Margulies gave an audiovisual presentation at our September sales meeting in Whistler, it went very well.
7. I'll have Tina call the main office, you ask Polsun to set up an appointment for the four of us tomorrow.
8. You know, many countries forbid talking on your cell while driving, Canadian provinces are adopting legislation to do the same, even non-handheld devices are going to be banned.
9. I like to make oral presentations, they're fun.
10. Sunil is our most experienced employee, he joined the department in 2005.

Check your answers to the odd-numbered exercises on page 551.

Communicating Across Cultures

Learning Objectives

After reading and applying the information in Module 3, you'll be able to demonstrate

Knowledge of

- The components of culture
- Workplace diversity
- The importance and variety of nonverbal communication symbols
- Bias-free language

Skills to

- Consider diversity as part of your audience analysis
- Apply your awareness of others' values to your spoken and written messages
- Use bias-free language and photos

Employability Skills 2000+ Checklist

In this module, the key skills from the Conference Board of Canada's Employability Skills 2000+ are

Communicate

○ write and speak so others pay attention and understand

○ listen and ask questions to understand and appreciate the points of view of others

Manage Information

○ access, analyze, and apply knowledge and skills from various disciplines (e.g., the arts, languages, science, technology, mathematics, social sciences, and the humanities)

Think & Solve Problems

○ assess situations and identify problems
○ seek different points of view and evaluate them based on facts

○ recognize the human, interpersonal, technical, scientific, and mathematical dimensions of a problem

Work with Others

○ understand and work within the dynamics of a group
○ be flexible: respect, be open to, and be supportive of the thoughts, opinions, and contributions of others in a group
○ recognize and respect people's diversity, individual differences, and perspectives

○ accept and provide feedback in a constructive and considerate manner
○ contribute to a team by sharing information and expertise

Learn Continuously

○ be willing to continuously learn and grow
○ assess personal strengths and areas for development

○ identify and access learning sources and opportunities

Participate in Projects & Tasks

○ adapt to changing requirements and information

All human beings conform to a culturally determined reality. Our culture shapes the way we "see" reality. Often we are unaware of our cultural biases until we come into contact with people whose cultural assumptions differ from ours. If we come from a culture where cows and pigs are raised to be food, for example, that may seem normal until we meet people whose cultures consider these animals sacred, or unclean, or people who consider raising any animal for consumption to be cruel and barbaric. As another example, North America's body-conscious and food-obsessed culture teaches us contempt for overweight people; however, Western Africans consider being fat praiseworthy.[1]

Regardless of our cultural convictions, our ability to communicate flexibly and sensitively with others is a necessary for our personal and professional success. Multicultural awareness makes sound economic, ethical, and legal sense.

What Is Culture?

Our culture is a learned set of assumptions that shape our perceptions of the world, and of appropriate values, norms, attitudes, and behaviours.

We learn our culture. Perceptions about gender, age, and social class are culturally based, as are our ideas about

- Race
- Ethnicity
- Religious practices
- Sexual orientation
- Physical appearance and ability
- Regional and national characteristics

No culture is monolithic. And cultural diversity is not restricted to ethnicity (Module 2). For example, studies on the effect of gender on language indicate that women "are more sensitive than men to being polite."[2] Indeed, linguistics professor and gender communications expert Deborah Tannen claims that women and men communicate according to very different cultural norms. A study of work team behaviours validates this hypothesis. Professors Jennifer Berdahl, University of Toronto, and Cameron Anderson, University of California, Berkeley, studied the teamwork and leadership behaviours of students enrolled in a course in organizational behaviour. Students were divided into teams. "The researchers found that all the teams [whether] predominantly male or female[,] started off with leadership concentrated in one person." However, the teams made up mostly of women evolved into shared leadership; "those with mostly men continued taking direction from one person." The teams with shared leadership performed better and received higher grades.[3]

Communication difficulties arise because we take our cultural behaviours for granted, and because we assume they are "normal." Culturally sophisticated communicators know better. They know that people's expectations of behaviours vary from culture to culture, and even within cultures.

What Is Canadian Culture?

Canada is a country of diverse cultures.

Our cultural diversity is very much a part of the Canadian identity. Indeed, Canada is becoming the most culturally diverse country in the world, home to more than 200 different ethnic groups,[4] and with a foreign-born population second only to Australia's.[5] Almost a quarter of a million people from all over the world choose to immigrate to Canada every year.

Because two out of three of these immigrants settle in our largest cities, Toronto is "the most ethnically diverse city in the world … home to more than 80 ethnic groups speaking 100 languages.[6] And our diversity is growing. According to Statistics Canada, if Canada's attraction to immigrations continues, by 2017 over 22 percent of Canada's population will be foreign-born, one-fifth of whom (over seven million) will be members of a visible minority. Presently, Chinese and South

Canada is home to a multitude of cultural realities.

Asian immigrants form the two largest of Canada's visible-minority populations. West Asian, Korean, and Arab populations will expand rapidly by 2017.[7]

Besides contributing to our architecture, visual and performing arts, fashion, festivals, festivities and food, health care, literature, medicine, music, science, and much more, immigrants to Canada are essential for business productivity. Without our immigrant population, Canada would not have had the labour force necessary to prosper during the boom times of the late 20th and early 21st centuries: "skilled immigrants who arrived in the past ten years accounted for 70 percent of the growth in Canada's labour force during the same period."[8]

Moreover, as the workforce continues to age (half of North America's Boomers will be 55 or older by 2011), skilled worker shortages will be filled by new Canadians.[9]

Diversity at work also includes Canada's aging population. In 2006, the ratio of potential young workers (15 to 24 years) to potential retirees (55 to 64 years) was about 1.2, half what it was in 1976.[10] According to population projections, by 2013, 55-to-64-year-olds will outnumber 15-to-24-year-olds.[11]

Current research makes much of age-related behavioural differences as a source of potential workplace conflict. In addition to Boomers, GenXers, and GenYs, Echos, or Millennials, the Canadian population apparently now includes Zoomers: "Boomers with Zip! The 14.5 million Canadians 45-plus."[12] "Zip" notwithstanding, supposedly most people over 30 are "immigrants" to the "new, instant satisfaction" Millennial culture (those born between 1979 and 1994). Although they can learn to adapt, people born before 1979 can never be "natives" like the Millennials, who are "a huge generation of impatient, experiential learners, digital natives, multitaskers, and gamers who ... expect nomadic connectivity, 24×7."[13]

Language FOCUS

Boomers (also known as baby boomers) are people born between 1946 and 1964. **GenXers** are those born between 1964 and 1981. **GenYs** are those born between 1981 and 1992; this group is also referred to as the Echos or the Millennials.

24/7 (or 24×7 as above) means 24 hours a day, 7 days a week. This has been expanded in some cases to 24/7/365, which includes 365 days a year, in reference to businesses or services available all the time.

Cultural diversity includes differing generational perspectives and values.

Millennial multitasking includes answering cell phones at a business lunch, in meetings, and even in the middle of a conversation. Regardless of age or culture, many people consider this behaviour blatantly rude. As a result, more and more workplaces and public spaces have rules in place to regulate cell phone use.

However, University of Toronto economics professor David Foot, author of *Boom, Bust and Echo*, claims that "regardless of the generation, age-based tensions have always existed in the workplace." These tensions arise from different perspectives ("older employees tend to forget what they were like as 20-year-olds").[14]

For both financial and psychological reasons, many of these older employees will remain in the workforce long after they turn 65; therefore, you will be working with and for people older than your grandparents. These older people will be an important audience demographic for you (Module 2), as their values (and expectations) continue to shape what is considered appropriate business communications and culture.

Therefore, cultural sensitivity is not only emotionally intelligent (see Expanding a Critical Skill, page 50), but also financially smart: people you work with and for are *not* just like you; being aware of others' norms and values enables you to shape your messages for positive results.

Recognition of and respect for the diverse views of others is also legally responsible behaviour. Legal support for the heterogeneous population in Canadian workplaces is articulated in the *Canadian Charter of Rights and Freedoms* (1982), the *Canadian Human Rights Act* (1985), the *Multiculturalism Act* (1985), the *Official Languages Act* (1988), the *Pay Equity Act* (1990), and the *Employment Equity Act* (1995). "Provinces and territories also have laws, human rights commissions and programs that promote diversity."[15]

Furthermore, the rapidity of change and the economic effects of globalization demand effective intercultural communication. Foreign trade is essential to the growth of both individual businesses and Canada's economy. Although the United States is our primary trading partner, the North American Free Trade Agreement (NAFTA) and the economic interests of countries worldwide, especially those of China and India, are the future for Canadian business.

How Does Culture Affect Business Communication?

Cultural assumptions and expectations determine both the form and the content of every business interaction.

Cultural anthropologist E. T. Hall theorized that people's cultural values and beliefs determine their communication style. Hall characterized these communication behaviours as high context and low context:

- In **high-context cultures**, most of the information is inferred from the context of a message; little is "spelled out." Chinese, Japanese, Arabic, and Latin American cultures might be considered high context.
- In **low-context cultures**, context is less important; most information is explicitly spelled out. German, Scandinavian, and the dominant North American cultures might be considered low context.

As David Victor points out in Table 3.1, high-context and low-context cultures value different kinds of communication and have different attitudes toward oral and written channels.[16] As the table shows, low-context cultures favour direct approaches and perceive indirectness as dishonest or manipulative. The written word is seen as more important than spoken agreements, so contracts are binding but promises may be broken. Details, logic, and time constraints matter. North American communication practices reflect these low-context preferences.

Cultural assumptions and expectations determine both the form and the content of every business interaction.

TABLE 3.1   Views of Communication in High-Context and Low-Context Cultures

	High Context (e.g., Japan, United Arab Emirates)	Low Context (e.g., Germany, Canada, United States)
Preferred communication strategy	Indirectness, politeness, ambiguity	Directness, confrontation, clarity
Reliance on words to communicate	Low	High
Reliance on nonverbal signs to communicate	High	Low
Importance of written word	Low	High
Agreements made in writing	Not binding	Binding
Agreements made orally	Binding	Not binding
Attention to detail	Low	High

Source: Adapted from David A. Victor, *International Business Communication* (New York: HarperCollins, 1992), Table 5.1, p. 148. Reprinted by permission of Addison-Wesley Educational Publishers, Inc.

Culture influences every single aspect of our personal and professional communication: how to dress; how to demonstrate politeness and respect, how much information to give; how to motivate people; when, how much, and how loudly to talk and laugh; how to organize a letter; even what size paper to use.

Communication is also influenced by the organizational culture and by personal culture, such as gender, race and ethnicity, social class, and so forth. As Figure 3.1 suggests, these cultures intersect to determine the communication needed in a given situation. Often one kind of culture assumption dominates another culture assumption. For example, in a study of aerospace engineers in Europe, Asia, and the United States, researchers John Webb and Michael Keene found that the similarities of the professional discourse community (one kind of culture) (Module 2) outweighed differences in national cultures.[17]

Technology also changes cultural assumptions. A Toronto university student faced expulsion for running a Facebook study group that the university said was a threat to academic integrity. The student and members of the study group argued that theirs was no different from any collaborative learning group—which the university encourages—except that the online information exchange made sense for their wired generation. Ultimately, the student was disciplined because the professor had stipulated that students were to work independently.[18] Technological innovation and accessibility will continue to challenge our cultural assumptions about everything, from how we learn to what constitutes private space.

FIGURE 3.1

National Culture, Organizational Culture, and Personal Culture Overlap

Source: Adapted from Farid Elashmawi and Philip R. Harris, *Multicultural Management 2000: Essential Cultural Insights for Global Business Success* (Houston: Gulf, 1998), p. 169.

Values, Beliefs, and Practices

Values and beliefs, often unconscious, affect our response to people and situations. Most Canadians, for example, value "fairness." "You're not playing fair" is a sharp criticism calling for changed behaviour. In some countries, however, people expect certain groups to receive preferential treatment. Most North Americans accept competition and believe that it produces better performance. The Japanese, however, believe that competition leads to disharmony. U.S. businesspeople believe that success is based on individual achievement and is open to anyone who excels. Many Canadians prefer cooperation to blatant competition.

In England and in France, success is more obviously linked to social class. And in some countries, the law prohibits people of some castes or races from participating fully in society.

Many North Americans value individualism. Other countries rely on group consensus for decision making. In Japan, for example, groups routinely work together to solve problems. In the dominant North American culture, quiet is a sign that people are working. In Latin American, Mediterranean, Middle Eastern, and Asian countries, people talk to get the work done.[19] Conversely, the extroverted behaviours rewarded in the classrooms and boardrooms of North America are considered rude and crazy in Japanese culture.

Cultural assumptions also affect people's spiritual, religious, and political beliefs, and these, in turn, shape personal and professional communications.

For example, Christianity coexists with a view of the individual as proactive. In some Muslim and Asian countries, however, it is seen as presumptuous to predict the future by promising action by a certain date. Some Mennonite and Jewish communities live and work in strict adherence to traditional customs. The Puritan work ethic, embraced as a cultural value throughout the northeastern United States regardless of race or religion, legitimizes wealth by seeing it as a sign of divine favour. In other cultures, a simpler lifestyle is considered closer to God.

These differences in values, beliefs, and practices lead to differences in the kinds of appeals that motivate people, as Table 3.2 illustrates.

Cultural FOCUS

Mennonites are a Christian religious group who live mostly in Southern Ontario and Manitoba. Some live without electricity and do not drive cars; you may see some using a horse and buggy for transportation.

The **Puritan work ethic** refers to the belief that hard work and success are important in order to be a good Christian, and that if you are successful it means God is happy with you.

TABLE 3.2   **Cultural Contrasts in Motivation**

	North America	**Japan**	**Arab Countries**
Emotional appeal	Opportunity	Group participation, company success	Religion, nationalism, admiration
Basis of recognition	Individual achievement	Group achievement	Individual status, status of class or society
Material rewards	Salary, bonus, profit sharing	Annual bonus, social services, fringe benefits	Gifts for self or family, salary
Threats	Loss of job	Loss of group membership	Demotion, loss of reputation
Values	Competition, risk taking, freedom	Group harmony, belonging	Reputation, family security, religion

Source: Reproduced by permission. From *Multicultural Management 2000.* © 1998, Gulf Publishing Company, Houston, Texas, 800-231-6275. All rights reserved.

Our cultural assumptions shape our perceptions of the world, and of appropriate values, norms, attitudes, and behaviours.

Nonverbal Communication

Nonverbal communication—communication that makes meaning without words—permeates our lives. Facial expressions, gestures, our use of time and space—even our pauses and vocal intonations—all communicate pleasure or anger, friendliness or distance, power, and status.

Nonverbal communication is older and more powerful than spoken language. And its symbols can be misinterpreted just as easily as can verbal symbols (words). For example, a woman brought a new idea to her boss, who glared at her, brows together in a frown, as she explained her proposal. The stare and lowered brows symbolized anger to her, and she assumed that he was rejecting her idea. Several months later, she learned that her boss always "frowned" when he was concentrating. The facial expression she had interpreted as anger had been intended to convey thinking.

Misunderstandings are even more common in communication across cultures, since nonverbal signals are culturally defined. An Arab student assumed that his North American

EXPANDING A CRITICAL SKILL

Building Emotional Intelligence

In his bestselling book *Emotional Intelligence*, Daniel Goleman claims that we can develop intrapersonal and interpersonal communication skills that can transform our lives. Golman's emotional intelligence (EQ) consists of knowing and managing your emotions, motivating yourself, recognizing the emotions of other people, and managing relationships productively. A strong EQ, audience awareness, and cultural sensitivity are interdependent.

The concept that we can build and apply emotional competencies to better understand and manage our own feelings and relationships has gained considerable currency. Indeed, studies show that having high EQ is a better predictor of personal, academic, and professional success than is having a high IQ. The best managers and top-performing employees all demonstrate a number of high-EQ competencies; many organizations use EQ tests to identify and nurture people with strong emotional competencies, since these people outperform employees with average or low EQ; organizations that train employees in EQ consistently outperform their competitors.

Strengthening your emotional intelligence is vital for survival in our wired world. You must consider carefully before you send: for, as social media expert Joan Vinall-Cox points out, whatever words or visuals you choose to post "are out there forever, for everyone, anywhere," as the "Cisco Fatty" masters student who twittered herself out of a great job opportunity found. And she is far from alone in her indiscretion. Failing to consider your audience (and to check your privacy box) leads to failure, period. Fortunately, plentiful print and electronic resources exist to help you assess and develop your EQ.

Sources: Daniel Goleman, *Emotional Intelligence* (New York: Bantam Books, 1995); Joan Vinall Cox, statement to Kathryn Braun, April 9, 2009; "Richard Boyatzis/Anita Howard Career Success Through Emotional Intelligence: Developing EI Competencies," http://www.careertrainer.com/Request.jsp?l View=ViewArticle&Article=OID%3A112423&Page=OID%3A112933; Cary Chernis, "The Business Case for Emotional Intelligence," http://www.eiconsortium.org/reports/business_case_for_ei.html; Michael E. Rock, "The 90% Factor EQ (Emotional Intelligence) and the NewWorkplace," http://www.canadaone.com/magazine/eq050198.html; "Emotional Intelligence May Be Good Predictor of Success in Computing Studies," *Science Daily*, October 5, 2005, http://www.sciencedaily.com/releases/2005/10/051005072152.htm.

roommate disliked him intensely because the roommate sat around the room with his feet up on the furniture, soles toward the Arab roommate. Arab culture sees the foot in general and the sole in particular as unclean; showing the sole of the foot is an insult.[20]

As is true of every communication situation, knowledge is power: learning about nonverbal symbols gives you the information you need to project the image you want, and makes you more conscious of the signals you are interpreting. Since experts claim that up to 93 percent of all our communication is based on nonverbal symbols, your awareness and correct interpretation of nonverbal communication is vital to your personal and professional development. Remember, however, that nonverbal communication is also culturally learned. Always check your perceptions before making assumptions about others' nonverbal signals.

Body Language

Posture and **body language** show self-concept, energy, and openness. North American **open body positions** include leaning forward with uncrossed arms and legs, with the arms away from the body. **Closed or defensive body positions** include leaning back, arms and legs crossed or close together, or hands in pockets. As the labels imply, "open" positions suggest that people are accepting and open to new ideas. "Closed" positions suggest that people are physically or psychologically uncomfortable, that they are defending themselves and shutting other people out.

People who cross their arms or legs claim that they do so only because the position is more comfortable. Certainly crossing one's legs is one way to be more comfortable in a chair that is the wrong height. Canadian women used to be taught to adopt a "ladylike" posture: arms close to their bodies and knees and ankles together. But notice your own body the next time you're in a perfectly comfortable discussion with a good friend. You'll probably find that you naturally assume open body positions. The fact that so many people in organizational settings adopt closed positions may indicate that many people feel at least slightly uncomfortable in school and on the job.

People of Eastern cultures value the ability to sit quietly. They may see the North American tendency to fidget and shift as an indication of a lack of mental or spiritual balance. Even Canadian interviewers and audiences usually respond negatively to nervous gestures such as fidgeting with a tie or hair or jewellery, tapping a pencil, or swinging a foot.

Eye Contact
Canadians of European background see eye contact as a sign of honesty. But in many cultures, dropped eyes are a sign of appropriate deference to a superior. Puerto Rican children are taught not to meet the eyes of adults.[21] The Japanese are taught to look at the neck.[22] In Korea, prolonged eye contact is considered rude. The lower-ranking person is expected to look down first.[23] In Muslim countries, women and men are not supposed to make eye contact.

These differences can lead to miscommunication in the multicultural workplace. Supervisors may infer from their eye contact that employees are being disrespectful, when, in fact, the employee is behaving appropriately according to the norms of his or her culture.

Gestures
Canadians sometimes assume that, if language fails, they can depend on gestures to communicate with non-English-speaking people. But Birdwhistell reported that "although we have been searching for 15 years [1950–65], we have found no gesture or body motion which has the same meaning in all societies."[24]

Gestures that mean approval in Canada may have very different meanings in other countries. The "thumbs up" sign that means "good work" or "go ahead" in Canada, the United States, and most of Western Europe is a vulgar insult in Greece. The circle formed with the thumb and first finger that means OK in Canada is obscene in Southern Italy and Brazil, and it can mean "You're worth nothing" in France and Belgium.[25]

Space   Concepts of space are also culturally understood. **Personal space** is the distance people want between themselves and other people in ordinary, non-intimate interchanges. Most North Americans, North Europeans, and Asians want a bigger personal space than do Latin Americans, French, Italians, and Arabs. People who are accustomed to lots of personal space and are forced to accept close contact on a crowded elevator or subway react in predictable and ritualistic ways: they stand stiffly and avoid eye contact with others.

Even within a culture, some people like more personal space than do others. One study found that men took up more personal space than women did. In many cultures, people who are of the same age and sex take less personal space than do mixed-age or mixed-sex groups. Latin Americans stand closer to people of the same sex than North Americans do, but North Americans stand closer to people of the opposite sex.

Touch   Humans crave touch. Babies need to be touched to grow and thrive, and older people are healthier both mentally and physically if they are touched. But some people are more comfortable with touch than others. Some people shake hands in greeting but otherwise don't like to be touched at all, except by family members or lovers. Other people, having grown up in families that touch a lot, hug as part of a greeting and touch even casual friends. Each kind of person may misinterpret the other. A person who dislikes touch may seem unfriendly to someone who's used to touching. A toucher may seem overly familiar to someone who dislikes touch.

In general, North Americans are much more casual about touch than Easterners and Middle-Easterners. Studies indicate that in North American culture, touch can be interpreted as power: more powerful people touch less powerful people. When the toucher has higher status than the recipient, both men and women liked being touched.[26] In Iran and Iraq, handshakes between men and women are seen as improper.[27] Handshakes between men and women are beginning to be accepted in India's larger cities because of their expanding young, urban, middle-class workers.[28]

Most parts of North America allow opposite-sex couples to hold hands or walk arm in arm in public, but frown on the same behaviour in same-sex couples. People in Asia, the Middle East, and South America have the opposite expectation: male friends or female friends can hold hands or walk arm in arm, but it is slightly shocking for an opposite-sex couple to touch in public.

Spatial Arrangements   In North America, the size, placement, and privacy of a person's office indicate status. Large corner offices have the highest status. An individual office with a door that closes suggests more status than a desk in a common area.

People who don't know each other well may feel more comfortable with each other if a piece of furniture separates them. For example, in most Canadian interviews, a desk, which both people perceive as part of the interviewer's space, separates the interviewer and the applicant. It's considered inappropriate for the applicant to place his or her property (notebook, purse) on a desk or to lean on the desk. In some situations, a group might work better sitting around a table than just sitting in a circle. In North America, a person sitting at the head of a table is generally assumed to be the group's leader. However, one experiment showed that when a woman sat at the head of a mixed-sex group, observers assumed that one of the men in the group was the leader.[29]

In low-context cultural settings, the size, placement, and privacy of a person's office connotes status.

Time

Canadian organizations—businesses, government, and schools—keep time by the calendar and the clock. Being "on time" is seen as a sign of dependability. Other cultures may keep time by the seasons and the moon, the sun, internal "body clocks," or a personal feeling that "the time is right."

Canadians who believe "time is money" are often frustrated in negotiations with people who take a much more leisurely approach. Part of the miscommunication stems from a major perception difference: people in many other cultures want to take the time to establish a personal relationship before they decide whether to do business with each other.

Miscommunication occurs because various cultures perceive time differently. Many Canadians measure time in five-minute blocks. Someone five minutes late to an appointment or a job interview feels called upon to apologize. If the executive or interviewer is running half an hour late, the caller expects to be told about the likely delay when he or she arrives. Some people won't be able to wait that long and will need to reschedule their appointments. But in Latin American and other cultures, 15 minutes or half an hour may be the smallest block of time. To someone who mentally measures time in 15-minute blocks, being 45 minutes late is no worse than being 15 minutes late.

Edward T. Hall distinguishes between **monochronic cultures**, where people do only one important activity at a time, and **polychronic cultures**, where people do several things at once.

Canada and the United States are predominantly monochronic cultures. When North American managers feel offended because a Latin American manager also sees other people during "their" appointments, the two kinds of time are in conflict. However, people who eat breakfast while they drive are doing more than one thing at a time. In a few organizations, it is even acceptable to do other work during a meeting. Such "multitasking" may indicate that some North American companies are evolving from a monochronic culture to a somewhat polychronic culture.

According to some scholars, Europeans schedule fewer events in a comparable period than North Americans. Perhaps as a result, Germans and German Swiss see North Americans as too time-conscious.[30]

Other Nonverbal Symbols

Many other symbols—clothing, colours, age, and height, to name a few—carry nonverbal meanings.

In Canada, certain styles and colours of clothing are considered more "professional" and more "credible." Certain cloths and fabrics—silk and linen, for example—carry nonverbal messages of success, prestige, and competence. In Japan, clothing denotes not only status but also occupational group. All students in junior and senior high school wear school uniforms. Company badges indicate rank within the organization. Workers wear different clothes when they are on strike than they do when they are working.[31]

Our clothing choices reflect our cultural assumptions.

Colours can also carry cultural meanings. In Canada, mourners wear black to funerals, while brides wear white at their wedding. In pre-Communist China and in some South American tribes, white is the colour of mourning. Purple flowers are given to the dead in Mexico.[32] In Korea, red ink is used to record deaths but never to write about living people.[33]

North American culture values youth. More and more individuals choose to colour their hair and have surgery to look as youthful as possible. In Japan, younger people defer to older people. North Americans attempting to negotiate in Japan are usually taken more seriously if at least one member of the team is noticeably grey-haired.

Height connotes status in many parts of the world. Executive offices are usually on the top floors; the underlings work below. Even being tall can help a person succeed. Studies have shown that employers are more willing to hire men who are over 1.85 metres tall than shorter men with the same credentials. Studies of real-world executives and graduates have shown that taller men make more money. In one study, every extra inch of height brought in an extra $600 a year.[34] But being too big can be a disadvantage. A tall, brawny football player complained that people found him intimidating off the field and assumed that he "had the brains of a Twinkie."

Language FOCUS

A **Twinkie** is a snack made of cake and frosting. However, when a person refers to another as "having the brain of a Twinkie" it is an insult, because it means the person is stupid.

Oral Communication

Effective oral communication also requires cultural understanding. As Table 3.3 shows, both purpose and content of business introductions differ across cultures.

TABLE 3.3   **Cultural Contrasts in Business Introductions**

	North America	**Japan**	**Arab Countries**
Purpose of introduction	Establish status and job identity; network	Establish position in group; build harmony	Establish personal rapport
Image of individual	Independent	Member of group	Part of rich culture
Information	Related to business	Related to company	Personal
Use of language	Informal, friendly; use first name	Little talking	Formal; expression of admiration
Values	Openness; directness; action	Harmony; respect; listening	Religious harmony; hospitality; emotional support

Source: Adapted from Farid Elashmawi and Philip R. Harris, *Multicultural Management 2000: Essential Cultural Insights for Global Business Success* (Houston: Gulf, 1998), p. 113.

Deborah Tannen uses the term *conversational style* to denote our conversational patterns and the meanings we give to them: the way we show interest, courtesy, social decorum.[35]

Your answers to the following questions reveal your own conversational style:

- How long a pause tells you that it's your turn to speak?
- Do you see interruption as rude? Or do you say things while other people are still talking to show that you're interested and to encourage them to say more?
- Do you show interest by asking lots of questions? Or do you see questions as intrusive and wait for people to volunteer whatever they have to say?

No conversational style is better or worse than any another, but people with different styles may feel uncomfortable without knowing why. A boss who speaks slowly may frustrate a subordinate who talks quickly. People who talk more slowly may feel shut out of a conversation with people who talk more quickly. Someone who has learned to make requests directly ("Please pass the salt") may be annoyed by someone who uses indirect requests ("This casserole needs some salt").

In the workplace, conflicts may arise because of differences in conversational style. GenXers often use a rising inflection on statements as well as questions. They see this style as gentler and more polite. But Boomer bosses may see this speech pattern as hesitant, as if the speaker wants advice—which they then proceed to deliver.[36]

Many middle-aged professionals consider certain speech patterns—"you know," "like," "basically," "right?"—to be eye-rolling irritants. According to University of Toronto sociolinguistics professor Sali Tagliamonte, however, our speech patterns reflect our age, and our cultural values. People under 40 "are much more likely to use 'like' when narrating a story, than those over 40." ("And I'm like, OK, I'm all over that.") Tagliamonte believes the use of "like" is a demographic identifier; migrating from California, it has become a fashionable "way to voice a speaker's inner experience."[37]

Daniel N. Maltz and Ruth A. Borker believe that differences in conversational style might be responsible for the miscommunication that sometimes occurs in male–female conversations. For example, researchers have found that women are much more likely to nod and to say yes or say "mm-hmm" than men are. Maltz and Borker hypothesize that to women, these symbols mean simply, "I'm listening; go on." Men, on the other hand, may decode these symbols as "I agree" or at least "I follow what you're saying so far." A man who receives nods and "mm"s from a woman might feel she is inconsistent and unpredictable if she then disagrees with him. A woman might feel that a man who doesn't provide any feedback isn't listening to her.[38]

To decrease conflict due to differences in conversational style, talk less and listen more (Module 14), and try to mirror the speaker's pace.

Understatement and Exaggeration   Closely related to conversational style is the issue of understatement and overstatement. The British have a reputation for understatement. Someone good enough to play at Wimbledon may say he or she "plays a little tennis." Or ask a Canadian how the meeting yesterday or last night's game went, and the answer will be "Not bad!" even if the event was a roaring success. On the other hand, many people in the United States exaggerate. A U.S. businessman negotiating with a German said, "I know it's impossible, but can we do it?" The German saw the statement as nonsensical: by definition, something that is impossible cannot be done at all. The American saw "impossible" as merely a strong way of saying "difficult," and assumed that with enough resources and commitment, the job could, in fact, be done.[39]

Compliments   The kinds of statements that people interpret as compliments and the socially correct way to respond to compliments also vary among cultures. The statement "You must be really tired" is a compliment in Japan, since it recognizes the other person has worked hard. The correct response is "Thank you, but I'm OK." A Canadian complimented on giving a good oral presentation will probably say, "Thank you." A Chinese or Japanese person, in contrast, will apologize: "No, it wasn't very good."[40]

Statements that seem complimentary in one context may be inappropriate in another. For example, businesswomen may feel uncomfortable if male colleagues or superiors compliment them on their appearance: the comments suggest that the women are being treated as visual decoration rather than contributing workers.

Silence   Silence also has different meanings in different cultures and subcultures. North Americans have difficulty doing business in Japan, because they do not realize that silence almost always means that the Japanese do not like the ideas.

Different understandings of silence can prolong problems with sexual harassment in the workplace. Women sometimes use silence to respond to comments they find offensive, hoping that silence will signal their lack of appreciation. But some men may think that silence means appreciation, or at least neutrality.

Writing to International Audiences

Most cultures are more formal than ours. When you write to international audiences, use titles, not first names. Avoid contractions, slang, and sports metaphors.

The patterns of organization that work for Canadian audiences might not work for international correspondence beyond the United States. As Table 3.4 suggests, you may need to adapt your style, structure, and strategy when writing to international readers. For most cultures, buffer negative messages (Module 12) and make requests (Module 13) more indirect. Make a special effort to avoid phrases your audience might interpret as arrogant or uncaring. Cultural mistakes made orally may float away on the air; those made in writing are permanently recorded.

TABLE 3.4   **Cultural Contrasts in Written Persuasive Documents**

	North America	**Japan**	**Arab Countries**
Opening	Request action or get reader's attention	Offer thanks; apologize	Offer personal greetings
Way to persuade	Immediate gain or loss of opportunity	Waiting	Personal connections; future opportunity
Style	Short sentences	Modesty; minimize own standing	Elaborate expressions; many signatures
Closing	Specific request	Desire to maintain harmony	Future relationship; personal greeting
Values	Efficiency; directness; action	Politeness; indirectness; relationship	Status; continuation

Source: Adapted from Farid Elashmawi and Philip P. Harris, *Multicultural Management 2000: Essential Cultural Insights for Global Business Success* (Houston: Gulf, 1998), p. 139.

Checkpoint

Culture is a learned set of assumptions about the norms and values that we internalize and accept as true. Our culture shapes our perceptions of the world around us and influences our communication styles and content.

With So Many Different Cultures, How Can I Know Enough to Communicate?

Focus on being sensitive and flexible.

The first step in understanding people of another culture is to realize that they may do things very differently and that they value their way as much as you do yours. Moreover, people within a single culture differ. The kinds of differences summarized in this module can turn into stereotypes, which can be just as damaging as ignorance. Don't try to memorize the material here as a rigid set of rules. Instead, use the examples to get a sense for the kinds of things that differ from one culture to another. Test these generalizations against your experience. When in doubt, research and ask.

If you work with people from other cultures, or if you plan to travel to a specific country, read about that country or culture and learn a little of the language. Also, talk to people; that's really the only way to learn whether someone is wearing black as a sign of mourning, as a fashion statement, or as a colour that slenderizes and doesn't show dirt.

As Brenda Arbeláez suggests, the successful international communicator is

- Aware that his or her preferred values and behaviours are influenced by culture and are not necessarily "right"
- Flexible and open to change
- Sensitive to verbal and nonverbal behaviour
- Aware of the values, beliefs, and practices in other cultures
- Sensitive to differences among individuals within a culture[41]

Use the PAIBOC questions shown in Figure 3.2 to prepare to communicate interculturally.

FIGURE 3.2   PAIBOC Questions for Analysis

> P   What are your **purposes** in communicating?
>
> A   Who is your **audience**? What are their values and expectations? How will they react to the content of your message? What form will make your message accessible to your audience? How should you frame your message to your audience's expectations?
>
> I   What **information** will meet the needs of your audience and your purposes?
>
> B   What reasons or audience **benefits** can you use to support your position?
>
> O   What **objections** can you expect from your audience? What negative content must you deemphasize or overcome?
>
> C   What is the **context** of the message, and how will the context affect your audience's response? What is your relationship with your audience? What time of day are you delivering your message? What cultural differences should you be sensitive to? What special circumstances should shape the form and content of your message?

How Can I Make My Documents Bias-Free?

Start by using non-sexist, non-racist, and non-ageist language.

Bias-free language is language that does not discriminate against people on the basis of sex, physical condition, race, age, or any other category. Bias-free language is fair and friendly; it complies with the law. It includes all readers; it helps to sustain goodwill. When you produce newsletters or other documents with photos and illustrations, choose a sampling of the whole population, not just part of it.

Making Language Non-sexist

Non-sexist language treats both sexes neutrally. Check to be sure that your writing is free from sexism in four areas: words and phrases, job titles, pronouns, and courtesy titles. Courtesy titles are discussed in Module 9 on format. Words and phrases, job titles, and pronouns are discussed in this module.

Words and Phrases
If you find any of the terms in the first column in Table 3.5 in your writing or your company's documents, replace them with terms from the second column.

TABLE 3.5   Eliminating Sexist Terms and Phrases

Instead Of:	Use:	For This Reason
The girl at the front desk	The woman's name or job title: Ms. Browning, Rosa, the receptionist	Call female employees women just as you call male employees men. When you talk about a specific woman, use her name, just as you use a man's name to talk about a specific man.
The ladies on our staff	The women on our staff	Use parallel terms for males and females. Therefore, use "ladies" only if you refer to the males on your staff as "gentlemen." Few businesses do, since social distinctions are rarely at issue.
Manpower Man-hours Manning	Personnel Hours or worker hours Staffing	The power in business today comes from both women and men. Use non-sexist alternatives.
Managers and their wives	Managers and their guests	Managers may be female; not everyone is married.
Businessman	A specific title: executive, accountant, department head, owner of a small business, men and women in business, businessperson	Gender-neutral title.
Chairman	Chair, chairperson, moderator	Gender-neutral title.
Foreman	Supervisor	Gender-neutral title.
Salesman	Salesperson, sales representative	Gender-neutral title.
Waitress	Server	Gender-neutral title.
Woman lawyer	Lawyer	Gender-neutral title. You would not describe a man as a "male lawyer."
Workman	Worker, employee, or use a specific title: crane operator, bricklayer	Gender-neutral title.

Not every word containing *man* is sexist. For example, *manager* is not sexist. The word comes from the Latin *manus*, meaning *hand*; it has nothing to do with maleness.

Avoid terms that assume everyone is married or is heterosexual.

Biased: You and your husband or wife are cordially invited to the dinner.

Better: You and your guest are cordially invited to the dinner.

Job Titles   Use neutral titles that imply that a person of either gender could hold the job. Many job titles are already neutral: *accountant, banker, doctor, engineer, inspector, manager, nurse, pilot, secretary, technician,* to name a few. Other titles reflect gender stereotypes and need to be changed. (See Table 3.5 for examples.)

Pronouns   When you write about a specific person, use appropriate-gender pronouns:

In his speech, John Jones said that …

In her speech, Judy Jones said that …

When you are not writing about a specific person, but about anyone who may be in a given job or position, avoid using traditional-gender pronouns.

Sexist:	a. Each supervisor must certify that the time sheet for his department is correct.
Sexist:	b. When the nurse fills out the accident report form, she should send one copy to the Central Division Office.

Business writing uses four ways to eliminate sexist generic pronouns: use plurals, use second person (*you*), revise the sentence to omit the pronoun, and use pronoun pairs. Whenever you have a choice of two or more ways to make a phrase or sentence non-sexist, choose the alternative that is smoothest and least conspicuous.

The following examples use these methods to revise sentences (a) and (b) above.

1. Use plural nouns and pronouns.

Non-sexist:	a. Supervisors must certify that the time sheets for their departments are correct.

Note: When you use plural nouns and pronouns, other words in the sentence may need to be made plural too. In the example above, plural supervisors have plural time sheets and departments.

Avoid mixing singular nouns and plural pronouns.

Non-sexist, but lacks agreement:	a. Each supervisor must certify that the time sheet for their department is correct.

Since *supervisor* is singular, it is incorrect to use the plural *they* to refer to it. The resulting lack of agreement is acceptable orally, but not yet acceptable to many readers in writing. Instead, use one of the four grammatically correct ways to make the sentence non-sexist.

2. Use *you*.

Non-sexist:	a. You must certify that the time sheet for your department is correct.
Non-sexist:	b. When you fill out an accident report form, send one copy to the Central Division Office.

You is particularly good for instructions and statements of the responsibilities of someone in a given position. Using *you* frequently shortens sentences, because you write "Send one copy" instead of "You should send one copy." It also makes your writing more direct.

3. Substitute an article (*a, an,* or *the*) for the pronoun, or revise the sentence so that the pronoun is unnecessary.

Non-sexist:	a. The supervisor must certify that the time sheet for the department is correct.

Non-sexist: b. The nurse will

                 1. Fill out the accident report form

                 2. Send one copy of the form to the Central Division Office

4. When you must focus on the action of an individual, use pronoun pairs.

Non-sexist: a. The supervisor must certify that the time sheet for his or her department is correct.

Non-sexist: b. When the nurse fills out the accident report form, he or she should send one copy to the Central Division Office.

Making Language Neutral

Language is as neutral as possible when it treats all races and ages fairly, avoiding negative stereotypes of any group. Use these guidelines to check for bias in documents you write or edit:

- *Avoid terms that assume everyone is married or is heterosexual.*

  Biased: You and your husband or wife are cordially invited to the dinner.

  Better: You and your guest are cordially invited to the dinner.

- *Give someone's race or age only if it is relevant to your story.* When you do mention these characteristics, give them for everyone in your story—not just the non-Caucasian, non-young-to-middle-aged adults you mention.

- *Refer to a group by the term it prefers. As preferences change, change your usage.* Sixty years ago, *Negro* was preferred as a more dignified term than *coloured* for North Americans of African origin. As times changed, *black person* and *African American* replaced it in the United States. In Canada, *black person* is generally preferred to *African Canadian*, which is more often used for recent immigrants from Africa and thus might not include, for example, black Canadians from Caribbean nations, or black Canadians who came to Nova Scotia as Loyalists in the late 18th century.

  Asian is preferred to *Oriental*, which may be considered offensive.

  East Indian is frequently misused to include people of non-Indian origin, such as new Canadians from Pakistan, Sri Lanka, and Bangladesh. *South Asian* is more accurate, and *Pakistani*, *Sri Lankan*, and *Bangladeshi* are preferred.

  Eskimo is a negative label. A better term is *Inuit*, which means *the people*.

  Aboriginal peoples is generally used to refer to Canada's indigenous peoples: First Nations, Inuit, and Métis. But usage will vary according to the preference of the individual or group referred to. For example, most Aboriginal peoples consider *Indian* offensive or at least a source of confusion with people from India. Where possible, consider referring to the specific band or nation of the individual (e.g., Métis, Mohawk, Cree, Haida).

Cultural FOCUS

First Nations has replaced *Indian* in North America, and **Inuit** has replaced *Eskimo*. **Métis** are also Aboriginal people in North America whose First Nations ancestors married Europeans.

Older people and *mature customers* are more generally accepted terms than *senior citizens* or *golden-agers*.

- *Avoid terms that suggest competent people are unusual in a group.* The statement "She is an intelligent Métis woman" suggests that the writer expects most Métis women to be stupid. "He is a credit to his race" suggests that excellence in the "race" is rare. "He is a spry 70-year-old" suggests that the writer is amazed that anyone that old can still move.

Talking About People with Disabilities and Diseases

A disability is a physical, mental, sensory, or emotional impairment that interferes with the major tasks of daily living. In 2006, approximately four-and-a-half "million (one in seven) Canadians ... reported having a disability." The number of people with disabilities will rise as social acceptance of reporting increases, and as the population ages.[42]

- *People-first language* focuses on the person, not the condition. Avoid outdated adjectives used as nouns that imply that the condition defines the person.
- *Avoid negative terms, unless the audience prefers them.* Preference takes precedence over positive emphasis: use the term a group prefers. People who lost their hearing as infants, children, or young adults often prefer to be called *deaf*. But people who lose their hearing as older adults often prefer to be called *hard of hearing*, even when their hearing loss is just as great as someone who identifies as part of deaf culture.

Just as people in a single ethnic group may prefer different labels based on generational or cultural divides, so differences exist within the disability community (see Table 3.6). Using the right term requires keeping up with changing preferences. If your target audience is smaller than the whole group, use the term preferred by that audience, even if the group as a whole prefers another term.

TABLE 3.6 **Eliminating the Use of Terms and Phrases to Define Persons with Disabilities**

Instead Of:	Use:
The mentally retarded	Developmentally delayed people
The blind	People with vision impairments
Cancer patients	People being treated for cancer

Some negative terms, however, are never appropriate. Negative terms such as *afflicted, suffering from, the victim of*, and *struck down by* also suggest an outdated view of illness.

Checkpoint

The successful international communicator is
- Aware that his or her preferred values and behaviours are influenced by culture and are not necessarily "right"
- Flexible and open to change
- Sensitive to verbal and nonverbal behaviour
- Aware of the values, beliefs, and practices in other cultures
- Sensitive to differences among individuals within a culture

Choosing Bias-Free Photos and Illustrations

When you produce a document with photographs or illustrations, check the visuals for possible bias. Do they show people of both sexes and all races? Is there a sprinkling of various kinds of people (younger and older, people using wheelchairs, etc.)? It's acceptable to have individual pictures of just one sex or one race; the photos as a whole do not need to show exactly 50 percent men and 50 percent women. But the general impression should suggest that diversity is welcome and normal.

Check relationships and authority figures as well as numbers. If all the men appear in business suits and the women in maids' uniforms, the pictures are sexist even if an equal number of men and women are pictured. If the only black people and Filipinos pictured are factory workers, the photos support racism even when equal numbers of people from each race are shown.

Don't use biased clip art or stock photos: look for alternatives, or create your own bias-free illustrations.

MODULE SUMMARY

- Culture is a learned set of assumptions that shape our perception of reality. No culture exits wherein all members adhere to one notion of reality, and in urban Canada, cultural diversity is the norm.

- Each of us belongs to a number of cultures, whose expectations are communicated through symbols, including language. Cultural assumptions and expectations shape the form and content of our communication.

- In high-context cultures, most of the meaning is inferred from the context of the message; little is explicitly conveyed. In low-context cultures, most information is explicitly stated.

- No gesture has a universal meaning across cultures, and nonverbal symbols can be misinterpreted as easily as verbal symbols (words).

- North Americans, who believe "time is money," are often frustrated in negotiations with people from

cultures with different values: people who want to establish a personal relationship before they decide whether to do business with each other, or people who measure time in 15- or 30-minute increments rather than the 5-minute intervals North Americans are used to.

- Conversational style denotes our conversational patterns, and the way we display age, interest, politeness, and appropriateness.

- Generational differences may affect perceptions, and lead to conflict in the workplace. Use empathy to try to see other points of view to adapt.

- In today's global marketplace, cultural awareness is vital to communication success. Analyzing your audience allows you to be sensitive to their cultural norms, and flexible about adapting to those norms. The most effective communicator mirrors others in form and content.

ASSIGNMENTS FOR MODULE 3

Questions for Critical Thinking

3.1 Is it sexist to put the male pronoun first in pronoun pairs (e.g., *he or she* rather than *she or he* or *s/he*)? Why do the authors of this book recommend that method as one alternative? Which method do you prefer? Why?

3.2 Suppose you know your audience is sexist, ageist, racist, or otherwise prejudiced. How should you adapt

your message to your audience? What are the ethical implications of your adapting?

3.3 You can't possibly learn what every symbol means in every culture. How can you avoid offending the people you work with?

3.4 What other cultures are you most likely to work with? How might you learn about those cultures?

Exercises and Problems

3.5   Revising Sexist Job Titles

Suggest non-sexist alternatives for each of the following:

cleaning lady	mailman
alderman	night watchman
garbage man	repairman
male nurse	salesman
mail boy	waitress
actress	stewardess

3.6   Eliminating Biased Language

Explain the source of bias in each of the following and revise to remove the bias.

1. We recommend hiring Jim Renker and Elizabeth Shuman. Both were very successful summer interns. Jim drafted the report on using rap music in ads, and Elizabeth really improved the look of the office.
2. All sales associates and their wives are invited to the picnic.
3. Although he is blind, Mr. Morin is an excellent group leader.
4. Unlike many Caribbean Canadians, Yvonne has extensive experience designing Web pages.
5. Chris Gottlieb Pacific Perspectives
   6300 West 12th Avenue
   Vancouver, BC
   Gentlemen:
6. Enrique Torres is very intuitive for a man.
7. Twenty-First-Century Parenting shows you how to persuade your husband to do his share of childcare chores.
8. Mr. Paez, Mr. O'Connor, and Tonya will represent our office at the convention.
9. Sue Corcoran celebrates her 50th birthday today. Stop by her cubicle at noon to get a piece of cake and to help us sing "The Old Grey Mare She Ain't What She Used to Be."
10. Because older customers tend to be really picky, we will need to give a lot of details in our ads.

3.7   Dealing with Discrimination

Despite Canada's reputation for tolerance, courtesy, and fair play, many of its citizens frequently experience discriminatory behaviour. Some believe that prejudice is systemic—that bias against visible minorities, women, people with disabilities, and seniors is built into our legal and judicial systems and demonstrated daily in our assumptions and attitudes.

Media attention has focused on such culturally sensitive issues as racism among members of the police force, and discriminatory hiring and promotion practices in Canadian postsecondary institutions.

Find a specific, relevant news story of cultural bias or discrimination. Or use your own experience to identify a serious miscommunication based on cultural assumptions. Write a summary of the news story or of your experience. Using what you have learned in Modules 1 and 2, write a memo to your classmates and your professor, providing specific ideas about how to deal positively with such a situation.

3.8   Identifying Sources of Miscommunication

In each of the following situations, identify one or more ways in which cultural differences may be leading to miscommunication.

a. Alan is a Canadian sales representative in Mexico. He makes appointments and is careful to be on time. But the person he's calling on is frequently late. To save time, Alan tries to get right to business. But his host wants to talk about sightseeing and his family. Even worse, his appointments are interrupted constantly, not only by business phone calls, but also by long conversations with other people and even the customer's children who come into the office. Alan's first progress report is very negative. He hasn't yet made a sale. Perhaps Mexico just isn't the right place to sell his company's products.

b. To help her company establish a presence in Japan, Susan wants to hire a local interpreter who can advise her on business customs. Kana Tomari has superb qualifications on paper. But when Susan tries to probe about her experience, Kana just says, "I will do my best. I will try very hard." She never gives details about any of the previous positions she's held. Susan begins to wonder whether Kana's résumé is inflated.

c. Stan wants to negotiate a joint venture with a Chinese company. He asks Tung-Sen Lee if the Chinese people have enough discretionary income to afford his product. Mr. Lee is silent for a time, and then says, "Your product is good. People in the West must like it." Stan smiles, pleased that Mr. Lee recognizes the quality of his product, and he gives Mr. Lee a contract to sign. Weeks later, Stan still hasn't heard anything. If China is going to be so inefficient, he wonders if he really should try to do business there.

d. Elspeth is very proud of her participatory management style. On assignment in India, she is careful not to give orders but to ask for suggestions. But people rarely suggest anything. Even a formal suggestion system doesn't work. And to make matters worse, she doesn't sense the respect and camaraderie of the plant she managed in Canada. Perhaps, she decides gloomily, people in India just aren't ready for a female boss.

3.9   Advising a Hasty Subordinate

Three days ago, one of your subordinates forwarded to everyone in the office a bit of email humour he'd received from a friend. The message, titled "You know you're a Newfie when …," poked fun at Newfoundland and Labrador speech, attitudes, and lifestyles. Today you get this message from your subordinate:

> Subject: Should I Apologize?
>
> I'm getting flamed left and right because of the New-foundland message. I thought it was funny, but some people just can't take a joke. So far I've tried not to re-spond to the flames, figuring that would just make things worse. But now I'm wondering if I should apologize. What do you think?

Answer the message.

3.10   Responding to a Complaint

You're the director of corporate communications; your office produces the employee newsletter. Today you get this email message from Caroline Huber:

> Subject: Complaint about Sexist Language
>
> The article about the "Help Desk" says that Martina Luna and I "are the key customer service representatives 'man-ning' the desk." I don't MAN anything! I WORK.

Respond to Caroline, and send a message to your staff, reminding them to edit newsletter stories as well as external documents to replace biased language.

3.11   Asking About Travel Arrangements

The CEO is planning a trip to visit colleagues in another country (you pick the country). As executive assistant to the CEO of your organization, it's your job to make travel plans. At this stage, you don't know anything except dates and flights. (The CEO will arrive in the country at 7 A.M. local time on the 28th of next month, and stay for three days.) It's your job to find out what the plans are and communicate any of the CEO's requirements.

Write an email message to your contact.

Hints:

- Pick a business, nonprofit organization, or government agency you know something about, making assumptions about the kinds of things its executive would want to do during an international visit.
- How much international travelling does your CEO do? Has he or she ever been to this country before? What questions will he or she want answered?

3.12   Sending a Draft to Japan

You've drafted instructions for a product that will be sold in Japan. Before the text is translated, you want to find out whether the pictures will be clear. So you send an email to your Japanese counterpart, Takashi Haneda, asking for a response within a week.

Write an email message; assume that you will send the pictures as an attachment.

3.13   Creating a Web Page

Create a Web page for managers who must communicate across cultures.

Assume that this page can be accessed from the organization's intranet. Offer at least seven links. (More are better.) You may offer information as well as links to other pages with information. At the top of the page, offer an overview of what the page covers. At the bottom of the page, put the creation and update date and your name and email address.

As your instructor directs,

a. Turn in two printed copies of your page(s). On another page, give the URLs for each link.

b. Turn in one printed copy of your page(s) and a disk with the HTML code and .gif files.

c. Write a memo to your instructor identifying the audience for whom the page is designed and explaining (1) what search strategies you used to find material on this topic, (2) why you chose the pages and information you've included, and (3) why you chose the layout and graphics you've used.

d. Post your memo in an email message to the class.

e. Present your page orally to the class.

Hints:

- Limit your page to just one culture or country.
- Try to cover as many topics as possible: history, politics, notable people, arts, conversational style, customs, and so forth. For a culture in another country, also include money, living accommodations, geography, transport, weather, business practices, and so forth.
- Chunk your links into small groups under headings.
- See Module 5 on Web page design.

3.14 Requesting Information About a Country

Use one or more of the following ways to get information about a country. You might focus on

- Business opportunities
- History and geography
- Principal exports and imports
- Dominant religions
- Holidays
- School system
- Political system

1. Visit Industry Canada's Strategis Web site for International Market Research and Country Commercial Guides at http://strategis.ic.gc.ca/epic/internet/inibi-iai.nsf/vwGeneratedInterE/Home, and click "Country/Region Information."
2. Check the country's trade office, if there is one in your city.
3. Interview someone from that country or someone who has lived there.
4. Read about the country.

As your instructor directs,

a. Share your findings orally with a small group of students.
b. Summarize your findings in a memo to your instructor.
c. Present your findings to the class.
d. Email your findings to the class.
e. Join with a group of classmates to write a group report on the country.

3.15 Answering an Inquiry About Photos

You've just been named vice-president for diversity, the first person in your organization to hold this position. Today, you receive the following memo from Sheila Lathan, who edits the employee newsletter:

Subject: Photos in the Employee Newsletter

Please tell me what to do about photos in the monthly employee newsletter. I'm concerned that almost no single issue represents the diversity of employees we have here.

As you know, our layout allows two visuals each month. One of those is always the employee of the month (EM). In the last year, most of those have been male and all but two have been white. What makes it worse is that people want photos that make them look good. You may remember that Ron Olmos was the EM two months ago; in the photo he wanted me to use, you can't tell that he's in a wheelchair. Often the EM is the only photo; the other visual is a graph of sales or something relating to quality.

Even if the second visual is another photo, it may not look balanced in terms of gender and race. After all, 62 percent of our employees are women, and 70 percent are non-white. Should the pictures try to represent those percentages? The leadership positions (both in management and in the union) are heavily male and white. Should we run pictures of people doing important things and risk continuing the imbalance?

I guess I could use more visuals, but then there wouldn't be room for as many stories—and people really like to see their names in print. Plus, giving people information about company activities and sales is important to maintaining goodwill. A bigger newsletter would be one way to have more visuals and keep the content, but with the cost-cutting measures we're under, that doesn't look likely.

What should I do?

As your instructor directs,

a. Work in a small group with students to come up with a recommendation for Sheila.
b. Write a memo responding to Sheila.
c. Write an article for the employee newsletter about the photo policy you recommend and how it relates to the company's concern for diversity.

POLISHING YOUR PROSE

Subject–Verb Agreement

Make sure the subjects and verbs in your sentences agree in number: singular subjects take singular verbs; plural subjects take plural verbs.

Correct: The laser printer no longer works.

Correct: The broken laser printers are in the storeroom.

Often, subject–verb errors occur when other words come between the subject and verb. Learn to correct errors by looking for the subject—who or what is doing the principal action—and the verb—the action itself:

Incorrect: A team of marketing researchers are reviewing our promotional campaign.

Correct: A team of marketing researchers is reviewing our promotional campaign.

Incorrect: The idea of tax rebates do not solve the growing gap between rich and poor.

Correct: The idea of tax rebates does not solve the growing gap between rich and poor.

Canadian and American usage treats company names and the words *company* and *government* as singular nouns. In England and countries adopting the British system, these nouns are plural:

Correct (Canada):   Clarica is headquartered in Waterloo, Ontario.

Correct (U.S.):   National Insurance is headquartered in Columbus, Ohio.

Correct (U.K.):   Lloyds of London are headquartered in London.

Use a plural verb when two or more singular subjects are joined by *and*.

Correct: Mr. Simmens, Ms. Lopez, and Mr. Yee were in Seoul for a meeting last week.

Use a singular verb when two or more singular subjects are joined by *or*, *nor*, or *but*.

Correct: Neither Dr. Hroscoe nor Mr. Jamieson is in today.

When the sentence begins with *There* or *Here*, make the verb agree with the subject that follows the verb:

Correct: There were blank pages in the fax we received.

Correct: Here is the information on the job candidate you requested.

Some words that end in *s* are considered singular and require singular verbs:

Correct: The World Series features advertisements of our product in the stadium.

When you encounter situations that don't seem to fit the rule, or when following the rules produces an awkward sentence, rewrite the sentence to avoid the problem:

Problematic: The grant coordinator in addition to the awarding agency (is, are?) happy with the latest proposal we submitted.

Better: The grant coordinator and the awarding agency are happy with the latest proposal we submitted.

Exercises

Choose the correct verb or rewrite the sentence.

1. Each of us (is, are) entitled to company healthcare benefits.
2. KPMG, a leading management consulting firm, (operate, operates) in nine Canadian provinces.
3. The price of our stocks (is, are) increasing.
4. Every project team (train, trains) for at least 90 days before projects (is, are) started.

5. We (order, orders) a dozen new toner cartridges each month.
6. A series of meetings (is, are) devoted to concerns about our office air quality.
7. Marina Schiff and her assistant (is, are) attending the conference in Halifax.
8. Make it a point to (has, have) your report ready by Monday.
9. Professor Beauparlant, Mr. Kincaid, and Ms. Carolla (is, are) on the guest list and (plan, plans) to sit at the same table.
10. The offices in Buenos Aries (report, reports) a 19 percent increase in employee turnover for the past year.

Check your answers to the odd-numbered exercises on page 551.

MODULE

4

Planning, Writing, and Revising

Learning Objectives

After reading and applying the information in Module 4, you'll be able to demonstrate

Knowledge of

- The activities in the writing process
- The process application

Skills to

- Begin to apply the activities in the writing process
- Begin to identify and analyze your own strategies
- Begin to use revision and editing techniques
- Get started writing

Employability Skills 2000+ Checklist

In this module, the key skills from the Conference Board of Canada's Employability Skills 2000+ are

Communicate

○ write and speak so others pay attention and understand

Think & Solve Problems

○ assess situations and identify problems
○ seek different points of view and evaluate them based on facts
○ recognize the human, interpersonal, technical, scientific, and mathematical dimensions of a problem
○ identify the root cause of a problem

○ be creative and innovative in exploring possible solutions
○ readily use science, technology, and mathematics as ways to think, gain and share knowledge, solve problems, and make decisions
○ evaluate solutions to make recommendations or decisions

Demonstrate Positive Attitudes & Behaviours

○ show interest, initiative, and effort

Be Adaptable

○ be innovative and resourceful: identify and suggest alternative ways to achieve goals and get the job done

○ be open and respond constructively to change
○ learn from your mistakes and accept feedback
○ cope with uncertainity

Learn Continuously

○ be willing to continuously learn and grow

○ identify and access learning sources and opportunities

Skilled performances may look easy and effortless. In reality, as all athletes and artists know, skilled performances are the product of hours of practice, attention to detail, and intense concentration. Like all skilful performances, business writing rests on a base of work: planning, researching, analyzing, drafting, and rewriting, as the changes in the memo shown in Figures 4.1a and 4.1b demonstrate.

FIGURE 4.1a   **Writing Is Rewriting: Draft Email**

November 10, 2010

To: Bartenders, wait servers, and bussing staff

From: Omar

Re: Christmas

While we're planning our Christmas party we should also be thinking about what we're going to do about who's going to be responsible for cleaning up and locking up after the party, if we start partying after closing time at 1 on the 21, and party until 3 or 4, that's fine with the managers, and some staff have already said they will taxi people home but we need people to stay to clean up and set up for the next day's lunch crowd. Also, somebody has to take the day's receipts and money for safekeeping, and bank it the next day.

Party includes free food and you can bring a guest. You need to bring your own booze

Can you let me know who will volunteer to do that? Thx

FIGURE 4.1b   **Writing Is Rewriting: Revised Email**

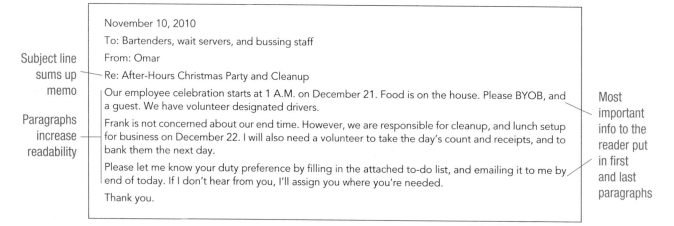

Subject line sums up memo

Paragraphs increase readability

November 10, 2010

To: Bartenders, wait servers, and bussing staff

From: Omar

Re: After-Hours Christmas Party and Cleanup

Our employee celebration starts at 1 A.M. on December 21. Food is on the house. Please BYOB, and a guest. We have volunteer designated drivers.

Frank is not concerned about our end time. However, we are responsible for cleanup, and lunch setup for business on December 22. I will also need a volunteer to take the day's count and receipts, and to bank them the next day.

Please let me know your duty preference by filling in the attached to-do list, and emailing it to me by end of today. If I don't hear from you, I'll assign you where you're needed.

Thank you.

Most important info to the reader put in first and last paragraphs

Language FOCUS

BYOB stands for "Bring Your Own Beverage" or "Bring Your Own Booze" (which means alcoholic beverages). Being asked to bring your own beverage to a party is common practice in Canada.

What Is the Writing Process?

The process of planning, drafting, and rewriting can include many activities.

Planning

- Analyzing the situation: What has the client asked for? Specifically, what is the assignment?
- Defining your purposes, and analyzing your audience needs.
- Thinking about the information: What "proof" will you need, and where can you find it?
- Gathering the information—through your own and others' observations and experiences, from the Internet, from articles.
- Making notes, creating outlines, considering how to organize the information: Are you writing in an academic or a business context? What are the reader's expectations? What do your audiences already know? What do they need to know?

Drafting

Putting notes on paper or on the screen: drafting can include purpose statements, visuals, lists, dot jots, stream-of-consciousness thoughts, or a formal draft.

Rewriting

- Assessing your work by measuring it against your criteria: What are your goals, and what are the requirements of the situation and the audience? You get the best results by seeing the draft from the reader's point of view: Is it clear? complete? convincing? tactful?
- Getting continuous feedback: Ask peers and colleagues to comment. Does it make sense? Does it flow? Is the organization appropriate and reader-friendly? Is the information convincing? What about mechanics—grammar and usage? What about typos?
- Deleting, adding, substituting, rearranging: rewriting can be changing large sections of the document, or revising sentences or single words.
- Editing the draft. Here you correct spelling and mechanical errors, and check word choice and format. Editing focuses on the surface of writing.
- Proofing the final copy to ensure it's error-free.

Note the following points about the writing process:

- Writers do not necessarily follow these activities in order. For example, some people compose completely in their heads, write a first draft, and then use a reader, revise, edit, and proofread. Many people gather information after writing a draft because only then do they see that they need to add more specific information to get results.
- You do not have to finish one activity to start another. Some writers continually interrupt their composing to assess, revise, and edit. They write a short section, assess and correct it, then write the next short section, assess and revise it, and so on through the whole document. This recursive process typifies freelancer Leslie Butler's activities: "I can't go forward unless I go backward: I may write two paragraphs; then I have to go back and reread what I've written, over and over again. Sometimes I read and revise and edit the first paragraph twelve to thirty times."[1]

The writing process can include many critical thinking strategies.

- You may do an activity several times for the same document. Maybe you'll compose and immediately post your microblogs to friends, but, depending on your purposes and audiences, you may compose a business-related blog, get feedback, revise, get more feedback, revise yet again, and so on.

Most writers do not use all the activities for every document they write. You'll use more of the activities when you write a new kind of document, about a new subject, or to a new audience.

Although there is no one *right* way to write, all writers agree that they write best when they know their topic, and understand the audience reading their work. Transactional writers (essayists, journalists, textbook authors, businesspeople) research their subject thoroughly, identify a story or point of view that they believe will attract and hold their audience's attention, and then compose, revise, and edit using techniques that work for them.

Does It Matter What Process I Use?

Know what the experts do, and use what works best for you.

Just as athletes improve their game by studying videotapes and focusing on exactly how they kick a ball or spin during a jump, so writers improve their writing by studying their own processes. No single writing process works for all writers all the time.

Experienced writers tend to

- Focus on their purpose and audience
- Identify a story, thesis, theme, or central idea related to their purpose and audience
- Assume that the first draft will be revised
- Break big writing jobs into a series of steps
- Read daily
- Write regularly
- Work to acquire a large vocabulary of concrete nouns and action verbs
- Discuss their writing with others
- Ask for and apply feedback
- Use a reader for revising, editing and proofing
- Use whatever rules work for them[2]

Practised writers spend more time identifying and analyzing the initial problem, understanding the task more broadly and deeply, drawing from a wider repertoire of strategies, and seeing patterns more clearly. Practised writers compose more slowly than novices, and spend more time evaluating their work.[3]

Thinking about the processes you currently use, and trying out experts' strategies can help you become a better writer.

Language FOCUS

Good writers do not rely on direct translations from dictionaries. If English is not your first language, it is important to use words and phrases as they are used in North America. Instead of directly translating from your first language, pay close attention to the way native speakers use the language and try to copy it.

How Should I Use My Time?

Make notes on your research and thinking. Save plenty of time for rewriting.

To get the best results, try to use only one-third of your time composing your first draft. Spend at least one-third of your time analyzing your purpose(s) and audience(s), gathering your information, and organizing what you want to say. Keep notes (electronic and hardcopy) on all your information. These jottings can stimulate your thinking and serve as your rough draft. Spend another third of your time revising and editing: assess your draft based on your analysis of purpose and audience; revise; get feedback, and revise again; edit for correct grammar and mechanics; proofread your final copy.

Different projects have different lead times. When you get an assignment, consider the steps you'll need to go through so you can timeline the project. Figure 4.2 provides samples timelines. Of course, different writers might need different amounts of time to produce the same-quality document.

What Planning Should I Do to Prepare to Write or Speak?

Do as much planning as you can, and keep a record.

Spend at least one-third of your time gathering ideas, researching, planning, and making notes. The more familiar you are with your ideas, the fewer drafts you'll need to produce a good document. Start by using the analysis questions from Module 1 to identify purpose and

FIGURE 4.2   Allocating Time to Write a Memo

	Total Time: 6 Hours
Planning	1.5 hours
Understand the policy.	
Answer the PAIBOC questions (Module 1).	
Think about document design (Module 5).	
Organize the message.	
Writing	1.5 hours
Create a draft.	
Revising	3.0 hours
Reread draft.	
Measure draft against PAIBOC questions and against principles of business communication.	
Revise draft.	
Ask for feedback.	
Revise draft based on feedback.	
Edit to catch grammatical errors.	
Run spell check.	
Proof by eye.	
Initial memo.	
Duplicate and distribute document.	

Source: Private communication, Joe Taleroski to Steve Kaczmarek, August 9, 2005.

audience. Use the strategies described in Module 2 to analyze audience and in Module 8 to develop reader benefits. Gather information you can use for your document.

If ideas won't come, try the following techniques:

- **Brainstorm.** Write down all your ideas without judging them. Consciously try to get at least a dozen different ideas before you stop.
- **Freewrite.**[4] Make yourself write, without stopping, for 10 minutes or so, even if you have to write "I will think of something soon." At the end of 10 minutes, read what you've written and identify the best point in the draft. Get a clean paper or screen and write for another 10 uninterrupted minutes. Read this draft, marking anything that's good and should be kept, and then write again for another 10 minutes. By the third session, you will probably produce several sections that are worth keeping—maybe even a complete draft that's ready to be revised.
- **Cluster.**[5] Write your topic in the middle of the page and circle it. Write down the ideas the topic suggests, circling them, too. (The circles are designed to tap into the nonlinear half of your brain.) When you've filled the page, look for patterns or repeated ideas. Use different-coloured pens to group related ideas (Modules 18 and 19). Then use these ideas to develop reader benefits in a memo, questions for a survey, or content for the body of a report. Figure 4.3 presents the clusters that one writer created about business communication in Canada and France.
- **Talk to your audiences.** Research shows that talking to internal and external audiences is invaluable. Talking to real audiences helped writers involve readers in the planning process, understand social and political relationships among readers, and negotiate conflicts orally rather than depending solely on the document. These writers were then able to think about content as well as about organization and style, appeal to common ground (such as reducing waste or increasing productivity) that several readers shared, and reduce the number of revisions needed before documents were approved.[6]

FIGURE 4.3   **Guidelines for Various Documents**

Email message answering a simple question. Total time: 15 minutes

5 minutes	5 minutes	5 minutes
Read the question Gather any information necessary for reply Plan the message	Draft the message	Reread the message Run the message through a spell checker Make small changes Send the message

Email message answering a question that requires simple research. Total time: 2 hours

1 hour	30 minutes	30 minutes
Read the question Think about what is needed to reply Do research (on the Web, ask people, etc.) Analyze the information Plan the message	Draft the message and any attachments	Reread the message Revise the message and attachments Run the message through a spell checker Send the message

Memo explaining a new policy. Total time: 6 hours

90 minutes	60 minutes	90 minutes	30 minutes	90 minutes
Understand the policy Answer the PAIBOC questions (Module 1) Think about document design Organize the message	Draft	Reread draft Measure draft against PAIBOC questions and principles of business communication Revise draft	Ask for feedback	Revise draft based on feedback Run a spell check Proof by eye Initial memo Duplicate and distribute document

Report recommending ways to improve customer service. Total time: 30 business days

6 days	1 day	2 days	9 days
Collect information about weaknesses in service Write working purpose statement Plan research to gather more information Revise purpose statement Get library sources; check the Web; plan survey or interview questions Write proposal to do research to find solution	Ask for feedback on proposal, research plan	Revise proposal	Conduct research Analyze data Create visuals for report Prepare appendices

5 days	1 day	5 days	1 day
Draft report Evelute draft against proposal and principles of business communication	Ask for feedback on recommendations, report design, and visuals	Revise report Revise visuals Plan oral presentation Edit document and visuals Run a spell check Proof by eye Duplicate document	Submit report Present results orally

FIGURE 4.4   Clustering Helps Generate Ideas

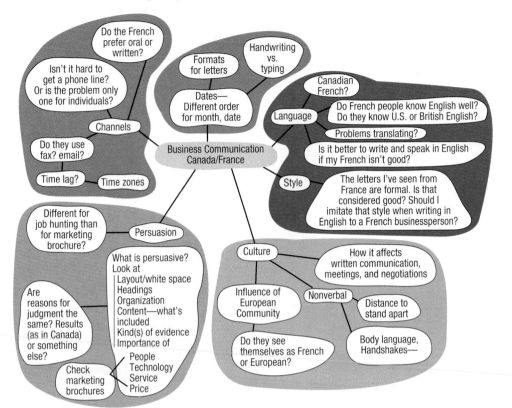

Thinking and talking to others about the content, layout, or structure of your document can also give you ideas. For long documents, *write out the headings you'll use.* For anything that's shorter than five pages, less formal notes will probably work. You may want to jot down ideas that you can use as the basis for a draft.

For an oral presentation, a meeting, or a document with lots of visuals, use your presentation software to create a storyboard, or make your own paper storyboard with a rectangle representing each page or unit. Draw a box with a visual for each main point. Below the box, write a short caption or label.

Letters and memos will go faster if you can visualise a basic organizational pattern before you start. Modules 10, 12, and 13 give detailed patterns of organization for the most common kinds of letters and memos. You may want to customize those patterns with a **planning guide**[7] to help you keep the big picture in mind as you write. Figure 4.5 shows planning guides developed for specific kinds of documents.

What Is Revision? How Do I Do It?

Revision means seeing the document new, from the reader's point of view.

Writers make their drafts better by revising, editing, and proofreading from the reader's point of view.

- **Revising** means making changes that will better satisfy your purposes and your audience.
- **Editing** means making surface-level changes that make the document grammatically correct.
- **Proofreading** means checking to be sure the document is free from typographical errors.

FIGURE 4.5   **Customized Planning Guides for Specific Documents**

Planning guide for a trip report

- The Big Picture from the Company's Point of View: We Can Go Forward on the Project
- Criteria/Goals
- What We Did
- Why We Know Enough to Go Forward

Planning guide for a proposal

- Customer's Concern #1 Our Proposal or Answer
- Customer's Concern #2 Our Proposal or Answer
- Customer's Concern #3 Our Proposal or Answer

Planning guide for an email message

- My Purpose
- Points I Want to Make
- Document(s) to Attach
- Next Steps

Planning guide for a credit rejection

- Reason
- Refusal
- Alternative (Layaway/ Co-signer/Provide more information)
- Goodwill Ending

Source: Email and proposal guides based on Fred Reynolds, "What Adult Work-World Writers Have Taught Me About Adult Work-World Writing," *Professional Writing in Context: Lessons from Teaching and Consulting in Worlds of Work* (Hillsdale, NJ: Lawrence Erlbaum Associates, 1995), pp. 18, 20.

FIGURE 4.6   **Checklist for Thorough Revision**

Content and Clarity

- ❑ Does your document meet the needs of the organization and of the reader—and make you look good?
- ❑ Have you given readers all the information they need to understand and act on your message?
- ❑ Have you organized your message for optimum positive audience impact? (Modules 2 and 11.)
- ❑ Is all the information accurate?
- ❑ Is each sentence clear? Is the message free from apparently contradictory statements?
- ❑ Are generalizations and benefits backed up with adequate supporting detail?

Organization and Layout

- ❑ Does the design of the document make it easy for readers to find the information they need? Is the document visually inviting?
- ❑ Are transitions between ideas smooth? Do ideas within paragraphs flow smoothly?
- ❑ Are the most important points emphasized?
- ❑ Are the first and last paragraphs effective?

Style and Tone

- ❑ Does the message build goodwill?
- ❑ Is the message easy to read?
- ❑ Is the message friendly and free from biased language?

When you're writing to a new audience or solving a particularly difficult problem, plan to revise the draft at least three times. The first time, look for content and clarity. The second time, check the organization and layout. Finally, check style and tone, using the information in the Revising and Editing Resources at the end of this book. Figure 4.6 summarizes the questions you might ask.

Often you'll get the best revision by setting aside your draft, getting a blank page or screen, and redrafting. This strategy takes advantage of the thinking you did on your first draft without locking you into the sentences in it. As you revise, be sure to read the document through from start to finish. This is particularly important if you've composed it in several sittings, or if you've used text from other documents. Researchers have found that such documents tend to be well organized but don't flow well.[8] You may need to add transitions (refer to the Revising and Editing Resources at the end of this book), cut repetitive parts, or change words to create unity throughout the document.

If you're really short on time, do a light revision (see Figure 4.7). The quality of the final document might not be as high as with a thorough revision, but even a light revision is better than nothing.

FIGURE 4.7   **Checklist for Light Revision**

❑ Are the first and last paragraphs effective?
❑ Does the design of the document make it easy for readers to find the information they need?
❑ Have I told the reader what to do?

Can a Grammar Checker Edit for Me?

No. You have to decide on each change.

Grammar checkers are good at finding missing halves. For example, if you open a parenthesis and never close it, a grammar checker will note that you need a second one. Of course, *you* have to decide where it goes. In terms of other errors, all a grammar checker can do is ask you about what you have done. A grammar checker can tell you that you've used a passive verb (refer to the Revising and Editing Resources at the end of this book) and ask whether you want to change it. But you have to decide whether the passive is justified. If it finds the word *well*, the grammar checker can tell you that *good* and *well* are sometimes confused. But you have to decide which word fits your meaning. You still need to know the rules so you can decide which changes to make.

Check for the most common grammar concerns:

- Sentence structure
- Subject–verb and noun–pronoun agreement
- Parallelism
- Punctuation
- Dangling or misplaced modifiers
- Passive verbs

Then check for correct word use, correct spelling—including spelling of names—and numbers accuracy.

You need to know the rules of grammar and punctuation to edit. Most writers make a small number of errors repeatedly. If you know that you have trouble with dangling modifiers or subject–verb agreement, for example, specifically look for them in your draft. Also look for any errors that especially bother your boss and correct them.

Grammar checkers frequently include an option for checking the readability of a selected passage. Microsoft Word's grammar checker will indicate readability on the basis of the Flesch-Kincaid Grade Level (corresponding to years of education required to comprehend the material) and a Flesch Reading Ease score (assessing the difficulty level on the basis of the average number of words per sentence and the average number of syllables per word). Table 4.1 sets out guidelines for interpreting these results.

TABLE 4.1   Interpreting Flesch Readability Scores

Flesch Reading Ease	Difficulty	Flesch-Kincaid Grade Level	Example
0–29	Very difficult	Postgraduate	
30–49	Difficult	College	32: *Harvard Law Review* 40–50: Standard score for insurance documents required by law in several U.S. states
50–59	Fairly difficult	High school	52: *Time*
60–69	Standard	Grade 8 to 9	60: "Plain English" (20 words per sentence, 1.5 syllables per word) 65: *Reader's Digest*
70–79	Fairly easy	Grade 7	
80–89	Easy	Grade 5 to 6	
90–100	Very easy	Grade 4 to 5	

Source: Tom McArthur, ed., *The Oxford Companion to the English Language* (Oxford: Oxford University Press, 1992), p. 407.

Most business writers strive for readability score of Grade 8 to 10, because clear and concise documents make it easier for the audience to read and understand the message. Saving the reader time and trouble has a positive impact (Modules 6 and 7), increasing the chances of you getting the results you want.

Try to edit *after* you revise. There's no point in taking time to fix a grammatical error in a sentence that may be cut when you clarify your meaning or tighten your style. Some writers edit more accurately when they print out a copy of a document and edit the hard copy.

I Use a Spell Checker. Do I Still Need to Proofread?

Yes.

Proofread every document both with a spell checker and by eye to catch the errors a spell checker can't find.

Employability Skills

Proofreading is hard, because writers tend to see what they expect should be there rather than what is really on the page or screen. Since it's always easier to proof something you haven't written, you may want to swap papers with a proofing buddy. (Be sure the person looks for typos, not for content.)

To proofread, follow these steps:

- Read once quickly for meaning to see that nothing has been left out.
- Read a second time, slowly. When you find an error, correct it and then reread that line. Readers tend to become less attentive after they find one error and may miss other errors close to the one they've spotted.

To proofread a document you know well, read the lines backward, or the pages out of order.

Always triple-check numbers, headings, first and last paragraphs, and the reader's name.

Checkpoint

Writing is a complex, time-consuming process that includes **planning**, **researching**, **composing**, **assessing**, **getting feedback**, **revising**, **editing**, and **proofreading**. Writers do not follow these activities in order, although the most successful writers focus their time on **planning**, **researching**, **revising**, and **proofreading**.

How Can I Get Good Feedback?

Ask for the kind of feedback you need.

Being asked to revise documents is a fact of life in businesses, government, and nonprofit organizations.

To improve the quality of the feedback you get, and of your revisions, tell people which aspects you'd especially like comments about. For example, when you give a reader the outline or planning draft,[9] you might want to know whether the general approach is appropriate. After your second draft, you might want to know whether reader benefits are well developed. When you reach the polishing draft, you'll be ready for feedback on style and grammar. Figure 4.8 lists questions to ask.

To get a fresh perspective, writers talk to others about their work.

It's easy to feel defensive when someone criticizes your work. If the feedback stings, put it aside until you can read it without feeling defensive. Even if you think that the reader has misunderstood what you were trying to say, the fact that the reader commented means the section could be improved.

EXPANDING A CRITICAL SKILL

Revising After Feedback

When you get feedback that you understand and agree with, make the change.

If you get feedback you don't understand, ask for clarification.

- Paraphrase: "So you're saying I need to give more information?"
- Ask for more information: "Can you suggest a way to do that?"
- Test your inference: "Would it help if I did this?"

Sometimes you may get feedback you don't agree with.

- If it's to do with grammar or usage, check this book or online (sometimes even smart people get things wrong).

- If it's about the content, recognize that something about the draft could be improved; something is leading the reader to respond negatively.
- If the reader thinks a fact is wrong (and you know it's right), show where the fact came from "According to ... ."
- If the reader suggests a change in wording you don't like, try another option.
- If the reader seems to have misunderstood or misread, think of ways to make the meaning clearer.

If the reader says "This isn't true" and you know that the statement is true, try rephrasing the statement, giving more information or examples, or documenting the source.

FIGURE 4.8 **Questions to Ask Readers**

Outline or Planning Draft

❑ Does the plan seem to be on the right track?
❑ What topics should be added? Should any be cut?
❑ Do you have any other general suggestions?

Revised Draft

❑ Does the message satisfy all its purposes?
❑ Is the message adapted to the audience(s)?
❑ Is the organization effective?
❑ Are any parts unclear?
❑ What ideas need further development?
❑ Do you have any other suggestions?

Polished Draft

❑ Are there any problems with word choice or sentence structure?
❑ Did you find any inconsistencies?
❑ Did you find any typos?
❑ Is the document's design effective?

Your supervisor's comments on a draft can help you improve that document, help you write better drafts the next time, and teach you about the culture of your organization. Look for patterns in the feedback you receive. Are you asked to use more formal language, or to make the document more conversational? Does your boss want to see an overview before details? Does your company prefer information presented in bulleted lists rather than in paragraphs? When the feedback is honest, even harsh criticism can be beneficial. Pay attention to the meaning of the criticism, rather than how it is delivered. You can choose to use any feedback as a source of information.

Can I Use Form Letters?

Yes, but make sure they're appropriate in form and content.

A **form letter** or **template** is a prewritten, fill-in-the-blanks document designed for routine situations. Some form letters have different paragraphs that can be inserted, depending on the situation.

For example, a form letter admitting students to university might add additional paragraphs for students receiving financial aid.

Boilerplate is language—sentences, paragraphs, even pages—from a previous document that a writer includes in a new document. In academic papers, material written by others must be quoted and documented. However, because businesses own the documents their employees write, text from those documents may be included without attribution.

In some cases, boilerplate may have been written years ago. For example, many legal documents, including apartment leases and sales contracts, are almost completely boilerplated. In other cases, writers might use boilerplate they themselves have written. For example, a section from a proposal describing the background of the problem situation might also be used in the final report after the proposed work was completed. A section from a progress report describing what the writer has done might be used with only a few changes in the methods section of the final report.

Many organizations encourage their employees to use templates and boilerplate to save time and energy, and to use language that has already been approved by the organization's legal staff. However, using templates and old text creates problems:[10]

- The template pattern may be inappropriate to the content you are adding, or outdated. For example, many organizations continue to send letters that place the subject above the salutation:

Re: Basement Flood Repairs

Dear Ms. Tuwawi:

- Unrevised boilerplate can be outdated, or can create a document with incompatible styles and tones. The salutations *Dear Sir/Madam* and *To Whom It May Concern* are examples of unacceptable boilerplate language.
- Form letters and boilerplate can encourage writers to see situations and audiences as identical when, in fact, they differ.

Before you use a form letter, make sure that it is well written, uses contemporary language and tone, and applies to the current situation.

Before you incorporate old language in a new document, check to see that the old section is well written.

Consciously look for differences between the two situations, audiences, or purposes that may require different content, organization, or wording.

Read through the whole document at a single sitting to be sure that style, tone, and level of detail are consistent.

How Can I Get Started?

Employability Skills

Talk, participate, and practise. Reward yourself for activities that encourage writing.

According to psychologist Robert Boice, a combination of actions works to get people writing.[11]

- **Participate actively in the organization and the community.** The more you talk to people, the more you communicate with some of your audiences, the more you learn about the company, culture and context (Module 2), the easier it will be to write—and the better your writing will be.
- **Practise writing regularly, and in moderation.**
- **Learn as many strategies as you can.** Good writers have a repertoire of strategies they draw on. They try a variety of techniques in each new situation. Research these strategies and patterns, and try them to see what works for you.
- **Talk positively to yourself.** "I can do this." "I write for 15 minutes, and see what happens." "It doesn't have to be perfect; I can make it better later."
- **Talk about writing with other people.** Talk to peers, colleagues, and supervisors about writing. Value the feedback you get. Ask your supervisor for models of good examples of writing. Talking to other people expands your repertoire of strategies, and helps you understand what is valued in the discourse communities (Module 2) in which you write.

To avoid procrastinating, modify your behaviour by rewarding yourself for activities that *lead* to writing:

- **Set a regular time to write.** Sit down and stay there for the time you planned, even if you write nothing usable.

- **Develop a ritual for writing.** Choose tools—laptop, pen and paper, chair—that you find comfortable. Use the same tools in the same place every time you write.
- **Freewrite.** Write for 10 minutes without stopping.
- **Write down your thoughts and fears as you write.** If your thoughts are negative, try to reframe them more positively: "I can do this." "I'll keep going and evaluate it later." "If I keep working, I'll produce something that's okay."
- **Identify the problem that keeps you from writing.** Deal with the problem; then go back to your writing.
- **Set modest goals** (a paragraph, not the whole essay or report) **and reward yourself for reaching them.**

MODULE SUMMARY

- Planning, writing, and revising can include analyzing, collecting information, composing, assessing, getting feedback, revising, editing, and proofreading.

- **Revising** means *reseeing* the document from the reader's point of view; you revise to maximize positive audience impact while satisfying your purposes.

- **Editing** means making surface-level changes for correct grammar, punctuation, and usage.

- **Proofreading** means checking to ensure the document is free from typographical errors.

- Practised writers expect to revise the first draft, read and write regularly, have clear goals, know many different strategies, wait to edit until the first draft is complete, and regularly ask for feedback.

- Writers use processes that work for them: these include expecting to revise, writing regularly, having clear goals, modifying the task if it's too easy or too hard, knowing many different strategies, using rules as guidelines, and waiting to edit until after the draft is complete. To think of ideas, try **brainstorming**, **freewriting** (writing without stopping for 10 minutes or more), and **clustering** (brainstorming using visuals).

- You can improve the quality of feedback you get by telling people which aspects of the draft you'd like comments about. Look for patterns in the feedback you get.

- If the writing task is new or difficult, plan to revise at least three times. The first time, look for clarity and content. The second time, check the layout and organization. Finally, check style and tone.

- **Form letters** are prewritten, fill-in-the-blanks documents designed for routine situations. **Boilerplate** is language from a previous document that writers include in new documents. Using templates (or form letters) and boilerplate indiscriminately can create documents that are inconsistent, outdated, or incompatible in tone and style.

- **To get started** writing,

  1. Participate actively in the organization, and the community.
  2. Follow a routine: practise writing regularly.
  3. Learn as many strategies as you can.
  4. Talk about your writing tasks with other people.

ASSIGNMENTS FOR MODULE 4

Questions for Critical Thinking

4.1 Of the processes that expert writers use, which do you already use? How could you modify your process to incorporate at least one more on the list?

4.2 Of the people who have seen your writing, which person(s) has (have) given you the most useful feedback? What makes it useful?

4.3 In what areas are you best at giving feedback to other people? How might you make your feedback even better?

4.4 Think about the form letters you have received. How could they be improved?

Exercises and Problems

4.5 Clustering or Mind-Mapping a Lecture

Use clustering to mind-map (see Figure 4.4) a classroom lecture or organizational meeting. Then convert your visuals into a summary of the lecture or meeting. To maximize your results, compare them with those of peers or colleagues. Where are the similarities? Where are the differences? How well does clustering as a form of note-taking work for you?

4.6 Interviewing Writers About Their Composing Processes

Interview someone who writes for a living about the composing process(es) he or she uses. You can find your source online through local writers' groups or through the Editors' Association of Canada.

Questions you might ask include:

- What kind of planning do you do before you write? Do you make lists? formal or informal outlines?
- When you need more information, where do you get it?
- How do you compose your drafts? Do you dictate? draft with pen and paper? compose on screen? How do you find uninterrupted time to compose?
- When you want advice about style, grammar, and spelling, what sources do you consult?
- Does your supervisor read your drafts and make suggestions?
- Do you ever work with other writers to produce a single document? Describe the process you use.
- Describe the process of creating a document that you felt reflected your best work.
- Describe the process of creating a document that you found difficult or frustrating. What sorts of things make writing easier or harder for you?

As your instructor directs,

- a. Share your results orally with a small group of students.
- b. Present your results in an oral presentation to the class.
- c. Present your results in a memo to your instructor.
- d. Post an email message to the class discussing your results.
- e. Share your results with a small group of students and write a joint memo reporting the similarities and differences you found.

4.7 Analyzing Your Own Writing Processes

Save your notes and drafts from several assignments so that you can answer the following questions:

- Which of the activities in the writing process do you use?

- How much time do you spend on each of the activities?
- What kinds of revisions do you make most often?
- Do you use different processes for different documents, or do you have one process that you use most of the time?
- Which practices of good writers do you follow?
- What parts of your process seem most successful? Are there any places in the process that could be improved? How?
- What relation do you see between the process(es) you use and the quality of the final document?

As your instructor directs,

- a. Discuss your process with a small group of students.
- b. Write a memo to your instructor analyzing in detail your process for composing one of the papers for this class.
- c. Write a memo to your instructor analyzing your process during the term. What parts of your process(es) have stayed the same throughout the term? What parts have changed?

4.8 Checking Spell Checkers and Grammar Checkers

Each of the following paragraphs contains errors in grammar, spelling, and punctuation. Which errors does your spelling or grammar checker catch? Which errors does it miss? Does it flag as errors any words that are correct?

1. Answer to an Inquiry

   Enclosed are the tow copies you requested of our pamphlet, "Using the Internet to market Your products. The pamphlet walks you through the steps of planning the Home Page (The first page of the web cite, shows examples of other Web pages we have designed, and provide a questionnaire that you can use to analyze audience the audience and purposes).

2. Performance Appraisal

   Most staff accountants complete three audits a month. Ellen has completed 21 audits in this past six months she is our most productive staff accountant. Her technical skills our very good however some clients feel that she could be more tactful in suggesting ways that the clients accounting practices could be improved.

3. Brochure

   Are you finding that being your own boss crates it's own problems? Take the hassle out of working at home with a VoiceMail Answering System. Its almost as good as having your own secretary.

POLISHING YOUR PROSE

Commas in Lists

Use commas in lists to separate items:

At the office supply store, I bought pens, stationery, and three-ring binders.

Commas show distinctions between items in a list. Technically, the comma before the coordinating conjunction *and* is optional, but the additional comma always adds clarity. Use commas consistently throughout your document. Missing or improperly placed commas confuse readers:

We bought the following items for the staff lounge: television cabinet computer desk refrigerator and microwave oven.

Does television describe cabinet or is it a separate item? Is computer desk one item? Or are computer and desk two separate things? Inserting commas makes the distinction clear:

We bought the following items for the staff kitchen: television, cabinet, computer, desk, refrigerator, and microwave oven.

Semicolons replace commas in lists in which the items themselves contain commas:

Our company has plants in Moncton, New Brunswick; Flin Flon, Manitoba; and Lethbridge, Alberta.

Exercises

Use commas to make these lists clearer.

1. Please send the "fruit of the month" in April May June and July.
2. At the weekly staff meeting we will be joined by Mr. Loomis Ms. Handelman Ms. Lang and Mr. Kim.
3. The special parts division is opening offices in Brampton Ontario Fredericton New Brunswick and Big Salmon Yukon.
4. Buy small medium and large paper clips at the office supply store.
5. I need to telephone Mary Frank and Paul to finish my report and mail copies of it to Ted Sam and Latanya.
6. Applicants should send copies of their résumés to Mr. Arthur Bramberger human resource director Ms. Tina Ramos vice-president of marketing and Ms. Ellen Choi administrative assistant in marketing.
7. The weather affects our offices in Montreal New York City and Philadelphia.
8. Interns will be rotated through the receiving claims adjustment customer service and shipping departments.
9. Elizabeth Tyrone Mark and Sara presented the team's recommendations.
10. We are open until 9 P.M. on Mondays Wednesdays Fridays and Saturdays.

Check your answers to the odd-numbered exercises on page 551.

Designing Documents, Slides, and Screens

Learning Objectives

After reading and applying the information in Module 5, you'll be able to demonstrate

Knowledge of

- The importance of document appearance, layout, and design
- Essential design principles
- The relationship between readability and your credibility

Skills to

- Apply design principles to paper pages, presentation slides, and Web pages
- Use computer software to increase document readability

Employability Skills 2000+ Checklist

In this module, the key skills from the Conference Board of Canada's Employability Skills 2000+ are

Communicate

- ○ listen and ask questions to understand and appreciate the points of view of others
- ○ share information using a range of information and communication technologies (e.g., voice, email, computers)

- ○ use relevant scientific, technological, and mathematical knowledge and skills to explain or clarify ideas

Think & Solve Problems

- ○ seek different points of view and evaluate them based on facts
- ○ recognize the human, interpersonal, technical, scientific, and mathematical dimensions of a problem

- ○ be creative and innovative in exploring possible solutions

Work with Others

- ○ recognize and respect people's diversity, individual differences, and perspectives

A well-designed document invites reading. Good document design saves time and money, builds goodwill, and reduces legal problems. Effective design also groups ideas visually, making the structure of the document more obvious and easier to read (see Figure 5.1b).

Easy-to-read documents enhance your credibility and build an image of you as a professional, competent person.[1]

Why Is Design Important?

Design is essential to meaning making.

Your audience brings expectations to and constructs meaning from the design of your message. Business audiences expect document and slide design to make it easy for them to read and understand the content. And readers' demands for readability grow as more and more information clamours for our attention.

Document design can transform the way audiences see and respond to your message. When FedEx redesigned its ground-operations manuals, for example, employees found the right answers more often, more quickly. The redesign saved the company $400 000 annually.[2]

Use PAIBOC analysis to create reader-friendly design.

PAIBOC Questions for Analysis

P What are your **purposes** for writing, or for creating slides or screens?

A Who will be reading your document, slide or screen? What physical, psychological, and emotional expectations does your **audience** bring to your document, slide or screen? What does your audience already know? What does your audience need to know? How can you design your message to meet your audience's needs?

I What **information** must your message include? What design will emphasize the vital information? What design will make your message most attractive and accessible to your audience?

B How can you use your design to emphasize reasons or reader **benefits**?

O How can you use design to deemphasize or eliminate potential reader **objections**?

C How will the **context** of the information affect reader response? What time of day will your presentation take place? What economic, environmental, cultural, and organizational realities will affect reader response to your message? How can you use design principles to attract and hold audience interest?

FIGURE 5.1a   Design Is an Essential Communication Tool: Before

When the Alberta government redesigned this form (see Figure 5.1b) to meet its audience's needs, reporting compliance jumped from 25 to 95 percent.

```
        GAME PRODUCTION ANIMAL REGISTRATION CERTIFICATE

                          ELK

Registration Number:      ABBB9999    Sex:        F

Genetic Status:           ELK         Birth Year: 93

Plastic Ear Tag Number:   9999C       Tag Colour: Purple

Sire Registration Number: TBIR045W

Dam Registration Number:  TALL011

Present Owner (please print): _____

Present Owner Signature:      _____

Located at Licensed Farm No.: 028

Farm Licensee:                John Carson

Licensee Signature:           _____

Date of Issue:                21-April-93

- - - - - - - - - - - - - - - - - - - - - - - - - - - - - -
            APPLICATION TO TRANSFER OWNERSHIP

Registration Number:      ABBB9999    Sex:        F
Plastic Ear Tag Number:   9999C       Tag Colour: Purple

Present Farm Licence No.:  028        Licensee: Carson

Present Owner (print):_____   Signature:_____

New Farm Licence No.:      ____       Licensee: _____

New Owner (print):    _____    Signature:_____

Date of Actual Transfer: _____
```

FIGURE 5.1b **Design Is an Essential Communication Tool: After**

Elk and Deer Registration Certificate

Information about the animal

Animal registration number   Dangle ear tag number

Species of animal   Sex of animal   Purebred or hybrid

Birth date (dd/mm/yy)   Origin

Sire's registration number   Dam's registration number

Location and ownership of animal

Licensed farm where animal is   Owner's name and address (if different
located   from owner of licensed farm)

Farm licence number   Date issued

When this animal is sold, give the certificate to the new owner. The new owner must complete
and mail the Notice to Change Registration on the back of this certificate. If the animal dies, is
slaughtered, or escapes, you must complete the back of this certificate and mail it to us.

Alberta
AGRICULTURE, FOOD AND
RURAL DEVELOPMENT

AG0499 Rev. 10/94

Notice to Change Registration

Please fill out the section below that applies to you, then date
and sign this notice. Mail it to the address below.

This animal (check ✓ one):

Sold to a new owner ❑

Licensed farm where animal is located	New owner's name and address (if different from owner of licensed farm)
Farm licence number	Date of sale

Moved to new location ❑

Licensed farm to where animal was moved	Farm licence number
	Date moved

**Exported or
sent to slaughter** ❑   **Escaped** ❑   **Died** ❑

Date sent	Date of escape	Date of death

Signature of farm operator	Date

AG0499 Rev. 10/94

You must send this notice
to the address below
within 30 days of the sale,
move, death, loss, or
escape of the animal.

Send this notice to:

Animal Industry Division
Alberta Agriculture, Food and
Rural Development
#204, 7000 - 113 Street
Edmonton, AB T6H 5T6
Tel: (403) 427-5083
Fax: (403) 427-1057

Alberta
AGRICULTURE, FOOD AND
RURAL DEVELOPMENT

Source: Adapted from Elk and Deer Inventory Certificates with permission of Alberta Agriculture and Rural
Development.

How Should I Design Paper Pages?

Follow these guidelines.

Here are a few guidelines to create visually attractive documents:

- Use white space to separate and emphasize points.
- Use headings to group points.
- Limit the use of words set in all-capitals.
- Use no more than two typefaces in a single document.
- Decide whether to justify margins on the basis of the situation and the audience.

Use White Space

White space—the empty space on the page—emphasizes the material that it separates from the rest of the text. This emphasis makes the material easier to read. Creating white space is also known as "menu writing," because the visual design principle—brief text highlighted by space—is the same as you find on restaurant menus.

You can create white space in several ways:

- Use headings.
- Use a mix of paragraph lengths (maximum six to seven typed lines).
- Use lists.
- Use tabs or indents—not spacing—to align items vertically.
- Use numbered lists when the number or sequence of items is exact.
- Use bullets (large dots or squares like those in this list) when the number and sequence are equal.

When you create a list, use parallelism: begin each item on the list with the same part of speech. If you begin your list with a verb, for example, begin every following item on the list with a verb. This parallel structure meets the reader's subconscious expectation. *And meeting reader expectations is the most important aspect of business writing.*

Not parallel: The following suggestions can help employers avoid bias in job interviews:
1. Base questions on the job description.
2. Questioning techniques
3. Selection and training of interviewers

Parallel: The following suggestions can help employers avoid bias in job interviews:
1. Base questions on the job description.
2. Ask the same questions of all applicants.
3. Select and train interviewers carefully.

Also parallel: Employers can avoid bias in job interviews by
1. Basing questions on the job description
2. Asking the same questions of all applicants
3. Selecting and training interviewers carefully

Figure 5.2 shows an original typed document. In Figure 5.3 the same document is improved by using shorter paragraphs, lists, and headings. These devices take space. When saving space is essential, it's better to cut the text and keep white space and headings.

FIGURE 5.2   A Document with Poor Visual Impact

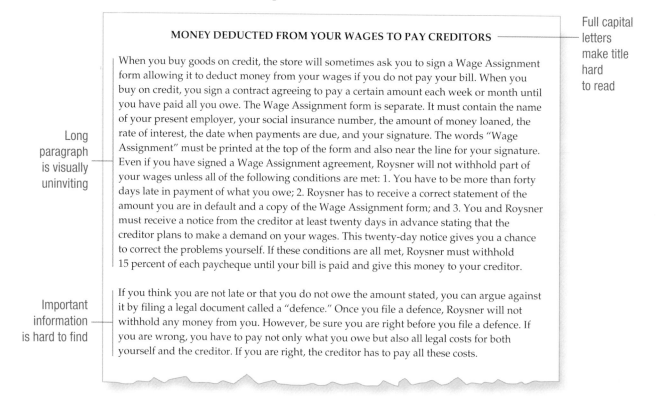

MONEY DEDUCTED FROM YOUR WAGES TO PAY CREDITORS — *Full capital letters make title hard to read*

When you buy goods on credit, the store will sometimes ask you to sign a Wage Assignment form allowing it to deduct money from your wages if you do not pay your bill. When you buy on credit, you sign a contract agreeing to pay a certain amount each week or month until you have paid all you owe. The Wage Assignment form is separate. It must contain the name of your present employer, your social insurance number, the amount of money loaned, the rate of interest, the date when payments are due, and your signature. The words "Wage Assignment" must be printed at the top of the form and also near the line for your signature. Even if you have signed a Wage Assignment agreement, Roysner will not withhold part of your wages unless all of the following conditions are met: 1. You have to be more than forty days late in payment of what you owe; 2. Roysner has to receive a correct statement of the amount you are in default and a copy of the Wage Assignment form; and 3. You and Roysner must receive a notice from the creditor at least twenty days in advance stating that the creditor plans to make a demand on your wages. This twenty-day notice gives you a chance to correct the problems yourself. If these conditions are all met, Roysner must withhold 15 percent of each paycheque until your bill is paid and give this money to your creditor.

Long paragraph is visually uninviting

If you think you are not late or that you do not owe the amount stated, you can argue against it by filing a legal document called a "defence." Once you file a defence, Roysner will not withhold any money from you. However, be sure you are right before you file a defence. If you are wrong, you have to pay not only what you owe but also all legal costs for both yourself and the creditor. If you are right, the creditor has to pay all these costs.

Important information is hard to find

Use Headings

Headings are words or short phrases that identify a complete idea and divide your letter, memo, or report into sections. Headings increase readability because they summarize what the reader is about to read and increase white space.

- Make headings specific.
- Make each heading cover all the material until the next heading.
- Keep headings at any one level parallel: all nouns, all complete sentences, or all questions.

In a letter or memo, type main headings flush with the left-hand margin in bold. Capitalize the first letters of the first word and other major words; use lowercase for all other words. (See Figure 5.3 for an example.) In single-spaced text, triple-space between the previous text and the heading; double-space between the heading and the text that follows.

In a long document, you may need more levels of headings.

Limit the Use of Words Set in All-Capitals

We recognize words by their shapes.[3] (For example, try reading each line in Figure 5.4.) With all-capitals, words look rectangular; letters lose the descenders and ascenders that make reading easier and faster. Use full capitals sparingly. Instead, bold text to emphasize it.

FIGURE 5.3   A Document Revised to Improve Visual Impact

**Money Deducted from Your Wages
to Pay Creditors**

First letter of each main word capitalized—title split onto two lines

When you buy goods on credit, the store will sometimes ask you to sign a Wage Assignment form allowing it to deduct money from your wages if you do not pay your bill.

Have You Signed a Wage Assignment Form?

Headings divide document into chunks

When you buy on credit, you sign a contract agreeing to pay a certain amount each week or month until you have paid all you owe. The Wage Assignment form is separate. It must contain the following:

- The name of your present employer
- Your social insurance number
- The amount of insurance
- The rate of interest
- The date when payments are due
- Your signature

List with bullets where order of items doesn't matter

The words "Wage Assignment" must be printed at the top of the form and also near the line for your signature.

When Would Money Be Deducted from Your Wages to Pay a Creditor?

Headings should be parallel. Here, all are questions.

Even if you have signed a Wage Assignment agreement, Roysner will not withhold part of your wages unless all of the following conditions are met:

Numbered list where number, order of items matter

1. You have to be more than 40 days late in payment of what you owe.
2. Roysner has to receive a correct statement of the amount you are in default and a copy of the Wage Assignment form.
3. You and Roysner must receive a notice from the creditor at least 20 days in advance stating that the creditor plans to make a demand on your wages. This 20-day notice gives you a chance to correct the problem yourself.

White space between items emphasizes them

If these conditions are all met, Roysner must withhold fifteen percent (15 percent) of each paycheque and give this money to your creditor until your bill is paid.

What Should You Do If You Think the Wage Assignment Is Incorrect?

Important information emphasized

If you think you are not late or that you do not owe the amount stated, you can argue against it by filing a legal document called a "defence." Once you file a defence, Roysner will not withhold any money from you. However, be sure you are right before you file a defence. If you are wrong, you have to pay not only what you owe but also all legal costs for both yourself and the creditor. If you are right, the creditor has to pay these costs.

FIGURE 5.4   **Full Capitals Hide the Shape of a Word**

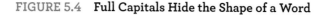

| Full | capitals | hide | the | shape | of | a | word | and | slow | reading | 19% . |

| FULL | CAPITALS | HIDE | THE | SHAPE | OF | A | WORD | AND | SLOW | READING | 19% . |

Use No More Than Two Fonts in a Single Document

Each font comes in several sizes and usually in several styles (bold, italic, etc.). Most computer fonts are **proportional**: wider letters (such as *w*) take more space than narrower letters (such as *i*). Times Roman, Palatino, Helvetica, Geneva, and Arial are proportional fonts. Fonts such as Courier and Prestige Elite, which were designed for typewriters and are still offered as computer fonts, are **fixed**. Every letter takes the same space, so that an *i* takes the same space as a *w*.

Serif fonts have little extensions, called *serifs*, from the main strokes. (In Figure 5.5, look at the feet on the *t* in Times Roman and the little flicks on the ends of the top bar of the *t*.) In hardcopy documents, serif fonts are easier to read, because the serifs help the eyes move from letter to letter. Courier, Times Roman, Palatino, and Lucinda Calligraphy are serif fonts. Helvetica, Geneva, and Arial are called **sans serif** fonts because they lack serifs (*sans* is French for "without"). Sans serif fonts are good for titles, tables, and narrow columns.

In magnified text, sans serif fonts are easier to read; therefore, use sans serif fonts for your PowerPoint™ presentations.

Most business documents use just one font—usually Times Roman, Palatino, Helvetica, or Arial in 11-point or 12-point. In a complex document, use bigger type for main headings and slightly smaller type for subheadings and text. If you combine two fonts in one document, choose one serif and one sans serif typeface.

FIGURE 5.5   **Examples of Different Fonts**

> This sentence is set in 12-point Times Roman.
>
> This sentence is set in 12-point Arial.
>
> This sentence is set in 12-point New Courier.
>
> *This sentence is set in 12-point Lucinda Calligraphy.*
>
> **This sentence is set in 12-point Broadway.**
>
> This sentence is set in 12-point Technical.

Decide Whether to Justify Margins on the Basis of the Situation and the Audience

Margins that are justified on the left are sometimes called **ragged right margins**. Lines end in different places because words are of different lengths. Left justification with ragged right margins are common in current business usage. However, computers allow you to use **full justification**, so that type on the both sides of the page is evenly lined up. Books, like this one, usually use full justification.

Use justified margins when you

- Can use proportional typefaces
- Want a more formal look
- Want to use as few pages as possible

Use ragged right margins when you

- Do not have proportional typefaces
- Want a less formal look
- Want to be able to revise an individual page without reprinting the whole document
- Use very short line lengths

How Should I Design Presentation Slides?

Keep slides simple, relevant, and interesting.

As you design slides for PowerPoint and other presentation programs, keep these guidelines in mind:

- Create slides that emphasize your key ideas.
- Emphasize visuals. Pictures, charts, and graphs have much greater impact: they appeal to the right, or creative, side of the brain; they are more easily accessible than text; and they are more memorable.
- Use audience-relevant photos or metaphoric illustrations to keep memorable images in your listeners' minds.
- Keep the text to an absolute minimum; give your audience slide handouts on which they can write notes.
- Use bullet-point phrases with concrete words.
- Contrast background and text: the rule is light on dark or dark on light.
- Use a big font: 44-point or 50-point for titles, 32-point for subheads, and 28-point for examples.
- Customize your slides with the company logo, charts, and scanned-in photos and drawings.
- Place illustrations at the top right of the slide for a stronger and longer impression.

Avoid death by PowerPoint: never, ever read text to your audience. Presenters who put plenty of text on their slides, and then *read* the text, only exasperate their audiences. People do not want presenters to read to them; they can read for themselves. The last thing they want to read is an uninterrupted block of text.

Use relevant animation, video, and/or sound files in your presentations only if these contribute to audience understanding, and meet your objectives. If you are a novice presenter, avoid these presentation hazards.

Use clip art only if the art is really appropriate to your points and only if you are able to find non-sexist and non-racist images.

FIGURE 5.6   **Effective and Ineffective Colours for Presentation Slides**

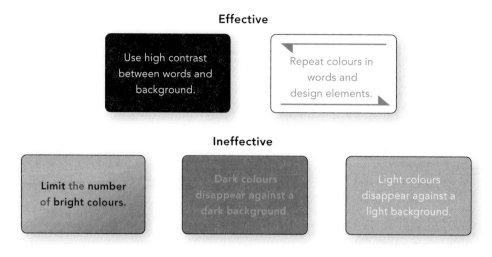

Choose a consistent template, or background design, for the entire presentation. Make sure that the template is appropriate for your subject matter. For example, use a globe only if your topic is international business and palm trees only if you're talking about tropical vacations. PowerPoint's basic templates may seem repetitive to people who see lots of presentations. Whenever possible, customize the basic template.

Choose a light background if the lights are off during the presentation, and a dark background if the lights are on. Slides will be easier to read if you use high contrast between the words and background. See Figure 5.6 for examples of effective and ineffective colour combinations.

 Cultural **FOCUS**

Pay close attention to the colours you use for presentations. Colour combinations that may be acceptable in your culture may not be accepted in North America. For example, the colours orange and brown were used together in the 1970s in fast-food restaurants in order to encourage customers to hurry in and out, as this colour combination was not considered pleasant by most people. Today, however, some businesses are using these colours in order to be "retro" and portray a 70s image. As another example, few businesses will use purple and orange together, as these are not pleasing colour combinations. Pay close attention to the slides your instructors use and examine Figure 5.6 carefully so that you understand the colour rules that businesses follow here. You can also go online and learn about colour psychology on various Web sites.

How Should I Design Web Pages?

Pay attention to content, navigation, and the first page.

Good Web pages incorporate accessible content and design.

Your home page is crucial. Author and Web-design specialist Jakob Nielsen says that only 10 percent of users scroll beyond the first page.[4] To make it more likely that visitors will scroll down, on the first page

- Provide an introductory statement orienting the reader to the organization.
- Offer an overview of the content of your page, with links to take readers to the parts that interest them.
- Include information that will be the most interesting and useful to the most readers.

The rest of the page can contain information that only a limited number of readers will want. When a document reaches four pages or more, think about dividing it into several documents. Specialized information can go on another page, which readers can click on if they want it.

Make it clear what readers will get when they click on a link.

Ineffective phrasing:	Employment. Openings and skills levels are determined by each office.
Better phrasing:	Employment. Openings listed by <u>skills level</u> and by <u>location</u>.

EXPANDING A CRITICAL SKILL

Using Computer Software to Create Good Design

Standard word-processing programs such as WordPerfect and Word help you create well-designed documents.

Different versions of each program handle commands differently. Look up the bolded terms below in a manual, a book about the program, or the online Help menu of your computer program to find out how to use each feature.

Letters and Memos

- Choose a businesslike **font** in 11-point or 12-point type. Times Roman, Palatino, Helvetica, and Arial are the most commonly used business fonts.
- Use **bold** headings. Avoid having a heading all by itself at the bottom of the page. If you can't have at least one line of text under it, move the heading to the next page. You can check this by eye or set your program to avoid **widows** and **orphans**.
- Use **tabs** or **indents** to line up the return address and signature blocks in modified block format (Module 9), the To/From/Subject line section of a memo, or the items in a list.
- Change your **tab settings** to create good visual impact. A setting at 0.6 inch (1.5 centimetre) works well for the Date/To/From/Subject line section of memos. Use 0.4 inch (1 centimetre) for paragraphs and 0.6 inch (1.5 centimetre) for the start of bulleted lists. For lists with 10 or more items, the setting will need to be a bit farther to the right—about 0.65 inch (1.65 centimetre).
- Choose the design for **bullets** under **Insert** or **Format**. Both WordPerfect and Word will create bulleted or numbered lists automatically. If you have lists with paragraphs, turn off the automatic bullets and create them with the bullets in **Symbols**. Use indent (not tab) to move the whole list in, not just a single line of it.
- Use a **header** (in the **Insert** or **View** menu) with automatic **page numbering** (pull down **Format** to **Page**) for second and subsequent pages. That way, when you delete a paragraph or expand your reader benefits, you don't have to move the header manually.

You can either delay the header until page 2 or create it on page 2. For best visual impact, make your header one point size smaller than the body type.

- For a two-page document, change the top **margin** of the second page to 0.5 inch (1.25 centimetre) so the header is close to the top of the page.
- Use the same side margins as your letterhead. If you aren't using letterhead, use 1 inch (2.5 centimetre) side margins.
- On a two-page document, make sure the second page has at least four to six lines of text for letters and at least 10 lines of text for memos. If you have less, either (1) add details, (2) start the message further down on page 1 so that there is more text on page 2, or (3) make the text fit on just one page by (a) tightening your prose, (b) using full justification to save space, or (c) using less white space.
- Word-processing programs have a **quick correct** or **auto correct** feature that changes *hte* to *the*, (c) to ©, and so forth. Go into the **Tools** or **Format** menus to find these features and edit them so they make only the changes you want.
- Hyphenation may be under **Format** or **Language** in **Tools**.
- Before you print, centre your document on the page like a picture in a frame. Go to **File**, **Page Setup**, **Layout**, **Vertical Alignment**, **Centre**.

Printing

- To save paper, check **Print Preview** on the **File** menu. You'll be able to see how your document will look on the page and make minor layout changes before you print.
- If you prepare your document on one computer and print it from another, be sure to open the document and check all of it before you print. Different printers may change margins slightly. Even the same-size font may differ from printer to printer: a document that fits on one page in 11-point on one computer may take up more room on a different one.

Minimize the number of links readers have to click through to get to the information they want.

Keep these points in mind as you design the pages:

- Use small graphics; keep animation to a minimum. Both graphics and animation take time to load, especially with a slow modem. Include a "Skip Intro" button if you have an animated introduction page.
- Provide visual variety. Use indentations, bulleted or numbered lists, and headings.
- Unify multiple pages with a small banner, graphic, or label so surfers know who sponsors each page.
- On each page, provide a link to the home page, the name and email address of the person who maintains the page, and the date when the page was last revised.
- If your Web pages include music or sound effects, put an "Off" button where users can find it immediately.

How Do I Know If My Design Works?

Test it.

A design that looks fine to you may not work for your audience. To know whether your design is functional, test it with your audience:

- Watch someone as he or she uses the document to do a task. Where does the reader pause, reread, or seem confused? How long does it take? Does the document enable the reader to complete the task accurately?
- Ask the reader to "think aloud" while completing the task: interrupt the reader at key points to ask what he or she is thinking, or ask the reader to describe his or her thought processes after completing the document and the task. Exploring the reader's thought processes is important, since a reader may get the right answer for the wrong reasons. You can thus identify where and how the design needs work.
- Test the document with the people most likely to have trouble with it: very young readers, people with little education, people who read English as a second language, and people who have little experience with Web pages.

Cultural FOCUS

Statistics predict that in Canada, the number of immigrants will continue to rise. Therefore, documents will need to be easy to read for all audiences. Make sure your design is accessible to the majority of people, not just you. Also, if you are creating documents for a specific cultural group, make sure you examine samples before you create your own. This way, you will ensure your documents meet the cultural expectations of that group.

When Should I Think About Design?

Think about design at each stage of the writing process.

Because layout and design make the first impression on readers, document design is a vital component of persuasion. Indeed, you create the best documents when you think about design at each stage of your writing process:

- As you plan, apply your PAIBOC audience analysis. Are your audience members skilled readers? Are they busy? Will they read the document straight through or skip around in it? Design the document to meet readers' needs and expectations.

- As you write, incorporate lists and headings. Use visuals to convey numerical data clearly and forcefully.
- Get feedback from people who will be using your document. What parts of the document do they find hard to understand? What additional information do they need?
- As you revise, check your draft against the guidelines in this module.

MODULE SUMMARY

- Your audience makes meaning first and foremost from the design of your message. Business audiences expect documents and slides to be easy to read and understand.
- An attractive document is inviting and easy to read. Visual grouping of ideas also makes the document easier to read.
- Good document design saves time, money, and legal problems.
- To create visually inviting documents,
  - Use white space
  - Use headings
  - Limit the use of words in all capital letters
  - Limit the number of fonts in a single document
  - Decide on whether to justify margins on the basis of your audience and situation analysis
- Keep presentation slides simple and relevant.
- To avoid slide overkill,
  - Use a large, sans-serif font
  - Use bullets
  - Use clear, concise language
  - Make only three to five points on a slide
  - Customize your slides to your audience

- Appealing Web pages offer both good content and interesting design:
  - Orient the reader to the site organization.
  - Offer an overview of the content, with links to take readers to the parts that interest them.
  - Make it clear what readers will get if they click on a link.
  - Keep graphics small.
  - Provide visual variety.
  - Unify multiple pages with a small banner, graphic, or label so surfers know who sponsors each page.
  - On each page, provide a link to the home page, the name and email address of the person who maintains the page, and the date when the page was last revised.
  - Include a "Skip Intro" button for animated introductions, and an "Off" button for sound.
- To test a document, observe readers, ask them to "think aloud" while completing the task, interrupt them at key points to ask them what they are thinking, or ask them to describe their thought processes after completing the document and the task.
- You create the best documents when you consider design throughout the writing process, and get feedback from people who will be using your document.

ASSIGNMENTS FOR MODULE 5

Questions for Critical Thinking

5.1 "Closed captions" for people with hearing impairments are almost always shown in full capitals. Why is that a bad idea? Are there any advantages to full capitals? What arguments might you use for changing the practice?

5.2 Suppose that, in one company, a worker says, "We don't need to worry about design. People pay a toll charge to call us, and we make a slight profit on each call. So if they have questions about the product, that's OK. If better design reduced the number of calls, we might actually lose money!" How would you

persuade such a person that good document design is worthwhile?

5.3 Royal College is preparing a brochure to persuade prospective students to consider taking classes. The school doesn't want to invest a lot of money in full-scale document testing. What free or almost-free things could it do to make the document as effective as possible?

5.4 Design choices have ethical implications. Indicate whether you consider each of the following actions ethical, unethical, or a grey area. Which of the actions would you do? Which would you feel uncomfortable doing? Which would you refuse to do? Why?

1. Putting the advantages of a proposal in a bulleted list, while discussing the disadvantages in a paragraph

2. Using a bigger type size so that a résumé fills a whole page

3. Putting the services not covered by your health plan in full capitals to make it less likely people will read the page

Exercises and Problems

5.5   Evaluating Page Designs

Use the guidelines in Module 5 to evaluate each of the following page designs. What are their strong points? What might be improved?

Source: Diane Burns and S. Venit, "What's Wrong with This Paper?," *PC Magazine* 17 (October 13, 1987): 174–75.

5.6 Evaluating PowerPoint Slides

Evaluate the following drafts of PowerPoint slides.

- Is the background appropriate for the topic?
- Do the slides use words or phrases rather than complete sentences?
- Is the font big enough to read from a distance?
- Is the art relevant and appropriate?
- Is each slide free from errors?

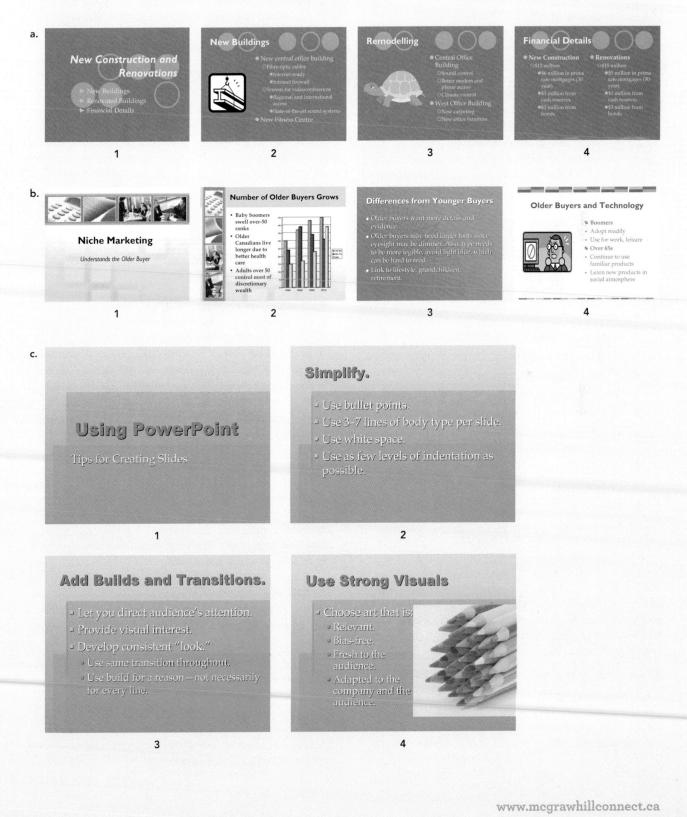

5.7   Using Headings

Reorganize the items in each of the following lists, using appropriate headings. Use bulleted or numbered lists as appropriate.

a. Rules and Procedures for a Tuition Reimbursement Plan

1. You are eligible to be reimbursed if you have been a full-time employee for at least three months.
2. You must apply before the first class meeting.
3. You must earn a C or better in the course.
4. You must submit a copy of the approved application, an official grade report, and a receipt for tuition paid to be reimbursed.
5. You can be reimbursed for courses related to your current position or another position in the company, or for courses that are part of a degree related to a current or possible job.
6. Your supervisor must sign the application form.
7. Courses may be at any appropriate level (high school, college or university, or graduate school).

b. Activities in Starting a New Business
- Getting a loan or venture capital
- Getting any necessary city or provincial licences
- Determining what you will make, do, or sell
- Identifying the market for your products or services
- Pricing your products or services
- Choosing a location
- Checking zoning laws that may affect the location
- Identifying government and university programs for small business development
- Figuring cash flow
- Ordering equipment and supplies
- Selling
- Advertising and marketing

5.8   Analyzing Documents

Collect several documents available to you as a worker, student, or consumer: letters and memos, newsletters, ads and flyers, reports. Using the guidelines in Module 5, your research, and your experience, create your own set of criteria to evaluate each of them.

As your instructor directs,
a. Form a group of three or four students.
b. Compare your design evaluation criteria.
c. Choose criteria you can all agree on.
d. Evaluate the collected documents using the group's criteria.

e. Write a memo to your instructor evaluating three or more of the documents. Include originals or photocopies of the documents you discuss as an appendix to your memo.
f. Write a memo to your supervisor recommending ways the organization can improve its documents.
g. In an oral presentation to the class, explain what makes one document good and another one weak. If possible, scan the documents so classmates can see them as you evaluate them.

5.9   Evaluating Web Pages

Compare three Web pages in the same category (e.g., non-profit organizations such as the Canadian Public Health Association, car companies, university departments, sports information). Using the guidelines in Module 5, your research, and your experience, create your own set of criteria to evaluate each of them.

Which pages are most effective? Why? What would you change? Why?

As your instructor directs,
a. Form a group of three or four students, and compare your design evaluation criteria.
b. Choose criteria you can all agree on.
c. Write a memo to your instructor evaluating the pages. Include the URLs of the pages in your memo.
d. In an oral presentation to the class, explain what makes one page good and another one weak. If possible, put the pages onscreen so classmates can see the pages as you evaluate them.
e. Post your evaluation of the pages in an email message or blog to the class. Include hot links to the pages you evaluate.

5.10   Analyzing a Document

Your municipal and provincial governments may offer internships and cooperative placements to postsecondary students. Research (visit, telephone, email, find someone who knows someone) the placement possibilities through your college/university co-op placement office, or contact the government department directly. Request a copy of the application or information documents for these positions. Write an analysis of the document's layout and page design.

5.11   Revising a Financial Aid Form

You've just joined the Financial Aid office at your school. The director gives you the accompanying form and asks you to redesign it.

"We need this form to see whether parents have other students in college or university besides the one requesting aid. Parents are supposed to list all family members that the parents support—themselves, the person here, any other kids in college or university, and any younger dependent kids.

"Half of these forms are filled out incorrectly. Most people just list the student going here; they leave out everyone else.

"If something is missing, the computer sends out a letter and a second copy of this form. The whole process starts over. Sometimes we send this form back two or three times before it's right. In the meantime, students' financial aid is delayed—maybe for months. Sometimes things are so late that they can't register for classes, or they have to pay tuition themselves and get reimbursed later.

"If so many people are filling out the form wrong, the form itself must be the problem. See what you can do with it. But keep it to a page."

As your instructor directs,

a. Analyze the current form and identify its problems.
b. Revise the form. Add necessary information; reorder information; change the chart to make it easier to fill out.

Hints:

- Where are people supposed to send the form? What is the phone number of the financial aid office? Should they need to call the office if the form is clear?
- Does the definition of *half-time* apply to all students or just those taking courses beyond high school?
- Should capital or lowercase letters be used?
- Are the lines big enough to write in?
- What headings or subdivisions within the form would remind people to list all family members whom they support?
- How can you encourage people to return the form promptly?

Please complete the chart below by listing all family members for whom you (the parents) will provide more than half support during the academic year (July 1 through June 30). Include yourselves (the parents), the student, and your dependent children, even if they are not attending college or university.

EDUCATIONAL INFORMATION, 2006–2007

FULL NAME OF FAMILY MEMBER	AGE	RELATIONSHIP OF FAMILY MEMBERS TO STUDENT	NAME OF SCHOOL, COLLEGE, OR UNIVERSITY SCHOOL YEAR	FULL-TIME	HALF-TIME* OR MORE	LESS THAN HALF-TIME
STUDENT APPLICANT						

*Half-time is defined as 6 credit hours or 12 clock hours a term.

When the information requested is received by our office, processing of your financial aid application will resume.

Please sign and mail this form to the above address as soon as possible. Your signature certifies that this information and the information on the FAF is true and complete to the best of your knowledge. If you have any questions, please contact a member of the needs analysis staff.

_____   _____
Signature of Parent(s)   Data

POLISHING YOUR PROSE

Active and Passive Voice

Because it depicts the action, the verb is the most important word in the sentence. Verbs indicate who or what is doing the action through "voice." When whoever is acting is also the subject of the sentence, the verb is active; in the passive voice, the subject is acted on by someone or something else.

Active:	The man bought grapes at the store.
Passive:	The grapes were bought at the store by the man.

In the active voice, the subject—the man—is doing the action—bought. In the passive version, "The grapes" is the subject, yet it is the man, not the grapes, actually doing the action. It is harder for the reader to follow who or what did the action. In addition, it takes more words to convey the same idea.

Contemporary communication prefers verbs in the active voice, because the resulting sentence is clearer and shorter. When writers want to avoid or downplay responsibility, they use the passive voice.

To change a passive voice construction into the active voice, start by identifying who or what is doing the action. If no agent ("by _____") is present in the sentence, you will need to supply it. A passive verb is usually accompanied by a copula verb, such as *is*, *are*, or *were*. Rewrite the sentence by putting the actor in the role of subject and dropping the helping verb:

Passive:	The plan was approved by our clients.
Active:	Our clients approved the plan.
Passive:	PowerPoint slides have been created.
Active:	Susan created the PowerPoint slides.
Passive:	It is desired that you back up your work daily.
Active:	Back up your work daily.

In business communication, active voice is usually better. However, passives are better in three situations:

1. Use passives to emphasize the object receiving the action, not the agent.

   Your order was shipped November 15.

   The customer's order, not the shipping clerk, is important.

2. Use passives to provide coherence within a paragraph. A sentence is easier to read if "old" information comes at the beginning of a sentence. When you have been discussing a topic, use the word again as your subject even if that requires a passive verb.

The bank made several risky loans in the late 1990s. These loans were written off as "uncollectible" in 2003.

Using "loans" as the subject of the second sentence provides a link between the two sentences, making the paragraph as a whole easier to read.

3. Use passives to avoid assigning blame.

   The order was damaged during shipment.

   An active verb would require the writer to specify who damaged the order. The passive here is more tactful.

Exercises

Identify whether the passives in the following sentences are acceptable, or whether the verb should be changed to active.

1. The contract was signed by the vice-president of finance.
2. New employees Ms. Taleroski, Mr. Franklin, and Ms. Holbreck were introduced at last week's staff meeting.
3. Two visitors are expected to arrive at headquarters tomorrow.
4. Outgoing correspondence was collected by the mailroom staff.
5. The proposal was turned in late.

Turn these passive-voice constructions into active-voice ones:

6. Correspondence was collected by the mailroom staff.
7. Phone calls were returned by the human resources administrator.
8. In April, budgets were amortized and files created for the project.
9. Phone calls need to be returned within 24 hours.
10. Packages are to be sent to the mailroom for delivery.

Check your answers to the odd-numbered exercises on page 551.

CASES FOR COMMUNICATORS

Minorities Need Apply

Canadians may feel complacent about Canadian multiculturalism. A closer look at our institutions, corporate boards and police forces, however, indicates that systemic prejudice still exists. The Royal Canadian Mounted Police (RCMP) is one of many Canadian institutions that must transform itself to reflect the diverse populations it serves.

At present, the RCMP is mostly made up of white males. Indeed, of the 1000 Mounties on the force, "just 6.4 percent ... are from minority backgrounds. Some 7.6 percent are aboriginal and 18 percent are women." Although visible minorities make up "about 13 percent" of officers on the Toronto and York police forces, "minority representation in Canadian police services averages around 5 percent." Since even our smaller cities are now attracting immigrants from all over the world, the RCMP recognizes it's time to recruit and hire people whose languages and cultures represent the diverse communities they serve.

But this goal is not as easy as it sounds. First, many recent immigrants do not know much about the RCMP; they don't know that the Mounties are a national police force with the same roles and responsibilities as provincial and municipal police officers. Secondly, the recruitment drive must be inclusive enough to attract applicants from Canada's widely diverse cultural mix.

How can the Mounties best reach their audiences?[5]

Individual Activity

You're the constable in charge of planning the RCMP diversity recruitment drive. Before you can devise any strategies, you need to apply the PAIBOC model to analyze the situation:

- **Purpose(s):** Why are we recruiting? What results do we want from our recruiting drive? How can we best attract the positive attention of our audiences?
- **Audiences(s):** Who are our target audiences? What groups are considered "diverse"? What do these groups know about the RCMP force? What do they need to know to be attracted to the force? How homogeneous are these target groups? What values of these disparate groups can we appeal to?
- **Information:** What information must our recruitment strategies convey? Why?
- **Benefits:** What are the many benefits, tangible and intangible, of joining the Mounties? What benefits would specifically attract our target groups?
- **Objections:** What objections about joining the RCMP might I expect? How can I best eliminate, overcome, or respond to those objections?
- **Context:** How do my target audiences feel about the RCMP? About policing in general? What current economic, political, legal and/or social events can I use to my advantage? What current events might deter members of my target audiences from joining the RCMP?

Write down your thoughts for future reference. Be as thorough as possible in your analysis.

Next, visit and tour the RCMP Web site, at www.rcmp-grc.gc.ca. How many of the groups identified as diverse do you see represented in the photos on the site? What is your opinion of the current recruitment drive strategies identified on the site? Jot down your impressions.

Group Activity

Form a recruitment drive committee with three other classmates. Compare notes on your PAIBOC analyses, and your analyses of the RCMP Web site. Together with your committee members, identify four recruitment strategies that will attract any/all of your four target groups.

Write a letter from your committee to Geoff Gruson, Executive Director of the Police Sector Council, in Ottawa, describing your recruitment drive strategies in detail.

Source: Reprinted with permission. Torstar Syndication Services.

One of Toyota Canada's top salespeople originally studied to become a nurse. However, completing the hospital practicum part of his course meant that Burt Townsend would have to quit the night security job where he worked to pay for his education. Burt had to leave college.

When he spied an automotive industry recruitment ad, he was intrigued by the promise of further education. A week's intensive training and scrutiny were required for both the career in the automotive industry and postsecondary education. "I've always been a car buff, and the opportunity appealed to me." Of the 1 000 applicants who showed up that first morning, only 10 graduated five days later. Burt was one of the graduates. Toyota hired him within a week of his interview.

Twelve years later, Burt continues to be his dealership's most successful salesperson. He is also the most accredited: the many Toyota University awards of achievement on his office wall attest to his belief that "you always have to be willing to learn, and to upgrade your skills.

"Toyota believes that quality sells, so my university courses focus on knowing the product. I learn everything I can about the vehicles, their engineering, technical, and functional operations, … about the competition, … I even learn about Toyota quality anecdotally, by listening to suppliers' stories. Toyota makes a quality product. That's why it's forecasted to lead car sales again this year. I couldn't sell the product if I didn't believe in it, and I've had plenty of other offers. So believing in what I'm selling, and having the product knowledge are big advantages. But that's not the whole story."

The dozens of client letters and emails that crowd his bulletin board tell the rest of the story. Customers want Burt—and Burt's boss—to know how his you-attitude has made them lifelong customers of this particular dealership.

"My focus is on the customer, and on building the relationship. I need to listen, to understand the other person's point of view: What does the purchase mean, from the customer's perspective? What are their expectations? What's their financial situation? What decision will meet their needs now and in the future?

"Anyone can sell that first car. What about the second, and the third? People don't want to buy the car and know that's the end of the transaction. What about after the sale? What if they need information or advice? What if they have an accident? My clients continue to depend and to call on me, five, six years after the initial sale. People want to establish that trust, to know someone will look after their interests, be there to take care of them, long after the sale.

"It's not about the sale. It's about building an ongoing relationship that's beneficial for both of us. At the end of the day, did I understand and do my best for my clients? Then I've done the job."

PAIBOC ANALYSIS

1. In what two ways does Burt influence his clients?

2. What methods does Toyota Canada use to create goodwill with its clients?

3. What you-attitude skills does Burt demonstrate?

4. What three of your values will determine the kind of car you buy?

6

Communicating You-Attitude

Learning Objectives

After reading and applying the information in Module 6, you'll be able to demonstrate

Knowledge of

- The importance of audience-focused messages

Skills to

- Adapt your message to the audience
- Begin to use persuasion strategies
- Emphasize what the reader wants to know
- Assess your messages for you-attitude

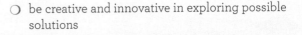

Employability Skills 2000+ Checklist

In this module, the key skills from the Conference Board of Canada's Employability Skills 2000+ are

Communicate

○ listen and ask questions to understand and appreciate the points of view of others

Think & Solve Problems

○ seek different points of view and evaluate them based on facts

○ recognize the human, interpersonal, technical, scientific, and mathematical dimensions of a problem

○ be creative and innovative in exploring possible solutions

Be Responsible

○ be accountable for your actions and the actions of your group

Work with Others

○ be flexible: respect, be open to, and be supportive of the thoughts, opinions, and contributions of others

○ recognize and respect people's diversity, individual differences, and perspectives

You-attitude is a way of communicating that demonstrates your ability to see another point of view. It means empathizing—"putting yourself in the other person's shoes."

Whether text messaging, emailing, or presenting, you-attitude

- Looks at the situation from the audience's point of view
- Treats the audience with courtesy
- Respects the audience's intelligence
- Protects the audience's ego
- Emphasizes what the audience wants to know

Communicating with you-attitude pays with positive results.

You-attitude also means making it easy for your audience to do what you want. For example, entrepreneur Kirk Layton, founder and president of Eservus.com Online Services Ltd., has made his online concierge services accessible and easy to use. His audience—property managers and building tenants across Canada— get exclusive access to "discounted sports, theatre and movie tickets, flower ... [and] travel services and a variety of other things usually associated with traditional in-house concierges at high-end properties." Layton markets his services by getting clients to register online; registrants' "weekly permission-based email newsletter" generates services sales and builds Eservus' client base. Layton has translated his you-attitude focus into a $3 million enterprise.[1]

Kirk Layton's online concierge products and services provide client recognition.

What Is You-Attitude in Writing?

You-attitude messages focus politely and positively on the audience.

Writers create you-attitude through their rhetorical (persuasive) choices (Module 5). Appearance, layout, visuals, content, and language all contribute to reader-centred documents, as Figure 6.1 demonstrates.[2]

Compare the authorial choices in Figure 6.1 with those of the writer in Figure 6.2. This writer-centred memo refers to the author throughout, and the last paragraph sounds condescending: no colleague or supervisor would appreciate being spoken to this way.

Language FOCUS

To be **condescending** means that you are speaking to someone as if they were younger, or not as smart as you are. It is often referred to as "talking down to" someone. When writing, if you are unsure if your tone is condescending, ask one of your classmates for feedback.

FIGURE 6.1   **Christmas Appeal from the Salvation Army Demonstrates You-Attitude Through Visuals, Layout, and Language Choices**

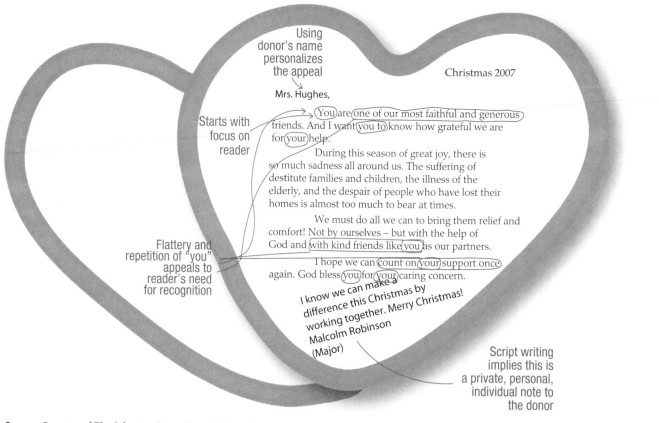

Source: Courtesy of The Salvation Army, Ontario Central Division. Reprinted with permission.

FIGURE 6.2   **Writer-Centred Memo Without You-Attitude**

Date: April 3, 2007

To: Li Zhou

From: Adrian Trin

Subject: Guest Speaker

I would like to take the opportunity to thank you for arranging to have Chris Bosh come to speak to my Grade 8 students. I have greatly admired Bosh's prowess on the court, so I was truly thrilled when I heard he was coming to our school.

I was amazed to hear how young Bosh was when he came to Canada to play for the Raptors, and I was also surprised to find out how far-reaching his foundation is. I was most gratified, however, by the opportunity to speak with Bosh after his presentation.

I want to say thanks again, and keep up the great work!

How Do I Create Reader-Focused, You-Attitude?

Talk about the reader—except in negative situations.

To create you-attitude,

1. Talk about the reader, not about yourself.
2. Avoid talking about feelings, except to congratulate or offer sympathy.
3. Use *you* more often than *I* in positive situations. Use *we* when it includes the reader.
4. Avoid the blaming *you* in negative situations.

1. Talk about the reader, not about yourself.

Readers want to know how they benefit or are affected. When you provide this information, you make your message more interesting and more compelling.

Lacks you-attitude: I have negotiated an agreement with Apex Rent-a-Car that gives you a discount on rental cars.

You-attitude: As a Sun Life employee, you now get a 20 percent discount when you rent a car from Apex.

Instead of focusing on what you are doing for the reader, it's important to stress how the reader will benefit. Any sentence that focuses on the writer's work or generosity lacks you-attitude, even if the sentence contains the word *you*. To change the emphasis, you may need to change the structure of the sentence.

Lacks you-attitude: We are shipping your order of September 21 this afternoon.

You-attitude: The two dozen print cartridges you ordered will be shipped this afternoon and should reach you by September 28.

Emphasize what the reader wants to know. The reader is more interested in when the order will arrive than when you shipped it. Note that the phrase "should reach you by" leaves room for variations in delivery schedules. If you can't be exact, give your reader the information you do have: "UPS shipment from Burnaby to Regina normally takes two business days." If you have absolutely no idea, give the reader the name of the carrier, so the reader knows whom to contact if the order doesn't arrive promptly.

2. Avoid talking about feelings, except to congratulate or offer sympathy.

Lacks you-attitude:	We are happy to extend you a credit line of $5 000.
You-attitude:	You can now charge up to $5 000 on your Bank of Montreal card.

In most business situations, your feelings are irrelevant. The reader doesn't care whether you're happy, bored stiff at granting a routine application, or worried about granting so much to someone who barely qualifies. *All the reader cares about is the situation from his or her point of view.*

It is appropriate to talk about your own emotions in a message of congratulations or condolences.

You-attitude:	Congratulations on your promotion to district manager! I was really pleased to read about it.
You-attitude:	I was sorry to hear that your father died.

In internal memos, it may be appropriate to comment that a project has been gratifying or frustrating. In the letter of transmittal that accompanies a report, it is permissible to talk about your feelings about doing the work. But other readers in your own organization are primarily interested in their own concerns, not your feelings.

Of course you-attitude also includes choosing the appropriate medium for your message. People prefer to get handwritten cards—not emails or text messages—on important occasions (births, deaths, marriages). Negotiations and conflict-resolution situations demand face-to-face dialogue.

Don't talk about the reader's feelings, either. It can be offensive to have someone else tell us how we feel—especially if the writer is wrong.

Lacks you-attitude:	You'll be happy to hear that Open Grip Walkway Channels meet Occupational Health and Safety requirements.
You-attitude:	Open Grip Walkway Channels meet Occupational Health and Safety requirements.

Maybe the reader expects that anything you sell meets government regulations. (Occupational Health and Safety, Canada's national centre for workplace safety, is a federal government agency) The reader may even be disappointed if he or she expected higher standards. Simply explain the situation or describe a product's features; don't predict the reader's response.

When you have good news for the reader, simply give the good news.

Lacks you-attitude:	You'll be happy to hear that your scholarship has been renewed.
You-attitude:	Congratulations! Your scholarship has been renewed.

> ### Checkpoint
>
> **You-attitude** is a style of writing that
> - Looks at things from the reader's point of view
> - Respects the reader's Intelligence
> - Protects the reader's ego
> - Emphasizes what the reader wants to know

3. Use *you* more often than *I* in positive situations.

Use *we* when it includes the reader.

Talk about the reader, not you or your company.

Lacks you-attitude:	We provide dental coverage to all employees.
You-attitude:	You receive dental coverage as a full-time Clairtone employee.

Depending on your audience, you may certainly use *I* in email messages, letters, and memos. However, avoid beginning the first sentence of any written message with *I*.

Edit external messages to ensure *I* is used rarely. *I* suggests that you're concerned about personal issues, not about the organization's problems, needs, and opportunities. *We* works well when it includes the reader. Avoid *we* if it excludes the reader (as it would in a letter to a customer or supplier, or as it might in a memo about what *we* in management want *you* to do).

4. Avoid *you* in negative situations.

To avoid blaming the reader, use an impersonal expression or a passive verb.

Lacks you-attitude:	You failed to sign your cheque.
You-attitude (impersonal):	Your cheque arrived without a signature.
You-attitude (passive)	The cheque was not signed.

Impersonal constructions omit people and talk only about things.

Passive verbs describe the action performed on something, without necessarily saying who did it. (See Module 5 on active and passive voice. See the Revising and Editing Resources at the end of this book for a full discussion of passive verbs.)

In most cases, active verbs are better. But when your reader is at fault, passive verbs may be useful to avoid assigning blame.

Normally, writing is most lively when it's about people, and most interesting to readers when it's about them. When you have to report a mistake or bad news, however, you can protect the reader's ego by using an impersonal construction—one in which things, not people, do the acting.

Lacks you-attitude:	You made no allowance for inflation in your estimate.
You-attitude (passive):	No allowance for inflation has been made in this estimate.
You-attitude (impersonal):	This estimate does not allow for inflation.

A purist might say that impersonal constructions are illogical. An estimate, for example, is inanimate and can't "allow" anything. In the practical world of business writing, however, impersonal constructions often help you convey potentially critical information tactfully.

Cultural FOCUS

Despite the perception that North Americans prefer openness and informality, members of low-context cultures (see Module 3) expect a respectful tone in business communication.

When you restrict the reader's freedom, talk about the group to which the reader belongs rather than about the reader as an individual.

Lacks you-attitude: You must get approval from the communications department before you speak with any media agency.

You-attitude: Conversations with the media require approval from the communications department.

When you have negatives, third person (*she, he, it*) is better you-attitude than second person (*you*), because third person shows that everyone is being treated the same way.

Employability Skills

Checkpoint

Four Ways to Create You-Attitude

1. Talk about the reader, not about yourself.
2. Avoid talking about feelings, except to congratulate or offer sympathy.
3. In positive situations, use *you* more often than *I*. Use *we* when it includes the reader.
4. Avoid *you* in negative situations.

Does You-Attitude Mean Using the Word *You*?

Communicating you-attitude means making deliberate choices in layout, content, language, and organization—choices to influence your audience to pay attention to and act on your message.

All reader-centred messages use you-attitude, but the words that achieve it change depending on the situation.

- In a positive message, focus on what the reader can do. "We give you" lacks you-attitude, because the sentence focuses on what *we* are doing.
- Avoid *you* when it criticizes the reader or limits the reader's freedom.
- In a job application letter, create you-attitude by showing how you can help meet the reader's needs, but keep the word *I* to a minimum (Module 25).

I've Revised My Sentences. Do I Need to Do Anything Else?

Emphasize what the reader wants to know.

Good messages apply you-attitude beyond the sentence level by using *content and organization* as well as style to build goodwill.

Consider the email letter in Figure 6.3. As the marginal notes indicate, many individual sentences in this letter lack you-attitude. The last sentence in paragraph one sounds both harsh and defensive. The language is stiff, harsh, repetitive, and filled with outdated jargon. Perhaps the most serious problem is that the fact most interesting to the reader is surrounded by negative-sounding statements. Since we have good news for the reader, we should put that information first, as the writer does in her revision, Figure 6.4. (See Module 11.)

EXPANDING A CRITICAL SKILL

Seeing Another Point of View

Imagine the job competition in the most populated country in the world: How would you differentiate yourself? For the Chinese, market differentiation lies in knowing how to speak English well, which translates into more job opportunities and an "estimated 70% higher" salary. Given the motivation, and the numbers of eager students, how would you proceed?

Canadian entrepreneur Michael Kraft (Lingo Media Corporation) designed the ideal solution: fun and free interactive English lessons at Speak2Me.cn.

Learners hold conversations with Lucy, the virtual language teacher; speech recognition software encourages learners to refine their English pronunciation. The site uses social networking software, like Facebook's, to target a potential 40 million postsecondary students.

The initial projection of 600 000 Speak2Me.cn users may be low. Research shows at least 250 million people want to learn conversational English, and China's ESL market is worth over $2 billion.

And how will Kraft make money from his venture? Again, audience analysis is key. Companies pay to place their products in a conversation scenario (buying a coffee), and have over 300 such scenarios to choose from. The advertiser is targeting a potential client base of millions.

PAIBOC analysis with a focus on you-attitude provided Michael Kraft with a perspective on how to encourage people to master a difficult skill: make it fun and free. That same analysis will pay back millions.

Sources: Fabrice Taylor, "How to Make Money Teaching English for Free," Report on Business, *The Globe and Mail*, June 20, 2008, retrieved June 25, 2008 from http://www.reportonbusiness.com/servlet/story/RTGAM. 20080619.wvox0620/BNStory/Business; BNET Business Network, retrieved July 11, 2008 from http://findarticles.com/p/articles/mi_pwwi/is_200803/ ai_n24368312; "Speak2Me Presents Business English Training Opportunity to Chinese Investors," Alpha Trade Finance, April 22, 2009, retrieved April 29, 2009 from http://finance.alphatrade.com/story/2009-04-22/CCN/2009042 20840CCNMATHWCANADAPR_0525498001.html.

FIGURE 6.3   **A Letter Lacking You-Attitude**

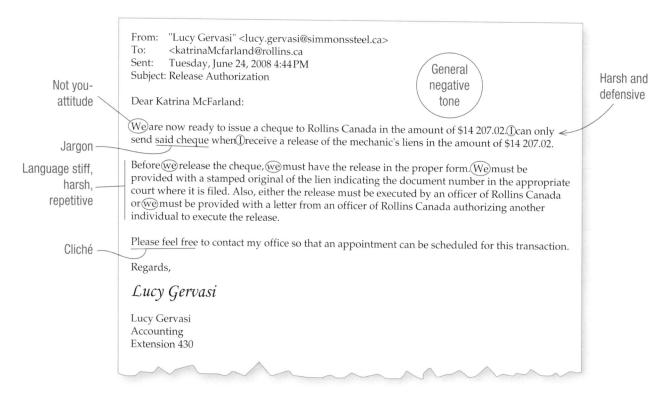

Not you-attitude

Jargon

Language stiff, harsh, repetitive

Cliché

General negative tone

Harsh and defensive

From: "Lucy Gervasi" <lucy.gervasi@simmonssteel.ca>
To: <katrinaMcfarland@rollins.ca>
Sent: Tuesday, June 24, 2008 4:44 PM
Subject: Release Authorization

Dear Katrina McFarland:

We are now ready to issue a cheque to Rollins Canada in the amount of $14 207.02. I can only send said cheque when I receive a release of the mechanic's liens in the amount of $14 207.02.

Before we release the cheque, we must have the release in the proper form. We must be provided with a stamped original of the lien indicating the document number in the appropriate court where it is filed. Also, either the release must be executed by an officer of Rollins Canada or we must be provided with a letter from an officer of Rollins Canada authorizing another individual to execute the release.

Please feel free to contact my office so that an appointment can be scheduled for this transaction.

Regards,

Lucy Gervasi

Lucy Gervasi
Accounting
Extension 430

FIGURE 6.4   **A Letter Revised to Improve You-Attitude**

You-attitude

No jargon; language more natural

Positive approach

Numbered/bulleted info makes it easy for reader to understand and comply.

From: "Lucy Gervasi" <lucy.gervasi@simmonssteel.ca>
To: <katrinaMcfarland@rollins.ca>
Sent: Tuesday, June 24, 2008 4:44 PM
Subject: Release Authorization

Dear Katrina McFarland:

With your help we can clean up the lien in the Allen contract.

Your company will receive a cheque for $14 207.02 as soon as you give us a release for the mechanic's lien of $14 207.02.

To ensure the release is in the proper form, please

1.   Give us a stamped original of the lien with the document's court number, and
2.   Either
   a.   Have an officer of your company sign the release
        or
   b.   Give us a letter from a Rollins officer authorizing someone else to sign the release.

Please call to tell me which way works best for you.

Sincerely,

Lucy Gervasi

Lucy Gervasi
Accounting
Extension 430

To create goodwill with *content*,

- Be concise and complete: give the reader the necessary information and *only* the necessary information to get the results you want.
- Consider using an appendix or attachment for information that the reader may want to see but that does not directly support your purpose.
- Anticipate and answer questions or objections the reader is likely to have.
- Show why information that the reader did not ask for, but that you've included, is important.
- Explain to readers how the subject of your message affects them.

To build goodwill with *organization*,

- Put the information that readers are most interested in first.
- Arrange the information to meet your reader's needs, not yours.
- Use headings and lists so that the reader can find key points quickly.

Use the checklist in Figure 6.5 to assess your messages for the you-attitude that builds goodwill.

FIGURE 6.5   You-Attitude Checklist

1. **The message is clear:**
   - ❑ Signals to the reader that it's a business message.
   - ❑ Defines the purpose of the message.
   - ❑ Organized so that form follows function.
   - ❑ Uses business language.
   - ❑ Provides specific details in concrete language.

2. **The message is concise:**
   - ❑ Provides all relevant information using the fewest possible words.

3. **The message is comprehensive:**
   - ❑ Uses a format appropriate to the purpose, the audience, and the situation.
   - ❑ Has a beginning, middle, and end.
   - ❑ Uses a thesis to establish unity and coherence.
   - ❑ Establishes rapport; is reader-centred.
   - ❑ Demonstrates that the writer knows, understands, and respects the audience.
   - ❑ Uses transitional words and phrases to lead the reader from one idea to the next.
   - ❑ Tells the audience what's in it for them.

4. **The message is complete:**
   - ❑ Gives all necessary proof, explanations, and examples.
   - ❑ Anticipates the audience's questions, concerns, and objections.
   - ❑ Tells the audience what to do next or what's going to happen next.

5. **The message is correct:**
   - ❑ Is error-free.
   - ❑ Demonstrates revision, editing, and proofreading.

MODULE SUMMARY

- Communicating with you-attitude means consciously writing and speaking in a way that
  - Looks at the situation from the audience's point of view
  - Treats the audience with courtesy
  - Respects the audience's intelligence
  - Protects the audience's ego
  - Emphasizes what the audience wants to know.
- You convey you-attitude when you choose organization, content, layout and style to build goodwill with your audience.

- You apply you-attitude in sentences when you
  - Talk about the reader/audience, not about yourself
  - Refer specifically to the audience's request or order
  - Don't talk about feelings, except to congratulate or offer sympathy
- In positive situations, use *you* more often than *I*. Use *we* when it includes the reader.
- Avoid the blaming *you* in negative situations.

ASSIGNMENTS FOR MODULE 6

Questions for Critical Thinking

6.1 Think of a time when you knew that a business or organization cared about you. What words and/or actions made you feel that way?

6.2 How does technology influence the you-attitude in communications? When texting, and/or creating voicemail messages, how do you convey you-attitude?

6.3 What strategies do you use to compensate for hastily sent messages that may sound curt, or contain grammar and spelling mistakes?

Exercises and Problems

6.4   The Ethical Consideration of You-Attitude: A Memo Report (See Modules 20 and 21)

In what situation(s) might you consider audience-focused messages unethical? Consider, for example, print and Internet advertising, and the persuasive tactics of telemarketers, or people selling energy savings door to door. When have you felt uncomfortable, or exploited, by you-attitude messages?

Write a two-page memo report for your teacher and fellow students describing in detail one such situation. What ethical boundaries did the message cross? If you were the speaker or writer, what would you do differently?

6.5   Using Passives and Impersonal Constructions to Improve You-Attitude

Revise each of these sentences to improve you-attitude, first using a passive verb, then using an impersonal construction (one in which things, not people, do the action). Are both revisions equally good? Why or why not?

1. You did not send us your cheque.
2. You did not include all the necessary information in your letter.
3. By failing to build a fence around your pool, you have created a health hazard.

4. Because your section is always late, we miss the deadline and lose marks.
5. You didn't look at the itinerary so you aren't prepared.
6. Your driving a Hummer is neither cost- nor environmentally effective.

6.6 Improving You-Attitude

Revise these sentences to improve you-attitude. Eliminate any awkward phrasing. In some cases, you may need to add information to revise the sentence effectively.

1. We are pleased to offer you the ability to sign up for dental coverage online on our intranet.
2. You will be happy to know that you can use your new cell phone number anywhere in Canada.
3. After hours of hard work, I have negotiated a new employee benefit for you.
4. I urge you to attend a meeting about the new benefits package so that we can inform you about your rights and responsibilities.
5. You will be happy to learn that additional cards for your spouse or child are free.
6. We have added another employee benefit for you.
7. Today, we shipped the book you ordered.
8. In your report, you forgot to tell how many people you surveyed.
9. I hope that it is obvious to you that we want to give you the very best prices on furniture.
10. You didn't order enough doughnuts for the meeting.

6.7 Improving You-Attitude

Revise these sentences to improve you-attitude. Eliminate any awkward phrasing. In some cases, you may need to add information to revise the sentence effectively.

1. Starting next month, the company will offer you a choice of three different health plans.
2. We provide dental coverage to all full-time employees.
3. At the meeting, we'll tell you about the team responsibilities and how we expect you to behave.
4. I have ordered a new computer for you. I expect it to arrive by the 15th, and I'll get it ready for you to use as soon as my schedule permits.
5. We are happy to enrol you in our stock-purchase plan.
6. You will be happy to learn that you can transfer credits from our business diploma programs to a university commerce degree.

7. We give you the following benefits when you join our "Frequent Flier" program.
8. We are pleased to send you a copy of "Investing in Stocks," which you requested.
9. Your audit papers did not convert U.S. revenue into Canadian dollars.
10. Of course we want to give you every possible service that you might need or want.

6.8 Revising a Form Letter for You-Attitude

You've taken a part-time job at a store that sells fine jewellery. In orientation, the manager tells you that the store photographs the jewellery it sells or appraises and mails the photo as a goodwill gesture after the transaction. However, when you see the form letter, you know that it doesn't build much goodwill—and you say so.

The manager says, "Well, you're in postsecondary. Suppose you rewrite it."

Rewrite the letter. Use square brackets for material (such as the customer's name) that would have to be inserted in the form letter to vary it for a specific customer. Add information that would help build goodwill.

> Dear Customer:
>
> We are most happy to enclose a photo of the jewellery that we recently sold you or appraised for you. We feel that this added service, which we are happy to extend to our fine customers, will be useful should you want to insure your jewellery.
>
> We trust you will enjoy this additional service. We thank you for the confidence you have shown by coming to our store.
>
> Sincerely,
>
> Your Sales Associate

6.9 Evaluating You-Attitude in Documents That Cross Your Desk

Identify three sentences that use (or should use) you attitude in documents you see as a student, consumer, or worker. If the sentences are good, write them down or attach a copy of the document(s) marking the sentence(s) in the margin. If the sentences need work, provide both the original sentence and a possible revision.

As your instructor directs,

a. Share your examples with a small group of students.

b. Write a memo to your instructor discussing your examples.

c. Post an email message or blog to the class discussing your examples.

d. Present two or three of your examples to the class in a short presentation.

e. With your small group, write a collaborative short report to your instructor about the patterns you see.

POLISHING YOUR PROSE

Using the Apostrophe for Contractions and *It's/Its*

The apostrophe replaces the missing letter in a contraction:

It is → it's

I have → I've

You will → you'll

We are → we're

You are → you're

They are → they're

With an apostrophe, *it's* is a contraction meaning *it is*. Without an apostrophe, *its* is a possessive pronoun meaning *belonging to it*.

Since *it's* and *its* sound the same, you have to look at the logic of your sentence to choose the right word: if you can substitute *it is*, and the sentence makes sense, use *it's*.

Exercises

Choose the right word in the set of parentheses.

1. (It's/its) too bad that the team hasn't finished (it's/its) presentation.

2. The company projected that (it's/its) profits would rise during the next quarter.

3. (It's/its) going to require overtime, because the data centre needs (it's/its) reports quickly.

4. I don't want responsibility for the project unless (it's/its) important.

5. The company will announce (it's/its) new name at a press conference.

6. I'm not sure whether (it's/its) a good idea to offer a conference.

7. (It's/its) a good idea to keep your travel receipts in a separate file.

8. (It's/its) good that our computer automatically backs up (it's/its) files.

9. The Saskatoon office will share (it's/its) findings with the other branch offices.

10. (It's/its) cash reserves protected the company from a hostile takeover.

Check your answers to the odd-numbered exercises on page 551.

Communicating with Positive Emphasis

Learning Objectives

After reading and applying the information in Module 7, you'll be able to demonstrate

Knowledge of

- Methods to reframe information positively
- The legal and practical advantages of doing business ethically
- Techniques to convey appropriate tone in your messages

Skills to

- Continue to build your persuasion skills
- Emphasize the positive
- Use positive emphasis ethically
- Choose an appropriate tone

Employability Skills 2000+ Checklist

In this module, the key skills from the Conference Board of Canada's Employability Skills 2000+ are

Communicate

○ write and speak so others pay attention and understand

Manage Information

○ assess, analyze, and apply knowledge and skills from various disciplines

Think & Solve Problems

○ assess situations and identify problems
○ seek different points of view and evaluate them based on facts
○ be creative and innovative in exploring possible solutions

○ recognize the human, interpersonal, technical, scientific, and mathematical dimensions of a problem
○ check to see if a solution works, and act on opportunities for improvement

Be Adaptable

○ be innovative and resourceful: identify and suggest alternative ways to achieve goals and get the job done

○ be open and respond constructively to change

Positive emphasis is a way of presenting, or framing a situation. Choosing to communicate positively through words, content, organization, and layout (Module 5) is a fundamental principle of successful negotiating. And positive emphasis is persuasive. Projecting the positive can favourably influence your audience's opinion of you and your message. Even when delivering negative messages, doing so clearly, briefly and honestly—as Maple Leaf Foods. President and CEO Michael McCain did in a variety of media throughout the listeria crisis—can positively influence your audiences.

What's the Point of Positive Emphasis?

Positive emphasis is part of creating goodwill.

A positive work environment is essential to recruit, retain, and motivate employees.[1] And, according to VanCity Savings Credit Union CEO Dave Mowatt, a positive workplace is more productive: "[Y]ou can draw a direct, straight-line relationship to the financial success of your company. It is just a fact that the higher the morale of your organization, the more money you make."[2]

Furthermore, people who choose to communicate positively tend to live longer and more healthily.[3] Positive emphasis is part of successful communication.

Indeed, positive emphasis is characteristic of successful entrepreneurs, since they perceive opportunities and are undaunted by failure.[4] CV Technologies' CEO and Chief Scientific Officer (CSO) Jacqueline Shan couldn't speak English when she emigrated from China "to pursue a PhD in physiology at the University of Alberta." Shan concentrated her research on the potential for scientifically validating herbal medicines. Together with partner Peter Pang, Shan developed Cold-fX, "the top-selling cold remedy in Canada."

Before Cold-fX attracted media attention and investors, CV Technologies floundered financially. Shan never gave up. She began managing CV's business and marketing operations, and sales grew. In the first half of 2005, CV Technologies' "net income [went] from a loss of $58,569 to a profit of $6.8 million." And Cold-fX's potential is such that "[a]n Edmonton-based study is ... examining whether it could become a 'standard of care' for the prevention of upper respiratory infections in Canadian nursing homes."[5]

Dr. Jacqueline Shan's positive outlook helped her find a herbal cold preventative.

What Should I Do If My Message Is Bad News?

Deliver the news responsibly: be clear and sensitive.

Legal and practical reasons demand that you deliver negative information sensitively.

Straightforward negatives build credibility when you have bad news to give the reader, such as announcements of layoffs, product defects and recalls, or price increases. Being honest about the drawbacks of a job situation increases motivation, morale, and the likelihood that employees will stay.

Furthermore, negatives may help people take a problem seriously. Wall Data improved the reliability of its computer programs when it eliminated the term *bugs* and used the term *failures* instead.

In some messages, such as negative performance appraisals, your purpose is to deliver a rebuke with no alternative. In these situations, you are legally responsible for ensuring that your language conforms to organizational and governmental regulations (in a union environment, to the rules in the collective agreement; in every workplace situation, to the province's *Employment Standards Act/Code* and to the Human Rights Commission mandates concerning issues of harassment and discrimination).

Employability Skills

Even in a rejection letter, good writers avoid negative words that insult or attack the reader.
PEANUTS reprinted with permission of United Features Syndicate.

In most situations, however, it's better to be positive. People respond more favourably to positive than to negative language, and are more likely to act on a positively worded request.[6]

How Do I Create Positive Emphasis?

Deemphasize or omit negative words and information.

The following five techniques deemphasize negative information:

1. Avoid negative words and words with negative connotations.
2. Focus on what the reader can do rather than on limitations.
3. Justify negative information by giving a reason or linking it to a reader benefit.
4. Omit the negative if it is unimportant.
5. Put the negative information in the middle and present it compactly.

You won't use all five techniques in every negative message (Module 12). Practise each of these techniques so that you can use whichever are appropriate to your purpose and the needs of your audience.

Language FOCUS

Connotation means an associated meaning for a word, not the literal meaning. For example, if you think of the word "dog," you may think of caring and loyalty if you like dogs, but if you are afraid of dogs the connotation is negative. Words have many connotations in different cultures, so it important to be aware of these as well as the literal meaning of words. If you are using a translation dictionary while composing, be sure to use a good English dictionary to check for both literal and connotative meanings.

Negative Words and Words with Negative Connotations

Table 7.1 lists some common negative words. If you find one of these words in a draft, substitute a more positive word. When you must use a negative, use the *least negative* term that will convey your meaning.

The following examples show how to replace negative words with positive words.

Negative: We have failed to finish taking inventory.

Better: We haven't finished taking inventory.

Still better: We will be finished taking inventory Friday.

Negative: If you can't understand this explanation, feel free to call me.

Better: If you have further questions, please call me.

Still better: (Omit the sentence.)

If a sentence has two negatives, substitute one positive term.

Negative: Do not forget to back up your disks.

Better: Always back up your disks.

TABLE 7.1   **Negative Words to Avoid**

Negative words			Some *dis-* Words	Some *mis-* Words
afraid	fail	objection	disapprove	misfortune
anxious	fault	problem	dishonest	missing
avoid	fear	reject	dissatisfied	mistake
bad	hesitate	reluctant		
careless	ignorant	sorry	**Many *in-*Words**	**Many *un-*Words**
damage	ignore	terrible	inadequate	unclear
delay	impossible	trivial	incomplete	unfair
delinquent	lacking	trouble	inconvenient	unfortunate
deny	loss	wait	injury	unfortunately
difficulty	neglect	weakness	insincere	unpleasant
eliminate	never	worry		unreasonable
error	no	wrong		unreliable
except	not			unsure

When you must use a negative term, use the least negative word that is accurate.

Negative: Your balance of $835 is delinquent.

Better: Your balance of $835 is past due.

Getting rid of negatives has the added benefit of making what you write easier to understand. Sentences with three or more negatives are very hard to understand.[7]

Beware of **hidden negatives**: words that are not negative in themselves but become negative in context. *But* and *however* indicate a shift; so, after a positive statement, they are negative. *I hope* and *I trust that* suggest you aren't sure. *Patience* may sound like a virtue, but it is a necessary virtue only when things are slow. Even positives about a service or product may backfire if they suggest that in the past the service or product was bad.

Negative: I hope this is the information you wanted. [Implication: I'm not sure.]

Better: Enclosed is a brochure about road repairs scheduled for 2009–10.

Still better: The brochure contains a list of all roads and bridges scheduled for repair during 2009–10. Call Gwen Wong at 604-555-3245 for specific dates when work will start and stop, and for alternative routes.

Hewlett-Packard's free recycling envelope positively emphasizes free and easy environmental awareness while reinforcing its brand.

Negative: Please be patient as we switch to the automated system.
[Implication: You can expect problems.]

Better: If you have questions during our transition to the automated system, call Melissa Morgan.

Still better: You'll be able to get information instantly about any house on the market when the automated system is in place. If you have questions during the transition, call Melissa Morgan.

Negative: Now Crispy Krisp tastes better.
[Implication: It used to taste terrible.]

Better: Now Crispy Krisp tastes even better.

Removing negatives does not mean being arrogant or pushy.

Negative: I hope that you are satisfied enough to place future orders.

Arrogant: I look forward to receiving all of your future business.

Better: Call Mercury whenever you need transistors.

When you eliminate negative words, be sure to maintain accuracy. Words that are exact opposites will usually not be accurate. Instead, use specifics to be both positive and accurate.

Negative: The exercycle is not guaranteed for life.

Not true: The exercycle is guaranteed for life.

True: The exercycle is guaranteed for 10 years.

Negative: Customers under 25 are not eligible for the Prime Time discount.

Not true: You must be over 25 to be eligible for the Prime Time discount.

True: If you're 25 or older, you can save 10 percent on all your purchases with RightWay's Prime Time discount.

Legal phrases also have negative connotations for most readers and should be avoided whenever possible. The idea will sound more positive if you use everyday English.

Negative: If your account is still delinquent, a second, legal notice will be sent to you informing you that cancellation of your policy will occur 30 days after the date of the legal notice if we do not receive your cheque.

Better: Even if your cheque is lost in the mail and never reaches us, you still have a 30-day grace period. If you do get a second notice, you will know that your payment hasn't reached us. To keep your account in good standing, stop payment on the first cheque and send a second one.

Focus on What the Reader Can Do Rather Than on Limitations

Sometimes, positive emphasis is a matter of the way you present something: Is the glass half empty or half full? Sometimes it's a matter of eliminating double negatives. When there are limits, or some options are closed, focus on the alternatives that remain.

Negative: We will not allow you to charge more than $1 500 on your Visa account.

Better: You can charge $1 500 on your new Visa card.

Or: Your new Visa card gives you $1 500 in credit that you can use at thousands of stores nationwide.

As you focus on what will happen, check for you-attitude (Module 6). In the last example, "We will allow you to charge $1 500" is positive, but it lacks you-attitude.

When you have a benefit, and a requirement the reader must meet to get the benefit, the sentence is usually more positive if you put the benefit first.

Negative: You will not qualify for the student membership rate of $25 a year unless you are enrolled for at least 10 hours.

Better: You get all the benefits of membership for only $25 a year if you're enrolled for 10 hours or more.

Justify Negative Information by Giving a Reason or Linking It to a Reader Benefit

A reason can help your reader see that the information is necessary; a benefit can suggest that the negative aspect is outweighed by positive factors. Be careful, however, to make the logic behind your reason clear and to leave no loopholes.

Negative: We cannot sell computer disks in lots of fewer than 10.

Loophole: To keep down packaging costs and to help you save on shipping and handling costs, we sell computer disks in lots of 10 or more.

EXPANDING A CRITICAL SKILL

Using Positive Emphasis Ethically

Several of the methods to achieve positive emphasis can be misused. Consider omission.

A bank notified customers that chequing account fees were being "revised" but omitted the amounts. Customers had to go into the bank and copy down the new (higher) fees themselves.

In another case, a condominium resort offered an "all-terrain vehicle" as a prize for visiting. (Winners had to pay $29.95 for "handling, processing, and insurance.") The actual "prize" was a lawn chair with four wheels that converted into a wheeled cart. The company claims it told the truth: "It is a vehicle. It's a four-wheel cart you can take anywhere—to the beach, to the pool. It may not be motorized, but [we] didn't say it was motorized."

In both cases, full disclosure might have affected decisions: some customers might have chosen to change banks; some customers would have declined the condominium visit. It isn't ethical to omit information that people need to make decisions. Presenting information compactly can also go too far. A credit card company mailed out a letter with the good news that the minimum monthly payment was going down. But a separate small flyer explained that interest rates (on the charges not repaid) were going up. The print was far too small to read: 67 lines of type were crowded into five vertical inches of text.

Ethicist Chris MacDonald suggests that making ethical choices, regardless of our motivation, leads to positive results. Even when businesses act ethically because doing so "is good for the bottom line," everyone benefits. An organization that treats its employees, clients, and shareholders ethically enhances its reputation and builds its business. Furthermore, even when it originates out of self-interest, ethical behaviour can be habit-forming.

Sources: Chris MacDonald, "Why Act Ethically? And Does the Answer a Company Gives Matter?," August 4, 2004, retrieved August 8, 2006 from http://www.ethicsweb.ca/bepubs.html; Carmella M. Padilla, "It's a ... a ... a ... All-Terrain Vehicle, Yeah, That's It, That's the Ticket," *The Wall Street Journal*, July 17, 1987, p. 17; Donna S. Kienzler, "Visual Ethics," *Journal of Business Communication* 34 (1997): 175–76.

Suppose the customer says, "I'll pay the extra shipping and handling. Send me seven." If you can't or won't sell in lots of fewer than 10, you need to write:

Better: To keep down packaging costs and to help customers save on shipping and handling costs, we sell computer disks only in lots of 10 or more.

If you link the negative element to a benefit, be sure that it is an audience-based benefit.

Avoid telling people that you're doing things "for their own good." They may have a different notion of what their own good is. You may think you're doing customers a favour by limiting their credit so they don't get in over their heads and go bankrupt. They may feel they'd be better off with more credit so they could expand in hopes of making more sales and more profits.

Omit the Negative If It Is Truly Unimportant

Omit negatives entirely only in three instances:

- The reader does not need the information to make a decision.
- You have already given the reader the information, and he or she has access to the previous communication.
- The information is trivial.

The following examples suggest the kind of negatives you can omit:

Negative: A one-year subscription to *Canada Business* is $49.97. That rate is not as low as the rates charged for some magazines.

Better: A one-year subscription to *Canada Business* is $49.97.

Still better: A one-year subscription to *Canada Business* is $49.97. You save 43 percent off the newsstand price of $87.78.

Negative: If you are dissatisfied with Sun Life Insurance, do not renew your policy.

Better: (Omit the sentence.)

Bury the Negative Information and Present It Compactly

The beginning and end of a message are always positions of emphasis. Put negatives there only if you want to emphasize the negative, as you may in a negative message (Module 12). To deemphasize a negative, put it in the middle of a paragraph rather than in the first or last sentence, or in the middle of the message rather than in the first or last paragraphs.

When a letter or memo runs several pages, remember that the bottom of the first page is also a position of emphasis, even if it is in the middle of a paragraph, because of the extra white space of the bottom margin. (The first page gets more attention since it is on top, and the reader's eye may catch some lines of the message even when he or she isn't consciously reading it; the tops and bottoms of subsequent pages don't get this extra attention.) If possible, avoid placing negative information at the bottom of the first page.

Giving a topic plenty of space emphasizes it. You can deemphasize negative information by giving it as little space as possible. Give negative information only once in your message. Don't list negatives vertically on the page, since lists take space and emphasize material.

Cultural FOCUS

In Canadian schools, students are trained to look at the first sentence of a paragraph and to try to guess what the rest of the paragraph will be about. If they are told to *skim* a document, they will read the first and last paragraph to determine what the essay or paper is about. Therefore, when people are looking at a business document, they will often look at the beginning and end to *scan* for the information they need. This is why negative news is placed in the middle. Customers will see the neutral information first and then continue to read on.

Why Do I Need to Think About Tone, Politeness, and Power?

Think about these factors so that you don't offend people by mistake.

No one likes to deal with people who seem condescending or rude. Poorly chosen words can create that sense, whether the sender "meant" to be rude or not. Tone is the implied attitude of the writer toward the reader. Tone is tricky, because it interacts with power: the words that might seem friendly from a superior to a subordinate may seem uppity if used by the subordinate to the superior. Norms for politeness are cultural and generational. Language that is acceptable within one group may be unacceptable if used by someone outside the group (Module 3).

Cultures that value group cohesiveness put much more emphasis on courtesy than the dominant North American culture does. Politeness spares others' feelings, and "saves face" for both message sender and receiver. A direct "no" response is rude in Pakistani and Chinese culture, for example, and such discourtesy might cost you a deal.

The desirable tone for business writing is businesslike but not stiff, friendly but not phoney, confident but not arrogant, polite but not grovelling. The following guidelines will help you achieve the tone you want:

- *Use courtesy titles for people outside your organization whom you don't know well.* Canadian organizations use first names for everyone, whatever their age or rank. But many people don't like being called by their first names by people they don't know or by someone much younger. When you talk or write to people outside your organization, use first names only if you've established a personal relationship. If you don't know someone well, use a courtesy title (Module 9):

  Dear Mr. Reynolds:
  Dear Ms. Lee:

- *Be aware of the power implications of the words you use.* "Thank you for your cooperation" is generous coming from a superior to a subordinate; it's not appropriate in a message to your superior.

Cultural FOCUS

In North America, many women, even if they are married, use *Ms.*, not *Mrs.* If you are unsure which to use, *Ms.* is best.

Different ways of asking for action carry different levels of politeness, as Table 7.2 shows.[8]

TABLE 7.2   **Forms of Request and Their Levels of Politeness**

Form of Request	Level of Politeness	Example
Order	Lowest politeness	Turn in your time card by Monday.
Polite order	Mid-level politeness	Please turn in your time card by Monday.
Indirect request	Higher politeness	Time cards should be turned in by Monday.
Question	Highest politeness	Would you be able to turn in your time card by Monday?

You need to be more polite if you're asking for something that will inconvenience the reader and help you more than the person who does the action. Generally, you need to be less polite when you're asking for something small, routine, or to the reader's benefit. Most readers and some discourse communities, however, prefer that even small requests be made politely.

Lower politeness: To start the scheduling process, please describe your availability for meetings during the second week of the month.

Higher politeness: Could you let me know what times you'd be free for a meeting the second week of the month?

Higher levels of politeness may be unclear. In some cases, a question may seem like a request for information to which it's acceptable to answer, "No, I can't." In other cases, it will be an order, simply phrased in polite terms.

Generally, requests sound friendliest when they are framed in conversational language.

Poor tone: Return the draft with any changes by next Tuesday.

Better tone: Let me know by Tuesday whether you'd like any changes in the draft.

When the stakes are low, be straightforward. Messages that beat around the bush sound pompous and defensive.

Poor tone: Distribution of the low-fat plain granola may be limited in your area. May we suggest that you discuss this matter with your store manager.

Better tone: Our low-fat granola is so popular that there isn't enough to go around. We're expanding production to meet the demand. Ask your store manager to keep putting in orders, so that your grocery is on the list of stores that will get supplies when they become available.

Or: Store managers decide what to stock. If your store has stopped carrying our low-fat granola, the store manager has stopped ordering it. Talk to the manager. Managers try to meet customer needs, so if you say something you're more likely to get what you want.

When you must give bad news, consider hedging your statement. Linguistic experts John Hagge and Charles Kostelnick have shown that auditors' suggestion letters rarely say directly that firms are using unacceptable accounting practices. Instead, they use three strategies to be more diplomatic: specifying the time ("Currently, the records are quite informal"), limiting statements ("It appears," "It seems"), and using impersonal statements that do not specify who caused a problem or who will perform an action.[9]

What's the Best Way to Apologize?

Apologize early, briefly, and sincerely.

When you are at fault, you build goodwill by admitting that fact promptly. However, apologies may have legal implications, so some organizations prefer that their employees do not offer apologies to customers.

When you have done everything you can for your customer, and when a delay or problem is due to circumstances beyond your control, you aren't at fault and don't need to apologize. It may be appropriate to include an explanation so the reader knows you weren't negligent. If the news is bad, put the explanation first. If you have good news for the reader, put it before your explanation.

Negative:	I'm sorry that I could not answer your question sooner. I had to wait until the sales figures for the second quarter were in.
Better (neutral or bad news):	We needed the sales figures for the second quarter to answer your question. Now that they're in, I can tell you that ...
Better (good news):	The new advertising campaign is a success. The sales figures for the second quarter are finally in, and they show that ...

If the delay or problem is long or large, it is good you-attitude to ask the reader whether he or she wants to confirm the original plan or make different arrangements.

Negative:	I'm sorry that the chairs will not be ready by August 25 as promised.
Better:	Because of a strike against the manufacturer, the desk chairs you ordered will not be ready until November. Do you want to keep that order, or would you like to look at the models available from other suppliers?

When an apology is appropriate, do so early, briefly, and sincerely.

Apologize only once, early in the message. Let the reader move on to other, more positive information.

Even if major trouble or inconvenience has resulted from your error, you don't need to go on about all the horrible things that happened. The reader already knows this negative information, and you can omit it. Instead, focus on what you have done to correct the situation.

If you don't know whether any inconvenience has resulted, don't raise the issue at all. Why draw attention to a negative your reader may not have thought of?

Negative:	I'm sorry I didn't answer your letter sooner. I hope that my delay has not inconvenienced you.
Better:	I'm sorry I didn't answer your letter sooner.

MODULE SUMMARY

- Beware of **hidden negatives**: words not negative in themselves that become negative in context.
- The best business communication tone is businesslike but not stiff, friendly not phoney, confident but not arrogant, polite but not grovelling.
  - Use courtesy titles for people outside your organization whom you don't know well.
  - Be aware of the power implications of the words you use.
  - When the stakes are low, be straightforward.

- When you must give bad news, consider hedging your statement.
- Don't apologize if the error is small and if you are correcting the mistake. Don't apologize if you are not at fault. If the delay is long, or the problem large, it is good you-attitude to ask your audience whether he/she wants to make different arrangements.
- When you do apologize, do it early, briefly, and sincerely. However, apologies may have legal implications, so some organizations prefer that their employees do not apologize to customers or the public.

ASSIGNMENTS FOR MODULE 7

Questions for Critical Thinking

7.1 Some negative phrases (such as "please do not hesitate") are business clichés. Why is it better to avoid them?

7.2 If you work for a company that claims to be egalitarian, do you still need to attend to tone, power, and politeness?

7.3 Can you think of situations in which positive emphasis might backfire or be inappropriate? What strategies would be most likely to meet the audience's needs in those situations?

Exercises and Problems

7.4   Analyzing Your Discourse Community for Tone, Courtesy, and Power

Analyze the cultural norms for tone, levels of courtesy, and use of power in your organization. Choose a discourse community of which you are a member—you can use a club, social, ethnic, religious, or academic organization, or your place of work.

Identify a minimum of three oral and three written messages that exemplify the norms and attitudes toward power in the organization. Write a memo to your instructor and class-mates about your findings.

7.5   Evaluating the Ethics of Positive Emphasis

The first word in each line at the right is negative; the second is a positive term that is sometimes substituted for it. Which of the positive terms seem ethical? Which seem unethical? Briefly explain your choices.

junk bonds	high-yield bonds
second mortgage	home-equity loan
tax	user fee
tax increase	revenue enhancement
nervousness	adrenaline
problem	challenge
price increase	price change

7.6   Focusing on the Positive

Revise each of the following sentences to focus on the options that remain, not those that are closed off.

1. As a first-year employee, you are not eligible for dental insurance.
2. I will be out of the country October 25 until November 10 and will not be able to meet with you until I return.
3. You will not get your first magazine for at least four weeks.
4. I'm sorry I'm away from my desk and cannot answer your call.

7.7 Identifying Hidden Negatives

Identify the hidden negatives in the following sentences and revise to eliminate them. In some cases, you may need to add information to revise the sentence effectively.

1. This publication is designed to explain how your company can start a recycling program.
2. I hope you find the information in this brochure beneficial to you and a valuable reference as you plan your move.
3. In thinking about your role in our group, I remember two occasions where you contributed something.

7.8 Revising Sentences to Improve Positive Emphasis

Revise the following sentences to improve positive emphasis. In some cases, you may need to add or omit information to revise effectively.

1. It will be necessary for you to submit Form PR-47 before you can be reimbursed for your travel expenses.
2. If you have further questions, please do not hesitate to contact me.
3. I'm sorry you were worried about your health insurance. It is not too late to sign up for a flexible spending account.
4. You cannot return this item for a full refund if you keep it more than 30 days.
5. When you write a report, do not make claims that you cannot support with evidence.
6. Although I was only an intern and didn't actually make presentations to major clients, I was required to prepare PowerPoint™ slides for the meetings and to answer some of the clients' questions.
7. You will pay $30 more if you wait till after October 1 to register for the conference.
8. To reduce unnecessary delays in processing your order, please check the form at the end of this letter to see that nothing is omitted or incorrect before you sign the form and return it.
9. The figures for budget changes made at the meeting may be wrong, as I got lost during John's presentation. Please check the figures and let me know if they need correction.
10. We cannot process your application to graduate, because you did not supply all of the necessary information.

7.9 Revising Sentences to Improve Positive Emphasis

Revise the following sentences to improve positive emphasis. In some cases, you may need to add or omit information to revise effectively.

1. No subcontractor shall be employed without the previous consent of the director.
2. To avoid unnecessary delays, call for an appointment before coming in to the office.
3. I realize that Wednesday at 10 A.M. is not a convenient time for everyone, but I was unable to arrange a time that is good for everyone.
4. I'm sorry you were worried about the résumé you emailed us. We did not have any problems scanning it into our system.
5. I am anxious to talk with you about the job.
6. People who come to work late may be perceived as unreliable.
7. I hope that you receive the April spreadsheet (three pages) that follows and that the fax quality isn't too poor.
8. I was treasurer of the accounting club. Of course, we didn't have much money so I didn't have much responsibility, but I was able to put into practice principles I learned in the classroom.
9. If you have any problems using your email account, I will try to explain it so that you can understand.
10. If you submitted a travel request, as you claim, we have failed to receive it.

7.10 Revising a Memo to Improve Positive Emphasis

Revise the following memo to improve the you-attitude and positive emphasis.

Subject: Status of Building Renovations

The renovation of the lobby is not behind schedule. By Monday, October 9, we hope to be ready to open the west end of the lobby to limited traffic.

The final phase of the renovation will be placing a new marble floor in front of the elevators. This work will not be finished until the end of the month.

Insofar as is possible, the crew will attempt to schedule most of the work during the evenings so that normal business is not disrupted.

Please exercise caution when moving through the construction area. The floor will be uneven and steps will be at unusual heights. Watch your step to avoid accidentally tripping or falling.

7.11 Identifying Positive Emphasis in Ads and Documents

Look at print advertisements and at documents you receive from your college or university, from your workplace, and from organizations to which you belong. Identify five sentences that either (a) use positive emphasis or (b) should be revised to be more positive.

As your instructor directs,

   a. Share your examples with a small group of students.

   b. Write a memo to your instructor discussing your examples.

   c. Post an email message to the class discussing your examples.

   d. Present two or three of your examples to the class in a short presentation.

   e. With your small group, write a collaborative short report to your instructor about the patterns you see.

POLISHING YOUR PROSE

Using the Apostrophe to Show Ownership

The apostrophe indicates ownership or possession:

   Sidwat's idea; Veronica's textbook; Verdun's report

When the noun doing the owning does not end in s, the apostrophe goes between the noun and the s:

   company's flagship (flagship of the company)

   student's text (text of the student)

   neighbour's complaint (complaint of the neighbour)

When the possessing noun ends in s, put the apostrophe after the s:

   companies' customers (customers of companies)

   students' texts (texts of students)

   neighbours' complaints (complaints of neighbours)

In names that end with s or an s sound, style books permit either form:

   Thomas'

   Thomas's

   Linux'

   Linux's

Look at the logic of your sentence to choose the right place for the apostrophe. Or turn the ownership phrase around to determine if the noun ends in an s:

   We welcome our employees opinions

becomes

   We welcome the opinions of our employees.

The noun *employees* ends in s, so if the apostrophe is used, it comes after the s:

   We welcome our employees' opinions.

Exercises

Choose the correct word in each set of parentheses.

   1. Research indicates most Canadians feel responsible for the (world's/worlds') global warming.

   2. The winter holiday season can account for one-quarter to one-half of a (store's/stores') annual profits.

   3. (Canadian's/Canadians') views of the economy reflect their confidence in the stock market.

   4. To sell in another country, you need to understand its (people's/peoples') culture.

   5. We meet the municipal, provincial, and federal (government's/governments') standards for quality control.

   6. Skirt's/skirts' lengths reflect the state of the economy: the maxi becomes popular during economic downturns.

   7. The (committee's/committees') duties will be completed after it announces its decision.

   8. Employees who have worked as Big Sisters have enjoyed seeing the (girl's/girls') progress.

   9. We'll decide whether to have more computer training sessions on the basis of (employee's/employees') feedback.

   10. The (company's/companies') benefit plan is excellent.

Check your answers to the odd-numbered exercises on page 551.

Communicating Reader Benefits

Learning Objectives

After reading and applying the information in Module 8, you'll be able to demonstrate

Knowledge of

- People's motivations and needs
- Elements of reader-centred messages
- The importance of identifying audience benefits

Skills to

- Use audience analysis to identify and choose reader benefits
- Develop reader benefits with logic and detail
- Match the benefit to the audience

Employability Skills 2000+ Checklist

In this module, the key skills from the Conference Board of Canada's Employability Skills 2000+ are

Communicate

○ listen and ask questions to understand and appreciate the points of view of others

○ write and speak so others pay attention and understand

Manage Information

○ access, analyze, and apply knowledge and skills from various disciplines (e.g., the arts, languages, science, technology, mathematics, social sciences, and the humanities)

Think & Solve Problems

○ assess situations and identify problems

○ seek different points of view and evaluate them based on facts

○ recognize the human, interpersonal, technical, scientific, and mathematical dimensions of a problem

○ be creative and innovative in exploring possible solutions

Demonstrate Positive Attitudes & Behaviours

○ deal with people, problems, and situations with honesty, integrity, and personal ethics

○ show interest, initiative, and effort

Learn Continuously

○ be willing to continuously learn and grow

○ identify and access learning sources and opportunities

Staples' brand reinforces the basic benefit of shopping at Staples: it makes life easy for the customer.

Reader benefits are benefits or advantages the reader gets by

- Using your services
- Buying your products
- Following your policies
- Adopting your ideas

Good reader benefits are

- Adapted to your audience
- Based on built-in advantages
- Supported by clear logic and explained in adequate detail
- Presented with you-attitude

How Do Reader Benefits Work?

Reader benefits appeal to the audience's attitudes and actions.

Reader benefits appeal to both the attitudes and the behaviour of your audience. When you provide benefits that focus on readers' needs and wants, people feel more positive about you and your request. Providing reader benefits makes it easier for you to accomplish your goals.

Most people try to do their best only when they believe that they can succeed and when they want the rewards that success brings. Indeed, studies reveal that how we think about a task determines our feelings about the task "and ultimately our willingness to put our heads down and work."[1]

Reader benefits tell readers that they can do the job successfully and that they will be rewarded.[2] Reader benefits help overcome two problems that reduce motivation: people may not think of all the possible benefits, and they may not understand the relationships among efforts, performance, and rewards.[3]

Checkpoint

Reader benefits are benefits or advantages that the reader gets from using your services, buying your products, following your policies, or adopting your ideas.

How Do I Identify Reader Benefits?

Analyze your reader and brainstorm!

Sometimes reader benefits are obvious and easy to describe. When they are harder to identify, brainstorm in two steps:

1. Think of the feelings, values, needs, and fears that may motivate your reader. Then identify features of your service, product, or policy that meet those values or needs.
2. Identify the obvious features of your product or policy. Then think how these features might benefit the audience.

Try to brainstorm three to five possible benefits for every informative message, and five to seven benefits for every persuasive message. The more benefits you think of, the easier it will be to choose ones that will directly appeal to your audience.

For example, supposing you want to start your own business: a window-washing service. What benefits does your service offer? Your brainstorming notes might look like those in Table 8.1.

1. Consider Your Readers' Needs

One of the best-known analyses of needs is Abraham H. Maslow's hierarchy of needs.[4] Physical needs are the most basic, followed by needs for safety and security, for love and a sense of belonging, for esteem and recognition, and finally for self-actualization or self-fulfilment. All of us go back and forth between higher-level and lower-level needs. Whenever lower-level needs make themselves felt, they take priority. When we're hungry for lunch, for example, we are much less motivated to pay attention to a lecture.

TABLE 8.1   Brainstorming to Identify Audience Benefits

Customer Feelings, Values, Needs	Service Offers	Service Features	Customer Benefits
Cleaning windows takes a lot of time.	Our time.	We do the work and guarantee results.	Save time for other household chores.
Takes a lot of energy.	We do the work.	We do the work and guarantee results.	Use energy on other projects.
It's a dirty job.	We get dirty.	We do the work and guarantee results.	Customer can forget about this dirty job, and does not have any mess to clean up.
Uses a lot of products.	We use our own cleaning products.	Materials are all green.	Save money on buying these products; save storage space; feel good about not harming environment.
Leaves streaks.	Trained employees do streak-free job.	We guarantee results.	Satisfaction.
Have to get the ladder out; have to climb up ladder.	We bring and climb ladder.	Customer safety.	Worry- and hassle-free job done for you.
Window-cleaning service costs money.	We offer competitive prices.	Money spent offers peace of mind and quality work.	Time and value: freedom from low-level chore = time to spend on more interesting, fun projects.

Maslow's model is a good starting point to identify the feelings, fears, and needs that may motivate your audience. Figure 8.1 shows organizational motivators for each of the levels in Maslow's hierarchy.

Compare the PAIBOC model with Maslow's hierarchy. Notice that you must define and refine your message **purpose(s)**, **information**, **benefits anticipated objections**, and **context** according to the needs of your **audience**.

Often a product or idea can meet needs on several levels. Focus on the ones that your audience analysis suggests are most relevant for your audience. But remember: even the best analysis may not reveal the most pressing of your reader's needs. For example, a well-paid manager may be worried about security needs if her spouse has lost his job, or if the couple is supporting children in college or an elderly parent.

Furthermore, age and culture influence motivation (Module 3). For example, Millennials (people born between 1980 and 2000) value inclusiveness and flexibility. In the workplace, "[t]hey want to make a meaningful contribution immediately, and they want their input to be taken seriously." Therefore, challenging work motivates them more than pay or security.[5]

2. Translate Features into Benefits

A feature by itself is not a benefit. For example, a store might promote its own brand of natural potato chips. But how does buying the store brand benefit the consumer? One benefit might be that the store brand is made on the premises, so the chips are always fresh.

FIGURE 8.1   Organizational Motivations for Maslow's Hierarchy of Needs

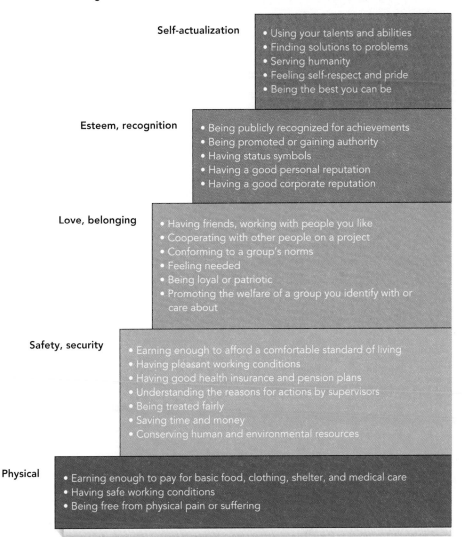

Self-actualization
- Using your talents and abilities
- Finding solutions to problems
- Serving humanity
- Feeling self-respect and pride
- Being the best you can be

Esteem, recognition
- Being publicly recognized for achievements
- Being promoted or gaining authority
- Having status symbols
- Having a good personal reputation
- Having a good corporate reputation

Love, belonging
- Having friends, working with people you like
- Cooperating with other people on a project
- Conforming to a group's norms
- Feeling needed
- Being loyal or patriotic
- Promoting the welfare of a group you identify with or care about

Safety, security
- Earning enough to afford a comfortable standard of living
- Having pleasant working conditions
- Having good health insurance and pension plans
- Understanding the reasons for actions by supervisors
- Being treated fairly
- Saving time and money
- Conserving human and environmental resources

Physical
- Earning enough to pay for basic food, clothing, shelter, and medical care
- Having safe working conditions
- Being free from physical pain or suffering

FIGURE 8.2   PAIBOC Questions for Analysis

Use the PAIBOC questions to analyze the communication situation and to identify reader benefits/appeals:

P What are your **purposes** in communicating? What results do you want?

A Who is your **audience**? What do they value? What are their needs?

I What **information** must your message include? What does your audience already know? What do they need to know?

B What reasons or reader **benefits** can you use to support your position?

O What **objections** can you expect your audience to have?

C How will the **context** affect audience response? Consider your relationship with the audience, and economic, political, social and cultural, and organizational factors that may influence audience perception.

Often, a feature has several possible benefits.

Feature: Lowering office air conditioning and lighting

Benefits: Saves energy
Reduces overhead costs
Is easy to do
Could reduce monitor glare
Encourages awareness
Encourages people to feel they can make a contribution

Feature: Carpooling

Benefits: Saves fuel costs and vehicle depreciation
Reduces greenhouse gas emissions
Enables carpoolers to use fastest highway lane: people can wake up later and get to work sooner
Reduces driving anxiety
Is easy to do
Encourages awareness
Encourages people to feel they can make a contribution

Feature: Flextime

Benefits: Enables workers to accommodate personal needs
Helps organizations recruit, retain workers
Makes more workers available in early morning and in evening
Enables office to stay open longer—more service to clients, customers
Enables workers to communicate with colleagues in different time zones more easily

Different features may benefit different subgroups in your audience. Depending on the features a restaurant offers, you might appeal to one or more of the subgroups shown in Table 8.2.

To develop your benefits, think about the details of each one. If your selling point is your relaxing atmosphere, think about the specific details that make the restaurant relaxing.

If your strong point is elegant dining, consider all the details that contribute to that elegance. Sometimes you may offer features that do not meet any particular need but are still good benefits. In a sales letter for a restaurant, you might also want to mention your free coatroom, your convenient location, free parking or a drive-up window, and speedy service.

Whenever you're writing to customers or clients about features that are not unique to your organization, present both the benefits of the features themselves and the benefits of dealing with your company. If you talk about the benefits of dining in a relaxed atmosphere but don't mention your own restaurant, people may go somewhere else!

TABLE 8.2   **Audience Subgroups**

Subgroup	Features to Meet the Subgroup's Needs
People who work outside the home	A quick lunch; a relaxing place to take clients or colleagues
Parents with small children	High chairs, child-sized portions, and activities to keep the kids entertained while they wait for their order
People who eat out a lot	Variety both in food and in décor
People on tight budgets	Economical food; a place where they don't need to tip (cafeteria or fast food)
People on special diets	Low-sodium and low-calorie dishes; vegetarian food; kosher food
People to whom eating out is part of an evening's entertainment	Music or a floor show; elegant surroundings; reservations so they can get to a show or event after dinner; late hours so they can come to dinner after a show or game

How Detailed Should Each Benefit Be?

Use concrete, vivid details. Paint a mental picture.

Develop reader benefits by linking each feature to the reader's needs—and provide details to make the benefit vivid! You'll usually need at least three to five sentences to give enough details about a reader benefit. If you develop two or three reader benefits fully, you can use just a sentence or two for less important benefits.

Weak: We have placemats with riddles.

Better: Answering all the riddles on Caesar's special placemats will keep the kids happy till your pizza comes. If they don't have time to finish (and they may not, since your pizza is ready so quickly), just take the riddles home—or answer them on your next visit.

Make your reader benefits specific.

Weak: You get quick service.

Better: If you only have an hour for lunch, try our Business Buffet. Within minutes, you can choose from a variety of main dishes, vegetables, and a make-your-own-sandwich-and-salad bar. You can put together a lunch that's as light or filling as you want, with time to enjoy it—and still be back to the office on time.

Psychological description is a technique you can use to develop vivid, specific reader benefits. Psychological description means creating a scenario rich with sense impressions—what the reader sees, hears, smells, tastes, feels—so readers can picture themselves using your product or service and enjoying its benefits. You can also use psychological description to describe the problem your product will solve. Psychological description works best early in the message to catch readers' attention.

Feature: Snooze alarm

Benefit: When you press the snooze button, the alarm goes off and comes on again nine minutes later.

Psychological description: Some mornings, you really want to stay in bed just a few more minutes. With the Sleepytime Snooze Alarm, you can snuggle under the covers for a few extra winks, secure in the knowledge that the alarm will come on again to get you up for that breakfast meeting with an important client. If you want to sleep in, you can keep hitting the snooze alarm for up to an additional 63 minutes of sleep. With Sleepytime, you're in control of your mornings.

Feature:	Tilt windows
Benefit:	Easier to clean
Psychological description:	No wonder so many cleaners "don't do windows." Balancing precariously on a rickety ladder to clean upper-story windows ... shivering outside in the winter winds and broiling in the summer sun as you scrub away ... running inside, then outside, then inside again to try to get the spot that always seems to be on the other side. Cleaning traditional windows really is a chore.

You'll find cleaning a breeze with Tilt-in Windows. Just pull the inner window down and pull the bottom toward you. The whole window lifts out! Repeat for the outer window. Clean inside in comfort (sitting down or even watching TV if you choose). Then replace the top of the outer window in its track, slide up, and repeat with the inner window. Presto! Clean windows!

With psychological description, you're putting your reader in a picture. If the reader doesn't feel that the picture fits, the technique backfires. To prevent this, psychological description often uses subjunctive verbs ("If you like ... ," "If you were ...") or the words *maybe* and *perhaps*.

> You're exhausted after a long day. You're hungry but too tired to cook. Perhaps you are having guests for dinner. Or it's your turn to bring Mom and Dad a meal. Or you only have a half-hour for lunch. Whatever the situation, foodathome.com cooks delicious, nutritious meals and delivers them to your door.
>
> If you want homemade, we have it. If you want plenty of choice, we have it. If you want free delivery, we have it. And the price is right.
>
> So why not make the convenient, budget-wise choice for your next dining dilemma: order online at foodathome.com.

How Do I Decide Which Benefits to Use?

Use the following three guidelines to decide.

Three principles guide your choice of reader benefits:

1. Use at least one benefit for each subgroup in your audience.
2. Use intrinsic benefits.
3. Use the benefits you can develop most fully.

1. Use at Least One Benefit for Each Subgroup in Your Audience

Most messages go to multiple audiences. In a memo announcing a company-subsidized day-care program, you want to describe benefits not only for parents who might use the service, but also for people who don't have children or whose children are older. Reader benefits for these last two audiences help convince them that spending money on day care is a good use of scarce funds.

In a letter to "consumers" or "voters," different people will have different concerns. The more of these concerns you speak to, the more persuasive you'll be.

FIGURE 8.3   A Promotional Handout with Both Intrinsic and Extrinsic Appeals

Please take a few minutes to give us your feedback about — Intrinsic
The Beer Store and the Ontario Deposit Return Program
and you could WIN a Grand Prize of a Napoleon Barbecue — Extrinsic
or 1 of 50 Gift Cards for various retailers*

www.navicomsurvey.com/TBS-C
Enter the following password: XXXXX-XXX

The Beer Store   *Please see contest rules and regulations for gift card retailers and more details. If you have any difficulty accessing the survey please contact Navicom Inc. at 1-800-463-2293 from 9-5 EST.

This survey request offers both intrinsic and extrinsic benefits.

2. Use Intrinsic Benefits

Intrinsic benefits are natural outcomes of doing something, or using a product. Such benefits appeal to our need to feel good about ourselves. For example, an intrinsic benefit of helping a friend in need is feeling kind. The Beer Store survey appeal (above) offers intrinsic benefits to meet such high-level needs as feeling needed, cooperating, loyalty, and recognition (see Maslow's Hierarchy of Needs, page 137).

Extrinsic benefits are "added on"; they do not necessarily come from using the product, or doing the action. The Beer Store appeal offers 51 chances to win a prize for completing the online survey. You may not win; chances are you won't, given the number of people who may choose to participate in the survey. But the extrinsic benefit is the added inducement of the chance to win.

Table 8.3 gives examples of extrinsic and intrinsic rewards for three activities.

TABLE 8.3   Extrinsic and Intrinsic Rewards

Activity	Intrinsic Reward	Extrinsic Reward
Making a sale	Pleasure in convincing someone; pride in using your talents to create a strategy and execute it	Getting a commission
Turning in a suggestion to a company suggestion system	Solving a problem at work; making the work environment a little pleasanter; feeling of pride for a job well done	Getting a monetary reward when the suggestion is implemented
Writing a report that solves an organizational problem	Pleasure in having an effect on an organization; pride in using your skills to solve problems; pleasure in solving the problem itself	Getting praise; a good performance appraisal, and maybe a raise

Intrinsic rewards or benefits are better than extrinsic benefits for two reasons:

1. There just aren't enough extrinsic rewards for everything you want people to do. You can't give a prize to every customer every time he or she places an order, or a promotion to every subordinate who does what he or she is supposed to do.
2. Research suggests that you'll motivate people more effectively by stressing the intrinsic benefits of following policies and adopting proposals. People prefer recognition and respect to more tangible rewards.

Indeed, in a groundbreaking study of professional employees, Frederick Herzberg found that the things people said they liked about their jobs were all intrinsic rewards—pride in achievement, an enjoyment of the work itself, responsibility. Extrinsic features—pay, company policy—were sometimes mentioned as things people disliked, but they were never cited as things that motivated or satisfied them. People who made a lot of money still did not mention salary as a good point about the job or the organization.[6]

Many family-friendly companies have discovered that a culture of care keeps turnover low. The higher salary that a competitor might pay just doesn't overcome the advantage of working at a supportive, flexible company that values its employees.[7] In the current competitive job market, different candidates want different things. But many accept lower salaries to get flextime, stock options, interesting work, or people they want to work with.[8]

EXPANDING A CRITICAL SKILL

Using You-Attitude, Positive Emphasis, and Audience Benefits to Create a Winning Corporation

Survey results for the fourth annual list of Canada's top small and medium-sized businesses prove that matching benefits to audience, and communicating with you-attitude and positive emphasis are the most productive business strategies.

The organizations that led the list, from Ontario and Vancouver, include two credit unions, a restaurant, and a software development business. Calgary's Axia NetMedia Corporation, a broadband developer and operator, got the number-one spot. However, all top 25 companies have a corporate culture of open and honest communication with their employees.

The survey, produced through the partnership of *The Globe and Mail*, Queen's Centre for Business Venturing (Queen's School of Business), and Hewitt Associates (a global human resources services company), identified five communication strategies the top 25 have in common.

First, every organization operates "an open-concept culture" wherein management and employers work together in the same physical space, people meet frequently informally and formally, and employees' comments and suggestions are encouraged and acted upon at once. Second, employees know exactly how their performance

is measured, and how it will be rewarded; they establish their own career objectives and receive priority information on company job postings; employees who excel "are offered a variety of resources for professional growth, including business coaching, tuition reimbursement, work experience, and training paths for management." Third, the companies offer a transparent environment: new hires receive full orientation, and employees get all company updates and information, including the same financial statements the board of directors and management get. Fourth, employee lifelong learning is part of the job: these organizations help their employees build individual professional development plans, review these plans regularly, and pay for work-related courses. The fifth communication strategy is the foundation of organizational success: managers consistently solicit employees' opinions and demonstrate through action that they are listening.

Identifying the intrinsic and extrinsic benefits that positively motivate employees, and communicating these benefits openly, positively, and with you-attitude create engaged employees and productive organizations.

Sources: Randy Ray, "The 25 Best Small Companies to Work For," January 16, 2008, retrieved June 27, 2008 from http://www.reportonbusiness.com/servlet/story/RTGAM.20080116.wxcasmb16/BNStory/specialSmallBusiness/home/?pageRequested=5.

Different audiences may value different intrinsic and extrinsic benefits.

PEANUTS reprinted with permission of United Features Syndicate.

Language FOCUS

Turnover refers to how quickly employees come and go at a company. A company with high turnover incurs many additional expenses, such as placing ads in newspapers or online for new candidates, spending time and money interviewing new people and training the new hires. Most companies try to keep turnover low.

3. Use the Benefits You Can Develop Most Fully

Employability Skills

One-sentence benefits don't do much. Use benefits that you can develop in three to five sentences or more.

A reader benefit is a claim that the reader will benefit if he or she does something. Convincing the reader, therefore, requires two steps: ensuring that the benefit appeals to your reader and really will happen, and explaining it to the reader.

Your benefit(s) have to be relevant and real. If the logic behind a claimed reader benefit is faulty or inaccurate, there's no way to make that particular reader benefit convincing. Revise the benefit to make it logical.

Faulty logic:	Using a computer will enable you to write letters, memos, and reports much more quickly.
Analysis:	If you've never used a computer, in the short run it will take you *longer* to create a document using a computer than it would to type it. Even after you know how to use a computer and its software, the real-time savings come when a document incorporates parts of previous documents or goes through several revisions. Creating a first draft from scratch still takes planning and careful composing; the time savings may or may not be significant.
Revised reader benefit:	Using a computer allows you to revise and edit a document more easily. It eliminates retyping as a separate step and reduces the time needed to proofread revisions. It allows you to move the text around on the page to create the best layout.

If the logic is sound, making that logic evident to the reader is a matter of providing enough evidence and showing how the evidence proves the benefit claim. Always provide enough detail to be vivid and concrete. You'll need more detail in the following situations:

- The reader may not have thought of the benefit before.
- The benefit depends on the difference between the long run and the short run.
- The reader will be hard to persuade, and you need detail to make the benefit vivid and emotionally convincing.

Does the following statement have enough detail?

> You'll save money by using our shop-at-home service.

Readers always believe their own experience. Readers who have never used a shop-at-home service may think, "If somebody else does my shopping for me, I'll have to pay that person. I'll save money by doing it myself." They might not think of the savings in gas and parking, in travel time, and in less car wear and tear. Readers who already use shop-at-home services may believe you if they compare your items and services with another company's to see that your cost is lower. Even then, you could make saving money seem more forceful and more vivid by telling readers how much they could save and mentioning some of the ways they might use your service.

What Else Do Reader Benefits Need?

Check for you-attitude.

If reader benefits aren't stated in you-attitude terms (see Module 6), they'll sound selfish and won't be as effective as they could be. A Xerox sales letter with strong you-attitude as well as reader benefits got a far bigger response than an alternative version with reader benefits but no you-attitude.[9] It doesn't matter how you phrase reader benefits while you're brainstorming and developing them, but in your final draft, edit for you-attitude.

Lacks you-attitude:	We have the lowest prices in town.
You-attitude:	At Abbotsford Toyota, you get the best deal in town.

The Beer Store survey request (Figure 8.3) uses you-based language throughout. Both the intrinsic appeal ([You] *Please take a few minutes ... your feedback ...*), and the extrinsic benefit (*you could WIN ...*) are emphatically reader-based.

MODULE SUMMARY

- Reader benefits are advantages the reader gets by using your services, buying your products, following your policies, or adopting your ideas. Reader benefits assure readers that they can do the job, and their success will be rewarded.

- Good reader benefits are adapted to the audience, based on innate advantages, supported by clear logic, detailed, and presented with you-attitude. There are not enough extrinsic (external) benefits to reward every desired behaviour; furthermore, extrinsic benefits reduce the high-level satisfaction in doing something for its own sake.

- To create reader benefits,
  - Identify the feelings, needs, and fears that may motivate your reader.

  - Describe how readers can meet their needs with the features of your service, product, or policy.

- Psychological description creates rich sense impressions—what the reader can see, hear, smell, taste, feel—so readers can picture themselves using your product and service and enjoying its benefits.

- Brainstorm twice as many reader benefits as you'll need for a message. Use the benefits you can develop most fully.

- Make sure you communicate reader benefits with you-attitude.

ASSIGNMENTS FOR MODULE 8

Questions for Critical Thinking

8.1 What three intrinsic benefits motivate you most strongly? Which of these, if any, are related to your age? Which are related to your culture?

8.2 Identify three ways you can apply your knowledge of Maslow's hierarchy of needs to improve your professional and/or interpersonal communications.

8.3 Why should you frame reader benefits using you-attitude?

Exercises and Problems

8.4 Identifying and Developing Reader Benefits

Listed here are five things an organization might like its employees to do:

1. Use less paper.
2. Attend a brown-bag lunch to discuss ways to improve products or services.
3. Become more physically fit.
4. Volunteer for community organizations.
5. Ease a new hire's transition into the unit.

As your instructor directs,

a. Identify the motives or needs that might be met by each of the activities.
b. Develop each need or motive as a reader benefit in a full paragraph. Use additional paragraphs for the other needs met by the activity. Remember to use you-attitude!

8.5 Identifying Objections and Reader Benefits

Think of an organization you know something about, and answer the following questions for it.

1. Your organization is thinking of creating a training video. What objections might people have? What benefits could videos offer your organization? Which people would be easiest to convince?
2. The advisory council of Nunavut Arctic College recommends that business faculty have three-month internships with local organizations to learn material. What objections might people in your organization have to bringing in faculty interns? What benefits might your organization receive? Which people would be easiest to convince?
3. Your organization is thinking of buying laptop computers for all employees who travel. What fears or objections might people have? What benefits might your organization receive? Which people would be easiest to convince?

As your instructor directs,

a. Share your answers orally with a small group of students.
b. Present your answers in an oral presentation to the class.
c. Email your answers to class members.
d. Write a paragraph developing the best reader benefit you identified. Remember to use you-attitude.

8.6 Identifying and Developing Reader Benefits for Different Audiences

Assume that you want to encourage people to do one of the activities listed below:

1. Hire a personal trainer

   Audiences: Professional athletes

   Busy managers

   Someone trying to lose weight

   Someone making a major lifestyle change after a heart attack

2. Buy a cell phone

   Audiences: People who do a lot of driving

   Older people

   People who do a lot of driving in rural areas

   People who do a lot of flying

3. Get advice about interior decorating

   Audiences: Young people with little money to spend

   Parents with small children

   People upgrading or adding to their furnishings

   Older people moving from single family homes into smaller apartments or condominiums

   Builders furnishing model homes

4. Get advice on investment strategies
   Audiences: New college or university graduates
                   People earning more than $100 000 annually
                   People responsible for investing funds for a church, synagogue, or temple
                   Parents with small children
                   People within 10 years of retirement

5. Garden
   Audiences: People with small children
                   People in apartments
                   People concerned about reducing pesticides
                   People on tight budgets
                   Retirees
                   Teenagers

6. Buy voice-activated computer software
   Audiences: College and university students
                   Financial planners who visit clients at home
                   Sales representatives who travel constantly
                   People who make PowerPoint presentations
                   Older people

7. Teach adults to read
   Audiences: Retired workers
                   Businesspeople
                   Students who want to become teachers
                   High school, college, and university students
                   People concerned about poverty

8. Vacation at a luxury hotel
   Audiences: Stressed-out people who want to relax
                   Tourists who like to sightsee and absorb the local culture
                   Businesspeople who want to stay in touch with the office even on vacation
                   Parents with small children
                   Weekend athletes who want to have fun

9. Attend a fantasy sports camp (you pick the sport), playing with and against retired players who provide coaching and advice.

10. Attend a health spa where clients get low-fat and low-calorie meals, massages, beauty treatments, and guidance in nutrition and exercise.

As your instructor directs,

a. Identify needs that you could meet for the audiences listed here. In addition to needs that several audiences share, identify at least one need that would be particularly important to each group.

b. Identify a product or service that could meet each need.

c. Write a paragraph or two of reader benefits for each product or service. Remember to use you-attitude.

d. Develop one or more of the benefits using psychological description.

Hints:

- For this assignment, you can combine benefits or programs as if a single source offered them all.
- Add specific details about particular sports, cities, tourist attractions, activities, and so on, as material for your description.
- Be sure to move beyond reader benefits to vivid details and sense impressions.
- Phrase your benefits using you-attitude.

POLISHING YOUR PROSE

Plurals and Possessives

Possessives and plurals usually sound the same but don't mean the same to your readers. And they are spelled differently. You add an apostrophe to show possession or ownership. You make nouns plural by adding s; when the noun ends in *y*, you drop the *y* and replace with *ies*. However, you almost never add an apostrophe to pluralize a noun.

Right: No cameras allowed in the theatre.

Wrong: No camera's allowed in the theatre.

Wrong: No cameras' allowed in the theatre.

Singular Possessive	Plural Possessive	Plural
company's	companies'	companies
computer's	computers'	computers
family's	families'	families

job's	jobs'	jobs
manager's	managers'	managers
team's	teams'	teams

When possessive nouns and plurals sound the same, you have to look at the logic of your sentence to choose the right word.

Exercises

Choose the right word in each set of parentheses.

1. Canadian (companies, company's) are competing effectively in the global market.
2. We can move your (families, family's) furniture safely and efficiently.
3. (Managers, manager's, managers') ability to listen is more important than their technical knowledge.
4. A (memos, memo's) appearance, word choice, paragraph length and subject heading can positively or negatively influence the reader.
5. The (community social workers, social worker's) tell clients about services available in their neighbourhoods.
6. Savvy employees check the (companies, company's, companies') benefits plan periodically to make sure it continues to serve their needs.
7. Information about the new community makes the (families, family's) move easier.
8. The (managers, manager's) all have open-door policies.
9. (Memos, memo's) are internal documents, sent to other workers in the same organization. (Letters', letters, letter's) are for external readers.
10. Burnout affects an (employees', employees, employee's) productivity and morale.

Check your answers to the odd-numbered exercises on page 551.

CASES FOR COMMUNICATORS

Green Commuting: The Newest Employee Benefit

For many Canadians, the financial downturn has moved environmental awareness into focus. Finding alternative fuels and changing the way we use our resources: these topics dominate conversations, social networks, our minds, and the media.

Right now only a few companies pay attention to the physical and financial pressures of their commuting employees. But as more and more Canadians assume responsibility for their own energy use (www.carbonfootprint.com/calculator.aspx), employers encouraging commuting alternatives, and offering commuting choices will be more attractive to prospective employees.

Individual Activity

You are a new hire for Wallace Financial Solutions, a small but flourishing financial services company offering accounting and investing advice to clients. You (a financial services advisor) have been hired to expand the client list.

The company is located in downtown Calgary. Its CAs, CGAs, CMAs, and accredited financial advisors have clients located all over downtown Calgary, its outskirts and suburbs. Few employees live in downtown Calgary. Most commute, as will you since you live about 43 kilometres away.

Competition in the financial services industry is tough; however, Wallace Financial's clients are loyal because of the company's reputation for superb customer service and sound financial solutions. Personal rapport and client trust matter most in the financial services sector. Advisors will spend hours of face time with prospects over several weeks—even months—before people feel confident enough to invest their money. Wallace Financial meets with established clients four times annually, more frequently during tax season. Advisors visit prospects and clients in their homes, at their request. This service has always differentiated Wallace from the competition. However, this important service now costs the company—in fuel costs and a reputation for social responsibility.

President Annette Wallace is offering bonuses to employees who provide practical options to the long-distance, fuel-guzzling commuting, and in-home client visits.

Brainstorm as many possibilities to reduce travel as you can. Research possibilities. (You can start with http://vehicles.gc.ca; www.tc.gc.ca/programs/Environment/Commuter/menu.htm; idealbite.com; treehugger.com.)

Identify and analyze your various audiences' reactions to your options.

- Who will gain from your ideas?
- What needs may motivate your colleagues to adopt your idea(s)
- What needs may motivate clients and prospects?
- What benefits will convince Wallace and your commuting colleagues that your suggestion(s) are workable?
- What benefits will convince clients?
- What benefits will convince prospects?

Group Activity

Exchange your ideas with two or three classmates. Combine your results to generate a list of workable options, with their benefits. As a group, select the best three ideas, with their audience benefits.

Write a memo report to President Annette Wallace and the management committee, describing your ideas, with their benefits.

Revise your report to

- Use you-attitude
- Include a benefit for each audience
- Justify negative information, focusing on what the reader can do rather than on limitations
- Omit unnecessary negative information

When you have finished your memo report, create a PowerPoint presentation highlighting your options and benefits for the management committee. Keep the presentation to six slides, maximum, since you have only five or ten minutes and intend to hand out the memo report after your presentation.

Source: Case idea based on Wallace Immen's article, "Easing Gas Pains, Fueling Loyalty," Globe Careers, *The Globe and Mail*, May 28, 2008, p. C1.

Composing Letters, Memos, and Emails

- **Module 9:**
  Formatting Hard Copy Letters and Memos

- **Module 10:**
  Writing Email and Electronic Messages

- **Module 11:**
  Composing Informative and Positive Messages

- **Module 12:**
  Composing Negative Messages

- **Module 13:**
  Composing Persuasive Messages

Arezoo Ghobadpour writes business messages all day, every day. Although her official title is Office Manager, Arezoo functions as human resources manager, recruiter, researcher, executive assistant to the company president, and as editor and proofreader for her company's electronic and hardcopy documents.

Arezoo works for ACS Incorporated, an international company specializing in carrier management services, including freight audit and payment. Her audiences include both internal and external customers: Arezoo uses email to write letters to other companies, including recruiting agencies, and to memo staff with policy and procedure updates, and responses to queries.

Most of her time is spent performing her HR duties, for which Arezoo feels a true affinity. "Because my position relates to every department and responsibility, I get a lot of variety, every day. I like the challenge of keeping on top of it all, and I like being busy and feeling useful. I am involved in everything and anything: from recruiting, interviewing and maintaining personnel records, to

managing group benefits and ensuring legislation compliance.

"Working in the HR field requires me to create and update job descriptions, and write letters of promotion and discipline. I also write human resource policies and standard operating procedures for jobs within my department. I use the job descriptions to create job postings, and to announce openings in the company."

Perhaps because she has had so much practice, Arezoo also likes researching and every part of the writing process: "I like the challenge of solving problems. I love the Internet for allowing me to research anything, instantly! I often research HR topics, such as new legislation, legal requirements, or answers to employees' questions.

"I enjoy everything about writing. I like the creativity when composing my first line, and I love the flow that follows that. Writing is very freeing for me.

"I am a bit of a perfectionist, so I edit and proof documents before they go to anyone outside the company. When we updated our Web site, I proofread all the

text before it was posted. I even helped edit our sales and marketing initiative."

Arezoo is also committed to furthering her formal education: "I learned the basics of my job through experience, working as a legal administrative assistant. Now I'm completing a Human Resources Management Certificate program for my CHRP designation. Then I am going to pursue a degree in communications or human resource management. My interest in researching and writing offers infinite possibilities."

PAIBOC ANALYSIS

1. For what purposes does Arezoo write?

2. Identify four different audiences Arezoo writes to.

3. Which of Arezoo's messages would you consider informative and positive? Why?

4. Which of Arezoo's messages would you consider negative? Why?

5. Which of Arezoo's messages would you consider persuasive? Why?

Formatting Hardcopy Letters and Memos

Learning Objectives

After reading and applying the information in Module 9, you'll be able to demonstrate

Knowledge of

- The basic design formula: Form follows function
- How to use PAIBOC to decide on your format
- Basic business formats

Skills to

- Use PAIBOC to choose appropriate formats
- Use non-sexist courtesy titles
- Create a business image

Employability Skills 2000+ Checklist

In this module, the key skills from the Conference Board of Canada's Employability Skills 2000+ are

Communicate

○ write and speak so others pay attention and understand

Manage Information

○ locate, gather, and organize information using appropriate technology and information systems

Think & Solve Problems

○ assess situations and identify problems
○ seek different points of view and evaluate them based on facts

○ recognize the human, interpersonal, technical, scientific, and mathematical dimensions of a problem

Participate in Projects & Tasks

○ work to agreed quality standards and specifications

○ adapt to changing requirements and information

Whether hardcopy or electronic, letters and memos are both brief business messages, similar in formality, length, style, and organization. **Letters** go to people outside the organization, whereas **memos** are internal messages sent to people within your organization. Because they have different **audiences**, letters and memos differ in format, signalling recipients that they are reading an external or internal message.

Format means the parts of a document and the way they are arranged on the page. Short reports use letter or memo format (Modules 20 and 21). Long reports can use the format described in Module 22. If your organization has its own formats for letters and memos, use them. Otherwise, choose one of the formats in this module.

When you are considering how best to deliver your message, remember the principle of all good design: *form follows function.* This design principle is essential to communication success: when you shape your message (format) to meet the needs of your audience and your purposes (function), you get the results you want. Use PAIBOC analysis to choose the right format for your message.

How Should I Set Up Letters?

Letters are written in block and modified block.

The two most common letter formats are block, sometimes called **full block**, and **modified block** or **semi-block**.

FIGURE 9.1   **PAIBOC Questions for Analysis**

P   What is the **purpose** of your communication? What do you hope to achieve? What results do you want?

A   Who is your **audience**? Are they inside or outside your organization? What are their expectations? What do they care about? What do they value? What do they know? What do they need to know? How will they feel about your message?

I   Based on your purpose and audience analysis, what **information** must your message include?

B   Based on your purpose and audience analysis, what **benefits** can you use to meet your audience's needs, and achieve your purpose?

O   Based on your audience and purpose analysis, what **objections** can you expect from your audience? What negative aspects of your message must you deemphasize, or overcome?

C   How does the **context** affect audience response? What circumstances—economic, environmental, legal, and/or organizational—might influence how your audience will perceive the message?

Figures 9.2 and 9.3 show block and semi-block formats.

FIGURE 9.2   **Block Format on Letterhead (mixed punctuation; collection letter)**

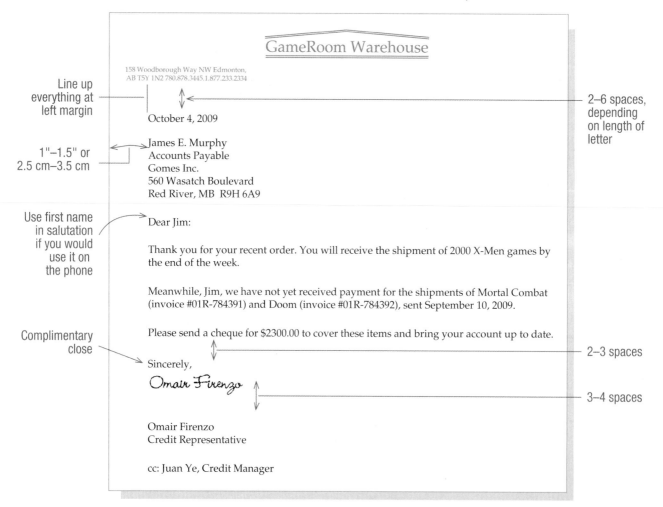

FIGURE 9.3   Indented Format on Letterhead (mixed punctuation; employee evaluation letter)

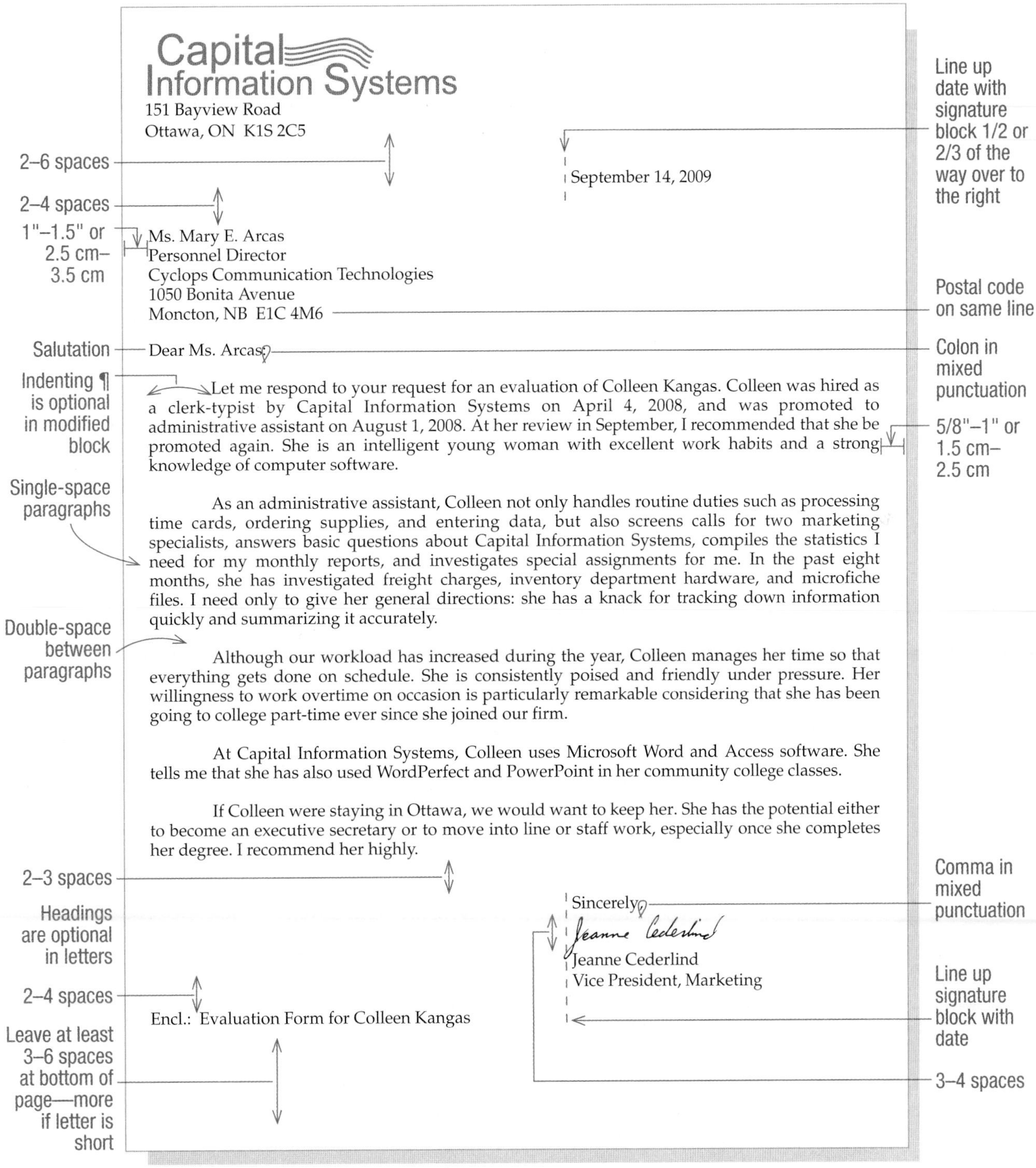

Capital Information Systems

151 Bayview Road
Ottawa, ON K1S 2C5

September 14, 2009

Ms. Mary E. Arcas
Personnel Director
Cyclops Communication Technologies
1050 Bonita Avenue
Moncton, NB E1C 4M6

Dear Ms. Arcas:

    Let me respond to your request for an evaluation of Colleen Kangas. Colleen was hired as a clerk-typist by Capital Information Systems on April 4, 2008, and was promoted to administrative assistant on August 1, 2008. At her review in September, I recommended that she be promoted again. She is an intelligent young woman with excellent work habits and a strong knowledge of computer software.

    As an administrative assistant, Colleen not only handles routine duties such as processing time cards, ordering supplies, and entering data, but also screens calls for two marketing specialists, answers basic questions about Capital Information Systems, compiles the statistics I need for my monthly reports, and investigates special assignments for me. In the past eight months, she has investigated freight charges, inventory department hardware, and microfiche files. I need only to give her general directions: she has a knack for tracking down information quickly and summarizing it accurately.

    Although our workload has increased during the year, Colleen manages her time so that everything gets done on schedule. She is consistently poised and friendly under pressure. Her willingness to work overtime on occasion is particularly remarkable considering that she has been going to college part-time ever since she joined our firm.

    At Capital Information Systems, Colleen uses Microsoft Word and Access software. She tells me that she has also used WordPerfect and PowerPoint in her community college classes.

    If Colleen were staying in Ottawa, we would want to keep her. She has the potential either to become an executive secretary or to move into line or staff work, especially once she completes her degree. I recommend her highly.

Sincerely,

Jeanne Cederlind

Jeanne Cederlind
Vice President, Marketing

Encl.: Evaluation Form for Colleen Kangas

Annotations (left):
- 2–6 spaces
- 2–4 spaces
- 1"–1.5" or 2.5 cm– 3.5 cm
- Salutation
- Indenting ¶ is optional in modified block
- Single-space paragraphs
- Double-space between paragraphs
- 2–3 spaces
- Headings are optional in letters
- 2–4 spaces
- Leave at least 3–6 spaces at bottom of page—more if letter is short

Annotations (right):
- Line up date with signature block 1/2 or 2/3 of the way over to the right
- Postal code on same line
- Colon in mixed punctuation
- 5/8"–1" or 1.5 cm– 2.5 cm
- Comma in mixed punctuation
- Line up signature block with date
- 3–4 spaces

How Are the Two Formats Similar?

Block and modified block business letters share many elements:

- Organizations include their return address in their **letterhead**.
- Written documentation is for the record, so the **date** is essential.

Employability Skills
2 0 +

- Readers are addressed by name in the **salutation**.
- Subject and reference lines direct readers' attention to your purpose.
- A standard **complimentary close** (*Sincerely*, *Best*, *Regards*) comes before your signature.
- Correct punctuation is essential for credibility.
- Continuation pages maintain coherence.
- "Enclosure" tells the reader that you have included additional material, like a duplicated document or a résumé.

Use the same level of formality in the **salutation**, or greeting, as you would in talking to that person on the phone: *Dear Ahmed* if you're on a first-name basis, and *Dear Mr. Guten* if you don't know the reader well enough to use a first name. When you are responding to a letter or memo, use a salutation that mirrors the original sender's signature, which reflects how the person wants to be addressed.

Sincerely and *Cordially* are standard complimentary closes. When you are writing to people in special groups or to someone who is a friend as well as a business acquaintance, you may want to use a less formal close. Depending on your reader's expectations, the following informal closes might be acceptable: *Yours for a better environment*, *Best*, *Regards*, or even *Ciao*.

In two-point or **mixed punctuation**, a colon follows the salutation and a comma follows the close. Today, many people use a comma after the salutation to make the letter look more personal. A few organizations use open punctuation because it's faster to type. In **open punctuation**, omit all punctuation after the salutation and the close.

A **subject line** tells readers what they are about to read. This "reader-redundancy," or repetition for reinforcement—an element of persuasion—demonstrates you-attitude (Module 6).

Subject lines are required in hardcopy memos, and all emails; they are optional in letters. If you do use a subject line in your letter, place it after the salutation. Good subject lines are specific, concise, and appropriate for your purposes and the response you expect from your reader.

- When you have good news, put it in the subject line.
- When your information is neutral, summarize it concisely in the subject line.
- When your information is negative, use a negative subject line if the reader may not read the message, or needs the information to act, or if the negative is your error.
- When you have a request that will be easy for the reader to grant, put either the subject of the request or a direct question in the subject line.
- When you must persuade a reluctant reader, use common ground, a reader benefit, or a directed subject line (Module 13) that makes your position on the issue clear.

For examples of subject lines in each of these situations, see Modules 11, 12, and 13.

A **reference line** refers the reader to the number used on previous correspondence, or the order or invoice number that this letter is about. Government organizations, such as Revenue Canada, use numbers on every piece of correspondence they send out, to quickly find the earlier document to which an incoming letter refers.

Both block and modified block formats use headings, lists, and indented sections (known as *telegraphing*, *highlighting*, *bulleting* or *dot-jotting*) for emphasis.

Each format has advantages. Block is the format most frequently used for business letters; readers expect it; and it can be typed quickly, since everything lines up at the left margin. Speed-readers say it is easier to read. *Modified* block format creates a visually attractive page by moving the date and signature block into what would otherwise be empty white space. Table 9.1 compares the two formats.

TABLE 9.1   **Differences Between Letter Formats**

	Block	**Modified Block**
Date and signature block	Lined up at left margin	Lined up ½ or ⅔ over to the right
Paragraph indentation	None	Optional
Subject line	Optional	Rare

Letterhead is pre-printed stationery with the organization's name, logo, address, and phone number. Figure 9.4 shows how to set up modified block format when you do not have letterhead. (It is also acceptable to use block format without letterhead.)

FIGURE 9.4   **Modified Block Format Without Letterhead (open punctuation; claim letter)**

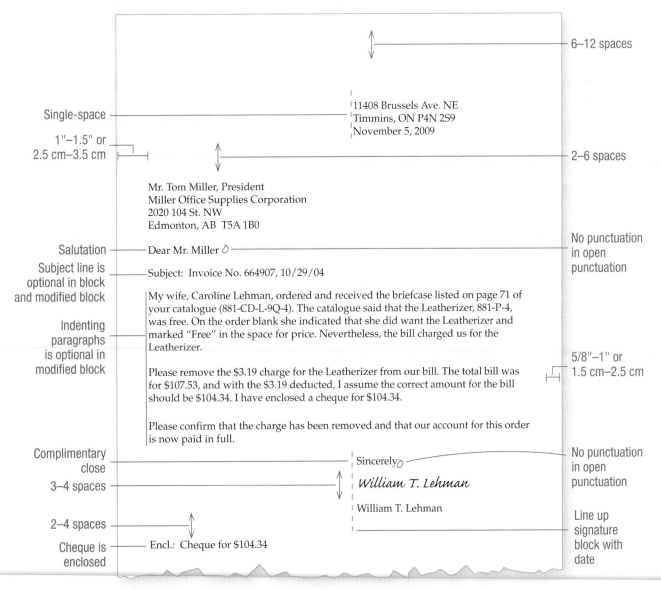

What If My Letter Is More Than a Page?

When your letter runs two or more pages, use a heading on the second page to identify it. Putting the reader's name helps the writer, who may be printing out many letters at a time, to make sure the right second page gets in the envelope. Note that even when the signature block is on the second page, it is still lined up with the date.

Reader's Name
Date
Page Number

or

Reader's Name   Page Number   Date

When a letter runs to two or more pages, use letterhead only for page 1. (See Figures 9.5 and 9.6.) For the remaining pages, use plain paper that matches the letterhead in weight, texture, and colour.

Set side margins of 2.5 to 3.5 centimetres (1 to 1.5 inch) on the left and 1.5 to 2.5 centimetres (0.75 to 1 inch) on the right. If your letterhead extends all the way across the top of the page, set your margins even with the ends of the letterhead for the most visually pleasing page. The top margin should be three to six lines under the letterhead, or 5 centimetres (2 inches) down from the top of the page if you aren't using letterhead. If your letter is very short, you might want to use bigger side and top margins so that the letter is centred on the page.

How Do I Indicate I Am Sending Additional Documents?

Many letters are accompanied by other documents. Whatever these documents may be—a multi-page report or a two-line note—in hardcopy letters they are called **enclosures**, since they are enclosed in the envelope. The writer should refer to the enclosures in the body of the letter: "As you can see from my résumé, …" The enclosure line is usually abbreviated: *Encl.* (see Figure 9.4). The abbreviation reminds the person who seals the letter to include the enclosure(s).

Sometimes you write to one person but send copies of your letter to other people. If you want the reader to know that other people are getting copies, list their names on the last page. The abbreviation *cc* originally meant "carbon copy" but now means "computer copy." Other acceptable abbreviations include *pc* for "photocopy" or simply *c* for "copy." You can also send copies to other people without telling the reader. These **blind copies** are not mentioned on the original; they are listed on the copy saved for the file with the abbreviation *bc* preceding the names of people getting these copies.

You do not need to indicate that you have shown a letter to your superior or that you are saving a copy of the letter for your own files. These are standard practices.

FIGURE 9.5 **Two-Page Letter, Block Format (mixed or two-point punctuation; informative letter)**

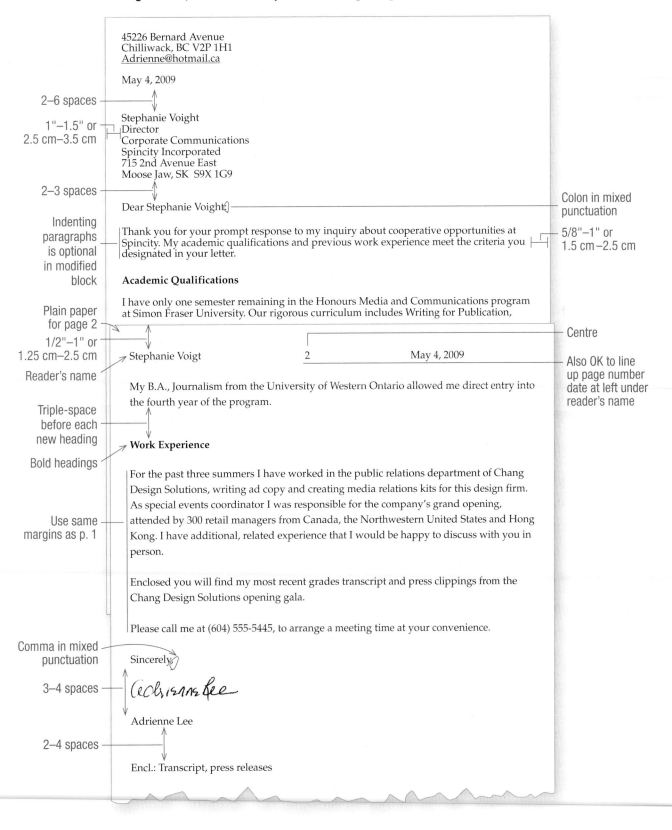

45226 Bernard Avenue
Chilliwack, BC V2P 1H1
Adrienne@hotmail.ca

May 4, 2009

2–6 spaces

1"–1.5" or
2.5 cm–3.5 cm

Stephanie Voight
Director
Corporate Communications
Spincity Incorporated
715 2nd Avenue East
Moose Jaw, SK S9X 1G9

2–3 spaces

Dear Stephanie Voight:

Colon in mixed punctuation

Thank you for your prompt response to my inquiry about cooperative opportunities at Spincity. My academic qualifications and previous work experience meet the criteria you designated in your letter.

5/8"–1" or
1.5 cm–2.5 cm

Indenting paragraphs is optional in modified block

Academic Qualifications

I have only one semester remaining in the Honours Media and Communications program at Simon Fraser University. Our rigorous curriculum includes Writing for Publication,

Plain paper for page 2
1/2"–1" or
1.25 cm–2.5 cm

Reader's name

Stephanie Voigt   2   May 4, 2009

Centre

Also OK to line up page number date at left under reader's name

My B.A., Journalism from the University of Western Ontario allowed me direct entry into the fourth year of the program.

Triple-space before each new heading

Bold headings

Work Experience

For the past three summers I have worked in the public relations department of Chang Design Solutions, writing ad copy and creating media relations kits for this design firm. As special events coordinator I was responsible for the company's grand opening, attended by 300 retail managers from Canada, the Northwestern United States and Hong Kong. I have additional, related experience that I would be happy to discuss with you in person.

Use same margins as p. 1

Enclosed you will find my most recent grades transcript and press clippings from the Chang Design Solutions opening gala.

Please call me at (604) 555-5445, to arrange a meeting time at your convenience.

Comma in mixed punctuation

Sincerely,

3–4 spaces

Adrienne Lee

2–4 spaces

Encl.: Transcript, press releases

FIGURE 9.6   Two-Page Letter, Modified Block Format (mixed or two-point punctuation; informative and goodwill letter)

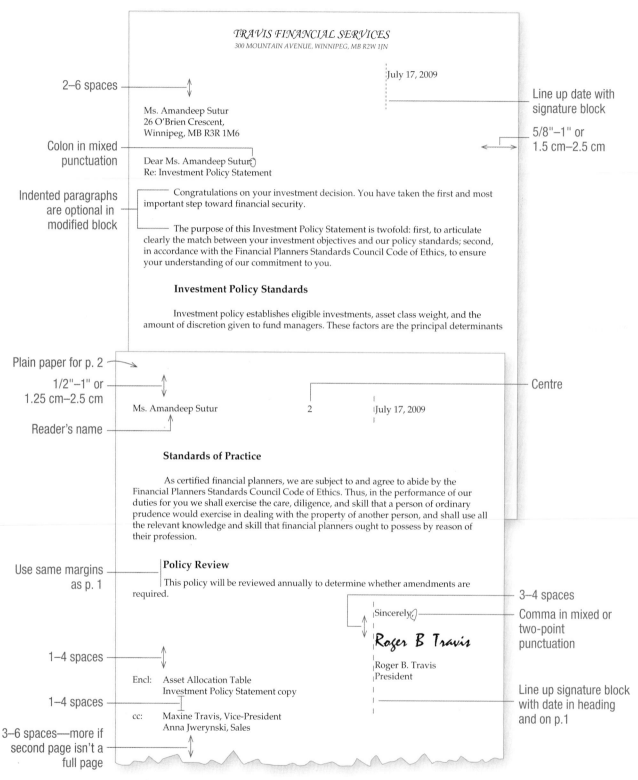

TABLE 9.2   Postal Service Abbreviations for Canadian Provinces, Territories, and U.S. States

Province/Territory Name	Postal Service Abbreviation	State/Territory Name	Postal Service Abbreviation
Alberta	AB	Maryland	MD
British Columbia	BC	Massachusetts	MA
Manitoba	MB	Michigan	MI
New Brunswick	NB	Minnesota	MN
Newfoundland and Labrador	NL	Mississippi	MS
Northwest Territories	NT	Missouri	MO
Nunavut	NU	Montana	MT
Nova Scotia	NS	Nebraska	NE
Ontario	ON	Nevada	NV
Prince Edward Island	PE	New Hampshire	NH
Quebec	QC	New Jersey	NJ
Saskatchewan	SK	New Mexico	NM
Yukon Territory	YT	New York	NY
		North Carolina	NC
State/Territory Name	**Postal Service Abbreviation**	North Dakota	ND
Alabama	AL	Ohio	OH
Alaska	AK	Oklahoma	OK
Arizona	AZ	Oregon	OR
Arkansas	AR	Pennsylvania	PA
California	CA	Rhode Island	RI
Colorado	CO	South Carolina	SC
Connecticut	CT	South Dakota	SD
Delaware	DE	Tennessee	TN
District of Columbia	DC	Texas	TX
Florida	FL	Utah	UT
Georgia	GA	Vermont	VT
Hawaii	HI	Virginia	VA
Idaho	ID	Washington	WA
Illinois	IL	West Virginia	WV
Indiana	IN	Wisconsin	WI
Iowa	IA	Wyoming	WY
Kansas	KS	Guam	GU
Kentucky	KY	Puerto Rico	PR
Louisiana	LA	Virgin Islands	VI
Maine	ME		

What Courtesy Titles Should I Use?

Research your reader's preference.

Today, most salutations use "Dear *first name last name*." Using *Dear* is a courteous, standard business convention and in no way implies a personal relationship with the recipient.

Some people and many cultures prefer their professional titles: Director Chadraba, President Mauricio. Use *Ms., Mr.,* or *Mrs.* when your audience has signed his or her correspondence that way.

1. Use professional titles when they're relevant.

> Dr. Kristen Sorenson is our new company physician.
> The Rev. Robert Townsley gave the invocation.

2. If a woman prefers to be addressed as *Mrs.* or *Miss*, rather than *Ms.*, use the title she prefers. (You-attitude [Module 6] takes precedence over non-sexist language: address the reader as she—or he—prefers to be addressed.) To find out whether a woman prefers a traditional title:
   a. Check the signature block in previous correspondence. If a woman types her name as *(Miss) Elaine Anderson* or *(Mrs.) Kay Royster*, use the title she designates.
   b. Notice the title a woman uses in introducing herself on the phone. If she says, "This is Robin Stine," use *Dear Robin Stine* when you write to her. If she says, "I'm Mrs. Stine," use the title she specifies.
   c. Check your company directory. In some organizations, women who prefer traditional titles list them with their names.
   d. When you're writing job letters or other crucial correspondence, call the company and ask the receptionist which title your reader prefers.

Ms. is particularly useful when you do not know a woman's marital status. However, when you know that a woman is married or single, use courtesy titles only when your audience requests them.

In addition to using parallel courtesy titles, use parallel forms for names. See Table 9.3.

TABLE 9.3   **Use Parallel Forms for Names**

Not Parallel	Parallel
Members of the committee will be Mr. Jones, Mr. Yacone, and Lisa	Members of the committee will be Mr. Jones, Mr. Yacone, and Ms. Melton
	or
	Members of the committee will be Irving, Ted, and Lisa

Employability Skills

When You Know the Reader's Name but Not the Gender

Never assume a person's gender by their name. When you know your reader's name but not the gender, you can do two things:

1. Call the company and ask the receptionist.
2. Use the reader's full name in the salutation.

> Dear Chris Crowell:
> Dear J. C. Meath:

When You Know Neither the Reader's Name Nor Gender

When you know neither the reader's name nor gender, you have four options:

1. Use an attention line:

   Attention Customer Service:
   Attention Human Resources:
   Attention Office of the Registrar:

2. Use the reader's position or job title:

   Dear Loan Officer:
   Attention Registrar:

3. Use a general group to which your reader belongs:

   Dear Investor:
   Attention Admissions Committee:

4. Omit the salutation and use a subject line in its place:

   Subject: Recommendation for Ben Wandell

Using bolded attention and subject lines is acceptable.

How Should I Set Up Hardcopy Memos?

The standard memo uses block format but has no salutation, close, or signature.

Hardcopy and electronic memos are messages sent within an organization. Hardcopy memos omit both the salutation and the close. Memos never indent paragraphs. Subject lines are required; headings are optional. If you use headings, make sure each heading covers all the information until the next heading. Never use a separate heading for the first paragraph. The simple request memo in Figure 9.7 uses a standard format.

FIGURE 9.7   **Simple Request Memo**

May 4, 2009

To: Noushad

From: Shantel   *SW*

Subject: Forgotten Password

Please accept my apologies: I have forgotten my new password to get into client files. Please reset, and call me (extension 5340) with the temporary password.

Thank you, Noushad.

Figures 9.8 and 9.9 illustrate the standard hardcopy memo format typed on a plain sheet of paper. Note that the first letters of the reader's name, the writer's name, and the subject phrase are lined up vertically. Note also that memos are usually initialled beside the To/From block. Initialling tells the reader that the memo's writer takes responsibility for the document.

FIGURE 9.8 **Memo Format (on plain paper; analytical proposal/short report)**

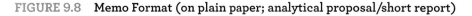

Everything lined up at left

Plain paper

October 8, 2009

2–4 spaces

Line up

To: Annette T. Califero

Double-space

Writer's initials added in ink

From: Kyle B. Abrams *KBA*

1"–1.5" or 2.5 cm–3.5 cm

Subject: A Low-Cost Way to Reduce Energy Use

Capitalize first letter of each major word in subject line

No heading for ¶ 1

As you requested, I've investigated low-cost ways to reduce our energy use. Reducing the building temperature on weekends is a change that we could make immediately, that would cost nothing, and that would cut our energy use by about 6 percent.

5/8"–1" or 1.5 cm–2.5 cm

Triple-space before each new heading

The Energy Savings from a Lower Weekend Temperature

Bold headings

Lowering the temperature from 20°C to 15.5°C from 8 p.m. Friday evening to 4 a.m. Monday morning could cut our total consumption by 6 percent. It is not feasible to lower the temperature on weeknights because many staff members work late; the cleaning crew is also on duty from 6 p.m. to midnight. Turning the temperature down for only four hours would not result in a significant heat saving.

Single-space paragraphs; double-space between paragraphs

Turning the heat back up at 4 a.m. on Mondays will allow the building temperature to be back to 20°C by 9 a.m. Our furnace already has computerized controls that can be set to automatically lower and raise the temperature.

Triple-space

How a Lower Temperature Would Affect Employees

Capitalize first letter of each major word of heading

A survey of employees shows that only seven people use the building every weekend or almost every weekend. Eighteen percent of our staff have worked at least one weekend day in the last two months; 52 percent say they "occasionally" come in on weekends.

Do not indent paragraphs

People who come in for an hour or less on weekends could cope with the lower temperature just by wearing warm clothes. However, most people would find 15.5°C too cool for extended work. Employees who work regularly on weekends might want to install space heaters.

Action Needed to Implement the Change

Would you also like me to check into the cost of buying a dozen portable space heaters? Providing them would allow us to choose units that our wiring can handle and would be a nice gesture toward employees who give up their weekends to work. I could have a report to you in two weeks.

No signature

We can begin saving energy immediately. Just authorize the lower temperature, and I'll see that the controls are reset for this weekend.

FIGURE 9.9 Memo Format (on memo letterhead; good news)

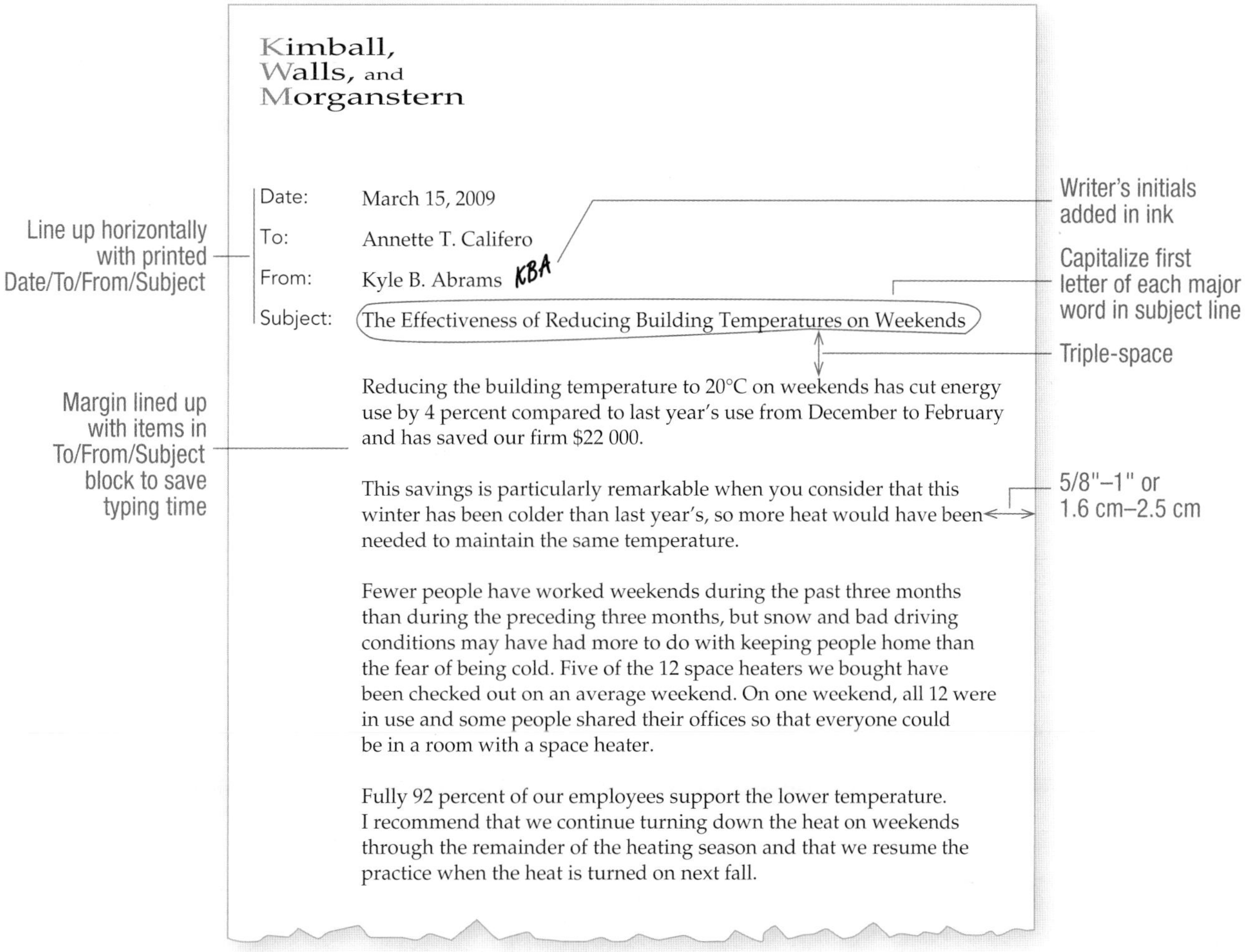

Kimball,
Walls, and
Morganstern

Line up horizontally with printed Date/To/From/Subject

Date: March 15, 2009

To: Annette T. Califero

From: Kyle B. Abrams *KBA*

Subject: (The Effectiveness of Reducing Building Temperatures on Weekends)

Writer's initials added in ink

Capitalize first letter of each major word in subject line

Triple-space

Margin lined up with items in To/From/Subject block to save typing time

Reducing the building temperature to 20°C on weekends has cut energy use by 4 percent compared to last year's use from December to February and has saved our firm $22 000.

This savings is particularly remarkable when you consider that this winter has been colder than last year's, so more heat would have been needed to maintain the same temperature.

5/8"–1" or 1.6 cm–2.5 cm

Fewer people have worked weekends during the past three months than during the preceding three months, but snow and bad driving conditions may have had more to do with keeping people home than the fear of being cold. Five of the 12 space heaters we bought have been checked out on an average weekend. On one weekend, all 12 were in use and some people shared their offices so that everyone could be in a room with a space heater.

Fully 92 percent of our employees support the lower temperature. I recommend that we continue turning down the heat on weekends through the remainder of the heating season and that we resume the practice when the heat is turned on next fall.

Some organizations have special letterhead for hardcopy memos. When *Date/To/From/Subject* are already printed on the form, the date, writer's and reader's names, and subject may be set at the main margin to save typing time (see Figure 9.9).

Some organizations alter the order of items in the Date/To/From/Subject block. Some organizations ask employees to sign memos rather than simply initialling them. The signature goes below the last line of the memo, starting halfway over on the page, and prevents anyone adding unauthorized information.

Checkpoint

Letters are business messages written to readers outside the company. Letters use **block** or **modified semi-block** format.

Memos are business messages sent between people in the same company. Memos begin with a **Date** line, a **To** line, a **From** line, and a **Subject** line.

If the hardcopy memo runs to two pages or more, consider breaking the text up with headings (Modules 20 and 21). Use an informative heading at the top of the second and subsequent pages (see Figure 9.10). Since many of your memos go to the same people, putting a brief version of the subject line will be more helpful than just using "All Employees."

Brief Subject Line
Date
Page Number

or

Brief Subject Line	Page Number	Date

Making it easy for your audiences to read, understand, and respond to your messages makes it much more likely they will comply.

Documents need to look professional, too. Now that most documents are keyed on computers and printed with laser printers, we don't need to worry about whited-out errors or uneven keystrokes. We do need to make sure that the ink or toner is printing evenly and that the document uses a standard format.

Some organizations prescribe a standard format for documents. If your organization does, follow it. If you have your choice, use one of the formats in this book. They're widely used in businesses, so they communicate a message of competence.

EXPANDING A CRITICAL SKILL

Creating a Business Image

The way you and your documents look affects the way people respond to you and to them. All discourse communities and organizations (Module 2) have a dress code. One young man was upset when an older man told him he should wear better shoes. He was wearing leather shoes but not the kind that said "I'm promotable" in that workplace. Dress codes are rarely spelled out; the older worker was doing the young man a favour by being direct.

If you have a mentor in the organization, ask him or her if there are other ways you can make your appearance even more professional. If you don't have a mentor, look at the people who rank above you. Notice clothing, jewellery, and hairstyles. If you're on a budget, go to stores that sell expensive clothing to check the kind of buttons, the texture and colours of fabric, the width of lapels and belts. Then go to stores in your price range and choose garments that imitate the details of expensive clothing.

Some urban, multicultural workplaces welcome clothing choices that reflect a person's ethnic background and/or religious beliefs, and accept personal artefacts, including tattoos and piercing. However, such choices may evoke negative assumptions; it's up to you to research the apparel choices considered appropriately professional in your organization.

Some organizations' dress codes are less formal than others'.

FIGURE 9.10 Two-Page Memo (analytical proposal/short report)

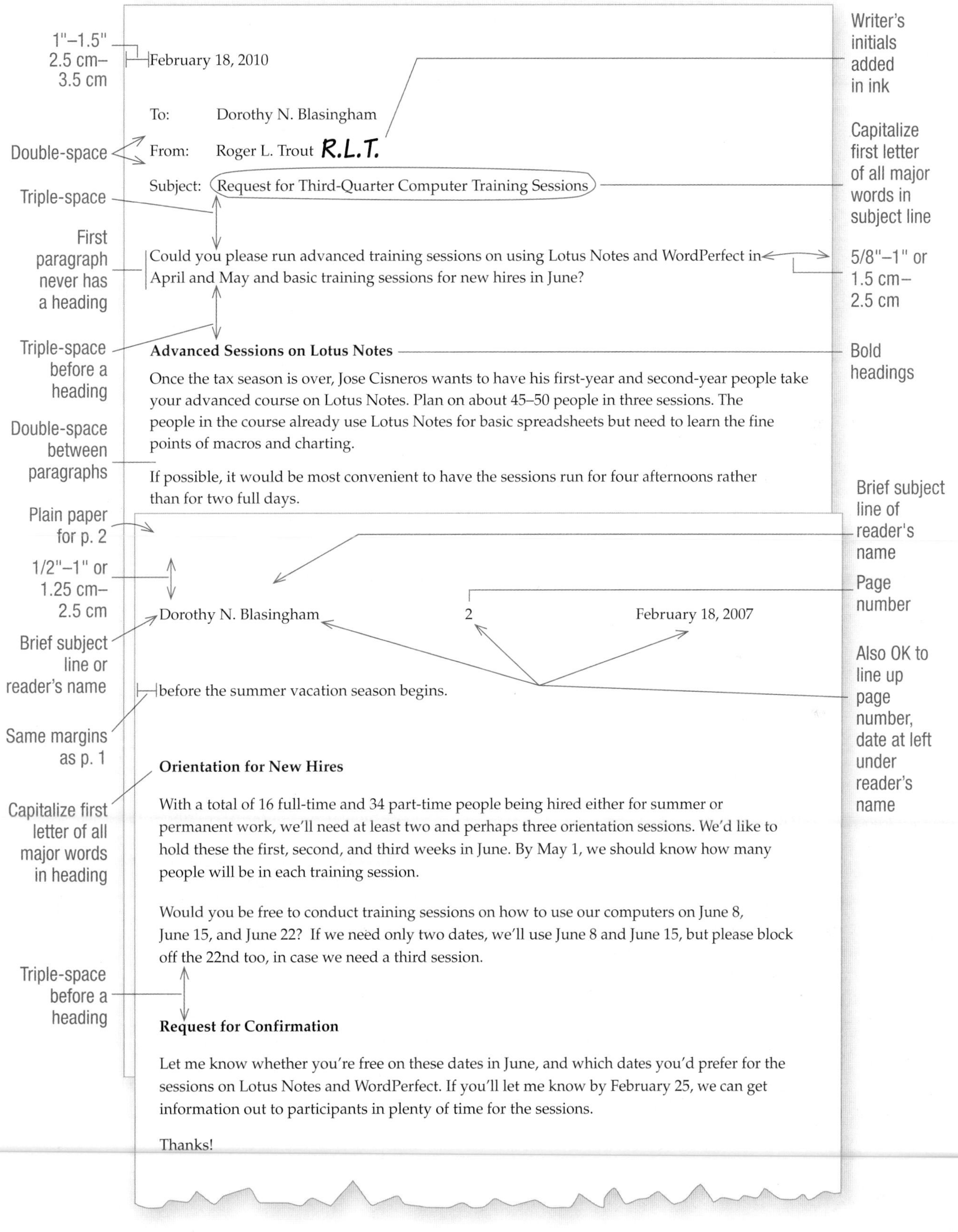
February 18, 2010

To: Dorothy N. Blasingham

From: Roger L. Trout R.L.T.

Subject: Request for Third-Quarter Computer Training Sessions

Could you please run advanced training sessions on using Lotus Notes and WordPerfect in April and May and basic training sessions for new hires in June?

Advanced Sessions on Lotus Notes

Once the tax season is over, Jose Cisneros wants to have his first-year and second-year people take your advanced course on Lotus Notes. Plan on about 45–50 people in three sessions. The people in the course already use Lotus Notes for basic spreadsheets but need to learn the fine points of macros and charting.

If possible, it would be most convenient to have the sessions run for four afternoons rather than for two full days.

Dorothy N. Blasingham 2 February 18, 2007

before the summer vacation season begins.

Orientation for New Hires

With a total of 16 full-time and 34 part-time people being hired either for summer or permanent work, we'll need at least two and perhaps three orientation sessions. We'd like to hold these the first, second, and third weeks in June. By May 1, we should know how many people will be in each training session.

Would you be free to conduct training sessions on how to use our computers on June 8, June 15, and June 22? If we need only two dates, we'll use June 8 and June 15, but please block off the 22nd too, in case we need a third session.

Request for Confirmation

Let me know whether you're free on these dates in June, and which dates you'd prefer for the sessions on Lotus Notes and WordPerfect. If you'll let me know by February 25, we can get information out to participants in plenty of time for the sessions.

Thanks!
1"–1.5" 2.5 cm–3.5 cm
Double-space
Triple-space
First paragraph never has a heading
Triple-space before a heading
Double-space between paragraphs
Plain paper for p. 2
1/2"–1" or 1.25 cm–2.5 cm
Brief subject line or reader's name
Same margins as p. 1
Capitalize first letter of all major words in heading
Triple-space before a heading
Writer's initials added in ink
Capitalize first letter of all major words in subject line
5/8"–1" or 1.5 cm–2.5 cm
Bold headings
Brief subject line of reader's name
Page number
Also OK to line up page number, date at left under reader's name

MODULE SUMMARY

- Letters are written to people outside the organization; memos are documents written to people inside your organization.

- Block and modified block are the two standard letter formats.

- Use the courtesy titles people prefer. If you don't know a person's gender or title preference, ask.

- In a list of several people, use parallel forms for names. Use courtesy titles and last names for everyone, or use first names for everyone.

- Traditional hardcopy memos omit both the salutation and the close. Memos never indent paragraphs. Memos require subject lines; headings are optional. Each heading must cover all the information until the next paragraph. Never use a separate heading for the first paragraph.

ASSIGNMENTS FOR MODULE 9

Questions for Critical Thinking

9.1 How do you decide whether you are writing a letter or a memo?

9.2 Microsoft Word offers dozens of templates for business documents. How would you decide what template to use? What are the advantages of using Word templates? What are the disadvantages?

9.3 How do you decide how to address your recipient when you write?

9.4 What two types of letter formats are used in business? Which letter format do you prefer? Why?

9.5 What are the advantages in telling your reader who is getting copies of your message? What are the disadvantages?

9.6 When is texting someone appropriate? How do you decide?

Exercises and Problems

9.7 Formatting a Message

Correct the format errors in the following hardcopy memo.

March 3,2009

To: Professor Hughes
From: Adele Cameron
Subject: My Writing Progress

Overview

Dear Professor Hughes. Thank you for the opportunity to review my writing progress so far. Because I have been using a reader to provide specific feedback, my writing has improved since the beginning of the semester.

Writing Strategies

When you encouraged us to find someone to read and respond to our writing, I asked my older brother, a recent university graduate, to do so. He and I sit together while he reads the first drafts of my writing assignments. He gives me specific feedback on my organization, content, word choice, and transitions.

Initially I felt very awkward and defensive when Daniel was reading my papers. He often stopped reading to ask me to clarify an argument, or to explain the meaning of a sentence that seemed pretty obvious to me. After a few such meetings, however, I found that my brother's feedback was forcing me to examine my writing in a new way. I was learning to move from the role of writer to the role of reader, in order to assess whether what I was trying to say made sense from the reader's point of view. Now I reread my papers from the reader's perspective.

Editing Strategies

Daniel also critiqued my grammar and punctuation, which have never been strong. After watching and listening to him, I was able to make some of these corrections myself. Although by no means an expert, I am learning how to edit and proofread my own work.

Thank you very much for the suggestion about using a reader. This practice, and my patient brother's assistance, have helped me to improve my writing skills.

Sincerely,

Adele Cameron

9.8 Analyzing and Revising Message Formats

As consumers, employees and/or students, we all receive hardcopy letters and memos regularly. Bring in two letters and two memos you have received recently.

As your instructor directs,

a. Share your examples with a small group of students.
b. Identify the formats the writers are using.
c. Identify any format errors.
d. Be prepared to present your results to the rest of the class.

POLISHING YOUR PROSE

Making Pronouns Agree with Their Nouns

Pronouns stand in for nouns, and must agree with the nouns they refer to, so that your meaning is clear to your reader. When your reader has to puzzle out what you are saying, you-attitude and positive emphasis disappear.

For the sake of clarity, make your pronouns agree in person (first, second, third) and number (singular, plural) with the nouns they replace.

	Singular	Plural
First person	I, my, mine, me, myself	we, our, us, ourselves
Second person	you, your, yourself	you, your, our, ours, yourselves
Third person	he, she, it, him, her, his, hers	they, their, them, themselves

Incorrect:	In my internship, I learned that you have to manage your time wisely.
Correct:	In my internship, I learned to manage my time wisely.
Incorrect:	The sales team reached their goal.
Correct:	The sales team reached its goal. (*Team* is a collective or group noun, and takes a singular verb and pronoun.)

In Canada and the United States, company names and the words *company* and *government* are singular nouns. In Great Britain, these nouns are plural and require plural pronouns:

Correct (Canadian):	Clarica trains its agents well.
Correct (U.S.):	Nationwide Insurance trains its agents well.
Correct (U.K.):	Lloyd's of London train their agents well.

Exercises

Identify and correct any errors. Note that some sentences do not contain errors.

1. An administrative assistant should help their boss work efficiently.
2. The mayor should give themselves credit for doing a good job.
3. The company announces their quarterly profits today.
4. Most new employees find that they need to learn a new culture.
5. A CEO's pay is often based on the performance of their company.
6. The union votes today on whether they will go on strike.
7. In my first month of work, I learned that you need to check email at least three times a day.
8. One of the features of my corporate culture is a willingness to share ideas.
9. The team will present its recommendations to the Executive Committee.
10. Every employee is interested in improving their technical skills.

Check your answers to the odd-numbered exercises on page 552.

Writing Email and Electronic Messages

Learning Objectives

After reading and applying the information in Module 10, you'll be able to demonstrate

Knowledge of

- Business netiquette basics
- Time management

Skills to

- Write business emails for the results you want
- Apply proven time management techniques

Employability Skills 2000+ Checklist

In this module, the key skills from the Conference Board of Canada's Employability Skills 2000+ are

Communicate

○ write and speak so others pay attention and understand
○ share information using a range of information and communications technologies (e.g., voice, email, computers)

○ use relevant scientific, technological, and mathematical knowledge and skills to explain or clarify ideas

Manage Information

○ locate, gather, and organize information using appropriate technology and information systems

Work with Others

○ contribute to a team by sharing information and expertise

Writing an email may feel as informal and spontaneous as speaking. However, email messages lack all the subtle symbols—facial expressions, gestures, tone, posture, use of space—we use to shape meaning. Communicating effectively by email, therefore, demands the same analytical thinking (PAIBOC), and the same writing processes (composing, revising, editing) as any document.

What Do I Need to Know About Email Messages?

While electronic communication continues to evolve, one reality is constant: when you post, you're published. Electronic privacy does not exist.

As you write email messages, keep these guidelines in mind:

- Writing email requires discretion. Email is neither private nor informal, as a conversation may be. Employers may legally check your messages. And any messages you send can be printed out or forwarded to others without your knowledge or consent. As is true of Facebook, Twitter—of all your electronic messages—what you put out there is forever. Even personal BlackBerry conversations are in the public domain, as the 2005 court case between CIBC and Genuity Capital Markets Technology demonstrated. CIBC was able to trace the BlackBerry users' private, PIN-to-PIN messages to use as evidence.[1]

- All the principles of good business writing apply to email. And because they are so easily misinterpreted, composing emails requires a heightened awareness of courtesy. Use you-attitude (Module 6) and positive emphasis (Module 7). Use reader benefits (Module 8) when appropriate. Choose a pattern of organization that fits the purpose of the message (Modules 11, 12, and 13).

- Because email seems to be as instantaneous as text messaging, some writers pay less attention to grammar, punctuation, and spelling. However, business emails should be as correct as paper documents. Use a spell checker; check for grammar and punctuation.
- Reread and proofread your message before you send it. Even better, get a reader.
- Use your subject line effectively. Take special care when writing to people who do not report to you, or to people outside your organization or unit. If your subject line and first paragraph are not interesting, readers will hit Delete.

FIGURE 10.1 Email Letter Request for Adjustment

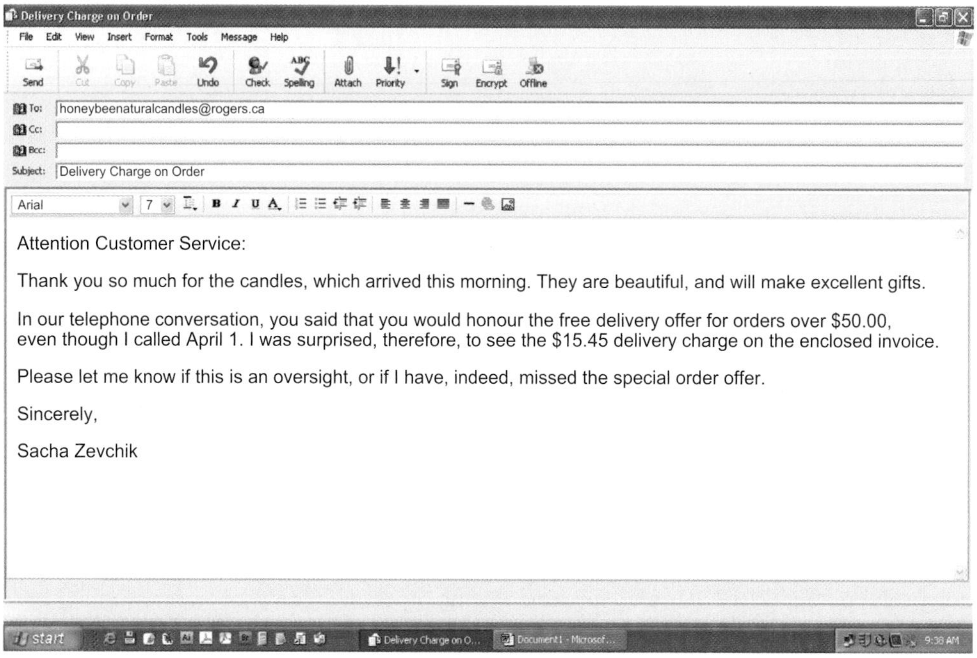

FIGURE 10.2 Email Letter/Sales Letter

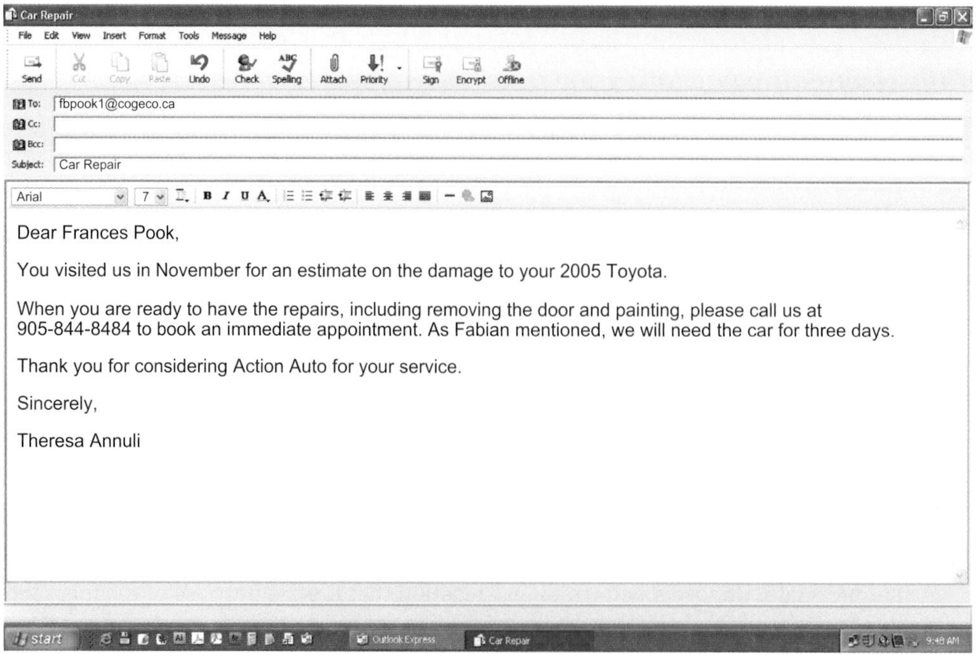

How Should I Set Up Email Messages?

Follow organizational formats, or use a software template.

Many organizations use boilerplate formats for their electronic and hardcopy documents. If you are unsure about how to format a document, research the expectations of your discourse community (Module 2).

Other resources include software and email programs that provide formats you can customize.

Although the email screen has a To line (as do memos), some writers still use an informal salutation, as in Figure 10.3. Most of us prefer a salutation; omitting *Dear (Name)*, *Good Morning (Name)*, even *Hi (Name)* or *Hey (Name)*, sounds brusque, even rude. A salutation is particularly important for readers of high-context cultures (Module 3) whose members value courtesy and formality.

The writer in Figure 10.4 ends the message with a signature block, but you can choose simply to type your name. These conventions depend on context: your relations to the reader and the assumptions and expectations of your company's culture. When in doubt, always err on the side of courtesy, since your respect for the reader conveys you-attitude (Module 6), and engenders respect for you.

You can store a signature block in the email program and set the program to insert the signature block automatically. In contrast, the writer in Figure 10.5 omits both the salutation and his name. When you send a message to an individual or a group you have set up, the From: line will have your name and email address. If you post a message to an email group someone else has set up, be sure to give at least your name and email address at the end of your message, as some programs strip out identifying information when they process messages.

When you hit Reply, the email program automatically uses *Re:* (Latin for "about") and the previous subject. To emphasize you-attitude (Module 6), change the subject line to make it appropriate for your message. When you change the subject line, you can include the original one in parentheses for the reader who sorts messages by thread. When you create a new subject line, delete the *Re:*.

If you prepare your document in a word processor, use 5 centimetre (2 inch) side margins to create short line lengths. If the line lengths are too long, they'll produce awkward line breaks. Use two- or three-space tab settings to minimize wasted space on the screen.

FIGURE 10.3   Outlook Express Email Memo Template

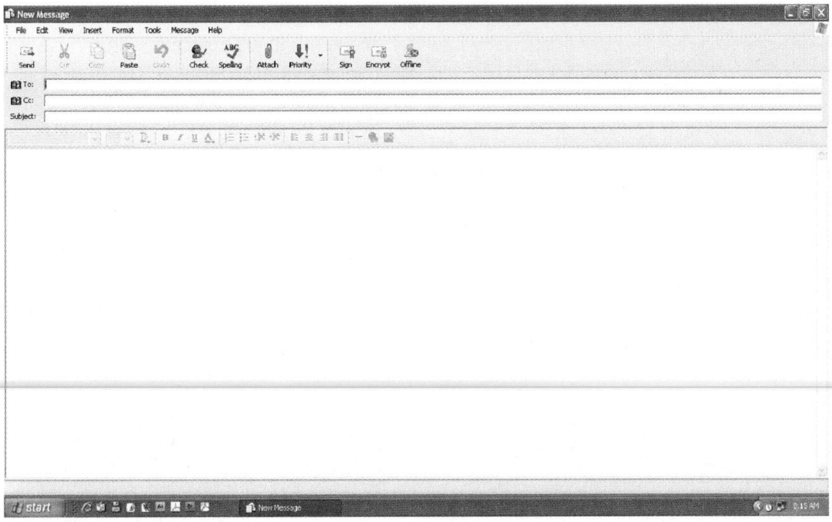

FIGURE 10.4 **A Basic Email Message in Eudora (direct request)**

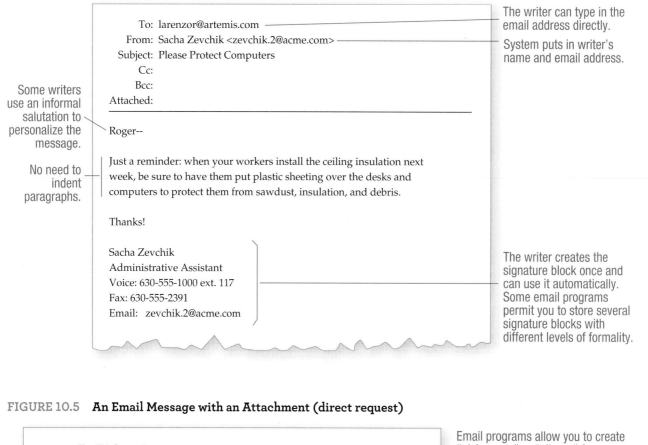

> To: larenzor@artemis.com
> From: Sacha Zevchik <zevchik.2@acme.com>
> Subject: Please Protect Computers
> Cc:
> Bcc:
> Attached:
>
> Roger--
>
> Just a reminder: when your workers install the ceiling insulation next week, be sure to have them put plastic sheeting over the desks and computers to protect them from sawdust, insulation, and debris.
>
> Thanks!
>
> Sacha Zevchik
> Administrative Assistant
> Voice: 630-555-1000 ext. 117
> Fax: 630-555-2391
> Email: zevchik.2@acme.com

The writer can type in the email address directly.

System puts in writer's name and email address.

Some writers use an informal salutation to personalize the message.

No need to indent paragraphs.

The writer creates the signature block once and can use it automatically. Some email programs permit you to store several signature blocks with different levels of formality.

FIGURE 10.5 **An Email Message with an Attachment (direct request)**

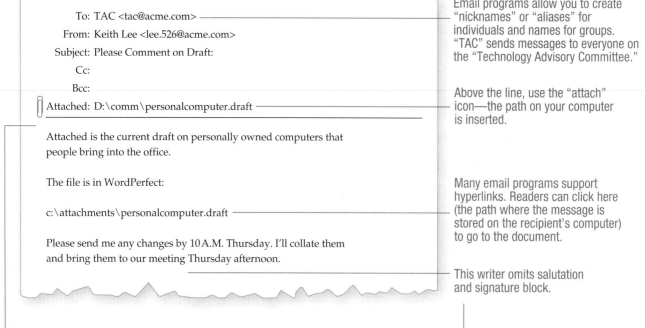

> To: TAC <tac@acme.com>
> From: Keith Lee <lee.526@acme.com>
> Subject: Please Comment on Draft:
> Cc:
> Bcc:
> Attached: D:\comm\personalcomputer.draft
>
> Attached is the current draft on personally owned computers that people bring into the office.
>
> The file is in WordPerfect:
>
> c:\attachments\personalcomputer.draft
>
> Please send me any changes by 10 A.M. Thursday. I'll collate them and bring them to our meeting Thursday afternoon.

Email programs allow you to create "nicknames" or "aliases" for individuals and names for groups. "TAC" sends messages to everyone on the "Technology Advisory Committee."

Above the line, use the "attach" icon—the path on your computer is inserted.

Many email programs support hyperlinks. Readers can click here (the path where the message is stored on the recipient's computer) to go to the document.

This writer omits salutation and signature block.

What Should I Know About Content and Tone?

Employability Skills

Use PAIBOC analysis: write to meet your audience's needs and your purposes.

York University professor Heather Lotherington, a multitechnological literacy expert, claims that as soon as people could chat in real time (what Lotherington calls "synchronous messages"), they developed a code to convey meaning instantaneously. This systematic email code includes such symbols as sound-based abbreviations ("c u ltr"), emoticons, sentence fragments, full caps (for shouting), and cyber names.[2] None of these belongs in business messages.

Indeed, although technology will continue to change how, what, where and when we communicate, business message formats and content remain relatively rigid. Furthermore, the lack of face-to-face symbols that characterize email messages means you have to consider your audience carefully. Humour, sarcasm, jokes, and chain letters do not travel well, especially in a global workplace: recipients find them incomprehensible, rude, and a waste of time and resources. Many people feel overwhelmed by the amount of email they receive daily; any part of your message that readers perceive as frivolous will negatively affect your purpose.

Remember to

Employability Skills

- *Deliver sensitive messages in person whenever possible.* Because of the limitations of electronic media, negative and persuasive messages (reprimands, negotiations) are more efficiently delivered face to face. The important nuances added through nonverbal communication speak volumes and can save time and energy. If you must deliver negative information electronically, write so that it's easy for readers to understand and act on the information quickly.
- *Be clear, courteous, and concise.* Unless your reader's expectations, your corporate culture, or your purposes dictate otherwise, compose and revise your messages to convey necessary information as politely, clearly, and briefly as possible. Your readers will appreciate this you-attitude (Module 6).
- *Format attachments appropriately.* Attached documents (letter, résumés, reports, invoices, etc.) standard paper formats (Module 9).

FIGURE 10.6 PAIBOC Questions for Analysis

Use the PAIBOC model to analyze business communication problems:

P Why are you writing? What is your **purpose**? What results do you want?

A Who is your **audience**? What do they know? What do they need to know? How will they react to your message? What's in it for them?

I Based on your audience and purpose analysis, what **information** must you include?

B What reasons or reader **benefits** can you use to support your position? What will motivate your audience to comply?

O What **objections** can you expect your reader to have, to your message, or to you? What negative elements must you deemphasize or overcome?

C How will the **context** affect your reader response? What cultural, organizational, economic, environmental, and/or seasonal circumstances might impact your reader's response to your message?

- *Compose and copy with discretion.* In email memos, *cc* denotes computer copies; your recipient can see the names of other people getting the message. *Bcc* denotes blind computer copies, usually used for mailing lists; the recipient does not see the names of these people (Module 9). Copying your supervisor and/or other people unnecessarily is inflammatory and unethical.
- *Count to ten before you SEND.* When you write, you are on the record. Emails sent in anger, to the wrong person, or to everyone on a list can damage your relationships, your reputation, or your future.

Employability Skills

How Should I Organize Email Messages?

Organize to meet readers' expectations. Deliver good news directly; give bad news indirectly.

Because they have to deal with so many email messages daily, readers read and reply to email rapidly. Write messages so that it's easy for people to understand and deal with them quickly: take time to plan, revise, and proofread, just as you would with paper messages. Figure 10.7 shows how a reader might allocate time to respond to a simple email request. Figure 10.8 lists the activities needed for a more complex email message.

Writing Positive and Informative Email Messages

Email is especially appropriate for positive and informative messages. Figures 10.4 and 10.5 are examples of an informative message and a request for feedback on a document, respectively.

FIGURE 10.7   Allocating Time in Writing an Email Answering a Simple Question (your time may vary)

	Total Time: 7 minutes
Planning	2 minutes
Read the question.	
Gather any information necessary for reply.	
Plan the message.	
Writing	2 minutes
Draft the message.	
Revising	3 minutes
Reread draft.	
Make small changes.	
Run spell check.	
Proof by eye.	
Send the message.	

FIGURE 10.8   Allocating Time in Writing a Persuasive Request with Attachments (your time may vary)

	Total Time: 3 hours
Planning	1 hour
Understand the situation.	
Answer the PAIBOC questions (Module 1).	
Think about document design (Module 5).	
Organize the message.	
Writing	½ hour
Draft the message and attachments.	
Revising	1½ hours
Reread draft.	
Measure draft against PAIBOC questions and checklist for problem-solving persuasive messages (Figure 13.10).	
Revise draft and attachments.	
Ask for feedback.	
Revise draft based on feedback.	
Edit to catch grammatical errors.	
Run spell check.	
Proof by eye.	
Send the message.	

Writing Negative Email Messages

Major negatives, such as firing someone, must be delivered in person, not by email. But email is appropriate for many less serious negatives.

- *Never send email messages when you're angry.* If a message infuriates you, wait till you're calmer before you reply—even then, reply only if you must. Writers using email are much less inhibited than they would be on paper or in person, sending insults, swearing, name-calling, and making hostile statements.[3] **Flaming** is the name given to this behaviour. Flaming reflects badly on the sender: it does not make you look like a mature, level-headed candidate for bigger things. And since employers have the right to read all email, flaming—particularly if directed at co-workers, regulators, suppliers, or customers—might cause an employee to be fired.
- *In the body of the email message, give a reason only if it is watertight and reflects well on the organization.* Give an alternative, if one exists.
- *Edit and proofread your message carefully.* An easy way for an angry reader to strike back is to attack typos or other errors.
- *Remember that email messages, like any written text, can become relevant documents in lawsuits.* When a negative email is hard to write, you may want to compose it offline so that you can revise and even get feedback before you send the message.

Writing Persuasive Email Messages

When you ask for something small or for something that it is part of the reader's job duties to provide, your request can be straightforward (see Figure 10.5).

- In the body of the message, give people all the information they need to act.
- At the end of the message, ask for the action you want. Make the action as easy as possible, and specify when you need a response. You may want an immediate response now ("Let me know ASAP whether you can write a story for the newsletter so that I can save the space") and a fuller one later ("We'll need the text by March 4").

Cultural FOCUS

Many writers feel that ending a message with an **end-date** (when you want a response by) might seem pushy. However, this is not the case. Readers often appreciate knowing a deadline, so they can plan accordingly.

When you ask for something big or something that is not a regular part of that person's duties, use the first paragraph to specify the request, and to make the reader view it positively. Use the second paragraph to provide an overview of the evidence that the rest of the message will provide: "Here's why we should do this. Let me describe the project. Then, if you're willing to be part of it, I'll send you a copy of the proposal" (Module 13).

Everyone feels busy, so you need to make the reader want to do as you ask. Use audience analysis (Module 2) to find a reason that the reader will find convincing to do as you ask. Be sure to provide all the information the reader will need to act on your request. Ask for the action you want.

Email is not an appropriate medium for major requests that require changes in attitudes, values, culture, or lifestyles.

What Kinds of Subject Lines Should I Use for Email Messages?

Use subject lines that are specific, concise, and catchy.

Subject lines in email are even more important than those in letters and memos, because it's so easy for the recipient to hit the Delete key. Subject lines must be specific, concise, and catchy. Many email users get so many messages that they don't bother reading messages if they don't recognize the sender, or if the subject doesn't catch their interest.

Try to keep the subject line short. If that's difficult, put the most important part into the first few words, because some email programs show only the first 28 characters of the subject line.

If your message is very short, you may be able to put it in the subject line. "EOM" (end of message) tells your reader there is no additional information in the body of the message.

Subject: Will Attend 3:00 P.M. Meeting EOM

Checkpoint

Try to keep the subject line short. If that's difficult, put the most important part into the first few words, because some email programs show only the first 28 characters of the subject line.

When you send emails just for information, put "FYI" at the end of the subject line.
© 1998 United Features Syndicate, Inc.

Subject Lines for Informative and Positive Email Messages

If you have good news to convey, be sure it's in the subject line. Be as brief as you can. The following subject lines would be acceptable for informative and good news email messages:

Subject: Travel Plans for Sales Meeting

Subject: Your Proposal Accepted

Subject: Reduced Prices During February

Subject Lines for Negative Email Messages

When you must say "no" to an email request, consider your purpose and audience to decide how to frame your message (Module 12). When you write, you will have to decide whether to use a neutral or negative subject line. The subject line should only contain the negative in three situations:

- *The negative is serious.* Many people do not read all their email messages. A neutral subject line may lead the reader to ignore the message.
- *The reader needs the information* to make a decision or act.
- *You report your own errors* (as opposed to the reader's).

The following would be acceptable subject lines in email messages:

Subject: We Lost Lick's Account

Subject: Power to Be Out Sunday, March 12

Subject: Error in Survey Data Summary

In other situations, a neutral subject line is appropriate.

Subject: Results of 360-Degree Performance Appraisals

Subject Lines for Persuasive Email Messages

Depending on your purpose and audience, a persuasive email subject line should make it clear that you're asking for something. If you're sure that the reader will read the message, a subject line as vague as "Request" may work. Most of the time, you'll improve readability and reduce reader aggravation by being specific.

Subject: Move Meeting to Tuesday?

Subject: Need an Extension

Subject: Want You for United Way Campaign

You'll find more information on how to structure informative, positive, negative and persuasive messages in Modules 11, 12, and 13.

Checkpoint

The subject line of a persuasive email message should make it clear that you're asking for something.

What "Netiquette" Rules Should I Follow?

Follow these guidelines to be a good netizen.

- *Never send angry messages by email.* If you have a conflict with someone, work it out face to face, not electronically.
- *Send people only messages they need.* Send copies to supervisors/bosses only if they have asked you to.
- *Avoid clichés* such as "Enclosed please find" and "Please don't hesitate to call," as you would when composing hardcopy documents.
- *Send cards, rather than emails, to express condolences and appreciation for hospitality.* When establishing business relationships internationally, research the protocols. When responding, mirror the sender's choice of medium, format, and language.
- *Before you hit Send, assume your email will appear on the front pages of the national newspaper,* because it very well could.
- *Avoid using full caps; use mixed case in subject lines and use full caps only if you have to emphasize a word or two.* Putting the whole message in full caps is considered shouting.
- *Find out how your recipient's system works, and adapt your messages to it.* Most people would rather get a separate short message on each of several topics, so that the messages can be stored in different mailboxes. But people who pay a fee to download each message might prefer longer messages that deal with several topics.
- *When you respond to a message, include only the part of the original message essential to your reply, so that the reader understands your posting.* Delete the rest. If the quoted material is lengthy, put your response first, then the original material.
- *When you compose a message in your word processor and call it up in email, use short line lengths (set the right margin at two inches or five centimetres).* That way you'll avoid awkward line breaks.

Language FOCUS

Netiquette is the short form for "Internet etiquette." Netiquette means the rules that you should follow when using the Internet for email, blogs, and discussion boards. Following these rules will help you be a good **netizen** (citizen of the Internet, or virtual world).

How and When Should I Use Attachments?

Send attachments when your PAIBOC analysis tells you that they meet the needs of your audience.

Any text document can be copied and pasted into the body of your email message.

Sending attachments makes sense when you send any of these:

- A business letter, or report
- A long text document

EXPANDING A CRITICAL SKILL

Managing Your Time

Do you feel you need more time? You are not alone! Although researchers claim that we have more leisure hours than we did 20 years ago, most of us feel more overworked than ever. And the number of things you'll need to do will only increase as you assume more job responsibilities.

The secret is to manage yourself, so that you feel more in control.

The first step in managing your time is to establish short- and long-term **SMART** goals, goals that describe your **S**pecific, **M**easurable, **A**chievable, **R**ealistic "to dos" in a definite **T**ime frame. "Starting today, I'm going to reserve a half-hour a day to read the paper, every day," is an example of a SMART goal. Identify your immediate and long-term SMART goals, write them down, and cross your daily SMART goals off as you achieve them. Following this process keeps you focused and positive.

As an immediate SMART time management goal, divide projects or incoming mail into three piles (real or imaginary). Put urgent items in the A pile, important items in the B pile, and other items in the C pile. Do the A items first. Most people find that they never get to their C piles.

At the end of the day, make a list of the two most important things you need to do the next day—this list is your SMART goal record—and leave the paper where you'll see it when you start work the next morning.

Initiate a systematic problem-solving approach to understanding how you currently manage yourself:

1. For at least a week, log how you spend your time. Record what you're doing in 15-minute intervals.
2. Analyze your log to identify patterns, time obligations, time wasters, and frustrations. You might be surprised to find how much time you spend "social notworking."

Or you might discover that answering email takes an hour every morning—not the five minutes or so that you'd estimated.

3. Clarify your SMART goals. What do you want to accomplish on the job and in your personal life? What strategies or steps (e.g., taking a course, learning a new skill, or sending out job applications) will you need to do to reach your goals?
4. Set short-term SMART priorities. For the next month, what do you need to accomplish? In addition to goals for school and work, think about building relationships, meeting personal obligations, and finding time to plan, to relax, and to think.
5. Ask for help or negotiate compromises. Maybe you and another parent can share babysitting so that you each have some time to yourselves. If your responsibilities at work are impossible, talk to your supervisor to see whether some of your duties can be transferred to someone else or whether you should stop trying to be excellent and settle for "good enough." You won't be willing or able to eliminate all your obligations, but sometimes dropping just one or two responsibilities can really help.
6. Schedule your day to reflect your priorities. You don't necessarily have to work on every goal every day, but each goal should appear on your schedule at least three times a week. Schedule some time for yourself, too.
7. Evaluate your new use of time. Are you meeting more of your goals? Are you feeling less stressed? If not, go back to step 1 and analyze more patterns, obligations, time wasters, and frustrations to see how you can make the best use of the time you have.

Source: "Social Notworking," Urban Dictionary site, retrieved May 6, 2009, from http://www.urbandictionary.com/define.php?term=Social%20Notworking &defid=3617456.

- A text document with extensive formatting
- A non-text file (e.g., PowerPoint slides, HTML file, spreadsheet)

When you send an attachment, remember that word-processing programs can generally open documents created in earlier versions of such programs but not later ones. Thus, WordPerfect 2003 can open documents created in Word 98 but not in Word 2007. In the text of your email, draw the reader's attention to the attachment—*Here is, I have attached, You'll see ...* —as you would in a hard-copy letter (*Enclosure*).

A computer **virus** is a script that harms your computer or erases your data. You can't get a virus through email, but viruses can infect files that are "attached" to email messages or that you download. You can do several things to stay virus-free:[4]

- Install an antivirus program on your computer, and keep it up to date.
- Ask people who send you attachments to include their names in the document titles. Virus titles aren't that specific.
- If you're in doubt about an attachment, don't open it.
- Forward email messages only when you're sure of the source and contents.

Employability Skills

Can I Use Blogging on the Job?

Yes, as long as you are professional.

Creating Web logs, or blogging, is an increasingly popular way of communicating. Millions of bloggers, in dozens of languages, post thoughts, images, and links in journal-like entries available through the Internet.

Businesses are using blogs to recruit employees, and CEOs are posting their own blogs to try to speak directly to customers and associates. And a few people have turned blogging into a career.

But blogging in a professional setting is different from blogging in a personal one. For example, some bloggers share deeply personal information, or unflattering opinions about people in their lives, or the companies they work for. Such behaviour in a business situation is inappropriate. In fact, some employees have been disciplined or fired for doing just that, such as programmer Mark Jen, whose complaints about the healthcare benefits and free-food policy of his employer, Google, got him fired. General Motors Vice-President Bob Lutz has joined the growing ranks of top executives who blog; his FastLane Blog attracts both supporters and detractors of GM vehicles, but Lutz's balanced responses have won him praise.[5]

If companies own or pay for computer resources, they are entitled to access email and blogs created by their employees on their systems. And blogs can be cached just like Web pages, meaning that years after the fact, someone can access an otherwise nonexistent blog.

To create a blog for business, Jeff Wuorio suggests these basics:[6]

- Identify your audience.
- Decide where your blog should live.
- Start talking.
- Get into the practice of "blog rolling," or linking to Web sites and other blogs.
- Emphasize key words.
- Keep it fresh.
- Watch your traffic closely.

What Else Do I Need to Know About Communicating Electronically?

Be discreet: you leave an electronic trail.

Evolving technology means that electronic capabilities will continue to grow in number and sophistication. However, new features will demand an ongoing learning curve for users. Many people are concerned about cell phone etiquette, as they are offended by interruptions and loud, or inappropriate conversations in such spaces as theatres, classrooms, and even restrooms.

Many people routinely use their cell phones and BlackBerrys for text messages. As with a telephone conversation, messaging requires you to respond quickly but also to think carefully about what you are going to say. Whatever you send electronically is retrievable, and can be permanent.

MODULE SUMMARY

- All the principles of good writing apply to email. Use you-attitude, positive emphasis, and reader benefits when you'd use them in paper messages. Because emails omit the thousands of nonverbal nuances present in face-to-face communication, humour, sarcasm, and sensitive interpersonal negotiations are not appropriate in emails.

- Create emails that are clear, concise, and courteous. Make sure you write messages that people can read and act on quickly.

- Compose important messages offline to give yourself time for thought and revision.

- Organize email messages as you would paper documents: give good news directly, and bad news indirectly.

- Write your subject lines last: make them specific, concise, and catchy.

- Use good writing principles for all your electronic communications. Use PAIBOC analysis to write for the results you want.

- If you blog on the job, keep it professional. Avoid sharing deeply personal information about yourself, or unflattering opinions about people in your life or the company you work for.

- Be discreet when you post or hit Send. All electronic communications can be shared without your permission; blogs, instant and text messages are all retrievable.

ASSIGNMENTS FOR MODULE 10

Questions for Critical Thinking

10.1 Why are spelling and punctuation still important in email?

10.2 Why should you compose important email messages offline?

10.3 When should writers avoid humour, sarcasm, and emoticons in their email content?

10.4 Why is it OK for your boss to send you a message with the subject line "To Do," even though that wouldn't work when you need to ask a colleague to do something?

Exercises and Problems

10.5 Telling an Employee That a Workshop Is Full

As director of human resources, you sponsor a variety of workshops for employees. You received this email message today:

Subject: Re: Oral Presentations Workshops

Please register me for the workshop on giving oral presentations next week. My supervisor has told me I should attend this.

The workshop is full, however, and you already have three people on a waiting list to fill vacancies if anyone should cancel.

You will repeat the workshop only if you have guarantees for at least 15 participants.

Write the message.

10.6 Saying No to the Boss

Today, you received this email from your boss:

Subject: Oversee United Way

I'm appointing you to be the company representative to oversee United Way. You've done a good job the last three years, so this year should be a piece of cake.

It's true that you know exactly what to do. The job wouldn't be hard for you. But that's just the problem. You wouldn't learn anything, either. You'd rather have an assignment that would stretch you, teach you new skills, or enable you to interact with new people. Continuing to grow is your insurance of continued employability and mobility. Three upcoming projects in your division might offer growth: creating DVDs for a "town meeting" for all employees to be held at the beginning of next quarter, creating an intranet for the company, or serving on the diversity committee. Any of these would be time-consuming, but no more time-consuming than running the United Way campaign.

Respond to your boss, asking for something more challenging to do.

10.7 Persuading the CEO to Attend Orientation

As the director of education and training of your organization, you run orientation sessions for new hires. You're planning next quarter's session (new quarters start in January, April, July, and October) for a big group of new college graduates. You'd really like the organization's president and CEO to come in and talk to the group for at least 15 minutes. Probably most of the employees have seen the CEO, but they haven't had any direct contact. The CEO could come any time during the three-day session. Speaking just before or after lunch would be ideal, because then the CEO could also come to lunch and talk informally with at least a few people. Next-best would be speaking just before or after the midmorning or midafternoon breaks. But the CEO is busy, and you'll take what you can get.

As your instructor directs,

a. Assume that your instructor is your CEO, and send an email message persuading him or her to come to orientation.

b. Send an email message to your instructor, asking him or her to address new members of a campus organization.

c. Address the CEO of your university, college, or workplace, asking him or her to speak to new employees.

10.8 Asking for More Time or Resources

Today, this message shows up in your email inbox from your boss:

Subject: Re: Want Culture Report

This request has come down from the CEO. I'm delegating it to you. See me a couple of days before the board meeting—the first Monday of next month—so we can go over your presentation.

I want a report on the culture for underrepresented groups in our organization. A presentation at the last board of directors' meeting showed that although we do a good job of hiring women and minorities, few of them rise to the top. The directors suspect that our culture may not be supportive and want information on it. Please prepare a presentation for the next meeting. You'll have 15 minutes to speak.

Making a presentation to the company's board of directors might really help your career. But preparing a good presentation and report will take time. You can look at exit reports filed by Human Resources when people leave the company, but you'll also need to interview people—lots of people.

And you're already working 60 hours a week on three major projects, one of which is behind schedule. Can one of the projects wait? Can someone else take one of the projects? Can you get some help? Should you do just enough to get by? Ask your boss for advice—in a way that makes you look like a committed employee, not a slacker.

10.9 Asking for Volunteers

You have an executive position with one of the major employers in town. (Pick a business, nonprofit organization, or government office you know something about.) Two years ago, your company "adopted" a local school. You've provided computers and paid for Internet access; a small number of workers have signed up to be mentors. Today you get a call from the school's principal, a friend of yours. "I'd like to talk to you about the mentoring program. You're providing some mentors, and we're grateful for them, but we need 10 times that number."

(You wince. This program has not been one of your successes. You reply:) "I know that part of the program hasn't worked out as well as we hoped it would. But people are really busy here. Not all that many people have two or three hours a week to spend with a kid."

Principal: "So you think the time it takes is really the problem."

(Maybe your friend will appreciate that you can't force people to do this. You say:) "Pretty much."

Principal: "Do you think people would be willing to be mentors if we could find a way for it to take less time?"

"Maybe," you say. (You sense a hook is coming, and you're wary.)

Principal: "Your people spend a lot of time on email, don't they?"

"Yes. Two to three hours a day, for most of them."

Principal: "What if we created a new mentoring structure in which people just emailed their mentees instead of meeting with them? That way they could still provide advice and support, but they could do it at any time of the day. And it wouldn't have to take long."

(That sounds interesting. You reply:) "So people would just have email conversations. That would be a lot easier, and we'd get more people. But can they really have a relationship if they don't meet the kids?"

Principal: "Maybe we could have a picnic or go to a game a couple of times a year so people could meet face to face."

"And all the kids have computers?," you ask.

Principal: "Not necessarily at home. But they all have access to email at school. Writing email to professionals will also give them more practice and more confidence. People like to get email."

"Not when they get 200 messages a day, they don't."

Principal: "Well, our kids aren't in that category. What do you say?"

"I think it will work. Let's try it."

Principal: "Great. Just send me a list of the people who are willing to do this, and we'll match them up with the kids. We'd like to get this started as soon as possible."

Write an email message to all employees asking them to volunteer.

10.10 Asking for Something Different for Administrative Professionals' Week

Your clerical job gives you the flexibility you need while you're in school. Administrative Professionals' (formerly Secretaries') Week is approaching, and you really don't want flowers or a free lunch. You'd much rather have a bonus or at least time off to attend an educational seminar (resourced by the company). You're interested in learning advanced features of a computer program or assertive behaviour techniques.

Write an email to the person who supervises clerical workers in your unit, asking that Administrative Professionals' Week give you something useful.

Hints:

- Assume that you work in an organization you know something about.
- Specify one or more seminars you'd like to attend.
- Some seminars may cost a lot more than flowers or lunch; some may cost less. How much financial flexibility does the organization have?
- Are there other clerical workers? Would they also like bonuses or seminars, or do some prefer flowers or lunch?
- How well does the person who will make the decision know you? How positively does he or she view you and any other clerical workers?

POLISHING YOUR PROSE

Correcting Dangling Modifiers

Modifiers are words or phrases that give more information about parts of a sentence. For instance, an adjective is a modifier that usually describes a noun (*top* performer), and an adverb modifies a verb (performs *brilliantly*).

Dangling modifiers confuse readers, because the word they modify is not in the sentence. If you diagrammed the sentence, the modifier would not be attached to anything; it would dangle.

Dangling: Confirming our conversation, your Hot Springs Hot Tub Spa is scheduled for delivery April 12. [This sentence seems to imply that the spa is doing the confirming.]

Correct a dangling modifier in either of these ways:

1. Rewrite the modifier as a subordinate clause.

Correct: As we agreed yesterday, your Hot Springs Hot Tub Spa is scheduled for delivery April 12.

2. Rewrite the main clause so its subject or object can be modified correctly.

Correct: Talking on the phone, we confirmed that your Hot Springs Hot Tub Spa is scheduled for delivery April 12.

Exercises

Correct the dangling modifiers in these sentences.

1. After working here a year, dental insurance covers you.
2. Using the fax machine, new orders are processed quickly.
3. At the age of 10, I bought my daughter her first share of stock.
4. Working in teams, projects can be completed quickly.
5. Calling ahead of time, the reservations can be made efficiently.
6. Before joining our company, your résumé shows a good deal of experience with computer software.
7. Posting risqué material on Facebook potential employers can access even years later.
8. A simple notebook filled with thoughts and ideas, you can keep a journal of your business experiences.
9. Sharing files with our legal department, our attorneys can work better with you.
10. As a new employee, your supervisor can answer your questions.

Check your answers to the odd-numbered exercises on page 552.

Composing Informative and Positive Messages

Learning Objectives

After reading and applying the information in Module 11, you'll be able to demonstrate

Knowledge of

- The criteria that define positive messages
- The "good news" message structure
- The persuasive element of all effective messages

Skills to

- Further analyze business communication situations
- Begin to organize and write informative and positive messages

Employability Skills 2000+ Checklist

In this module, the key skills from the Conference Board of Canada's Employability Skills 2000+ are

Communicate

○ write and speak so others pay attention and understand
○ share information using a range of information and communications technologies (e.g., voice, email, computers)

○ use relevant scientific, technological, and mathematical knowledge and skills to explain or clarify ideas

Manage Information

○ locate, gather, and organize information using appropriate technology and information systems

Think & Solve Problems

○ assess situations and identify problems
○ seek different points of view and evaluate them based on facts
○ recognize the human, interpersonal, technical, scientific, and mathematical dimensions of a problem
○ identify the root cause of a problem

○ be creative and innovative in exploring possible solutions
○ readily use science, technology, and mathematics as ways to think, gain and share knowledge, solve problems, and make decisions
○ evaluate solutions to make recommendations or decisions

You can categorize messages by analyzing your purposes and the initial response you expect from the reader. In an informative or positive message, you expect the audience to respond neutrally to the message, or to be pleased. Negatives are minor; they are not the point of the message. You must convey information, but are not asking the audience to do anything—although you may want the audience to save the information and act on it later. You usually do want to build positive attitudes about yourself and the information you are presenting, so, in that sense, even informative messages have persuasive elements.

Informative or "good news" messages usually have several purposes.

Primary purposes:

- To give information or good news to the reader, or to reassure the reader
- To have the reader read the message, understand it, and view the information positively
- To deemphasize any negative elements

Underlying purposes:

- To reduce or eliminate future correspondence on the same subject
- To build a good image of the writer
- To build a good image of the writer's organization
- To initiate or build a good relationship between the writer and reader

Language FOCUS

All business messages have both a **primary purpose** and an **underlying** (or **secondary**) **purpose**. In order to be an effective writer, you must always think about both purposes and address them in your message.

Checkpoint

You want to build positive attitudes toward the information you are presenting, so in that sense, even an informative message has a persuasive element.

Examples of informative and positive messages are

- Acceptances
- Announcements of changes that the reader will see as positive or neutral
- Information about procedures, products, services, or options
- Positive answers to reader requests
- News that benefits the reader

How Should I Organize Informative and Positive Messages?

Consider your audience's needs: put the good news and a summary of the information first.

We all share similar needs and fears. Putting good news up front meets your audience's recognition and esteem needs (Module 8).

Present informative and positive messages in the following order:

1. *Give any good news and summarize the main points.* Share good news immediately. Include details such as the date that policies begin and the percent of a discount. If the reader has already raised the issue, make it clear that you're responding.
2. *Give details, clarification, and background.* Don't repeat information from the first paragraph. Do answer all the questions your reader is likely to have; provide all the information necessary to achieve your purposes. Present details in *the order of importance to the reader.*
3. *Present any negative elements as positively as possible.* A policy might have limits; information might be incomplete; or the reader might have to satisfy requirements to get a discount or benefit. Make these negatives clear, but present them as positively as possible.
4. *Explain any reader benefits.* Most informative memos need reader benefits. Show that the policy or procedure helps readers, not just the company. Give enough detail to make the benefits clear and convincing. In letters, you may want to give the benefits of dealing with your company as well as the benefits of the product or policy (Module 8). In a good news message, it's often possible to combine a short reader benefit with a *goodwill ending* in the last paragraph.
5. *Use a goodwill ending: positive, personal, and forward-looking.* Shifting your emphasis away from the message to the specific reader suggests that serving the reader is your real concern.

Figure 11.1 summarizes the pattern. Figures 11.2 and 11.3 illustrate two ways to apply the pattern.

FIGURE 11.1

How to Organize an Informative or Positive Message

FIGURE 11.2 An Informative Email

Dear Dennis Baronski,

Thank you for shopping at goodbooks.ca. We are pleased to confirm that the item(s) listed below has been shipped from your order, OR141133149. Any item(s) remaining in your order will ship as they become available. If you paid for your order by credit card, we are now processing a charge to your card for the shipped item(s).

To check your order's status, sign in to your Online Account and reference your Order History.

ITEM(S) SHIPPED
1. Bob Dylan: In His Own Words - 1 @ 29.88
2. Down the Highway: The Life of Bob Dylan - 1 @ 49.35

Item(s) Subtotal: $79.23
Shipping: $0.00
GST: $5.55

_____

_____

TOTAL: $84.78

Knowing the appropriate organizational pattern can help you compose messages more quickly and create a more effective final product. The organization patterns described in this module and the modules that follow will work in most business writing situations.

- Be sure you understand the rationale behind each pattern so that you can modify the pattern if necessary. (For example, when you write instructions, any warnings should go up front, in a place of emphasis.) See Figure 11.4.
- Sometimes you can present several elements in one paragraph. Sometimes you'll need several paragraphs for just one element.

When Should I Use Reader Benefits in Informative and Positive Messages?

Use reader benefits when you want readers to view your policies and your organization positively.

Not all informative and positive messages need reader benefits (Module 8). Use reader benefits when you want readers to view your policies and your organization positively.

You don't need reader benefits when

- You're presenting factual information only
- The reader's attitude toward the information doesn't matter
- Stressing benefits may make the reader sound selfish
- The benefits are so obvious that to restate them insults the reader's intelligence

You do need reader benefits when

- You are presenting policies
- You want to shape readers' attitudes toward the information or toward your organization
- Stressing benefits presents readers' motives positively
- Some of the benefits may not be obvious to readers

FIGURE 11.3 A Positive Memo

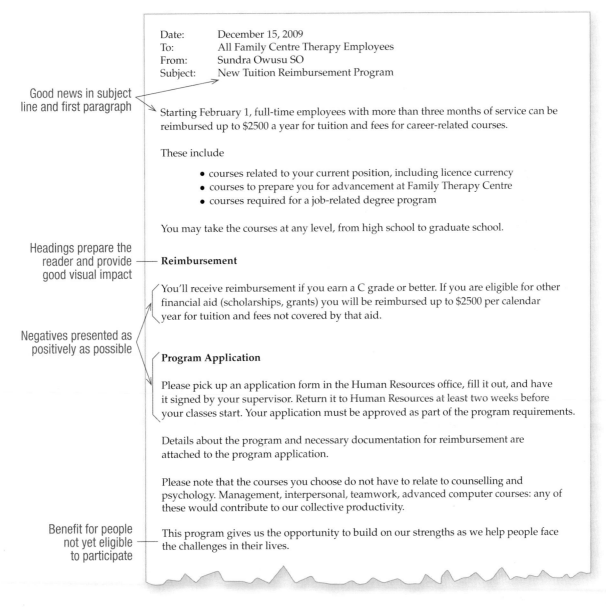

Good news in subject line and first paragraph

Headings prepare the reader and provide good visual impact

Negatives presented as positively as possible

Benefit for people not yet eligible to participate

Date: December 15, 2009
To: All Family Centre Therapy Employees
From: Sundra Owusu SO
Subject: New Tuition Reimbursement Program

Starting February 1, full-time employees with more than three months of service can be reimbursed up to $2500 a year for tuition and fees for career-related courses.

These include

- courses related to your current position, including licence currency
- courses to prepare you for advancement at Family Therapy Centre
- courses required for a job-related degree program

You may take the courses at any level, from high school to graduate school.

Reimbursement

You'll receive reimbursement if you earn a C grade or better. If you are eligible for other financial aid (scholarships, grants) you will be reimbursed up to $2500 per calendar year for tuition and fees not covered by that aid.

Program Application

Please pick up an application form in the Human Resources office, fill it out, and have it signed by your supervisor. Return it to Human Resources at least two weeks before your classes start. Your application must be approved as part of the program requirements.

Details about the program and necessary documentation for reimbursement are attached to the program application.

Please note that the courses you choose do not have to relate to counselling and psychology. Management, interpersonal, teamwork, advanced computer courses: any of these would contribute to our collective productivity.

This program gives us the opportunity to build on our strengths as we help people face the challenges in their lives.

Checkpoint

Use reader benefits when

- Presenting policies
- Shaping readers' attitudes toward the information or toward your organization
- Stressing benefits to present readers' motives positively
- Describing benefits that may not be obvious to readers

Messages to customers or potential customers sometimes include a sales paragraph promoting products or services you offer, in addition to the product or service that the reader has asked about. For example, when not-for-profits and charitable organizations write to thank

FIGURE 11.4   **A Safety Procedures Memo**

Date: May 11, 2007
Memo to: All chefs, sous-chefs, wait staff, staff
From: Franco
Re: Procedures for Spills

To comply with Health and Safety legislation, and to protect your own safety and the safety of all employees and patrons, please ensure that you read, understand, and comply with the following instructions for dealing with spills:

1. STOP! whatever you are doing immediately.

2. Alert the person closest to you.
    Indicate to that person
       a.   The exact location of the spill
       b.   The nature of the spill (e.g., grease, juice, water, gravy, sauce, etc.)

3. WHILE THAT PERSON WAITS IN PLACE, get the yellow warning sign, and a pail and mop from cupboard #3.

4. Place the sign and clean the spill immediately.

5. Ensure floor/area is completely clean.

6. Ensure the floor/area is completely dry.

7. Return the sign, mop, and pail to cupboard #3.

Your cooperation is essential for the safety, security, and comfort of us all.

donors for a contribution, and to send a tax receipt, they often include a form for monthly giving, or for another donation.

Be careful about up-selling in writing: consumers tend to be both sophisticated and cynical. Sales promotion in an informative or positive message should be low-key, not "hard sell."

Reader benefits are hardest to develop when you are announcing policies. The organization has probably decided to adopt the policy in its own interests; the people who made the decision may not have thought about whether it would help or hurt employees. Yet reader benefits are most essential in this kind of message so readers can see the reason for the change, and support it.

When you present reader benefits, be sure to present the advantages *for the reader*. Most new policies help the organization in some way, but few employees will see their own interests as identical with those of the organization. Even if the organization saves money or increases its profits, workers will benefit directly only if they own stock in the company, if they are to receive bonuses, if the savings enable a failing company to avoid layoffs, or if all the savings go directly to employee benefits. In many companies, any money saved will go to executive bonuses, shareholder profits, or research and development.

To develop reader benefits for informative and positive messages, use the steps suggested in Module 8. Be sure to think about the intrinsic benefits (see Module 8, page 141) of your policy: what benefits come from the activity or policy itself, apart from any financial benefits? For example, how does a new policy mandating "green" practices benefit employees?

What Kinds of Informative and Positive Messages Am I Likely to Write?

You will likely write instructions, transmittals, confirmations, summaries, adjustments, and thank-you notes.

Messages are informative, negative, or persuasive depending on how the reader perceives what you have to say.

- Readers may feel neutral about assembly, safety, and fire drill instructions (unless, of course, these are badly written and therefore hard to understand and follow; then readers may feel irritated or frustrated).
- A transmittal can be positive when you're sending glowing sales figures, or persuasive when you want the reader to act on the information.
- A performance appraisal is positive when you evaluate someone who's doing superbly, negative when you want to compile a record to justify firing someone, and persuasive when you want to motivate a satisfactory worker to continue to improve.
- A collection letter is persuasive; it becomes negative in the last stage when you threaten legal action.

Each of these messages is discussed in this module for the pattern it uses most frequently. However, in some cases you will need to use a different pattern (Modules 12 and 13).

Checkpoint

Organizing Informative and Positive Messages

1. Give any good news and summarize the main points.
2. Give details, clarification, background.
3. Present any negative elements—as positively as possible.
4. Explain any reader benefits.
5. Use a goodwill ending: positive, personal, and forward-looking.

Instructions

Information on new procedures may generate hostility, since most of us are reluctant to change. You can use placement, language, and font size for effective emphasis. Instructions for complicated procedures (electronic application, machine assembly) require diagrams right beside the text.

Transmittals

When you send someone in an organization a hardcopy message, attach a memo or letter of transmittal explaining what you're sending. A transmittal can be as simple as a small yellow Post-it™ note with "FYI" ("for your information") written on it, or it can be a separate typed document, especially when it transmits a formal document such as a report (Module 22).

Organize a memo or letter of transmittal in this order:

1. Tell the reader what you're sending.
2. Summarize the main point(s) of the document.
3. Indicate any special circumstances or information that would help the reader understand the document. Is it a draft? Is it a partial document that will be completed later?

4. Tell the reader what will happen next. Will you do something? Do you want a response? If you do want the reader to act, specify exactly what you want the reader to do and give a deadline.

Frequently, transmittals have important secondary purposes, such as showing readers that you're working on projects they value, and building goodwill.

Confirmations

Many informative messages are for the record: they go to the other party in the conversation to summarize the conversation. These messages should be brief, and give only the information shared orally. Start the message by indicating that it is a confirmation, not a new message:

> As we discussed on the phone today, ...
>
> As I told you yesterday, ...
>
> Attached is the meeting schedule we discussed earlier today.

Summaries

You may summarize a team meeting, a dialogue with a client, or a conversation, document, or an outside meeting for colleagues or superiors. (Minutes of an internal meeting are usually more detailed. See Module 16 for advice on writing minutes of meetings.)

In a summary of a conversation for internal use, apply PAIBOC analysis: to meet your needs, and the needs of your audience, identify

- Who was present
- What was discussed
- What was decided
- Who does what next

FIGURE 11.5 **Informative Email Letter Summarizing Meeting**

From:	www.tutoringtalent.ca
To:	dtravers@metroluge.ca
Cc:	jholmes@metroluge.ca
Sent:	Friday, July 10, 2008 12:50 PM
Subject:	Coaching Debra Travers

Dear Janice and Debra:

Thank you for our conversation yesterday.

Debra, as we discussed, I can begin your coaching sessions a week this Thursday, July 17, 2009. The three-hour session will include SMART goal setting, so you can identify specifically what objectives you want to meet, and how you will demonstrate that you have met them. Then we can meet once a week, for five more weeks, three hours a session, customizing the coaching content each week.

Janice, please send me a copy of the contract at your convenience.

Again, thank you for your time. Debra, I look forward to working with you.

Sincerely,

Martha

Martha Grimes
TutoringTalent Inc.
www.tutoringtalent.ca
905.847.3395

To summarize a document,

- Start with the main point.
- Give supporting evidence and details.
- Evaluate the document, if your audience asks for evaluation.

Identify the actions that your organization should take on the basis of the document. Should others in the company read this blog? Should someone in the company write a letter to the editor responding to this newspaper article? Should your company try to meet with someone in the organization that the story is about?

Adjustments and Responses to Complaints

A study showed that when people had gripes but didn't complain, only 9 percent would buy from the company again. But when people did complain—and their problems were resolved quickly—82 percent would buy again.[1]

Sean Lerner left his corporate job as a computer systems designer to work for himself. Lerner's first design creation—the TTC Subway Rider Efficiency Guide—shows passengers where to sit to access their exits most quickly. Get your guide free at www.ttcrider.ca.

Language FOCUS

To **gripe** is an informal way of saying that someone is complaining continually. Often, when we say someone is griping, we mean they are complaining about something to friends and colleagues, but they are not complaining to the correct person. For example, someone may have been unhappy about the service at a local restaurant. However, instead of complaining to the restaurant manager, who is the proper person to complain to, the person goes to work the following day and complains to everyone there about the terrible service.

When you grant a customer's request for an adjusted price, discount, replacement, or other benefit to resolve a complaint, do so in the very first sentence.

> Your Visa bill for a night's lodging has been adjusted to $63. Next month a credit of $37 will appear on your bill to reimburse you for the extra amount you originally paid.

Don't talk about your own process in making the decision. Don't say anything that sounds grudging. Give the reason for the original mistake only if it reflects credit on the company. (In most cases, it doesn't, so the reason should be omitted.)

Thank-You and Congratulatory Notes

Sending a **thank-you note** recognizes and acknowledges a person's contribution (see Maslow's Hierarchy of Needs in Module 8) and is invaluable in fostering the recipient's goodwill. Furthermore, your recognition of others will make people more willing to help you again in the future.

Thank-you letters are prompt and short. They need to be specific to sound sincere. Most of us appreciate any sincere thank-you; when you put it in writing, however, you demonstrate that you feel grateful enough to take the time to write, and you give the recipient a record of your appreciation.

Congratulating someone sincerely and respectfully can build good feelings between you and the reader, and enhance your own visibility.

Employability Skills

What's the Best Subject Line for an Informative or Positive Message?

The best subject line contains the basic information or good news.

A **subject line** is the title of a document. It aids in filing and retrieving the document, tells readers why they need to read the document, and provides a framework or context in which to set what you're about to say.

Try composing the subject line after writing the message. Because you now know what you want to say, you can compose a subject line that sums up and previews the message content for the reader.

Subject lines are standard in memos. Letters are not required to have subject lines (Module 9). However, since a subject line saves the reader's time (and builds the writer's credibility), most businesspeople consider a subject line in a letter to be very important. A good subject line meets three criteria: it is specific, concise, and appropriate to the kind of message (positive, negative, persuasive).

Making Subject Lines Specific

The subject line needs to be specific enough to differentiate that message from others on the same subject, but broad enough to cover everything in the message.

Too general:	Training Sessions
Better:	Technical Training Sessions Dates
or:	Evaluation of Training Sessions on Conducting Interviews
or:	Should We Schedule a Short Course on Proposal Writing?

Making Subject Lines Concise

Most subject lines are relatively short—usually no more than 10 words, often only three to seven words.[2]

Wordy:	Survey of Student Preferences in Regard to Various Pizza Factors
Better:	Students' Pizza Preferences
or:	The Feasibility of a Pizza Pizza Branch on Campus
or:	What Students Like and Dislike About Pizza Pizza

If you can't make the subject both specific and short, be specific.

Making Subject Lines Appropriate for the Pattern of Organization

In general, do the same thing in your subject line that you would do in the first paragraph.

When you have good news for the reader, build goodwill by **highlighting** it in the subject line. When your information is neutral, summarize it concisely for the subject line.

Subject: Discount on Rental Cars Effective January 2

Starting January 2, as an employee of Amalgamated Industries you can get a 15 percent discount on cars you rent for business or personal use from Roadway Rent-a-Car.

Subject: Update on Arrangements for Videoconference with Montreal

In the last month, we have chosen the participants and developed a tentative agenda for the videoconference with our Montreal office scheduled for March 21.

The checklist in Figure 11.6 summarizes the points to remember when writing informative and positive messages.

Sharing information is crucial to business success. To drive that point home, Siemens sent 60 managers from around the world to the shores of a lake south of Munich, Germany, and told them to build rafts. They weren't allowed to talk: they had to write messages and diagrams on flip charts. Back in the office, ShareNet lets employees around the world ask questions and share answers.

FIGURE 11.6   Checklist for Informative and Positive Messages

❏ In positive messages, does the subject line give the good news? In either message, is the subject line specific enough to differentiate this message from others on the same subject?

❏ Does the first paragraph summarize the information or good news? If the information is too complex to fit into a single paragraph, does the paragraph list the basic parts of the policy or information in the order in which the memo discusses them?

❏ Is all the information given in the message? (The information needed will vary depending on the message, but information about dates, places, times, and anything related to money usually needs to be included. When in doubt, ask!)

❏ In messages announcing policies, is there at least one reader benefit for each segment of the audience? Do all reader benefits seem likely to occur in this organization?

❏ Is each reader benefit developed, showing how the benefit will come from the policy and why the benefit matters to this organization? Do the benefits build on the job duties of people in this organization and on the specific circumstances of the organization?

❏ Does the message end with a positive paragraph—preferably one that is specific to the readers, not a general one that might fit any organization or policy?

Originality in a positive or informative message may come from

❏ Creating good headings, lists, and visual impact

❏ Developing reader benefits

❏ Thinking about readers and giving details that answer their questions and make it easier for them to understand and follow the policy

And, for all messages, not just informative and positive ones,

❏ Does the message use you-attitude and positive emphasis?

❏ Is the style easy to read and friendly?

❏ Is the visual design of the message inviting?

❏ Is the format correct?

❏ Does the message use standard grammar? Is it free from typos?

How Can PAIBOC Analysis Help Me Write Informative and Positive Messages?

PAIBOC analysis helps you identify a reader-centred organizational pattern, and the information you should include.

Before you tackle the assignments for this module, examine the following problem. See how the PAIBOC questions probe the basic points required for a solution. Study the two sample solutions to see what makes one unacceptable and the other one good. Note the recommendations for revision that might make the good solution excellent.[3] The checklist in Figure 11.6 can help you evaluate a draft.

Employability Skills

A PAIBOC Problem for Analysis

CanWest Insurance's payments and billings system is computerized. Often there's a time lag between receiving a payment from a customer, and recording it on the computer. Sometimes, while the payment is in line to be processed, the computer sends out additional notices: past-due notices, collection letters, even threats to sue. Customers are frightened or angry and write asking for an explanation. In most cases, if customers just waited a little longer, the situation would be straightened out. But policyholders are afraid that they'll be without insurance because the company thinks the bill has not been paid.

CanWest doesn't have the time to check every individual situation to see whether the cheque did arrive and has been processed. It wants you to write a letter that will persuade customers to wait. If something is wrong and the payment never reaches CanWest, the company sends a legal notice to that effect, saying that the policy will be cancelled by a certain date (which the notice would specify) at least 30 days after the date on the original premium bill. Continuing customers always get this legal notice as a third chance (after the original bill and the past-due notice).

Prepare a form letter that can go out to every policyholder who claims to have paid a premium for automobile insurance and resents getting a past-due notice. The letter should reassure readers and build goodwill for CanWest.

Analysis of the Problem

P   What are your **purposes** in writing or speaking?

To reassure readers: they're covered for 30 days; to inform them they can assume everything is OK unless they receive a second notice; to avoid further correspondence on this subject; to build goodwill for CanWest: (a) we don't want to suggest CanWest is error-prone or too cheap to hire enough people to do the necessary work; (b) we don't want readers to switch companies; (c) we do want readers to buy from CanWest when they're ready for more insurance.

A   Who is your **audience**? How do the members of your audience differ from one another? What audience characteristics are relevant to this particular message?

The audience is automobile insurance customers who say they've paid but still got a past-due notice. They're afraid they're no longer insured. Since it's a form letter, different readers will have different situations: in some cases payment did arrive late, in some cases the company made a mistake, in some the reader never paid (cheque lost in mail, unsigned, bounced, etc.)

I   What **information** must your message include?

Readers are still insured. We cannot say whether their cheques have now been processed (company doesn't want to check individual accounts). Their insurance will be cancelled only if they do not pay after receiving the second past-due notice (the legal notice).

B   What reasons or reader **benefits** can you use to support your position?

Computers help us provide personal service to policyholders. We offer policies to meet all their needs. Both of these points would need specifics to be interesting and convincing.

O   What **objections** can you expect your readers to have? What negative elements of your message must you deemphasize or overcome?

Computers appear to cause errors. We don't know whether the cheques have been processed. We will cancel policies if their cheques don't arrive.

C   How will the **context** affect the reader's response? Think about your relationship to the reader, the morale in the organization, the economy, the time of year, and any special circumstances.

The insurance business is highly competitive—other companies offer similar rates and policies. The customer might be able get a similar policy for about the same money from someone else. Most people find that money is tight, so they want to keep insurance costs low. On the other hand, the fact that prices are steady or rising means that the value of what they own is higher—they need insurance more than ever.

Many insurance companies are refusing to renew policies (car, liability, malpractice insurance). These refusals to renew have received lots of publicity, and many people have heard horror stories about companies and individuals whose insurance has been cancelled or not renewed after a small number of claims. Readers don't feel very kindly toward insurance companies.

In Canada, drivers are legally required to have car insurance. If their insurance policies are cancelled because of a computer error, drivers have a legitimate worry.

Discussion of the Sample Solutions

The solution in Figure 11.7 is unacceptable. The marginal comments show problem spots. Since this is a form letter, we cannot tell customers we have their cheques; in some cases, we may not. The letter is far too negative. The explanation in paragraph 2 makes CanWest look irresponsible and uncaring. Paragraph 3 is far too negative. Paragraph 4 is too vague; there are no reader benefits; the ending sounds selfish.

FIGURE 11.7   **An Unacceptable Solution to the Sample Problem**

Need date.

Not personalized: not you-focused.

This explanation makes company look bad.

Need to present this positively.

Dear Customer:

Relax. We got your cheque.

There is always a time lag between the time payments come in and the time they are processed. While payments are waiting to be processed, the computer with super-human quickness is sending out past-due notices and threats of cancellation.

Cancellation is not something you should worry about. No policy would be cancelled without a legal notice to that effect giving a specific date for cancellation which would be at least 30 days after the date on the original premium notice.

If you want to buy more insurance, just contact your local Canwest Life Insurance agent. We will be happy to help you.

Sincerely,

Not necessarily true. Reread problem.

Too negative.

This paragraph isn't specific enough to work as a reader benefit. It lacks you-attitude and positive emphasis.

A major weakness with the solution is that it lifts phrases straight out of the problem; the writer does not seem to have thought about the problem or about the words he or she is using. Measuring the draft against the answers to the questions for analysis suggests that this writer should start over.

The solution in Figure 11.8 is much better. Most of the marginal comments show the letter's strong points. The message opens with the good news that is true for all readers. (Whenever possible, one should use the good news pattern of organization.) Paragraph 2 explains CanWest's policy. It avoids assigning blame and ends on a positive note. The negative information is buried in paragraph 3 and is presented positively: the notice is information, not a threat; the 30-day extension is a grace period. Telling the reader what to do if a second notice arrives eliminates the need for a second exchange of letters. Paragraph 4 offers benefits for using computers, since some readers may blame the notice on computers, and offers benefits for being insured by CanWest. Paragraph 5 promotes other policies the company sells and prepares for the last paragraph.

As the red comments indicate, this good solution might be improved by including the name and number of the local agent. Computers could make both of those insertions easily. This good letter can become an excellent letter by revising paragraph 4 to include more reader benefits. For instance, do computers help agents advise clients of the best policies for them? Does CanWest offer good service—quick, friendly, non-pressured—that might be stressed? Are agents well trained? All these might yield ideas for additional reader benefits.

EXPANDING A CRITICAL SKILL

Writing a Goodwill Ending

Goodwill endings focus on establishing or building business relationships. When you write to one person, tailor the last paragraph to that person specifically. When you write to someone who represents an organization, the last paragraph can refer to your company's relationship with the reader's organization. When you write to a group (e.g., to "All Employees") your ending should apply to the whole group.

Possibilities include complimenting the reader for a job well done, describing a reader benefit, or looking forward to something positive that relates to the subject of the message.

For example, consider possible endings for responding to an information query about tours of Wikwemikong Indian reserve on Manitoulin Island. The People of the Three Fires community offer group tours for special-interest groups.

Weak closing paragraph: Should you have any questions regarding this matter, please feel free to call me.

Goodwill ending: Upon request, the People of the Three Fires Tours can develop custom tours for educational institutions and corporate retreats. Please contact us at threefires tours@rogers.ca for further information.

Some writers end every message with a standard invitation:

If you have questions, please do not hesitate to ask.

This sentence lacks positive emphasis (Module 7). But saying "feel free to call"—though more positive—is rarely a good idea. Most of the time, the writer should omit the sentence. Don't make more work for yourself by inviting calls to clarify simple messages. And avoid clichés.

One of the reasons you write is to save the time needed to tell everyone individually. People in business aren't shrinking violets; they will call if they need help. Do make sure your phone number is in the letterhead or is typed below your name. You can also add your email address below your name.

FIGURE 11.8   **A Good Solution to the Sample Problem**

Need date

Good paragraph #1; true for all readers

Good to treat notice as information, tell reader what to do if it arrives

Benefits of using computers

Use computer to personalize. Put in name and address of a specific reader.

Good you-attitude

Good specifics

Acceptable ending

Dear Amjit Sunder:

Your auto insurance is still in effect.

Past-due notices are mailed out if the payment has not been processed within three days after the due date. This may happen if a cheque is delayed in the mail or arrives without a signature or account number. When your cheque arrives with all the necessary information, it is promptly credited to your account.

Even if a cheque is lost in the mail and never reaches us, you still have a 30-day grace period. If you do get a second notice, you'll know that we still have not received your cheque. To keep your insurance in place, just stop payment on the first cheque and send a second one.

Computer processing of your account guarantees that you get any discounts you're eligible for: multicar, accident-free record, good student. If you have a claim, your agent uses computer tracking to find matching parts quickly, no matter what kind of car you drive. You get a cheque quickly—usually within three working days—without having to visit dealer after dealer for time-consuming estimates.

Today, your home and possessions are worth more than ever. You can protect them with Canwest Insurance's homeowners' and renters' policies. Let your local agent show you how easy it is to give yourself full protection. If you need a special rider to insure a personal computer, a coin, or stamp collection, or a fine antique, you can get that from Canwest, too.

Whatever your insurance needs—auto, home, life, or health—one call to Canwest can do it all.

Sincerely,

MODULE SUMMARY

- You decide how to organize your message on the basis of your purpose and audience analysis.

- Use PAIBOC analysis to identify what you want your message to achieve, how your audience will feel about your message, and what information you should include.

- If your audience will feel neutral or pleased about your message, use the direct, or good news organizational pattern:

  1. Give the good news, and summarize the main points.

  2. Give details.

  3. Give any reader benefits.

  4. End positively.

- Use reader benefits in informative and positive messages when

  ○ You are presenting policies.

  ○ You want to influence readers' attitudes toward the information, or your organization.

  ○ Stressing benefits presents readers' motives positively.

  ○ Some of the benefits may not be obvious to readers.

- For informative and positive documents, use a subject line that highlights the good news, and/or concisely summarizes the information.

ASSIGNMENTS FOR MODULE 11

Questions for Critical Thinking

11.1 What's wrong with the subject line "New Policy"?

11.2 Is it unethical to "bury" any negative elements in an otherwise positive or informative message?

11.3 Why is it important to analyze and identify the secondary and the primary purposes of your message?

11.4 Are you more likely to need reader benefits in informative letters or memos? Why? Or why not?

Exercises and Problems

11.5 Revising a Letter

Your colleague emails you the following draft letter attachment, asking for your feedback before she sends it:

Dear Ms. Hebbar:

I received your request to send a speaker to participate in "Career Day" at King Elementary School next month. I am pleased to be able to send Audrey Lindstrom to speak at your school about her job at the childcare centre.

Audrey has been working in the childcare centre for over five years. She trains contracted centre personnel on policies and procedures of the department.

Another commitment later that day will make it impossible for her to spend the whole day at your school. She will be happy to spend two hours with your class participating in the event.

Call Audrey to coordinate the time of the program, the expected content, and the age group of the audience.

Your students will see the importance of trained daycare providers in our neighbourhoods.

Thank you for asking our agency to be part of your school's special event. Our future lies in the hands of today's students.

Sincerely,

This draft definitely needs some work. It lacks you-attitude and positive emphasis, it isn't well organized, and it doesn't have enough details. "Ms. Lindstrom" would be more professional than "Audrey." And more information is needed. Exactly when should she show up? Will she be giving a speech (how long?), speaking as a member of a panel, or sitting at a table to answer questions? Will all grade levels be together, or will she be speaking to specific grades? Will all students hear each speaker, or will there be several concurrent speakers from which to choose?

As your instructor directs,

  a. Write an email to your colleague, explaining what revisions are necessary.

  b. Revise the letter.

11.6 Responding to a Supervisor's Request

You've received this email from your supervisor. Answer the message, describing something that you or others in your unit do well.

Subject: Need "Best Practices"

Our organization is putting together something on "Best Practices" so that good ideas can be shared as widely as possible. Please describe something our unit does well—ideally something that could be copied by or at least applied to other units.

Be specific. For example, don't just say "serve customers"—explain exactly what you do and how you do it to be effective. Anecdotes and examples would be helpful.

Also indicate whether a document, a videotape, or some other format would be the best way to share your practice. We may use more than one format, depending on the response.

I need your answer ASAP so that I can send it on to my boss.

11.7 Accepting Suggestions

Your municipal government encourages money-saving suggestions to help balance the city budget. The suggestion committee, which you chair, has voted to adopt five suggestions:

1. Direct-deposit paycheques to save distribution and printing costs. Suggested by Poh-Kim Lee, in Recreation and Parks.
2. Buy supplies in bulk. Suggested by Jolene Zigmund, in Maintenance.
3. Charge nearby towns and suburbs a fee for sending their firefighters through the city fire academy. Suggested by Charles Boxell, in Fire Safety.
4. Set up an honour system for employees to reimburse the city for personal photocopies or phone calls. Suggested by Maria Echeverria, in Police.
5. Install lock boxes so meter readers don't have to turn off water valves when people move. This causes wear

and tear, and broken valves must be dug up and replaced. Suggested by Travis Gratton, in Water Line Maintenance.

Each suggester gets $100. The Accounting Department will cut cheques the first of next month; cheques should reach people in interoffice mail a few days later.

As your instructor directs,

  a. Write to one of the suggesters, giving the good news.
  b. Write to all employees, announcing the award winners.

11.8   Giving Good News

Write to a customer or client, to a vendor or supplier, or to your boss announcing good news. Possibilities include a product improvement, a price cut or special, an addition to your management team, a new contract.

11.9   Easing New Hires' Transition into Your Unit

Prepare an orientation document to help new hires adjust quickly to your unit. You may want to focus solely on work procedures; you may also want to discuss aspects of the corporate culture.

11.10   Announcing a Change in Group Life Insurance Rates

Your organization provides group life insurance to your salaried employees, worth 2.5 times the employee's annual salary. Hourly employees who worked 30 hours or more a week in the last year receive life insurance equal to what the person was paid in the last year. The premium that the organization pays has been considered taxable income. The exact value is listed on the pay stub in the box labelled "Employer-Paid Benefits." Now, the Ministry of Finance has announced a reduction in the rates used to calculate the taxable value of this employer-provided life insurance. As a result, the value of the insurance will be slightly lower, and all the taxes based on pay will be slightly lower: federal, provincial, city, provincial hospitalization insurance, and school district taxes. These changes will be effective in the paycheque issued at the end of this month for employees paid monthly and in the paycheque issued 10 days from now for employees paid biweekly.

Write a memo to all employees, explaining the change.

11.11   Introducing a Wellness Program

Your company has decided to launch a wellness program in an effort to get employees to adopt healthier lifestyles. Studies show that people who smoke, who are moderate or heavy drinkers, who are overweight, and who do not exercise regularly have higher rates of absence due to illness. They visit doctors more often, need more prescription drugs, and are hospitalized more often and for longer periods of time.

You'll give a $100 rebate (annually) to each employee who doesn't smoke or use chewing tobacco. Employees who don't drink to excess (more than an average of 170 millilitres of beer, 85 of wine, or 42 of hard liquor a day) and who don't use illegal drugs can also get $100, as can those whose cholesterol isn't over 150. Employees who exercise at least 30 minutes a day, three times a week, will get rebates of $50. Exercise doesn't have to be difficult: walking and gardening count. Another rebate of $50 is available for a waist-to-hip ratio under 0.8 for women or 0.95 for men.

As part of the wellness program, the company cafeteria will focus on serving healthier foods and the company will offer twice-yearly health fairs with free routine immunizations and flu shots for employees and dependants. These parts of the program will begin next month.

Write to all employees informing them about the wellness program.

Hints:

- Choose an organization you know something about to use for this message.
- If the organization saves money through reduced absenteeism, will employees benefit?
- Why don't people already follow healthy practices? What can you do to overcome these objections?
- Saving money may not motivate everyone. Offer intrinsic benefits as well.
- Use the analysis that you developed for Exercise 2.6 in Module 2.

11.12   Explaining Packing Material

Your organization ships thousands of boxes to fill orders from catalogues and from your Web site. To cushion items, you fill the empty spaces around the items with plastic "popcorn." Some customers have written to complain about the plastic, which is not biodegradable. Some have asked you to use real popcorn, paper, or starch (which will degrade when wet). However, these materials do not cushion as well as plastic does (so that more items are damaged during shipment) and weigh more (so that shipping costs are higher). In addition, popcorn is subject to Canadian Food Inspection Agency regulations, which you do not want to monitor; paper fill creates dust and thus is a health hazard for packers; and starch doesn't work in very humid or very dry climates. You want to use one packing material for all boxes, wherever they are going.

Customers could save and reuse the plastic packaging material. If they can't reuse it, they may be able to recycle it.

They can call their local solid waste department to find out. Or they could check The Internet Consumer Recycling Guide, an online guide for Canadian and U.S. consumers, at www.obviously.com/recycle/guides/hard.html.

As your instructor directs,

a. Write one customer who has complained, showing why you are continuing to use plastic fill.

b. Prepare a one-page insert to be included in every package, explaining your decision about packaging.

11.13   Reminding Guests About the Time Change

Twice a year the switch to and from daylight saving time affects people in Canada. The time change can be disruptive for hotel guests, who may lose track of the date, forget to change the clocks in their rooms, and miss appointments as a result.

Prepare a form letter to leave in each hotel room reminding guests of the impending time change. What should guests do?

Write the letter.

Hints:

- Use an attention-getting page layout so readers don't ignore the message.
- Pick a specific hotel or motel chain you know something about.
- Use message to build goodwill for your hotel or motel chain. Use specific references to services or features the hotel offers, focusing not on what the hotel does for the reader, but on what the reader can do at the hotel.

11.14   Confirming a Reservation

You work in reservations at Basin Hot Springs Lodge in Banff National Park. Most travellers phone 13 months in advance to reserve a room and once you process the credit card payment for the first night, you then write to them to confirm the reservation.

The confirmation contains the amount charged to the credit card, the date on which the reservation was made, the confirmation number, the kind of room (Lakefront Retreat or Mountainview Retreat), and the dates the guest will be arriving and leaving.

In addition, the letter needs to give several pieces of general information. The amount of the deposit and the amount quoted per night are the rates for the current calendar year. However, room rates change annually; in general, rates increase by about 4 percent to 5 percent, per year. Guests need to know that they will pay the new rate for each additional night after the first night.

Anyone who wants a refund must cancel the reservation in writing four days before the scheduled arrival date. Cancellations may be faxed: the fax number is on the letterhead the letter will be printed on.

Parking is limited. People who bring big motor homes, boats, or camp trailers may have to park in the main parking area rather than right by their cabins.

All the rooms are cabin style with three to four rooms in each building. There are no rooms in a main lodge. People will need to walk from their cabins to the restaurants, unless they do their own cooking.

Both Lakefront and Mountainview Retreats have kitchenettes with microwaves, but guests have to bring their own cooking utensils, dishes, supplies, and food. The bedroom area (with a king-size bed in the Lakefront Retreats and a queen-size bed in the Mountainview Retreats) has a sliding divider that can separate it from the sitting area, which has a sofa bed.

Since the deposit pays for the first night, the room will be held regardless of the time of arrival. Check-in time is 3 P.M.; earlier room availability cannot be guaranteed. Checkout time is 11 A.M.

All cabins are nonsmoking. Smoking is permitted on the decks of the Lakefront Retreats or the porches of the Mountainview Retreats.

The guest should present the confirmation letter when checking in.

As your instructor directs,

a. Write a form letter that can be used for one type of room (either Lakefront or Mountainview Retreat). Indicate with square brackets material that would need to be filled in for each guest: for instance, arriving [date of arrival] and departing [date of departure].

b. Write a letter to Stephanie Lafleur, who has reserved a Lakefront Retreat room arriving September 18 and departing September 20. Her credit card is being billed for $187.25 ($175 plus GST—the current rate). Her address is 3122 Rue Laurier, Quebec City, QC, G1R 3M7.

11.15   Lining Up a Consultant to Teach Short Courses in Presentations

As director of education and training, you oversee all in-house training programs. Five weeks ago, Runata Hartley, vice-president for human resources, asked you to set up a training course on oral presentations. After making some phone calls, you tracked down Brian Barreau, a professor of communications at a nearby college.

"Yes, I do short courses on oral presentations," he told you on the phone. "I would want at least a day and a half with participants—two full days would be better. They need time to practise the skills they'll be learning. I'm free Thursdays and Fridays.

"I'm willing to work with up to 20 people at a time. Tell me what kind of presentations they make, whether they know how to use PowerPoint™, and what kinds of things you want me to emphasize. I'll need a digital video camera to record each participant's presentations and a DVD for each person. My fee is $2 000 a day."

You told him you thought a two-day session would be feasible, but you'd have to get back to him after you got budget approval. You wrote a quick memo to Runata explaining the situation and asking about what the session should cover.

Two weeks ago, you received this memo:

> I've asked for budget approval of $4000 for a two-day session plus no more than $500 for all expenses. I don't think there will be a problem.
>
> We need some of the basics: how to plan a presentation, how to deal with nervousness. Adapting to the audience is a big issue: our people give presentations to varied audiences with very different levels of technical knowledge and interest. Most of our people have PowerPoint on their computers, but the slide shows I've seen have been pretty amateurish.
>
> I don't want someone to lecture. We need practical exercises that can help us practise skills that we can put into effect immediately.
>
> Attached is a list of 18 people who can attend a session Thursday and Friday of the second week of next month. Note that we've got a good mix of people. If the session goes well, I may want you to schedule additional sessions.

Today, you got approval from the vice-president to schedule the session, pay Professor Barreau's fee, and reimburse him for expenses to a maximum of $500. He will have to keep all receipts and turn in an itemized list of expenses to be reimbursed; you cannot reimburse him if he does not have receipts.

You also need to explain the mechanics of the session. You'll meet in the Conference Room, which has a screen and flip charts. You have an overhead projector, a laptop, a digital video camera, and a monitor, but you need to reserve these if he wants to use them. Will he bring his own laptop computer, or does he want you to provide the computer?

Write to Professor Barreau. You don't have to persuade him to come since he's already informally agreed, but you do want him to look forward to the job and to do his best work.

Hints:

- Choose an organization you know something about.
- What audiences do people speak to? How formal are these talks? What are their purposes?
- Is this session designed to hone the skills of people who are competent, or is it designed to help people who are very weak, perhaps even paralyzed with fright?
- What role do presentations play in the success of the organization and of individuals in it?
- Check the calendar to get the dates. If there's any ambiguity about what "the second week of next month" is, call Runata to check.

11.16   Answering an International Inquiry

Your business, government, or nonprofit organization has received the following inquiries from international correspondents. (You choose the country the inquiry originated from.)

1. Please tell us about a new product, service, or trend so that we can decide whether we want to buy, license, or imitate it in our country.
2. We have heard about a problem [technical, social, political, or ethical] that occurred in your organization. Could you please tell us what really happened and estimate how it is likely to affect the long-term success of the organization?
3. Please tell us about college or university programs in this field. We are interested in sending some of our managers to your country to complete a degree.
4. We are considering setting up a plant in your city. We have already received adequate business information. However, we would also like to know how comfortable our nationals would feel. Do people in your city speak our language? How many? What opportunities exist for our nationals to improve their English? Does your town already have people from a wide mix of nations? Which are the largest groups?
5. Our organization would like to subscribe to an English-language trade journal. Which one would you recommend? Why? How much does it cost? How can we order it?

As your instructor directs,

a. Answer one or more of the inquiries. Assume that your reader either reads English or can have your message translated.
b. Write a memo to your instructor explaining how you've adapted the message for your audience.

Hints:

- Even though you can write in English, English may not be your reader's native language. Write a letter that can be translated easily.
- In some cases, you may need to spell out background information that might not be clear to someone from another country.

11.17   Writing a Thank-You Message

Write a thank-you message to someone who has helped you achieve your goals.

As your instructor directs,

    a. Turn in a copy of the letter.
    b. Mail the letter to the person who helped you.
    c. Write a memo to your instructor explaining the choices you made in writing the thank-you letter.

11.18   Evaluating Web Pages

Today you received this email from your boss:

> Subject: Evaluating Our Web Page
>
> Our CEO wants to know how our Web page compares to those of our competitors. I'd like you to do this in two steps. First, send me a list of your criteria. Then give me an evaluation of two of our competitors' pages and of our own pages. I'll combine your memo with others on other Web pages to put together a comprehensive evaluation for the next executive meeting.

As your instructor directs,

    a. List the generic criteria for evaluating a Web page. Think about the various audiences for the page and the content that will keep them coming back, page organization and navigation, the visual design, and the details, such as a creation or update date.
    b. List criteria for pages of specific kinds of organizations. For example, a nonprofit organization might want information for potential and current donors, volunteers, and clients. A financial institution might want to project an image both of trustworthiness and optimism.
    c. Evaluate three Web pages of similar organizations. Which is best? Why?

Hint:

- Review the information on Web page design in Module 5.

11.19   Creating a Human Resources Web Page

As firms attempt to help employees balance work and family life (and as employers become aware that personal and family stresses affect performance at work), human resource departments sponsor an array of programs and provide information on myriad subjects. However, some people might be uncomfortable asking for help, either because the problem is embarrassing (who wants to admit needing help to deal with drug or spousal abuse or addiction to gambling?) or because they feel that focusing on non-work issues (e.g., child care) might lead others to think they aren't serious about their jobs. The World Wide Web allows organizations to post information that employees can access privately—even from home.

Create a Web page that could be posted by human resources to help employees with one of the challenges they face. Possible topics include

- Appreciating an ethnic heritage
- Buying a house
- Caring for dependants: child care, helping a child learn to read, living with teenagers, elder care, and so forth
- Dealing with a health issue: exercising, having a healthy diet, and so on
- Dealing with an environmental situation: energy prices, conserving resources, recycling and/or reusing items
- Dealing with a health problem: alcoholism, cancer, diabetes, heart disease, obesity, and so on
- Dressing for success or dressing for casual days
- Managing finances: basic budgeting, deciding how much to save, choosing investments, and so on
- Nourishing the spirit: meditation, religion, mindfulness
- Planning for retirement
- Planning vacations
- Reducing stress
- Resolving conflicts on the job or in families

Assume that this page can be accessed from another of the organization's pages. Offer at least seven links. (More are better.) You may offer information as well as links to other pages with information. At the top of the page, offer an overview of what the page covers. At the bottom of the page, put the creation and update date and your name and email address.

As your instructor directs,

    a. Turn in two printed copies of your page(s). On another page, give the URLs for each link.
    b. Turn in one printed copy of your page(s) and a disk with the HTML code and .gif files.
    c. Write a memo to your instructor identifying the audience for which the page is designed and explaining (1) how you found material on this topic, (2) why you chose the pages and information you've included, and (3) why you chose the layout and graphics you've used.
    d. Present your page orally to the class.

Hints:

- Pick a topic you know something about.
- Realize that audience members will have different needs. You could explain the basics of choosing day care or stocks, but don't recommend a specific daycare centre or a specific stock.

- If you have more than nine links, chunk them in small groups under headings.
- Create a good image of the organization.
- Review the information on Web page design in Module 5.

POLISHING YOUR PROSE

Applying Parallel Structure

Use parallel structure in lists, headings, and subheadings by using the same grammatical form for ideas that have the same relationship in your sentence.

Not parallel:	Good reports are factual, logical, and demonstrate clarity.

It may be easier to see faulty parallelism by listing parts that need to be parallel. Check to make sure each component fits with the words that introduce the list.

Not parallel: Good reports are

Factual

Logical

Demonstrate clarity

Parallel: Good reports are

Factual

Logical

Clear

Make sure all of the list is horizontal or vertical. Don't start a list horizontally and finish it vertically.

Incorrect: As department manager, I supervised eight employees.

- Wrote the department budget
- Presented our sales strategy to the board of directors

Correct: As department manager, I supervised eight employees, wrote the department budget, and presented our sales strategy to the board of directors.

Also correct: As department manager, I

- Supervised eight employees
- Wrote the department budget

- Presented our sales strategy to the board of directors

Headings have to be parallel throughout the document, but subheads need only be parallel to other subheads in the same section.

Not parallel: Should Ogden Industries Purchase Blue Chip International in 2010?

- Short-Term Costs
- What Are the Long-Term Gains?

Parallel: Should Ogden Industries Purchase Blue Chip International in 2010?

- Short-Term Costs
- Long-Term Gains

In addition to grammatical parallelism, also check your sentences for logical parallelism.

Incorrect: The group ranges from males and females to people in their 20s, 30s, and 40s.

Better: We interviewed men and women ranging in age from 20 to 50.

Gender is one category; age is another.

Exercises

Rewrite the following sentences or headings to make them parallel.

1. Last week, Alain and Rochelle flew to Toronto, Montreal, Quebec City, and the capital of the state of Michigan.
2. Ask Ms. Liken, Mr. Fitzgerald, Bill Anderson, and Professor Timmons to join us for the meeting.
3. To ship a package

   1. Fill out an address form.
   2. Specify on the form how the package should be sent.
   3. If you want to send a package by overnight mail, your supervisor must initial the appropriate box on the address form.

4. Make sure benefits announcements get routed to managers, supervisors, and the folks in the Human Resources Department.

5. Appointments can be scheduled in 5-minute, 10-minute, quarter-hour, or 20-minute intervals.

6. The project's fixed costs include material, salaries, advertising, bonus packages for anyone who goes above and beyond the call of duty, and the cost of travel to different cities.

7. This report discusses Why We Should Upgrade Capital Equipment, Why We Should Increase Staff by 25 percent, The Benefits of Decreasing Employee Turnover, and The Importance of Identifying New Product Markets.

8. The selection committee reviews each job applicant on the basis of education, experience, extracurricular activities, the awards the employee has received, and the strength of the applicant's personal statement.

9. Use the telephone to answer customer questions, email to send order confirmations, and take orders using our Web page.

10. Each agency should estimate Annual Costs, Costs per Month, Salaries, New Equipment Costs, and How Much You Need in a Reserve Fund for Unexpected Expenses.

Check your answers to the odd-numbered exercises on page 552.

Composing Negative Messages

Learning Objectives

After reading and applying the information in Module 12, you'll be able to demonstrate

Knowledge of

- The criteria that define negative messages
- The bad news message structure
- The legal and ethical implications of your messages

Skills to

- Organize negative messages
- Give bad news while retaining goodwill
- Write common kinds of negative messages
- Further analyze business communication situations

Employability Skills 2000+ Checklist

In this module, the key skills from the Conference Board of Canada's Employability Skills 2000+ are

Communicate

- ○ read and understand information presented in a variety of forms (e.g., words, graphs, charts, diagrams)
- ○ write and speak so others pay attention and understand

- ○ share information using a range of information and communications technologies (e.g., voice, email, computers)
- ○ use relevant scientific, technological, and mathematical knowledge and skills to explain or clarify ideas

Manage Information

- ○ locate, gather, and organize information using appropriate technology and information systems

Use Numbers

- ○ decide what needs to be measured or calculated
- ○ observe and record data using appropriate methods, tools, and technology

- ○ make estimates and verify calculations

Think & Solve Problems

- ○ assess situations and identify problems
- ○ seek different points of view and evaluate them based on facts
- ○ recognize the human, interpersonal, technical, scientific, and mathematical dimensions of a problem
- ○ identify the root cause of a problem

- ○ be creative and innovative in exploring possible solutions
- ○ readily use science, technology, and mathematics as ways to think, gain and share knowledge, solve problems, and make decisions
- ○ evaluate solutions to make recommendations or decisions

Work with Others

- ○ understand and work within the dynamics of a group

Negative or bad news messages contain information that will cost the reader comfort, time, money, esteem, or resources. Few people like to give bad news—and fewer still like to get it. However, negative messages are common in business. How we present negatives, and what we write or say can affect how audiences respond to our messages, and how they see our organization and us.

A negative message always has several purposes:

Primary purposes

- To give the reader the bad news
- To have the reader read, understand, and accept the message
- To maintain as much goodwill as possible

Secondary purposes

- To build a good image of the writer
- To build a good image of the writer's organization
- To reduce or eliminate future correspondence on the same subject so the message doesn't create more work for the writer

Even when readers will be unhappy with the news we must convey, we still want readers to feel several positive things:

- They have been taken seriously.
- Your decision is fair and reasonable.
- If they were in your shoes, they would make the same decision.

Negative messages include

- Rejections and refusals
- Announcements of policy changes that do not benefit customers or consumers
- Requests the reader will see as bothersome, insulting, or intrusive
- Negative performance appraisals and disciplinary notices
- Product recalls or notices of defects

How Should I Organize Negative Messages?

It depends on your purposes and audiences.

Use **PAIBOC** analysis and **Maslow's hierarchy** (Module 8) to identify your audience's needs. Whether saying no to a request, notifying a client about a price increase, or emailing colleagues about extra work they must do, you want to give the necessary information while maintaining goodwill. Otherwise, you'll waste time and money in lost customers and disruptive work relationships.

Choose your pattern of organization on the basis of the situation.

- Letters to people outside your organization should be indirect to build goodwill.
- When you write to supervisors, propose solutions when you report a problem.
- When you write to peers and subordinates, ask for their input in dealing with negative situations.

Giving Bad News to Customers and Other People Outside Your Organization

The following pattern helps writers maintain goodwill:

1. *Start with a neutral statement, or buffer.* These openings are meant to orient readers and psychologically prepare them for news that they are not going to like. Whether writing or speaking, the best buffers begin with areas that both you and your audience can agree on. Buffer statements such as "Thank you for your letter," in response to a

complaint or query, acknowledge that you have read, understood, and are responding to your reader's concern.

2. *Give the reason for the refusal before the refusal itself* when you have a reason that readers will understand and accept. A good reason prepares the reader to expect the refusal.

3. *Give the negative just once, clearly.* Inconspicuous refusals can be missed, making it necessary to say no a second time.

4. *Always present an alternative or compromise, if one is available.* An alternative gives readers another way to get what they want; it also suggests that you care about the readers and want to help them solve their problems.

5. *End with a positive, forward-looking statement.*

Figure 12.1 uses the basic pattern. Figure 12.2 includes the buffer, the reason, and the refusal in the first paragraph.

FIGURE 12.1 **A Negative Letter**

Nature's Lifesource Inc
111 Pleasant Street
Stephan, NB E3L 1B4
www.naturlif@origin.ca

May 8, 2009

Alyssa Scarangella
72 Rue Windermere
Montreal, PQ H9A 2C4

Dear Alyssa Scarangella:

Subject: **Shipments # 3101-3105 inclusive**

Buffer:
Neutral — Thank you for the information you provided yesterday.
statement

Explanation: As we discussed, the last three shipments have arrived with product damage. Both our
Reasons transportation service suppliers and warehouse personnel have expressed concerns about the security of the loading. The quality of the pallets supporting the products and of the equipment fastenings could lead to load shifts, creating dangerous highway conditions.

Explanation: As you requested, I am enclosing photographs of the damage to shipments # 3103, 3104,
Proof and 3105. These photographs show the condition of the pallets and the manner in which the load was secured. Since our research indicates that these two factors led to the damage, I would appreciate your help in recouping our costs for the damaged products.

Positive Thank you for your assurance that the quality of the pallets and the fastenings of all
ending future shipments will provide a safe, secure load.

When you have reviewed the photographs, please let me know what additional information you will need.

Sincerely,

Leovee Yang

Leovee Yang

Enclosure

FIGURE 12.2   **A Refusal with Alternative**

AlbertaFilmInstitute

8th floor Commerce Place 10155 102 Street Edmonton AB T5J 4L6
T: 780.415.0200 F. 780.415.0201 E. stephanblackbird@gov.ab.ca

November 22, 2009

Mr. Marco Novelli
319 Sweetwater Bay
Winnipeg, MB R2J 3G4

Dear Mr. Novelli:
Subject: Submission, Original Screenplay *Doubtful*

Buffer: Beginning clause — Although your play is highly original and well crafted, we have found that film noir themes do not attract a large box office. Therefore we cannot use your story for next year's festival. — **Explanation / Refusal**

With your permission, however, we would like to send your treatment on to Jessie Prynne, chair of the Alberta Arts Foundation. Foundation members are always looking for original works to stage. — **Alternative**

If this is agreeable to you, please let me know by email, letter, or phone.

Meanwhile, please keep writing, and please continue to send us your work. — **Positive, forward-looking ending**

Sincerely,

Stephan Blackbird

Stephan Blackbird
Script Supervisor

The Buffer

A **buffer** is a neutral or positive statement that allows you to delay the negative. You'll want to begin messages with a neutral statement or buffer when the reader (individually or culturally) values harmony, or when the buffer serves another purpose. For example, when you have to thank the reader somewhere in the letter, putting the "thank you" in the first paragraph allows you to start on a positive note.

To be effective, a buffer must put the reader in a good frame of mind—not give the bad news but not imply a positive answer either—and provide a natural transition to the body of the letter. The kinds of statements most often used as buffers are good news, facts and chronologies of events, references to enclosures, thanks, and statements of principle, as the examples below illustrate.

1. Start with any good news or positive elements the letter contains.

   Starting Thursday, June 26, you'll have access to your money 24 hours a day at TD Canada Trust.

Letter announcing that the drive-up windows will be closed for two days while new automatic teller machines are installed

2. State a fact or provide a chronology of events.

> A new, graduated dues schedule, determined by delegate assembly vote last December, has been endorsed by the executive council. Members are now asked to establish their own dues rate and to calculate the total amount of their remittance.

Announcement of a new dues structure that will raise most members' dues

3. Refer to enclosures in the letter.

> Enclosed is a new sticker for your car. You may pick up additional ones in the office if needed. Please destroy old stickers bearing the signature of "L. S. LaVoie."

Letter announcing an increase in parking rental rates

4. Thank the reader for something he or she has done.

> Thank you for scheduling appointments for me with so many senior people at the Bank of Montreal. My visit there March 14 was very informative.

Letter refusing a job offer

5. State a general principle.

> Good drivers should pay substantially less for their auto insurance. The Good Driver Plan was created to reward good drivers (those with five-year accident-free records) with our lowest available rates. A change in the plan, effective January 1, will help keep those rates low.

Letter announcing that the company will now count traffic tickets, not just accidents, in calculating insurance rates—a change that will raise many people's premiums

Buffers are hard to write. Even if you think the reader would prefer to be let down easily, use a buffer only when you can write a good one.

FIGURE 12.3 How to Organize a Negative Message

It's better *not* to use a buffer (1) if the reader might ignore a letter with a bland first paragraph, (2) if the reader or the organization prefers "bottom-line-first messages," (3) if the reader is suspicious of the writer, or (4) if the reader "won't take no for an answer."

Buffer
Explanation
Negative
Alternative
Goodwill Ending

Checkpoint

To be effective, a **buffer** has to put the reader in a good frame of mind, not give the bad news but not imply a positive answer either, and provide a natural transition to the body of the letter.

Employability Skills

Reasons

Make the reason for the refusal clear and convincing in terms of the audience's needs and wants (Modules 3 and 8). The following reason is inadequate.

Weak reason: The goal of the ValuDrug CHARGE-ALL Centre is to provide our customers with faster, more personalized service. Since you now live outside the Halifax ValuDrug CHARGE-ALL service area, we can no longer offer you the advantages of a local CHARGE-ALL Centre.

If the reader says, "I don't care if my bills are slow and impersonal," will the company let the reader keep the card? No. The real reason for the negative is that the drugstore's franchise allows it to have cardholders only in a given geographical region.

Better reason:	Each local CHARGE-ALL Centre offers accounts to customers in a specific regional area. The Nova Scotia ValuDrug CHARGE-ALL Centre serves customers east of Quebec. Your current card is good until it expires. When that happens, please open an account with a CHARGE-ALL Centre that serves Quebec.

Don't hide behind "company policy": readers will assume the policy is designed to benefit you at their expense. If possible, show how the readers benefit from the policy. If they do not benefit, don't mention policy.

Weak reason:	I cannot write an insurance policy for you because company policy does not allow me to do so.
Better reason:	General Insurance insures cars only when they are normally garaged at night. Standard insurance policies cover a wider variety of risks and charge higher fees. Limiting policies gives General's customers the lowest possible rates for auto insurance.

Avoid saying that you *cannot* do something. Most negative messages exist because the writer or company has chosen certain policies or cutoff points. In the example above, the company could choose to insure a wider variety of customers if it wanted to do so.

Often you will enforce policies that you did not design. Don't pass the buck by saying, "This is a terrible policy." Carelessly criticizing your superiors is never a good idea. If you really think a policy is bad, try to persuade your superiors to change it. If you can't think of convincing reasons to change the policy, maybe it isn't so bad after all.

If you have several reasons for saying no, use only those that are strong and watertight. If you give five reasons and readers dismiss two of them, readers may feel that they've won and should get the request.

Weak reason:	You cannot store large bulky items in the dormitory over the summer: moving them into and out of storage would tie up the stairs and the elevators right at the busiest times when people are moving in and out.
Way to dismiss the reason:	We'll move large items before or after the two days when most people are moving in or out.

If you do not have a good reason, omit the reason rather than use a weak one. Even if you have a strong reason, omit it if it reflects poorly on your organization.

Reason that reflects poorly on company:	Our company is not hiring at the present time because profits are down. In fact, the downturn has prompted top management to reduce the salaried staff by 5 percent just this month, with perhaps more reductions to come.
Better:	Our company does not have any openings now.

Checkpoint

Organizing Negative Letters to Customers

1. Provide a buffer, if possible.
2. Give the reason for the refusal before the refusal itself when you have a reason that readers will understand and accept.
3. Give the negative just once, clearly.
4. Present an alternative or compromise, if one is available.
5. End with a positive, forward-looking statement.

Refusals

Deemphasize the refusal by putting it in the same paragraph as the reason, rather than in a paragraph by itself. Sometimes you may be able to imply the refusal rather than stating it directly.

Direct refusal:	You cannot get insurance for just one month.
Implied refusal:	The shortest term for an insurance policy is six months.

Be sure that the implication is clear. Any message can be misunderstood, but an optimistic or desperate reader is particularly likely to misunderstand a negative message. One of your purposes in a negative message is to close the door on the subject. You do not want to have to write a second letter saying that the real answer is no.

EXPANDING A CRITICAL SKILL

Thinking About the Legal and Ethical Implications of What You Say

Any message that is recorded—on paper (even a napkin), on a disk or hard drive, on a cell phone, or in voice mail—can be used in a legal case, as former CIBC employees who used their BlackBerrys assuming total confidentiality found to their chagrin. Even an erased electronic message can be recovered by experts. In any message you write, however informal or hurried, you need to be sure to say exactly what you mean. The Supreme Court of Canada and provincial defamation legislation protect individuals' dignity, right to privacy, and reputation. Libel and slander liability can include everyone who participates in disseminating injurious material.

Thinking about the legal implications of what you say is particularly important in negative messages. In an effort to cushion bad news, writers sometimes give reasons that create legal liabilities. For example, as Elizabeth McCord has shown, the statement that a plant is "too noisy and dangerous" for a group tour could be used as evidence against the company in a worker's compensation claim. In another case, a writer telling a job candidate that the firm had hired someone else said that he thought she was the best candidate. She sued and won.

Although you may choose the direct or indirect bad news pattern organization—depending on your audience's expectations—you also need to think about the ethical implications of your messages. People prefer to do business with someone they trust; therefore, it's good business to deliver negative message honestly and sensitively.

Acting ethically means acting out of enlightened self-interest: treating others as you want to be treated. You need to assume your audience's point of view to figure out what to say—or not to say. Think about how a reasonable person might interpret your words. If that interpretation isn't what you mean, revise the passage so that it says what you mean, in a way you would find acceptable.

Sources: Sinclair Stewart and Richard Bloom, "BlackBerry Battle Chills Bay St. Gossips," July 7, 2005, http://www.theglobeandmail.com/servlet/ArticleNews/TPStory/LAC/20050107/BLACKBERRY07/TPNational/TopStories, retrieved August 8, 2006; and Javad Heydary (May 26, 2005), "Is Your Boss Monitoring Your BlackBerry?," *E-Commerce Times*, May 26, 2005, http://www.ecommercetimes.com/story/43376.html, retrieved August 8, 2006; Elizabeth A. McCord, "The Business Writer, the Law, and Routine Business Communication: A Legal and Rhetorical Analysis," *Journal of Business and Technical Communication* 5(2) (1991): 173–99.

Alternatives

Giving the reader an alternative or a compromise, if one is available, does several things:

- It offers the reader another way to get what he or she wants.
- It suggests that you really care about the reader, and about meeting his or her needs.
- It enables the reader to reestablish the psychological freedom you limited when you said no.
- It allows you to end on a positive note and to present yourself and your organization as positive, friendly, and helpful.

When you give an alternative, give readers all the information they need to act on it, but let readers decide whether to try the alternative.

Negative messages limit the reader's freedom. People may respond to a limitation of freedom by asserting their freedom in some other arena. University of Kansas psychology professor Jack W. Brehm calls this phenomenon **psychological reactance**.[1] Psychological reactance is at work when a customer who has been denied credit no longer buys even on a cash basis, or a subordinate who has been passed over for a promotion gets back at the company by deliberately doing a poor job.

Psychological reactance in action.

An alternative allows the reader to react in a way that doesn't hurt you. By letting readers decide for themselves whether they want the alternative, you allow them to reestablish their sense of psychological freedom.

The specific alternative will vary depending on the circumstances. In Figure 12.2, the script supervisor of the Alberta Film Institute refuses to accept *Doubtful*, but tells the filmmaker he is sending his film on to someone who might use it.

Endings

If you have a good alternative, refer to it in your ending: "We are offering 10% off all treatments in March."

The best endings look to the future, as in this example of refusing to continue a charge account for a customer who has moved:

> Wherever you have your account, you'll continue to get all the service you've learned to expect from CHARGE-ALL and the convenience of charging items at more than a thousand ValuDrugs stores in Canada—and in Halifax, too, whenever you come back to visit!

To maintain goodwill and retain a positive business relationship, end sincerely:

> Please call me at 403-555-7700 if you need further clarification.

Avoid endings that seem insincere or clichéd:

> We are happy to have been of service, and should we be able to assist you in the future, please do not hesitate to contact us.

This ending lacks you-attitude and would not be good even in a positive message. In a situation where the company has just refused to help, it sounds sarcastic.

Giving Bad News to Superiors

Your superior expects you to solve minor problems by yourself. But sometimes, solving a problem requires more authority or resources than you have. When you give bad news to a superior, try to recommend a way to deal with the problem. Turn the negative message into a persuasive one.

1. *Describe the problem.* Say what's wrong, clearly and unemotionally.
2. *Tell how it happened.* Provide the background. What underlying factors led to this specific problem?
3. *Describe the options for fixing it.* If one option is clearly best, you may need to discuss only one. But if the reader will think of other options, or if different people will judge the options differently, describe all the options, giving their advantages and disadvantages.
4. *Recommend a solution and ask for action.* Ask for approval so that you can go ahead to make the necessary changes to fix the problem.

Checkpoint

Organizing Bad News to Superiors

1. Describe the problem.
2. Tell how it happened.
3. Describe the options for fixing it.
4. Recommend a solution and ask for action.

Giving Bad News to Peers and Subordinates

When giving serious bad news to peers and subordinates, use a variation of the pattern to superiors:

1. *Describe the problem.* Say what's wrong, clearly and unemotionally.
2. *Present an alternative or compromise, if one is available.* An alternative gives readers another way to get what they want, and suggests that you care about the readers and want to help them meet their needs.
3. *If possible, ask for input or action.* People in the audience may be able to suggest solutions. And workers who help make a decision are far more likely to accept the consequences.

No serious negative (such as being downsized or laid off) should come as a complete surprise. Managers can prepare for possible negatives by giving full information as it becomes available. It is also possible to let the people who will be affected by a decision participate in setting the criteria. Someone who has bought into the criteria for awarding cash for suggestions or retaining workers is more likely to accept decisions using such criteria. And in some cases, the synergy of groups may make possible ideas that management didn't think of or rejected as unacceptable. Some workplaces, for example, might decide to reduce everyone's pay slightly rather than laying off some individuals.

When the bad news is less serious, as in Figure 12.6, use the bad news organizational pattern (buffer, explanation, bad news, positive ending) unless your knowledge of the reader suggests that another pattern will be more effective.

FIGURE 12.4   **A Negative Memo to Subordinates**

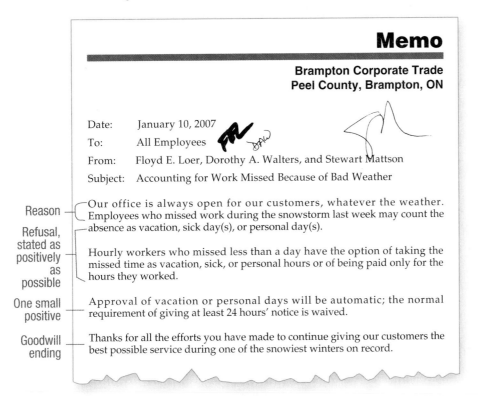

Whatever the medium, the context of communication is crucial. The reader's reaction is influenced by the answers to these questions:

- Do you and the reader have a good relationship?
- Does the organization treat people well?
- Have readers been warned of possible negatives?
- Have readers "bought into" the criteria for the decision?
- Do communications after the negative build goodwill?

Checkpoint

Organizing Bad News to Peers and Subordinates

1. Describe the problem.
2. Present an alternative or compromise, if one is available.
3. If possible, ask for input or action.

What Are the Most Common Kinds of Negative Messages?

Rejections and refusals, disciplinary notices, negative performance appraisals, and layoffs and firings are common negative messages.

Three of the most difficult kinds of negative messages to write are rejections and refusals, disciplinary notices, negative performance appraisals, and layoffs and firings.

Rejections and Refusals

When you refuse requests, try to use a buffer. Give an alternative if one is available. For example, if you are denying credit, it might still be possible for the reader to put an item on layaway.

Politeness and length help. An experiment using a denial of additional insurance found that subjects preferred a rejection letter that was longer, more tactful, and more personal. The preferred letter started with a buffer, used a good reason for the refusal, and offered sales promotion in the last paragraph.[2]

Since many Canadians, especially those of high-context cultures (Module 3), value courtesy, they prefer this organizational pattern.[3]

When you refuse requests within your organization, use your knowledge of the culture and of the specific individual to craft your message. In some organizations, it may be appropriate to use company slogans, offer whatever help already established departments can give, and refer to the individual's good work. In less personal organizations, a simple negative without embellishment might be more appropriate.

Disciplinary Notices and Negative Performance Appraisals

Present disciplinary notices and negative performance appraisals directly, with no buffer. A buffer might encourage the recipient to minimize the message's importance—and might even become evidence in a court case that the employee had not been told to shape up "or else." Cite quantifiable observations of the employee's behaviour, rather than generalizations or inferences based on it. If an employee is disciplined by being laid off without pay, specify when the employee is to return.

Performance appraisals are discussed in detail in Module 13 on persuasive messages. Performance appraisals will be positive when they are designed to help a good employee improve. But when an employee violates a company rule or fails to improve after repeated appraisals, the company may discipline the employee or build a dossier to support firing him or her.

Layoffs and Firings

Information about layoffs and firings is normally delivered orally but accompanied by a written statement explaining severance pay or unemployment benefits that may be available. The written statement should start either with the reason or with the decision itself. A buffer would not be appropriate.

If a company is in financial trouble, management needs to communicate the problem clearly long before it is necessary to lay anyone off. Sharing information and enlisting everyone's help in finding solutions may make it possible to save jobs. Sharing information also means that layoff notices, if they become necessary, will be a formality; they should not be new information to employees.

Before you fire someone, double-check the facts. Make sure that the employee has been told about the problem and that he or she will be fired if the problem is not corrected. Give the employee the real reason for the firing. Offering a face-saving reason unrelated to poor performance can create legal liabilities. But avoid broadcasting the reason to other people: doing so can leave the company liable to a defamation suit.[4]

What's the Best Subject Line for a Negative Message?

Only use negative subject lines if you think the reader might otherwise ignore the message.

Letters don't require subject lines (Module 9). Omit a subject line in negative letters unless you think readers might ignore what they think is a routine message. (See, for example, Figure 12.1.)

When you give bad news, use a subject line that focuses on solutions, not problems:

> Subject: Improving Our Subscription Letter

Or you can put the topic (but not your action on it) in the subject line:

> Subject: Status of Conversion Table Program
>
> Because of heavy demands on our time, we have not yet been able to write programs for the conversion tables you asked for.

How Can PAIBOC Help Me Write Negative Messages?

Employability Skills

The PAIBOC questions help you examine the points your message should include.

Before you tackle the assignments for this module, examine the following problem. As in Module 11, the PAIBOC questions probe the basic points required for a solution. Study the two sample solutions to see what makes one unacceptable and the other one good.[5] The checklist in Figure 12.8 on page 223 can help you evaluate a draft.

Problem

You're director of employee benefits for a Fortune 500 company. Today, you received the following memo:

> From: Michelle Jagtiani
>
> Subject: Getting My Retirement Benefits
>
> Next Friday will be my last day here. I am leaving [name of company] to take a position at another firm.
>
> Please process a cheque for my retirement benefits, including both the deductions from my salary and the company's contributions for the last three and a half years. I would like to receive the cheque by next Friday if possible.

You have bad news for Michelle. Although the company does contribute an amount to the retirement fund equal to the amount deducted for retirement from the employee's paycheque, employees who leave with fewer than five years of employment get only their own contributions. Michelle will get back only the money that has been deducted from her own pay, plus 4 percent interest compounded quarterly. Her payments and interest come to just over $17 200; the amount might be higher depending on the amount of her last paycheque, which will include compensation for any unused vacation days and sick leave. Furthermore, since the amounts deducted were not considered taxable income, she will have to pay income tax on the money she receives.

You cannot process the cheque until after her resignation is effective, so you will mail it to her. You have her home address on file; if she's moving, she needs to let you know where to send the cheque. Processing the cheque may take two to three weeks.

Write a memo to Michelle using PAIBOC analysis.

FIGURE 12.5   **Allocating Time for Writing a Negative Memo (memo denying matching funds; time may vary)**

	Total Time: 3 hours
Planning	1 hour
Understand the situation.	
Answer the PAIBOC questions (Module 1).	
Think about document design (Module 5).	
Organize the message.	
Writing	½ hour
Draft the memo.	
Revising	1½ hours
Reread draft.	
Measure draft against PAIBOC questions and checklist for negative messages (Figure 12.8).	
Revise draft.	
Ask for feedback.	
Revise draft based on feedback.	
Edit to catch grammatical errors.	
Run spell check.	
Proof by eye.	
Initial memo.	
Put in interoffice mail.	

Analysis of the Problem

P   What are your **purposes** in writing or speaking?

- To tell Michelle that she will get only her own contributions, plus 4 percent interest compounded quarterly; that the cheque will be mailed to her home address two to three weeks after her last day on the job; and that the money will be taxable as income
- To build goodwill so that she feels that she has been treated fairly and consistently; to minimize negative feelings she may have
- To close the door on this subject

A   Who is your **audience**? How do the members of your audience differ from each other? What audience characteristics are relevant to this particular message?

The audience is Michelle Jagtiani. Unless she's a personal friend, you probably wouldn't know why she's leaving and where she's going.

There's a lot you don't know. She may or may not know much about taxes; she may or may not be able to take advantage of tax-reduction strategies. You can't assume the answers, because you wouldn't have them in real life.

I   What **information** must your message include?

Your message must tell Michelle when the cheque will arrive; the facts that the cheque will be based on her contributions, not her employer's, and that the money will be taxable income; how lump-sum retirement benefits are calculated; and the fact that you have her current address on file but need a new address if she's moving.

B   What reasons or reader **benefits** can you use to support your position?

Stating the amount currently in her account might make Michelle feel that she is getting a significant sum of money. Suggesting someone who can give free tax advice (if the company offers this as a fringe benefit) reminds her of the benefits of working with the company. Wishing her luck with her new job is a nice touch.

O   What **objections** can you expect your readers to have? What negative elements of your message must you deemphasize or overcome?

Michelle is getting about half the amount she expected, since she won't receive any matching funds.

She might have been able to earn more than 4 percent interest if she had invested the money herself. Depending on her personal tax situation, she may pay more tax on the money as a lump sum than would have been due had she paid it each year as she earned the money.

C   How will the **context** affect the reader's response? Think about your relationship to the reader, the morale in the organization, the economy, the time of year, and any special circumstances.

The stock market has not been doing well; 4 percent interest is looking good.

Discussion of the Sample Solutions

The solution in Figure 12.6 is not acceptable. The subject line gives a negative with no reason or alternative. The first sentence has a condescending tone that is particularly offensive in negative messages. The last sentence focuses on what is being taken away rather than what remains. Paragraph 2 lacks you-attitude and is vague. The memo ends with a negative. There is nothing anywhere in the memo to build goodwill.

The solution in Figure 12.7, in contrast, is very good. The policy serves as a buffer and explanation. The negative is stated clearly but is buried in the paragraph to avoid overemphasizing it. The paragraph ends on a positive note by specifying the amount in the account and the fact that the sum might be even higher.

Paragraph 3 contains the additional negative information that the amount will be taxable, but offers the alternative that it might be possible to reduce taxes. The writer builds goodwill by suggesting a specific person the reader might contact.

Paragraph 4 tells the reader what address is in the company files (Michelle might not know whether the files are up to date), asks that she update it if necessary, and ends with the reader's concern: getting her cheque promptly.

FIGURE 12.6 **An Unacceptable Solution to the Sample Problem**

Give reason before refusal.

This is lifted straight from the problem. The language in problems is often negative and stuffy; information is disorganized.

Think about the situation and use your own words to create a satisfactory message.

April 20, 2009

To: Michelle Jagtiani

From: Lisa Niaz *LN*

Subject: Denial of Matching Funds ————————————— Negative!

You cannot receive a cheque the last day of work and you will get only your own contributions, not a matching sum from the company, because you have not worked for the company for at least five full years.

Better to be specific.

Your payments and interest come to just over $17 200; the amount could be higher depending on the amount of your last paycheque, which will include compensation for any unused vacation days and sick leave. Furthermore, since the amounts deducted were not considered taxable income, you will have to pay income tax on the money you receive.

How will reader know what you have on file? Better to give current address as you have it.

The cheque will be sent to your home address. If the address we have on file is incorrect, please correct it so that your cheque is not delayed.

Negative

FIGURE 12.7 **A Good Solution to the Sample Problem**

April 20, 2009

To: Michelle Jagtiani

From: Lisa Niaz *LN*

Subject: Receiving Employee Contributions from Retirement Accounts ————— Neutral

Good to state reason in third person to deemphasize negative.

Employees who leave the company with at least five full years of employment are entitled both to the company contributions and to the retirement benefit paycheque deductions contributed to retirement accounts. Those employees who leave the company with fewer than five years of employment will receive the employee paycheque contributions made to their retirement accounts.

Good to be specific.

You now have $17 240.62 in your account, which includes 4% interest compounded quarterly. The amount you receive could be even higher since you will also receive payment for any unused sick leave and vacation days.

Good to show how company can help.

Because you now have access to the account, the amount you receive will be considered taxable income. Beth Jordan in Employee Financial Services can give you information about possible tax deductions and financial investments that can reduce your income taxes.

Good to be specific.

The cheque will be sent to your home address on May 16. The address we have on file is 2724 Merriman Road, Kingston, ON K7L 3N7. If your address changes, please let us know so you can receive your cheque promptly.

Positive

Forward-looking

Good luck with your new job!

The final paragraph ends on a positive note. This generalized goodwill is appropriate when the writer does not know the reader well.

FIGURE 12.8   **Checklist for Negative Messages**

❏ Is the subject line appropriate?
❏ If a buffer is used, does it invite a neutral or affirmative response?
❏ Is the reason presented before the refusal? Is the reason clear and relevant to the reader?
❏ Is the negative information clear and concise?
❏ Is an alternative given, if a good one is available? Does the message provide all the information needed to act on the alternative, but leave the choice up to the reader?
❏ Is the last paragraph forward-looking?
❏ Is the tone appropriate—positive, confident, and respectful?

Checklist for All Effective Messages

❏ Does the message use you-attitude and positive emphasis?
❏ Is the style easy to read and friendly?
❏ Is the visual design of the message inviting?
❏ Is the format correct?
❏ Does the message use standard grammar? Is it free from typos?

Add Originality in a Negative Message

❏ Use an effective buffer, if one is appropriate.
❏ Include a clear, complete statement of the reason for the refusal.
❏ Offer a good, clear alternative showing that you're thinking about what the reader really needs.
❏ Add details that show you're thinking about a specific organization and the specific people in that organization.

MODULE SUMMARY

- Organize negative messages in this way:
  1. Begin with a buffer or neutral statement when possible.
  2. Explain the refusal.
  3. Give the negative once, clearly.
  4. End with a positive, forward-looking statement.
- Use a buffer when the reader values harmony, or when the buffer serves a purpose in addition to simply delaying the negative.
- Organize negative messages to superiors this way:
  ○ Describe the problem.
  ○ Explain how it happened.
  ○ Describe options for fixing it.
  ○ Recommend a solution, and ask for action.
- When giving bad news to peers or subordinates,
  ○ Describe the problem.

  ○ Present an alternative or compromise, if one is available.
  ○ If possible, ask for input.
- Make sure your reason for refusing is valid. Omit the reason if it is weak, or makes your organization look bad.
- Giving an alternative or compromise
  ○ Offers the audience another way of getting what they want
  ○ Suggests you care about the audience and helping to meet their needs
  ○ Enables the reader to reestablish the psychological freedom limited when you said no
  ○ Lets you end on a positive note, and to present your organization and you as positive, friendly and helpful
- Use PAIBOC analysis and Maslow's hierarchy to analyze how best to compose negative messages that meet your purposes and your audience's needs.

ASSIGNMENTS FOR MODULE 12

Questions for Critical Thinking

12.1 How do specific varieties of negative messages adapt the basic pattern?

12.2 How do you use positive emphasis in a negative message?

12.3 How do you decide whether to give the negative directly or to buffer it?

Exercises and Problems

12.4 Rejecting Employees' Suggestions

For years, businesses have had suggestion programs, rewarding employees for money-saving ideas. Now your city government has adopted such a program, but not all the suggestions are adopted. Today, you need to send messages to the following people. Because their suggestions are being rejected, they will not get any cash award.

1. *Diane Hilgers, secretary, Mayor's office.* Suggestion: Charge for 911 calls. Reason for rejection: "This would be a public relations disaster. People call because they have emergencies. We already charge for ambulance or paramedic trips; to charge just for the call will offend people. And it might not save money. It's a lot cheaper to prevent a burglary or murder than to track down the person afterward—to say nothing of the trauma of the loss or death. Bad idea."

2. *Steve Rieneke, building and grounds supervisor.* Suggestion: Fire the city's public relations specialists. Reason for rejection: "Positive attitudes toward city workers and policies make the public more willing to support public programs and taxes. In the long run, we think this is money well spent."

3. *Jose Rivera, Accountant I.* Suggestion: Schedule city council meetings during the day to save on light bills and staff overtime. Reason for rejection: "Having the meetings in the evening enables more citizens to attend. People have to be able to comment. Open meetings are essential so that citizens don't feel that policies and taxes are being railroaded through." Write the messages.

12.5 Telling the Boss About a Problem

In any organization, things sometimes go wrong. Tell your supervisor about a problem in your unit and recommend what should be done.

As your instructor directs,

a. Prepare notes for a meeting with your supervisor.

b. Write an email to your supervisor.

c. Give an oral presentation on the problem.

d. Write an email to your instructor explaining the problem, the corporate culture, and the reasons for your solution.

12.6 Telling Customers That Prices Are Going Up

Periodically, organizations raise prices or impose separate fees for services that were previously free. Think of an increase in the prices your customers pay.

As your instructor directs,

a. Write an email to customers, telling them about the new fees or higher prices.

b. Examine your organization's files for messages sent out the last time prices were raised. Are the messages effective? Why or why not? Include copies of the messages with your analysis of them.

12.7 Refusing a Gift

As the head of a charitable organization, you spend a lot of your time asking for money. But today, you're turning down a gift: a timeshare condominium in Florida. Timeshares are so difficult to sell that regular real-estate agents do not list them. Places that list timeshares frequently charge an upfront fee (not just a commission, which is paid if and when the unit sells). If you accepted the gift, your organization would have to pay maintenance fees charged by the homeowners' association and taxes until the unit sold (if it sold). And you'd probably have to hire someone to check on the property occasionally, since the maintenance fee covers general building maintenance, not repairs for a specific unit. You don't want the expense and hassle of something that might not ever yield funds for your organization, so you're going to refuse the gift.

Write a letter to the would-be donors, Benjamin and Sarah Mellon, refusing the gift.

As your instructor directs,

Write letters for one or more of the following situations.

a. Yours is a well-known national charity. You have never met the Mellons, but your records show that they have given small gifts (under $100) in three of the last five years.

b. Yours is a local religious organization; the Mellons are prominent members. They don't give much money, but they're active and faithful.

c. Yours is a local charitable organization that struggles to stay open. The Mellons are major contributors. Sarah Mellon served on your board of directors, in a term ending three years ago.

d. Yours is a national charity. No one in the office has ever heard of the Mellons. They haven't contributed in the last three years—your records don't go back further.

Hints:

- Choose a charitable organization you know something about.
- Give the real reason for the refusal. You would accept real estate that seemed easy to sell.
- In situations (a) to (c) above, thank the Mellons for their past support. Be specific about what they've done.
- Use a salutation and complimentary close that are appropriate to the situation.
- In all the situations, encourage the donor to give other (more liquid) gifts to you in the future. Tell about upcoming opportunities for giving.

12.8 Refusing to Participate on a Panel

As a prominent speaker, you get many requests to appear before various groups. Today, you've received a request to participate in a panel of three to five professionals who will talk about "Succeeding in the Real World." The session will run from 2 to 5 P.M. on the second Sunday of next month.

You're trying to cut back on outside commitments. Work continues to take much of your time; you have major obligations in a volunteer organization; and you want some time for yourself and your family. This request does not fit your priorities. Decline the invitation.

As your instructor directs,

Assume that the request is from one of the following:

a. A university business honour society that expects 250 students at the session

b. The youth group at the church, synagogue, temple, or mosque you attend

c. The Chinese Student Association at the local college or university

12.9 Announcing Cost-Saving Measures

Your company has to cut costs but would prefer to avoid laying off workers. Therefore, you have adopted the following money-saving ideas. Some can be implemented immediately; some will be implemented at renewal dates. The company will no longer pay for

- Flowers at the receptionist's desk and in executive offices
- Skyboxes for professional sporting events
- Employees' dues for professional and trade organizations
- Liquor at business meals

Only essential business travel will be approved. The company will pay only for the lowest cost of air travel (coach, reservation 7 to 14 days in advance, stay over Saturday night).

The company will no longer buy tables or blocks of tickets for charitable events and will not make any cash donations to charity until money is less tight.

Counters will be put on the photocopiers. People have to have access numbers to make photocopies; personal photocopies will cost $0.10 a page.

As the chief financial officer, write an email to all employees, explaining the changes.

12.10 Closing Bill-Payment Offices

For many years, Chilliwack Public Utilities Commission had five office locations where people could take their payments. On the first of the month following next month, you're closing these offices. On that date, 100 local merchants, such as grocers, will begin to accept utility payments. Closing the freestanding offices will save your municipality almost $1 million a year. Customers will still be able to mail in payments or have them deducted automatically from their bank accounts.

Write a notice that can be inserted in utility bills this month and next month.

12.11 Giving a Customer Less Credit Than She Wants

Yang-Ming Lee applied for your VISA card, asking for a credit limit of $15 000 and a separate card for her husband, Chad Hoang. You've checked the credit references, and they're good enough to merit granting a credit card. But you generally give new customers only a $7 500 limit, even when the family income is very high, as it is in this case. You might make an exception if your bank had a previous relationship with the client, but no such relationship exists here. Although you have no set policy for reviewing and raising credit limits, normally you would expect at least six months of paying the minimum amount promptly.

Write a letter to Ms. Lee, granting her a credit card with a $7 500 limit.

12.12 Rejecting a Member's Request

All non-supervisory public service workers in your province are union members. As a paid staff person for the union, you spend about a third of your time writing and editing the monthly magazine, *Public [Your Province] Employee*. You receive this letter:

Dear Editor:

Every month, we get two copies of the union magazine—one addressed to me, one to my husband. We have different last names, so your computer might not realize that we're connected, but we are, and we don't need two copies. Sending just one will save printing and postage costs and reduce environmental waste. My name is Dorothy Livingston; my husband is Eric Beamer. Please combine our listings to send just one copy.

Sincerely,

Dorothy Livingston

As it happens, a couple of years ago you investigated possible savings of sending just one mailing to couples who both work for the province. Sophisticated computerized merge/purge programs to eliminate duplicates are far too expensive for the union's tight budget. And going through the mailing list manually to locate and change duplications would cost more than would be saved in postage. Printing costs wouldn't necessarily drop either, since it actually costs less for each copy to print big runs. But you want to build goodwill—both with this writer and for the union in general. Extra copies of the magazine (whether a double mailing or simply a copy someone is finished with) might be given to a nonmember, or taken to a doctor's or dentist's waiting room or a barber or beauty shop. Such sharing would help spread public support for the union and provincial government workers.

Write an email to Ms. Livingston, explaining why you can't combine mailings.

POLISHING YOUR PROSE

Finding Your Narrative Voice

Narrative voice refers to the "personality" of the writer. Words, phrases, expressions, and tone convey narrative voice. Just as fiction and composition do, business communication uses narrative voice. The "voice" in memos, letters, and reports can be friendly, assertive, bureaucratic, threatening, or confident, to name just a few possibilities. You'll get the results you want, however, if you *speak* to your reader the way you would want to be spoken to.

Consider the following email message from a student to his instructor: If you were the instructor, how persuasive would you judge this memo?

To: Kathryn

From: Dave

Subject: report

i am sending my final report. i cant remember when its do but here it is.iknow ive missed alot of classes but i have to work. im going to keep on sending this message until you tell me you got it. Whats my final grade.

Narrative voice is as individual as personality. However, we have control over narrative voice, because we can choose the language we use to make meaning. Knowing your own voice can help you to understand the "personality" it demonstrates.

Exercises

How would you characterize the narrative voice in each of the following messages? Which voices appeal to you as appropriate for business communication? How could you communicate the same message in a more appropriate voice?

1. Employees will clock in at their designated hour. Employees will follow their assigned schedules to the letter. There will be NO EXCEPTION to these rules.

2. Hi, Mr. Mills! Just stop in to pick up your order when you get a chance. Give us a ring if you want delivery. Thanks!

3. Attention *Balance and Wellness Magazine* Subscriber:

    Thank you for your interest in our magazine. I hope you have enjoyed your two free issues. As you can read in November's Letters to the Editor, subscribers have responded enthusiastically to October's article on the health benefits of keeping a journal.

    Perhaps you have already sent your annual subscription fee of $29.98 (plus 5% GST). If so, please accept my thanks. If not, please take a few minutes to enclose your cheque in the postage-paid envelope, to enjoy a whole year of healthful reading.

    Sincerely,

    Joe Malone, Editor-in-chief

4. Please find enclosed my résumé, which speaks to my superlative and most relevant qualities as candidate for the advertised position of account executive with your illustrious organization.

5. Dear Homeowner,

    It has been brought to our attention that your hydro meter is obstructed by dense shrubbery. This makes it difficult for our technician to read your hydro meter, and represents a potential safety hazard.

    We would ask that you cut back or remove the obstructing shrubbery to allow ease of access.

6. Dear Client,

    I am now spending up to four hours a day responding to emails, telephone calls, faxes, tax assessments, etc. As I'm sure you can appreciate, this correspondence contributes to an already overly long day. Please be advised, therefore, that effective immediately, your annual accounting fee will include a correspondence fee of $ 150.00 plus GST every six months ($25.00 per month).

    Alternatively, I can measure actual time spent and bill accordingly (expensive & time-consuming)

    I enclose a self-addressed envelope.

    Sincerely,

    George Estrada, CA

7. Pertaining to the party of the first part, hereafter called "party first," and excepting any and all objections from the party of the second part, hereafter called "party second," this amendment shall be considered null and void with proper written notice three (3) days prior to the execution of the original agreement.

8. Congratulations on your recent promotion to district manager, Rita. All of us in accounting look forward to working with you.

9. Martina,

    I've spent at least three hours looking for the invoice, which is a complete waste of my time. Where would you suggest I look NOW??!!

10. In the event of catastrophic LAN failure, users will
    1. Perform SYS/MD-3 shutdown for affected systems.
    2. Engage standard recovery matrix (SRM), per #4105.1 in SYS/MD Manual (2000: H3-H12).

3. Record time and date, RE: LAN Failure, in compliance log, cc. MEISNER.

4. Notify Data Services at ext. 5547, ATTN: J.J. MEISNER.

11. Nope. This idea won't work. It's not very good. I'm not sure the project is even worth our time anymore.

I'm definitely not interested in having a meeting to discuss it. Don't call me unless you guys have something better.

Check your answers to the odd-numbered exercises on page 552.

Composing Persuasive Messages

Learning Objectives

After reading and applying the information in Module 13, you'll be able to demonstrate

Knowledge of

- Persuasive appeals
- Persuasive patterns of organization

Skills to

- Choose and use persuasive strategies
- Organize persuasive messages
- Identify and overcome objections
- Write common kinds of persuasive messages
- Write effective subject lines for persuasive messages
- Further analyze business communication situations

Employability Skills 2000+ Checklist

In this module, the key skills from the Conference Board of Canada's Employability Skills 2000+ are

Communicate

○ share information using a range of information and communications technologies (e.g., voice, email, computers)

○ write and speak so others pay attention and understand

○ use relevant scientific, technological, and mathematical knowledge and skills to explain or clarify ideas

Manage Information

○ locate, gather, and organize information using appropriate technology and information systems

Think & Solve Problems

○ recognize the human, interpersonal, technical, scientific, and mathematical dimensions of a problem

○ readily use science, technology, and mathematics as ways to think, gain and share knowledge, solve problems, and make decisions

Be Responsible

○ set goals and priorities, balancing work and personal life

○ plan and manage time, money, and other resources to achieve goals

Be Adaptable

○ be innovative and resourceful: identify and suggest alternative ways to achieve goals and get the job done

○ cope with uncertainty

Participate in Projects & Tasks

○ work to agreed quality standards and specifications

○ adapt to changing requirements and information

All successful communication contains a persuasive element. Knowing how to appeal to your audiences will help you to influence them positively.

Businesses depend on persuasion to get quality work done and to build relationships with customers. And people are more readily persuaded by intrinsic benefits, such as superior customer service, than by incentives like lower costs. External motivation doesn't last (Module 8, extrinsic vs. intrinsic benefits). Some people may buy a certain brand of pizza if they have a coupon. But when the coupon expires, or if another company offers the same deal, customers may leave. However, if customers like your pizza better—if they are intrinsically motivated to choose it—then you will keep your customers even if another company comes in with a lower price.

What Are Persuasive Appeals?

People are persuaded by their perceptions of (1) the trustworthiness of the messenger, and (2) the emotional and logical resonances of the message.

Your audience will pay attention to your message if they perceive you to be a trustworthy or credible person; they will act on your message if the facts and the way you present those facts appeal to their deepest values and beliefs. And people are more easily persuaded by what they perceive as familiar. Maple Leaf Foods used all these elements of persuasion to restore public trust during the Listeria crisis. The company used high-profile executives in a media blitz to apologise, announce product recalls, and explain next steps. The result was renewed public confidence.[1]

Persuasive messages have several purposes.

Primary purposes

- To have the reader act
- To provide enough information so that the reader knows exactly what to do
- To overcome any objections that might prevent or delay action

Secondary purposes

- To establish a good impression of the writer
- To build a good image of the writer's organization
- To build a good relationship between the writer and reader
- To reduce or eliminate future correspondence on the same subject

Persuasive messages include the following:

- Orders and requests
- Proposals and recommendations
- Sales and fundraising letters
- Job application letters
- Reports, if they recommend action
- Efforts to change people's behaviour, such as collection letters, criticisms or performance appraisals where you want the subordinate to improve behaviour, and public service ads designed to reduce drunk driving, drug use, and so on.

What Is the Best Persuasive Strategy?

It depends on how much and what kinds of resistance you expect.

You can use any of four persuasive strategies: direct request, problem-solving persuasion, sales,[2] and reward and punishment. This book will focus on the first two strategies. Rewards and punishment have limited use, in part because they don't produce permanent change and because they produce psychological reactance (Module 12). To effect a major change, no single message will work, as antismoking lobbyists are well aware. To change attitudes and behaviours, you will need a campaign like Maple Foods', with a series of messages, from a variety of sources.

Making a positive first impression is the most important persuasive technique of all. First impressions establish credibility. When you write, your audience's first impression comes from your choice of medium, document layout, organizational pattern, and readability (clarity, conciseness, correctness). Your organizational pattern is part of your message's persuasive element, because specific patterns meet the audience's expectations, and are, therefore, logically and emotionally appealing.

Use the direct (deductive or good news) request pattern (Module 11) in these situations:

- The audience will do as you ask without any resistance.
- You need a response only from the people who are willing to act.
- The audience is busy and may not read all the messages received.
- Your organization's culture prefers direct requests.

Use the indirect (problem-solving, inductive, bad news) pattern (Module 12) in the following cases:

- The audience is likely to object to doing as you ask.
- You need action from everyone.
- You trust the audience to read the entire message.

To choose the best persuasive content, analyze your audience. The most persuasive argument is the one that best meets your audience's needs (Module 8, Maslow's Hierarchy of Needs). Your message strategy must also conform to the values and norms of your corporate culture. A persuasive strategy that works in one organization may be unacceptable elsewhere.

You can learn the corporate culture (Module 2), through observing and imitating. Observe the style of powerful people in your organization: When you show a draft to your boss, are you told to tone down your statements or to make them stronger? Role models and advice are two ways organizations communicate their cultures to newcomers.

Different ethnic and national cultures also have different preferences for gaining compliance. Canada's international reputation as a welcoming nation of courteous peacekeepers is reflected in English Canadians' cultural preference for indirect requests, even though Canada is a low-context culture (Module 3). Canadian newcomers emigrating from Southeast Asia, India, Pakistan, and the Philippines also communicate using indirect requests: high-context cultures see direct requests as rude and aggressive.

Employability Skills

How Should I Organize Persuasive Messages?

In direct requests, start with the request. In a problem-solving message, start with the problem you share.

Start with the request only when you anticipate ready agreement, when you fear that a busy reader may not read a message whose relevance isn't clear, or when your organization's culture prefers direct requests.

Writing Direct Requests

When you expect quick agreement, save the reader's time by presenting the request directly.

1. *Consider asking immediately for the information or service you want.* Delay the request if it seems too abrupt or if you have several purposes in the message.
2. *Give readers all the information and details they will need to act on your request.* Number your questions or set them off with bullets so the reader can check to see that all of them have been answered.

   In a claim (in which a product is under warranty or a shipment was defective), explain the circumstances so that the reader knows what happened. Be sure to include all the relevant details: date of purchase, model or invoice number, and so on.

   In more complicated direct requests, anticipate possible responses. Suppose you're asking for information about equipment meeting certain specifications. Explain which

FIGURE 13.1   **A Direct Request**

Request topic in subject line —

Appeals to recognition, esteem needs

Request in para. 1

Specifics/ explanation

Ask for action; make action easy

> Suggestion # 97204
>
> File   Edit   View   Insert   Format   Tools   Message   Help
>
> Send   Cut   Copy   Paste   Undo   Check   Spelling   Attach   Priority   Sign   Encrypt   Offline
>
> To: mantonucci@bcs.com
> Cc:
> Bcc:
> Subject: Suggestion # 97204
>
> Arial   8
>
> Good morning, Michael,
>
> Please evaluate the attached suggestion by May 29.
>
> • Should BCS adopt it? Why or why not?
> • Will the company save money? If so, how much annually?
> • If we adopt the suggestion, what kind of award should we give?
>
> Please send your responses and brief reasons to me by May 29 for the committee meeting May 30.
>
> Thanks!
>
> start   Outlook Exp…   Seggestion….   11:34 AM

criteria are most important so that the reader can recommend an alternative if no single product meets all your needs. You may also want to tell the reader what your price constraints are and ask whether the item is in stock or must be special-ordered.

3. *Ask for the action you want.* Do you want a cheque? a replacement? a catalogue? answers to your questions? If you need an answer by a certain time, say so. If possible, show the reader why the time limit is necessary.

Figure 13.1 illustrates the pattern. Figure 13.2 summarizes this pattern. Note that direct requests do not contain reader benefits and do not need to overcome objections: they simply ask for what is needed.

Direct requests should be direct. Don't make the reader guess what you want.

| **Indirect request:** | Is there a newer version of the 2009 *Accounting Reference Manual*? |
| **Direct request:** | If there is a newer version of the 2009 *Accounting Reference Manual*, please send it to me. |

FIGURE 13.2   **How to Organize a Direct Request**

Request for Action

Details

Request for Action

In some direct requests, your combination of purposes may suggest a different pattern. For example, in a letter asking a prospective employer to reimburse you for expenses after a job interview, you'd want to thank your hosts for their hospitality and reinforce the good impression you made at the interview. To do that, you'd spend the first two paragraphs talking about the trip and the interview. Only in the last third of the letter (or even in the postscript) would you make your request for reimbursement.

Similarly, in a letter asking about a graduate program, a major purpose might be to build a good image of yourself so that your application for financial aid will be viewed positively. To achieve that goal, you would provide information about your qualifications and interest in the field before you ask questions.

Organizing Problem-Solving Messages

Use an indirect (inductive or bad news) approach and the problem-solving pattern or organization when you expect resistance from the reader, but you can show that doing what you suggest will solve the problem. This pattern allows you to anticipate and overcome objections by showing all the reasons in favour of your position before you give your readers a chance to say no.

1. *Mention the problem you share (which your request will solve).* Because you're interested in solving the problem, mention the problem objectively: it's a waste of time and ink to assign blame or mention personalities.
2. *Detail the results of the problem as they affect your reader.* Be specific about the cost in money, time, lost goodwill, inconvenience, and so on. Persuade your readers that *something* has to be done before you convince them that your solution is the best one.
3. *Explain the solution to the problem.* If you know that the reader will favour another solution, start with that solution and show why it won't work before you present your solution. Present your solution, focusing on practicality, workability, and desirability without using the words *I* or *my*. Appeal to the reader's wallet or sense of enlightened self-interest.
4. *Prove that any negative elements (cost, time, concerns, disruptions) are outweighed by the advantages.*
5. *Summarize any additional benefits of the solution.* You can present the main benefit—solving the problem—briefly, since you have described the problem in detail. However, if there are any additional benefits, mention them.
6. *Ask for the action you want.* Often your reader will authorize or approve something; other people will implement the action. Give your reader a reason to act promptly, perhaps offering a new reader benefit. ("By buying now, we can avoid the next quarter's price hikes.")

Figure 13.3 summarizes the pattern. Figure 13.4 uses the pattern. Reader benefits can be brief in this kind of message, since the biggest benefit comes from solving the problem.

How Do I Identify and Overcome Objections?

Know your audience. Talk to your audience. Then try these strategies.

The easiest way to learn about objections your audience may have is to ask knowledgeable people in your network, or organization.

FIGURE 13.3   How to Organize a Problem-Solving Persuasive Message

Shared Problem

Details

Solution

Negatives

Reader Benefits

Request for Action

FIGURE 13.4   **A Problem-Solving Persuasive Message**

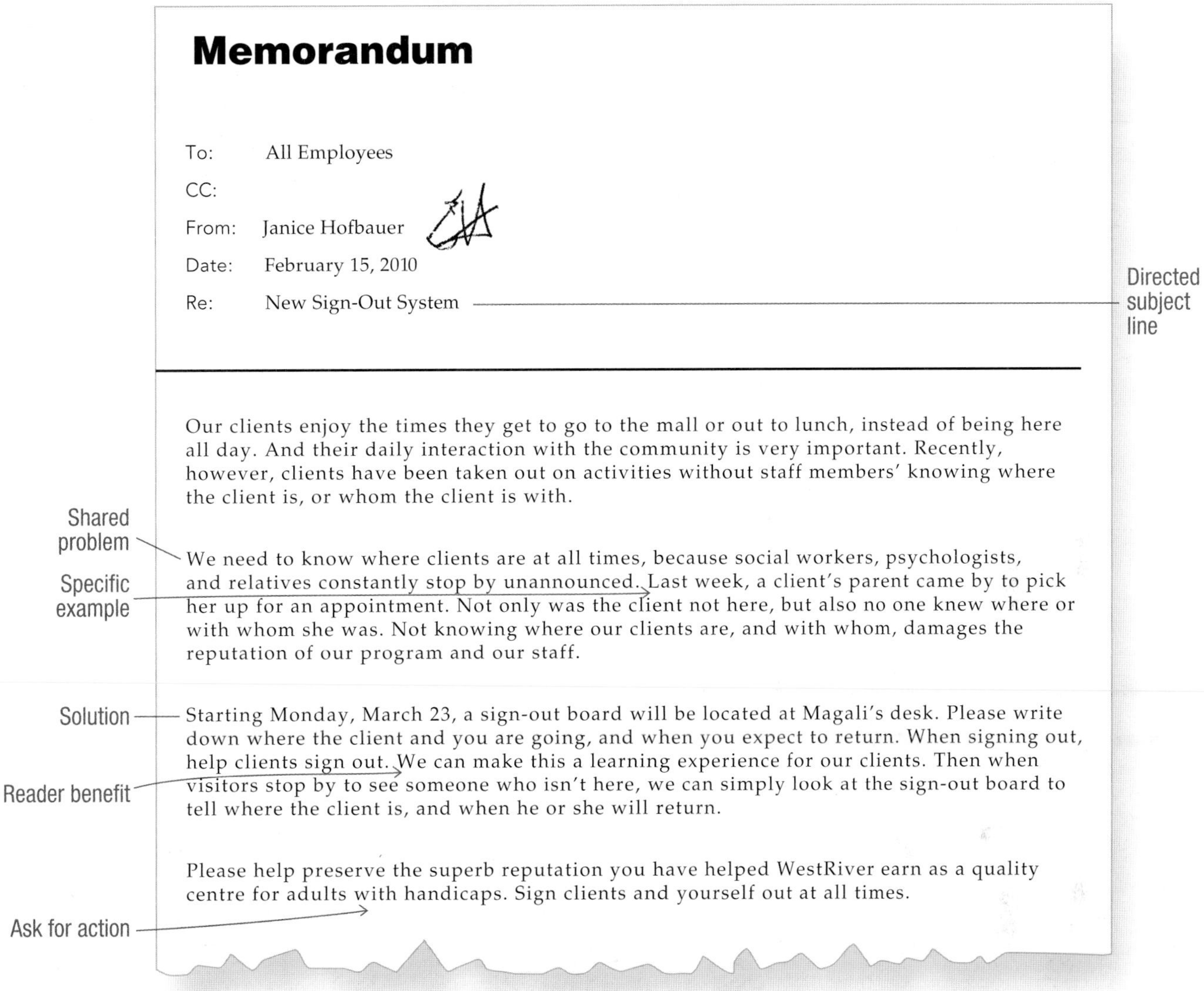

Memorandum

To: All Employees

CC:

From: Janice Hofbauer

Date: February 15, 2010

Re: New Sign-Out System ———————————————————— Directed subject line

Our clients enjoy the times they get to go to the mall or out to lunch, instead of being here all day. And their daily interaction with the community is very important. Recently, however, clients have been taken out on activities without staff members' knowing where the client is, or whom the client is with.

Shared problem

We need to know where clients are at all times, because social workers, psychologists, and relatives constantly stop by unannounced. Last week, a client's parent came by to pick her up for an appointment. Not only was the client not here, but also no one knew where or with whom she was. Not knowing where our clients are, and with whom, damages the reputation of our program and our staff.

Specific example

Solution — Starting Monday, March 23, a sign-out board will be located at Magali's desk. Please write down where the client and you are going, and when you expect to return. When signing out, help clients sign out. We can make this a learning experience for our clients. Then when visitors stop by to see someone who isn't here, we can simply look at the sign-out board to tell where the client is, and when he or she will return.

Reader benefit

Please help preserve the superb reputation you have helped WestRiver earn as a quality centre for adults with handicaps. Sign clients and yourself out at all times.

Ask for action

- *Use open questions and phrase your questions neutrally*, so that people feel encouraged to express their opinions openly: "What concerns would you have about a proposal to do X?" "Who makes a decision about Y?" "What do you like best about [the supplier or practice you want to change]?"
- *Ask follow-up questions* to be sure you understand: "Would you be likely to stay with your current supplier if you could get a lower price from someone else? Why?"

People are most aware of and willing to share objective constraints such as time and money. We are all less willing to acknowledge emotional anxieties. We have a **vested interest** in something when we benefit directly from keeping things as they are.

For example, during his summer job, an engineering student saw how his company's waste treatment system could be redesigned to save the company more than $200 000 a year. He wrote a report recommending the change and gave it to his boss. Nothing happened. Why not? His supervisor wasn't about to send up a report that would require him to explain why *he'd* been wasting more than $200 000 a year of the company's money.[3] The supervisor's low-level security needs took precedence over such high-level needs as esteem, recognition, and self-actualization (Module 8). His emotional investment in retaining the old system overrode any logical considerations.

To avoid situations such as these, you need to probe to find out the real reasons for your audience's objections.

The best way to deal with an objection is to eliminate it. To sell Jeep Cherokees in Japan, Mitsuru Sato convinced Chrysler to put the driver's seat on the right side, to make an extra pre-shipment quality check, and to rewrite the instruction booklet in Japanese style, with big diagrams and cartoons.[4]

If an objection is false, based on misinformation, give the response to the objection without naming the objection. In a brochure, you can present responses in a "question/answer" format. When objections have already been voiced, you might want to name the objection so your audience realizes you are responding to that specific objection. However, to avoid solidifying the opposition, don't attribute the objection to your audience. Instead, use a less personal attribution and neutral language: "Some people wonder ..."; "Some clients are concerned that ..."

If real objections remain, try one or more of the following strategies to counter objections:

1. Specify how much time or money is required—it may not be as much as the reader fears.

    > Distributing flyers to each house or apartment in your neighbourhood will probably take two afternoons.

2. Put the time or money in the context of the benefits they bring.

    > The additional $152 500 will (1) allow the Open Shelter to remain open 24 rather than 16 hours a day, (2) pay for three social workers to help men find work and homes, and (3) keep the neighbourhood bank open, so that men don't have to cash welfare cheques in bars, and so that they can save the $800 they need to have up front to rent an apartment.

3. Show that money spent now will save money in the long run.

    > By replacing the boiler now, we'll no longer have to release steam that the overflow tank can't hold. Depending on how severe the winter is, we will save $100 to $750 a year in energy costs. If energy costs rise, we'll save even more.

4. Show that doing as you ask will benefit a group or a cause the reader supports, although the action may not help the reader directly.

    > By being a Big Brother or a Big Sister, you'll give a child the attention he or she needs to become a well-adjusted, productive adult.

5. Show the reader that the sacrifice is necessary to achieve a larger, more important goal to which he or she is committed.

    > These changes will mean more work for all of us. But we've got to cut our costs 25 percent to keep the plant open and to keep our jobs.

Toyota responded to North American brand loyalty by customizing its automotive products, promotions, and services to the Canadian market. Besides the products developed specifically for Canadian winters, the company's Canadian investments include financial support for local community organizations and Canada's Special Olympics, and partnerships with the Evergreen Learning Grounds Program and community colleges' technical training programs.

6. Show that the advantages as a group outnumber or outweigh the disadvantages as a group.

> None of the locations is perfect. But the Quebec City location gives us the most advantages and the fewest disadvantages.

7. Turn a disadvantage into an opportunity.

> With the hiring freeze, every department will need more lead time to complete its own work. By hiring a freelance worker, the Planning Department could provide that lead time.

What Other Techniques Make My Messages More Persuasive?

Build credibility and emotional appeal. Use the right tone, and offer a reason to act promptly.

Persuasive messages—whether short-term or long-term—will be more effective if you build credibility and emotional appeal, use the right tone, and offer a reason to act promptly.

Build Credibility

Credibility is the audience's response to the source of the message. People are more easily persuaded by someone they see as expert, powerful, attractive, or trustworthy. We are also more easily persuaded by people whom we perceive to be like us (similar in class, values, and age) and by those who are articulate, confident, and likeable.

Build Rational Appeal

When you don't yet have the credibility that comes from being an expert or being powerful, build credibility by the language and strategy you use:

- *Be factual.* Use concrete language, supportive statistics, and exact dollar or time requirements. Don't exaggerate.
- *Be specific.* If you say "X is better," detail how it is better. Show the reader exactly where the savings or other benefits come from so that it's clear that the proposal really is as good as you say it is.
- *Be reliable.* If you suspect that a project will take longer to complete, cost more money, or be less effective than you originally thought, tell your audience *immediately*. Negotiate a new schedule that you can meet.

Build Emotional Appeal

Emotional appeal means making the reader want to do what you ask. People make decisions—even business decisions—both logically and emotionally.

Finding common ground with people is one way of building emotional appeal. To find a common ground, you must analyze your audience: understand their biases, needs, and fears. And you must identify with your audience to help them identify with you. Finding this common ground must be based on a respect for, and sensitivity to your audience's position.

People are highly sensitive to manipulative emotional appeals. No matter how much you disagree, you must respect your audience's intelligence to begin to understand why they believe or do something, and why they may object to your position. When you can understand your readers' point of view, you'll be more effective. And you won't alienate your readers by talking down to them.

The best common grounds are specific, and focus on something the reader cares about. Often a problem the reader will want to solve makes a good common ground.

Weak common ground:	We all want this plant to be profitable.
Improved common ground:	We lost about $186,000 profits last summer due to a 17% drop in productivity.

In your common ground, emphasize the parts of your idea that fit with what your audience already believes or knows. An employee of 3M wanted to develop laser disks. He realized that 3M's previous successful products were thin and flat: Scotch Tape, Post-it Notes™, magnetic tape. When he made his presentation to the group that chose new products for development, he held his prototype disk horizontally, so his audience saw a flat, thin object rather than a large, round, record-like object. Making his project fit with the audience's previous experience was a subtle and effective emotional tool to make it easier for the audience to say yes.

Stories and psychological description (Module 8) are also effective ways to build emotional appeal. Research suggests that stories are more persuasive because people remember them.[5] Emotional appeal works best when people want to be persuaded. Even when you need to provide statistics or numbers to convince the careful reader that your anecdote is a representative example, telling a story first makes your message more persuasive. For example, many charities send out letters describing how a person's life has changed as a result of donors' generosity. These stories motivate people to give.

Visuals create stories too. The size, illustrations, layout, and lettering of the design-winning promotional brochure pictured in Figure 13.5 tell a story before you read a word of text.

Use the Right Tone

When you ask for action from people who report directly to you, you have several choices. Although orders ("Get me the Ervin file") and questions ("Do we have the third-quarter numbers yet?") might work, you'll get greater compliance with courtesy. When you need action from co-workers, superiors, or people outside the organization, you may need to be firm but you must always be polite.

Avoiding messages that sound parental or preachy is often a matter of tone. Saying *please* is important, especially to people on your level or outside the organization. Tone works better when you give reasons for your request.

Parental:	Everyone is expected to comply with these regulations. I'm sure you can see that they are common-sense rules needed for our business.
Better:	Even on casual days, visitors expect us to be professional. So please let's leave the gym clothes at home!

When you write to people you know well, humour can work. Just make sure that the message isn't insulting to anyone who doesn't find the humour funny. And remember that humour does not travel well via email (Module 10).

FIGURE 13.5 Marketing Brochure Tells a Story

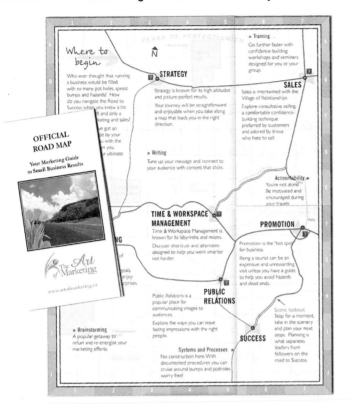

Source: Imagine Creative Communications Inc. © 2008 *The Art of Marketing*.

Writing to superiors is trickier. You may want to tone down your request by using subjunctive verbs and explicit disclaimers that show you aren't taking a yes for granted.

Arrogant: Based on this evidence, I expect you to give me a new computer.

Better: If department funds permit, I would like a new computer.

Passive verbs and jargon sound stuffy. Use active imperatives—perhaps with "Please" to create a friendlier tone.

Stuffy: It is requested that you approve the above-mentioned action.

Better: Please authorize us to create a new subscription letter.

To persuade, be prepared to appeal to emotions as well as to logic.
©1998 Scott Adams/Dist. by United Features Syndicate, Inc.

Offer a Reason for the Reader to Act Promptly

The longer people delay, the less likely they are to carry through with the action they had decided to take. In addition, you want a fast response so you can go ahead with your own plans.

Request action by a specific date. Always give people at least a week or two: they have other things to do besides respond to your requests. Set deadlines in the middle of the month, if possible. If you say, "Please return this by March 1," people will think, "I don't need to do this until March." Ask for the response by February 28 instead. If you can use a response even after the deadline, say so. Otherwise, people who can't make the deadline may not respond at all.

EXPANDING A CRITICAL SKILL

Preparing for a Performance Appraisal

We all give and get performance appraisals every day as we communicate with other people, even complete strangers. Every time you honk your horn, or comment on others' appearance or behaviour, you are assessing their performance. The grade you receive on an assignment; friends' feedback on your style of dress, choice of music, manners: all of these express assessments of you. We incorporate this feedback into our concepts of ourselves.

Most of us respond best to positive appraisals. However, if we cannot get positive responses, we'll even behave badly, just to get feedback: because we are social animals, we crave any kind of attention.

Throughout your years at school, and while you are working, you will get and give performance appraisals. As is true of all meaning exchange, the more you know and use conscious, audience-focused strategies, the more successful your communication will be.

On the job, your performance appraisal can be a persuasive transaction for both you and the savvy supervisor: formative evaluation is a key retention technique. If your organization does not appraise or evaluate your performance at least once a year, ask for this feedback.

Use the occasion to accomplish three goals:

- Identify your boss's specific opinions about your performance.
- Communicate your ambitions.
- Ask for the training and experience you want.

Some supervisors don't know how to talk about subordinates' performance strengths and the skills they need to improve. If your supervisor doesn't specify them, ask,

"What am I doing well?" and "Specifically, what are the two or three things I could do that would most improve my performance?"

In the twenty-first century, most of us will change employers a minimum of seven times. Even supposedly staid accountants will job-hop an average of five times during their careers. "Employers are impressed by people who make strategic career moves at various stages of their careers to improve or broaden their skills," according to Kathryn Bolt, district president of the Canadian division responsible for recruiting and placing accountants at Robert Half International Inc. To remain employable, therefore, you need to add to your current skills and get new experiences (not just keep doing the same old thing). Be ready to name one or two training programs you'd like to take in the next six months. Indicate the kinds of projects you'd like a chance to try.

Let your boss know that you want to contribute even more to the organization; make it clear that you're interested in lateral or vertical moves. Ask, "What kinds of things should I do now so that I'm promotable a year (or two) from now?"

Having frequent discussions about work is a sign that your supervisor sees you as promotable. If your supervisor just asks you yes/no questions, he or she may not think of you as someone who has the ability or desire to advance. Use the performance appraisal to change the way your supervisor sees you and to prepare for the job you really want.

Source: Virginia Galt, "Job-Hopping Now an Accepted Principle," *The Globe and Mail,* May 29, 2001.

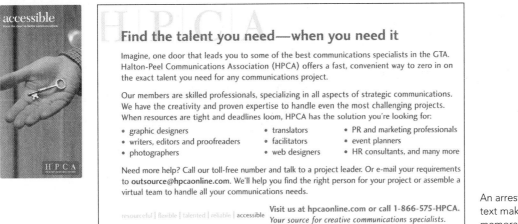

An arresting image and concise text make this marketing postcard memorable.

Show why you need a quick response:

- *Show that the time limit is real.* Perhaps you need information quickly to use it in a report that has a due date. Perhaps a decision must be made by a certain date to catch the start of the school year, the holiday selling season, or an election campaign. Perhaps you need to be ready for a visit from out-of-town or international colleagues.
- *Show that acting now will save time or money.* If business is slow and your industry isn't doing well, then your company needs to act now (to economize, to better serve customers) in order to be competitive. If business is booming and everyone is making a profit, then your company needs to act now to get its fair share of the available profits.
- *Show the cost of delaying action.* Will labour or material costs be higher in the future? Will delay mean more money spent on repairing something that will still need to be replaced?

What Are the Most Common Kinds of Persuasive Messages?

Orders, collection letters, performance appraisals, and letters of recommendation are the most common persuasive messages.

Orders

Orders may be written on forms, phoned in, or made by clicking boxes on the Web. When you write an order, be sure to do three things:

- Be specific. Give model or page numbers, colours, finishes, and so forth.
- Tell the company what you want if that model number is no longer available.
- Double-check your arithmetic, and add sales tax and shipping charges.

Collection Letters

Most businesses find that phoning rather than writing results in faster payment. But as more and more companies install voicemail systems, you may sometimes need to write a collection series of letters when leaving messages doesn't work.

Collection letters ask customers to pay (as they have already agreed to do) for the goods and services they have already received. Good credit departments send a series of letters. Letters

FIGURE 13.6   **An Initial Collection Letter**

Saki's

October 23, 2007

Eva Pavlinic
532 Heath Street East
Toronto, ON M5W 3M1

Card Number: 503 913 248 1 ——————————— Request topic
Balance: $36.28   in subject line.
Payment Required: $33.00

                                                                            Courteous
                                                                            opening saves
                                                                            reader's face.

Dear Eva Pavlinic

Perhaps you missed making your recent payment because the balance on your account is so
small. It is not difficult to do and many of us overlook small balance accounts.

                                                                            Ask for actions.
However, we would appreciate it if you would take a few minutes to mail us your cheque —— Make action
for $33.00.   easy.

If your payment has already been made, thank you. —————————— Positive, friendly
                                                                            close.
Credit Department
Tel: 416-555-4567

in the series should be only a week or two apart. Waiting a month between letters implies that you're prepared to wait a long time—and the reader will be happy to oblige you.

Early letters are gentle, assuming that the reader intends to pay but has met with temporary problems or has forgotten. However, the request should assume that the cheque has been mailed but did not arrive. A student who had not yet been reimbursed by a company for a visit to the company's office put the second request in the P.S. of a letter refusing a job offer:

> P.S. The cheque to cover my expenses when I visited your office in March hasn't come yet. Could you check to see whether you can find a record of it? The amount was $490 (airfare, $290; hotel room, $185; taxi, $15).

If one or two early letters don't result in payment, call the customer to ask whether your company has created a problem. It's possible that you shipped something the customer didn't want or sent the wrong quantity. It's possible that the invoice arrived before the product and was filed and forgotten. It's possible that the invoice document is poorly designed, so customers set it aside until they can figure it out. If any of these situations apply, you'll build goodwill by solving the problem rather than arrogantly asking for payment.[6]

Middle letters are more assertive in asking for payment. Figure 9.2 (page 152) gives an example of a middle letter. Middle letters offer to negotiate a schedule for repayment if the reader is not able to pay the whole bill immediately, remind the reader of the importance of a good credit rating (which will be endangered if the bill remains unpaid), educate the reader about credit, and explain why the creditor must have prompt payment.

Unless you have firm evidence to the contrary, assume that readers have some legitimate reason for not yet paying. Even people who do not have enough money to pay all their bills, or who put payment off as long as possible, will respond more quickly if you do not accuse them. If a reader is offended by your assumption that he or she is dishonest, that anger can become an excuse to continue delaying payment.

Late letters threaten legal action if the bill is not paid. However, the writer cannot threaten legal action unless he or she actually intends to sue. Other regulations also spell out what a writer may and may not do in a late letter.

Many small businesses find that establishing personal relationships with customers is the best way to speed payment.

Performance Appraisals

At regular intervals, supervisors evaluate or appraise the performance of their subordinates. In most organizations, employees have access to their own files; sometimes they have to sign the appraisal to show that they've read it. The supervisor normally meets with the subordinate to discuss the appraisal.

As a subordinate, you should prepare for the appraisal interview by listing your goals and achievements. Where do you want to be in one year? five years? What training and experience do you need to reach your goals? What skills would you like to improve? If you need training, advice, or support from the organization to build on your strengths, the appraisal interview is a good time to ask for these resources.

Appraisals motivate the employee and protect the organization. But these two purposes may conflict. People need praise and reassurance to believe that they're valued and can do better. But the praise that motivates someone to improve can come back to haunt the company if the person does not eventually do acceptable work. An organization is in trouble if it tries to fire someone whose evaluations never mention mistakes.

Avoid labels (*wrong, bad*) and inferences. Instead, cite specific observations that describe behaviour.

Inference:	Sam is an alcoholic.
Vague observation:	Sam calls in sick a lot. Subordinates complain about his behaviour.
Specific observation:	Sam called in sick 12 days in the past two months. After a business lunch with a customer last week, Sam was walking unsteadily. Two of his subordinates have said that they would prefer not to make sales trips with him because they find his behaviour embarrassing.

Sam might be an alcoholic. He might also be having a reaction to a physician-prescribed drug; he might have a mental illness; he might be showing symptoms of a physical illness other than alcoholism. A supervisor who jumps to conclusions creates ill will, closes the door to solving the problem, and may provide grounds for legal action against the organization.

Be specific in an appraisal.

Too vague:	Sue does not manage her time as well as she could.
Specific:	Sue's first three weekly sales reports have been three, two, and four days late, respectively; the last weekly sales report for the month is not yet in.

Without specifics, Sue won't know that her boss objects to late reports. She may think that she is being criticized for spending too much time on sales calls or for not working 80 hours a week. Without specifics, she might change the wrong behaviours in a futile effort to please her boss.

Good managers try not only to identify the specific problems in subordinates' behaviour but also to discover the causes of the problem and to provide resources for change. Does the employee need more training? Perhaps a training course or a mentor will help. Does he or she need to work more effectively? Perhaps this is a communication, time-management, or motivation problem.

Performance appraisals are motivational and therefore useful when they occur frequently and regularly, when managers' behaviours are consistent with organizational values and when employees feel engaged in the process. Persuasive performance appraisals focus on specific attitudes and behaviours relevant to department and company goals. When evaluating others' performances, it's vital to clarify the most important areas and to elicit specific recommendations for improvement from the employee. No one can improve 17 weaknesses at once. Which two should the employee work on this month? Is getting reports in on time more important than increasing sales? Supervisors should explicitly identify these priorities during the appraisal interview.

Identify goals and benchmarks in **specific, measurable, achievable, relevant,** and **timelined** terms. Achieving "considerable progress toward completing" a report could mean anything when the manager thinks that "considerable progress" means 50 or 85 percent of the total work. When the manager and employee articulate and agree on concrete goals, both the employee and the organization benefit.

Letters of Recommendation

In an effort to protect themselves against lawsuits, some companies state only how long they employed someone and the position that person held. Such bare-bones letters have themselves been targets of lawsuits when employers did not reveal relevant negatives. Whatever the legal climate, there may be times when you want to recommend someone for an award or for a job.

Letters of recommendation must be specific. General positives that are not backed up with specific examples and evidence are seen as weak recommendations. Letters of recommendation that focus on minor points also suggest that the person is weak.

Either in the first or the last paragraph, summarize your overall evaluation of the person. To establish your credibility, show early in the letter how well and how long you've known the person, perhaps in the first paragraph. In the middle of the letter, offer specific details about the person's performance. At the end of the letter, indicate whether you would be willing to rehire the person and repeat your overall evaluation. See Figure 9.3 (page 153).

Experts are divided on whether you should include negatives. Some people feel that any negative weakens the letter. Other people feel that presenting but not emphasizing honest negatives makes the letter more convincing.

To help pay his way through UBC, Brian Scudamore persuaded people to pay him to take out the trash. The CEO and founder of 1-800-GOT-JUNK now runs an international franchise worth millions.

What's the Best Subject Line for a Persuasive Message?

For direct requests, use the request, the topic, or a question. For problem-solving messages, use a directed subject line or a reader benefit.

In a direct request, put the request, the topic of the request, or a question in the subject line.

Direct request subject line:	Subject: Request for Updated Software
	My copy of HomeNet does not accept the aliases for Magnus accounts.
Direct request subject line:	Subject: Status of Account #3548-003
	Please send me the following information about account #3548-003.
Direct request subject line:	Subject: Do We Need an Additional Training Session in October?
	The two training sessions scheduled for October will accommodate 40 people. Last month, you said that 57 new staff accountants had been hired. Should we schedule an additional training session in October? Or can the new hires wait until the next regularly scheduled session in February?

When you have a reluctant reader, putting the request in the subject line just gets a quick no before you've had a chance to give all your arguments. One option is to use a directed subject line that makes your stance on the issue clear. In the following examples, the first is the most neutral. The remaining two increasingly reveal the writer's preference.

Directed subject line:	Subject: A Proposal to Change the Formula for Calculating Retirees' Benefits
Directed subject line:	Subject: Arguments for Expanding the Bramalea Plant
Directed subject line:	Subject: Why Cassano's Should Close Its West-Side Store

Another option is to use common ground (page 238) or a reader benefit—something that shows readers that this message will help them.

Reader benefit subject line:	Subject: Reducing Energy Costs in the Office
	Energy costs in our office have risen 12 percent in the past three years, although the cost of gas has risen only 8 percent and the cost of electricity has risen only 5 percent.

Although your first paragraph may be negative in a problem-solving message, your subject line should be neutral or positive, to show that you are solving a problem, not just reporting one.

Both directed subject lines and benefit subject lines can also be used as report titles.

How Can PAIBOC Help Me Write Persuasive Messages?

The PAIBOC questions help you examine the points your message should include.

Before you tackle the assignments for this module, examine the following problem. As in Modules 11 and 12, the PAIBOC questions probe the basic points required for a solution. Study the two sample solutions to see what makes one unacceptable and the other one good.[7] The checklists in Figures 13.9 and 13.10 can help you evaluate your draft.

Problem

In one room in the production department of Golden Electronics Company, employees work on computer monitors in conditions that are scarcely bearable because of the heat. Even when the temperature outside is only 23°C, it is more than 30°C in the monitor room. In June, July, and August, 24 out of 36 workers quit because they couldn't stand the heat. This turnover happens every summer.

In a far corner of the room sits a quality control inspector in front of a small fan (the only one in the room). The production workers, in contrast, are carrying 10 kilogram monitors. As production supervisor, you tried to get air conditioning two years ago, before Golden acquired the company, but management was horrified at the idea of spending $500 000 to insulate and air condition the warehouse (it is impractical to air condition the monitor room alone).

You're losing money every summer. Write a memo to Jennifer M. Kirkland, operations vice-president, renewing your request.

Analysis of the Problem

P   What are your **purposes** in writing or speaking?

You need to persuade Kirkland to authorize insulation and air-conditioning, and you want to build a good image.

A   Who is your **audience**? How do members of your audience differ? What audience characteristics are relevant to this particular message?

The operations vice-president will be concerned about keeping costs low and keeping production running smoothly. Kirkland may know that the request was denied two years ago, but another person was vice-president then; Kirkland wasn't the one who said no.

I   What **information** must your message include?

You need to include the cost of the proposal and the effects of the present situation.

B   What reasons or reader **benefits** can you use to support your position?

Cutting turnover may save money and keep the assembly line running smoothly. Experienced employees may produce higher-quality parts. Putting in air conditioning would relieve one of the workers' main complaints; it might make the union happier.

O   What **objections** can you expect your readers to have? What negative elements of your message must you deemphasize or overcome?

The cost, including the cost of the time that operations will be shut down while installation is taking place will be the main objection.

C   How will the **context** affect reader response? Think about your relationship to the reader, the morale in the organization, the economy, the time of year, and any special circumstances.

Prices on computer components are falling; interest rates are low. Nonetheless, the company will be reluctant to make a major expenditure. Although people are looking for jobs, filling vacancies in the monitor room is hard; we are getting a reputation as a bad place to work. Summer is over, but the problem will recur next year.

Discussion of the Sample Solutions

Solution 1, shown in Figure 13.7 is unacceptable. By making the request in the subject line and the first paragraph, the writer invites a no before giving all the arguments.

The writer does nothing to counter the objections that any manager will have to spending a great deal of money. By presenting the issue in terms of fairness, the writer attempts a manipulative emotional appeal. The writer doesn't use details or find common ground to show that the problem is indeed serious. The writer asks for fast action but doesn't show why the reader should act now to solve a problem that won't occur again for eight months.

Solution 2, shown in Figure 13.8, is an effective persuasive message. The writer chooses a positive subject line. The opening sentence catches the reader's attention by focusing on a problem the reader and writer share. The paragraph makes it clear that the memo offers a solution to the problem. The problem is spelled out in detail. The writer creates emotional impact by taking the reader through the day as the temperature rises. The solution is presented impersonally. There are no *I*'s in the memo.

FIGURE 13.7   An Unacceptable Solution to the Sample Problem

Date: October 12, 2009

To: Jennifer M. Kirkland, Operations Vice-President

From: Arnold M. Morgan, Production Supervisor *AMM*

Subject: Request for Air Conditioning in the Monitor Room ———

Request in subject line stiffens resistance when reader is reluctant.

Please put air conditioning in the monitor room. This past summer, 2/3 of our employees quit because it was so hot. It's not fair that they should work in unbearable temperatures when management sits in air-conditioned comfort.

Inappropriate emphasis on writer.

Attacks reader.

I propose that we solve this problem by air-conditioning the monitor room to bring down the temperature to 26°C.

Insulating and air-conditioning the monitor room would cost $500 000. ———

Cost sounds enormous without a context.

Please approve this request promptly.

Memo sounds arrogant. Logic isn't developed. This attacks reader instead of enlisting reader's support.

The memo stresses reader benefits: the savings that will result once the investment is recovered. The last paragraph tells the reader exactly what to do and links prompt action to a reader benefit. The memo ends with a positive picture of the problem solved.

Figures 13.9 and 13.10 provide checklists for direct requests and problem-solving persuasive messages.

FIGURE 13.8   A Good Solution to the Sample Problem

Reader benefit in subject line

Date: October 12, 2009

To: Jennifer M. Kirkland, Operations Vice-President

From: Arnold M. Morgan, Production Supervisor   AMM

Subject: Improving Summer Productivity

Shared problem

Golden forfeited a possible $186 000 in profits last summer because of a 17 percent drop in productivity. That's not unusual: Golden has a history of low summer productivity. We can, however, reverse the trend and bring summer productivity in line with the rest of the year's.

Good to show problem can be resolved

Cause of problem

The problem starts in the monitor room. Because of high turnover and reduced efficiency from workers who are on the job, we just don't make as many monitors as we do during the rest of the year.

Additional reason to solve problem

Both the high turnover and reduced efficiency are due to the unbearable heat in the monitor room. Temperatures in the monitor room average 20°C higher than the outside temperature. During the summer, when work starts at 8:00 A.M., it's already 29°C in the tube room. By 11:30 A.M., it's at least 30°C. On six days last summer, it hit 35°C. When the temperatures are that high, we may be violating Occupational Health and Safety regulations.

Production workers are always standing, moving, or carrying 10 kg monitors. When temperatures hit 30°C, they slow down. When no relief is in sight, many of them take sick days or quit.

We replaced 24 of the 36 employees in the monitor room this summer. When someone quits, it takes an average of five days to find and train a replacement; during that time, the trainee produces nothing. For another five days, the new person can work at only half speed. And "full speed" in the summer is only 90 percent of what we expect the rest of the year.

More details about problem

Here's where our losses come from:

Normal production = 50 units a person each day (upd)

Loss due to turnover:
    loss of 24 workers for 5 days =   6 000 units
    24 at 1/2 pace for 5 days =   3 000 units
        Total loss due to turnover =   9 000 units

Shows detail— set up like an arithmetic problem

Loss due to reduced efficiency:
    loss of 5 upd × 12 workers × 10 days =   600 units
    loss of 5 upd × 36 × 50 days =   9 000 units
        Total loss due to reduced efficiency =   9 600 units

Total loss =   18 600 units

FIGURE 13.8   **A Good Solution to the Sample Problem (continued)**

Shows where numbers in para. 1 come from

Additional benefit

Tells reader what to do

Ends on positive note of problem solved, reader enjoying benefit

Reason to act promptly

Jennifer M. Kirkland   2   October 12, 2007

According to the accounting department, Golden makes a net profit of $10 on every monitor we sell. And, as you know, we sell every monitor we make. Those 18 600 units we don't produce are costing us $186 000 a year.

Bringing down the temperature to 25°C (the minimum allowed under provincial guidelines) from the present summer average of 30°C will require an investment of $500 000 to insulate and air-condition the warehouse. Extra energy costs for the air conditioning will run about $30 000 a year. We'll get our investment back in less than three years. Once the investment is recouped, we'll be making an additional $150 000 a year—all without buying additional equipment or hiring additional workers.

By installing the insulation and air conditioning this fall, we can take advantage of lower off-season rates. Please authorize the Purchasing Department to request bids for the system. Then, next summer, our productivity can be at an all-time high.

FIGURE 13.9   **Checklist for Direct Requests**

- ❏ If the message is a memo, does the subject line indicate the request? Is the subject line specific enough to differentiate this message from others on the same subject?
- ❏ Does the first paragraph summarize the request or the specific topic of the message?
- ❏ Does the message give all the relevant information? Is there enough detail?
- ❏ Does the message answer questions or overcome objections that readers may have without introducing unnecessary negatives?
- ❏ Does the last paragraph ask for action? Does it give a deadline if one exists and a reason for acting promptly?

Checklist for All Messages, Not Just Direct Requests

- ❏ Does the message use you-attitude and positive emphasis?
- ❏ Is the style easy to read and friendly?
- ❏ Is the visual design of the message inviting?
- ❏ Is the format correct?
- ❏ Does the message use standard grammar? Is it free from typos?

Add Originality to a Direct Request

- ❏ Provide good lists and visual impact.
- ❏ Think about readers and give details that answer their questions, overcome any objections, and make it easier for them to do as you ask.
- ❏ Add details that show you're thinking of a specific organization and the specific people in that organization.

FIGURE 13.10   Checklist for Problem-Solving Persuasive Messages

❏ If the message is a memo, does the subject line indicate the writer's purpose or offer a reader benefit? Does the subject line avoid making the request?

❏ Is the problem presented as a joint problem both writer and reader have an interest in solving, rather than as something the reader is being asked to do for the writer?

❏ Does the message give all the relevant information? Is there enough detail?

❏ Does the message overcome objections that readers may have?

❏ Does the message avoid phrases that sound dictatorial, condescending, or arrogant?

❏ Does the last paragraph ask for action? Does it give a deadline if one exists and a reason for acting promptly?

Checklist for All Messages, Not Just Persuasive Ones

❏ Does the message use you-attitude and positive emphasis?

❏ Is the style easy to read and friendly?

❏ Is the visual design of the message inviting?

❏ Is the format correct?

❏ Does the message use standard grammar? Is it free from typos?

Add Originality to a Problem-Solving Persuasive Message

❏ Use a good subject line and common ground.

❏ Include a clear and convincing description of the problem.

❏ Be sure the content reflects readers' interests, gives details that answer their questions, overcomes objections, and makes it easier for them to do as you ask.

❏ Include details that show you're thinking of a specific organization and the specific people in that organization.

MODULE SUMMARY

- All successful communication contains an element of persuasion: you can only get what you need and want when you recognize and try to meet your audience's needs and wants.

  ○ Use your PAIBOC analysis when considering how to organize your messages for best results.

- The direct approach works well when you anticipate that your audience will feel positively or neutrally about you and/or your message.

- The indirect, problem-solving approach works best when you anticipate your audience will be resistant to you and/or the message.

- People have a **vested interest** in something if they benefit directly from keeping things as they are.

- Analyze your audience members to better understand their positions, and to establish common ground.

- To counter objections, use sound logical and emotional appeals.

- To encourage readers to act promptly, give a deadline. Show that the time limit is real, and that acting now will save time or money.

ASSIGNMENTS FOR MODULE 13

Questions for Critical Thinking

13.1 What do you see as the advantages of positive and negative appeals? Illustrate your answer with specific messages, advertisements, or posters.

13.2 Is it dishonest to "sneak up on the reader" by delaying the request in a problem-solving persuasive message?

13.3 Think about a persuasive message (or a commercial) that did not convince you to act. Could a different message have convinced you? How?

Exercises and Problems

13.4   Revising a Form Memo

You've been hired as a staff accountant; one of your major duties will be processing expense reimbursements. Going through the files, you find this form memo:

Subject: Reimbursements

Enclosed are either receipts that we could not match with the items in your request for reimbursement, or a list of items for which we found no receipts, or both. Please be advised that the Accounting Department issues reimbursement cheques only with full documentation. You cannot be reimbursed until you give us a receipt for each item for which you desire reimbursement. We must ask that you provide this information. This process may be easier if you use the Expense Report Form, available in your department.

Thank you for your attention to this matter. Please do not hesitate to contact us with questions.

You know this is not a persuasive memo. In addition to wordiness, a total lack of positive emphasis and you-attitude, and a vague subject line, the document design and organization of information bury the request.

Create a new memo that could be sent to people who do not provide all the documentation necessary to be reimbursed.

13.5   Recommending a Co-worker for a Bonus or an Award

Recommend someone at your workplace for a bonus or an award. The award can be something bestowed by the organization itself (Employee of the Month, Dealership of the Year, and so forth), or it can be a community or campus award (Business Person of the Year, Volunteer of the Year, an honorary degree, and so forth).

As your instructor directs,

  a. Create a document or presentation to achieve the goal.
  b. Write a memo to your instructor describing the situation at your workplace and explaining your rhetorical choices (medium, strategy, tone, wording, organization, graphics or document design, and so forth).

13.6   Asking for a Raise or Reclassification

Do you deserve a raise? Should your job be reclassified to reflect your increased responsibilities (with more pay, of course!)? If so, write a memo to the person with the authority to determine pay and job titles, arguing for what you want.

As your instructor directs,

  a. Create a document or presentation to achieve the goal.
  b. Write a memo to your instructor describing the situation at your workplace and explaining your rhetorical choices (medium, strategy, tone, wording, organization, graphics or document design, and so forth).

13.7   Persuading Guests to Allow Extra Time for Check-Out

Your hotel has been the headquarters for a convention, and on Sunday morning you're expecting 1 000 people to check out before noon. You're staffing the checkout desk to capacity, but if everyone waits till 11:30 A.M. to check out, things will be a disaster.

So you want to encourage people to allow extra time. And they don't have to stand in line at all: by 4:00 A.M., you'll put a statement of current charges under each guest's door. If that statement is correct and the guest is leaving the bill on the credit card used at check-in, the guest can just leave the key in the room and go. You'll mail a copy of the final bill, together with any morning charges, by the end of the week.

Write a one-page message that can be put on pillows when the rooms are made up Friday and Saturday night.

13.8   Persuading an Organization to Expand Flextime

Municipal government offices are open from 9:00 A.M. to 5:00 P.M. Employees have limited flextime: they can come in and leave half an hour early or half an hour late. But employees want much more flexible hours. Some people want to start at 6:00 A.M. so they can leave at 2:00 P.M.; others want to work from 11:00 A.M. to 7:00 P.M.

When the idea has been proposed, supervisors have been very negative. "How will we hold staff meetings? How can we supervise people if everyone works different hours? We have to be here for the public, and we won't be if people work whatever hours they please."

But conversations with co-workers and a bit of research show that there are solutions. Many firms that use flextime require everyone to be at work (or at lunch) between 10:00 A.M. and 2:00 P.M. or 11:00 A.M. and 2:00 P.M., so that staff meetings can be scheduled. Right now, when clients call, a representative is frequently on the phone and has to call back. Voicemail and better message forms might solve the problem. And flextime might actually let offices stay open longer hours—say 8:00 A.M. to 6:00 P.M., which would be helpful for taxpayers who themselves work 9:00 A.M. to 5:00 P.M. and now can come in only on their own lunch hours. Write a memo to the mayor and municipal council, persuading them to approve a change in work hours.

Hints:

- Assume that this situation is happening in your own municipal government. What services does the municipality offer?
- Use any facts about your municipality that are helpful (e.g., being especially busy right now, having high turnover, dealing with tax issues).
- Use what you know about managing to allay managers' fears.
- Use the analysis that you developed for Exercise 2.7 on page 39.

13.9   Persuading Disability Services to Increase the Handivan's Hours

The local community college has a "Handivan" that takes students who use wheelchairs from their residences or apartments to campus locations and back again. But the van stops at 6:00 P.M. (even though there are evening classes, lectures, and events). And it doesn't take people to off-campus restaurants, movies, grocery stores, or shopping centres. Write to the director of disability services, urging that the Handivan's services be increased.

13.10   Handling a Sticky Recommendation

As a supervisor in a not-for-profit provincial agency, you have a dilemma. You received this email message today:

From: John Inoye, Director of Personnel, Communications

Subject: Need Recommendation for Peggy Chafez

Peggy Chafez has applied for a position in the Communications Department. On the basis of her application and interview, she is the leading candidate. However, before I offer the job to her, I need a letter of recommendation from her current supervisor.

Could you please let me have your evaluation within a week? We want to fill the position as quickly as possible

Peggy has worked in your office for 10 years. She designs, writes, and edits your office's monthly newsletter; she designed and maintains the department Web site. Her designs are creative; she's a very hard worker; she seems to know a lot about computers.

However, Peggy is in many ways an unsatisfactory staff member. Her standards are so high that most people find her intimidating. Some find her abrasive. People have complained to you that she's only interested in her own work; she seems to resent requests to help other people with projects. And yet both the newsletter and the Web page are projects that need frequent interaction. She's out of the office a lot. Some of that is required by her job (she takes the newsletters to the post office, for example), but some people don't like the fact that she's out of the office so much. They also complain that she doesn't return voicemail and email messages.

You think managing your office would be a lot smoother if Peggy weren't there. You can't fire her: employees' jobs are secure once they get past the initial six-month probationary period. Because of budget constraints, you can hire new employees only if vacancies are created by resignations. You feel that it would be easy to find someone better.

If you recommended that John Inoye hire Peggy, you would be able to hire someone you want. If you recommended that John hire someone else, you might be stuck with Peggy for a long time.

As your instructor directs,

- **a.** Write an email message to John Inoye.
- **b.** Write an email to your instructor listing the choices you've made and justifying your approach.

Hints:

- What are your options? Consciously look for more than two.
- Is it possible to select facts or to use connotations so that you are truthful but still encourage John to hire Peggy? Is it ethical? Is it certain that John would find Peggy's work as unsatisfactory as you do? If you write a strong recommendation and Peggy doesn't do well at the new job, will your credibility suffer? Why is your credibility important?

13.11   Writing Collection Letters

You have a small desktop publishing firm. Today, you've set aside some time to work on overdue bills.

As your instructor directs,

Write letters for one or more of the following situations.

- **a.** A $750 bill for producing three monthly newsletters for a veterinarian to mail to her clients. The agreement was that you'd bill her $250 each month. But somehow you haven't sent out bills for the last two months, so they'll go on this month's bill. You'd like payment for the whole bill, and you want to continue this predictable income of $250 a month.

b. A $200 bill for creating flyers for a local rock band to post. You've called twice and left messages on an answering machine, but nothing has happened. The bill is only three weeks overdue, but the band doesn't seem very stable. You want to be paid now.

c. A $3 750 bill, three weeks past due, for designing and printing a series of brochures for Creative Interiors, a local interior decorating shop. When you billed Creative Interiors, you got a note saying that the design was not acceptable and that you would not be paid until you redesigned it (at no extra charge) to the owner's satisfaction. The owner had approved the preliminary design on which the brochures were based; he did not explain in the note what was wrong with the final product. He's never free when you are; indeed, when you call to try to schedule an appointment, you're told the owner will call you back—but he never does. At this point, the delay is not your fault; you want to be paid.

13.12   Getting Permission from Parents for a School Project

As part of a community cleanup program, all public school students will spend the afternoon of the second Friday of April picking up trash. Younger students will pick up trash on school grounds, in parks, and in parking lots; older students will pick up trash downtown. Teachers will supervise the students; where necessary, school buses will transport them. After students are finished, they'll return to their school's playground, where they'll be supervised until the end of the school day. Each school will maintain a study hall for any students whose parents do not give them permission to participate. Trash bags and snacks have been donated by local merchants.

Write a one-page cover letter that students can take home to their parents telling them about the project and persuading them to sign the necessary permission form. You do not need to create the permission form but do refer to it in your letter.

Hints:

- What objections may parents have? How can you overcome these?
- Where should parents who drive their kids to school pick them up?
- Should students wear their normal school clothing?
- When must the form be returned? Who gets it? Whom can parents call if they have questions before they sign the form?

13.13   Asking an Instructor for a Letter of Recommendation

You're ready for the job market or for transfer to a college or university, and you need letters of recommendation.

As your instructor directs,

a. Assume that you've asked an instructor for a recommendation, and he or she has agreed to write one. "Why don't you write up something to remind me of what you've done in the class? Tell me what else you've done, too. And tell me what they're looking for. Be sure to tell me when the letter needs to be in and whom it goes to."

b. Assume that you've been unable to talk with the instructor whose recommendation you want. When you call, no one answers the phone; you stopped by once and no one was in. Write asking for a letter of recommendation.

c. Assume that the instructor is no longer on campus. Write him or her a letter asking for a recommendation.

Hints:

- Detail the points you'd like the instructor to mention.
- How well will this instructor remember you? How much detail about your performance in his or her class do you need to provide?
- Specify the name and address of the person to whom the letter should be written; specify when the letter is due. If there's an intermediate due date (e.g., if you must sign the outside of the envelope to submit the recommendation), say so.

13.14   Recommending Investments*

Recommend whether your instructor should invest in a specific stock, piece of real estate, or other investment. As your instructor directs, assume that your instructor has $1 000, $10 000, or $100 000 to invest.

Hints:

- Pick a stock, property, or other investment you can research easily.
- What are your instructor's goals? Is he or she saving for a house? For retirement? For the kids' postsecondary education expenses? To pay off his or her own student loans? When will the money from the investment be needed?
- How much risk is your instructor comfortable with?
- Is your instructor willing to put time into the investment (as managing a rental house would require)?

*Based on an assignment created by Cathy Ryan, The Ohio State University.

13.15　Retrieving Your Image

As director of business communication, you get this letter from Sharon Davis, a member of your college advisory board and a major donor:

> My bank received this letter from one of your soon-to-be-graduates. It seems as though a closer look at writing skills is warranted.
>
> > To Whom It May Concern:
> >
> > This is in reference to the loan soliciation that I received in the mail. This is the second offer that I am now inquiring about. The first offer sent to my previous address I did not respond. But after some careful thought and consideration I think it wise to consolidate my bills. Therefore I hope the information provided is sufficient to complete a successful application. I think the main purpose of this loan is to enable me to repair my credit history. I have had problems in the past because of job status as part-time and being a student. I will be graduating in June and now I do have a full-time job. I think I just need a chance to mend the past credit problems that I have had.

(The next two inches of the letter are blocked out, and both the signature and typed name are crossed out so that they cannot be read.)

As your instructor directs,

   a. Write to the faculty who teach business communications, reminding them that the quality of student writing may affect fundraising efforts.
   b. Write to Ms. Davis, convincing her that indeed your school does make every effort to graduate students who can write.

13.16　Persuading Employees to Join the Company Volleyball Team

Your company has decided to start a company volleyball team to play in the city recreation league. Now you need to get people to sign up for the team. Ideally, you'd like to have several teams to involve as many people as possible and build company loyalty. If you have enough teams, they can play each other once a week in a round-robin company tournament.

Write a memo to all employees persuading them to sign up.

Hints:

- How young and how athletic are your employees? How busy are they? Will this be an easy or a difficult thing to persuade them to do?
- Some people may be reluctant to join because their skills are rusty. How can you persuade people that you want everyone to participate even if they're not athletic?

- Will the people who sign up have to pay anything or buy uniforms?
- How do people sign up? Is there a deadline?
- What other perks or positives might team members enjoy?

13.17　Persuading Tenants to Pay the Rent

As the new manager of an apartment complex, you find this message in the files:

> ATTENTION!
>
> DERELICTS
>
> If you are a rent derelict (and you know if you are) this communiqué is directed to you!
>
> RENT IS DUE THE 5TH OF EACH MONTH AT THE LATEST!
>
> LEASE HAS A 5-DAY GRACE PERIOD UNTIL THE 5TH OF THE MONTH NOT THE 15TH.
>
> If rent is not paid in total by the 5th, you will pay the $25 late charge. You will pay the $25 late charge when you pay your late rent or your rent will not be accepted.
>
> Half of you people don't even know how much you pay a month. Please read your lease instead of calling up to waste our time finding out what you owe per month! Let's get with the program so I can spend my time streamlining and organizing maintenance requests. My job is maintenance only.
>
> RENT PAYMENT IS YOUR JOB!
>
> If you can show up for a test on time, why can't you make it to the rental office on time or just mail it?
>
> P.S. We don't take cash any longer due to a major theft.

This message is terrible. It lacks you-attitude and may even encourage people who are now paying on the 1st to wait until the 5th.

Write a message to go to people who have been slow to pay in the past.

13.18　Writing a Performance Appraisal for a Member of a Collaborative Group

During your collaborative writing group meetings, keep a log of events. Record specifics of both effective and ineffective behaviours of group members. Then evaluate the performance of the other members in your group. (If there are two or more other people, write a separate appraisal for each of them.)

In your first paragraph, summarize your evaluation. Then, in the body of your memo, give the specific details that lead to your evaluation by answering the following questions:

- What specifically did the person do in terms of the task? Brainstorm ideas? Analyze the information? Draft the text? Suggest revisions in parts drafted by others? Format the document or create visuals? Revise? Edit? Proofread? (In most cases, several people will have done each of these activities together. Don't overstate what any one person did.) What was the quality of the person's work?
- What did the person contribute to the group process? Did he or she help schedule the work? raise or resolve conflicts? make other group members feel valued and included? promote group cohesion? What roles (page 275–277) did the person play in the group?

Support your generalizations with specific observations. The more observations you have and the more detailed they are, the better your appraisal will be.

As your instructor directs,

a. Write a midterm performance appraisal for one or more members of your collaborative group. In each appraisal, identify the two or three things the person could try to improve during the second half of the term.

b. Write a performance appraisal for one or more members of your collaborative group at the end of the term. Identify and justify the grade you think each person should receive for the portion of the grade-based group process.

c. Give a copy of your appraisal to the person about whom it is written.

Correcting Run-On Sentences

A sentence with too many ideas, strung together by coordinating conjunctions that lack the required comma, is a run-on. (Remember that coordinating conjunctions such as *and*, *or*, *for*, *yet*, and *but* need a comma to connect independent clauses.)

Although most run-on sentences are long, length is not the real problem. Don't confuse run-ons with grammatically correct long sentences whose ideas are still clear to readers.

Run-ons confound readers, because there are too many ideas competing for attention, and because the missing commas make the ideas harder to follow.

The effect is similar to listening to a speaker who does not pause between sentences: Where does one point begin and another end?

Test for run-ons by looking for more than two main ideas in a sentence and a lack of commas with coordinating conjunctions:

We installed the new computers this morning and they are running fine but there aren't enough computers for everyone so we are going to purchase more on Wednesday and we will install them and then the department will be fully operational.

Count the number of things going on in this sentence. Where are the commas?

Fix a run-on in one of three ways:

1. For short run-ons, add the missing commas:

Incorrect: The purchasing department sent order forms but we received too few so we are requesting more.

Correct: The purchasing department sent order forms, but we received too few, so we are requesting more.

2. Rewrite the sentence using subordination:

Correct: Because we received too few order forms, we are requesting more from the purchasing department.

3. For longer run-ons, break the run-on into two or more sentences, add missing commas, and subordinate where appropriate.

Correct: We installed the new computers this morning. They are running fine, but because there aren't enough computers for everyone, we are going to purchase more on Wednesday. We will install them, and then the department will be fully operational.

Exercises

Fix the following run-on errors.

1. The marketing department ordered new brochures that are really nice and the brochures are in four-colour.

2. All expense accounts should be itemized based on type and cost so remember to include the appropriate shipping confirmation number.

3. Work into your schedule some time to meet next week and we can talk about your promotion so you can transition easily into the new job.

4. We will take a final product inventory on December 1 and managers will report any lost stock so employees should make sure any broken items are reported and managers should record this information in their computer databases.

5. Employees may request benefits changes during the annual enrolment period and supervisors should pass out the required forms and employees should have them completed by the deadline on the form.

6. Ian leaves his computer on overnight but Aaron turns his off and Marilyn leaves hers on, too, and so does Tashi.

7. Mohammed should make sure he specifies 20-lb. rather than 15-lb. paper stock and Jenna should call the print shop and ask them whether they need anything and Bruce needs to tell Ms. Winans we appreciate her letting us know we originally ordered the wrong stock.

8. The Halifax office is planning a new marketing campaign so the St. John's office will help with the promotion but the Fredericton office is coordinating the product show.

9. A few customers are concerned about the shipping date but the mailroom is sure we can ship overnight and I think there's no reason to be concerned.

10. Last week I went to Montreal and Haj went to Miami and this week Tony took a trip too so our travel budget is almost gone.

Check your answers to the odd-numbered exercises on page 552.

CASES FOR COMMUNICATORS

Wikipedia: What's the Plan?*

In March 2008 alone, over "11 million Canadians visited Wikipedia, … Wikimedia Foundation's free, online encyclopedia."[8] Global users number in the hundreds of millions, and Wikipedia's potential growth is inestimable. Herein lies the problem: Wikipedia's success has grown beyond the expectations of both enthusiasts and detractors. Now the collaborative, not-for-profit, information source has to develop a business plan to say what it is, and where it is going. If, for example, Wikipedia were to accept advertising revenues, devotees insist the site would be irremediably compromised: the interests of big business would reduce the free flow of ideas, and eventually discourage or distort the democratic exchange of contributors and users.

Others argue that advertising would generate billions of dollars, which could be used in vital national and global research and development initiatives.

*Based on Kimberly White's article "The Wiki Business Plan," *The Globe and Mail*, May 26, 2008, p. B1.

What direction would be best for Wikipedia and its users? Wikipedia directors need your help in defining the online encyclopedia's new identity.

Individual Activity

Consider your experience with Wikipedia. When and how have you used the online resource?

What about family, friends and colleagues? What do they know about Wikipedia? What are the benefits for them? How useful do they find the site? Who contributes to updating the information?

Research others' experience and opinions of Wikipedia. What do other people think is valuable about the site as it is? Who is in favour of commercializing Wikipedia? What are their reasons? Who would benefit from this decision?

Suggested sites

http://www.alleyinsider.com/2008/3/better_idea_for_wiki
pedia_go_private_give_away_profits

http://slashdot.org/article.pl?sid=08/03/11/0610216&from=rss

http://en.wikipedia.org/wiki/User:Luigifan/What_good_is_
Wikipedia%3F

http://www.cbsnews.com/stories/2006/12/10/sunday/
main2244008.shtml

http://wikipediareview.com/blog/20080104/criticisms-of-
wikipedia

Group Activity

Exchange ideas with two or three classmates. Combine your research and opinions to decide whether Wikipedia should accept advertising or not. Use PAIBOC analysis to compose an email letter to Wikimedia Foundation head Sue Gardner, detailing your plan and its benefits.

Prepare a five-minute presentation for your instructor and students persuading them to support your plan.

Building Emotional Intelligence: Interpersonal Communication

- **Module 14:**
Listening Actively

- **Module 15:**
Working and Writing in Teams

- **Module 16:**
Planning, Managing, and
Recording Meetings

- **Module 17:**
Making Oral Presentations

Collen Bowen and his brother Cory started in the foundation repair business with one small truck, subcontracting repairs from other companies. Today their corporation, Bowen Foundation Inc, operates ten trucks, employs fifteen people, and owns the company building. Bowen Foundation flourishes because the company culture values building and maintaining client relationships.

"Foundation repair is a growth industry; there's always a need. We decided to go into business for ourselves because we felt we could provide better service. We looked at competitors' Web sites, and asked them to quote for work. We analyzed their sales and estimate presentations, and their proposed materials and warranties: we knew we could do a better job."

Collen equates business success with specific interpersonal skills: "Listening comes first. Customers must feel confident that I understand and will solve the problem. Our business is not the same as home renovation or landscaping, where people can look forward to esthetically pleasing results. I am very

aware that our customers would rather not spend their money on a home repair; therefore, I must listen empathetically, to ensure that we give the customer the optimum solution. I follow up on every job, and ask for feedback to ensure that customers feel their money has been well spent."

Collen considers every contact to be a networking opportunity: "Paying attention, listening to people: you establish a network for all your business needs, and you become a contact for others. For example, I met Mike Holmes while subcontracting a job; then Mike saw the quality of our work: next thing, Bowen Repair Foundation is featured on *Holmes on Homes*, and now on his new show."

Collen left school in Grade 10. When he was 25, he returned as a mature student, earning a Business Marketing diploma. "The college courses reinforced my lifetime experience: put people first; then you get the chance to do the quality job.

"The most important business trademarks are being honest, keeping your

word, and being on time. Sometimes, in the short term, being honest and keeping your word can translate into financial loss. For example, if I go to a potential customer's house to quote on a job, and find a minor problem, I suggest an inexpensive solution. And some jobs may require more materials and additional labour than I anticipated in the quote. Long-term, however, keeping the trust pays off: the client becomes an advocate for our company, and refers us to family and friends.

"And, of course, being on time demonstrates you value the customer's time. It's the first, and lasting impression."

PAIBOC ANALYSIS

1. What interpersonal communication and emotional intelligence skills does Collen use to influence customers positively, and to build the business?

2. Visit the Bowen Foundation Repair website at www.bfr.ca. How did Collen use PAIBOC analysis to design the site?

3. Go to www.youtube.com/watch?v= EKrleXSmXMM. Using PAIBOC analysis, identify four improvements Collen could make to the video.

MODULE

14

Listening Actively

Learning Objectives

After reading and applying the information in Module 14, you'll be able to demonstrate

Knowledge of

- The fundamentals of good listening practice
- Active listening as a core communication skill

Skills to

- Begin to listen actively
- Begin to listen for understanding
- Continue to learn how to influence others positively

Employability Skills 2000+ Checklist

In this module, the key skills from the Conference Board of Canada's Employability Skills 2000+ are

Communicate

○ listen and ask questions to understand and appreciate the points of view of others

○ share information using a range of information and communications technologies (e.g., voice, email, computers)

Think & Solve Problems

○ seek different points of view and evaluate them based on facts

○ recognize the human, interpersonal, technical, scientific, and mathematical dimensions of a problem

Be Adaptable

○ cope with uncertainty

○ be open and respond constructively to change

Learn Continuously

○ be willing to continuously learn and grow

○ assess personal strengths and areas for development

Work with Others

○ be flexible: respect, be open to, and be supportive of the thoughts, opinions, and contributions of others in a group

○ recognize and respect people's diversity, individual differences, and perspectives

○ accept and provide feedback in a constructive and considerate manner

Listening means decoding and interpreting both verbal and nonverbal symbols, as the speaker intends them. In study after study, employers rank listening skills first among the most critical communication skills.[1] Yet we rarely receive formal training in this key skill.

Good listening is active, and demands energy and practice. Good listening is active because you must focus on accurately interpreting the speaker's words, gestures, and tone *in the moment*. Actively listening to another person requires energy because, to truly listen, you must work to reduce physical, emotional, and psychological distractions; you must clear your mind of your own preoccupations and biases. Obviously, good listening demands practice because focusing on another person in an open, uncritical way does not come naturally to any of us.

The payback, however, is well worth the effort: active listening is integral to providing the feedback essential to communication (Module 2). Active listening enables you to identify and solve problems. And since you must really pay attention to understand someone else's point of view, active listening helps you identify what motivates the speaker. Active listening, therefore, provides clues on how to influence others, and is essential in successful negotiating.[2]

Demonstrating that you are actively listening to customers is part of doing business in our wired world. Today's customers are better informed, and shop with high expectations of both products and services. Most important, customers use the Internet to "control the conversation." They "expect to be heard," and want "individual treatment."[3] And when they feel

FIGURE 14.1   **Active Listening Includes Giving Feedback**

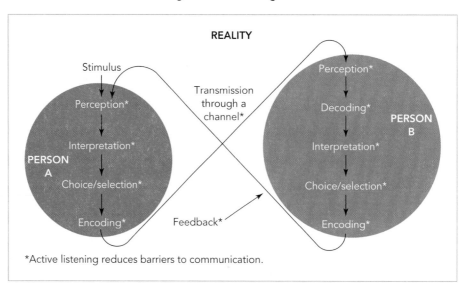

*Active listening reduces barriers to communication.

mistreated, they don't just go elsewhere; they post their negative experiences for a global audience.

In response, savvy organizations use the Web to welcome conversations with their customers, and to demonstrate that they are listening. Home Depot has "a dedicated team to reply to every message sent to wearelistening@homedepot.com."[4] Calgary's Memory Express Computer Products' CEO "encourages customers to post comments about his products directly on his website."[5] Active listening is essential business practice in our digital society.

What Do Good Listeners Do?

They prepare by analyzing (PAIBOC) the situation. Then they consciously follow four practices.

After analyzing the listening situation, good listeners pay attention, focus on the other speaker(s) in a generous way, avoid making assumptions, and listen for feelings as well as for facts.

1. Good Listeners Pay Attention

Good listening requires energy. You have to resist distractions and tune out noise (Module 2), whether it's another conversation nearby, or worry about your parking meter expiring.

You can do several things to avoid listening errors caused by not paying attention:

- Before the conversation, anticipate the information you need. Make a list of your questions. When is the project due? What resources do you have? What is the most important aspect of this project from the other person's point of view? During a conversation, listen for answers to your questions.
- At the end of the conversation, check your understanding with the other person. Especially check who does what next.
- During or after the conversation, write down key points that affect deadlines or work assessment.

FIGURE 14.2   **Use PAIBOC to Activate Your Listening**

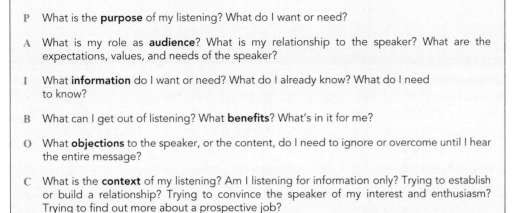

P	What is the **purpose** of my listening? What do I want or need?
A	What is my role as **audience**? What is my relationship to the speaker? What are the expectations, values, and needs of the speaker?
I	What **information** do I want or need? What do I already know? What do I need to know?
B	What can I get out of listening? What **benefits**? What's in it for me?
O	What **objections** to the speaker, or the content, do I need to ignore or overcome until I hear the entire message?
C	What is the **context** of my listening? Am I listening for information only? Trying to establish or build a relationship? Trying to convince the speaker of my interest and enthusiasm? Trying to find out more about a prospective job?

2. Good Listeners Focus on the Other Speaker(s) in a Generous Way

Most of us miss meaning because we attend to our own internal monologues. We focus on factors incidental to the topic, or look for flaws: "What an ugly tie." "She sounds like a little girl." "There's a typo in that slide." Often we listen only for the pause that signifies it's our turn to speak, or, as if the discussion were a competition, collect weapons to attack the other speaker. "Ah-ha! You're wrong about *that*!"

Good listeners, in contrast, use enlightened self-interest to block out the noise inside their heads. They focus on the message, not on the messenger's shortcomings. They concentrate on what's in the message for themselves: *What's going on here?*

Good listeners know that even people who are poor speakers may have something worthwhile to say. Rather than pouncing on the first error they hear and tuning out the speaker while they wait impatiently for their own turn to speak, good listeners weigh all the evidence before they make a judgment. They realize that they can learn and use something even from people they do not like, or do not agree with.

You can avoid listening errors caused by self-absorption:

- Focus on the content: on what the speaker says, not his or her appearance or delivery.
- Spend your time evaluating what the speaker says, not just planning your rebuttal.
- Consciously work to learn something from every speaker.

3. Good Listeners Avoid Making Assumptions

Each of us brings our own perceptions to the communication process. Many listening errors, therefore, come from making faulty assumptions, based on a natural tendency to focus on our own ego needs, and to interpret the speaker's meaning according to our own experiences. Furthermore, we perceive experience through our own cultural biases. We are socialized to communicate the way we do. People from different cultures speak and listen very differently

(Modules 2 and 3). The most adept listeners strive to listen for understanding without making assumptions.[6]

Indeed, good listeners wait to ask questions to elicit and clarify information. Superb sales-people, for example, listen closely to client questions and objections, to better identify and respond to the sticking points of a sale. Magazine advertising account representative Beverly Jameson received a phone call from an ad agency saying that a client wanted to cancel the ad space that client had bought. Jameson saw the problem as an opportunity: "Instead of hearing 'cancel,' I heard, 'There's a problem here—let's get to the root of it and figure out how to make the client happy.'" Jameson met with the client, asked questions, and discovered that the client wanted more flexibility. She made some changes, kept the business, and turned the client into a repeat customer.[7]

You can avoid listening errors caused by faulty assumptions:

- Focus on the other person's background and experiences. Why is this point important to the speaker? What might he or she mean by it? How can its importance to the speaker benefit you?
- Query instructions you think are unnecessary. Before you do something else, check with the order giver to see whether there is a reason for the instruction.
- Paraphrase what the speaker has said, giving him or her a chance to correct your understanding.

4. Good Listeners Listen for Feelings *and* Facts

Sometimes, someone just needs to blow off steam, to vent (page 278). Sometimes, people just want to have a chance to fully express themselves: "winning" or "losing" does not matter. Sometimes, people may have objections that they can't quite put into words.

You can learn to avoid listening errors caused by focusing solely on facts by

- Consciously listening for feelings
- Paying attention to tone of voice, facial expression, and body language
- Paraphrasing what the speaker has said, and acknowledging the feelings you are observing
- Not assuming that silence means consent and inviting the other person to speak

What Is Active Listening?

Active listening involves feeding back the literal meaning, or the emotional content, or both.

In **active listening**, receivers actively demonstrate that they've heard and understood by feeding back to the speaker either the literal meaning or the emotional content, or both. Other techniques in active listening are asking for more information, and stating your own feelings.

After listening without interrupting, use these five strategies to create active responses:

1. Paraphrase the content. Feed back the meaning, as you understand it, in your own words.
2. Mirror the speaker's feelings. Identify the feelings you think you hear.
3. State your own feelings. This strategy works especially well when you are angry (Modules 14, 15).
4. Ask for information or clarification.
5. Ask how you can help.

TABLE 14.1   **Blocking Responses Versus Active Listening**

Blocking Response	Possible Active Response
Ordering, threatening	**Paraphrasing content**
"I don't care how you do it. Just get that report on my desk by Friday."	"You're saying that you don't have time to finish the report by Friday."
Preaching, criticizing	**Mirroring feelings**
"You should know better than to air the department's problems in a general meeting."	"It sounds like the department's problems really bother you."
Interrogating	**Stating one's own feelings**
"Why didn't you tell me that you didn't understand the instructions?"	"I'm frustrated that the job isn't completed yet, and I'm worried about getting it done on time."
Minimizing the problem	**Asking for information or clarification**
"You think that's bad. You should see what I have to do this week."	"What parts of the problem seem most difficult to solve?"
Advising	**Offering to help solve the problem together**
"Well, why don't you try listing everything you have to do and seeing which items are most important?"	"What can I do to help?"

Source: The five responses that block communication are based on a list of 12 in Thomas Gordon and Judith Gordon Sands, *P.E.T. in Action* (New York: Wyden, 1976), pp. 117–18.

Instead of mirroring what the other person says, many of us respond to our own needs by attempting to analyze, solve, or dismiss the problem. People with problems need to know above all that we hear that they're having a rough time. Table 14.1 lists some of the responses that block communication. Ordering others around, or interrogating them tells speakers that the listener doesn't want to hear what they have to say.

Preaching attacks the other person. Minimizing the problem suggests that the other person's concern is misplaced. Even advising shuts off discussion. Giving a quick answer minimizes what the person feels and puts him or her down for not seeing (what is to us, because it's not our problem) the obvious answer. Even if it is a good answer from an objective point of view, the other person might not be ready to hear it. And sometimes, the off-the-top-of-the-head solution doesn't address the real problem.

Clearly, active listening takes time and energy. Even people who are skilled listeners can't do it all the time, because the listener's feelings interfere with open reception. Furthermore, as experts have pointed out, active listening works only if you genuinely accept the other person's ideas and feelings. Active listening can reduce the conflict that results from miscommunication, but it alone cannot reduce the conflict that comes when two people want apparently inconsistent things, or when one person wants to change someone else.

How Do I Show People That I'm Listening to Them?

Acknowledge their comments in words, in non-verbal symbols, and in actions.

Employability Skills

Active listening is a good way to show people that you are listening. Referring to another person's comment is another way: "I agree with Diana that ..."

Acknowledgment responses or **conversation regulators**—nods, uh-huhs, smiles, frowns—also help carry the message that you're listening. Remember, however, that listening responses vary from culture to culture.

European Canadians indicate attention and involvement by making eye contact, leaning forward, and making acknowledgment responses. However, as Module 3 shows (page 51), some cultures show respect by looking down. In a multicultural workforce, you won't always know whether a colleague who listens silently agrees with what you say or disagrees violently but is too polite to say so. The best thing to do is to observe the behaviour, without assigning a meaning to it: "You aren't saying much." Then let the other person speak.

Of course, if you go through the motions of active listening but then act with disrespect, people will feel that you have not heard them. Acting on what people say is necessary for people to feel completely heard.

Can I Use These Techniques If I Really Disagree with Someone?

Most of us do our worst listening when we are in highly charged emotional situations, such as talking with someone with whom we really disagree, getting bad news, or being criticized. But at work, you need to listen even to people with whom you have major conflicts.

At a minimum, good listening enables you to find out why your opponent objects to the programs or ideas you support. Understanding the objections to your ideas is essential if you are to create a persuasive campaign to overcome those objections.

Good listening is crucial when you are being criticized, especially by your boss. You need to know which areas are most important, and exactly what kind of improvement counts. Otherwise, you might spend your time and energy changing your behaviour, but changing it in a way not valued by your organization.

Listening can do even more. Listening to people is an indication that you're taking them seriously. If you really listen to the people you disagree with, you show that you respect them. And taking that step may enable them to respect you and listen to you.

EXPANDING A CRITICAL SKILL

Learning by Listening

The most effective managers lead by listening. Listening for understanding creates environments where people flourish. Indeed, listening to, and meeting the needs of their employees distinguishes the culture of the Greater Toronto Area's best 75 organizations.

Enormous energy, stamina, and curiosity characterize the habits of the best managers. And they draw on these skills ceaselessly, since at least 90 percent of their day is spent communicating. Canadian, American, British, and Swedish managers demonstrate a marked preference for gathering information by word of mouth, and through conversations, telephone calls, and meetings, rather than by reading documents. These managers lead by putting themselves in the centre of the organization's

information flow. Listening to "soft" data, including opinions and gossip, allows them to recognize problems and opportunities, make decisions, motivate, and negotiate. To accumulate and disseminate the information necessary to do their job, these leaders spend most of their day listening.

The key to active listening is preparedness. Being prepared and receptive can transform our lives.

For example, active listening created a business for out-of-work stagehand Sam Holman. In a conversation with Holman, friend Bill MacKenzie—a baseball scout—commented on the number of bats that major-leaguers broke each season. He challenged Holman to use his

When I am tutoring, I must listen closely

carpentry skills to solve the problem: "Why don't you start making bats?" Hundreds of hours of research later, Holman carved the prototype Sam Bat, the first Maple bat in the history of baseball. Although its original price didn't cover production costs, the Sam Bat attracted important converts: the Blue Jays' Joe Carter loved the bat and began to lobby the league to approve it. In 1998, the Sam Bat received approval—the first Maple bat in major-league history to do so. Meanwhile heavy hitters on all the major league teams began ordering Holman's bats, which many credited for their improved batting averages. Today Holman's The Original Maple Bat Corporation continues to flourish.

You don't have to be in business to start to develop listening skills. After graduating with a Business Accounting college diploma, University of Waterloo student Kim Aitken found listening to lectures and note-taking difficult. Kim began listening to understand the lecturer; instead of taking verbatim notes, Kim started writing down the key ideas so that they made sense to her.

Fortunately, Kim has had plenty of listening practice. In her accounting firm co-op job, Kim had learned that it was important to listen and remember what "partners and seniors would tell me [about] a client or file so as not to have to ask them to repeat themselves later." Kim started to take a note pad with her everywhere, "so that I can not only listen but write down notes for later."

In her third year, Kim applied for and won a coveted place in Waterloo University's School of Accounting and Finance Fellowship program. As ambassadors for Waterloo and the School of Accounting and Finance program, fellows receive leadership training and opportunities. They must maintain their 80 percent average while tutoring and coaching other students. "When I am tutoring, I must listen closely. We are not there to give students answers; instead I must encourage students to tell me what they think, then figure out what they know so I can help them discover the answer. I must listen to their questions and pay attention to their thought processes, so as not to confuse them with an explanation they do not understand."

Fellowship Program participants receive a $2 000 scholarship for their third and fourth years. Kim's place in the Program will be a fine addition to her résumé. Her listening habits will prove a lifetime benefit.

Sources: "The Honour Roll," *Toronto Star*, October 18, 2008, pp. R8–11; Henry Mintzberg, "The Manager's Job: Folklore and Fact," http://www.uu.edu/personal/bnance/318/mintz.html, retrieved August 14, 2006; Alex Gillis, "Bat Man," *National Post*, October 1999, pp. 60–69.

MODULE SUMMARY

- Hearing means having the physical ability to perceive sounds. Listening means decoding these sounds, and interpreting them the way the speaker intended.

- Good listeners pay attention, focus on the speaker rather than themselves, avoid making assumptions, and listen for feelings as well as facts.

- To avoid listening errors caused by inattention,
  - Be conscious of the points you need to know, and listen for them.
  - At the end of the conversation, check your understanding with the speaker.
  - During or after the conversation, make notes: write down key points, deadlines, and evaluation procedures.

- To avoid listening errors caused by self-absorption,
  - Focus on what the speaker says, not on his/her appearance or delivery.
  - Focus on understanding and assessing what the speaker says, not on your rebuttal.
  - Consciously work to learn something from every speaker.

- To reduce errors caused by misinterpretation,
  - Pay attention to instructions.
  - Assess the speaker's background and experiences: Why is this point important to the speaker?

- Paraphrase what the speaker's has said, giving him/her a chance to correct your understanding.

- To avoid listening errors caused by focusing solely on the facts,
  - Consciously listen for feelings.
  - Pay attention to tone of voice, pauses, facial expression, and body language.
  - Don't ever assume that silence means agreement; invite the other person to speak.

- In active listening, you demonstrate that you have heard and understood a speaker by feeding back the literal meaning or the emotional meaning, or both. To do this, you can
  - Paraphrase the content.
  - Mirror the speaker's feelings.
  - State your own feelings.
  - Ask for information or clarification.
  - Ask how you can help solve the problem.

ASSIGNMENTS FOR MODULE 14

Questions for Critical Thinking

14.1 Think about someone you know who is a good listener. List all the other qualities this person possesses. Why do you think this person is a "good listener"? How does being a good listener enhance this person's other qualities?

14.2 Why is active listening such hard work?

14.3 Think about a time when you really felt that the other person listened to you, and a time when you felt unheard. How did you know the other person was listening? What behaviours and words caused you to feel unheard? What was different in each situation?

Exercises and Problems

14.4   Reflecting on Your Own Listening

Keep a listening log for day. Note how you listened, for how long, what barriers you encountered, and what strategies you used to listen more actively and more effectively. What situations were easiest? Which were most difficult? What cultural assumptions affected how and when you listened? What discourse communities have influenced your listening habits? Which parts of listening do you need to work hardest on?

As your instructor directs,

a. Share your information with a small group of students in your class.

b. Present your findings orally to the class.

c. Present your findings in a memo to your instructor.

d. Join with other students to present your findings in a group report or presentation.

14.5   Diagramming Your Active Listening

Choose a lecture class, or any other one-way communication situation that requires you to listen. Instead of taking linear notes of the speaker's ideas, cluster or mind-map (see Figure 4.4 in Module 4) the lecture.

As your instructor directs,

a. Share your information with a small group of students in your class.
b. Present your findings orally to the class.
c. Present your findings in a memo to your instructor, with your cluster diagram.
d. Join with other students to present your findings in a group report or presentation.

14.6   Responding to an Expert's Opinion

Entrepreneur, author, and business expert Seth Godin gives his opinion of the value of social networking at www.openforum.com/marketing/video_socialgood.html. Watch and listen to the tape, then summarize Godin's main idea in a single sentence.

Write a response (two to three paragraphs), either supporting or refuting Godin's ideas, and post it on his blog: http://sethgodin.typepad.com. In your argument, include specific examples from your own experience and research.

As your instructor directs,

a. Share your writing with a small group of students in your class.
b. Present your opinion in a memo to your instructor.
c. Join with other students to present your opinions in a group report or presentation.

14.7   Interviewing Workers About Listening

Interview someone about his or her on-the-job listening. Possible questions to ask are

- Whom do you listen to as part of your job? your superior? subordinates? (How many levels down?) customers or clients? Who else?
- How much time a day do you spend listening?
- What people do you talk to as part of your job? Do you feel they hear what you say? How do you tell whether they're listening?
- Do you know of any problems that came up because someone didn't listen? What happened?
- What do you think prevents people from listening effectively? What advice would you have for someone on how to listen more accurately?

As your instructor directs,

a. Share your information with a small group of students in your class.
b. Present your findings orally to the class.
c. Present your findings in a memo to your instructor.
d. Join with other students to present your findings in a group report or presentation.

14.8   Interviewing Workers About Listening

Interview an employee or employer (preferably in an organization where you would like to work) about his or her on-the-job listening. Possible questions include:

- Whom do you listen to as part of your job? Subordinates? Managers? Peers? Customers or clients? Who else?
- How much time a day do you spend listening? What people do you talk to as part of your job? How do you tell whether they are listening?
- What strategies do you use to encourage others to listen to you?
- What strategies do you use to listen effectively?
- What prevents people from listening effectively? What advice do you have on how to listen more accurately?

As your instructor directs,

a. Share your information with a small group of students in the class.
b. Present your findings orally to the class.
c. Present your findings in a memo to your teacher.
d. Join with other students to present your findings in a group report or presentation.

14.9   Reflecting on Acknowledgment Responses

Try to be part of at least three conversations involving people from more than one culture. What acknowledgment responses do you observe? Which seem to yield the most positive results? If possible, talk to the other participants about what verbal and nonverbal cues show attentive listening in their cultures.

As your instructor directs,

a. Share your information with a small group of students in your class.
b. Present your findings orally to the class.
c. Present your findings in a memo to your instructor.
d. Join with other students to present your findings in a group report or presentation.

14.10   Listening for Understanding

Do this exercise as a class. Let each student complain about something (large or small) that really bothers him or her. Then the next student(s) will

a. Check his or her understanding of what the speaker said

b. Paraphrase the statement

c. Check for feelings that might lie behind the statement

d. Ask questions to better identify the problem

Note: The instructor should choose a group (four or five) of student "assessors" to note and comment on the accuracy of the paraphrasing and questioning responses.

POLISHING YOUR PROSE

Using Colons and Semicolons

Using colons and semicolons can help you to combine sentences efficiently. Indeed, colons and semicolons contribute to a sophisticated writing style. The trick is to learn to use them correctly.

Colons introduce lists, explanations, or qualifications.

Think of it this way: only the informed citizen can be part of a democracy.

His best feature was his fairness: all encompassing, just, and charitable.

CA, CPA or CMA: after your work placement you'll have a better idea of which certification would be best for you.

Note that when you use a colon, you need only one complete thought: either before or after the colon.

Semicolons have the same emphasis as periods; however, you can use them only between two complete thoughts. Using a semicolon suggests that the thoughts are connected. Often writers use a transitional word after the colon to further emphasize this connection. The result: the semicolon contributes to the unity and flow of the sentence, and allows the reader to write longer sentences without losing readers.

Jasmine has spent two hours searching for the lade bill; she's reviewed the customer's last six months, checked for incorrect entry, and done a manual search.

Toyota cannot keep up with the demand for its hybrid cars; apparently Canadians have finally woken up and smelled the gas fumes.

Most people appear delighted to use online banking services; for example, they pay bills, make deposits, and even invest electronically.

Facebook holds plenty of problems for the uninformed: you can be the object of bullying; you can be taken off someone's list; perhaps most important, your past is globally open to any potential employer.

Exercises

Use appropriate punctuation to combine the following sentences.

1. That file on the Richman proposal. Can you send me a copy by tomorrow, please?
2. Ms. Amarotti will arrive tomorrow. Nevertheless we have enough time to find her a great space.
3. Watch out. some people think there's a certain "ick" factor to social networking.
4. Take a moment to read the instructions before completing the form. Then bring it to the processing desk
5. Strange. I thought I already signed up for another six months.
6. Darcy got the promotion he's been working for. Now he's human resources assistant manager.
7. Remember. When we turn on the break room lights, everyone is to yell, "Happy Birthday, Susharita"
8. You have to make three copies for three different departments. Accounting, legal, and sales.
9. The best gig he ever has was his ten-month posting in Amsterdam. The night life is spectacular. Everything's open. Museums, pubs, shops. He was sad to come home.
10. Here's another effective career search question. What do you most enjoy doing?

Check your answers to the odd-numbered exercises on page 552.

Working and Writing in Teams

Learning Objectives

After reading and applying the information in Module 15, you'll be able to demonstrate

Knowledge of

- The ground rules for working well with others
- Roles people play in groups
- The characteristics of successful work teams

Skills to

- Work productively in a team
- Begin to resolve conflicts constructively
- Write collaboratively

Employability Skills 2000+ Checklist

In this module, the key skills from the Conference Board of Canada's Employability Skills 2000+ are

Communicate

○ write and speak so others pay attention and understand

Think & Solve Problems

○ assess situations and identify problems
○ seek different points of view and evaluate them based on facts
○ recognize the human, interpersonal, technical, scientific, and mathematical dimensions of a problem

○ check to see if a solution works, and act on opportunities for improvement

Demonstrate Positive Attitudes & Behaviours

○ deal with people, problems, and situations with honesty, integrity, and personal ethics

○ recognize your own and other people's good efforts
○ show interest, initiative, and effort

Be Adaptable

○ work independently or as part of a team
○ carry out multiple tasks or projects
○ be innovative and resourceful: identify and suggest alternative ways to achieve goals and get the job done

○ be open and respond constructively to change
○ cope with uncertainty

Work with Others

○ understand and work within the dynamics of a group
○ ensure that a team's purpose and objectives are clear
○ be flexible: respect, be open to, and be supportive of the thoughts, opinions, and contributions of others in a group
○ recognize and respect people's diversity, individual differences, and perspectives
○ accept and provide feedback in a constructive and considerate manner

○ contribute to a team by sharing information and expertise
○ lead or support when appropriate, motivating a group for high performance
○ understand the role of conflict in a group to reach solutions
○ manage and resolve conflict when appropriate

Participate in Projects & Tasks

○ work to agreed quality standards and specifications
○ select and use appropriate tools and technology for a task or project

○ adapt to changing requirements and information

Teamwork is fundamental to doing business today. People work in teams to create new products, streamline processes, hire employees, identify and solve problems, and brainstorm, articulate, and implement strategic organizational goals. Increasingly, people also work in teams to produce documents.

In an ideal world, we get to work in teams whose members share our values. In reality, we often work with people who hold very different ideas from ours, and who believe in the rightness of these ideas as insistently as we do in our own.

The most effective teams agree on and adopt explicit ground rules, and outcomes. Team members operate on two basic behavioural principles: *What gets rewarded gets repeated; what gets measured gets done.*

Table 15.1 lists some of the most common behavioural ground rules used by workplace teams.

TABLE 15.1   Possible Group Ground Rules

Start on time; end on time.	Practise NOSTUESO ("No one speaks twice until everyone speaks once").
Come to the meeting prepared.	If you have a problem with another person, tell that person, not everyone else.
Focus comments on the issues.	Everyone must be 70% comfortable with the decision and 100% committed to implementing it.
Avoid personal attacks.	If you agree to do something, do it.
Listen to and respect members' opinions.	Communicate immediately if you think you may not be able to fulfil an agreement.

Sources: Nancy Schullery and Beth Hoger, "Business Advocacy for Students in Small Groups," Association for Business Communication Annual Convention, San Antonio, November 9–11, 1998; "An Antidote to Chronic Cantankerousness," *Fast Company*, February/March 1998, p. 176; John Grossmann, "We've Got to Start Meeting Like This," *Inc.*, April 1998, p. 70; Gary Dessler, "Winning Commitment," quoted in *Team Management Briefings*, preview issue (September 1998), p. 5; and 3M Meeting Network, "Groundrules and Agreements," http://www.3M.com/meetingnetwork/readingroom/meetingguide_grndrules.html, retrieved October 25, 2006.

Table 15.2 lists some of the most common task-focused outcomes workplace teams focus on.

TABLE 15.2   Group Task Outcomes

- Define, articulate and agree on the goal(s) of the project.
- Describe the goal(s) in writing.
- Create time-management guidelines (**who** does **what when**) to reach desired goal(s).
- Create measurements that describe both (1) successful products (proposals, interviews, visuals) that work toward the goal and (2) the successful final product (an A+ on the report, the sales contract).
- Ensure every team member has a copy of the goals, the timeline, individual responsibilities, and the criteria for success.

What Kinds of Communication Happen in Groups?

Different messages occur at different points in a group's development.

Group messages fall into three categories: both *information* messages and *procedural* messages relate to getting the task done; *interpersonal* messages focus on maintaining group norms and fostering group cohesion.

1. **Informational messages** focus on content: the problem or challenge, data, and possible solutions.
2. **Procedural messages** focus on method and process. How will the group make decisions? Who will do what? When will assignments be due?
3. **Interpersonal messages** focus on people, promoting friendliness, cooperation, and group loyalty.

Effective work teams encourage open communication among members.

Different messages dominate during the various stages of group development.

During **orientation**, when members meet and begin to define their task, people who want to work well together consciously communicate in ways that foster mutuality and interdependence. Group members work toward some sort of social cohesiveness, and develop procedures for meeting and acting. Interpersonal and procedural messages reduce the tension that exists in a new group. Insisting on information at this stage of the process can impede the group's productivity.

Conflicts almost always arise when the group chooses a leader, and defines the problem. In this **formation** phase, people use interpersonal communication to resolve the conflicts that surface. Good leaders clarify procedures and roles, so that each person understands what he or she is supposed to do. Successful groups define, analyze, and agree on the problem carefully before they begin to search for solutions.

Coordination is the longest phase, during which most of the group's work is done. Procedural and interpersonal communications maintain the trust necessary to gather and focus on the task information. Creative conflict reoccurs as the group members debate alternative solutions.

In **formalization** the group seeks consensus. In this stage, the group tries to forget earlier conflicts as members focus on agreeing to the solution. The success of this phase determines how well the group's decision will be implemented.

Developing team unity depends on understanding different cultural values. Collective (high-context) cultures (Module 3) focus more strongly on relationship building (the formation and coordination stages) to ensure mutual understanding and respect among team members. Establishing and fostering this respect are vital processes for team productivity.

Indeed, businesses that incorporate the group dynamics of collective cultures enjoy higher employee retention and productivity rates. The "network group" adapts "Aboriginal community-building concepts such as talking circles, collective decision making, holistic approaches to life, cooperation, and respect for others and respect of self" to retain valuable Aboriginal employees. In our increasingly diverse and complex workplace, building relationships must be the first order of team business.[1]

Eagle's Flight® is a leader in experiential training for the business community. Here, participants investigate a realistic crime scene—an environment designed to teach the critical elements of effective communication through sharing, evaluation, and organization of information.

Technology also contributes to building workplace relationships, as interactive media replace traditional communication methods. Company-managed social networking sites and blogs foster a sense of community, and let even the most reticent employee voice his or her concerns. The success of McDonald's Station M., created as "an online meeting place for … staff … feedback and engagement" has surpassed management's expectations: "more than 14,000" crew members "from all over North America" log in daily to chat, ask questions or give/get peer advice.[2] More and more organizations are using digital media as a team-building tool.

Talking circles help build the relationships that make teams work.

What Roles Do People Play in Groups?

People play both group maintenance and task roles, and every role can be positive or negative.

Positive *maintenance* roles and actions that help the group build loyalty, resolve conflicts, and function smoothly to achieve task goals include[3]

Employability Skills

- *Listening actively.* Showing group members that they have been heard and that their ideas are being taken seriously (Module 14)
- *Encouraging participation.* Demonstrating openness and acceptance, recognizing the contributions of members, calling on quieter group members
- *Relieving tensions.* Joking and suggesting breaks and activities
- *Checking feelings.* Asking members how they feel about group activities and sharing one's own feelings with others
- *Solving interpersonal problems.* Opening discussion of interpersonal problems in the group and suggesting ways to solve them

Positive roles and actions that help the group achieve its *task* goals include

- *Seeking information and opinions.* Asking questions, identifying gaps in the group's knowledge
- *Giving information and opinions.* Answering questions, providing relevant information
- *Summarizing.* Restating major points, pulling ideas together, summarizing decisions
- *Evaluating.* Comparing group processes and products to standards and goals
- *Coordinating.* Planning work, giving directions, and fitting together contributions of group members

Negative roles and actions that hurt the group's *products* and *processes* include

- *Blocking*—disagreeing with everything proposed. Criticizing ideas is necessary if the group is to produce the best solution, but criticizing every single idea without suggesting possible solutions blocks a group.
- *Dominating*—trying to run the group by ordering, shutting out others, and insisting on one's own way. Active listening (Module 14) strategies build relationships, defuse conflict, and encourage participation. Authoritarian, tyrannical people don't just alienate others; they reduce or eliminate productivity.
- *Clowning*—making unproductive jokes and diverting the group from the task. Jokes can defuse tension and make the group more creative, but too many or inappropriate jokes can frustrate or offend team members, or impede progress.
- *Withdrawing*—being silent in meetings, not contributing, not helping with the work, not attending meetings. Silently listening encourages others to contribute; passive-aggressive behaviours can create a dysfunctional team.

Leadership in Groups

You may have noted that "leader" was not one of the roles listed above. Leadership is based on communication and interpersonal effectiveness. Several studies have shown that people who talk a lot, listen effectively, and respond nonverbally to other members in the group are considered leaders.[4]

Being a leader, however, does not mean doing all the work yourself. Indeed, someone who implies that he or she has the best ideas and can do the best work is likely playing the negative roles of blocking and dominating.

Effective groups balance three kinds of leadership, which parallel the three group development dimensions:

1. **Informational leaders** generate and evaluate ideas and text.
2. **Interpersonal leaders** monitor the group's process, check people's feelings, and resolve conflicts.
3. **Procedural leaders** set the agenda, make sure that everyone knows what's due for the next meeting, communicate with absent group members, and check to be sure that assignments are carried out.

Although it's possible for one person to take on all these responsibilities, in many groups, three (or more) different people take on the three kinds of leadership. Some groups formally or informally rotate or share these responsibilities, so that everyone—and no one—is a leader. Groups that rotate or share leadership roles are more productive, because more members assume responsibility for the group's success.

Characteristics of Successful Student Groups

A case study of six student groups completing class projects found that students in successful groups were not necessarily more skilled or more experienced than students in less successful groups. Instead, successful and less successful groups communicated differently in three ways:[5]

1. In the successful groups, the leader set clear deadlines, scheduled frequent meetings, and dealt directly with conflict that emerged in the group. In less successful groups, members had to ask the leader what they were supposed to be doing. The less successful groups met less often, and they tried to pretend that conflicts didn't exist.
2. The successful groups listened to criticism and made important decisions together. Perhaps as a result, everyone in the group could articulate the group's goals. In the less successful groups, a subgroup made decisions and told other members what had been decided.
3. The successful groups had a higher proportion of members who worked actively on the project. The successful groups even found ways to use members who didn't like working in groups. For example, one student who didn't want to be a "team player" functioned as a "freelancer" for her group, completing assignments by herself and giving them to the leader. The less successful groups had a much smaller percentage of active members and each had some members who did very little on the final project.

Student groups produce better projects when they openly disagree over substantive issues of content and document design. The disagreement does not need to be angry: a group member can simply say, "Yes, and here's another way we could do it." Deciding between two (or more) alternative options forces the group member to explain the rationale for an idea. Even when the group adopts the original idea, considering alternatives rather than quickly accepting the first idea produces better writing.[6]

Writer Kimberly Freeman found that the students who spent the most time meeting with their groups had the highest grades—on individual as well as on group assignments.[7]

Peer Pressure and Groupthink

Groupthink is the tendency for groups to put such a high premium on agreement that they directly or indirectly punish dissent. Groups whose members never express conflict may be experiencing groupthink. Groups that "go along with the crowd" and suppress conflict ignore the full range of alternatives, seek only information that supports the positions they already favour, and fail to prepare contingency plans to cope with foreseeable setbacks. A business suffering from groupthink may launch a new product that senior executives support but for which there is no demand. Student groups suffering from groupthink turn in inferior documents.

The best correctives to groupthink are the following:

- Brainstorm for additional alternatives.
- Test assumptions against those of a range of other people.
- Encourage disagreement, perhaps even assigning someone to be "devil's advocate."
- Protect the right of people in a group to disagree.

EXPANDING A CRITICAL SKILL

Leading with Integrity

According to Harvard Business School professor Amy Edmondson, teams fail because (1) some members don't believe their knowledge is interesting or relevant, (2) people are oblivious to others members' opposing interests, and (3) some members deliberately withhold information. Conversely, people who work together well tend to consult one another openly, honestly, and frequently. Members of successful teams act with integrity: they take responsibility for both task and maintenance functions; they tend to share power; and as team leaders or members, they act on the assumption that every person has a valuable contribution to make to the team.

In their book *Integrity Works*, authors Adrian Telford and Dana Gostick identify 10 behaviours that characterize leaders with integrity:

- You know that the little things count.
- You find the white when others see the grey.
- In a situation you mess up, you fess up.
- You create a culture of trust.
- You keep your word.
- You care about the greater good.
- You're honest but modest.
- You act like you're being watched.
- You hire integrity.
- You stay the course.

You can begin to lead your team with integrity by putting some of these behaviours into action:

- *Smile.* Get to know the other members of your group as individuals. Invite members to say something about themselves, perhaps what job they're hoping to get and one fact about their lives outside schoolwork.

- *Share.* Tell people about your own work style and obligations, and ask others to share their styles and obligations. Savvy group members play to each other's strengths and devise strategies for dealing with differences. The earlier you know what those differences are, the easier it will be to deal with them.
- *Suggest.* "Could we talk about what we see as our purposes in this presentation?" "One of the things we need to do is...." "One idea I had for a project is...." Presenting your ideas as suggestions gets the group started without suggesting that you expect your views to prevail.
- *Think.* Leaders look at the goal and identify the steps needed to get there. "Our proposal is due in two weeks. Let's list the tasks we need to do in order to write a rough draft."
- *Volunteer.* Volunteer to take notes, to gather some of the data the group will need, or to prepare the charts after the data are in. Volunteer not just for the interesting parts of the job (such as surfing the Web to find visuals for your presentation) but also for some of the dull but essential work, such as proofreading.
- *Ask.* Bring other people into the conversation. Learn about their knowledge, interests, and skills so that you'll have as much as possible to draw on as you complete your group projects.

Sources: Amy C. Edmondson, James R. Dillon, and Kathryn S. Roloff, "Three Perspectives on Team Learning Outcome Improvement, Task Mastery, and Group Process," 2006, Harvard Business School site, http://www.hbs.edu/research/pdf/07-029.pdf, retrieved October 29, 2008; Jared Sandberg, "Teamwork: When It's a Bad Idea," *The Globe and Mail*, October 1, 2004, p. C7; Harvey Schachter, "Where Integrity Leads, and Where It Lags," *The Globe and Mail*, June 15, 2005, p. C3.

How Can Team Members Handle Conflict?

Listen actively to get at the real issue, and repair bad feelings.

Conflicts will arise in any group of intelligent people who care about the task. Many of us feel so uncomfortable with conflict that we pretend it doesn't exist. However, unacknowledged conflicts rarely go away: they fester, impeding progress and productivity.

Try the following ways to reduce the number of conflicts in a group:

- Make responsibilities and ground rules clear at the beginning.
- Acknowledge verbal and nonverbal messages of discomfort, anger, or hostility.
- Discuss problems as they arise, rather than letting them fester until people explode.
- Realize that group members are not responsible for each other's feelings.

Table 15.3 suggests several possible solutions to frequent sources of group conflict. Often the symptom arises from a feeling of not being respected or appreciated by the group. Problems can be averted if people advocate for their ideas in a positive way. The best time to advocate for an idea is when the group has not yet identified all possible options, seems dominated by one view, or seems unable to choose among solutions. A tactful way to advocate for the position you favour is to recognize the contributions others have made, to summarize, and then to hypothesize: "What if ...?" "Let's look six months down the road." "Let's think about this."[8]

Groups whose members take the time necessary to analyze and agree on the task, objectives, and group norms (expected, acceptable, and unacceptable behaviours) have less destructive conflict. Many groups articulate these objectives and behaviours in a contract, with defined rewards and penalties, which all members sign.

Steps in Conflict Resolution

Negotiating and resolving conflict start with active listening (Module 14). Dealing successfully with conflict requires attention to both the issues and to people's feelings, which you cannot understand unless you stop talking and listen. Taking notes helps you focus your listening.[9]

Then follow this five-step procedure to help you resolve conflicts constructively.

1. Make Sure That the People Involved Really Disagree

Sometimes someone who's under a lot of pressure may appear upset. But the speaker may just be **venting** anger and frustration; he or she may not in fact be angry at the person who receives the explosion. One way to find out whether a person is just venting is to ask, "Is there something you'd like me to do?"

2. Check to See That Everyone's Information Is Correct

Sometimes different conversational styles (Module 3) or cultural differences create apparent conflicts when no real disagreement exists. Similarly, misunderstanding can arise from faulty assumptions. Ask open questions (*Who? What? Why? When? Where? How?*) to clarify concerns.

3. Discover the Needs Each Person Is Trying to Meet

Sometimes identifying the real need makes it possible to see a new solution. The **presenting problem** (the subject of the conflict) may or may not be the real problem. For example, a worker who complains about the hours he's putting in may in fact be complaining not about the hours themselves but about not feeling appreciated. A supervisor who complains that the other supervisors don't invite her to meetings may really feel that the other managers don't accept her as a peer.

TABLE 15.3   **Troubleshooting Group Problems**

Behaviour	Possible Solutions
We can't find a time to meet that works for all of us.	a. Find out why people can't meet at certain times. Some reasons suggest their own solutions. For example, if someone has to stay home with small children, perhaps the group could meet at that person's home. b. Assign out-of-class work to "committees" to work on parts of the project. c. Meet virtually to share, discuss, and revise drafts.
One person isn't doing his or her fair share.	a. Ask for information. Is the person overcommitted? Does he or she feel unappreciated? Those are different problems you'd solve in different ways. b. Early on, do things to build group loyalty. Get to know each other as writers and as people. Sometimes, do something interesting together. c. Encourage the person to contribute. "Maria, what do you think?" "Savio, which part of this would you like to draft?" Then find something to praise in the work. "Thanks for getting us started." d. If someone misses a meeting, assign someone else to bring the person up to speed. People who miss meetings for legitimate reasons (job interviews, illness) but don't find out what happened may become less committed to the group. e. Consider whether strict equality is the most important criterion. On a given project, some people may have more knowledge or time than others. Sometimes the best group product results from letting people do different amounts of "work." f. Even if you divide up the work, make all decisions as a group: what to write about, which evidence to include, what graphs to use, what revisions to make. People excluded from decisions become less committed to the group.
I seem to be the only one in the group who cares about quality.	a. Find out why other members "don't care." If they received low grades on early assignments, stress that good ideas and attention to detail can raise grades. Perhaps the group should meet with the instructor to discuss what kinds of work will pay the highest dividends. b. Volunteer to do extra work. Sometimes people settle for something just OK because they don't have the time or resources to do excellent work. They might be happy for the work to be done—if they didn't have to do it. c. Be sure that you're respecting what each person can contribute. Group members sometimes withdraw when one person dominates and suggests that he or she is "better" than other members.
People in the group don't seem willing to disagree. We end up going with the first idea suggested.	a. Appoint someone to be a "devil's advocate." b. Brainstorm so you have several possibilities to consider. c. After an idea is suggested, have each person in the group suggest a way it could be improved. d. Have each person in the group write a draft. It's likely the drafts will be different, and you'll have several options to mix and match. e. Talk about ways to offer positive and constructive feedback. Sometimes people don't disagree because they're afraid other group members won't tolerate disagreement.
One person just criticizes everything.	a. Ask the person to follow up the criticism with a suggestion for improvement. b. Talk about ways to express criticism tactfully. "I think we need to think about X" is more tactful than "You're wrong." c. If the criticism is about ideas and writing (not about people), value it. Ideas and documents need criticism to improve them.

Sometimes people have trouble seeing beyond the problem because they've been taught to suppress their anger, especially toward powerful people. One way to tell whether the presenting problem is the real problem is to ask, "If this were solved, would I be satisfied?" If the answer is no, then the problem that presents itself is not, in fact, the real problem. Solving the presenting problem won't solve the conflict. Keep probing until you get to the real conflict.

4. Search for Alternatives

Sometimes people get into conflict because they see too few alternatives. Indeed, people often see only two polarized choices—known as the *either-or logical fallacy*.

Creative people train themselves to think in terms of possibilities—the more the better. This technique, known as **brainstorming**, is an essential part of every step in the problem-solving process!

5. Repair Bad Feelings

Conflict can emerge without anger and without escalating the disagreement, as the next section shows. But if people's feelings have been hurt, the group needs to deal with those feelings to resolve the conflict constructively. Only when people feel respected and taken seriously can they take the next step of trusting others in the group.

Employability Skills

Responding to Criticism

Conflict is particularly difficult to resolve when someone else criticizes or attacks us directly. When we are criticized, our natural reaction is to defend ourselves—perhaps by counterattacking. The counterattack prompts the critic to defend him or herself. The conflict escalates; feelings are hurt; and issues get muddied and more difficult to resolve.

Just as resolving conflict depends on identifying the needs each person is trying to meet, dealing with criticism depends on understanding the real concern of the critic. Constructive ways to respond to criticism and get closer to the real concern include

- Paraphrasing
- Checking for feelings
- Checking for inferences
- Buying time with limited agreement

Paraphrasing

To **paraphrase**, repeat in your own words, in a neutral tone, the verbal content of the critic's message. The purposes of paraphrasing are (1) to be sure that you have heard the critic accurately, (2) to let the critic know what his or her statement means to you, and (3) to communicate the feeling that you are taking the critic and his or her feelings seriously.

Criticism:	You guys are stonewalling my requests for information.
Paraphrase:	You're saying that we don't give you the information you need quickly enough.

Checking for Feelings

When you **check the speaker's feelings**, you identify the emotions that the critic seems to be expressing verbally or nonverbally. The purposes of checking feelings are to try to understand (1) the critic's emotions, (2) the importance of the criticism for the critic, and (3) the unspoken ideas and feelings that may actually be more important than the voiced criticism.

Criticism:	You guys are stonewalling my requests for information.
Feeling check:	You sound pretty angry. Are you angry?

Always *ask* the other person if you are right in your perception. Even the best reader of nonverbal cues is sometimes wrong.

Checking for Inferences

When you **check the inferences** you draw from criticism, you identify the implied meaning of the verbal and nonverbal content of the criticism. You take the statement a step further than the words of the speaker, to try to understand why the person is bothered by the action or attitude under discussion. The purposes of checking inferences are (1) to identify the real (as opposed to the presenting) problem and (2) to communicate the feeling that you care about resolving the conflict.

Criticism:	You guys are stonewalling my requests for information.
Inference:	Are you saying that you need more information from our group?

Inferences can be faulty. In the above interchange, the critic might respond, "I don't need more information. I just think you should give it to me without my having to send you three emails every time I want some data."

Buying Time with Limited Agreement

Buying time is a useful strategy for dealing with criticisms that really sting. When you buy time with limited agreement, you avoid escalating the conflict (as an angry statement might do) but also avoid yielding to the critic's point of view. To buy time, restate the part of the criticism that you agree is true. (This is often a fact, rather than the interpretation or evaluation the critic has made of that fact.) *Then let the critic respond, before you say anything else.* The purposes of buying time are (1) to allow you time to think when a criticism really hits home and threatens you, so that you can respond to the criticism rather than simply reacting defensively, and (2) to suggest to the critic that you are genuinely listening to what he or she is saying.

Criticism:	You guys are stonewalling my requests for information.
Limited agreement:	It's true that the cost projections you asked for last week still aren't ready.

Do *not* go on to justify or explain. A "Yes, but ..." statement is not a time-buyer.

You-Attitude in Conflict Resolution

You-attitude (Module 6) means looking at the situation from the audience's point of view, respecting the audience, and protecting the audience's ego. The critical *you* statements that many of us use when we are upset do not illustrate respect for the audience. These statements make recipients feel attacked and defensive, destroying any possibility for dialogue.

In conflict resolution, **I-based** statements **about your own feelings and perceptions** can initiate positive conversation. I-based statements show good you-attitude.

Inflammatory (Lacks positive you-attitude):	You never do your share of the work.
I-based statement:	I feel that I'm doing more than my share of the work on this project.
Inflammatory (Lacks positive you-attitude):	Even you should be able to run the report through a spell checker.
I-based statement:	I'm not willing to have my name on a report with so many spelling errors. I did lots of the writing, and I don't think I should have to do the proofreading and spell checking, too.

How Can Teams Co-author Good Documents?

Employability Skills

Talk about your purposes and audiences; discuss drafts and revisions as a group.

Whatever your career choices, many of the documents you produce will be written as part of a group. Business, government and academic organizations use collaboration because

- The task is too big or the time is too short for one person to do all the work.
- No one person has all the knowledge required to do the task.

- A group representing different perspectives must reach a consensus.
- The organization wants the best efforts of as many people as possible.
- Technology facilitates the process.[10]

Collaborative writing can be done by two people or by a much larger group. The group can be democratic or run by a leader who makes decisions alone. The group may share or divide responsibility for each of the eight stages in the writing process (Module 4).

Research in collaborative writing is beginning to tell us about the strategies that produce the best writing. Rebecca Burnett found that student groups that voiced disagreements as they analyzed, planned, and wrote a document produced significantly better documents than those that suppressed disagreement, going along with whatever was first proposed.[11] A case study of two collaborative writing teams in an agency found that the successful group distributed power equally, worked to soothe hurt feelings, and was careful to involve all group members. In terms of the writing process, the successful group understood the task as a response to a rhetorical situation, planned revisions as a group, saw supervisors' comments as legitimate, and had a positive attitude toward revision.[12]

Professors Ede and Lunsford's detailed case studies of collaborative teams in business, government, and science create an "emerging profile of effective collaborative writers." The profile reflects those interpersonal competency skills so sought after by employers: "They are flexible; respectful of others; attentive and analytical listeners; able to speak and write clearly and articulately; dependable and able to meet deadlines; able to designate and share responsibility, to lead and to follow; open to criticism but confident in their own abilities; ready to engage in creative conflict."[13]

Planning the Work and the Document

Collaborative writing is complicated because it is both a social and intellectual process, as Figure 15.1 illustrates. To be successful, members must focus on building the team, and establishing norms and roles, before beginning to plan the document.

When you plan a collaborative writing project, put the plan in writing:

- Make your analysis of the problem, the audience, and your purposes explicit so you know where you agree and where you disagree.
- Articulate and agree on the organization, format, and style of the document before anyone begins to write, to make it easier to blend sections written by different authors.
- Establish project-management time lines that meet members' needs, and maximize individual's communications' strengths. Consider your work styles, and other commitments. A writer working alone can stay up all night to finish a single-authored document. But members of a group need to work together to accommodate each other's styles and to enable members to meet other commitments.
- Consider creating a team contract which defines members' roles and responsibilities.
- Use computer applications and platforms—Google Wave, for example—that enable frequent virtual meetings, and real-time composing, revising, and editing collaboration.
- Build some leeway into your deadlines. It's harder for a group to finish a document when one person's part is missing than it is for a single writer to finish the last section of a document on which he or she has done all the work.

Composing the Drafts

Most writers find that composing alone is faster than composing in a group. However, composing together may reduce revision time later, since group members can examine every choice as it is made. Plenty of choices of software, including Google Wave, Google Docs, and Think Free, allow members to meet, write, and provide feedback immediately and accurately.

FIGURE 15.1 **Collaborative Writing Activities**

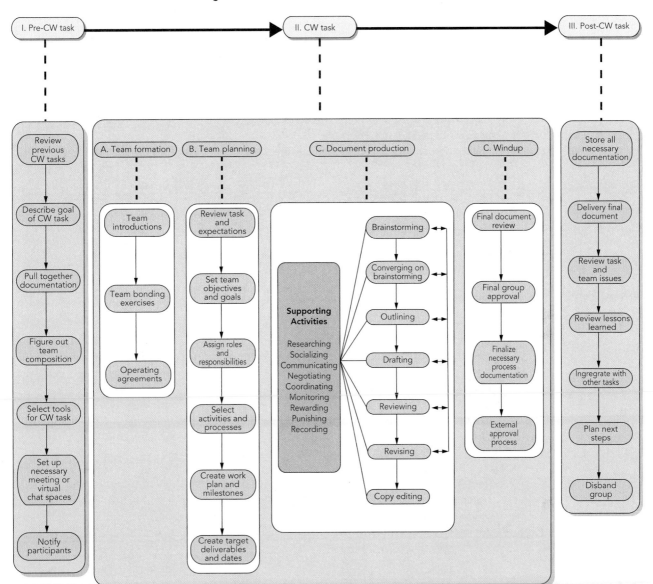

Source: Paul Benjamin Lowry, Aaron Curtis, and Michelle Rene Lowry, "Building a Taxonomy and Nomenclature of Collaborative Writing to Improve Interdisciplinary Research and Practice," *Journal of Business Communications* 41(1) (January 2004): 84, DOI: 10.1177/0021943603259363, retrieved October 22, 2009, from http://job.sagepub.com/cgi/reprint/41/1/66.pdf.

Encourage each member to choose task and maintenance roles (leader, summariser, reviser, editor) that best use his and her strengths. Have the best writer(s) draft the document after everyone has gathered the necessary information.

Revising the Document

Revising a collaborative document requires attention to content, organization, and style. The following guidelines can make the revision process more effective:

- Evaluate the content and discuss possible revisions as a group. Brainstorm ways to improve each section so the person doing the revisions has some guidance.
- Recognize that different people favour different writing styles. If the style satisfies the demands of standard English and the conventions of business writing, accept it even if you wouldn't say it that way.

- When the group is satisfied with the content of the document, one person—probably the best writer—should make any changes necessary to make the writing style consistent throughout.

Editing and Proofreading the Document

Since writers' mastery of standard English varies, a group report needs careful editing and proofreading.

- Have at least one person read the whole document for consistency of appearance and tone (e.g., formatting, numbering).
- Have another group member check the whole document for correct grammar, spelling, and usage.
- Use a spell checker.
- Have all group members proofread the document one last time, because spell checkers cannot think, and therefore cannot catch out-of-context misspellings (e.g., "there," "their," and "they're").

Making the Group Process Work

Employability Skills

Collaborative writing requires special attention to group process:

- Allow plenty of time to discuss problems and find solutions. Successful collaborative writing demands hours of communicating to manage project activities, and to keep members aware and engaged.[14] Students writing group reports spend six to seven hours a week outside class in group meetings—not counting the time they spend gathering information and writing their drafts.[15]
- Take the time to get to know group members, and to build group loyalty. Group members will work harder and the final document will be better if the group is important to members.
- Be a responsible group member. Attend all the meetings; do what you've committed to do, and plan so you will meet deadlines.
- Be aware that people have different ways of experiencing reality and of expressing themselves.
- Because talking is "looser" than writing, people in a group can think they agree when they don't. Don't assume that because the discussion went smoothly, a draft written by one person will necessarily be acceptable.

MODULE SUMMARY

- Effective groups balance informational leadership, interpersonal leadership, and procedural leadership.

- In productive groups, members communicate often, establish clear goals, define deadlines, deal directly with conflict, have an inclusive decision-making style, allow for others' individual working styles, actively contribute, and assume responsibility for meeting deadlines. Shared leadership is also characteristic of productive teams.

- Groupthink is the tendency for members to put such a high premium on agreement that they directly or indirectly punish dissent. To avoid groupthink, consciously brainstorm alternatives, test your assumptions against those of a range of other people, and protect the right of people in a group to disagree.

- To negotiate conflict, first make sure that the people involved really disagree. Next, ensure that everyone has the correct information. The problem causing dissention may not be the real problem. Encourage people to voice their real concerns, and brainstorm alternatives.

- Constructive ways to respond to criticism include paraphrasing, checking for feelings and inferences, buying time through limited agreement, and using I-based statements to express observable behaviours and feelings.

- Collaborative writing is a complex social and intellectual process. Writers producing a collaborative document are most productive when they first focus on the processes of group orientation and formation.

ASSIGNMENTS FOR MODULE 15

Questions for Critical Thinking

15.1 Why are so many people so afraid of conflict in groups? Why is it better for groups to deal with conflicts, rather than just trying to ignore them?

15.2 How can teams successfully manage cultural differences among members?

15.3 What do you find most difficult about collaborative writing? What strategies have you developed to make your contributions more effective?

Exercises and Problems

15.4 Assessing Your Negotiating Style

To get an idea of your negotiating style and skills, go to www.cpep-net.ca/system/files/Negotiating+Styles.pdf. Read the overview and click on the self-assessment link, www.swlearning.com/management/holley/lrp8e/Negotiating_Style-Final.rtf. After answering the questions, and reading the analysis of your style,

a. Ask a minimum of two close friends and/or family member how accurate your results are.

b. Consider a group or team you have been a member of. How did you deal with conflict in that situation? What similarities exist between your behaviours in the group and your results on the self-assessment?

Write a memo to your instructor describing your results, analyzing their accuracy, and providing a specific example that proves (or disproves) the results.

15.5 Identifying and Analyzing Group Roles

Observe your behaviours and the behaviours of others in the group to identify and analyze team roles and interpersonal leadership qualities.

a. Each group member writes his/her answers to the following questions after each group meeting.

b. Each member shares his/her perceptions with the group.

c. Each member identifies one leadership or positive team role he/she has demonstrated.

d. Each member identifies one leadership or positive team role he/she wants to develop.

Group Process Analysis

- How do you help others in the group talk and give their opinions? How do other members encourage your opinions? What could group members do to encourage greater participation?

- Describe your active listening techniques. Describe how other group members demonstrate they are listening. What could other members do to improve their listening techniques? What could you do?

- What kinds of questions are you asking each other: open-ended? encouraging? paraphrasing? interested? closed? Who asks the most questions? the fewest?

- How does the group keep track of discussions and tasks to be done? Who takes notes? How was that person chosen? What happens to those notes?

- Describe how the group reaches agreement. Describe what happens when members disagree.

- Describe how you usually deal with conflict. Describe how every other member deals with conflict. Assess how well these strategies work. In Exercises 15.6 through 15.9, assume that your group has been asked to recommend a solution.

As your instructor directs,

a. Send email messages to group members identifying your initial point of view on the issue and discussing the various options.

b. Meet as a group to come to a consensus.

c. As a group, answer the message.

d. Write a memo to your instructor telling how satisfied you are with

- The decision your group reached
- The process you used to reach it

e. Write a memo describing your group's dynamics.

15.6   Recommending a Fair Way to Assign Work Around the Holidays

You are on the labour–management committee. This email arrives from the general manager:

Subject: Allocating Holiday Hours

As you know, lots of people want to take extra time off around holidays to turn three-day weekends into longer trips. But we do need to stay open. Right now, there are allegations that some supervisors give the time off to their friends. But "fair" systems, such as giving more senior workers first choice at time off, or requiring that workers with crucial skills work, also create problems. And possibly we need a different system in December, when many people want to take off a week or more, than we do for other holidays, when most people take only an extra day or two.

Please recommend an equitable way to decide how to assign hours.

Write a group response recommending the best way to assign hours.

Hint: Agree on an office, factory, store, hospital, or other workplace to use for this problem.

15.7   Recommending an Internet Use Policy

You're on the information technology integration committee. You get this message from your manager:

Subject: Need Internet Use Policy

We have no policy on Internet use. Is it OK for people to play games, tweet, or surf the Web during work hours? Should we block access to certain Web sites?

The biggest problem may be responses to email lists, online shopping, and comments on blogs. There's no problem when people log on from home. But if they post responses from their workstations here, people might think the comment represents the official organizational stance on the issue—and it doesn't.

Write a group response recommending a policy.

Hint: Agree on an office, factory, store, hospital, or other workplace to use for this problem.

15.8   Recommending Ways to Retain Workers

You are on the recruitment and retention committee. This email arrives from the Vice-President, Human Resources:

Subject: Retaining Workers

As you know, it's a challenge to find employees with the skills we want. To limit the need to hire new people, we want to reduce turnover. What could we do to keep people happy? Please divide your recommendations into low-cost and high-cost solutions.

Write a group response recommending ways to retain workers.

Hint: Agree on an office, factory, store, hospital, or other workplace to use for this problem.

15.9   Judging Suggestions

You're on the suggestion committee. Employees submit suggestions that will save money or improve quality, procedures, or morale. Your committee must decide whether to accept, partially accept, or reject each suggestion.

Write a message to each employee, informing him or her of your decision.

1.   From: Elena Kusznirewicz, Human Resources

Subject: Suggestion to Change Sick Leave Policy

Right now, employees can "cash in" their unused sick-leave days each year and many people do that. The trouble is that people have too few days left if they need to have major surgery or chemotherapy. I recommend that we change the policy to allow people to "cash in" unused sick-leave days only when they retire or leave their jobs.

2.   From: Ivan Lin, Call Centre

Subject: Suggestion—Open Corporate Store

We should have a store. I visited a friend whose company had a store with company-logo clothing, toys, and sundries (mugs, mouse pads, etc.) as well as greeting cards, snacks, and so forth.

3.   From: Mohammed Chaar, Accounts Receivable

Subject: Suggestion: Allow Pets at Work

We should let people bring pets to work. Pets reduce stress and blood pressure. People like Justin's seeing-eye dog.

15.10 Planning a Game*

Many companies are using games and contests to solve problems in an enjoyable way. One company promised to give everyone $30 a month extra if they reduced the error rate below 0.5 percent. The rate improved immediately. After several successful months, the incentive went to $40 a month for getting it under 0.3 percent and finally to $50 a month for getting it under 0.2 percent. Another company offered workers two "well hours" if they got in by 7 A.M. every day for a month. An accounting and financial-services company divided its employees into two teams. The one that got the most referrals and new accounts received a meal prepared and served by the losing team (the firm paid for the food). Games are best when the people who will play them create them. Games need to make business sense and give rewards to many people, not just a few. Rewards should be small.

Think of a game or contest that might improve productivity or quality in your classroom, on campus, or in a workplace you know well.

As your instructor directs,

   a. Write a message to persuade your instructor, boss, or other decision maker to authorize the game or contest.
   b. Write a message announcing the game and persuading people to participate in it.

*Based on John Case, *The Open-Book Experience: Lessons from Over 100 Companies Who Successfully Transformed Themselves* (Reading, MA: Addison-Wesley, 1998), pp. 129–201.

15.11 Creating Brochures

In a collaborative group, create a series of brochures for an organization, and present your design and copy to the class in a group oral presentation. Your brochures should work well as a series but also be capable of standing alone if a reader picks up just one. They should share a common visual design and be appropriate for your purposes and audience. You may use sketches rather than photos or finished drawings. Text, however, should be as it will appear in the final copy.

As you prepare your series, talk to a knowledgeable person in the organization. For this assignment, although the person is knowledgeable, he or she does not have to have the power to approve the brochures.

As your instructor directs,

   1. Submit two copies of each brochure
   2. Submit a narrative explaining (a) how you responded to the wishes of the person in the organization who was your contact and (b) five of the choices you made in terms of content, visuals, and design, and the reasons that you made these choices

15.12 Analyzing the Dynamics of a Group

Analyze the dynamics of a group of which you are or were a member. Answer the following questions:

   1. Who was the group's leader? How did the leader emerge? Were there any changes in or challenges to the original leader?
   2. Describe the contribution each member made to the group and the roles each person played.
   3. Did any members of the group officially or unofficially drop out? Did anyone join after the group had begun working? How did you deal with the loss or addition of a group member, both in terms of getting the work done and in terms of helping people work together?
   4. What planning did your group do at the start of the project? Did you stick to the plan or revise it? How did the group decide that revision was necessary?
   5. How did your group make decisions? Did you vote? Reach decisions by consensus?
   6. What problems or conflicts arose? How did the group deal with them? To what extent did conflicts interfere with the group's task?
   7. Evaluate your group both in terms of its task and in terms of the satisfaction members felt. How did this group compare with other groups you've been part of? What made it better or worse?

As you answer the questions,

   - *Be honest.* You won't lose points for reporting that your group had problems or did something "wrong."
   - *Show your knowledge of good group dynamics.* That is, if your group did something poorly, show that you know what should have been done. Similarly, if your group worked well, show that you know why it worked well.
   - *Be specific.* Give examples or anecdotes to support your claims.

As your instructor directs,

   a. Discuss these questions with the other group members.
   b. Present your findings orally to the class.
   c. Present your findings in an individual memo to your instructor.
   d. Join with the other group members to write a collaborative memo to your instructor.

POLISHING YOUR PROSE

Delivering Criticism

No one likes to be told that his or her work isn't good. But criticism is necessary if people and documents are to improve.

Depending on the situation, you may be able to use one of these strategies:

1. Notice what's good as well as what needs work.

    The charts are great. We need to make the text as good as they are.

    I really like the ideas you've used in the slides. We need to edit the bulleted points so they're parallel.

2. Ask questions.

    Were you able to find any books and articles, in addition to sources on the Internet?

    What do you see as the most important revisions to make for the next draft?

3. Refer to the textbook or another authority.

    The module on design says that italic type is hard to read.

    Our instructor told us that presentations should have just three main points.

4. Make statements about your own reaction.

    I'm not sure what you're getting at in this section.

    I wouldn't be convinced by the arguments here.

5. Criticize what's wrong, without making global attacks on the whole document or on the writer as a person.

    There are a lot of typos in this draft.

    You begin almost every sentence with um.

Exercises

Rewrite each criticism to make it less hurtful. You may add or omit information as needed.

1. This is the worst report I've ever seen.
2. My 10-year-old can spell better than you do.
3. I can't believe that you didn't go to the library to get any sources.
4. You've used four different fonts in this report. Didn't you read the book? Don't you know that we're not supposed to use more than two?
5. This design is really lame. It looks like every other brochure I've ever seen.
6. There's no way we'll get a passing grade if we turn this in.
7. Were you asleep? Didn't you hear our instructor say that we had to use at least five sources?
8. This is really creative. You've written the perfect illustration for "How to Fail This Course."
9. This proposal makes no sense.
10. This clip art is sexist. There's no way we should use it.

Check your answers to the odd-numbered exercises on page 552.

Planning, Managing, and Recording Meetings

Learning Objectives

After reading and applying the information in Module 16, you'll be able to demonstrate

Knowledge of

- Meeting management
- Opportunities and challenges of virtual meetings

Skills to

- Plan a meeting
- Lead a meeting
- Participate in meetings
- Take good meeting minutes
- Participate in virtual meetings

Employability Skills 2000+ Checklist

In this module, the key skills from the Conference Board of Canada's Employability Skills 2000+ are

Communicate

○ write and speak so others pay attention and understand
○ listen and ask questions to understand and appreciate the points of view of others
○ share information using a range of information and communications technologies (e.g., voice, email, computers)

○ use relevant scientific, technological, and mathematical knowledge and skills to explain or clarify ideas

Manage Information

○ locate, gather, and organize information using appropriate technology and information systems

Demonstrate Positive Attitudes & Behaviours

○ feel good about yourself and be confident
○ deal with people, problems, and situations with honesty, integrity, and personal ethics

Be Responsible

○ plan and manage time, money, and other resources to achieve goals
○ be accountable for your actions and the actions of your group

○ be socially responsible and contribute to your community

Be Adaptable

○ work independently or as a part of a team
○ carry out multiple tasks or projects
○ be innovative and resourceful: identify and suggest alternative ways to achieve goals and get the job done

○ cope with uncertainty

Work with Others

○ understand and work within the dynamics of a group
○ ensure that a team's purpose and objectives are clear
○ be flexible: respect, be open to, and be supportive of the thoughts, opinions, and contributions of others in a group

○ recognize and respect people's diversity, individual differences, and perspectives

Participate in Projects & Tasks

○ work to agreed quality standards and specifications
○ select and use appropriate tools and technology for a task or project

○ adapt to changing requirements and information

People spend more time in meetings today than ever before. Although meetings have always made up the largest proportion of the average manager's day, emphasis on teamwork and collaboration (Module 15) means even more frequent meetings for all employees. Furthermore, the combustible combination of technological innovation, environmental concerns, and fossil fuel depletion will increase people's time in virtual meetings. Regardless of the meeting medium, however, when people perceive their meetings as organized, with productive results, they feel their time has been well spent.[1]

Business, nonprofit, and government organizations hold several types of meetings:

Employability Skills

- **Informal**, **one-on-one**, or **hall meetings** are the most significant meetings; people see them as an opportunity to exchange meaningful information. Employees talk by the photocopier or the refrigerator. One person walks into a colleague's office or cubicle to ask a question. A supervisor stops to chat with an employee, to ask how things are going and thereby "manage by walking around." These informal meetings create or reinforce company culture, support networking, and can facilitate career advancement.

    Indeed, according to experts, informal meetings that include gossip serve as vital organizational arteries; gossip "can be a powerful way to spread information, boost bonding and morale, and release stress.... [G]ossip in the office, over the Internet or on the phone ... causes us to relax ... and tell[s] [us] something about the underlying" organizational culture.[2]

- **Team meetings** bring people together to manage projects, solve problems, and collaborate on documents (Module 15). Recorded agendas and minutes formalize these meetings.

- **Regular staff meetings** are held to provide information, announce new policies and products, answer questions, share ideas, and motivate people. Recorded agendas and minutes formalize these meetings.

- Other frequent **organizational** meetings include **sales meetings**, **staff training sessions**, **conventions**, and **retreats**. These sessions allow people to develop themselves professionally, to team-build, and/or to do long-range planning.

- **Parliamentary proceedings** are the most formal types of meetings, run according to strict rules, like the rules of parliamentary procedure summarized in *Robert's Rules of Order*. These meetings are common only for boards of directors and legislative bodies.

Meetings today are usually supported by technology. Some organizations display proceedings for all the participants to see. "People literally see themselves being heard. Related comments are identified, linked, and edited on screen. The digressions and tangents quickly become apparent." The resulting document can be posted on the company intranet for further discussion and comments.[3]

Other organizations use group support software. Each person sits at a workstation. Participants key in their own brainstorming ideas and comments. People can vote by ranking items on a 1-to-10 scale; the software calculates the averages.[4]

Speakerphones, conference calls, and VoIP software like Skype allow people in different, even remote locations to participate in the same conversation. Online meetings, such as those hosted by WebEx (www.webex.com), allow you to bring together five other participants for a simultaneous email conversation in your own private chat room. Videoconferences provide high-quality video and audio transmissions. And now blogging allows a "chairperson" to initiate the worldwide cyber-meeting, and air his or her opinion without interruption.

The length and purposes of the meeting, the number of people attending, the budget, and the available technology all affect outcomes. However, as either initiator or attendee, you can prepare to ensure more productive meetings.

Many important meetings are informal.

What Planning Should Precede a Meeting?

Identify your purpose(s), and create an agenda.

Identify Your Purpose

Meetings can have at least six purposes:

- To share information
- To brainstorm ideas
- To evaluate ideas
- To make decisions
- To create a document
- To motivate members

When meetings combine two or more purposes, it's important to make the purposes explicit. For example, in the meeting of a university student government or a company's board of directors, some items are presented for information. Discussion is possible, but the group will not be asked to make a decision. Other items are presented for action; the group will be asked to vote. A business meeting might specify that the first half-hour will be allotted for brainstorming, with the second half-hour devoted to evaluation. Telling participants how their input will be used clarifies expectations and focuses the conversation.

Intel's agendas also specify *how* decisions will be made. The company uses four different decision-making processes:

- Authoritative (the leader makes the decision alone)
- Consultative (the leader hears group comments but then makes the decision alone)
- Voting (the majority wins)
- Consensual (discussion continues until everyone can "buy into" the decision)[5]

The most successful peer-group team meetings use consensual decision making, and share leadership roles (Module 15).

FIGURE 16.1   Use PAIBOC Analysis to Plan Successful Meetings

P Why are you holding/attending the meeting? What is the **purpose**? What specific outcomes do you want/need?

A Who is **attending**? Why? What is your relationship to attendees? What are their expectations, values and needs? What action(s) do you want/expect from attendees? How can you expect them to react? If it's a virtual meeting, what technology will maximize participation?

I What **information** do people already know? What do they need to know for you to achieve your intended purpose(s)? What's the best way to prepare them?

B How can participating in the meeting **benefit** your attendees? What's in it for them? Who else will benefit from the meeting, should you realize your purpose(s)?

O What **objections** might attendees have to the meeting content, time, length, medium, outcome(s), or to you? How can you overcome or reduce these objections?

C What is the meeting **context**? How long is the meeting? What time is the meeting? How will the meeting length and time of day affect attendees and outcome? What economic, environmental, political, and organizational realities will influence attendees' attitudes, feelings and beliefs? How can you use technology to realize your intended outcomes?

Create an Agenda

Once you've identified your purposes, think about how you can make them happen. If you want a participatory meeting, make sure attendees receive all the necessary information before the meeting. Be explicit in your expectations: ask people to read materials in advance, or to bring drafts to the meeting so that collaborative writing can go more quickly.

For team meetings called on short notice, the first item of business is to create an agenda. This kind of agenda can be informal, simply listing the topics or goals.

For meetings with more lead time, distribute an agenda several days before the meeting. (*Agenda* is Latin for "to be done.") If possible, give participants a chance to comment; then revise the agenda in response to those comments. A good agenda answers five questions:

- Where and when: time and place of the meeting
- What: agenda items
- Why: each item flagged for purpose—information, discussion, or decision
- Who: participants and individuals sponsoring or introducing each item
- How: meeting duration and time allotted for each item

Figure 16.2 shows an example of a meeting agenda.

FIGURE 16.2   Sample Meeting Agenda

Distribute the agenda early.

Some groups approve the agenda and the minutes of the last meeting.

People don't vote on information items.

Realistic time estimates help keep a meeting on track.

The decision will be made during the meeting.

Many groups use the last five minutes to review what went well and what needs to be improved.

Marketing Committee Agenda

September 9, 10 AM
Conference Room 410

10:00	1. Updates on Projects (For information)	Everyone!
10:15	2. Budget Report (For information)	Tim
10:20	3. Report from the Web Subcommittee (For <u>decision</u>: choose one of the three prototypes)	Lori
10:45	4. Planning the Subsidiary Web Pages (For decision: brainstorm; then assign responsibility)	Lori
11:00	5. Report from the Diversity Committee (For decision: approve hiring plan)	Hiroshi
11:25	6. Report from the Research Committee (For decision: assign research topics)	Amanda
11:45	7. Evaluation	
11:50	8. Adjourn	

Specify when and where the meeting will be held.

Specify who is responsible for presenting each item.

Agendas don't have to give this much detail. But referring to documents reminds participants to bring them to the meeting.

Some groups leave a slot for "new business."

Many groups put routine items first because getting agreement will be easy. Schedule controversial items early in the meeting, when people's energy levels are high, and to allow enough time for full discussion. Giving a controversial item only half an hour at the end of the meeting leads people to suspect that the leaders are trying to manipulate them.

The best meetings encourage participation, creativity, and fun. If you are organizing a long meeting, a training session or conference for example, make time for networking and socializing. These activities are vital to participants' perceptions of the value of the meeting. Allow for short breaks at least every two hours, and generous breaks twice a day so participants can chat informally with each other. Include some social functions so people can get to know each other.

You might want to leave five minutes at the end of the meeting to evaluate it. What went well? What could be better? What do you want to change next time?

When I'm in Charge, How Do I Keep the Meeting on Track?

Pay attention both to task and to process.

Your goal as chair is to clarify the meeting's significance and goals, and help participants deal with agenda items timely and adequately.

- When people are new to the group, make the ground rules explicit (Module 15). Ground rules might cover whether it is acceptable to check email, send messages, or answer cell phones during the meeting, and whether people must stay for the whole meeting, or may drop in and out.
- Introduce newcomers, and each person as he or she covers an agenda item.
- Use positive reinforcements—seeking opinions, giving information, summarizing, evaluating and coordinating (Module 15)—to remind the group of its progress: "We're a bit behind schedule. Let's try to get through the committee reports quickly."
- Acknowledge and negotiate conflict; shape the discussion or summarize issues when the issues are complex, or when members have major disagreements: "We're really talking about two things: whether the change would save money and whether our customers would like it. Does it make sense to keep those two together, or could we talk about customer reaction first, and then deal with the financial issues?"
- If the issue is contentious, ask speakers for and against a recommendation to alternate. If no one remains on one side, you can stop the discussion.
- Pay attention to people and process. In small groups, invite everyone to speak.
- If conflict escalates, focus on ways the group could deal with the conflict (Module 15), before getting back to the issue.
- If the group doesn't formally vote, summarize the group consensus after each point so that everyone knows what the decision is, who is responsible for implementing or following up, and when.

Meeting norms vary, depending on the corporate culture.

Meetings depend on social interaction as well as a good agenda.

What Decision-Making Strategies Work Well in Meetings?

Try the standard agenda or dot planning.

Probably the least effective decision-making strategy is to let the person who talks first, last, loudest, or most determine the decision. Voting is quick but may leave people in the minority unhappy with and uncommitted to the majority's plan.

Coming to consensus takes time but results in speedier implementation of ideas. Two strategies that are often useful in organizational groups are the standard agenda and dot planning.

The **standard agenda** is a seven-step decision-making process for solving problems:

1. Clarify and reach agreement on the task: what the group has to deliver, in what form, by what due date. Identify available resources.
2. Identify and reach agreement on the problem or the situation: What question is the group trying to answer? What exactly is the issue?
3. Gather information, share it with all group members, and examine it critically.

EXPANDING A CRITICAL SKILL

Building an Online Community

People spend more time meeting virtually than on any other Internet activity. Social media sites are now "the number one platform for creating and sharing content";[6] and as blogs and Wikis morph into ever-more-sophisticated digital applications, users' demand for participation in online communities will increase. And for employee communication, that's a good thing.

Organizations can use digital media to build on online community of interdependent teams. As is true of all team-building, however, success depends on careful planning. The project managers must consider their purposes, and prospective audiences, content and culture. When they have decided why they want to encourage virtual networking, companies have to consider how to encourage

employees to engage, what content will keep people coming back, what guidelines will communicate appropriate behaviours, who will manage the technological and staffing logistics, and how they will measure success.

Online communities can truly democratize the workplace, facilitate interdisciplinary knowledge sharing, and foster team-building. But the community can only be as good as its blueprint and its members.

Sources: Jason Falls, "Seven Questions to Ask Before Starting an Online Community"; Dave Wilkins and Drew Darnbrough, "Developing an Online Community"; Michael Wilson, "Best Practices for Building Successful Online Communities," *IABC CW Bulletin* 7(4) (April 2009), retrieved September 18, 2009, from http://www.iabc.com/cwb/archive/2009/0409/#feature1.

4. Establish criteria: What would the ideal solution include? Which elements of that solution would be part of a less-than-ideal but still acceptable solution? What legal, financial, ethical, or other limitations might keep a solution from being implemented?
5. Generate alternative solutions: brainstorm and record ideas for the next step.
6. Measure the alternatives against the criteria.
7. Choose the best solution.[7]

Dot planning offers a way for large groups to choose priorities quickly.

1. First, the group brainstorms ideas, recording each on pages that are put on the wall.
2. Each individual gets three to five adhesive dots in two colours. One colour represents high priority, the other lower priority.
3. People walk up to the pages and affix dots beside the points they care most about. Some groups allow only one dot from one person on any one item; others allow someone who is really passionate about an idea to put all of his or her dots on it.

As Figure 16.3 shows, the dots make it easy to see which items the group believes are most important.

How Can I Be an Effective Meeting Participant?

Employability Skills

Be prepared.

Take the time to prepare for meetings. Read the materials distributed before the meeting; think about the discussion topics. Bring those materials to the meeting, along with something

FIGURE 16.3   Dot Planning Allows Groups to Set Priorities Quickly

Here, green dots mean "high priority"; blue dots mean "low priority." Group members can see at a glance which items have widespread support, which are controversial, and which are low-priority.

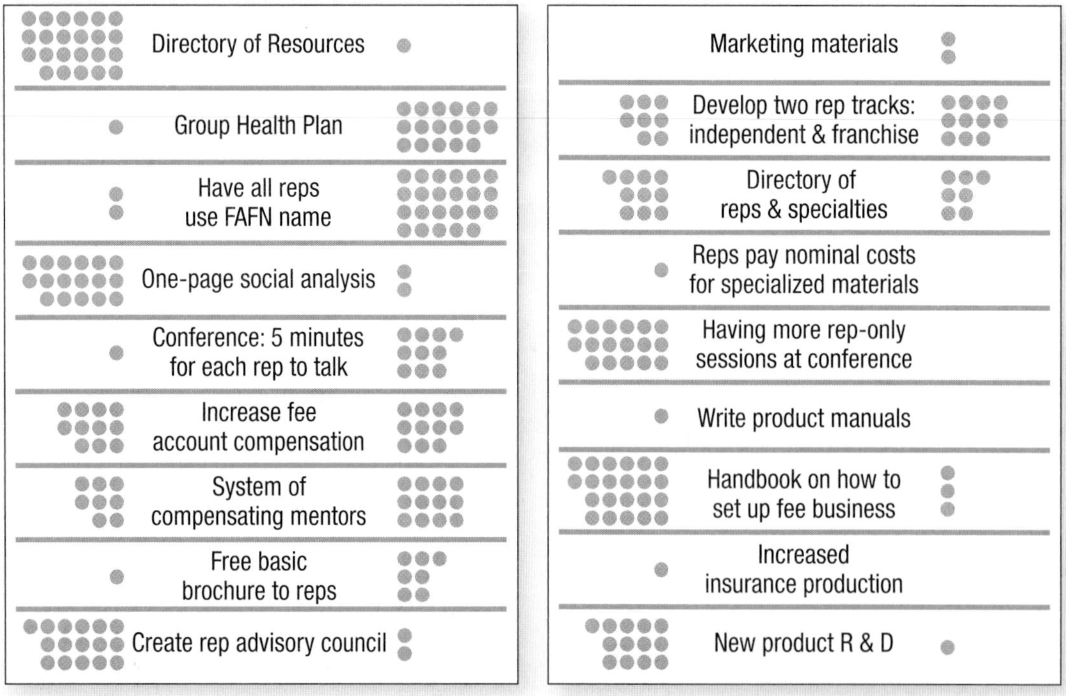

Source: Christopher Caggiano, "The Color-Coded Priority Setter," *Inc.*, June 1, 1995, pp. 70–71, http://www.inc.com/magazine/19950601/2300.html, retrieved September 18, 2009.

to write on and with. Taking notes enhances recall, and your notes may capture important nuances that meeting minutes do not.

Arrive on time: five to ten minutes early. Your timely attendance shows respect for other participants, and for the meeting content. Furthermore, you get your choice of seats; the best place is directly opposite the meeting chairperson because (1) you can make direct eye contact and (2) you can observe subtle nonverbal messages.

In a small meeting, you'll probably get several chances to speak. Research indicates that the most influential people in a meeting are those who say something in the first five minutes of the meeting (even just to ask a question), who talk most often, and who talk at greatest length.[8]

In a large meeting, you may get just one chance to speak. Make notes of what you want to say so that you can be concise, fluent, and complete.

What Should Be in Meeting Minutes?

Minutes should include attendees' names, discussion topics, and action items: lists of who does what next.

Meeting expert Michael Begeman suggests recording three kinds of information:

Employability Skills

1. Decisions reached
2. Action items, where someone needs to implement or follow up on something
3. Open issues—issues raised but not resolved[9]

Minutes of formal meetings include who was present and absent, the wording of motions and amendments, and the votes. Committee reports are often attached for later reference. For less formal meetings, brief minutes are fine.

The most important items are the decisions and action assignments. Long minutes are most helpful when assignments are set off visually from the narrative:

> We discussed whether we should initiate an online company social network.
>
> **Action**: Menhua will research options and best practices for next month's meeting.
>
> **Action**: Sophie will survey employees online to get their opinion.

Most people, however, file meeting minutes under "G" for garbage. If you want to write meeting minutes to be read, keep them to a page or less, write in the active voice, and highlight the most important information (**who** *does* **what next**).

What Should I Know About Virtual Meetings?

Be aware of the limitations of you communication medium. For important projects, build in some real meetings as well as some virtual ones. People still prefer to meet face to face.

When you meet technologically, you lose the informal interaction: going to lunch or chatting during a break. These personal meetings create bonds, so that people are more willing to work together. Face time also gives people a chance to work out many small misunderstandings. However, global environmental and budget concerns mean you'll spend more time in virtual meetings. In response, meeting technology will continue to evolve.[10]

Employability Skills

FIGURE 16.4   **Sample Meeting Minutes**

Finance Team Presentation Meeting, Course 20028: Reports and Presentations	Agreed
Wednesday, October 29, 2008, 8–11 am, Room C122	Anita introduces speaker.
Present: C. Cardiff, A. Borne, L. Monahan, M. Sidwath	Guest speaks for 3 minutes.
Regrets: None	Anita thanks speaker; does icebreaker; introduces us; gives overview.
Acting Chair: Martina	We give guest bottle of wine, end of presentation.
Acting Secretary: Lawrence	
1. Martina called the meeting to order, and we approved last week's minutes.	In intro, Anita stresses quiz and prizes.
2. New business.	Lawrence introduces short video for his part.
Mohammed asked about the guest speaker: when should the guest speak, for how long, who was taking responsibility for introducing the guest, and what gift would we be giving the speaker. We discussed.	We will all find at least two relevant videos; bring to next week's meeting.
3. Old business:	We rehearse twice after next week's meeting.
a. We discussed how to involve the class. b. We discussed rehearsal dates and times.	
4. We adjourned the meeting at 11 am.	Lawrence will to send a copy of the minutes to everyone by 5 pm today.

At present, electronic meetings have their limitations. When you are limited to email, you lose both tone of voice and body language. In addition, email messages are often more brusque than comments in person (Module 10). Audio messages provide tone of voice but not the non-verbal signals that tell you whether someone wants to make a comment or understands what you're saying. Videoconferencing and VoIP give you only the picture in the camera's lens. With all of these technologies, you'll need to attend specifically to your interpersonal skills: active listening, encouraging participation, positive team roles, and negotiating conflict.

Differences among national cultures create "significant challenges" for global virtual teams.[11] Culture and management consultants Salvador Apud and Talis Apud-Martinez maintain that team success depends not only on "a knowledgeable multicultural leader, ... assessment and alignment of both national and organizational cultures, and the proper use of the technology available[,]" but also on an "[i]nitial face-to-face teambuilding meeting."[12]

MODULE SUMMARY

- People in private- or public-sector, profit or not-for-profit, and small, medium, and large organizations meet frequently as part of their routine responsibilities.
- If you are calling the meeting, plan carefully to make the meeting productive.
  - Analyze your purpose(s).
  - Consider how you can best engage participants.
  - Determine what meeting medium, time of day, and meeting duration would make the meeting most effective.

- Distribute an agenda ahead of time.
- State the purpose of the meeting at the beginning.
- Attend to people and process as well as the task.
- Allow enough time for people to discuss controversial items.
- A good agenda indicates
  - The meeting date, time, and place
  - Items for information, discussion, and decision, and the time allotted for each
  - The person introducing or sponsoring each item

- If you don't take formal votes, summarize the group's consensus after each point. At the end of the meeting, summarize all decisions and action items, and remind the group who is responsible for doing what, when.
- The **standard agenda** is a seven-step process or solving problems. In **dot planning**, group members brainstorm ideas; then each person puts adhesive dots beside the points or proposals he or she cares most about.

- Minutes should record
  - ○ Decisions reached
  - ○ Action items, in which someone needs to do something
  - ○ Open issues—topics raised but not resolved
- Participants in virtual meetings have to pay particular attention to their interpersonal skills, to compensate for the limitations of the technology.

ASSIGNMENTS FOR MODULE 16

Questions for Critical Thinking

16.1 Think about an effective meeting you attended. What specifically made it effective?

16.2 Describe the decision-making strategies used in the meetings you attend most frequently. How well do these strategies work?

16.3 In the groups of which you're a member (at school, at work, and in volunteer organizations), what kinds of comments are most valued in meetings?

16.4 What online communities do you belong to? What criteria do you use to decide to join a social network? What career benefits do social networks offer you?

Exercises and Problems

16.5 Writing an Agenda

Write an agenda for your next collaborative group meeting.

As your instructor directs,

  a. Write a memo to your instructor, explaining the choices you made.
  b. Share your agenda with ones developed by others in your group. Use the agendas as drafts to help you create the best possible agenda.
  c. Present your best agenda to the rest of the class in a group oral presentation.

16.6 Taking Minutes

As your instructor directs,

Have two or more people take minutes of each class or collaborative group meeting for a week. Compare the accounts of the same meeting.

- To what extent do they agree on what happened?
- Does one contain information missing in other accounts?
- Do any accounts disagree on a specific fact?
- How do you account for the differences you find?

16.7 Writing a Meeting Manual*

Create a procedures manual for students next term, describing how to have effective meetings while they work on collaborative projects.

16.8 Planning Scripts for Informal Meetings

Create a script for a 90-second statement to your boss for each of the following:

  1. Describe the progress on a project you're working on.
  2. Provide an update on a problem the boss already knows about.
  3. Tell about a success or achievement.
  4. Tell about a problem and ask approval for the action you recommend.
  5. Ask for resources you need for a project.
  6. Ask for training you'd like to receive.
  7. Lay the groundwork for a major request you need to make.

As your instructor directs,

  a. Discuss your scripts with a small group of students.
  b. Present your script to the class.
  c. Write a memo to your instructor explaining the choices you have made in terms of content, arrangement, and word choice.

*Adapted from Miles McCall, Beth Stewart, and Timothy Clipson, "Teaching Communication Skills for Meeting Management," 1998 Refereed Proceedings, Association for Business Communication Southwestern United States, ed. Marsha L. Bayless (Nacogdoches, TX), p. 68.

POLISHING YOUR PROSE

Using Hyphens and Dashes

Hyphens and dashes are forms of punctuation used within sentences. Use a hyphen to do the following:

1. Indicate that a word has been divided between two lines.

   Correct: Our biggest competitor announced plans to introduce new models of computers into the European market.

Divide words only at syllable breaks. If you aren't sure where the syllables break, look up the word in a dictionary. When a word has several syllables, divide it after a vowel or between two consonants.

Although many word-processing programs automatically hyphenate for you, knowing where and when to divide words is important for words the program may not recognize or for special cases. For instance, don't divide words of one syllable (e.g., *used*), and don't divide a two-syllable word if one of the syllables is only one letter long (e.g., *acre*).

2. Join two or more words used as a single adjective.

   Correct: After a flurry of requests, we are marketing new lines of specialty dinners for Asian- and Jamaican-Canadian customers.

   Order five 10- or 12-m lengths.

Here, hyphens prevent misreading. Without the hyphen, readers might interpret *Asian-Canadian* incorrectly as Asian. (Typically, compound adjectives such as *Asian-Canadian* and *Jamaican-Canadian* are not hyphenated when used as nouns.) In the second sentence, five lengths are needed, not lengths of 5, 10, or 12 metres.

3. Use a dash to emphasize a break in thought.

   Correct: Despite our best efforts—which included sending a design team to Paris and increasing our promotional budget—sales are lagging.

Create a dash by typing the hyphen key twice. With some word processors, if you set up the Options that way, this double hyphen will automatically be replaced with a longer, single dash (called an "em dash"), which is used in typesetting. (See it above in the example.)

Exercises

Supply necessary dashes or hyphens in the following sentences. If no punctuation is needed—if a space is correct—leave the parentheses blank.

1. Our biggest competitors( )including those in the Asian and European markets( )introduced more product models during the fourth quarter.
2. Our cutting( )edge fashions sell best in French( ) Canadian cities like Montreal.
3. Please pick up three( )2( )by( )4 posts at the lumberyard.
4. Next Monday, *The Aboriginal Times* magazine will do a cover story on a thriving new business created by native( )Canadians.
5. Painters from the building( )services department plan to give Tarik's office two( )coats of paint.
6. Our gift certificates come in 5( ), 10( ), and 15( )dollar denominations.
7. The latest weather reports suggest that travel over South( ) and Latin( )America may be interrupted by storms.
8. We need to work on more cost( )effective versions of our best( )selling software( )programs.
9. You can email the results to my office in the early( ) morning.
10. Katrina gave us four( )options during the sales( ) meeting on Friday afternoon.

Check your answers to the odd-numbered exercises on page 552.

Making Oral Presentations

Learning Objectives

After reading and applying the information in Module 17, you'll be able to demonstrate

Knowledge of

- The differences between written and oral messages
- Types of presentations
- The criteria for effective presentations

Skills to

- Reframe written material into an oral presentation
- Plan and deliver oral presentations
- Develop a good speaking voice
- Prepare and deliver group presentations

Employability Skills 2000+ Checklist

In this module, the key skills from the Conference Board of Canada's Employability Skills 2000+ are

Communicate

- ○ write and speak so others pay attention and understand
- ○ share information using a range of information and communications technologies (e.g., voice, email, computers)

- ○ use relevant scientific, technological, and mathematical knowledge and skills to explain or clarify ideas

Manage Information

- ○ locate, gather, and organize information using appropriate technology and information systems

Participate in Projects & Tasks

- ○ plan, design, or carry out a project or task from start to finish with well-defined objectives and outcomes
- ○ develop a plan, seek feedback, test, revise, and implement

- ○ select and use appropriate tools and technology for a task or project
- ○ adapt to changing requirements and information

In every new communication situation, you have fewer than 90 seconds to make that first—and lasting—impression. How are you going to make that a positive one? Effective speakers make that 90 seconds work for them.

Most presentations serve more than one purpose, and every presentation contains an element of persuasion: you must know how to attract and hold your audience's attention if you want to achieve your purposes. The best oral presentations inform and influence people positively.

What Kinds of Presentations Are There?

Informative presentations inform or teach the audience. For example, health and safety training sessions are primarily informative. Secondary purposes may be to conform to legislation, to meet ISO standards, to persuade employees to follow organizational procedures, and to orient new employees (Module 2).

Persuasive and **sales presentations** motivate the audience to act or to believe. Giving information and evidence persuades through appeals to credibility and reason (Module 13). Moreover, the speaker must build goodwill by appearing to be credible and sympathetic to the audience's needs. The goal of most presentations is to get to *yes*. In business presentations, speakers want to persuade the audience to buy their product, proposal, or idea. Sometimes the goal is to change attitudes and behaviours, or to reinforce existing attitudes. Thus, a speaker at a workers' compensation and benefits information meeting might stress the importance of following safety procedures; a speaker at

All successful presentations are persuasive.

FIGURE 17.1   PAIBOC Questions to Plan Powerful Presentations

> P   What is the **purpose** of your presentation? What do you want to happen as a result of your presentation? What do you want your audience to think, say, or do?
>
> A   Who is your **audience**? What do they already know? What do they need to know? What do they care about? What will motivate them to do as you want? How do members of your audience differ? What cultural/corporate values and norms shape their perceptions? How can you grab your audience's attention positively? What's in it for them?
>
> I   What is your key message? What idea do you want the audience members to take away with them? What do you have to say that is important to them? How can you make the **information** relevant, and achieve your purpose(s)? How long is your presentation? What information can you omit?
>
> B   What **benefits** does your message offer the audience? How can you highlight these benefits?
>
> O   What **objections** will your audience have to your message? How will you overcome those objections? What are the negative aspects of your message? How can you deemphasize, compensate for, or overcome these negatives?
>
> C   What is the **context** of your message? What economic, environmental, professional, and/or personal realities will affect how your audience perceives your message? What time of day is your presentation? In what kind of room is it? How can you make your presentation interactive, engaging, and stimulating? What technology will you use, and why?

a city council meeting might talk about the problem of homelessness in the community to try to build support for homeless shelters.

Goodwill presentations entertain and validate the audience. In an after-dinner speech, the audience wants to be entertained. Presentations at sales meetings may be designed to stroke the audience's egos and to validate their commitment to organizational goals.

Regardless of the presentation purpose, the best presenters plan, prepare, and practise. They develop a strategy by analyzing the situation. They prepare stories and examples relevant to their audience. They practise until they are completely comfortable with the content. All this preparation increases confidence, and reduces the anxiety most speakers feel.

What Decisions Do I Need to Make as I Plan a Presentation?

Choose your main point, the kind of presentation, and ways to involve your audience.

An oral presentation needs to be simpler than a written message to the same audience. Identify the one idea—or critical takeaway—you want the audience to take away. Then phrase your idea so that it offers a specific benefit to the audience.

Employability Skills

Weak:	The purpose of my presentation is to discuss saving for retirement.
Better:	The purpose of my presentation is to persuade my audience to put their retirement funds in stocks and bonds, not in money market accounts and CDs.

or

> The purpose of my presentation is to explain how to calculate how much money someone needs to save in order to maintain a specific lifestyle after retirement.

Note: Your purpose is *not* the introduction of your talk; it is the principle that guides your decisions as you plan your presentation.

Michael Goldman is president and senior consultant of Facilitation First, a professional consulting firm specializing in expert meeting facilitation and training. Michael has edited several leading books on facilitation and team interventions. He also acts as a contributing editor for *the training report* and the Banff Centre of Management's *Leadership Compass*. Visit his Web site at www.facilitationfirst.com.

Now reinforce that idea through clarity, repetition, and emphasis: simplify your supporting detail so it's easy to follow; use visuals that can be taken in at a glance; choose concrete words and brief sentences so they're easy to understand.

Analyze your audience for an oral presentation just as you do for a written message. If you'll be speaking to co-workers, talk to them about your topic or proposal to find out what questions or objections they have. For audiences inside the organization, the biggest questions are often practical ones: Will it work? How much will it cost? How long will it take?[1] And answer: What's in it for them?

Before you begin planning your presentation, you need to know *for how long*, *where*, and *when* you will be speaking. Your time and the audience's expectations shape both the content and the kind of presentation you will give. The size and comfort of the room will affect the success of your presentation, as will the time of day. What size is the room? What equipment will be available? Will the audience be tired at the end of a long day of listening? Sleepy after a big meal? Will the group be large or small? The more you know about your audience and your environment, the better you can shape your presentation for maximum persuasive impact. And that knowledge is power: the more you know, the more in-control you will feel.

Choosing the Kind of Presentation

When you have identified your *purpose*, including the results you want to achieve, analyzed your audience's needs, and considered your time, you can decide on the kind of presentation you will give. Table 17.1 identifies the speaker's role in three kinds of presentations: monologue, guided discussion, and sales.

TABLE 17.1   **Michael Goldman's Guidelines for Choosing Your Presentation Role**

Chair When You Want To:	Facilitate When You Want To:
Exchange information	Increase participation
Get informal feedback	Deal with group dynamics
Hear members report back	Have members problem solve
Overview the current agenda	Have members make decisions
Set the parameters of the discussion	Have members create action plans
Review meeting objectives with members	Shift ownership and commitment levels

Source: Michael Goldman, "To Chair or to Facilitate, That Is the Question," *the training report*, January/ February 2001, p. 13.

In a **monologue presentation**, the speaker functions as an expert, speaks without interruption, and solicits questions at the end of the presentation. The speaker plans the presentation in advance and delivers it without deviation. This kind of presentation may represent the most common educational situation, but it's often boring for the audience. Good delivery skills are crucial, since the audience is comparatively uninvolved.

Guided discussions offer a better way to present material and encourage an audience to really engage. In a guided discussion, the speaker presents the questions or issues that both speaker and audience agree on. Rather than functioning as an expert with all the answers, the speaker serves as a facilitator to help the audience tap its own knowledge. This kind of presentation works well for adult training and for presenting the results of consulting projects, when the speaker has specialized knowledge, but the audience must implement the solution if it is to succeed. Guided discussions need more time than monologue presentations but produce more audience response, more responses involving analysis, and more commitment to the result.[2]

A **sales presentation** is a *conversation*, even if the salesperson stands up in front of a group and uses charts and overheads. The sales representative uses questions to determine the buyer's needs, probe objections, and gain temporary and then final commitment to the purchase. Even in a memorized sales presentation, the buyer might talk at least 30 percent of the time. In a problem-solving sales presentation, the buyer might talk 70 percent of the time.

Checkpoint

Three Purposes of Presentations

- **Informative presentations** inform or teach the audience.
- **Persuasive presentations** motivate the audience to act or to believe.
- **Goodwill presentations** entertain and validate the audience.

Most oral presentations have more than one purpose.

How Should I Organize a Presentation?

Usually you start with the main point. Then choose one of five standard organizational patterns.

Most presentations use a direct pattern of organization, even when the goal is to persuade a reluctant audience. In a business setting, the audience members are in a hurry and know that you want to persuade them. Be honest about your goals, and prepare your opening to demonstrate that your goal dovetails with the audience's needs.

In a persuasive presentation, start with your strongest point, your best reason. If time permits, give other reasons as well and respond to possible objections. Put your weakest point in the middle and end on a strong note.

Based on your purpose and audience analysis, use one of five standard patterns of organization:

1. **Chronological**. Start with the past, move to the present, and end by looking ahead.
2. **Problem-causes-solution**. Explain the symptoms of the problem, identify its causes, and suggest a solution. This pattern works best when the audience will find your solution easy to accept.
3. **Exclude alternatives**. Explain the symptoms of the problem. Explain the obvious solutions first and show why they won't solve the problem. End by discussing a solution that will work. This pattern may be necessary when the audience will find the solution hard to accept.
4. **Pro-con**. Give all the reasons in favour of something, then those against it. This pattern works well when you want the audience to see the weaknesses in its position.
5. **1-2-3**. Discuss three aspects of a topic. This pattern works well to organize short informative briefings. "Today I'll review our sales, production, and profits for the last quarter."

Early in your talk—perhaps immediately after your opener—provide an agenda or overview of the main points you will make. Include a presentation duration time, and end when you promised you would.

> In the next 20 minutes, I'm going to describe how you can make our city a safer, saner place. First, I'd like to talk about who the homeless on Vancouver's East Side are. Second, I'll talk about the services the Open Shelter provides. Finally, I'll talk about what you—either individually or as a group—can do to help.

An overview provides a mental peg that hearers can hang each point on. It can also prevent someone missing what you are saying because he or she wonders why you aren't covering a major point that you've saved for later.[3]

Offer a clear signpost or transition as you come to each new point. A signpost is an explicit statement of the point you have reached. Choose wording that fits your style. The following statements are four different ways that a speaker could use to introduce the last of three points:

> Now we come to the third point: what you can do as a group or as individuals to help homeless people in Vancouver.
>
> So much for what we're doing. Now let's talk about what you can do to help.
>
> You might be wondering, what can I do to help?
>
> As you can see, the Shelter is trying to do many things. We could do more with your help.

Checkpoint

Overviews and Signposts

Immediately after your opener, provide an **overview** of the main points you will make. Offer a clear **signpost** as you come to each new point. A signpost is an explicit statement of the point you have reached.

How Can I Adapt My Ideas to the Audience?

Employability Skills

Remember that *people can take in only so much information before they shut down!* Measure the message you'd like to send against where your audience is now. If your audience is indifferent, skeptical, or hostile, focus on the part of your message the audience will find most interesting and easiest to accept.

Don't seek a major opinion change in a single oral presentation. If your audience has already decided to hire a financial advisor, a strong presentation can convince them that you are the one to hire. However, if you're talking to a prospect who is not convinced that he/she needs investment advice, limit your purpose. You may simply strive to prove that expert advice can make the investor more money and free up his/her precious time for other activities. Only *after* the audience is receptive would you make the second sales presentation to prove that your investor should hire you rather than the competition.

Make your ideas relevant to your audience by linking what you have to say to the audience's experiences, interests, and needs. Showing your audience members that the topic affects them directly is the most effective strategy. When you can't do that, at least link the topic to some everyday experience.

When was the last time you were hungry? Maybe you remember being hungry while you were on a diet, or maybe you had to work late at a lab and didn't get back to the dorm in time for dinner. [Speech about world hunger to an audience of college students.]

How Can I Create a Strong Opening and Close?

Use your introduction and your conclusion as points of emphasis.

The beginning and the end of a presentation, like the beginning and end of a written document, are positions of emphasis. Use those key positions to interest the audience and emphasize your main point. You'll sound more natural and more effective if you write out your opener and close in advance and memorize them. (They'll be short: just a sentence or two.)

Employability Skills

Your introduction is particularly important. To catch and hold audience attention, try these strategies:

- Stand still.
- Focus on your audience.
- Attract their interest with a **dramatic statement**, **story**, **question**, or **quotation**.
- Make the hook or grabber relevant to them.

The more you can do to personalize your opener for your audience, the better. Recent events are better than things that happened long ago; local events are better than events at a distance; people they know are better than people who are only names.

Dramatic Statement

Twelve of our customers have cancelled orders in the past month.

This presentation to a company's executive committee went on to show that the company's distribution system was inadequate, and to recommend an additional warehouse located in the west.

Story

A mother was having difficulty getting her son up for school. He pulled the covers over his head.

"I'm not going to school," he said. "I'm not ever going again."

"Are you sick?" his mother asked.

"No," he answered. "I'm sick of school. They hate me. They call me names. They make fun of me. Why should I go?"

"I can give you two good reasons," the mother replied. "The first is that you're 42 years old. And the second is you're the school principal."[4]

This speech given at a seminar for educators went on to discuss "the three knottiest problems in education today." Educators had to face those problems; they couldn't hide under the covers.

Question

> Are you going to have enough money to do the things you want to when you retire?

This presentation to a group of potential clients discusses the value of using the services of a professional financial planner to achieve retirement goals.

THE FAR SIDE® BY GARY LARSON

© 1984 FarWorks, Inc. All Rights Reserved/Dist. by Creators Syndicate

The Far Side® by Gary Larson © 1984 FarWorks, Inc. All Rights Reserved. Used with permission.

Don't start a speech with a joke unless it fits the occasion, won't offend anyone, and is really funny.

Quotation

> According to Towers Perrin, the profits of Fortune 100 companies would be 25 percent lower—they'd go down $17 billion—if their earnings statements listed the future costs companies are obligated to pay for retirees' health care.

This presentation on options for health care for retired employees urges executives to start now to investigate options to cut the future cost.

Your opener must interest the audience and establish rapport. Some speakers use humour to achieve those goals. However, an inappropriate joke can turn the audience against the speaker. Never use humour that's directed against the audience. In contrast, speakers who make fun of themselves almost always succeed:

> It's both a privilege and a pressure to be here.[5]

Humour isn't the only way to put an audience at ease and establish a positive emotional connection. Smile at your audience before you begin; let them see that you're a real person and a pleasant one.

The end of your presentation should be as strong as the opener. For your close, do one or more of the following:

- Restate your main point.
- Refer to your opener to create a frame for your presentation.
- End with a vivid, positive picture.
- Tell the audience exactly what to do to solve the problem you've discussed.

The following close from a fundraising speech combines a restatement of the main point with a call for action, telling the audience what to do.

> Plain and simple, we need money to run the foundation, just like you need money to develop new products. We need money to make this work. We need money from you. Pick up that pledge card. Fill it out. Turn it in at the door as you leave. Make it a statement about your commitment ... make it a big statement.[6]

Checkpoint

An inappropriate joke can turn the audience against the speaker. Never use humour that's directed against the audience. In contrast, speakers who can make fun of themselves almost always succeed.

When you write out your opener and close, remember that listeners can take in only so much information; then they disengage and tune out. When preparing your presentation, apply the *KISS* formula: *Keep it short and simple.* As you can see in the example close just shown, speaking style uses shorter sentences and shorter, simpler words than writing does. Oral style can even sound a bit choppy when it is read. Oral style uses more personal pronouns, a less varied vocabulary, and much more repetition.

How Should I Use Visuals?

Use visuals to emphasize your main points. Keep them simple and specific.

People understand and retain information better when they both *see* and *hear* the facts; they understand and remember best when they *see*, *hear*, and *do*. However, your topic or your time may preclude having your audience practise what you're preaching.

Whatever your topic, visual support is vital. North American audiences expect business presentations to be supported by attractive visuals. Moreover, visuals can give your presentation

EXPANDING A CRITICAL SKILL

Finding Your Best Voice

Paralanguage—*how* we say what we say—accounts for more than 30 percent of the meaning in our messages. Next to your face, therefore, your voice is your most important presentation aid! Effective speakers use their voices to support and enhance content. Your best voice will vary pitch, intonation, tempo, and volume to express energy and enthusiasm.

Pitch

Pitch measures whether a voice uses sounds that are low (like the bass notes on a piano) or high. Low-pitched voices project more credibility than do high-pitched voices. Low-pitched presenters are perceived as being more authoritative, and more pleasant to listen to. Most voices go up in pitch when the speaker is angry or excited; some people raise pitch when they increase volume. People whose normal speaking voices are high might need to practise projecting their voices to avoid becoming shrill when they speak to large groups.

To find your best pitch, try humming. The pitch at which the hum sounds loudest and most resonant is your best voice.

Intonation

Intonation marks variation in pitch, stress, or tone. Speakers who use many changes in pitch, stress, and tone usually seem more enthusiastic; often they also seem more energetic and more intelligent. Someone who

speaks in a monotone may seem apathetic or unintelligent. Speakers whose first language does not use tone, pitch, and stress to convey meaning and attitude may need to practise varying these voice qualities.

Avoid raising your voice at the end of a sentence, since in English a rising intonation signals a question. Therefore, speakers who end sentences on a questioning or high tones—known as *uptalk*—sound immature or uncertain of what they're saying.

Tempo

Tempo is a measure of speed. In a conversation, match your tempo to the other speaker's to build rapport. In a formal presentation, vary your tempo. Speakers who speak quickly and who vary their volume during the talk are more likely to be perceived as competent.

Volume

Volume is a measure of loudness or softness. Very soft voices, especially if they are also breathy and high-pitched, give the impression of youth and inexperience. People who do a lot of speaking to large groups need to practise projecting their voices so they can increase their volume without shouting.

Sources: George B. Ray, "Vocally Cued Personality Prototypes: An Implicit Personality Theory Approach," *Communication Monographs* 53(3) (1986): 266–76; and Jacklyn Boice, "Verbal Impressions," *Selling Power*, March 2000, p. 69.

PowerPoint slides aren't the only or necessarily the best way to involve the audience. Dan Leebar persuaded UPS to switch to Valeo clutches by disassembling the competitor's clutch and showing part by part why Valeo's product was better.

a professional image (Module 5). However, the best presentations depend on the speaker's preparedness and rapport with the audience, not on visual pyrotechnics.

Design and rhetoric experts agree that PowerPoint™ slides—once attention-grabbers—are now misused and overused in presentations.[7] The best visuals are simple, clear, and specific. Illustrations should honestly and ethically reinforce your message. Whenever possible, put people in the picture—doing or using whatever you're selling. Keep text to a minimum. Use images and graphics immediately familiar to your audience. And when in doubt ... leave it out.[8]

Plan a maximum of one visual for every minute of your talk, plus two visuals to serve as title and conclusion. Don't base your whole talk on visuals. Use well-designed visuals as memory devices for your audience.

To create effective presentation visuals, use these guidelines:

- Use a sans-serif font (e.g., Arial, Helvetica, Technical) to maximize text readability.
- Use a minimum 24-point type to maximize readability (Module 5).
- Keep it simple.
- Use clear illustrations—charts, graphs, tables—whenever possible.
- Make only one point with each visual. Break a complicated point down into several visuals.
- Give each visual a title that makes a point connected to your presentation's main point.
- Limit the amount of text: no more than five lines per slide or five words per line.

To present your visuals effectively, use these guidelines:

- Use a friend/colleague to manage the visuals for you, so you can concentrate on your ideas and your delivery.
- Use your visuals as enhancement, not competition.
- Use no more than one visual or slide per minute.
- Put up your visual (or have your friend/colleague put up the visual) only when you are ready to talk about it.
- Leave the visual up until your next point.

See Module 23 for information on how to present numerical data through visuals.

Visuals work only if the technology they depend on works. When you give presentations in your own office, check the equipment in advance. When you make a presentation in another location or for another organization, arrive early so that you'll have time not only to check the equipment but also to track down a service worker if the equipment isn't working. Be prepared with a backup plan if you're unable to show your slides or videotape.

FIGURE 17.2   PowerPoint Slides for an Informative Presentation

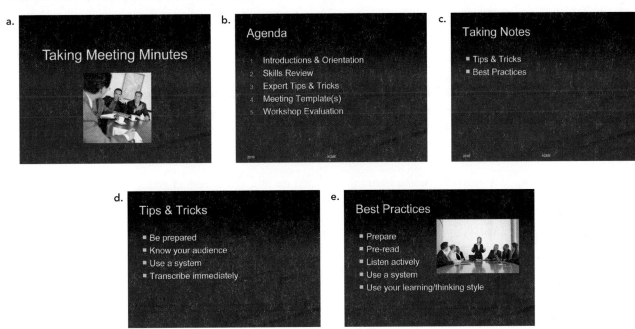

And because PowerPoint presentations have become commonplace, you must engage your audience in a variety of other ways:

- Students presenting on intercultural business communications demonstrated the way Chinese, Japanese, and Canadians exchange business cards by asking audience members to role-play the differences.
- Another student discussing the need for low-salt products brought in a container of salt, a measuring cup, a measuring spoon, and two plates. As he discussed the body's need for salt, he measured out three teaspoons onto one plate: the amount the body needs in a month. As he discussed the amount of salt the average diet provides, he continued to measure out salt onto the other plate, stopping only when he had 500 grams of salt—the amount in the average North American diet. The demonstration made the discrepancy clear in a way words or even a chart could not have done.[9]
- Some presenters use quizzes, game formats, and dramatizations to encourage audience members to share their expertise with others.
  - To make sure that his employees understood where money went, the CEO of a specialty printing shop printed up $2 million in play money and handed out big cards to employees marked "Labour," "Depreciation," "Interest," and so forth. Then he asked each "category" to come up and take its share of the revenues. The action was more dramatic than a colour pie chart could ever have been.[10]
  - Another speaker who was trying to raise funds used the simple act of asking people to stand to involve them, to create emotional appeal, and to make a statistic vivid:

[A speaker] was talking to a luncheon club about contributing to the relief of an area that had been hit by a tsunami. The news report said that 70 percent of the people had been killed or disabled. The room was set up with ten people at each round table. He asked three persons at each table to stand. Then he said, "You people sitting are dead or disabled. You three standing have to take care of the mess. You'd need help, wouldn't you?"[11]

What Are the Keys to Delivering an Effective Presentation?

Turn your nervousness into energy, look at the audience, and use natural gestures.

Audience members want you to succeed in your presentation out of a vested self-interest: they don't want to feel uncomfortable for you. They also want the sense that you're talking directly to them, that you've taken the time and trouble to prepare, that you're interested in your subject and that you care about their interest.

They'll forgive you if you get tangled up in a sentence and end it ungrammatically. They won't forgive you if you seem to have a "canned" talk that you're going to deliver no matter who the listeners are or how they respond. You convey a sense of caring to your audience by making direct eye contact, and by using a conversational style.

Putting Your Nervousness to Work

Feeling nervous is normal. Indeed, we are genetically programmed to feel anxious about speaking in public: being aware of other community members' perceptions of them was an essential survival mechanism for our ancestors.[12]

But you can harness that nervous energy to do your best work. As one student said, you don't need to get rid of your butterflies. All you need to do is make them fly in formation.

To calm your nerves as you prepare to give an oral presentation,

- Be prepared: analyze your audience, organize your thoughts, prepare visual aids, practise your opener and close, check out the arrangements.
- Practise, practise, practise.
- Use positive emphasis to reframe what you're feeling. Instead of saying, "I'm scared," try saying, "My adrenaline is up." Adrenaline sharpens our reflexes and helps us do our best.
- Visualize your success: see yourself moving naturally and confidently around the room; see people jumping up, smiling and clapping, as you end your presentation.
- Focus on what you know you have done to succeed. "I've practised the presentation; I know it really well; I've checked out the room, know where to put the screen; I've prepared for most questions."
- Use only the amount of caffeine you normally use. More or less may make you jumpy.
- Avoid alcoholic beverages.

Just before your presentation, use relaxation techniques:

- Consciously contract and then relax your muscles, starting with your feet and calves and going up to your shoulders, arms, and hands.
- Take several deep breaths from your diaphragm.

During your presentation, be sure to do the following:

- Pause and look at the audience before you begin speaking.
- Concentrate on communicating well.
- Channel your body energy into emphatic gestures and movement.

Using Eye Contact

Look directly at the people you're talking to. Speakers who looked the most at the audience during a seven-minute informative speech were judged to be better informed, more experienced, more honest, and friendlier than speakers who delivered the same information with less eye contact.[13] An earlier study found that speakers judged sincere looked at the audience 63 percent of the time, while those judged insincere looked at the audience only 21 percent of the time.[14]

The point in making eye contact is to establish one-on-one contact with the individual members of your audience. People want to feel that you're talking to them. Looking directly at individuals also enables you to be more conscious of feedback from the audience, so that you can modify your approach if necessary.

Standing and Gesturing

Stand with your feet far enough apart for good balance, with your knees flexed. Unless the presentation is very formal or you're on camera, you can walk if you want to. Some speakers like to come out from the lectern to remove that barrier between themselves and the audience.

Build on your natural style for gestures. Gestures usually work best when they're big and confident.

Using Notes and Visuals

Unless you're giving a very short presentation, you'll probably want to use notes. Even experts use notes. The more you know about the subject, the greater the temptation to add relevant points that occur to you as you talk. Adding an occasional point can help to clarify something for the audience, but adding too many points will overwhelm the audience, destroy your outline, and put you over the time limit.

Put your notes on cards or on sturdy pieces of paper. Use prompts (opening and closing sentences, then your points, large font, highlighting, reference to visuals) that work for you. Practise your presentation using your notes, and make whatever changes increase your comfort level.

During your presentation, look at your notes infrequently. Direct your eyes to members of the audience. Hold your notes high enough so that your head doesn't bob up and down like a yo-yo as you look from the audience to your notes and back again.

If you know your topic well, you won't need to look at your notes, and you'll feel more confident. You can focus on being yourself, and establishing rapport with your audience.

Get out of the way of your visuals: stand to the side of the screen, and *face the audience, not the screen*. Never read your visuals; the audience members can read for themselves. If your talk is lengthy, and the topic complicated, prepare handouts for your audience. Many people expect speakers to provide a copy of their slides at the end of the presentation.

Keep the room lights on if possible; turning them off makes it easier for people to fall asleep and harder for them to concentrate on you.

How Should I Handle Questions from the Audience?

Use PAIBOC to anticipate audience questions. Be honest. Rephrase biased or hostile questions.

Prepare for questions by listing every fact or opinion you can think of that challenges your position. Treat every objection seriously and try to think of a way to deal with it. If you're talking about a controversial issue, you may want to save one point for the question period, rather than making it during the presentation. Speakers who have visuals to answer questions seem especially well prepared.

During your presentation, tell the audience how you'll handle questions. If you have a choice, save questions for the end. In your talk, answer the questions or objections that you expect your audience to have.

During the question period, acknowledge questions by looking directly at the questioner. As you answer the question, expand your focus to take in the entire group.

If the audience may not have heard the question or if you want more time to think, repeat the question before you answer it. Link your answers to the points you made in your presentation. Keep the purpose of your presentation in mind, and select information that advances your goals.

If a question is hostile or biased, rephrase it before you answer it. "You're asking whether ... ." Or suggest an alternative question: "I think there are problems with both the positions you describe. It seems to me that a third possibility is ... ."

Sometimes people will ask a question really designed to state the their own position. Respond to the question if you want to. Another option is to say, "I'm not sure what you're asking" or "That's a clear statement of your position. Let's move to the next question now." If someone asks about something that you already explained in your presentation, simply answer the question without embarrassing the questioner. Even when actively participating, audiences remember only about 70 percent of what you say.

If you don't know the answer to a question, say so and promise to get the information and respond as soon as possible. Write down the question so that you can look up the answer before the next session. You may want to refer the question to your audience, which both involves and flatters them. If it's a question to which you think there is no answer, ask whether anyone in the room knows. When no one does, your "ignorance" is vindicated.

At the end of the question period, take two minutes to summarize your main point once more. (This can be a restatement of your close.) Questions may or may not focus on the key point of your talk. Take advantage of having the floor to repeat your message briefly and forcefully.

What Are the Guidelines for Group Presentations?

In the best presentations, voices take turns within each point.

Employability Skills

Plan carefully to involve as many members of the group as possible in speaking roles. The easiest way to make a group presentation is to outline the presentation and then divide the topics, giving one to each group member. Another member can be responsible for the opener and the close. During the question period, each member answers questions that relate to his or her topic.

In this kind of divided presentation, be sure to do the following:

- Plan transitions.
- Strictly enforce time limits.
- Coordinate your visuals so that the presentation seems a coherent whole.
- Choreograph the presentation: plan each member's movement and seating arrangements as the group transfers from speaker to speaker. Take turns managing the visual support so that each speaker can focus on content and delivery, without worrying about changing slides or transparencies.
- Practise the presentation as a group at least once; more is better.

The best group presentations are even more fully integrated; together, the members of the group complete the important tasks:

- Writing a very detailed outline
- Choosing points and examples
- Creating visuals

Then, *within* each point, speakers take turns. This presentation is most effective because each voice speaks only a minute or two before a new voice comes in. However, it works only when all group members know the subject well, and when the group plans carefully and practises extensively.

Whatever form of group presentation you use, introduce each member of the team to the audience at the beginning of the presentation and at each transition: use the next person's name when you change speakers: "Now, Jason will explain how we evaluated the Web pages."

As a team member, pay close attention to your fellow speaker; don't ever have sidebar conversations with others in the group. If other members of the team seem uninterested in the speaker, the audience gets the sense that that speaker isn't worth listening to.

MODULE SUMMARY

- Most oral presentations have more than one purpose. People present to inform, persuade, and build goodwill.
- Oral presentations need to be simpler than written messages.
- In a **monologue presentation**, the speaker delivers the content without deviation. In a **guided discussion**, the speaker presents the questions or topics that both speaker and audience have agreed on in advance. The speaker serves as facilitator to help the audience tap its members' own knowledge. A **sales presentation** is a conversation using questions to determine the buyer's needs, probe objections, and gain commitment to the purchase.
- Adapt your message to your audience's experiences, beliefs, and interests.
- Use the beginning and end of your presentation as points of emphasis.
- Use visuals to reinforce your main idea; make the visuals clear, simple and relevant.
- Use a direct pattern of organization: put your strongest reason first.
- Limit your talk to three main points. After your opener, **provide an overview of the main points** you will make. Give a clear signpost as you transition to each new point This verbal signal is an explicit statement of the point you have reached.
- Even the most seasoned speakers feel nervous when giving a presentation. Such anxiety is natural and normal. To reduce apprehension about presenting,

- Be prepared: analyze your audience; plan your content; prepare visuals; practise; create notes; check out the presentation room and arrangements.
- Drink your usual amount of coffee, and avoid alcohol.
- Visualize scenarios of your presentation success.
- Reframe your nervousness into positive affirmations.
- Just before your presentation,
  - Consciously contract, then relax your muscles, starting with your feet and calves, and moving up to your shoulders, arms, and hands.
  - Take several deep breaths from your diaphragm.
- During your presentation,
  - Pause and look at your audience before you begin to speak.
  - Concentrate on communicating confidently.
  - Use your energy in strong gestures and movement.
- Establish rapport with the audience members by making direct eye contact, and using a conversational style.
- Treat questions as opportunities to give more detailed information. Connect your answers to the points you made in your presentation.
- Repeat the question before answering it if you think that the audience may not have heard it, or you want more time to think. Rephrase hostile or biased questions before you answer them.
- The most effective group presentations result when the group writes a very detailed outline; chooses points and examples; creates visuals collaboratively; and, within each point, allows members' voices to trade off one another.

ASSIGNMENTS FOR MODULE 17

Questions for Critical Thinking

17.1 Think about why are you nervous before giving a presentation. What is the source of the nervousness? What can you do to reduce or eliminate it?

17.2 Why are PowerPoint slides effective? When are they inappropriate?

17.3 What visuals do you find work best? Why?

17.4 What's the most important part of any presentation? Why?

17.5 How can you use humour appropriately?

Exercises and Problems

17.6   Making a Short Oral Presentation

As your instructor directs,

Make a short (two-to-five-minute) presentation, with three to eight slides, on one of the following topics:

a. Explain how what you've learned in classes, in campus activities, or at work will be useful to the employer who hires you after graduation.

b. Profile someone who is successful in the field you hope to enter and explain what makes him or her successful.

c. Describe a specific situation in an organization in which communication was handled well or badly.

d. Make a short presentation based on another problem in this book, such as the following:

   1.8   Discuss three of your strengths.

   2.9   Analyze your boss.

   11.6 Explain a "best practice" in your organization.

   12.5 Tell your boss about a problem in your unit and recommend a solution.

   24.7 Explain one of the challenges (e.g., technology, ethics, international competition) that the field you hope to enter is facing.

   24.8 Profile a company you would like to work for and explain why you think it would be a good employer.

   27.7 Explain your interview strategy.

17.7   Making a Longer Oral Presentation

As your instructor directs,

Create a 5-to-12-minute individual or group presentation on one of the following. Use any appropriate visual communication, *excluding slides*, to make your talk powerful.

a. Show why your unit is important to the organization and either should be exempt from downsizing or should receive additional resources.

b. Persuade your supervisor to make a change that will benefit the organization.

c. Persuade your organization to make a change that will improve the organization's image in the community.

d. Persuade classmates to donate time or money to a charitable organization (Module 13).

e. Persuade an employer that you are the best person for the job.

f. Use another problem in this book as the basis for your presentation.

17.8   Making a Group Oral Presentation

As your instructor directs,

Make a 5-to-12-minute presentation using communication visuals on one of these topics:

   3.8   Show how cultural differences can lead to miscommunication.

   5.9   Evaluate the design of three Web pages.

   13.14 Recommend an investment for your instructor.

   15.8 Recommend ways to retain workers.

   15.11 Present brochures you have designed to the class.

   18.9 Summarize the results of your research.

   24.6 Share the advice of students currently in the job market.

17.9   Creating a Presentation Skills Evaluation Matrix

As your instructor directs,

Together with four peers, create an evaluation guide to evaluate your class presentations. Begin by brainstorming the components of a presentation, such as content, delivery, visuals, time, organization, audience relevance, and so on. Create a table with headings (e.g., *Excellent, Good, Needs Improvement*) and beside the criteria describe the behaviours you would expect to see.

Be prepared to explain your evaluation guide to the rest of the class.

POLISHING YOUR PROSE

Choosing Levels of Formality

Some words are more formal than others. Generally, business messages call for a middle-of-the-road formality, not too formal, but not so casual as to seem sloppy.

Formal and Stuffy	Short and Simple
ameliorate	improve
commence	begin, start
enumerate	list
finalize	finish, complete
prioritize	rank
utilize	use
viable option	choice
Sloppy	**Casual**
befuddled	confused
diss	criticize
guess	assume
haggle	negotiate
nosy	curious
wishy-washy	indecisive, flexible

What makes choosing words so challenging is that the level of formality depends on your purposes, the audience, and the situation. What's just right for a written report will be too formal for an oral presentation or an advertisement. The level of formality that works in one discourse community might be inappropriate for another.

Listen to the language that people in your discourse community use. What words seem to have positive connotations? What words persuade? As you identify these terms, use them in your own messages.

Exercises

In each sentence, choose the better word or phrase. Justify your choice.

1. On Monday, I [took a look at/inspected] our [stuff/inventory].
2. [Starting/commencing] at 5 P.M., all qualifying employees may [commence/begin] their [leave times/vacations].
3. Though their [guy/representative] was [firm/stubborn], we eventually [hashed out/negotiated] a settlement.
4. Call to schedule [some time/a meeting] with me to [talk about/deliberate on the issues in] your memo.
5. The manager [postponed making/waited until she had more information before making] a decision.
6. Rick has [done his job/performed] well as [top dog/manager] of our sales department.
7. In my last job, I [ran lots of errands/worked as a gofer] for the marketing manager.
8. Please [contact/communicate with] [me/the undersigned] if you [have questions/desire further information or knowledge].
9. This report [has problems/stinks].
10. In this report, I have [guessed/assumed] that the economy will continue to grow.

Check your answers to the odd-numbered questions on page 552.

CASES FOR COMMUNICATORS

A Business Lesson in Technology and Goodwill

Many companies offer training programs to improve performance among their employees. The programs develop better communication skills, creativity, and teamwork—all of which are crucial to success in an organization.

Traditional exercises, such as corporate golf outings and boot-camp rope courses, are becoming a thing of the past. Increasingly, companies are searching for entertaining programs that challenge minds, develop confidence, and encourage dependence on other participants rather than focus on individual achievement.

Two of the fastest-growing programs incorporate either philanthropy or technology. Those centred on public welfare often volunteer their participants' time for activities like building bicycles for charities or helping organizations such as Habitat for Humanity. High-tech activities, such as geocaching, use cell phones and hand-held global positioning systems, giving participants the ability to contact outside sources as they pursue a team goal.

In a unique combination of technology and goodwill, Best Buy recently trained employees in the use of a new video camera while also "giving back" to the community. During their training program, employees held a dinner for families with relatives in the military. After the meal, participants helped guide families through the use of the new camera and then showed them how to send movies to loved ones stationed overseas. The exercise gave Best Buy employees an opportunity to sharpen people skills, gain knowledge of the product, and boost both personal and company morale.

Source: Terry Trucco, "A New Kind of Business Conference Bonding," *The New York Times*, April 16, 2007, http://www.nytimes.com/2007/04/16/business/businessspecial3/16active.html.

Individual Activity

Imagine you are the director of corporate training at Best Buy. You have been given the task of developing an unconventional training plan for 50 sales employees to improve interpersonal communication. The training plan should include group exercises designed to develop trust, encourage participation, and relieve tension among group members. The training will take up a regular workday and take place in the location of your choice that will complement the goals of your unconventional training plan.

Create an agenda for your plan. Consider the following topics as you organize your day of training:

- What aspects of interpersonal communication are important to address?
- What interpersonal communication problems could develop between employees and customers?
- What are some creative ways to address these problems?
- What roles do people play in groups?
- In which kind of role-playing exercises could the group address problems?
- What are some exercises the group could do to learn how to work together effectively?
- What kind of group activity would address the importance of listening?

Group Activity

Your group has been asked to write a 500-word report on how unconventional training can be used to teach stronger teamwork skills. As a team, create and polish this document.

Plan the work and document as a group. In this process, discuss the following questions:

- What is the purpose of this document?
- Who is the audience?
- What organization, format, and style should the report have (Modules 20 and 21)?

When you have finished planning, decide how you will begin drafting the report together. Evaluate the content and discuss possible revisions as a group. If your discussions stall over questions of style, remember that business writing can embrace different styles, but the document should have a unified voice.

With a solid revision in hand, you are ready to edit and proofread. This stage is very important because of the writing styles and levels of expertise involved. Be sure to have at least one person check the document for grammar, mechanics, accuracy, and completeness.

After you have completed the document, discuss the following questions as a team:

- Did the majority of team members work actively on the project?
- Can you identify the positive roles and actions demonstrated during the writing process? (For example, who encouraged participation?)
- Can you identify any negative roles and actions demonstrated during the writing process? (For example, who attempted to dominate the group?)
- Can you identify an informational leader, interpersonal leader, and procedural leader in your group?

Finally, reflect as a group on the issue of conflict. Did conflict arise during the project? If so, how did you work as a team to identify the source and type of conflict and then follow the appropriate steps to resolve the issue?

Researching and Reporting

Environmental consultant Lee-Anne Bell researches and writes reports every day. Her specialty is soil and groundwater assessment and remediation, often related to property transactions. Her audiences include individuals, private companies, and municipal, provincial, and federal government ministries.

Lee-Anne does a great deal of research. "I often research the history of various properties. I may conduct interviews, refer to environmental databases, place formal inquiries with regulators, and/or review historical aerial photographs, city street directories, historical fire insurance plans, land title documents, and facility/property records."

Lee-Anne also uses her own observations and experiences: "I have seen how two-bite brownies and Chrysler cars are built. If I am going to visit a manufacturing plant, I might research the industry of the company to learn what I may encounter during my visit. To determine the environmental condition of a property I visit the property, collect soil or groundwater samples, or samples of any one of a variety of surface or sub-surface matrices.

"I often interview property owners and/or operators regarding the current and historical operations on their

properties. Sometimes I interview regulators regarding incidents that may have occurred on a property of interest. Once in a while I interview candidates for employment.

"About 95 percent of the research materials I use are electronic, and 5 percent literary (textbooks)."

Lee-Anne uses email for her letters and memos. She writes her reports in Word, and then transfers the documents to Adobe PDF files to send to clients.

Although Lee-Anne writes two-page reports, most of her reports are 10 to 20 pages long. "The purposes, audiences, and amount of information determine the medium. The one-page Executive Summary covers purpose, scope, methods, and results. Here the client finds immediate answers to his or her questions: 'Do I have a compliance issue or not? Is there contamination or not?'

"The report Body covers methodology, results, and interpretation (conclusions).

"Supplementary materials can include a variety of items such as figures and photos, data tables (showing analytical results, for example), supporting documentation (letters of response from regulators, database search results). Often the pages in a report's

appendices outnumber the pages in the up-front text. The detailed information demonstrates the methodology, makes an easy reference for readers, and is vital for ethical and legal reference."

Lee-Anne revises for clarity and conciseness; a colleague might peer-review her work.

Lee-Anne's education—a B.Sc. in Environmental Sciences from Guelph University, and a post-diploma course in Environmental Control—polished her technical expertise. However, she attributes her writing skills to her grade-school French immersion program, and her love of reading, which "enhanced my vocabulary and appreciation of various styles of writing."

PAIBOC ANALYSIS

1. Identify four primary sources Lee-Anne uses to gather information.

2. What specific information could Lee-Anne find online?

3. Why does Lee-Anne convert her reports to PDF files to send to clients?

4. How does Lee-Anne prepare to interview experts?

Researching Information

Learning Objectives

After reading and applying the information in Module 18, you'll be able to demonstrate

Knowledge of

- How and where to get information
- What quantitative and qualitative information are
- How to begin to analyze information
- How to prepare to take good notes

Skills to

- Identify primary and secondary sources
- Find electronic and print information
- Use the Internet for research
- Analyze sources
- Write questions for surveys and interviews
- Prepare to take good notes

Employability Skills 2000+ Checklist

Communicate

- ○ read and understand information presented in a variety of forms (e.g., words, graphs, charts, diagrams)
- ○ use relevant scientific, technological, and mathematical knowledge and skills to explain or clarify ideas

Manage Information

- ○ locate, gather, and organize information using appropriate technology and information systems
- ○ access, analyze, and apply knowledge and skills from various disciplines (e.g., the arts, languages, science, technology, mathematics, social sciences, and the humanities)
- ○ observe and record data using appropriate methods, tools, and technology

Think & Solve Problems

- ○ assess situations and identify problems
- ○ seek different points of view and evaluate them based on facts
- ○ recognize the human, interpersonal, technical, scientific, and mathematical dimensions of a problem
- ○ be creative and innovative in exploring possible solutions
- ○ readily use science, technology, and mathematics as ways to think, gain and share knowledge, solve problems, and make decisions

Be Adaptable

- ○ be innovative and resourceful: identify and suggest alternative ways to achieve goals and get the job done
- ○ cope with uncertainty

Learn Continuously

- ○ identify and access learning sources and opportunities

Participate in Projects & Tasks

- ○ plan, design, or carry out a project or task from start to finish with well-defined objectives and outcomes
- ○ develop a plan, seek feedback, test, revise, and implement
- ○ work to agreed quality standards and specifications
- ○ select and use appropriate tools and technology for a task or project
- ○ adapt to changing requirements and information
- ○ continuously monitor the success of a project or task and identify ways to improve

---

Researching may be as simple as getting a computer printout of sales for the last month; it may involve finding online material, or interviewing people. **Secondary research** retrieves information that someone else has gathered. Library research and online searches are well-known kinds of secondary research. **Primary research** gathers new information. Personal observations, experiences and experiments, and interviews and surveys are common methods for gathering and analyzing new information.

To research effectively, you need to know

- Where and how to find information
- How to evaluate and analyze the information you find
- How to use that information professionally and ethically

This module covers how to research and evaluate primary and secondary research. Module 19 describes how to synthesize the information, and credit your sources.

How Do I Begin My Research?

Focus your search: identify your objective, and draft a purpose statement.

To narrow your search for relevant information, identify your objective: What are you looking for, and why? Use PAIBOC analysis to identify your objective.

Next, draft a thesis or **working purpose statement** to clarify your objective. Your working purpose statement

- Narrows your research parameters: you search for and find the right information more efficiently
- Structures your document or presentation
- Becomes part of the your document or presentation introduction

In your working purpose statement, include the situation and your rhetorical purposes. (Figure 18.2 gives examples of working purpose statements; for more details on writing purpose statements, see Module 20, page 354.)

You might change your purpose statement when you have gathered and analyzed your information. However, with a working thesis, you can begin your search.

FIGURE 18.1 **PAIBOC Questions for Analysis**

P What's the **purpose** of your research? Why are you looking for information? Are you reporting or updating information? Justifying a request for funding to attend a conference? Writing a proposal to sell a product or service? Creating a business plan to attract investors? Are you writing a report to describe a problem and recommend solutions? Are you making a decision? exploring possibilities? preparing for a test?

Your purposes come from you and your organization. You must clearly define your purpose(s) before you can begin to research efficiently.

A Who is your **audience**? Who will read/view/hear your plan, request, report, or idea? What are your audience's expectations? What proof or evidence does your audience value? What proof will convince them? What kind of information would maximize your audience's understanding? Why?

I What **information** will achieve your purpose(s)? by meeting your audience's needs? What information will cause your readers to think or act as you want them to? Where can you find the relevant information? What primary sources are available? How can you use your own experiences and observations? Whom can you interview to get answers? What secondary resources are available, online and in print?

B What reasons or reader **benefits** can you find to meet your purpose(s)? What kind of information will emphasize those benefits?

O What audience **objections** do you anticipate? What information can you find, and how can you use that information to deemphasize or overcome audience objections?

C What **context** will affect your research? What environmental, economic, organizational, professional and personal factors will influence why, where and how you collect information?

FIGURE 18.2   **Working Purpose Statements**

I need to

- Inform my manager and colleagues about the most relevant information I learned at the conference
- Explain why we should review our report templates
- Describe how we can increase productivity by moving Human Resources upstairs
- Examine the property's soil for contamination, and report the results
- Prove that we need to hire another salesperson to improve customer service
- Convince my professor that I can find the information to write a good research report

How Can I Find Information?

Learn what resources are available, and how to use them.

Libraries and the Internet (electronic) offer billions of bytes of information. Searchable databases of journals, periodicals, magazines, and newspapers are free online through your local and university/college library. See Table 18.1 for examples. Ask your reference librarian about the free resources available.

TABLE 18.1   **Examples of Searchable Online Databases**

Business Source Premier

Full-text journals on business, marketing, accounting, economics, finance and management. Includes *Harvard Business Review* and country economic reports.

Canadian Business and Current Affairs Complete

Collection of journals, magazines, newspapers, and newsletters searchable in full text, including *Canadian Business* and *Maclean's*.

Canadian Business Online

Directory information on more than 1.5 million Canadian businesses, primarily in the wholesale, retail, and manufacturing sectors. Great for market research and sales prospecting.

Canadian Encyclopedia Online

Online access to the full text of the *Canadian Encyclopedia* courtesy of Historica.

Canadian Periodical Index Quarterly

Many full-text Canadian magazines and newspapers, including selected articles from the *Globe and Mail*.

Countries and Cultures eBooks

Encyclopedias devoted to the world's countries: their history, geography, peoples, and cultures.

Source: "Online Databases," Oakville Public Libraries site, http://www.opl.on.ca/research/databases, retrieved September 18, 2009.

Knowledge Ontario (www.knowledgeontario.ca), a provincially funded "collaboration of libraries, cultural heritage organizations and educational institutions," provides local and educational libraries access to hundreds of databases.[1] The site also provides video tutorials explaining what databases are, and how to use them efficiently.[2] Similar access exists in most other provinces.

How Can I Search Efficiently?

Use keyword searches. Keywords are the terms the computer looks for in a database or on the Web. The ABI/Inform Thesaurus lists synonyms and the hierarchies that index information in various databases.

At the beginning of a search, you might use all the synonyms and keywords you can think of. Skim several of the first sources you find; if they use additional or different terms, search for these new terms as well. You're looking for the keyword or phrase that will yield the specific information you need.

Refine your search:

- Use root words to find variations. A root word such as *stock* followed by the plus sign (*stock+*) will yield *stock, stocks, stockmarket*, and so forth.
- Use quotation marks for multi-word terms. If you want only sites that use the term "business communication," put quotes around the term.
- Use a Boolean search to get more specific hits. For example, to study the effect of the minimum wage on employment in the restaurant industry, you might specify

> (minimum wage) *and* (restaurant *or* fast food) *and* (employment rate *or* unemployment)

Without *and*, you'd get articles that discuss the minimum wage in general, articles about every aspect of restaurants, and every article that refers to unemployment, although many of these would not be relevant to your topic. The *or* calls up articles that use the term *fast food* but not *restaurant*, and vice versa. An article that used the phrase *fast food industry* would be eliminated unless it also used the term *restaurant*. Figure 18.3 illustrates this Boolean search example.

- Use a variety of search engines: you can google "search engine directories" for an alpha list of search engines and directories that can both widen and deepen your resources.[3]
- Use all available resources. Search engines and databases offer search tips, topic browsing, advanced searches, and refined search topic phrases to help you navigate, and focus your search. Databases also provide citation styles, with examples, and pop-ups that format the citation for you (Module 19).
- Create an **RSS (really simple syndication) Feed** for the most current information available. RSS sends subscribers up-to-date news articles: you get all the latest news right away without having to search the Web. "You set up your preferences once and the content comes to your desktop. Your subscription is anonymous."[4] Many feeds are free, and you can subscribe immediately on databases and search engines.

Employability Skills

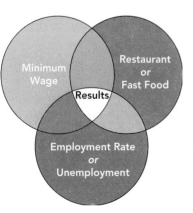

FIGURE 18.3   **Example of a Boolean Search**

Where Else Can I Find Information?

Powerful as it is, the Internet is just one search tool. Ask your reference librarian for research ideas, including print sources. And remember that textbooks and on-file company information are useful sources.

You can also do primary research to get new information. You can use your own observations and experiences, and consult topic experts and colleagues for information through interviews and surveys.

How Do I Decide Whom to Survey or Interview?

Use a random sample for surveys, if time and money permit. Use a judgment sample for interviews.

The **population** is the group you want to make statements about. Depending on the purpose of your research, your population might be all *Report on Business* Top 1000 companies, all business students at your college or university, or all consumers.

Defining your population correctly is crucial to getting useful information. For example, suppose you wanted to research and report on why people use social networking sites. First, you would have to define your parameters. What do you mean by "use"? Are you considering frequency of visits? the number of hours spent on such sites? the number of contacts? the amount of shared information?

Next, you would have to identify the demographic you want to interview: Facebook and MySpace attract very different users from LinkedIn, ZoomInfo, and XpressBook.

Random Sample   Because it is not feasible to survey everyone, you select a **sample**. If you take a true random sample, you can generalize your findings to the whole population from which your sample comes. In a **random sample**, each person in the population theoretically has an equal chance of being chosen. When people say they did something *randomly* they often mean *without conscious bias*. However, unconscious bias always exists. Someone passing out surveys in front of the library will be more likely to approach people who seem friendly, and less likely to ask people who seem intimidating, in a hurry, much older or younger, or of a different race, class, or sex. True random samples rely on random-digit tables generated by computers and published in statistics texts and books such as *A Million Random Digits*.

Convenience Sample   A **convenience sample** is a group of respondents who are easy to reach: students who walk through the student centre, people at a shopping mall, workers in your own unit. Convenience samples are useful for a rough pre-test of a questionnaire. However, you cannot generalize from a convenience sample to a larger group.

Judgment Sample   A **judgment sample** is a group of people whose views seem useful. Someone interested in surveying the kinds of writing done on campus might ask each department for the name of a faculty member who cares about writing, and then send surveys to those people. Judgment samples are often good for interviews, where your purpose is to talk to someone whose views are worth hearing.

How Do I Create Surveys and Write Questions for Interviews?

Test your questions to make sure they're clear and neutral.

A **survey** questions a large group of people, called **respondents** or subjects. The easiest way to ask many questions is to create a **questionnaire**, a written list of questions that people respond to. Figure 18.4 shows an example of a questionnaire.

Employability Skills 2000+

FIGURE 18.4 **A Student Questionnaire**

In your introductory paragraph, ① Tell how to return the survey; ② How the information will be used.

Start with easy-to-answer questions.

Branch questions allow readers to skip questions.

Put directions in parentheses to separate them from the question itself.

Give readers information they need to understand your question.

These abbreviations are OK when you survey skilled readers.

Make sure to break up the lines. Leaving an extra space makes it more likely that the respondent will check the right line.

Using columns gets the survey on one side, saving money in copying and eliminating the problem of people missing questions on the back. But it leaves almost no room to write in comments.

Repeat where to turn in or mail completed surveys.

Survey on Internships

Please answer the following questions and return the completed survey to the person who gave it to you. All information will be confidential and used only for a class project examining the feasibility of establishing an internship program for a particular business.

1. Major _____

2. Rank: First Year _____
           Sophomore _____
           Junior _____
           Senior _____

3. How important it is to you to have one or more internships before you graduate?
   ___ Very important
   ___ Somewhat important
   ___ Not important

4. Did you have an internship last summer?
   ___ Yes   ___ No (Skip to Question 6.)

5. What were the most beneficial aspects of your internship? (Check all that apply.)
   ___ Work related to my major
   ___ Likely to get a job offer/got a job offer
   ___ Chance to explore my interests
   ___ Made connections
   ___ Worked with clients
   ___ Looks good on my résumé
   ___ Other (Please explain.)

6. How much money did you make last summer? (Approximate hourly rate, before taxes.)

   _____

   ❑ Check here if you did not make any money last summer.

7. For next summer, could you afford to take an unpaid internship?
   ___ Yes   ___ No

8. For next summer, could you afford to take an internship paying only the minimum wage?
   ___ Yes   ___ No

9. How important is each of the following criteria in choosing whether to accept a specific internship?

	Very impt.	Some impt.	Not impt.
a. Money	❑	❑	❑
b. Prestige of company	❑	❑	❑
c. Location near where you live now	❑	❑	❑
d. Quality of mentoring	❑	❑	❑
e. Building connections	❑	❑	❑
f. Chance of getting a job with that company	❑	❑	❑
g. Gaining experience	❑	❑	❑

10. How interested are you in a career in managed care?
    ___ Very interested
    ___ Somewhat interested
    ___ Not interested

11. Could you take a job in Edmonton next summer?
    ___ Definitely
    ___ Maybe
    ___ No

12. Have you heard of FFI Rx Managed Care?
    ___ Yes
    ___ No

13. I invite any other comments you would like to make regarding internships.

Thank you for taking the time to answer this survey. Please return it to the person who gave it to you.

An interview is a structured conversation with someone able to give you useful information. However, surveys and interviews are useful only if the questions are well designed.

Although survey and interview queries are based on your ideas and a theory—or *working purpose statement*—it's important to phrase questions in a way that won't lead the respondent to the answer you want, or bias the response. Remember that *people tend to answer the questions they are asked.* Poor questions yield poor data.

Phrase questions clearly. Use words that mean the same thing to your respondents as they do to you. Whenever you can, use concrete, quantitative, measurable language. Words like *important* and *often* are open to anyone's interpretation.

Vague: Do you use the Web to research often?

Better: How many hours a week do you spend researching on the Web?

Avoid questions that make assumptions about your subjects, unless you are seeking to qualify your respondents. The question "Does your spouse have a job outside the home?" assumes that the respondent is married.

Closed questions—those questions to which people can answer only *yes* or *no*—limit information. **Open questions**—the journalism or "W" questions (*what, who, why, where, when, how*)—encourage information and do not lock the subject into any sort of response. Closed questions are faster for subjects to answer and easier for researchers to score. However, since all answers must fit into chosen categories, closed questions cannot probe the complexities of a subject. You can improve the quality of closed questions by conducting a pre-test with open questions to find categories that matter to respondents.

When you use multiple-choice questions, make sure that only one answer fits in any one category. In the following example of overlapping categories, a person who worked for a company with exactly 25 employees could check either *a.* or *b.* The resulting data would be unreliable.

Overlapping categories: Indicate the number of full-time employees in your company on May 16:

___ a. 0–25

___ b. 25–100

___ c. 100–500

___ d. more than 500

Discrete categories: Indicate the number of full-time employees in your company on May 16:

___ a. 0–25

___ b. 26–100

___ c. 101–500

___ d. more than 500

Branching questions direct different respondents to different parts of the questionnaire on the basis of their answers to earlier questions.

10. Have you talked to an academic advisor this year?

Yes _____ No _____

(If "no," skip to question 14.)

Use closed, multiple-choice questions for potentially embarrassing topics (e.g.: Formal education: (a) high school, (b) college diploma, (c) university undergraduate degree, (d) graduate degree). Seeing their own situation listed as one response can help respondents feel that it is acceptable. However, very sensitive issues are perhaps better asked in an interview, where interviewers can build trust and reveal information about themselves to encourage the interviewee to answer.

Poor questions yield poor data.

Put questions that will be easy to answer (like gender or program of study) early in the questionnaire. Put questions that are harder to answer, or that people may be less willing to answer (e.g., age and income) near the end of the questionnaire. Even if people choose not to answer such questions, you'll still have the rest of the survey filled out.

How Should I Design the Document?

Pay careful attention to the physical design of the document. Use indentations and white space effectively; make it easy to mark and score the answers. Include a brief statement of purpose if you (or someone else) will not be available to explain the questionnaire, or answer questions. Pre-test the questionnaire to make sure the directions are clear. A training facilitator handed out a double-sided questionnaire without mentioning it was double-sided; thirty percent of respondents answered only the questions on the first side.

How Should I Analyze the Data I Collect?

Evaluate your sources; understand your sources; look for patterns and emerging stories.

You are responsible for the validity of your data, and for your data analysis. You need to evaluate and understand your sources, and analyze the information you have gathered.

Look for answers to your research questions, and for interesting nuggets that may not have been part of your original focus, but that emerge from the data. Such stories can be more convincing in reports and oral presentations than pages of computer printouts.

Evaluating Your Sources

To expand your critical thinking and bolster your research, evaluate your sources and seek alternative views. Here are some guidelines for finding and evaluating sources:

- *Use reputable sources.* Start with sites produced by universities and established companies or organizations. Be aware, however, that such organizations are not going to post information that makes them look bad. To get the other side of the story, monitor blogs, bulletin boards, and email lists, or access pages critical of the organization. (Search for "consumer opinion" and the name of the organization.)
- *Look for an author.* Do individuals take "ownership" of the information? What are their credentials? Are they subject experts? Where do they work? How can you contact them with questions? Remember that ".edu" sites might be owned by students not yet experts on a subject.

- *Look for the date.* How relevant is the information?
- *Check the source.* Is the information adapted from other sources? If so, try to get the original.
- *Compare the information with other sources.* Internet sources should complement print sources. When facts are correct, you'll likely find them recorded elsewhere.

Evaluating online sources, especially Web pages, is absolutely vital, since anyone can post pages on the Web, create a blog, tweet, or contribute to Wikipedia. Can you find at least one credible online or print source that agrees with the Web information?

If you want to use citizen journalism, social networking, and community sites like Wikipedia,

- First check with your professor or supervisor; many organizations do not accept information from Wikipedia, How Stuff Works, or any encyclopaedia or ".com" (sales) Web sites.
- If you get approval, find other reliable sources that support the information.

By contrast, many online and print sources, especially academic, and peer-reviewed articles, periodicals, and journals, have an editorial board that reviews material for accuracy and truthfulness. Peer experts often review these sources before they are accepted. The review process helps ensure that information meets high standards.

EXPANDING A CRITICAL SKILL

Preparing to Make Notes

Recording information efficiently and effectively enables you remember, understand and retrieve your research. Creating useful notes is a critical information-processing skill.

To begin the process, and save time and energy, prepare:

- *Define your purpose.* We take different notes for different purposes. Why are you making notes? How are you going to use the notes? How is the information important? What is valuable, and why?
- *Listen.* Defining your purpose helps you focus on what you need to listen to. What do you want to take away? What's the situation? Will you be writing a report? Taking an exam? What will you make notes about? What do you want to remember?
  - Listen for understanding: What ideas does the speaker emphasize? If you're listening to a prepared lecture or presentation, what ideas does the speaker highlight in the introduction? What does the speaker repeat or stress in the conclusion? What examples and details are relevant to your purpose?
- *Pre-read.* What are you reading? Will it be relevant to your purpose? Save time and energy by browsing the material to ensure that it's going to be useful. Look for the
  - Information context, or medium: Is it an intranet Web page? newspaper? magazine article? textbook? reference book?

- Organizational pattern: Information is organized (Module 22) according to the expectations of the discourse community (Module 2). Newspapers and well-written Web pages use the inverse pyramid pattern: all the important information is up front, in the first paragraph; details follow. Scan that paragraph to see if you need or want to read further.
- Scan reports, journals, periodicals and magazines for summaries, overviews, abstracts, headings, and subheadings: These synthesize key ideas.
- Illustrations and visuals: These can condense and clarify text (Module 23). Scan to increase understanding and retention.
- Level of technical difficulty: If the material is incomprehensible, making notes won't do you much good. Scan for references to other texts. Pre-read these first.
- *Read to understand.* With your purpose in mind, focus only on relevant information.
  - Look for the main ideas in the topic sentences in each paragraph (usually the first or second sentence).
  - Look carefully at visuals: What information can you use?
- Decide what you're going to record.

Module 19, page 341 describes how to create useful notes.

As electronic information sources and access has increased, so has the need for critical assessment. A number of sites offer tutorials on how to use and evaluate Web sources. Before you accept any information as credible, do your homework. You can find excellent assessment tools online at www.vuw.ac.nz/staff/alastair_smith/evaln/evaln.htm, http://owl.english. purdue.edu/handouts/research/r_evalsource4.html, and www.lib.berkeley.edu/TeachingLib/ Guides/Internet/FindInfo.html.

Understanding Your Sources

When you use secondary data from library and online research, look at the sample, the sample size, and the exact wording of questions to see what the data actually measure. Some studies bias results by limiting the alternatives. For example, in one survey, 90 percent of students surveyed by Levi Strauss & Co. said Levi's 501 jeans would be the most popular clothes that year. But Levi's was the only brand of jeans on the list of choices.[5]

Identify the assumptions used in collecting and analyzing the data. When Nielson Media Research estimates the number of people who watch television stations, it must make assumptions: how well its People Meter actually tracks whether people are watching, and how best to count groups that are hard to measure.

Neilson reported that 18-to-34-year-old males are watching less television, in part because they spend more time with video games and DVDs. However, television stations complained that the company was underreporting this group's viewing. For example, they said, Neilson was not counting young people who leave for postsecondary, and its sample did not include homes with TiVo or other personal video recorders. Thus, Neilson, the networks and advertisers disagree about whether young men are losing interest in television programming.[6]

Analyzing Quantitative Data

Many reports analyze numbers—numbers either from databases and sources, or from a survey you conduct.

If you've conducted a survey, your first step is to transfer the responses on the survey form into numbers. For some categories, you'll assign numbers arbitrarily. For example, you might record men as "1" and women as "2" or vice versa. Such assignments don't matter, as long as you're consistent throughout your project. In these cases, you can report the number and percentage of men and women who responded to your survey, but you can't do anything else with the numbers.

When you have numbers for salaries or other figures, start by figuring the average, or mean, the median, and the range. The **average** or **mean** is calculated by adding up all the figures and dividing by the number of samples. The **median** is the number that is exactly in the middle. When you have an odd number of observations, the median will be the middle number. When you have an even number, the median will be the average of the two numbers in the centre. The **range** is the high and low figures for that variable.

Finding the average takes a few more steps when you have different kinds of data. For example, it's common to ask respondents whether they find a feature "very important," "somewhat important," or "not important." You might code "very important" as "3," "somewhat important" as "2," and "not important" as "1." To find the average in this kind of data,

1. Multiply the code for each response by the number of people who gave that response.
2. Add up the figures.
3. Divide by the total number of people responding to the question.

For example, suppose you have surveyed 50 people about the features they want in a proposed apartment complex.

The average gives an easy way to compare various features. If a party room averages 2.3 while extra parking for guests is 2.5, you know that your respondents would find extra parking more important than a party room. You can now arrange the factors in order of importance:

"How Important Is Each Factor to You in Choosing an Apartment?"

$n = 50$; 3 = "Very Important"

Extra parking for guests	2.5
Party room	2.3
Pool	2.2
Convenient to bus line	2.0

Often it's useful to simplify numerical data: round it off and combine similar elements. Then you can see that one number is about 2.5 times another. Charting can also help you see patterns in your data. Look at the raw data as well as at percentages. For example, a 50 percent increase in shoplifting incidents sounds alarming—but an increase from two to three shoplifting incidents sounds well within normal variation.

Checkpoint

Analyzing Numbers

The **average** or **mean** is calculated by adding up all the figures and dividing by the number of samples. The **median** is the number that is exactly in the middle. The **range** is the distance between high and low figures for that variable.

Analyzing Qualitative Data

When your survey contains words, explore what the words mean to the people who responded. Respondents to Whirlpool's survey of 180 000 households said they wanted "clean refrigerators." Whirlpool asked more questions. The company discovered that what people wanted was refrigerators that *looked* clean, so the company developed models with textured fronts and sides to hide fingerprints.[7]

Look for patterns.

- On which points do experts agree? Which disagreements can be explained by early theories or numbers that have now changed? by different interpretations of the same data? by different values and criteria? In your interviews and surveys, what patterns do you see?
- Have things changed over time?
- Do geography, gender, or education account for differences?
- What similarities do you see?
- What differences do you see?
- What confirms your hunches?
- What surprises you?

Checking Your Logic

As you analyze your data, differentiate between causation and correlation. **Causation** means that one thing causes or produces another. **Correlation** means that two things happen at the same time. One might cause the other, but both might be caused by a third.

Employability Skills

For example, suppose that you're writing a report to justify the purchase of a BlackBerry for every salesperson in your company. Your survey results indicate that employees who currently have BlackBerrys are more productive than people who don't. Does having a BlackBerry lead to higher productivity? Perhaps. But perhaps productive people are more likely to push to get BlackBerrys from company funds, while less productive people are more passive. Perhaps productive people earn more and are more likely to be able to buy their own Blackberrys if the organization doesn't provide them.

Consciously search for at least three possible causes for each phenomenon you've observed and at least three possible solutions for each problem. The more possibilities you brainstorm, the more likely you are to find good options. In your report, mention all the possibilities; discuss in detail only those that will occur to readers and that you think are the real reasons and the best solutions.

When you have identified patterns that seem to represent the causes of the problem or the best solutions, check these ideas against reality. Can you find support in the quotes or in the numbers? Can you answer counterclaims? If you can, you will be able to present evidence for your argument in a convincing way.

If you can't prove the claim you originally hoped to make, you will need to revisit your working thesis or modify your conclusions to fit your data. Even when your market test is a failure, you can still write a useful report.

- Identify changes that might yield a different result (e.g., selling the product at a lower price might enable the company to sell enough units).
- Discuss circumstances that may have affected the results.
- Summarize your negative findings in progress reports to let readers down gradually and to give them a chance to modify the research design.
- Remember that negative results are not always disappointing to the audience. A report demonstrating that an idea isn't feasible can save people's time and money.

MODULE SUMMARY

- **Primary research** gathers new information: personal observations, interviews, and surveys are common methods for gathering new information for business documents.

- **Secondary research** retrieves information that someone else has gathered. Library research and online searches are well-known kinds of secondary research.

- Begin your research by narrowing your focus. What are you looking for, and why?

- Draft a **working purpose statement** to clarify your objectives. This purpose statement
  - Narrows your research parameters
  - Structures your document or presentation
  - Becomes part of your document or presentation introduction

- Next, ask your reference librarian about the free resources available in your library.

- To research efficiently online, use
  - Keyword and Boolean searches
  - Suggested topics searches
  - Advanced searches
  - A variety of search engines
  - RSS feeds
  - Online tools, topics, and tutorials to navigate, and narrow your quest

- A **survey** questions a large group of people, called **respondents** or **subjects**. A **questionnaire** is a written list of questions people fill out. An **interview** is a structured conversation with someone who can give you useful information.

- When creating a questionnaire or interview questions, define your terms, and phrase questions clearly. Use words that mean the same thing to your respondents as they do to you. Use concrete, quantitative, measurable language.

- Closed questions limit answers to yes or no. Open questions encourage more information. Branching questions direct different respondents to different parts of the questionnaire on the basis of their answers to earlier questions.
- To find credible information sources
  - Check the source: look for an author.
  - Look for credentials.
  - Look for the date.
  - Is the information adapted from other sources? If so, try to get the original.

- Compare the information with other sources. Internet sources should complement print sources. When facts are correct, you'll likely find them recorded elsewhere.
- To take and create good notes, prepare:
  - Define your purpose.
  - Listen actively.
  - Pre-read materials.
  - Focus on the material you want to record.

ASSIGNMENTS FOR MODULE 18

Questions for Critical Thinking

18.1 What are the advantages to creating a working purpose statement before beginning your research?

18.2 What ethical considerations could face researchers collecting primary information?

18.3 Why look for alternative explanations for your research findings?

18.4 Why should you know the exact way a question was phrased before using results from the study as evidence?

Exercises and Problems

18.5 Finding and Using Web Resources

Visit the Web resources[8] listed below. Evaluate each resource based on the following questions:

1. What information does the site offer?
2. How can you use this information?
3. How reliable is the site, and the information? How do you know?
4. How accessible is the site? Is it easy to navigate? moderately difficult? difficult?

Make notes summarizing your findings: based on these questions, which sites are helpful to you? Why? Which are not helpful?

Web Tutorials

http://www.internettutorials.net/finding-scholarly-content.asp

http://www.internettutorials.net/best-bet-search.asp

http://www.internettutorials.net/choose.asp

http://www.lib.berkeley.edu/TeachingLib/Guides/Internet/MetaSearch.html

Alternative Engine Searches Information Access

http://www.virtualprivatelibrary.com

http://www.cuil.com

http://www.uduko.com

As your instructor directs,

  a. Post your results to the class on a blog or file-sharing application.
  b. Present your results in a memo to your instructor.
  c. Present your results to the class in an oral presentation.

18.6 Evaluating Survey Questions

Evaluate each of the following questions. How acceptable are they? How can you improve them?

  a. Questionnaire on grocery purchases:
  1. Do you usually shop at the same grocery store?
     a. Yes
     b. No
  2. Do you buy locally?
     a. Yes
     b. No
  3. Do you buy organic produce?
     a. Yes
     b. No
  4. Do you buy organic meat?
     a. Yes
     b. No

5. How much is your average grocery bill?

    a. Under $25

    b. $25–50

    c. $50–100

    d. $100–150

    e. More than $150

b. Survey on technology:

    1. Would you generally welcome any technological advancement that allowed information to be sent and received more quickly and in greater quantities than ever before?

    2. Do you think that all people should have free access to all information, or do you think that information should somehow be regulated and monitored?

c. Survey on job skills:

How important are the following skills for getting and keeping a professional-level job in Canadian business and industry today?

	Low				High
Ability to communicate	1	2	3	4	5
Leadership ability	1	2	3	4	5
Public presentation skills	1	2	3	4	5
Selling ability	1	2	3	4	5
Teamwork capability	1	2	3	4	5
Writing ability	1	2	3	4	5

18.7   Evaluating Web Sites

Evaluate seven Web sites related to the topic of your report. For each, consider

- Author(s)
- Objectivity
- Information
- Revision date

On the basis of these criteria, which sites are best for your report? Which are unacceptable? Why?

As your instructor directs,

    a. Share your results with a small group of students.

    b. Present your results in a memo to your instructor.

    c. Present your results to the class in an oral presentation.

18.8   Designing Questions for an Interview or Survey

Submit either a one-to-three-page questionnaire or questions for a 20-to-30-minute interview and the information listed below for the method you choose.

Questionnaire

1. Purpose(s), goal(s)
2. Subjects (who, why, how many)
3. How and where to be distributed
4. Rationale for order of questions, kinds of questions, wording of questions

Interview

1. Purpose(s), goal(s)
2. Subject (who and why)
3. Proposed site, length of interview
4. Rationale for order of questions, kinds of questions, wording of questions, choice of branching or follow-up questions

As your instructor directs,

    a. Create questions for a survey on one of the following topics:

- Survey students on your campus about their knowledge of, and interest in the programs and activities sponsored by a student organization.

- Survey students about their knowledge and use of campus services, such as the counselling, health, career, or tutoring centres.

- Survey workers at a company about what they like and dislike about their jobs.

- Survey people in your community about their willingness to pay more to buy products that use recycled materials and to buy products that are packaged with a minimum of waste.

- Survey students and faculty on your campus about their environmental awareness, habits, and concerns.

- Survey two groups on a topic that interests you.

    b. Create questions for an interview on one of the following topics:

- Interview an international student about the form of greetings and farewells, topics of small talk, forms of politeness, festivals and holidays, meals at home, size of families, and roles of family members in his or her county.

- Interview the owner of a small business about the problems the business has, the strategies the owner has already used to increase sales and profits and the success of these strategies, and the owner's attitudes toward possible changes in product line, decor, marketing, hiring, advertising, and money management.

- Interview someone who has information you need for a report you're writing.

18.9 Reporting your Survey Results*

Together with three of your peers,

- Form a research team and decide on a relevant investigation topic.
- Choose a topic related to your audience's interests and that will elicit interesting and varied responses (tuition fees, transportation to school, part-time work, dating trends, career plans, hobbies, gender miscommunication, postsecondary choices, quality of teaching)
- Create a survey questionnaire (minimum five questions: see Exercise 18.8) to interview people (20) who would have the information or opinions you seek.
- Use closed, open, and probing questions to provide you with enough data for analysis.

As your instructor directs,

a. Using your findings, prepare a short oral report for the class, with headings and topic sentences; arrange your information to reflect the way you want your readers to think about the data:

Introduction: *topic/purpose, scope, method (number of people interviewed, who)*

b. Create PowerPoint™ slides to summarize your data.

c. Draw conclusions based on your information. *You might want to use your questions as headings throughout the report.*

Conclusion: What did you discover? Why might your audience care?

d. Use APA in-text citations and end with a Reference page (Module 19) indicating your sources.

*Thanks to Professor Kathryn Voltan, University of Toronto, for this exercise.

POLISHING YOUR PROSE

Combining Sentences

Combining sentences is a powerful tool to make your writing more concise and more forceful.

When too many sentences in a passage have fewer than 10 words and follow the same basic pattern, prose is *choppy*. Choppy prose seems less unified and either robotic or frenzied in tone.

Combining short sentences to create longer flowing ones can eliminate this problem.

Choppy: I went to the office supply store. I purchased a computer, a fax machine, and a laser printer. I went to my office. I installed the equipment. I am more efficient.

Better: At the office supply store, I purchased a computer, a fax machine, and a laser printer. After installing the equipment in my office, I am more efficient.

There are several ways to combine sentences.

1. Use **transitions**: words and phrases that signal connections between ideas. Common transitions are *first, second, third, finally, in addition, likewise, for example, however, on the other hand, nevertheless, because, therefore, before, after, while,* and *in conclusion.*

Choppy: Neil drove the truck to the warehouse. Charlie loaded it with cement. Phil supervised the work.

Better: First, Neil drove the truck to the warehouse. Then Charlie loaded it with cement, while Phil supervised the work.

2. Rewrite sentences using **subordinate clauses**. A clause with one of the following words will be subordinate: *after, although, though, because,* or *since.*

Better: After Neil drove the truck to the warehouse, Charlie loaded it with cement. Phil supervised the work.

3. Join simple sentences together with *coordinating conjunctions,* such as *and, but,* and *or.* These conjunctions can also function as transitional words. Be sure to use the comma before the conjunction when combining two independent clauses.

Better: Neil drove the truck to the warehouse, Charlie loaded it with cement, and Phil supervised the work.

4. Create a list using commas and coordinating conjunctions.

Choppy: Sam put our old files in the storeroom. Sam placed extra copies of the company telephone directory in the storeroom. Sam put boxes of three-ring binders in the storeroom.

Better: Sam put old files, extra copies of the telephone directory, and boxes of three-ring binders in the storeroom.

Exercises

Combine the following sentences to make them easier to read.

1. You can get promoted quickly at our company. Being organized and on time will help. Not meeting deadlines will not help.

2. There are many reasons to choose Canadian Human Resource Planners as your human resources consulting firm. Our organization has more than 20 years in the business. We have regional offices in Calgary and Toronto. Canadian Human Resource Planners has an international membership of members from industry, government, nonprofit groups, educational institutions, and consulting firms.

3. Changing the toner cartridge on the photocopier is simple. Open the front panel. Find the green tabs. Depress the green tabs with your thumbs. Pull the black toner cartridge out. Put the toner cartridge in the recycling box. Slide a new toner cartridge into the compartment. The green tabs will snap back into place. Close the panel.

4. The development team members took a plane to Victoria. That was on Friday. They attended a conference. That was on Saturday. They came home. That was on Sunday. On Friday it rained. The team members used umbrellas. The other two days it did not rain. They did not need umbrellas on those days.

5. The tornado plan for our building has five parts. One part is to go to your designated shelter area in the basement of the building. One part is to listen for the tornado alert siren. One part is to sit down on the floor. One part is to take the stairs and not the elevator. One part is to cover your head with your arms.

Check your answers to the odd-numbered exercises on page 553.

Synthesizing and Documenting Information

Learning Objectives

After reading and applying the information in Module 19, you'll be able to demonstrate

Knowledge of

- How to summarize and paraphrase information
- How to create good notes
- Why researchers document their sources of information
- How to cite and document sources correctly

Skills to

- Begin to write summaries and précis
- Begin to take useful notes
- Document sources legally, ethically, and correctly

Employability Skills 2000+ Checklist

Communicate

○ read and understand information presented in a variety of forms (e.g., words, graphs, charts, diagrams)

○ use relevant scientific, technological, and mathematical knowledge and skills to explain or clarify ideas

Manage Information

○ locate, gather, and organize information using appropriate technology and information systems

○ access, analyze, and apply knowledge and skills from various disciplines (e.g., the arts, languages, science,

technology, mathematics, social sciences, and the humanities)

○ observe and record data using appropriate methods, tools, and technology

Think & Solve Problems

○ assess situations and identify problems

○ seek different points of view and evaluate them on the basis of facts

○ recognize the human, interpersonal, technical, scientific, and mathematical dimensions of a problem

○ be creative and innovative in exploring possible solutions

○ readily use science, technology, and mathematics as ways to think, gain and share knowledge, solve problems, and make decisions

Be Adaptable

○ be innovative and resourceful: identify and suggest alternative ways to achieve goals and get the job done

○ cope with uncertainty

Learn Continuously

○ identify and access learning sources and opportunities

Participate in Projects & Tasks

○ plan, design, or carry out a project or task from start to finish with well-defined objectives and outcomes

○ develop a plan, seek feedback, test, revise, and implement

○ work to agreed quality standards and specifications

○ select and use appropriate tools and technology for a task or project

○ adapt to changing requirements and information

○ continuously monitor the success of a project or task and identify ways to improve

---

Researching encompasses more than finding and analyzing data (Module 18). Research skills also include

- Knowing how to summarize the information
- Using it effectively
- Giving credit to the source of the information correctly

This module describes how to note and synthesize information, how to use in-text citations for business reports, and how to document sources using APA and MLA styles.

How Do I Summarize Information?

Read and listen for meaning; then write a synopsis, paraphrase, or précis.

We process information by sorting it into meaningful patterns. This pattern making includes summarizing and paraphrasing. When you **summarize**, you condense the data you're hearing or reading. You omit all details extraneous to your purpose, which is to capture and compress the meaning.

Summarizing Documents

To summarize text,

- Pre-read, skim and scan the article, document, or visual (Module 18).
- Identify and analyze the context; use PAIBOC analysis to answer:
  - What's the medium? Research report? Scholarly journal? Newspaper? Magazine? Blog? University Web page? Intranet page? Social network page? The medium frames the meaning: every discourse community (Module 2) has its own language rules, dependent on purpose and audience. Academic writing, for example, is often longer, denser, and more formal than business writing. Scientific and technical report writers often use the passive voice (see the Revising and Editing Resources, page 517) to meet audience expectations.
  - What's the purpose of the document, and who is the intended audience?
  - Who wrote it? What are the author's credentials? What's the evidence of expertise?
  - How does the writer develop the argument, or thesis? What is the pattern of organization? Comparison/contrast? Problem/solution? Elimination of alternatives? (Module 21.)
  - When was it published? How current is it?
  - What's the language level?
- Find the thesis, or main idea, which is usually in the introduction.
- Read the concluding paragraph: Does it sum up the information? What does it suggest the reader think or do?
- Find the topic sentences that control each paragraph. How are they related to the thesis?
- Look for proof. How does the author support his or her thesis? What's the evidence? Examples? Statistics? Studies? Experiments? Personal experience? Interviews?
- Set the text aside, and jot down or cluster (Module 4) an overview of the material: note (1) the main idea, (2) the medium, (3) the author's name, (4) an example, or proof, (5) your questions about the material. Figure 19.1 illustrates a cluster summary of these points.

Language FOCUS

Paraphrasing means that you are condensing the information you have and putting it *all* in your own words. You cannot just use synonyms for a few words and call it a précis or paraphrase. A paraphrase is also shorter than the original piece, so you leave out examples and illustrations that the original writer or speaker used. Also, when you summarize information, you are still using another person's ideas; therefore, you must always cite your source, telling who wrote it, what the title of the document is, and where the document (or oral information) came from. See the documentation formats, presented at the end of this module, for more help with this.

- Reread the document to ensure your summary information is accurate.
- Find the answers to your questions. If it suits your purpose, add them to your summary.
- Record all biographic data if you are using the summary in your report or presentation.
- Ask a peer or friend to check your summary against the original text.
- Add anything relevant.

Table 19.1 lists some of the Internet information resources you can research and summarize.

Summarizing Oral Communications

To summarize a lecture, presentation, interview, or speech,

- Listen for understanding; identify and analyze the context (Module 18):
  - Whenever possible, pre-read on the topic.

FIGURE 19.1   Clustering Information

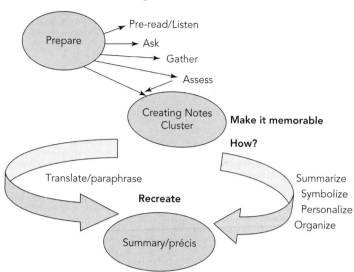

○ Listen for an overview. Use PAIBOC analysis: What? Why? Who? When? Where? Why?
○ Identify the speaker's purpose. Note it.
○ Identify the speaker's expectations of his or her audience. Note them.
○ Listen for the thesis. Note it.
○ Identify and analyze the organizational pattern. How does the speaker develop the argument, or thesis (Module 21)?
○ Listen for the proof. Note examples, statistics, evidence.
○ Listen for points of emphasis. Note them.
○ Listen for the close: How does the speaker sum up? What does the speaker want the audience to think, or do? Note that.
○ Read the handouts, or supplementary material if provided.

TABLE 19.1   Sources for Web Research, Analysis, and Synthesis

Canadian Government Information

Statistics Canada
http://www.statcan.ca

Most recent five years of data, constantly updated
http://www40.statcan.ca/ol/esto1

Profile of Canadian Communities, tables for more than 5 000 Canadian communities from most recent census, with the ability to create local base maps
http://www12.statcan.ca/english/census01/home/index.cfm

Canada Business Service Centres
http://www.cbsc.org

Canada's Business and Consumer Site
http://www.strategis.ic.gc.ca

Environment Canada
http://www.ec.gc.ca

Subject Matter Directories

AccountingNet
http://www.acountingnet.com

The Computer User High Tech Dictionary
http://www.computeruser.com/resources/dictionary/Dictionary.html

Education Index
http://www.educationindex.com

International Business Kiosk
http://www.calintel.org/kiosk

Management and entrepreneurship
http://www.lib.lsu.edu/bus/management/html

The WWW Virtual Library: Marketing
http://www.knowthis.com

Reference Collections

Britannica Online
http://www.eb.com

CEO Express
http://www.ceoexpress.com

Hoover's Online (information on more than 13 000 public and private companies worldwide)
http://www.hoovers.com/free

Reference Desk
http://www.refdesk.com

Interactive Atlas of Canada
http://atlas.nrcan.gc.ca/site/english/maps/topo/map

News Sites

Most Popular Business Websites EBizMBA
http://www.ebizmba.com/articles/business-sites

CBC News
http://www.cbc.ca/news

CBC Radio
http://cbc.ca/programguide

Business Week Online
http://www.businessweek.com

Canadian Business Online
http://www.canadianbusiness.com

The Globe and Mail Online
http://www.globeandmail.com

Maclean's Online
http://www.macleans.ca

The National Post Online
http://www.nationalpost.com

The New York Times on the Web
http://www.nyt.com

The Wall Street Journal Interactive Edition
http://www.wsj.com

- ○ Note your questions. What is unclear? What else do you need to know to understand?
- ○ Ask your questions, if appropriate to the situation
- Jot down or cluster (Figure 19.1) an overview of the material: (1) the thesis or main idea, (2) the speaker's name, if relevant to your purpose, (3) evidence and examples, (4) points of emphasis, (5) the conclusion.
- Check your summary for accuracy.
  - ○ If possible, ask the speaker to confirm that you have heard, understood, and synthesized all relevant information.
  - ○ Read related documents.
  - ○ If possible, compare your summary with that of another audience member.
- Add any relevant information.

Paraphrasing

When you paraphrase, you put information you're recording or reporting *into your own words*, while keeping the integrity of the meaning.

You write a **précis** when you paraphrase and summarize information. During a presentation, lecture or interview, for example, or when reading material you want to learn, you take notes that both translate and synthesize the information.

You don't need quotation marks when you include summaries and paraphrases in a report, but you must *cite and document the source of the information*.

For example, you might write "You cite your sources even when you use your own words" as

> u cte yr srcs evn whn u uz yr wn wrds

- Use common symbols: use symbols that let you "write rapidly and interpret easily" (Jensen, 2003, p. 119):

TABLE 19.2   Note-Taking Symbols

>	greater than	(+)	positive, good
<	less than	(−)	negative, against
=	the same, equals	c̄,w/	with
≠	different	w/o	without
X	times, cross	↓	down, under, decreasing
→	toward, going	↑	above, up, increasing
←	from	w/	with
∴	therefore, because	$	dollars, money
∞	infinity	Q	question

- Create your own code. Make your own symbols to summarize, organize, and emphasize information.
  - Use mind mapping (Module 4) to note patterns, sequences, hierarchies, and relationships.
  - Use spacing, different-size fonts, and different colours to highlight information you want to emphasize.
  - Keep a separate section to note what you want to follow up: questions, unclear information, and additional resources.

Creating purposeful notes is an acquired skill that depends on your understanding of both content and context. Learning to take great notes is easier when you practise daily, read widely and frequently, and have an extensive vocabulary. Competent note-takers use PAIBOC to analyze purpose and audience, and to understand the pattern the writer or speaker is using to organize the information.

Language FOCUS

When taking notes, it is best to record them in the language they are given in. If the lecturer is using English, record your notes in English. Do not try to translate into your own language while taking notes, as this might lead to mistakes later when you are studying or writing a report. For example, if you have incorrectly translated a word during a lecture or in a meeting, it will affect the accuracy of your report when you are writing it later and not able to double-check on your translation accuracy.

Why Should I Document My Sources?

Citing your sources of information demonstrates your honesty, enhances your credibility, and protects you from charges of plagiarism.

Employability Skills

Copyright laws protect people's creative output: "Copyright applies to all original literary, dramatic, musical and artistic works" (www.cipo.ic.gc.ca/eic/site/cipointernet-internetopic. nsf/eng/wr00506.html#no1). Ideas can't be owned, but the expression of those ideas can be. So Shakespeare can't own the idea that we should be true to ourselves, but he owns the phrase, "To thine own self be true."

Legally, therefore, researchers are required to identify the source of information that they do not originate. You must credit the source even when you put that information in your own words, or recreate a visual with your own software. Not doing so—intentionally or unintentionally—means you are plagiarizing. Stealing someone else's work has serious legal, academic, and personal consequences (http://plagiarism.org).

Academic penalties can include a grade failure or expulsion. In business, you can be sued for damages and lost revenue.

And since our laws express our social values (L. Butler, personal communication, July 8, 2008), you are also ethically responsible for crediting others' ideas, facts, figures, symbols, and words. Using someone else's work without giving him or her credit violates the individual's personal and professional rights. Doing so, even unintentionally, can damage your reputation.

Correctly documenting your sources also makes you look good. Investigating and citing a wide range of sources on your topic demonstrate your competence, and your analytical and critical thinking skills. Using a variety of authoritative research can suggest alternative points of view that lead to new insights, and provide you with the evidence you need to develop and prove your thesis. Documenting this research ethically proves your professionalism.

 Cultural **FOCUS**

In some cultures, perhaps your own, repeating word for word what a scholar has said is considered the best way to show you have understood and agree with certain points. It is also considered the best way to show respect for that scholar. However, for documents to be acceptable in North America (and many other Western cultures), you have to cite the source and also integrate the points into your own writing. This is how respect for the original writer or thinker is shown; it also demonstrates your own understanding of the ideas. By following the expected rules here, you are showing respect for and understanding of the cultural norms, just as you would expect others to show the same respect while working in your culture.

How Should I Document My Sources?

Use APA or MLA format.

The two most widely used formats for endnotes and bibliographies are those of the **American Psychological Association** (APA) and the **Modern Language Association** (MLA). (This module uses APA in-text citations.) Figure 19.2 shows the APA and MLA crediting the sources for this module.

"MLA ... style is most commonly used to write papers and cite sources within the liberal arts and humanities" (http://owl.english.purdue.edu/owl/resource/747/01/). MLA in-text citations give the author's last name and page number in parenthesis in the text. Example: (Gilsdorf and Leonard 118). If you use the author's name in the sentence, give only the page number (118). The Works Cited provides the full bibliographic citation, arranged alphabetically by author's last name.

APA style is used to cite and document sources in business, technology, and the sciences. APA in-text citations give authors' last names and the date of the work in parenthesis in the text. Put commas and an ampersand between multiple author names, then a comma and the date (Gilsdorf & Leonard, 2010). Only give the page number for a direct quotation (Cross, 2008, p. 74). If you use the author's name(s) in the sentence, give only the date in parenthesis. The References provide the full bibliographic citations, arranged alphabetically by the first author's last name.

FIGURE 19.2A **APA Format for Documenting Sources**

References

American Psychological Association. (2009). Electronic references. Retrieved July 8, 2009, from http://www.apastyle.org/elecref.html

British Science Association. (n.d.). Welcome to the honesty lab. *Dishonestylab.com.* Retrieved July 25, 2009, from http://www.britishscienceassociation.org/web/

Industry Canada. (2009). A guide to copyrights: Copyright protection. Ottawa: Canadian Intellectual Property Office. Retrieved July 17, 2009, from http://www.cipo.ic.gc.ca/eic/site/cipointernet-internetopic.nsf/eng/wr00506.html

Grossman, J. (1976). *Quickhand™.* New York: John Wiley & Sons, Inc.

Jensen, E. (2003). *Student success secrets.* New York: Barron's Educational Series, Inc.

Knowledge Ontario. (2008). *Welcome to Knowledge Ontario.* Retrieved January 27, 2009, from http://www.knowledgeontario.ca/

Mind Tools Ltd. (1995–2009). Mind maps, a powerful approach to note taking. Retrieved July 17, 2009, from http://www.mindtools.com/pages/article/newISS_01.htm

Modern Language Association of America. (2009). *MLA handbook for writers of research papers.* (7th ed.). New York: The Modern Language Association of America.

Plagiarism.org. (2009). What is plagiarism? *PlagiarismdotOrg.* Retrieved January 26, 2009, from http://www.plagiarism.org/learning_center/what_is_plagiarism.html

Purdue University Online Writing Lab (OWL). (2009, July). APA formatting and style guide. The OWL at Purdue. Retrieved July 23, 2009, from http://owl.english.purdue.edu/owl/resource/560/01/

PRESSfeed Co. (2009). RSS feeds—A tutorial. *PRESSfeed.* Retrieved July 9, 2009, from http://www.press-feed.com/howitworks/rss_tutorial.php#whatarewebfeeds

St. Francis Xavier University. (2009). Plagiarism. Angus L. Macdonald Library. Retrieved July 20, 2009, from http://library.stfx.ca/help/plagiarism.php

U Ottawa. (2009, June). Study skills—Note taking. *Student Academic Success Service.* Retrieved July 21, 2009, from http://www.sass.uottawa.ca/mentorship/undergraduate/note-taking.php

York University. (2008, February 25). Note taking at university. The Cornell note-taking system. *Skill-building online.* Retrieved July 15, 2009, from http://www.yorku.ca/cdc/lsp/skillbuilding/notetaking.html#cornell

---

Note: Emails and interviews by researcher are not listed in References. Identify emails and your interviews in the text as personal communications. Give name of author or interviewee and as specific a date as possible. Examples: (S. Mansour, personal communication, July 9, 2009). (J. Fear, personal communication, January 27, 2008).

Formatting styles, like language itself, constantly evolve; you can find MLA and APA updates on their respective home pages. Moreover, many databases and libraries offer free PLA and MLA formatting software:

> RefWorks is a web based tool that students, faculty and ... staff can use to create personal files of citations and bibliographies that can be integrated into research papers. Citations can be exported from many of the Library databases directly into RefWorks. (http://library.stfx.ca/help/plagiarism.php)

In a good report, sources are cited and documented smoothly and unobtrusively. **Citation** means attributing an idea or fact to its source in the body of the report: "According to the 2006 Census ..."; "Jane Bryant Quinn argues that...." **Documentation** means providing the biographic information readers would need to find the original source.

To maintain your professional credibility, demonstrate your research skills, and substantiate your ideas, credit your sources correctly. When you use the source's exact words, use quotation marks, and identify the source in the body of the report; put the source in parentheses, and in a list of **References** (APA style) or **Works Cited** (MLA style).

FIGURE 19.2B   **MLA Format for Documenting Sources**

Works Cited

American Psychological Association. Electronic References, 2009. Web. 8 July 2009.

Fear, Janet. "Re: CAAT Databases." Message to the author. 27 Jan. 2009.

Fear, Janet. Personal interview. 29 Jan. 2009.

Industry Canada. Canadian Intellectual Property Office. *A Guide to Copyrights: Copyright Protection*. Ottawa: Government of Canada, 2009. Web. 17 July 2009.

Grossman, Jeremy. *Quickhand™*. New York: John Wiley & Sons, Inc., 1976. Print.

Isaac, Brad. "A Beginner's Guide to Mind Mapping Meetings." *Lifehacker*, 13 Aug. 2007. Web. 17 July 2009.

Jensen, Eric. *Student Success Secrets*. New York: Barron's Educational Series, Inc., 2003. Print.

Knowledge Ontario. *Welcome to Knowledge Ontario*, 2008. Web. 27 Jan. 2009.

Mansour, Sherine. "Best Research Sites." Message to the author. 10 July 2009.

Mansour, Sherine. Personal interview. 8 July 2009.

Mind Tools Ltd. "Mind Maps, a Powerful Approach to Note Taking." *Mind Tools™*, 1995–2009. Web. 17 July 2009.

Modern Language Association of America. *MLA Handbook for Writers of Research Papers*. 7th ed. New York: The Modern Language Association of America, 2009. Print.

PRESSfeed Co. "RSS Feeds—A Tutorial." *Pressfeed*, 2009. Web. 9 July 2009.

Purdue OWL. "MLA Formatting and Style Guide." The Purdue OWL. Purdue U Writing Lab, 15 July 2009. Web. 23 July 2009.

St. Francis Xavier University. "Integrating Quotations." *StFX University. The Writing Centre*. n.d. Web. 17 July 2009.

"What Is Plagiarism?" *PlagiarismdotOrg*, 2009. Web. 26 Jan. 2009.

York University. "Note Taking at University. The Cornell Note-Taking System." *Skill-Building Online*, 25 Feb. 2008. Web. 15 July 2009.

When you put the source's idea into your own words, or synthesize the information, you don't use quotation marks, but you still have to document whose idea it is and where you found it.

Using Quotations

When you quote words and phrases, "integrate them [into your text] as smoothly as possible" to ensure consistent voice (www.stfx.ca/resources/writingcentre/Integrating%20Quotations.htm).

Introduce a full sentence quote with a colon:

> Journalist and professor Leslie Butler is adamant about the ethical ramifications of plagiarism: "It's a personal violation" (L. Butler, July 8, 2008).

Introduce a word or phrase with a comma:

> As journalist and professor Leslie Butler insists, "plagiarism is a personal violation" (L. Butler, July 8, 2008).

Indent long quotations on the left and right to set them off from your text. Indented quotations do not need quotation marks; the indentation shows the reader that the passage is a quotation. Since many readers skip quotations, always summarize the main point of the quotation in a single sentence before the quotation. If the last sentence before the quotation is a complete sentence, end the sentence with a colon, not a period, since it introduces the quotation.

Create an **RSS** Feed for the most current information available. **Really Simple Syndication** sends subscribers up-to-date news articles:

> You get all the latest news right away without having to search the web. You set up your preferences once and the content comes to your desktop. Your subscription is anonymous (http://www.press-feed.com/howitworks/rss_tutorial.php#whatarewebfeeds).

Interrupt a quotation to analyze, clarify, or question it. When you add or change words to clarify the quotation, or to make the quotation fit the grammar of your sentence, use square brackets around the new or changed words. Omit any words in the original source that are not essential for your purposes. Use ellipses (spaced dots) to indicate omissions.

MODULE SUMMARY

- To summarize and/or paraphrase information effectively,
  - Prepare: identify your purposes; pre-read; clarify the context.
  - Listen or read for a broad overview. Look for meaning.
  - Make sure you understand the material; if you don't, keep reading, read other sources, and ask questions until you do.
  - Create your own memorable and meaningful notes.
- To summarize and/or paraphrase information legitimately, ethically, and professionally, document your sources.
- Identifying your sources of information demonstrates your honesty, enhances your credibility, and protects you from charges of **plagiarism**—the conscious or unconscious theft of others' work.
- **Copyright laws** protect people's creative output; you are legally responsible for attributing intellectual property to its owner.
- Using someone else's work without giving credit is also unethical, since it violates the author's personal and professional rights.

- Academic penalties can include a grade failure or expulsion; in business, you can be sued for damages and revenue.
- As you research, document your sources immediately; this habit will save you hours of time and labour when composing your final copy.
- **Citation** means providing the source in the body of the report. When citing sources,
  - Pay attention to the order of the words and the punctuation. For example, when you use a short quotation (39 words or fewer), the sentence period goes outside the parentheses with the page number. In a long indented quotation (40 words or more), the parentheses and the page number follow the period at the end of the sentence.
- **Documentation** means giving the biographic information readers need to find the original source.
  - **APA** and **MLA** are the most commonly used formats for documenting references and endnotes.
  - Free online software on your local, college, or university library sites automatically formats your bibliographic information.

ASSIGNMENTS FOR MODULE 19

Questions for Critical Thinking

19.1 What kind of information would you find most difficult to summarize or paraphrase? Why?

19.2 What is unintentional plagiarism? What three strategies can you use to avoid it?

19.3 During a casual lunch conversation, a person at your table makes a comment that gives you a brilliant idea you can use in your report. Should you credit the person? Why or why not?

19.4 How can a researcher using only secondary sources come up with original material?

Exercises and Problems

19.5 Participating in an International Ethics Assessment

Together with the Brunel University Law School, the British Science Association (www.britishscienceassociation.org) has initiated a global "study to explore public concepts of honesty" (www.honestylab.com).

Go to www.honestylab.com to participate in the study. Watch the videos, answer the questions, and participate in the activities. Create whatever notes you will need to summarize your responses, and your reactions to the questions and activities.

As your instructor directs,

a. Together with two peers, discuss the experience: What surprised you? How similar were your answers? Where were the differences? How do you and your peers account for these differences?

b. Together with your two peers, draft an email memo to your instructor and the class. In your memo

  1. Sum up some of the similarities and differences in responses among the members of your triad.
  2. Offer explanations for the differences.
  3. In your final paragraph, summarize your team members' individual reactions to the honesty study, and the questions and activities. Do you think the study will provide relevant, reliable data? Why or why not?

19.6 Creating Notes on a Document Resource

Create notes on any of the following resources:

http://www.academicintegrity.uoguelph.ca/plagiarism_avoiding.cfm

http://www.alysion.org/handy/althandwriting.htm

http://backpack.blackboard.com/NoteTakingTutorial.aspx

http://www.bridgewater.edu/WritingCenter/Workshops/paraphrastips.htm

http://www.bridgewater.edu/WritingCenter/Workshops/summariztips.htm

http://www.cipo.ic.gc.ca/eic/site/cipointernet-internetopic.nsf/eng/wr00506.html#no1

http://www.lib.sfu.ca/help/writing/plagiarism

http://lifehacker.com/software/note-taking/a-beginners-guide-to-mind-mapping-meetings-288763.php

http://www.princeton.edu/pr/pub/integrity/08/cite/

http://www.socialresearchmethods.net/kb/ethics.php

http://www.utoronto.ca/ucwriting/paraphrase.html

http://www.yorku.ca/cdc/lsp/skillbuilding/notetaking.html#cornell

Before you begin, be sure to

1. Know your purpose: you are making notes to *write a précis* of the information (see Exercise 19.7).
2. Know your audiences: you are creating notes *for your peers, your instructor, and yourself.*
3. *Read all these directions* and all of the document material *before* making your notes.
4. *Pre-read the document.* Skim and scan for context and meaning: skim the material; scan headings, subheadings, and visuals; note white space, bold, italics, and underlining.
5. *Read the document again* as you make your notes.

Identify and note the most important information:

- The author, his or her credentials, evidence of expertise
- The purpose of and audiences for the document
- The organizational pattern: How does the author develop the argument: direct or indirect pattern? chronological? problem/solution? functional? spatial? elimination of alternatives? (Module 21.)
- The controlling idea or thesis of the document
- Three different ways the author proves or demonstrates his or her argument
- The level of difficulty: Is the document easy to understand? moderately easy? difficult? impossible? Note why you think this way.
- The most significant idea you learned by reading the document
- One way you will apply what you learned
- Your questions or information you want to follow up

Now create notes, manually or digitally, on any one of the resources.

As your instructor directs,

a. Use APA or MLA style to credit the source you choose.

b. Exchange notes with at least one peer (more is better) who has created notes on a different source. Read his or her notes. Provide feedback: (1) Do you understand the information based on reading the notes? What information is unclear? Why? (2) What note-taking strategies strike you as unusual, innovative, or particularly useful? Why? Now listen to the other person's feedback about your notes.

c. Reread and revise your notes based on the feedback, if necessary.

d. If you created electronic notes, send these as an email attachment to your instructor and the rest of the class. Be sure to include your APA or MLA documentation.

e. If you created handwritten notes, scan and send these as an email attachment to your instructor and the rest of the class. Be sure to include your APA or MLA documentation.

19.7   Writing a Précis on a Document

Précis the original document you chose in Exercise 19.6, using only the notes you created and revised.

- Use a word processor to draft a summary of the text in your own words.
- Summarize in sentences and paragraphs.
- Rewrite the summary until it is one-third the length of the original material.

As your instructor directs,

a. Use APA or MLA style to credit the source.

b. Exchange your précis with at least one peer (more is better) who has made a précis of a different source. Read his or her précis. Read the original source. Provide feedback: (1) How clear is the précis? Does the précis capture the meaning of the original? What information is missing? Does the précis writer use his or her own words? If not, what words or phrases would have to be put in quotations? Why? (2) How concise is the précis? Is it a third of the original? If not, does the précis writer have good reasons for the length? What are the reasons? Now listen to the other person's feedback on your précis.

c. Reread and revise your précis based on the feedback, if necessary.

d. Send your précis as an email attachment to your instructor and the rest of the class. Be sure to include your APA or MLA documentation.

e. In the email itself, describe what you found most difficult about writing the précis. Identify one specific way you can apply précis writing.

19.8   Creating Notes and a Précis on a Multimedia Source

Find a multimedia or interactive Web tutorial on any of the topics mentioned in Modules 18 and 19. (Possibilities include copyright; the legal, ethical, or professional implications of research; academic versus business research; and how to add in-text citations, document styles, paraphrase, avoid plagiarism, use quotations, write a précis, take notes, write summaries, or synopsize.)

1. Prepare to take handwritten or digital notes on the material.
2. Watch, listen to, and read the resource at least three times. Take notes.
3. Using only your notes, précis the material for the class, your instructor, and yourself.

As your instructor directs,

a. Use APA or MLA style to credit the source.

b. Send your précis as an email attachment to your instructor and the rest of the class. Be sure to include your APA or MLA documentation.

c. In the email itself, write a paragraph describing any differences between writing a précis of a written document and writing a précis of a multimedia source. How was it different? Was the difference due to content? To the medium? To your experience of having already done summaries and paraphrases? Explain.

POLISHING YOUR PROSE

Using APA and MLA Style

For examples of APA and MLA style, see Figure 19.2. Quick reference tips are available online at www.apastyle.org/faqs.html (APA) and http://owl.english.purdue.edu/owl/resource/557/01/ (MLA).

Identify and correct the errors in APA format in the following References items.

1. Andrew, Nikiforuk. **Alternatives**, Slip Sliding Away. Volume 34. Number 6. 2008. pages 14, 15. (2008) November 2008.

2. Morgan, G. (1997). Images of Organizations. London, UK. Sage Publications.

3. Mark Cox, "Business Courtesy Declining, Many Executives Say," Human Resources Professionals Association of Ontario (2004): http://www.hrpao.org/HRPAO/HRResource

4. Centre/KnowledgeCentre/newscluster2/Business+Courtesy+Declining.htm, retrieved August 30, 2010.

5. John Loomis, telephone conversation with author, June 20, 2009.

6. 1995 Michael C. Labossiere. The Nizkor Project, 1991–2009. retrieved January 30, 2009 from http://www.nizkor.org/features/fallacies/

Identify and correct the errors in MLA format in the following Works Cited items.

1. Andrew, Nikiforuk. **Alternatives**, Slip Sliding Away. Volume 34. Number 6. 2008. pages 14, 15. (2008)
2. Schryer Catherine "Walking a fine line: writing negative letters in an insurance company," Journal of Business and Technical Communication 14 (October 2000): 445–97
3. John Loomis, telephone conversation with author, June 20, 2009.
4. http://www.hrpao.org/HRPAO/HRResource Centre/KnowledgeCentre/newscluster2/ Business+Courtesy+Declining.htm, retrieved August 30, 2006.
5. Mark Cox, "Business Courtesy Declining, Many Executives Say," Human Resources Professionals Association of Ontario (2004):
6. Morgan, G. (1997). Images of Organizations. London, UK. Sage Publications.

Check your answers to the odd-numbered exercises on page 553.

Writing Information Reports

Learning Objectives

After reading and applying the information in Module 20, you'll be able to demonstrate

Knowledge of

- Types of reports
- Specific kinds of information reports
- The importance of writing good purpose statements
- Informal report writing style

Skills to

- Begin to write purpose statements
- Compose information reports
- Begin to develop a good writing style

Employability Skills 2000+ Checklist

Communicate

- ○ read and understand information presented in a variety of forms (e.g., words, graphs, charts, diagrams)
- ○ share information using a range of information and communications technologies (e.g., voice, email, computers)
- ○ use relevant scientific, technological, and mathematical knowledge and skills to explain or clarify ideas

Manage Information

- ○ locate, gather, and organize information using appropriate technology and information systems

Think & Solve Problems

- ○ assess situations and identify problems
- ○ seek different points of view and evaluate them based on facts
- ○ recognize the human, interpersonal, technical, scientific, and mathematical dimensions of a problem
- ○ identify the root cause of a problem
- ○ be creative and innovative in exploring possible solutions
- ○ readily use science, technology, and mathematics as ways to think, gain and share knowledge, solve problems, and make decisions

Be Adaptable

- ○ work independently or as a part of a team
- ○ carry out multiple tasks or projects
- ○ be innovative and resourceful: identify and suggest alternative ways to achieve goals and get the job done
- ○ be open and respond constructively to change
- ○ learn from your mistakes and accept feedback
- ○ cope with uncertainty

Learn Continuously

- ○ be willing to continuously learn and grow
- ○ assess personal strengths and areas for development
- ○ set your own learning goals
- ○ identify and access learning sources and opportunities
- ○ plan for and achieve your learning goals

Participate in Projects & Tasks

- ○ plan, design, or carry out a project or task from start to finish with well-defined objectives and outcomes
- ○ develop a plan, seek feedback, test, revise, and implement
- ○ work to agreed quality standards and specifications
- ○ adapt to changing requirements and information
- ○ continuously monitor the success of a project or task and identify ways to improve

Reports provide the information that people in organizations need to record information, and to plan, make decisions, and solve problems. Usually, reports are written *up* in an organization: supervisors and managers assign report topics and timelines to subordinates.

Your workplace may have templates for this documentation. However, these templates may include audience-inappropriate language, and redundant sections.[1] Whenever you can, use clear language and a report style format that meets the needs of your audiences, and achieves the report's purposes.

Whether following a template or creating your own, being able to write effective reports gets rewards: recognition for your competence, promotions and pay increases.[2]

What Is a Report?

Many different kinds of documents are called reports.

In some organizations, one- and two-page memos are called *reports*. In other organizations, a report is a long document with illustrations and numerical data. Still other companies produce PowerPoint™ slides as a report. **Informal reports** may be letters and memos, slide presentations, Web site summaries, business cases, or even computer printouts of production or sales figures. **Formal reports** contain formal elements such as a title page, a letter or memo transmittal page, a table of contents, and a list of illustrations.

Reports can provide information, provide information and analyze it, or provide information and analysis to support a recommendation (see Table 20.1). Reports can be called **information reports** if they collect data for the reader, **analytical reports** if they interpret data but do not recommend action, and **recommendation reports** if they recommend action or a solution.

TABLE 20.1   Types of Reports

Reports Can Provide:

Information only

- **Progress, conference, trip, periodic reports** provide information and summaries.
- **Incident reports** describe health and safety transgressions.
- **Sales reports** give sales figures for the week or month.
- **Quarterly reports** show productivity and profits for the quarter.

Information plus analysis

- **Annual reports** detail financial data and an organization's accomplishments over the past year.
- **Audit reports** interpret facts revealed during an audit.
- **Make-good or payback reports** calculate the point at which a new capital investment will pay for itself.
- **Technical reports** describe scientific/technical processes.
- **Business plans** describe and analyze business, market and financial projections.
- **Proposals** analyze a need and recommend a solution.

Information plus analysis plus a recommendation

- **Feasibility and yardstick reports** analyze and evaluate possibilities, and recommend what the organization should do.
- **Justification reports** justify the need for a purchase, an investment, a new personnel line, or a change in procedure.
- **Problem-solving reports** identify the causes of an organizational problem and recommend a solution.

Writers decide on the type of report, its format, organizational pattern, and information, its length, language, level of formality, and channel of distribution on the basis of PAIBOC analysis, and of the expectations of their organization and intended audiences (Module 2).

FIGURE 20.1 **PAIBOC Questions for Analysis**

> **P** Why are you writing the report? What is the report's **purpose**? What is the situation? What results do you want? Are you updating your supervisor on your progress? introducing a new initiative? reporting a health and safety issue? asking for time and money to attend a conference? justifying buying an expensive piece of equipment? analyzing the feasibility of an idea?
>
> **A** Who is your **audience**? What are your audience's expectations? What does your audience want and need? Updates? Information? Analysis? Justification? What does your audience value? What is important to your audience? What evidence will convince them?
>
> **I** What **information** must your message include? What does your audience already know? What do they need to know? What kind of information will your audience find most persuasive?
>
> **B** What reasons or reader **benefits** can you use to support your position? If your solution will cost the reader (in time or money), what benefits—to the organization, the audience, your colleagues—can you use to rationalize or outweigh those costs?
>
> **O** What **objections** can you expect your readers to have? What negative elements of your message must you deemphasize or overcome? *One important objection is time*: how long will it take your audience to read your report? To overcome that objection, revise your report for clarity and conciseness, edit it for correctness, and use a reader (a friend, colleague, or family member) to proof it.
>
> **C** How will the **context** affect the reader's response? Think about your relationship to the reader, the organizational culture, and morale, the current economic situation, the time of year, and any special circumstances.

What Do Reports Have in Common?

All reports contain three distinct sections: **Introduction**, **Body**, and **Conclusion**:

- The *Introduction* section puts the report in context for readers; it includes
  - A lead-in sentence: "This report describes ..."
  - A purpose statement: "The purpose of this report is to ..."
  - The scope of the report: "In this report, I explain the need for the program, and its structure and costs."
  - A summary of findings or results: "Employee feedback for the program was overwhelmingly positive."
- The *Body* section presents specifics (facts, figures, statistics, examples, visuals) the audience needs to understand a situation, and, in some cases, to make a decision.
- The *Conclusion* section summarizes the most important information covered in the Body, and can include
  - Recommendations, if the report's purpose is to effect change or solve a problem
  - Supplementary material the audience may want (appendices, questionnaires)
  - References, when the report uses secondary sources of information (Modules 18 and 19)

What Should I Do Before I Write Any Report?

Do your research. Define the situation. Draft a good purpose statement.

Creating a report includes

- Defining the situation
- Gathering and analyzing the necessary information

- Organizing the information
- Drafting the report
- Revising and editing the report
- Submitting the report

Before you begin to draft your report, you'll need to analyze your purposes and audiences. You also need to complete part of your research, in order to define the situation your report will discuss, and to identity the topics you will cover.

Your supervisor's direction and your analysis will help you to define the situation, or problem. However, you may need to narrow your focus. For example, the topic "using social media to improve business" is far too broad. Instead, use the following example to narrow the perspective and find your purpose:

- Choose one type of social media.
- Identify the specific situation or problem: what do you want the report to accomplish?
- Identify the specific audience with a vested interest in the situation, or with the power to support or implement your suggestions.

Your purpose statement might then be "Our Company can use Twitter to build business." Your audience might be your boss, colleagues, or aspiring entrepreneurs.

Remember that *how you define the problem shapes the solutions you find*. For example, suppose that a manufacturer of frozen foods isn't making money. If the researcher defines the situation as a marketing problem, he or she may analyze the product's price, image, advertising, and position in the market. But perhaps the real problem is that overhead costs are too high due to poor inventory management, or that an inadequate distribution system does not get the product to its target market. Defining the problem accurately is essential to finding an effective solution.

Writing Purpose Statements

Employability Skills

Once you've defined your problem or situation, you're ready to write a purpose statement. The purpose statement goes in the introduction, and is the organizing principle of every report. A good **purpose statement** makes three things clear:

- The situation or problem
- The specific information that must be explored, or questions that must be answered to resolve the situation or solve the problem
- The rhetorical purpose (to explain, to inform, to recommend, to propose, to request) the report is deigned to achieve

The following purpose statements have all three elements.

Scope: information report explores

Current management methods keep the elk population within the carrying capacity of the habitat but require frequent human intervention. Both wildlife conservation specialists and the public would prefer methods that controlled the elk population naturally.
 This report will compare the current short-term management techniques (hunting, trapping and transporting, and winter feeding) with two long-term management techniques, habitat modification and the reintroduction of predators. The purpose of this report is to recommend which techniques or combination of techniques would best satisfy the needs of conservationists, hunters, and the public.

Report Audience: Parks Canada Agency, responsible for Alberta's Elk Island National Park

Situation or problem

Organization pattern, method of development

Purpose: To recommend

When banner ads on Web pages first appeared in 1994, the initial response, or "click-through" rate, was about 10%. However, as ads have increased on Web pages, the click-through rate has dropped sharply. Rather than assuming that any banner ad will be successful, we need to ask, "What characteristics do successful banner ads share? Are ads for certain kinds of products and services, or for certain kinds of audiences, more likely to be successful on the Web?" The purpose of this report is to summarize the available research and anecdotal evidence and to recommend what Leo Burnett should tell its clients about whether and how to use banner ads.

Report Audience: Leo Burnett Advertising Agency

— Situation

Questions report examines and answers

— Purpose: To summarize research and make recommendation(s)

Situation and purpose: Proposal written in response to a request

Your request for a communications audit proposal reflects the City of Fredericton's commitment to its employees. A recent article in *The Globe and Mail* ("What Employees Care About," February 27, 2010, p. C1) details how poor communications cost organizations time and money. Good communication practices, however, have a proven 100 percent return on investment—in employee and customer satisfaction, employee retention, and improved productivity. My colleagues and I welcome the opportunity to work with you in identifying, developing, and implementing your communications' best-practices tools.

Report Audience: City of Fredericton HR Director

Focus of proposal: Vendor's proposal describes what vendor will do

To write a good purpose statement, you have to understand the basic situation, or problem, and have some idea of the questions that your report will answer. Note, however, that you can (and should) write a working purpose statement before researching the specifics the report will discuss (Module 18).

Checkpoint

A good **purpose statement** makes three things clear:

- The organizational problem or conflict
- The specific technical questions that must be answered to solve the problem
- The rhetorical purpose the report is designed to achieve

What Types of Short Reports Will I Write?

You will write summary reports, documenting information.

Supervisors expect employees to report information using short, informal documents. These internal reports summarize work, conferences, and sales trips, and describe work progress, and health and safety incidents, using memo format (Modules 9 and 10).

Information and Closure Reports

An **information report** summarizes your work or research to date. Similarly, a **closure report** summarizes a project, and assesses the results.

Information and closure reports include

- An *introduction paragraph*, summarizing the report topic, purposes, and most important outcomes, from the reader's perspective
- A *chronological account* (Module 21) of problem identification, actions, and results
- A *concluding paragraph* assessing the success of the project or work

Depending on the writer's mandate, the conclusion might include suggestions for further action.

See Figures 20.2 and 20.3 for examples of these two types of reports.

Conference and Trip Reports

Conference reports update your supervisor on industry trends, and justify the organizational expenditure (in your time and travel costs) by explaining the benefits to the audience. If your organization does not use templates, put the most significant information (for the audience) up front, and try to keep your report to a page or less. An example of a conference report appears in Figure 20.4.

Managers may accompany novice salespeople on client calls, and record their observations about the representative's performance. These follow-up **trip reports** are kept in the rep's file for reference, and may be copied to sales directors. Figure 20.5 shows an example of a trip report.

FIGURE 20.2   **Information Report, Memo Format**

From:	Shobana Kunella, Dennis MacDonald
Date:	April 20, 2009
To:	Doug Perrin, Operations Manager
Subject:	Employee Writing Needs Assessment

Hi Doug,

Over the last month, Dennis and I collected and assessed the information you requested about employees' writing concerns. We created a two-page, online survey, and sent it to all employees. We held eight interdepartmental focus groups, and interviewed managers of five departments: Accounting, Engineering, Human Resources, Sales and Marketing, and Research and Development. Altogether, we spoke to 76 people, and received 383 surveys.

In this report, I summarize the findings, and suggest next steps.

What We Write

The survey results and interviews indicate that every employee writes emails.

Additionally, employees write any or all of

- Letters
- Reports, including project and final project reports, proposals, RFPs, technical descriptions, feasibility, audits, studies, and formal technical reports
- Contracts
- Research papers
- Articles
- Manuals
- Meeting minutes

What We Want

People were consistent in their concerns. Everyone wanted support in grammar, proofreading, editing, and tone. Additionally, employees said they wanted help with

- Formatting, consistency, and unity
- Writing concisely
- Writing clearly
- Organizing information
- Using appropriate language

Employees had very different opinions about how to learn these skills. The majority liked the idea of onsite training. Others would prefer to take a course, or get individual coaching.

We need more information to make a decision. Dennis and I need to research the costs for people's preferences. Please let me if we should go ahead, and when you would like the information.

FIGURE 20.3   Closure Report, Memo Format

Date: March 15, 2010

To: Rob Dhillon, Human Resource Director

From: Irene Kaushansky, Staff Training and Development

Subject: Coaching Elisa Roberts

During our meeting of January 11, Elisa, you, and I agreed that Elisa would receive training in how to make successful accounts receivable calls. We agreed to hire a professional coach to help Elisa with the skills she needed to be successful in her new role. Further, we agreed that Elisa would identify the coach she felt she could work well with, and begin the training as soon as possible.

The purpose of this report is to describe the coaching program, and assess the results so far.

Coaching Elisa in Accounts Receivable Calls

In the week of January 18, Elisa and I interviewed three consultants about the coaching. We agreed that Mara Brady, of Brady and Associates, would be the right person to work with Elisa. Mara offered suggestions, and together she and Elisa decided on the program.

Coaching Parameters

Elisa, Mara, and I agreed on the training objectives:

1. To build Elisa's competence in AR calling
2. To identify AR calling best practices so that Elisa can train two other employees in successful AR calls

Mara recommended three coaching sessions of three hours each, a week apart, to begin January 25. In the first session, Elisa and Mara agreed to

- Analyze the current AR calling process
- Identify Elisa's telephone communication strengths
- Create SMART goals to build on those strengths

Coaching Methods

Mara suggested she observe Elisa making AR calls, and note (in writing) communication strengths and challenges. Together they would identify strategies (including active listening and negotiating techniques) to increase AR calling productivity, measured in

- Elisa's increased confidence
- Increased collection rate; amount to be determined after initial session
- Tips and techniques sheet

Further, they agreed that Elisa would keep a journal reflecting her learning experiences.

At the end of each session, Elisa and Mara would create a list of strategies for a best practices tip sheet. At the end of the three sessions, Elisa would evaluate the coaching experience, and decide if she needed additional training.

Coaching Results

By the end of the second coaching session, I saw noticeable improvement in Elisa's AR calls. A week after the third session, I sat with Elisa during her AR calls, and saw that she could

- Identify which clients would be motivated by AR calls
- Script a variety of calls
- Be courteous, calm, and confident throughout the call
- Listen to get results
- Control the tone and time of the call
- Ask for a commitment
- Produce written results, including suggestions for follow-up

Elisa has increased her collection rate by 30 percent, and is developing the tip sheet and a coaching program for Janine and Armand. She feels she doesn't need more coaching sessions right now, but would like the option of calling Mara in for a follow-up session in a few months.

The cost of the coaching sessions was $1 800 plus GST. On the basis of Elisa's feedback and her increased productivity, we are very pleased with the results.

FIGURE 20.4   Sample Conference Report: Email Attachment

Trip Report: Fuel Cell Seminar and Exposition

Vancouver, BC November 16 to 19, 2009

This conference focused on high-temperature fuel cell research and development, and fuel processing and hydrogen development. Approximately 1 500 people attended, with international participants from Ireland, Denmark, Korea, Japan, and Germany.

The exhibition ran for four days, and was very well attended; ten fuel cell cars were available for test drives. After the plenary session and short technical presentations on Monday, participants could choose any of six parallel sessions, both mornings and afternoons, over the next three days.

The conference provided me with client networking opportunities and industry updates. I will be making use of both during client visits over the next month.

Highlights

Despite the recession, fuel cell shipments have increased globally, with greatest demand in Denmark, Europe, the Middle East, and Southeast Asia.

- Fuel cell power is now a recognized alternative energy source with universal applications.
- Greenhouse gas emission reductions are significant (up to 65% in large vehicles).
- The U.S., British, German, Korean, and Danish governments are committed to investing a billion dollars in funding for hydrogen and fuel cell R&D over the next two years.
- Canadian government support has increased since last year; the federal government has promised $3 million in R&D investment over the next five years.
- Hydrogen fuelling stations continue to be built in the United States—eight were built in 2009 alone. The American presenter said that poor infrastructure continues to plague the industry, and suggested that governments and the private sector needed to be encouraged to understand the importance of hydrogen as the alternative energy source.
- One session examined alternative hydrogen sources production. Denmark is leading the world in biomass experimentation in this field.
- Cost reduction remains the priority: two sessions were devoted to panel discussions on possibilities. Since last year's conference, the emphasis has shifted from reducing material costs to improving manufacturing processes.

Approximately 110 more Canadian representatives attended than last year. Canada was also a significant presence in the exhibition. Perhaps the renewed enthusiasm is a result of the government's growing recognition of the importance of fuel cell technology.

FIGURE 20.5   Sample Trip Report, Email Attachment

Hi Lewis,

This email is long overdue; in future I'll get my follow-up email to you in a timelier manner!

I had a great two days calling with you. You have made a very positive impact on your clients in such a short time.

I notice that you are very prompt with follow-up emails. This is excellent—its one of the ways you can make yourself stand out as a sales rep. And you are making a good effort to meet as many people as possible when you are on campus, also great, especially at your travel schools.

As we discussed on Wednesday, one way to determine how important service is to instructors is to ask, "What do you look for in a sales rep?" It's another great question to set you apart. I am impressed that you are incorporating this line of questioning in your calls.

You were very strong in the presentation: you hit all the points you wanted to get across, and you took control of the room. You checked for questions, interest, and understanding, with challenges like "How do you see yourself using this in your course?" Your questions made the presentation very engaging. I know you were a little nervous leading up to it, but I suspect that as you get more practice, you'll feel more confident. And as always, the more you prep, the more confident you'll feel.

I'd like to see you continue to dig in your departments and get into areas where you haven't yet spent a lot of time. You'll pick up a lot of units with a lot less work than in those big committee situations. Working both big and small will ensure you have a solid year. Push yourself out of your comfort zone, and you'll increase your sales.

I'd also like to see you get really comfortable questioning around technology, and demonstrating on the fly. Let's talk after Closers to see where your comfort level is with the technologies for B&E and HSSL, and make plans accordingly.

I hope you found Closers helpful in developing strategies in all the different disciplines. Since you are the lead HSSL/B&E rep, I am going to arrange some extra product training for you. Let me know the areas where you would like more help.

Thanks again, Lewis. It's great to know I have such a strong rep in place in Man/Sask!

Incident Report

To protect employees, and themselves, most Canadian organizations comply with federal and provincial health and safety regulations. These regulations include WHMIS training and incident reporting. Usually, your organization will have a template you follow for an **incident report**. When you record an incident, use bullets or brief sentences to describe exactly what happened. Put the information in chronological order; note only observable behaviours; do not record your inferences, assumptions, or feelings. See Figure 20.6 for an example.

FIGURE 20.6   Incident Report

MediGroup Centre
945 Bradshaw Place
Prince Albert, SK S6V 2P5
306.566.5555

Accident/Incident Report

Date of Incident: *Mar. 13, 2010*   Time: *2:13*   AM/(PM)

Name of Injured Person: *Delphanie Hess*

Male: ____   Female: ✓

Date of Birth: *November 19, 1985*

Address: *22 Longboat Ave., Prince Albert, ON*

Contact Phone Number: *416.232.1093*

Type of injury: *Verbal abuse*

Describe Incident: *Patient F. Baum arrived for app't 37 mins. late. When I explained he had missed his app't, he began yelling and swearing at me. He leaned over reception desk and said he would "punch" me. I apologized and asked "May I give you another app't?" Client turned and walked out door, still yelling. Slammed door.*

Required physician/hospital?   Yes___ No ✓

Name of physician/hospital: *N/A*

Address: *N/A*

Physician/hospital phone number: *N/A*

Follow-up: *Written incident report: reported to Dr. Phillips*

Signature of injured person/parent/guardian: *D. Hess*   Date: *March 13, 2010*

Witness's signature: *Joanne Turbot (patient)*   Date: *March 13, 2010*

Reporter's signature: *D. Hess*   Date: *March 13, 2010*

Language FOCUS

WHMIS stands for **Workplace Hazardous Materials Information System**. WHMIS is a Canadian standard that companies have to follow for the use, storage, handling, and disposing of controlled substances and hazardous materials, such as cancer-causing chemicals. See www.hc-sc.gc.ca/ewh-semt/occup-travail/whmis-simdut/index-eng.php for more information.

Progress Reports

In **progress reports**, you report on what you've done, why it's important, and what you will do next.

When you're assigned to a single project that will take a month or more, you may be asked to file one or more progress reports. A progress report assures the employer or funding agency that you're making progress, and allows you and the employer or agency to resolve problems as they arise.

Different readers may have different concerns. An instructor may want to know whether you'll have your report in by the due date. A client may be more interested in what you're learning about the problem. Adapt your progress report to meet the needs of the audience.

You can use progress reports to do more than just report progress:

- *Suggest alternatives.* Explain, "I could continue to do X [what you approved]; I could do Y instead [what I'd like to do now]." The detail in the progress report can help back up your claim. Even if the idea is rejected, you don't lose face because you haven't made a separate issue of the alternative.
- *Minimize potential problems.* As you do the work, you may find that implementing your recommendations will be difficult. In your regular progress reports, you can alert your boss or the funding agency to the challenges, preparing your audience psychologically to act on your recommendations.

A study of the progress reports in a large research and development organization found that less successful writers tended to focus on what they had done and said very little about the value of their work. Good writers, in contrast, spent less space writing about the details of what they'd done but much more space explaining the value of their work for the organization.[3]

Subject lines for progress reports are straightforward. Specify the project on which you are reporting your progress.

Subject: Progress on Developing a Marketing Plan for Compact Hybrids

Subject: Progress on Organizing IABC Toronto Chapter Annual Conference

If you are submitting weekly or monthly progress reports on a long project, number your progress reports, or include the time period in your subject line. Include dates for the work completed since the last report and to be completed before the next report.

Report as positively as you honestly can. You build a better image of yourself when you show that you can take minor problems in stride, and that you're confident of your own abilities.

Negative: I have not deviated markedly from my schedule, and I feel that I will have very little trouble completing this report by the due date.

Positive: I am back on schedule and expect to complete my report by the due date.

Progress reports can be organized in three ways: by chronology, by task, and to support a recommendation.

Chronological Progress Reports

Chronological progress reports focus on what the writer has done and what work remains. Organize the report this way:

1. *Summarize your progress in terms of your goals and your original schedule.* Use measurable statements.

   Poor: My progress has been slow.

   Better: The research for my report is about one-third complete.

2. *Under the heading "Work Completed," describe what you have already done.* Be specific, both to support your claims in the first paragraph, and to allow the reader to appreciate your hard work. Acknowledge the people who have helped you. Describe any serious obstacles you've encountered and tell how you've dealt with them.

   Poor: I have found many articles about Procter & Gamble on the Web. I have had a few problems finding how the company keeps employees safe from chemical fumes.

   Better: On the Web, I found Procter & Gamble's home page, its annual report, and its mission statement. No one whom I interviewed could tell me about safety programs specifically at P&G. I have found seven articles about ways to protect workers against pollution in factories, but none mentions P&G.

3. *Under the heading "Work to Be Completed," or "Next Steps," describe the work that remains.* If you're more than three days late (for school projects) or two weeks late (for business projects), submit a new schedule, showing how you will be able to meet the original deadline. You may want to discuss "Observations" or "Preliminary Conclusions" if you want feedback before writing the final report, or if your reader has asked for substantive interim reports.

4. *Either express your confidence that you'll have the report ready by the due date or request a conference to discuss extending the due date or limiting the project.* If you are behind your original schedule, show why you think you can still finish the project on time.

Figure 20.7 shows a chronological progress report.

Task Progress Reports

In a task progress report, organize information under the various tasks you have worked on during the period. For example, a task progress report for a group report project might use the following headings:

> Finding Background Information on the Web and in Print
>
> Analyzing Our Survey Data
>
> Working on the Introduction of the Report and the Appendices

Under each heading, the group might discuss the tasks it has completed and those that remain.

Recommendation Progress Reports

Recommendation progress reports recommend action: resourcing a new idea, increasing the funding for a project, changing its direction, cancelling a project that isn't working out. When the recommendation will be easy for the reader to accept, use the direct request pattern of organization from Module 11. If your recommendation is likely to meet strong resistance, the problem-solving pattern (Module 12) might be more effective.

FIGURE 20.7   **Sample Chronological Progress Report**

Date: March 2, 2010

To: Kathryn Hughes

From: Sheema Khan

Subject: Formal Report Progress

As you requested, this report summarizes the work I have completed on my formal report topic. I have found several excellent sources for current information on the status of women working in the building trades. Therefore, I have met the timelines stated in my proposal, and anticipate submitting the report on the required due date.

Work Completed

Because I was able to access so many sound resources, I finished writing the first draft of the report Body yesterday. A *Toronto Star* article about the lack of women in the trades helped focus my topic. This article provides information on Canada's current labour shortage, on apprentices and journeymen, and on the many construction jobs available that are not "in the field." The article includes a self-assessment quiz to help people recognize if they might want to work in construction trades. All of this information proved invaluable in drafting the Body.

Through Internet research I found the National Association of Women in Construction (NAWIC), and StatsCan, with relevant data on jobs and women's representation in the skilled trades.

By far the most important resource, however, has been my sister Maria, who graduated in engineering but now works as a superintendent for Schell Construction Canada. Through interviewing Maria, I learned about the barriers women face in the construction industry, and about the roles education, legislation, and restructuring can play in favourably transforming the industry.

Work in Progress

For the next six days, while revising the first draft, I will be inserting in-text citations and preparing the References page, using the *APA Formatting and Style Guide*. Then I will draft the Conclusions and Summary sections of the report.

Final Steps

By March 18 I will have drafted the first and last parts of the report. I have allotted another ten days for revising and editing. Maria will read the second draft to ensure my facts and citations are correct. And two friends have agreed to read this draft for unity and organization. All three will also be reading for correct grammar and punctuation. I intend finishing the final draft by March 31, for submission April 3.

All the information I have gathered while researching has proven to me that my topic is both personally and socially relevant. Thank you for providing this opportunity.

EXPANDING A CRITICAL SKILL

Writing with Style

People's writing style conveys their attitudes about the subject and their audience. Good business writing is natural, polite, and concise, and correct, indicating respect for readers. You develop your own writing style through knowledge and practice.

Make Your Writing Natural

Natural style is not spontaneous, but the result of critical thinking and revision.

- Use PAIBOC to analyze your purpose and your audience's expectations. In informal reports,

○ Use first person (*I*) and second person (*you*).
○ Put your readers in your sentences ("Thank you for …," "As you requested.…"
○ Keep your paragraphs short.
○ Vary sentence structure and length. Remember, however, that the most readable sentences are between 14 and 20 words, and structured subject+verb+object.
○ Use active, action verbs (Writing and Editing Resources, page 517).
○ Use concrete nouns.

- ○ Avoid jargon and technical language.
- ○ Use parallel structure (Writing and Editing Resources, page 523).

Make Your Writing Polite

- Address your audience by name: people want to be recognized and treated as individuals.
- Research the names and preferred courtesy titles (Module 9) of the people whom you write to, and for, and use them.
- Include the information your audience needs to know (purpose, scope, results) up front, in your introduction.
- Use neutral or positive language; avoid the negative.
- Rewrite as the reader: reader-centred writing uses an organization pattern, sentence structure, and language that meets the audience's needs for clarity and understanding.

Make Your Writing Concise and Correct

- Compose drafts and sections of longer documents as soon you can; make notes on your research; summarize; paraphrase (Module 19).
- Save most of your time for revision; use proven revision strategies:
  - ○ Apply WIRMI (What I Really Mean Is …) as you read your sentences and paragraphs.
  - ○ Eliminate every unnecessary word.
  - ○ Use readers: ask colleagues or friends to read your writing; ask for specific feedback; revise.
- Edit for correct spelling, grammar, and punctuation.
- Ask a friend to proof your final copy.

MODULE SUMMARY

- Any kind of document or slide show can be a report. Usually, supervisors assign report topics and timelines to subordinates.
- **Information reports** collect data for the reader; **analytical reports** present and interpret data; **recommendation reports** recommend action or a solution.
- Creating a report includes
  - ○ Defining the situation
  - ○ Gathering and analyzing the necessary information
  - ○ Organizing the information
  - ○ Drafting the report
  - ○ Revising and editing the report
  - ○ Submitting the report
- Before you write any report,
  - ○ Do your research.
  - ○ Define the situation.
  - ○ Draft a good purpose statement.
- A good **purpose statement** frames your message for the reader. A good purpose statement clarifies
  - ○ The organizational situation or problem

- ○ The specific questions that must be answered to resolve the situation, or solve the problem
- ○ The rhetorical purposes (to describe, explain, to request, to propose, to recommend) the report is written to achieve
- In information, closure, conference and incident reports, provide the information chronologically.
- In progress reports, focus the reader on what you have done, and what work remains:
  - ○ Summarize your progress in terms of your goals and original work schedule.
  - ○ Use headings "Work Completed," "Next Steps"— describe what you have done, and will do.
  - ○ Express your confidence in meeting the due date, or request a meeting to discuss extending the due date, or limiting the project.
- Use **positive emphasis** in progress reports, to demonstrate confidence and competence.
- Good business writing style is natural, polite, concise, and correct. You develop your own style through knowledge and practice.

ASSIGNMENTS FOR MODULE 20

Questions for Critical Thinking

20.1 What do you have to know to identify the kind of report you are writing? Why?

20.2 Why is it often challenging to write good purpose statements? What strategies can you use to make it easier?

20.3 In what circumstances might you use technical terms in a report?

20.4 Is it ethical to use positive emphasis in your writing? Why or why not?

Exercises and Problems

20.5   Writing an Incident Report

Write an incident report to your supervisor describing a recent organizational or workplace accident, or health and safety transgression that you observed. If your organization has a template, use it; if not, create your own. For ideas go to McGill University Services Environmental Health and Safety site, at www.mcgill.ca/ehs/forms/forms/accident_incident_report.

As your instructor directs,

Attach the completed report to an email. Send the email to

a. Your supervisor
b. Your instructor

20.6   Writing a Chronological Progress Report

Write a memo report summarizing your progress on your report.

In the introductory paragraph, summarize your progress in terms of your schedule and your goals. Under a heading titled "Work Completed," list what you have already done. (This is a chance to toot your own horn: if you have solved problems creatively, say so! You can also describe obstacles you've encountered that you have not yet solved.) Under "Work to Be Completed," list what you still have to do. If you are more than two days behind the schedule you submitted with your proposal, include a revised schedule, listing the completion dates for the activities that remain.

In your last paragraph, either indicate your confidence in completing the report by the due date, or ask for a conference to resolve the problems you are encountering.

As your instructor directs,

Send the email or paper progress report to

a. The other members of your group
b. Your instructor

20.7   Writing a Task Progress Report

Write a memo report summarizing your progress on your report in terms of its tasks.

As your instructor directs,

Send the email or paper progress report to

a. The other members of your group
b. Your instructor

20.8   Writing a Chronological Progress Report for a Group Project (Module 15)

Write a memo to your instructor summarizing your group's progress on a project. Use an informal business style, and include headings (Modules 21, 22, and 23). In the introductory paragraph, summarize the group's progress in terms of its goals and its schedule, your own progress on the tasks for which you are responsible, and your feelings about the group's work thus far.

Under your first heading, list what has already been done. Use subheadings to specify what you have done. Describe briefly the chronology of group activities: number, time, and length of meetings; topics discussed and decisions made at meetings.

In the next section, describe the group's challenges. Use headings and subheadings to lead the reader. In these sections, you can also comment on problems that the group has faced, and whether or not they've been solved. You can comment on things that have gone well and have contributed to the smooth functioning of the group.

Under another heading, clarify what you personally and other group members still have to do. Indicate the schedule for completing the work.

In your last paragraph, either indicate your confidence in completing the report by the due date or ask for a conference to resolve the problems you are encountering.

POLISHING YOUR PROSE

Who/Whom and *I/Me*

Even established writers sometimes get confused about when to use *who* versus *whom* and *I* versus *me*. These pronouns serve different functions in a sentence or part of a sentence.

Use *who* or *I* as the subject of a sentence or clause.

Correct: Who put the file on my desk?

(*Who* did the action, *put*.)

Correct: Keisha and I gave the presentation at our annual meeting.

(Both *Keisha* and *I* did the action, *gave*.)

Correct: Ai-Lan, who just received a Ph.D. in management science, was promoted to vice-president.

(*Who* is the subject of the clause "who just received a Ph.D. in management science.")

Use *whom* and *me* as the object of a verb or a preposition.

Correct: Whom did you write the report for?

(*Whom* is the object of the preposition *for*.)

Correct: She recommended Thuy and me for promotions.

(*Me* is an object of the verb *recommended*.)

Though some print sources may use *who* and *whom* interchangeably, stick to the rules until this practice becomes widely acceptable.

If you're not sure whether a pronoun is being used as a subject or object, try substituting *he* or *him*. If *he* would work, the pronoun is a subject. If *him* sounds right, the pronoun is an object.

Correct: He wrote the report.

Correct: I wrote the report for him.

Exercises

Choose the correct word in each set of brackets.

1. Karen and [I/me] visited St. Francis Xavier University last week.
2. For [who/whom] is this letter intended?
3. Dr. Jacobsen, [who/whom] serves on the board of directors, is retiring.
4. Take it from Les and [I/me]: it pays to be prepared in business.
5. [Who/Whom] is the most experienced person on your staff?
6. There was only about an hour for Kelly, Maria, and [I/me] to get to the airport.
7. Between you and (I/me), my supervisor told me the committee will decide [who/whom] gets the promotion.
8. It is the customer for [who/whom] we make our product.
9. Three people at the firm [who/whom] can speak a second language are Van, Chang, and [I/me].
10. Trust [I/me]: it's not a good idea to begin a letter with "To [who/whom] it may concern," even if people frequently do.

Check your answers to the odd-numbered exercises on page 553.

Writing Proposals and Analytical Reports

Learning Objectives

After reading and applying the information in Module 21, you'll be able to demonstrate

Knowledge of

- How to compose more complex reports
- How to organize report information
- How to choose a pattern of organization
- How to increase document readability

Skills to

- Draft and revise analytical reports
- Choose an appropriate organizing pattern
- Increase document readability

Employability Skills 2000+ Checklist

Communicate

○ write and speak so others pay attention and understand

○ listen and ask questions to understand and appreciate the points of view of others

Manage Information

○ locate, gather, and organize information using appropriate technology and information systems

Think & Solve Problems

○ assess situations and identify problems
○ identify the root cause of a problem
○ be creative and innovative in exploring possible solutions

○ evaluate solutions to make recommendations or decisions

Be Adaptable

○ work independently or as a part of a team
○ carry out multiple tasks or projects
○ be innovative and resourceful: identify and suggest alternative ways to achieve goals and get the job done

○ be open and respond constructively to change
○ learn from your mistakes and accept feedback
○ cope with uncertainty

Learn Continuously

○ be willing to continuously learn and grow
○ assess personal strengths and areas for development
○ set your own learning goals

○ identify and access learning sources and opportunities
○ plan for and achieve your learning goals

Participate in Projects & Tasks

○ plan, design, or carry out a project or task from start to finish with well-defined objectives and outcomes
○ work to agreed-upon quality standards and specifications

○ adapt to changing requirements and information
○ continuously monitor the success of a project or task and identify ways to improve

People want to read clear, concise documents. Easy-to-read messages motivate people to do as you ask. When you write reports, organize the information to meet readers' expectations. Audiences usually want answers up front: Is the soil contaminated or not? Is the plan going to work? How and why? Should we expand or not?

As you revise, include only the information your reader needs, and organize that information to influence your readers positively.

What Other Kinds of Reports Will I Be Asked to Write?

You'll be asked to write reports that analyze and justify information.

Analytical reports—including feasibility, yardstick, and justification reports, and proposals—organize and analyze information to persuade readers to accept the suggestions or recommendations of the writer.

These reports may be brief, and use letter or memo format, depending on their purpose, and audience expectations. All reports, regardless of length, include an *introduction paragraph* stating the report's purpose and scope, and summarizing the problems or successes of the project (Module 20). And all reports *conclude* with a summary of the writer's key findings: this summary suggests next steps, or *recommends* action, depending on the writer's mandate, and audience expectations (Module 20).

Feasibility Reports

Feasibility or **yardstick reports** assess the practicality of a plan or idea based on a set of criteria established by the organization, or the writer. (Doing nothing or delaying action can be one of the conclusions of a feasibility report.) Organizations use feasibility studies to evaluate the doability of myriad ideas, including new toy designs, according to Peter Pook, Vice-President, Research and Development for Fisher Price Toys.[1]

Feasibility and yardstick reports normally open by explaining the decision to be made, listing available alternatives, and explaining the criteria.

In the body of the report, evaluate each alternative according to the criteria:

- Discuss each alternative separately when one alternative is clearly superior, when the criteria interact, and when each alternative is indivisible.
- Discuss each alternative under each criterion when the choice depends on the weight given to each criterion.

Business plans are developed in feasibility reports: the purpose is to prove that the business idea is so sound that the audience—banks, angel investors, or venture capitalists—should invest in it. (See Figure 21.1.)

Language FOCUS

Angel investors are people who are usually wealthy and invest in new companies, often in exchange for benefits from the company.

Venture capitalists are people who also invest in new companies, or in companies that are experiencing financial difficulties but have potential to make great profits.

FIGURE 21.1   Criteria Discussed in a New Business Venture Feasibility Study

A. Business Description (Summary)

   The Company
- Mission Statement
- Vision
- Values
- Brand Personality
- Location
- The Market
- Strategic Positioning

B. Products and Services
- Products
- Services

C. Location
- Test Market
- Channels

D. Market Analysis
- Economic Factors
- Environmental Factors
- Political/Legal Factors
- Social/Cultural Factors
- Demographic Factors
- Primary Customers
- Secondary Customers

E. Competitive Analysis
- Direct Competitors
- Indirect Competitors

F. Financials

G. Conclusions

H. Appendix

I. References

Whether recommendations should come at the beginning or the end of the report depends on the reader. Most readers want the "bottom line" up front. However, if your solution will cost time or money, provide all your evidence before giving the recommendation (Module 12).

Language FOCUS

A **mission statement** explains the purpose of the company or organization.

A **vision** is a statement describing the goals and objectives your company tries to meet or exceed.

Values are a written list of the goals and objectives your company tries to meet or exceed.

Justification Reports

Justification reports recommend or justify a purchase, investment, hire, or change in policy. If your organization has a standard format for justification reports, follow that format. If you can choose your headings and organization, use the *direct, deductive, or good news pattern* (Module 11) when your recommendation is easy for your reader to accept:

Employability Skills

1. *Indicate what you're asking for and why it's needed.* When the reader has not asked for the report, you must link your request to organizational goals.
2. *Briefly give the background of the problem or need.*
3. *Explain each of the possible solutions.* For each, give the cost and the advantages and disadvantages.
4. *Summarize the action needed to implement your recommendation.* If several people will be involved, indicate who will do what, and how long each step will take.
5. *Ask for the action you want.*

When the reader is reluctant to grant your request because action will cost time or money, use the *indirect, inductive, or bad news* variation of the problem-solving pattern described in Modules 12 and 13:

1. *Describe the organizational problem (which your request will solve).* Provide specific examples (results) to demonstrate the seriousness of the problem.
2. *Prove that easier or less expensive solutions will not solve the problem.*

3. *Present your solution impersonally.*
4. *Show that the disadvantages of your solution are outweighed by the advantages.*
5. *Summarize the action needed to implement your recommendation.* If several people will be involved, indicate who will do what and how long each step will take.
6. *Ask for the action you want.*

The amount of detail you need to give in a justification report depends on your reader's knowledge of and attitude toward your recommendation, and on the corporate culture. Many organizations expect justification reports to be short—only one or two pages. Other organizations may expect longer reports with much more detailed budgets and a full discussion of the problem and each possible solution.

What Should Go into a Proposal?

What you're going to do, how and when you'll do it, and evidence that you'll do it well.

Proposals are reports that describe a method for finding information, or solving a problem. Proposals have two goals: to get the project accepted, and to get the writer accepted to do the job. Proposals have to stress reader benefits and provide specific supporting details.

TABLE 21.1   Relationship Among Situation, Proposal, and Final Report

Company's Current Situation	The Proposal Offers To:	The Final Report Will Provide:
We don't know whether we should change.	Assess whether change is a good idea.	Insight, recommending whether change is desirable
We need to/want to change, but we don't know exactly what we need to do.	Develop a plan to achieve the desired goal.	A plan for achieving the desired change
We need to/want to change, and we know what to do, but we need help doing it.	Implement the plan, increase (or decrease) measurable outcomes.	A record of the implementation and evaluation process

Source: Adapted from Richard C. Freed, Shervin Freed, and Joseph D. Romano, *Writing Winning Proposals: Your Guide to Landing the Client, Making the Sale, Persuading the Boss* (New York: McGraw-Hill, 1995), p. 21.

To write a good proposal, you need to have a clear view of the problem you hope to solve and the kind of research or other action needed to solve it. A proposal must answer the following questions convincingly:

- What problem are you going to solve?
- How are you going to solve it?
- What exactly will you provide?
- How can you deliver what you promise?
- What benefits can you offer?
- When will you complete the work?
- How much will you charge?

Figure 21.2 shows a sample proposal selling services.

FIGURE 21.2 **Proposal for Services**

November 12, 2010

Sen Lee Chang, President

Tel-Direct Systems INC

1011 Bloor Street West

Oshawa, ON L1H 7K6

Dear Sen Lee Chang

Thank you for considering **communicore** for your training needs. Based on our conversation last Friday, I am pleased to propose this preliminary outline of the customer service workshop, and to suggest ways to maximize your return on investment.

Workshop Overview

The two-day Customer Service Strategies workshop encourages participants to define and refine the criteria for superior customer service. During the workshop, participants will

- Begin with an ice-breaker, self-assessment, and goal-setting exercises
- Role-play active listening, questioning, and problem-solving strategies
- Analyze and identify excellent customer service attitudes and behaviours
- Identify and apply two conflict negotiating models
- Articulate best-practices behaviours as the organizational standard
- Set a goal for further development

Depending on participants' preference, we can begin at 8 or 8:30 A.M., and finish at 4 or 4:30 P.M. I've attached a proposed agenda for your approval.

Methods

Using a variety of interactive exercises—including case analysis, taped role-play, peer feedback, and peer and self-assessment—your employees will review, describe, and apply behaviours that build customer relationships.

Since customized content contributes to learning transfer, I would like to visit your locations for a few hours to observe your service representatives before the training dates. This complimentary needs assessment will allow me to gather information about current practices, and to see your training facilities.

Resources

As we discussed, your employees will need uninterrupted time to review and practise customer serve techniques. Because participants will be working together, and moving around, they will need group seating, four to a table, and enough room to comfortably accommodate 16 people.

You mentioned that the room is equipped with a laptop, projector, and screen; participants will need writing materials, a USB key, and one flip chart per table. We will be bringing our own camera.

Qualifications

Our facilitators offer over 20 years' training experience, and expertise and accreditation in adult education principles, business, and interpersonal communications skills. As we agreed, I am attaching client reviews for our most recent training in customer service skills. Please visit our Web site: http://www.communicore.on.ca for more reviews.

Costs

The needs assessment is free. The cost for the training, including tailoring materials and exercises to participant's experiences, material printing and copying, two-day interactive facilitation, workshop evaluation sheet and summary, and written best-practices recommendations specific to your organization is $6 000, plus GST.

Again, thank you for your interest and consideration. At your convenience, please call or email me about your proposed employee training.

Sincerely

Kathryn Hughes

Kathryn Hughes

President

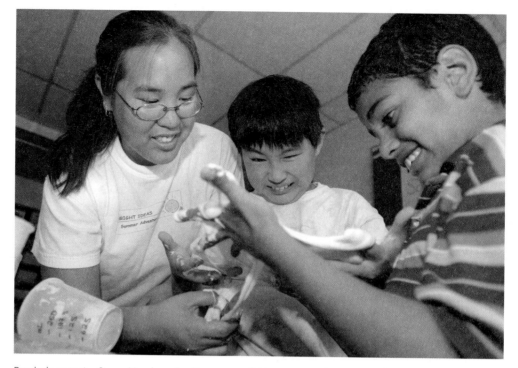

Psychology major Susan Ngo launched her successful business Bright Ideas Summer Adventure Camp with a $1 500 Ministry of Economic Development and Trade Grant, garnered through her winning business plan.

More on Sales Proposals

Decision makers routinely ask for proposals when purchasing expensive goods or services. For everything you offer, show the reader benefits (Module 8), using you-attitude (Module 6). Use content and language appropriate for your audience. Even if buyers want a state-of-the-art system, they may not appreciate or understand minute details, or technical jargon.

Attention to details—including good visual impact and proofreading—helps establish your professional image and suggests that you'll give the same care to the project if your proposal is accepted. (See Figure 21.3.)

Provide a one-page cover letter with long proposals. Organize the cover letter this way:

1. Catch the reader's attention and summarize up to three major benefits you offer.
2. Discuss each of the major benefits in the order in which you mention them in the first paragraph.
3. Deal with any objections or concerns the reader may have.
4. Mention other benefits briefly.
5. Ask the reader to approve your proposal, and provide a reason for acting promptly.

Government agencies and companies issue **Requests for Proposals**, known as **RFPs**, when contracting out work. The RFP details the project and vendor requirements in "a formal document describing ... how the contract companies should respond, how the proposals will be reviewed, and contact information."[2]

You follow the RFP exactly when you respond. Competitive proposals are often scored by giving points in each category. Evaluators look only under the headings specified in the RFP. If information isn't there, the proposal gets no points in that category.

FIGURE 21.3 **Proposal for House Repair**

Contract/EST#: <u>7565</u>

Bowen Foundation Repair Inc.
2486 Kingston Rd.; Scarborough, ON M1N 1V3
Tel: 416-288-0547 Fax: 416-288-1275 www.bfr.ca
LIC# B-19658

Date: <u>November 19, 2010</u>

Client Name: <u>Judy Green</u>   **Cell Phone No:**_____   **Home Phone No:** <u>905-844-5267</u>

Work Phone No:_____   **Email:**_____

Jobsite: <u>24 Queen Mary Rd.</u>_____

The undersigned proposes to furnish all materials and provide all material and labour necessary to complete all repairs described below.

Exterior Waterproofing Repair:

Trench 51' linear ft from 1' to 2' deep, sloping toward rear of property. Place filter-cloth in bottom of trenched area. Install 4" perforated weeping tile with nylon sock. Pour ¾" gravel over weeping tile system. Remove and dispose of all soil. Clean up work area. Remove and dump all debris. All material and labour included.

20-year transferable warranty against leakage in repaired area.
(Please retain this contract for warranty purposes.)

<u>No deposit required. Payment due in full upon completion of work.</u>

All of the above work to be completed in a good and workmanlike manner for the sum of:

_____   ($990.00) DOLLARS

GST# 85151766 RT0001_____   ($49.50) GST

_____   **($1,039.50) TOTAL**

All changes in the work to be charged for same shall be made in writing.
   This estimate is made on the basis of current material and labour costs. This estimate is valid for 90 days from date above. Any delay in acceptance of this estimate beyond 90 days shall void this estimate, and a review of this estimate shall be performed before any agreement between the Client and Bowen Foundation Repair Inc. becomes binding.
   All warranties are based on normal weather conditions.
   BFR is not responsible for ground settlement.
   BFR is not responsible for leakage due to grade change and or acts of God, i.e., tornadoes, flooding, hurricane, and the like.

ACCEPTANCE

You are hereby authorized to furnish all materials and labour to complete the work mentioned in the above proposal, for which the undersigned agrees to pay the amount mentioned in said proposal, and according to the terms thereof.

Date: _____

_____   *Collen Bowen*
_____

INDIVIDUAL/COMPANY NAME   BOWEN FOUNDATION REPAIR INC.

Proposals for Class Reports

A proposal for a student report usually has the following sections:

1. **Purpose statement**. In your first paragraph (no heading), summarize in a sentence or two the topic and purpose(s) of your report.
2. **Problem**. What organizational problem exists? What is the situation? What needs to change? Why? What background or history is relevant?

3. **Feasibility**. Can a solution be found in the time available? How do you know?

4. **Audience**. Who in the organization has the power to implement your recommendation? What secondary audiences might be asked to evaluate your report? What audiences would be affected by your recommendation? Will anyone serve as a gatekeeper, determining whether your report is sent to decision makers? What watchdog audiences might read the report? (Module 2.)

   For each of these audiences and for your initial audience (your instructor), give the person's name, job title, and business address and answer the following questions:

   - What is the audience's major concern or priority?
   - What will the audience see as the advantages of your proposal?
   - What objections, if any, is the reader likely to have?
   - How interested is the audience in the topic of your report?
   - How much does the audience know about the topic of your report?
   - What terms, concepts, equations, or assumptions might one or more of your audiences need to have explained? Briefly identify ways in which your audiences may affect the content, organization, or style of the report.

5. **Topics to investigate**. List the questions and sub-questions you will answer in your report, the topics or concepts you will explain, and the aspects of the problem you will discuss. Indicate how deeply you will examine each aspect you plan to treat. Explain your rationale for choosing to discuss some aspects of the problem and not others.

6. **Methods/procedure**. How will you get answers to your questions? Whom will you interview or survey? What published sources will you use? What Web sites will you consult? (Module 18.) Give the full bibliographic references (Module 19). Your methods section should clearly indicate where and how you will get the information you need to answer the questions in the Topics to Investigate section.

7. **Qualifications/facilities/resources**. What attitudes, knowledge, and skills qualify you to conduct this study? Do you work in the organization? Do you have a contact or source for information? What's your professional or personal interest? Do you have access to the resources you will need to conduct your research (computer, books, etc.)? Where will you turn for help if you hit an unexpected snag?

   You'll be more convincing if you have already scheduled an interview, checked out books, or identified online sources.

8. **Work schedule**. Create a timeline to plan your work. (See Figure 21. 4 for an example.) List both the total time you plan to spend on, and the date when you expect to finish each of the following activities:

   - Gathering information
   - Analyzing information
   - Preparing the progress report
   - Organizing information
   - Writing the draft
   - Revising the draft
   - Preparing the visuals
   - Editing the draft
   - Proofreading the report

FIGURE 21.4   Create a Timeline to Plan Your Schedule

Jan. 19	Feb. 9	Feb. 18	Mar. 1	Mar. 10	Mar. 15	Mar. 20	Mar. 23	Apr. 5	Apr. 17
Choose report topic; start research; draft proposal	Revise and submit proposal	Get approval; research	Begin first draft of body	Finish body draft; draft conclusions	Have peer read; revise	Draft summary	Have peer read; revise	Edit and proof	Submit report

Put your timeline into a work schedule in either a chart or in a calendar. A good schedule provides realistic estimates for each activity, allows time for unexpected problems, and indicates that you can manage a project and complete the work on time.

9. **Close/call to action**. In your final paragraph, indicate that you'd welcome any suggestions your instructor may have for improving the research plan. Ask your instructor to approve your proposal so that you can begin work on your report. Provide a contact number or email address for confirmation.

Figure 21.5 shows a draft student proposal for writing a research report using primary and secondary sources.

Checkpoint

When writing a **proposal for a student report**, include the following sections:

- Controlling statement or summary
- Problem
- Feasibility
- Audience
- Topics to investigate
- Methods
- Qualifications
- Work schedule
- Call to action

FIGURE 21.5   **Draft Proposal for a Student Report Using Primary and Secondary Sources**

Date: January 20, 2010

To: Professor Marcus Stawski

From: Teresa Amirud

Re: My Formal Report Topic

Costing is possibly the most vital aspect of the manufacturing process, since companies must use the most effective system in order to reduce costs and increase profits. In the manufacturing sector, different variations on costing systems can be tailored to suit the needs of any specific company. In my formal report I plan to research the costing system used by EcoSound Inc. in its paint manufacturing process. I will research the strengths and weaknesses of the costing system used during the paint manufacturing process, up to the completion of each unit. Using this research, I will analyze the company's cost system to determine if this system is suitable for the product line.

Topic Rationale

In deciding what to research and analyze for my formal report, I tried to incorporate what I already know, what I would like to learn more about, and what interests me. I decided to focus on EcoSound operation paint production costing for two reasons:

- Having worked part-time at Rona's in Milton for several years, I have the contacts needed to get primary information about the manufacturing of EcoSound's paint products.
- I mix and sell this paint to my customers daily; I thought it would be interesting to learn more about the manufacturing side of the products I am selling. Furthermore, the more knowledge I have about a product, the easier it is to sell the product, and answer any questions customers have.

Operations costing also appeals to me as a formal report topic because the research and writing will help me with my Cost and Budgets course. Not only will I learn how to write a formal report, but I will also be applying a real world example to the Cost and Budgets curriculum. Learning more about the actual application of operation costing within a real company will increase my understanding of the concepts being discussed in Cost and Budgets.

FIGURE 21.5   Draft Proposal for a Student Report Using Primary and Secondary Sources (continued)

Formal Report Focus

In my preliminary research, I was able to learn some of the basics of EcoSound paint production, which I will use to formulate research questions. In my report I will

- Examine where costs are added to the product, for example
  - Overhead costs added to each product based on the time spent at each work centre
  - Labour costs added by working out the number of employees at each work centre and their salary to get a labour rate at each work centre
- Create a flow chart of the production process, listing the "work stations" that each unit goes through before completion
- Analyze why there is such a large retail profit margin on paint products
  - 40–45% on EcoSound name-brand paints
- Discuss whether EcoSound's costing system is effective

Through my research and analysis I will determine the effectiveness and any weaknesses of the EcoSound system manufacturing process.

Research Sources

Primary Sources

- Josef Usdan—EcoSound sales representative
- Mario Eccles—EcoSound marketing representative
- Katrina Glausiusz—EcoSound accountant (Brampton plant)
- Myself
- Marian Feierabend—Cost and Budget instructor
- The knowledge I have gained about EcoSound paint products through my employment at Rona

Secondary Sources

- Internet—www.ecosystems.ca; www.highbeam.com/doc/1G1-146498025.html; ezinearticles.com/?Activity-Based-Costing-(ABC)-And-Traditional-Costing-Systems&id=2297443.mindtools.com/pages/article/newTED_08.htm
- *Managerial Accounting—Cost and Budget* textbook

Tentative Research and Writing Schedule

To remain on schedule in researching and writing my formal report, I have created a tentative work schedule:

- February 18   Get approval for my proposal; begin research
- March 1   Complete research; begin first draft of report Body
- March 10   Finish draft of Body; draft Conclusions
- March 15   Have peer read drafts; make necessary changes
- March 20   Begin draft of Summary
- March 23   Have peer read Summary; make necessary changes
- April 5   Edit report
- April 10   Proofread report

As you can see, I have selected an appropriate formal report topic for which I will be able to find relevant information. Please let me know at tamirud@ryerson.ca if my plan meets with your approval.

With long proposals, provide a one-page cover letter:

1. Catch the reader's attention and summarize up to three major benefits you offer.
2. Discuss each of the major benefits in the order in which you mention them in the first paragraph.
3. Deal with any objections or concerns the reader may have.
4. Mention other benefits briefly.
5. Provide a reason for acting promptly, and ask the reader to approve your proposal.

Proposals for Funding

If you need money for a new or continuing public service project, you may want to submit a proposal for funding to a foundation, a corporation, a government agency, or a religious agency. In a proposal for funding, stress the needs your project will meet, and show how your project helps fulfil the goals of the organization you are asking to fund it. Every funding source has certain priorities; most post lists of the projects they have funded in the past.

Estimating the Budget

A good budget is crucial to making the winning bid. Ask for everything you need to do a quality job. Asking for too little may backfire, leading the decision maker to assume you don't understand the scope of the project.

Read the RFP to find out what is and isn't fundable. Talk to the program officer and read successful past proposals to find out three things:

- What-size projects will the organization fund in theory?
- Does the funder prefer making a few big grants or many smaller grants?
- Does the funder expect you to provide in-kind or matching funds from other sources?

Think about exactly what will be done and who will do it. What will it cost to get that person? What supplies or materials will he or she need? Also think about indirect costs for office space, retirement and health benefits and salaries, and office supplies, administration, and infrastructure.

Detail the specifics of your estimates.

Weak:	75 hours of transcribing interviews	$1 500
Better:	25 hours of interviews; a skilled transcriber can complete an hour of interviews in 3 hours; 75 hours @ $20/hour	$1 500

Without inflating your costs, give yourself a cushion. For example, if the going rate for skilled transcribers is $20 an hour, but you think you might be able to train someone and pay only $17 an hour, use the higher figure. Then, even if your grant is cut, you'll still be able to do the project well.

How Should I Organize Reports?

You can organize information in any of seven patterns. Use PAIBOC analysis to determine the pattern that best achieves your purposes, and meets your audience's needs.

Any of these patterns can be used for all or part of a report:

1. General-to-particular or particular-to-general
2. Comparison or contrast
3. Problem–solution
4. Elimination of alternatives
5. Geographic or spatial
6. Functional
7. Chronological

Employability Skills
2 +

1. General-to-Particular or Particular-to-General

General-to-particular starts with the situation as it affects the organization, or as it exists in general, and then moves to a discussion of the parts of the situation, and solutions to each of these parts.

Particular-to-general starts with the problem as the audience defines it and moves to larger issues of which the problem is a part. Both are useful patterns when you need to redefine the reader's perception of the problem to solve it effectively.

For example, the directors of a student volunteer organization, Students Mentoring Students (SMS), have defined their problem as "not enough volunteers."

After doing their research, the writers are convinced that poor training, an inadequate structure, and low campus awareness are responsible both for a high dropout rate and low recruitment rate. The general-to-particular pattern helps the audience see the problem in a new way:

Why Students Helping Students (SMS) Needs More Volunteers
Why Some SMS Volunteers Drop Out

    Inadequate Training
    Feeling That SMS Takes Too Much Time
    Feeling That the Work Is Too Emotionally Demanding

Why Some Students Do Not Volunteer

    Feeling That SMS Takes Too Much Time
    Feeling That the Work Is Too Emotionally Demanding
    Preference for Volunteering with Another Organizations
    Lack of Knowledge About SMS Operations

How SMS Are Trained
Emotional Demands on SMS Volunteers
Ways to Increase Volunteer Commitment and Motivation

    Improving Training
    Improving the Flexibility of Volunteers' Hours
    Providing Emotional Support to Volunteers
    Providing More Information About Community Needs and SMS Services

2. Chronological

A chronological report records events in the order in which they happened or are planned to happen. Many information and progress reports use a chronological pattern:

Revisions Completed in October
Revisions Completed In November
Work Planned for December

3. Comparison or Contrast

Comparison or contrast examines each alternative in turn, discussing strengths and weaknesses. Feasibility studies and yardstick reports usually use this pattern.

A variation of the divided pattern is the **pro–con pattern**. In this pattern, under each specific heading, give the arguments for and against that alternative.

Whatever information comes second will carry more psychological weight. This pattern is least effective when you want to deemphasize the disadvantages of a proposed solution, for it does not permit you to bury the disadvantages between neutral or positive material.

A report recommending new plantings for a garden over an expressway uses the pro–con pattern:

Advantages of Ornamental Grasses
    High Productivity
    Visual Symmetry
Disadvantages of Ornamental Grasses
    Investments and Replacement Costs
    Visual Monotony

4. Problem–Solution

Identify the problem; explain its background or history; discuss its extent and seriousness; identify its causes. Discuss the factors (criteria) that affect the decision. Analyze the advantages and disadvantages of possible solutions. Conclusions and recommendations can go either first or last, depending on the length of the report, and preferences of your reader. This pattern works well when the reader is neutral.

A report recommending ways to eliminate solidification of granular bleach during production uses the problem–solution pattern:

> Recommended Reformulation for Alpha Bleach
> Problems in Maintaining Alpha's Granular Structure
>   Solidifying During Storage and Transportation
>   Customer Complaints About "Blocks" of Alpha in Boxes
>
> Why Alpha Bleach "Cakes"
>
>   Alpha's Formula
>   The Manufacturing Process
>   The Chemical Process
>   Modifications Needed to Keep Alpha Flowing Freely

5. Elimination of Alternatives

After discussing the problem and its causes, discuss the *impractical* solutions first, showing why they will not work. End with the most practical solution. This pattern works well when the solutions the reader is likely to favour will not work, while the solution you recommend is likely to be perceived as expensive, intrusive, or radical.

A report on toy commercials eliminates alternatives:

> Effect of TV Ads on Children
> Camera Techniques Used in TV Advertisements
> Alternative Solutions to Problems in TV Toy Ads
>   Leave Ads Unchanged
>   Mandate Ad Blockers on All TV Production
>   Ask the Industry to Self-Regulate
>   Give CRTC Authority to Regulate TV Ads Directed at Children

6. Geographic or Spatial

In a geographic or spatial pattern, you discuss problems and solutions in units by their physical arrangement. Move from office to office, building to building, factory to factory, province to province, region to region, and so on.

Sales and market research reports may use a geographic pattern of organization:

> Sales Have Risen in the European Economic Community
> Sales Have Fallen Slightly in Asia
> Sales Have Fallen in North America

7. Functional

Functional patterns discuss the problems and solutions of each functional unit. For example, a report on a new plant might divide data into sections on the costs of land and building, on the availability of personnel, on the convenience of raw materials, and so on. A government report might divide data into the different functions an office performed, taking each in turn.

PST Plant Move
- Manufacturing
  Equipment
  Offices
- Sales and Marketing
  Furniture
  Filing Cabinets
- Executive Offices
  Furniture
  Filing Cabinets

Checkpoint

Seven Ways to Organize Information

1. General-to-particular or particular-to-general
2. Chronological
3. Comparison or contrast
4. Problem–solution
5. Elimination of alternatives
6. Geographic or spatial
7. Functional

EXPANDING A CRITICAL SKILL

Increasing Readability

Readers do not want to read every word in a business document. They want instantaneous meaning; they want to skim and scan for the information they need. They want business documents to be as eye-easy as the best Web writing.[3]

What Makes Documents Easy to Read?

Increase readability with blueprints, transitions, topic sentences, white space, and headings that "talk."

Blueprints forecast what you will discuss in a section, or in the entire report. In an overview paragraph, blueprints tell the reader how many points there are, and number them. This overview paragraph establishes **repetition for reinforcement**: the blueprint establishes a contract with readers, who now know what they are going to read, and in what order:

Paragraph without blueprint

Employee Stock Ownership Programs (ESOPs) have several advantages. They provide tax benefits for the company. ESOPs also create tax benefits for employees and for lenders. They provide a defence against takeovers. In some organizations, productivity increases because workers now have a financial stake in the company's profits. ESOPs help the company hire and retain good employees.

Revised paragraph with blueprint

> Employee Stock Ownership Programs (ESOPs) provide four benefits. First, ESOPs provide tax benefits for the company, its employees, and lenders to the plan. Second, ESOPs help create a defence against takeovers. Third, ESPOs may increase productivity by giving workers a stake in the company's profits. Fourth, as an attractive employee benefit, ESOPs help the company hire and retain good employees.

Transitions are words, phrases, and sentences that tell the reader the discussion is continuing on the same point, or shifting points.

> There are economic benefits, too.

(Tells the reader that the discussion is still on advantages, and now moving to economic advantages.)

> An alternative plan is ...

(Tells the reader that a second option is coming up.)

> These advantages, however, only apply in the case of short-term patients, and not to those in long-term care.

(Prepares reader for a shift from short-term patients to those in long-term care.)

The **topic sentence** introduces or summarizes the main idea of a paragraph. Competent readers skim documents by searching for topic sentences at the beginning of paragraphs, because that's where competent writers put them.

Revised paragraph without summarizing topic sentence

> Another main use of ice is to keep the fish fresh. Each of the seven different kinds of fish served at the restaurant requires almost 3.78 L twice a day, for a total of 52.9 L. An additional 22.7 L a day are required for the salad bar.

Revised paragraph with summarizing topic sentence

> Seventy-six litres of ice a day are needed to keep food fresh. Of this, the largest portion (52.9 L) is used to keep the fish fresh. Each of the seven varieties requires almost four litres twice a day (7×7.56) = 52.9 L. The salad bar requires an additional 22.7 L a day.

White space increases reading ease because it separates and emphasizes ideas (Modules 5 and 10). To create white space, use

- Headings and subheadings
- Short paragraphs
- Tabs or indents
- Lists—with numbers or bullets

Headings are signposts that divide your letter, memo, or report into sections. **Subheadings** signal a subsection: the writer is providing specifics within the section. The best headings and subheadings "talk" to the reader; they

- Are short and specific
- Use highlighting: bold or italics
- Are differentiated: subheadings use a smaller or different font
- Summarize what the reader is about to read
- Cover all the material until the next heading
- Are parallel (i.e., use the same grammatical structure):

> The following suggestions can help employers avoid bias in job interviews:
>
> 1. Base questions on the job description.
> 2. Ask the same questions of all applicants.
> 3. Select and train interviewers carefully.

Revising for readability (using blueprints, transitions, topic sentences, white space, and "talking" headings and subheadings) creates a story line your readers can readily follow.

MODULE SUMMARY

- **Feasibility**, **yardstick**, and **justification** reports analyze and evaluate information readers need to make decisions.

- **Proposals** are reports that describe a method for finding information, or solving a problem.

- PAIBOC analysis will help you choose the **content** and **organizational pattern** that best meets your audience's needs and expectations, and serves your purpose(s). You can organize your information using any of seven patterns:

  - **General-to-particular** begins with the situation as it affects the organization, or manifests itself in general. Then the report discusses the parts of the problem, and offers solutions to each of these parts.

  - **Particular-to-general** starts with specifics, and then discusses the larger implications for the organization.

  - **Comparison or contrast** examines each alternative in turn; the **pro–con pattern**, a variation of the divided pattern, gives the arguments for and against that alternative under each specific heading.

  - The **problem–solution** pattern identifies the situation, explains causes, and analyzes the advantages and disadvantages of possible solutions.

  - **Elimination of alternatives** identifies the situation, explains causes, and discusses the least practical solution first, ending with the solution the writer favours.

  - **Geographic or spatial** patterns discuss the problems and solutions by units.

  - **Functional pattern** examines the problems and solutions of each functional unit.

- Revising for readability (using blueprints, transitions, topic sentences, white space, and "talking" headings and subheadings) makes your writing reader-friendly.

ASSIGNMENTS FOR MODULE 21

Questions for Critical Thinking

21.1 How do you decide what information to include in your report, and what to omit?

21.2 How do you decide on the level of formality you should use in your report?

21.3 How can you write headings in reports that are actually useful to readers?

21.4 How do you decide how to organize your report?

Exercises and Problems

21.5 Writing a Yardstick Report

Write a two-page yardstick report to your instructor and peers suggesting how users can protect themselves from cyber-crime on social networking sites. Choose a specific site (Facebook, MySpace, etc.) and research specific examples (fraud, identity theft, scams). Using primary and secondary sources (your own observations and experience and experts' advice), identify three possible solutions. Establish specific criteria by which to measure the solutions. Evaluate each based on your criteria. Conclude your report by identifying the best way users can protect themselves.

21.6 Writing a Justification Report

Write a two-page report to your supervisor justifying a change in policy, or a purchase, investment, or hire. Choose a topic that you can cover in two pages, and use an organizational pattern that your reader will find convincing. Possible topics are

- Introducing flex hours
- Extending breaks
- Funding a course you would like to take
- Purchasing a new coffee machine
- Bringing pets to work
- Hiring an new employee

21.7 Explaining "Best Practices"

Write a report describing the "best practices" of a unit or team of which you are a member. Convince your reader that other teams in your organization/college/university should adopt these practices.

21.8 Feasibility or Yardstick Report Recommending Action

Write a report identifying alternative actions your unit or organization could take, evaluating each solution, and recommending the best choice. Address your report to the person who has the power to approve your recommendation. Possibilities are

- Making your organization more eco-friendly
- Finding an additional worker for your department
- Making your organization more employee-friendly
- Making a change to improve efficiency
- Making changes to improve accessibility for customers or employees with disabilities

21.9 Writing a Proposal for a Student Report

Write a proposal to your instructor to do the research for a formal or informal report. The headings and questions in the section "Proposals for Class Reports" are your RFP; be sure to answer every question and to use the headings exactly as stated in the RFP.

Exception: Where alternative headings are given, combine them (Qualifications and Facilities), or use them as separate headings.

POLISHING YOUR PROSE

Writing Subject Lines and Headings

Subject lines are the title of a letter, memo, or email message. Headings within a document tell the reader what information you will discuss in that section.

Good subject lines are specific, concise, and appropriate for your purposes and the response you expect from the reader. Subject lines are required in memos, optional in letters.

- Put in good news if you have it.
- If information is neutral, summarize it.
- Use negative subject lines if the reader may not read the message or needs the information to act, or if the negative is your error.
- In a request that is easy for the reader to grant, put the subject of that request, or a direct question, in the subject line.
- When you must persuade a reluctant reader, use a common ground, a reader benefit, or a directed subject line that makes your stance on the issue clear.

Headings are single words, short phrases, or complete sentences that indicate the topic in a document section. Headings must be *parallel*—that is, they must use the same grammatical structure—and must cover all the information until the next heading.

The most useful headings are **informative or talking heads**, which sum up the content of the section.

Weak:	*Problem:*
	Cause 1
	Cause 2
	Cause 3

Better:	*Communication Problems Between Air Traffic Controllers and Pilots:*
	Selective Listening
	Indirect Conversational Style
	Limitations of Short-Term Memory

Exercises

Write a good subject line for each of the following situations.

1. I'm your new boss.
2. I wanted those annual enrolment forms back from you last week.
3. Blood drive
4. Not that it will really affect you, but starting next week there will be an opportunity for nonhourly workers (you're hourly) to also get overtime compensation for extra hours worked.
5. We're going to raise your insurance rates!

Make the following statements into effective headings using parallel form.

6. Making the Most of Undergraduate Years; Making the Most of Graduate School; Now What?
7. Research; Logistics: What's in It for Us?
8. Pros of Investing in Short-Term Mutual Funds; Cons of Investing in Short-Term Mutual Funds; The Market
9. Clemente Research Group's Five-Year Goals; What We Want to Accomplish in Ten Years; Our Fifteen-Year Goals
10. Overview: Budget; The Problem of Avondale Expanding into Europe

Check your answers to the odd-numbered exercises on page 553.

Writing Formal Reports

Learning Objectives

After reading and applying the information in Module 22, you'll be able to demonstrate

Knowledge of

- The parts of a formal report
- The importance of summaries
- Report formats and style choices

Skills to

- Create a formal report
- Begin to write summaries
- Use PAIBOC to analyze and identify audience-appropriate report formats and style

Employability Skills 2000+ Checklist

In this module, the key skills from the Conference Board of Canada's Employability Skills 2000+ are

Communicate

○ write and speak so others pay attention and understand

○ use relevant scientific, technological, and mathematical knowledge and skills to explain or clarify ideas

Manage Information

○ locate, gather, and organize information using appropriate technology and information systems

Think & Solve Problems

○ assess situations and identify problems
○ recognize the human, interpersonal, technical, scientific, and mathematical dimensions of a problem
○ identify the root cause of a problem
○ be creative and innovative in exploring possible solutions

○ readily use science, technology, and mathematics as ways to think, gain, and share knowledge, solve problems, and make decisions
○ evaluate solutions to make recommendations or decisions

Participate in Projects & Tasks

○ plan, design, or carry out a project or task from start to finish with well-defined objectives and outcomes
○ work to agreed quality standards and specifications

○ adapt to changing requirements and information

Employees in government and scientific organizations produce longer, more formal reports: multiple audiences, greater accountability, and recommendations that may be expensive and lengthy to implement demand more pages of supporting information. Formal reports differ from informal letter and memo reports in length, layout, and their additional components.

What Does a Formal Report Look Like?

A full formal report *may* contain the following components, also shown in Figure 22.1:

Formal reports are longer, often written in more formal language with illustrations, and begin with an Executive Summary.

- Cover
- Letter or Memo of Transmittal
- Title Page
- Table of Contents
- List of Illustrations
- Executive Summary
- Report Body
  - Introduction (Purpose and Scope; may also cover Limitations, Assumptions, and Methods.)
  - Background/History of the Problem (Serves as a record for later readers of the report.)
  - Body (Presents and interprets data in words and visuals. Analyzes the situation or problem, identifies and describes solutions, or evaluates possible solutions. Specific headings depend on the topic of the report.)

FIGURE 22.1   **Parts of the Formal Report**

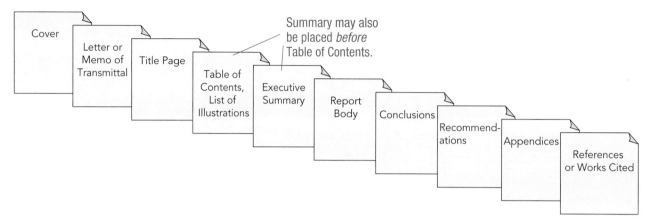

- Conclusions (Summarizes main points of the report.)
- Recommendations (Recommends actions to solve the problem. May be combined with Conclusions; may be put before body rather than at the end.)
- Appendices (Provides additional material the careful reader may need: transcript of an interview, copies of questionnaires, tallies of all the questions, computer printouts, previous reports.)
- References or Works Cited (Lists sources of information used in the report.)

How Should I Organize My Time?

Write parts as soon as you can. Spend most of your time on sections that support your recommendations.

Begin by analyzing and identifying your purposes and audiences: PAIBOC analysis will help you decide on the length, structure, organization, content, and language of your report.

FIGURE 22.2   **PAIBOC Questions for Analysis**

P   What are the **purposes** of the report? Are you providing information? Justifying a plan or decision? Providing information and analysis? Rationalizing and recommending change?

Your purposes come from your organization and your audiences.

A   Who will read/view your report? What are your **audiences'** expectations? What do they already know? What do they need to know? How are they going to use your report?

I   What **information** must the report cover? What is your evidence? What primary research can you use: observations? experiments? experience? discussions with colleagues, clients or managers, other department personnel? What information will your audience find relevant? What information will convince your audience? Where will you get this information? Will your report include visuals? How can you organize this information for maximum clarity and influence (Module 21)?

B   What reasons or reader **benefits** support your position? What reasons will best appeal to your audience? How do these benefits meet your audience's needs, or reinforce your audience's perceptions?

O   What **objections** will occur to your audience as they read your report? What information will your audience perceive as negative? How costly are your recommendations—in time and money? How can you organize the report to overcome audience objections, or deemphasize negative elements (Modules 12 and 21)?

C   What **context** will affect reader response? Consider your relationship to the reader, the reader's values and expectations, the economy, the environment, organizational culture, current morale, social mores, and the time of year.

When you've decided what kind of report you're writing (Modules 20 and 21), break the project into manageable pieces. Use a timeline to plan work on the whole project; start with your report due date, and work backwards, establishing specific, realistic dates for each process and product (see Figure 22.3).

FIGURE 22.3   Plan Your Report

May 4	May 12	May 20	May 25	May 27	May 28	May 31	June 4
Report assigned; write working thesis and begin research	Do PAIBOC analysis; draft body	Draft visuals	Have peer read body; start revisions; begin Conclusions and Recommendations	Finish Conclusions, Recommendations, and References	Start Summary	Have peer read Summary, Conclusions, and Recommendations; revise and proof	Report due

To use your time efficiently, think about the parts of the report, and jot down draft headings. Mark those that are most important to your reader and your proof, and spend most of your researching and writing time on them. Draft the important sections early. That way, you won't spend all your time on the background or history of the problem. Instead, you'll get to the meat of your report.

How Do I Draft the Report?

Start in the middle: write the body first; then draft the ending sections; then write the beginning parts of the formal report: the summary and transmittal.

You may want to start by composing the report body, because every other part of the report depends your findings, backed by research. Draft the Conclusions and Recommendations next, because these sections flow naturally out of your research and findings.

As you revise for clarity and conciseness, organize the different report sections to serve your purposes and meet your audience's needs.

For example, you might organize the proof in your body section using a comparison/contrast, problem–solution, or elimination of alternatives pattern. However, in your beginning and ending report sections (Transmittal, Summary, Introduction, Conclusions and Recommendations) you will probably find a chronological development most useful to your purposes and readers (Module 21).

As you read about the content in each section below, you might want to turn to the corresponding pages of the long report in Figure 22.4, starting on page 393, to see how the section is organized, and how it relates to the total report.

Report Body

Introduction

Employability Skills

The report body Introduction pulls the reader into the situation, and previews the body; the Introduction contains a statement of purpose and scope, and may include all the following:

- **Purpose**. Identify the organizational problem the report addresses, the technical investigations it summarizes, and the rhetorical purpose(s): to explain, to analyze, to evaluate, to solve, to recommend.

As policy advisor for the National Round Table on the Environment and the Economy (NRTEE: www.nrtee-trnee.com), Annika Tamlyn researches and writes formal reports that may take up to a year to complete.

- **Scope**. Identify the topics the report covers. For example, Company TSC is losing money on its line of customized, home-cooked meals. Does the report investigate the quality of the meals? the advertising campaign? the cost of cooking? the demand for home-cooked meals? When you define the scope, you contain the content of the report: if the report is to examine only advertising, then readers cannot fault the report for not considering other factors.

- **Limitations**. Limitations usually arise because time or money constraints don't permit full research, and such limitations make the recommendations less valid, or valid only under certain conditions. For example, a campus pizza restaurant considering expanding its menu might not have enough money to take a random sample of students and non-students. Without a random sample, the writer cannot generalize from the sample to the larger population.

Many feasibility studies and report recommendations remain valid only for a limited time. For example, in a business plan, the business location might be ideal at the time of writing, but economic or demographic changes may cause the location to lose its lustre. Or a store may want to investigate the kinds of clothing that will appeal to college men. The recommendations will remain in force only for a short time: a year from now, styles and tastes may change.

- **Assumptions**. Assumptions are statements whose truth you assume and that you use to support your conclusions and recommendations. If they are wrong, the conclusion will be wrong too. For example, recommendations about what cars appeal to drivers aged 18 to 34 would be on the basis of assumptions about the economy and gas prices. In a major recession, people wouldn't buy new cars. When gas prices radically rise or fall, young adults want different kinds of cars.

- **Methods**. Here writers describe how they found the report data: what they observed, whom they chose to survey, and interview, and how, when, and where respondents were interviewed. Omit methods if your report is based solely on library and online research. Instead, simply cite your sources in the text and document them in the References or Works Cited section. See Module 19 on how to cite and document sources.

Background or History

Although the current audience for the report probably knows the situation, reports are filed and then consulted years later. These later audiences will probably not know the background, although it may be crucial for understanding the options possible.

In some cases, the history section might cover many years. For example, a report recommending that a Quebec consortium purchase an Ontario superhighway will probably provide the history of the highway ownership from its construction date, several years before. In other cases, the background or history is much briefer, covering just the immediate situation.

Findings

The Findings section of the report provides the proof of your position. Here you present the facts, gathered through primary and secondary research (Modules 18 and 19), to demonstrate that your conclusions are accurate, and your recommendations inevitable.

Spend most of your time composing, rewriting and revising this section. Pay particular attention to the organization: you want to frame the situation, and your solutions, to influence your readers to your point of view. Through your PAIBOC analysis, you identify reader benefits, and objections. Use this information to structure your argument: emphasize benefits through placement and talking headings (Module 21); deemphasize negatives by offering alternatives (Module 12).

In the sample report (Figure 22.4), the writer's purpose is to prove that she is thoroughly prepared to sell the financial product. The writer demonstrates that she is so knowledgeable that she can recommend the sales approach that other representatives should take. The writer uses the chronological, the general-to-particular, and the particular-to-general organization patterns to describe the industry in general, and her organization's product in particular (Module 21).

To develop her argument the writer uses the comparison/contrast pattern: her tables highlight the unique features of her product, and detail its advantages over the competition. The chronological pattern of her recommendations tell readers exactly how to make the sales presentation.

The Report Ending

Conclusions and Recommendations

All communication is an act of creation: after all, when we make meaning, we create order out of chaos. Reports, too, can be creative. However, unlike fiction writing, your report does not contain any surprises for your intended audiences.

The best reports offer no surprises for their audiences.

Because formal reports are so lengthy, they use a great deal of repetition for reinforcement. Therefore, the ending sections do not introduce any new information; your conclusions and recommendations concisely and clearly summarize information covered in the body.

The Conclusions section sums up the key ideas proven by the facts in the body of the report. Note that you may present your conclusions in paragraphs or single sentences, depending on how full an explanation you have offered in the body, and on your reader's expectations. Use "should" throughout ("The Bay should hire one full-time staff for the holiday season") because the writer and reader share the assumption that the points have been proven.

The Recommendations section identifies action items to solve or partially solve the problem. Again, you have already explained these actions in the Body, where your skill in finding, organizing, and presenting the relevant facts lead the reader to the inevitability of your recommendations.

Be sure to number the recommendations to make them easy to discuss. If your readers will find your recommendations expensive, difficult, or controversial, give a brief rationale paragraph after each recommendation. If your recommendations are easy for the audience to accept, simply list them without comments or reasons.

Depending on audience's expectations, some recommendations use the imperative. ("Do this.")

1. Choose Positions for Co-op Students
2. Set Salaries
3. Choose Supervisors and Mentors
4. Publicize the Program
5. Recruit Students

Formal reports contain a great deal of repetition because of their length, and because repeated information increases readability and retention. Therefore, your recommendations also go in the Summary, and, if possible, in the Title and the Transmittal.

Appendices and References, or Works Cited

Place supplemental information, including visuals, questionnaires, scientific and survey data, historical documents, and even glossaries in your appendix, at the end of the report, before your bibliography. When deciding whether you need an appendix, follow the norms of your discourse community: if your readers expect plenty of supporting documentation, provide it.

If you are undecided about where to place such documentation, assess its value to the reader, and to your proof. If the data are necessary to prove your point of view, place them in the body. If the information is superfluous to your argument, omit it.

Your report's credibility, and your reputation, depend on your careful documentation of sources and resources (Module 19). Again, follow the norms of your discourse community when deciding whether to use endnotes or in-text citations, and PLA or MLA formats for your bibliography.

The Report Beginning

Title Page

The title page of a report contains four items: the title of the report, for whom the report is prepared, by whom it is prepared, and the release date.

The title of the report should be as informative as possible.

Poor title: New Office Site

Better title: Why St. John's Is the Best Site for the New Info.com Office

In many cases, the title states the recommendation in the report: "Improving Productivity at Cambridge International: Updating Communications Policies." However, omit the recommendations in the title when

- The reader will find the recommendations hard to accept.
- The recommendations in the title would make the title too long.
- The report does not offer recommendations.

If the title does not contain the recommendation, it usually indicates the problem that the report solves: "Best-Practices Analysis, City of Montreal: The Communications Audit."

Checkpoint

Report Titles

Normally, the title of the report should give the recommendation. Omit the recommendation in three cases:

- The reader will find the recommendations hard to accept.
- The recommendations in the title would make it too long.
- The report does not offer recommendations.

If the title does not contain the recommendation, it normally indicates what problem the report tries to solve.

Letter or Memo of Transmittal

The Transmittal has several purposes: to send the report, to orient the reader to the report, and to influence the reader favourably toward the report and the writer. Use a *memo of transmittal* if you are a regular employee of the organization for which you prepare the report; use a *letter of transmittal* if you are not.

Organize the transmittal in this way:

1. Tell when and by whom the report was authorized and the report's purpose.
2. Summarize your conclusions and recommendations.
3. Indicate minor problems you encountered in your investigation and show how you overcome them. Thank people who helped you.
4. Point out additional research necessary (if any).
5. Thank the reader for the opportunity to do the work, and offer to answer questions. Even if you did not enjoy writing the report, readers expect some positive acknowledgment about the experience.

Table of Contents

In the table of contents, list the headings exactly as they appear in the body of the report. If the report is shorter than 25 pages, list all the headings. In a very long report, list the two or three highest levels of headings. Include your List of Illustrations in your Table of Contents.

List of Illustrations

Report visuals comprise both tables and figures. **Tables** are words or numbers arranged in rows and columns. **Figures** are everything else: bar graphs, pie graphs, maps, drawings, photographs, computer printouts, and so forth (Module 23). Number tables and figures independently, so you may have both a "Table 1" and a "Figure 1." In a report with maps and graphs but no other visuals, the visuals are sometimes called "Map 1" and "Graph 1." Whatever you call the illustrations, list them in the order in which they appear in the report; give the name of each visual as well as its number.

See Module 23 for information about how to design and label visuals.

Executive Summary

An Executive Summary provides a précis (Module 19) of the whole report. The Summary includes the recommendations, and the reasons for the recommendations. For many readers, the Summary is the most important part of the report; here audiences find immediate answers to their questions.[1]

To write the Summary, you must know the report's recommendations, methods, and results. Write and revise the Summary last, as a stand-alone document.

1. In the first paragraph, identify the report's recommendations or main point (purpose). State the situation briefly:

> This report describes the competitive advantages of President's Choice Financial No Fee Daily Banking Account. The report's purpose is to provide the information PC sales representatives need to make a successful sales presentation to prospective customers.

2. In the summary body, identify the major supporting points for your argument. Include all the information decision makers will need.
3. Briefly describe your research methods.
4. If your report ends with conclusions, provide the conclusions section in the Summary.
5. If your report includes recommendations, provide the recommendations in the Summary.

Recommendations are up front in first paragraph of Summary.

> To market life insurance to mid-40s urban professionals, Great North Insurance should advertise in upscale publications and use direct mail.
>
> Network TV and radio are not cost-efficient for reaching this market. This group makes up a small percentage of the prime-time network TV audience and a minority of most radio station listeners. They tend to discard newspapers and general-interest magazines quickly, but many of them keep upscale periodicals for months. Magazines with high percentages of readers in this group include *Architectural Digest, Bon Appétit, Canadian Home, Canadian Gardening, Golf Digest,* and *Smithsonian.* Most urban professionals in their mid-40s already shop by mail and respond positively to well-conceived and well-executed direct-mail appeals.

Conclusions include focus of the report and findings.

Checkpoint

Report Style

Reports use the same style as other business documents, with three exceptions:

1. Reports use a more formal style than do many letters and memos.
2. Reports rarely use the word *you.*
3. Reports should be all-inclusive.

FIGURE 22.4 **A Formal Report**

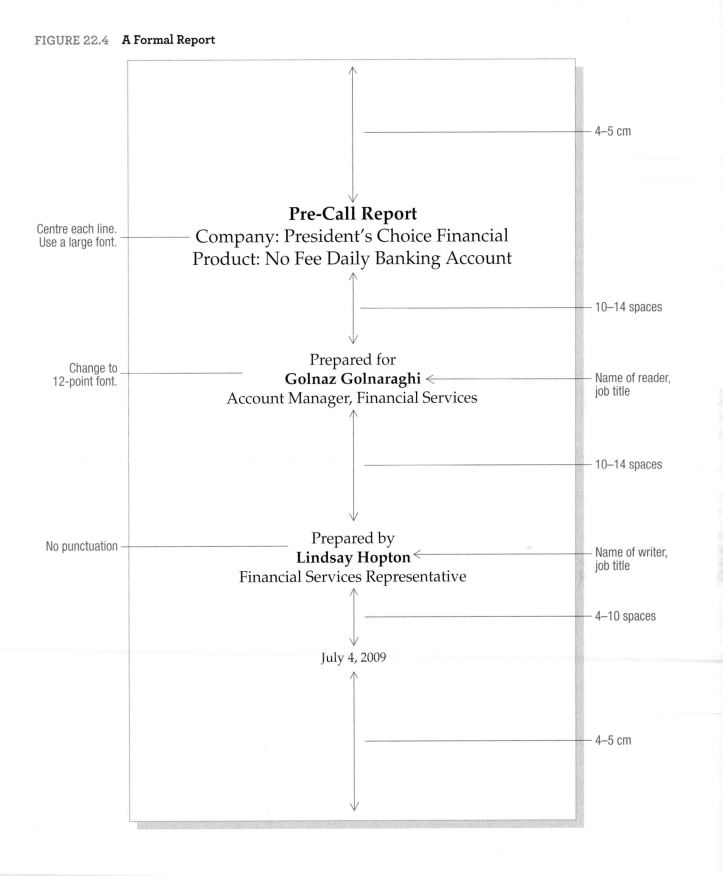

4–5 cm

Centre each line.
Use a large font.

Pre-Call Report
Company: President's Choice Financial
Product: No Fee Daily Banking Account

10–14 spaces

Change to
12-point font.

Prepared for
Golnaz Golnaraghi
Account Manager, Financial Services

Name of reader,
job title

10–14 spaces

No punctuation

Prepared by
Lindsay Hopton
Financial Services Representative

Name of writer,
job title

4–10 spaces

July 4, 2009

4–5 cm

FIGURE 22.4   **A Formal Report (continued)**

Writer chooses to position Executive Summary before Table of Contents.

President's Choice Financial No Fee Daily Banking Account ──────────

Report title

Executive Summary

This report describes the competitive advantages of President's Choice Financial No Fee Daily Banking Account. The report's purpose is to provide the information PC sales representatives need to make a successful sales presentation to prospective customers.

Executive Summary of whole report; includes purpose, focus and findings, and recommendations.

President's Choice Financial is an innovative and flexible company offering a variety of banking products and services to Canadian consumers. Surveys and client testimonials indicate that President's Choice Financial ranks highest in customer satisfaction among Canada's mid-size retail banks.

Findings

The President's Choice Financial No Fee Daily Banking Account offers customers a variety of benefits, including savings in interest and groceries, immediacy, and convenience. Most important, the PC Financial No Fee Daily Banking Account is the only free Canadian bank account with no hidden fees or requirements. Using this account can save customers hundreds of dollars annually.

President's Choice Financial's Primary target markets are students and young families, people who are looking for bank accounts that are cost-effective, convenient, and easy to use.

To ensure a successful sales presentation, PC Financial representatives should

1. Introduce President's Choice Financial No Fee Daily Bank Account to the household financial decision makers.

2. Target household decision makers in young families, and students.

3. Demonstrate the competitive advantages and financial savings that the President's Choice Financial No Fee Daily Bank account offers.

4. Obtain a completed application form by the end of the meeting.

Recommendations sequenced

5. Arrange for a follow-up meeting within a week to review the details of the new account once the application has been processed (processing takes up to two days).

6. Provide new clients with contact information so that they can get in touch with questions or concerns before the next meeting.

7. After the sales presentation is complete, provide customers with information regarding other President's Choice Financial products and services; arrange to meet in two weeks' time to review their additional financial needs.

All information in Executive Summary comes from the report.

i

FIGURE 22.4   A Formal Report (continued)

Table of Contents does not list itself.

Use lowercase roman numerals for frontmatter.

Report body Introduction begins on page 1.

Indent subheads.

Headings are parallel.

Subheads within each section are parallel.

Differentiate sub-subheads.

Table of Contents

List of Illustrations

ii

FIGURE 22.4   A Formal Report (continued)

President's Choice Financial No Fee Daily Banking Account ——————— Report title

Introduction to the Banking and Financial Services Industry ——— Talking Head

Intro paragraph summarizes all the content in this section.

A variety of factors impact the products and services offered in daily banking (chequing) accounts in Canada. These include business and economic factors, legal, political, and tax factors, technological factors, competitive factors, social and environmental factors, demographic factors, and current trends.

Business and Economic Factors

Canada's financial services sector is an essential contributor to the country's economic growth and well-being. "Banks are leading taxpayers, progressive employers and major purchasers of goods and services from Canadian suppliers" (http://www.cba.ca/en/content/general/080605%20-%20Contributions%20EN%20FINAL(1).pdf). ⟵ *Document sources.*

The banking industry influences the business industry as a whole. Businesses rely on banks and financial institutions for loans, credit, and lower interest rates. The recent drop in interest rates has helped many Canadian merchants, and businesses will look for low interest rates to remain constant during economic recovery.

Although Canada hasn't seen the same devastation in the banking and financial services industry as the U.S., consumers are wary. Increasingly Canadians are investing conservatively or putting their money in savings accounts.

Legal, Political, and Tax Factors

Privacy and confidentiality legislation control the financial services sector. Banks and other financial institutions are required to follow strict guidelines regarding clients' information. Canada has strict privacy policies and confidentiality regulations, and banks must enforce these regulations vigorously (http://www.cdic.ca/1/5/9/8/index1.shtml).

The Canada Deposit Insurance Corporation (CDIC) also protects Canadians' money. The CDIC, a federal Crown corporation, insures Canadians' bank savings against bank failure or bankruptcy. "The CDIC reports to Parliament through the federal Minister of Finance, and works at arm's length from the government" (http://www.cdic.ca/1/5/9/8/index1.shtml). ⟵ *Period follows the in-text citation.*

Canadian banks and other financial institutions stimulate the economy through their annual tax dollars. Furthermore, banks have made increasing number of tax credits available to both businesses and consumers in Canada to help alleviate the tax burden (http://www.cba.ca/en/content/general/080618%20-%20Tax%20BackgrounderEN%20FINAL.pdf).

Technological Factors

Topic sentences begin each paragraph.

Technological advancements continue to make it more convenient for consumers to access their money and perform daily banking activities that previously were time-consuming and inefficient.

According to the Canadian Bankers Association, Canadians have been "enthusiastic and early adopters of new banking technologies," and Canadian banks have revolutionized the banking industry and banking products. The Automated Banking Machine (ABM) introduced access to daily banking activities, and electronic statements and bills have made banking easy and organized. Now most banking activities occur online or over the telephone at consumer convenience. The Interac (debit) system also makes access to chequing accounts immediate, and future technology will see debit being used internationally on Canadian bank accounts (http://www.cba.ca/en/content/stats/fastfacts/Technology_and_Banking.pdf).

1

FIGURE 22.4 **A Formal Report (continued)**

Competitive Factors

A number of competitive factors affect the financial services industry, and specifically daily banking accounts. "Canadians have a wide choice of providers, and the number of financial and banking service providers is constantly increasing." More than 70 domestic and foreign banks operate in Canada. Although the "Big Six" are the best known, the industry is becoming increasingly competitive as new banks enter the market.

Consumers also have more choice in banking products. More than 100 bank account packages are available, and companies must strive to differentiate their banking services from those of the competition. For example, service fees and rate spreads in Canada are low compared to those in other countries. As the industry becomes more competitive, fees and rates on a variety of banking products, including chequing accounts, will decrease (http://www.cba.ca/en/content/stats/fastfacts/080604% 20-%20Competition%20FINAL%20EN.pdf).

Social and Environmental Factors

Environmental sustainability is a key part of Canadian banks' social responsibility efforts. Banks have established environmental policies, goals, and practices to ensure that they are doing their part in their respective communities:

Use bullets for readability.

- *Sustainable operations*—From recycling programs to energy conservation in offices and branches, banks are working to reduce their operational footprints on the environment.
- *Sustainable lending*—Banks take environmental protection into account when making lending decisions. In commercial and wholesale banking, this means "incorporating environmental due-diligence ..., which may include site visits, assessments of a client's environmental record, or third-party reporting on proposals."
- *Green products & services*—Banks are developing new products and services "that respond to consumer demand for ..., from paperless statements to co-branded credit cards."
- *Community activities*—Banks give generously to support environmental organizations and projects in cities and towns across the country (http://www.cba.ca/en/ViewDocument.asp? fl=2&sl=386&tl=&docid=836).

Ellipsis indicates missing words.

Demographic Factors

The Canadian population continues to grow and change due to immigration. These changes are reflected in the banking industry: international institutions are entering the Canadian market, and new products and services are available. Meanwhile, Canadians are now waiting longer to have children, and are having fewer children than ever before. Raising fewer children provides consumers with access to larger disposable incomes, and raises demand for ease and convenience in looking after that income. Furthermore, Canadians' life expectancy is longer, which means that Canadians will have to save and invest more in order to live comfortably for a longer period after retirement.

The Canadian population continues to age due to the large number of baby boomers. This aging population will impact every aspect of the country's social, cultural, and business landscape, including the banking industry. Most Canadians live in large urban centres across the country: in Toronto, Montreal, and Vancouver. These areas will continue to be the origin for new banks and product offerings (http://www.statcan.ca/english/freepub/91-003-XIE/91-003-XIE2007001.pdf).

According to Statistics Canada, the gap between Canada's wealthy and poor is widening. The financial services sector will expand traditional discounts—such as no fees with a minimum balance—to attract low-wage consumers (http://www.statcan.ca/Daily/English/061213/d061213c.htm).

Current Trends

A number of trends in the banking and financial industry will affect the future of banking. Consumers are tired of paying high fees for their banking; a new wave of products and services offer no fees or low fees. A recent trend toward high-interest savings products encourages customers to save their money. Consumer savings mean banks have access to more money to loan to other customers and businesses. A higher number of bank loans equals increased interest earnings.

Today's busy consumer expects easy and convenient banking, leading to growth in online and telephone banking products and services, and increased hours of operation. Today consumers can apply for accounts and loans online or over the phone, and stop in to the branch only to sign the paperwork. Technological innovation will continue to transform how and where people bank.

FIGURE 22.4   A Formal Report (continued)

Subheadings
within each section
are parallel.

Company Knowledge—President's Choice Financial

Size

According to CIBC, President's Choice Financial has nearly three million clients (http://www.canadabanks.net/default.aspx?article=PC+Financial).

While not part of the "Big Six" Canadian banks, President's Choice Financial is considered one of the larger mid-size domestic banks. Estimates of actual number of customers range from 2.4 to 2.7 million, and the number of PC Financial customers continues to grow.

Reputation

PC Financial has a reputation for offering innovative and cost-effective banking products and services without the "bricks and mortar" of traditional banking institutions. According to the J. D. Power and Associates' 2007 Canadian Retail Banking Customer Satisfaction Study, President's Choice Financial ranked the highest among mid-size retail banks in satisfying customers in Canada in 2007 (http://www.investmentexecutive.com/client/en/News/DetailNews.asp?id=40805&IdSection=147&cat=147).

History

Loblaw Companies Limited and CIBC founded President's Choice Financial in 1998. With this joint venture, Loblaws was the first major Canadian retailer to offer full-fledged banking. CIBC provided the banking services from 1998 to 2001. From January 2001 to October 2005, Amicus Bank, a subsidiary of CIBC, provided banking services for PC Financial. Amicus is now a division of CIBC Retail Markets; thus President's Choice Financial continues its partnership with CIBC (http://www.banking.pcfinancial.ca/a/helpful/faq.page?refId=quicklink).

Industry Image

The image of President's Choice Financial has changed dramatically since its market entry. At first, customers were wary about not having access to tellers. However, President's Choice Financial demonstrated that it could provide competitive products and services, and excellent customer service. Today the financial institution is a key player in the banking and financial industry. Not only is President's Choice Financial perceived as innovative and customer-oriented, but it also enjoys the highest customer satisfaction of all Canada's mid-size banks.

Pricing and Discount Policies

President's Choice Financial offers lower-priced products than its competitors. It is the only bank offering free accounts without a required minimum balance, and maintains competitive interest rates on loans and mortgages (although the rate pricing is primarily determined by the applicant's credit score). President's Choice offers no discounts to customers, because its policy is to maintain the best possible prices so that there is no need for discounting or exceptions. Even employees do not receive any special discounts or rates on President's Choice products (M. MacDonald, personal communication, June 25, 2008).

Some banks offer preferential pricing—a higher interest rate on investments or a lower interest rate on loans—if customers use more of their products or services, or bundle their services to provide discounted rates (http://www.banking.pcfinancial.ca/a/helpful/aboutTiedSelling.page).

But President's Choice Financial does not offer product bundles or preferential pricing. All pricing is based on the credit assessment provided by Equifax, and based on the customer's information (M. MacDonald, personal communication, June 25, 2008).

Credit and Terms of Sale

President's Choice Financial has specific guidelines for its products and services. Potential customers are screened based on identification requirements, income requirements, and credit history requirements. To determine if a potential customer is a good fit for a PC Financial product or service, Equifax Canada obtains the prospect's credit history. Customers are approved based on the requirements and Equifax information. Approved customers receive credit limits and interest rates for loans and bank accounts based on their credit rating with President's Choice. The terms of sale for PC Financial are

- Proper personal identification
- Personal information regarding finances, income, debt, assets/liabilities, employment history

3

FIGURE 22.4 A Formal Report (continued)

APA uses in-text citations for personal communications. These are not listed in the References.

This information determines customers' credit standing with PC and identifies the products and services appropriate for them. All potential clients submit a signature card in person at one of the kiosk locations before they can begin using their President's Choice banking products (M. MacDonald, personal communication, June 25, 2008).

Customer Channels

President's Choice Financial products and services are available via a variety of channels. The most easily accessible are website and telephone banking options. The website provides online banking for existing customers and the option of applying for new products. The website also provides an option for contacting President's Choice via email with questions or concerns (M. MacDonald, personal communication, June 25, 2008).

President's Choice telephone banking is similar to the online banking: it also offers application for new products and telephone banking for existing customers. And telephone banking offers the option to speak with a live person on the phone. Representatives are available almost 24/7 to answer questions about products or services, or to assist customers with banking requests.

President's Choice Financial has its own ABMs, usually located in or near a Loblaws-owned grocery store. PC Financial's partnership with CIBC allows customers to perform the same ABM banking activities at a CIBC ABM free of charge. Access to the ABM provides a variety of services, including

- Withdrawals
- Deposits
- Bill payments

These ABMs are only available to customers with an existing President's Choice account and debit card.

In place of traditional banks and tellers, President's Choice Financial offers face-to-face contact with representatives at kiosks located in Loblaws-owned grocery stores (http://www.banking.pcfinancial.ca/a/helpful/helpfulInfo.page?refId=topnav).

Normally located near the front entrance, all grocery stores in the Loblaws chain have personal banking representatives available during a variety of hours. Kiosks are open anywhere from 9:00 A.M. to 9:00 P.M., depending on location. Personal banking representatives are primarily available to help clients set up new services, and to provide information about President's Choice products. These representatives are not tellers, and no money is kept in the kiosks. All monetary transactions must be completed through the ABM, telephone, or Internet banking.

Service and Support

President's Choice Financial offers service and support through its Personal Banking Representatives in stores, and through telephone and Internet banking. Assistance is also available through mail service. Internet banking provides a contact feature that allows customers to send online messages directly to a PC Financial representative. Because of privacy and confidentiality concerns, not all requests can be handled in this manner (M. MacDonald, personal communication, June 25, 2008).

PC Financial primarily uses the telephone to maintain its service and support. Support representatives are available almost 24/7, and hold times are relatively short ("5 minutes or less even during peak calling times"). Personal banking representatives in store kiosks are also available for assistance, but the in-store representatives can resolve relatively few issues. Often representatives put customers on the phone with a telephone representative. Mail assistance is also available, but used primarily for mailing documents or paperwork (http://www.banking.pcfinancial.ca/a/helpful/helpfulInfo.page?refId=topnav).

4

FIGURE 22.4   **A Formal Report** (continued)

Competitive Knowledge—Scotiabank

Size

The Bank of Nova Scotia, or Scotiabank, is one of Canada's "Big Six" banks, and the third-largest bank in Canada by assets:

> Scotiabank Group and its affiliates serve more than 12.5 million customers in some 50 countries around the world. Scotia's Domestic Banking provides a comprehensive range of banking and investment services to over 7 million retail, wealth management, small business, and commercial customers across Canada. (http://www.scotiabank.com/cda/content/0,1608, CID821_LIDen,00.html)

Longer quotations are indented.

Period comes before the citation in a longer quotation.

Reputation

Scotiabank's asset value and market capitalization have earned it a spot in Canada's top six banks. However, some financial services industry employees perceive the credit requirements of Canada's traditional banking institutions as an impediment to customer access to products and services (M. MacDonald, personal communication, June 25, 2008).

History

The Bank of Nova Scotia (Scotiabank) "opened for business in 1832 in Halifax, Nova Scotia to support the thriving trans-Atlantic trade between Britain, North America, and the West Indies" (http://www.scotiabank.com/cda/content/0,1608,CID8399_LIDen,00.html).

Agents were "assigned to New York, Boston, and London, an early indication of the bank's global aspirations." By the late 1800s, Scotiabank had expanded internationally to the United States and Jamaica. By the early 1900s, a coast-to-coast Canadian branch network existed. "Scotiabank has substantially grown its international presence to become Canada's most international bank" (http://www.scotiabank.com/cda/content/0,1608,CID8399_LIDen,00.html).

Industry Image

The Bank of Nova Scotia is an established and reputable financial institution, viewed by loyal clients as a "one-stop shop" for all banking and financial services needs. Scotiabank continues to grow beyond the Canadian borders, and prides itself on being a community bank. The Scotia brand is major sponsor for a variety of community events (http://www.scotiabankcr.com/acercade_responsabilidad_social_ing.shtml).

Pricing and Discount Policies

Scotiabank strives to offer cost-effective products that are easy and convenient to use. Scotiabank provides a variety of different price ranges for customers such as students, youths, seniors, high transaction users, and non-branch users. Its student account pricing is the lowest out of all the major banks (http://scotiabank.com/cda/content/0,1608,CID478_LIDen,00.html).

Moreover, Scotiabank's pricing is competitive with, if not below that for similar products offered by the competition. Although Scotiabank does not have a specific or advertised discount policy, some of the major six banks will offer discounts to customers who are dissatisfied with their bank's services and are considering switching to another financial institution. While not an official discount policy, it is becoming increasingly popular for financial and banking institutions to provide discounts to existing clients to maintain the relationship (http://www.highinterest savings.ca/canadian-chequing-accounts).

5

FIGURE 22.4   **A Formal Report (continued)**

Credit and Terms of Sale

Scotiabank also has specific guidelines for offering products and services to prospective customers. Potential customers are screened based on identification requirements, income requirements, and credit history requirements. Credit history is obtained through Equifax Canada in order to determine if a potential customer is a good fit for Scotiabank products or services. Customers who are approved for Scotiabank services receive credit limits and interest rates for loans and bank accounts, based on their credit rating through Equifax and on the information in the Scotiabank system. The terms of sale for Scotiabank are

- Proper personal identification
- Personal customer information regarding finances, income, debt, assets/liabilities, employment history

This information determines client credit standing with Scotia and identifies the appropriate products and services. Scotiabank also requires consent to view the customer's information through Equifax, and also requires customers to "disclose any past credit history involving fraud or other illegal activity" (http://www.scotiabank.com/cda/content/0,1608,CID456_LIDen,00.html).

Customer Channels

Scotiabank products and services are available through a variety of channels. The most easily accessible are Scotia's website and telephone banking options. The website offers new products and online banking options. The website also provides an option for contacting Scotiabank via email with questions or concerns.

The Bank's telephone banking is similar to its online banking: it offers application for new products, and provides telephone banking for existing customers. However, the telephone banking also offers the option to speak with a live person on the phone. Representatives are available 24/7 to answer questions about products or services, or to assist existing customers with banking requests.

Scotiabank also offers the traditional physical branch locations with tellers and personal banking representatives. Branches tend to be open between 9:00 A.M. and 4:00 P.M., and some branches are open until 6:00 P.M. on Thursday and Friday evenings.

At the branch, customers can perform all of their banking activities. Scotiabank branches also offer ABM service to customers, with ABMs in other locations, such as malls, and convenience stores, where there is no access to a Scotiabank branch (http://www.scotiabank.com/scotialocator/locator.html).

Service and Support

Scotiabank offers service and support through its tellers and Personal Banking Representatives in branches, and through telephone and Internet banking. The Internet banking provides a contact feature, allowing customers to send an online message directly to a Scotiabank representative. Due to privacy and confidentiality concerns, not all requests can be handled this way, but it is an excellent source of general information about products and services.

Scotiabank also maintains service and support through an automated telephone system: customers can access support representatives and do their own banking (view account balances and pay bills) 24/7. Hold times vary due to increased call volume throughout the day.

In-branch tellers and Personal Banking Representatives are Scotia's primary service and support means. Customers can go into any branch of Scotiabank and receive a variety of services and support. Customers can also get sound financial advice, or speak with a branch manager about a concern, or about an existing product or service.

FIGURE 22.4   A Formal Report (continued)

Repetition for reinforcement

Tell the reader about the visuals in the text.

Start major headings on a new page for emphasis.

Tell a story with the visual's title.

Provide a source for data when you get information from somewhere or someone else.

Product Knowledge—No Fee Daily Banking Account

The President's Choice Financial No Fee Daily Banking Account is the only account of its kind. The account offers customers a daily chequing account with no monthly fees, and no minimum required balance. The account offers unlimited transactions such as withdrawals, deposits, bill payments, Interac purchases, pre-authorized payments, and unlimited access to telephone and online banking.

The President's Choice Financial No Fee Daily Banking Account is the only chequing account available in the banking industry without monthly fees, regardless of the size of the customer's account balance.

The President's Choice Financial No Fee account is also the only account to offer only telephone and online banking service. In-person representatives are available at in-store kiosks located in many Loblaws-owned grocery stores, but President's Choice does not offer traditional teller banking services. Thus, the institution eliminates operating "bricks and mortar" costs, and passes these savings on to customers in the form of higher interest rates on savings, and free daily banking.

The PC Financial No Fee Account features are outlined in Table 1. Table 2 compares PC Financial No Fee Account features with a similar product offered by Scotiabank, one of PC Financial's many competitors.

Features, Advantages, and Benefits

The following chart illustrates a number of features, advantages, and benefits of the President's Choice Financial No Fee Daily Bank Account.

Table 1: President's Choice Financial No Fee Daily Bank Account: Features, Advantages, and Benefits

Feature	Advantage	Benefit
No-fee daily banking	No monthly fees to pay	Save a minimum of $150 a year to spend elsewhere
No minimum balance	Not required to keep money in the account to waive fees	Have extra money to spend on other things
Internet and Telephone banking	The most convenient and easy way to bank	Save time and effort for more important things
Free ABM transactions	Use of over 3,700 PC Financial and CIBC ABM's	Easy to locate and don't have to pay other banks' ABM fees
Online statements available	Access to account statements 24/7	Stay organized and eliminate paper clutter
PC Points	Earn reward points on everyday purchases and transactions	Redeem points to receive free groceries and other offers
Unlimited banking transactions	Use account for whatever type of transaction required	No need to keep track of number of transactions or worry about extra fees
No bricks and mortar branches	Eliminates costly branch operating costs	Savings are passed on to customers in interest earnings and no fee accounts
CDIC Registered	Protects deposits in case of bank failure	Eliminates worry, deposits are safe and accessible

Source: http://www.banking.pcfinancial.ca/a/helpful/helpfulInfo.page?refId=topnav.

7

FIGURE 22.4   **A Formal Report (continued)**

Comparison of President's Choice Financial and Scotiabank Accounts

President's Choice Financial No Fee Bank Account compares favourably with the Scotiabank Power Chequing Account, the most comparable in terms of price and available features. No other completely free chequing accounts are available in the Canadian banking industry. This account offered through Scotiabank is the only chequing account with minimal fees that can be used without maintaining a minimum balance.

Table 2: President's Choice Financial and Scotiabank Product Comparison

	President's Choice Financial	Scotiabank
Account Name	No Fee Bank Account	Scotia Power Chequing Account
Monthly Fee	$0	$3.95
Daily Banking		
ABMs	Free at CIBC machine or President's Choice terminal	Free at Scotiabank machines
Teller Assisted Transactions	Not available	$0.65 each
Withdrawals per month	Unlimited	15 self-serve transactions
Charge for Additional Withdrawals	None	$0.65 each
Withdrawals—Maximum Withdrawal per day	Based on credit assessment, $200 to $3,000 per day	Based on credit assessment
Account Minimum Balance	Not required	$2,000 to waive monthly fees
Interac Direct Payments	Free—unlimited	15 self-serve transactions per month, $0.65 per additional transaction
Pre-authorized Payments		
Online Banking		
Telephone Banking		
Bill Payments		
Overdraft Protection		
Monthly Charge	$4.97	$5.00
Interest Rate	19% per annum	Scotia Prime + 5%
Cheques		
Cheques	Free, personalized	Must purchase
Support and Service		
Tellers	Not available	Available during bankers' hours
Online	24 hours	24 hours
Telephone	7:00 AM to 12:00 AM	24 hours
Extra Info		
Other	Earn PC points	Access to Global ATM Alliance ABM's when travelling

Source: http://www.banking.pcfinancial.ca/a/helpful/helpfulInfo.page?refId=topnav; http://www.scotiabank.com/cda/content/0,1608,CID456_LIDen,00.html.

As the comparison makes clear, President's Choice Financial No Fee Daily Bank Account offers several advantages, including

Bulleted list sums up visual.

- No monthly fees
- No account minimum balance
- Free and unlimited withdrawals
- Free and unlimited online and telephone transactions
- Free personalized cheques
- PC points for Loblaws Companies purchases

FIGURE 22.4   A Formal Report (continued)

Sub-subheading
are differentiated
from subheading.

Evidence and Differentiating Factors, and Testimonials

Evidence

President's Choice Financial ranks highest among mid-size retail banks in customer satisfaction, according to the J. D. Power and Associates 2007 Canadian Retail Banking Customer Satisfaction Study. With a score of 830 out of a possible 1,000 points, President's Choice Financial was the clear winner among consumers (http://www.jdpower.com/corporate/news/releases/pressrelease.aspx?ID=2007157).

President's Choice Financial was the only bank to score as "among the best" in all of the scorecard areas. PC Financials competitors were mainly scored as "the rest," an average-to-below-average rating, according to the J. D. Power survey.

President's Choice Financial scored a perfect "among the best" score in the following areas: "Account set-up and product offerings, Fees, Account statements, Facility, Overall transactions experiences, and Overall experience" (http://corp.jdpower.com/jdpcc/global/canada/content/ratings/retail-banking/index-midsize.jsp).

Differentiating Factors

- President's Choice Financial is the only institution to offer a truly free daily banking account, saving customers hundreds of dollars annually.
- Over the last 10 years President's Choice Financial has become the 11th-largest bank in Canada.
- In 2007 alone, PC Financial saved its customers $160 million in fees with Canada's only true no-fee daily bank account.
- Over the course of its ten-year history, President's Choice Financial has paid customers $811 million in interest.
- PC Financial has awarded $447 million in free groceries and rewards for health, beauty, home, and living with its PC Points program.
- 78% of President's Choice Financial customers say that free services were the main reason for selecting the bank (http://www.tradingmarkets.com/.site/news/Stock%20News/1207196).
- 77% of Canadians use online banking capabilities, and for 50% of retail banking customers this service is considered extremely important.
- 33% of Canadian banking customers already do all of their banking outside of traditional bricks-and-mortar bank facilities (http://www.jdpower.com/corporate/news/releases/pressrelease.aspx?ID=2006223).

9

FIGURE 22.4   **A Formal Report (continued)**

Customer Knowledge

President's Choice pursues two primary target customers most frequently.

Ideal Target Market #1—Students

Students are an ideal target market for President's Choice Financial for a number of reasons:

- Students tend to have lower incomes, and need to take advantage of opportunities to save money.
- They tend to be technologically savvy, and willing to take on technologically innovative products and services.
- Students use their bank cards frequently.
- Students do not maintain a minimum balance.
- Students rely on access to ABMs and Interac service.

President's Choice Financial lets students save on bank fees, and its online and telephone banking make it a good fit for students.

PC Financial is ideal because it allows students to use their debit cards without limitations or additional fees. President's Choice provides access to thousands of ABMs across the country through its partnership with CIBC. Students can access their cash quickly and conveniently.

Most students are generally unable to keep a large minimum balance in their chequing account in order to waive bank fees. The PC Financial No Fee Banking Account is a perfect fit, given that it does not require customers to keep a minimum balance for free banking.

The President's Choice No Fee Account eliminates the need for tedious tracking. Students can use the account as much as they want over the course of the month without worrying about additional fees or costly transactions.

Ideal Target Market #2—Young Families

Young families are an ideal target market for the President's Choice Financial No Fee Daily Banking Account for a number of reasons:

- Young families tend to be starting their careers, and have lower incomes; they haven't yet been promoted or reached their full earning potential.
- With children and a mortgage, young families want to save money and lower expenses.
- Young families tend to use their debit card frequently.
- Young families do not maintain a minimum account balance.
- Young families make Interac purchases for a variety of items, such as fuel, groceries, and household and children's items.
- Young families do not want to worry about or track the number of Interac transactions they use monthly.
- They are more comfortable using online and telephone banking than visiting their local bank branch every week.
- Young families want banking services that are easy, convenient, and cost-effective.

The PC Financial No Fee Bank account gives young families the potential to save nearly $1,000 over the course of the year, just on their daily banking activities. Young families also tend to be more familiar with technology and computers. President's Choice works well for them because they are able to take advantage of their technological knowledge, and save themselves time through immediate, anywhere access.

The President's Choice No Fee Account works perfectly for young families; not only can they use their debit card freely as many times as they need to, but they can also forget about minimum balances and transaction limits. This freedom eliminates unnecessary stress. President's Choice Financial is a perfect fit for their needs.

Bullets sum up relevant information and break up text.

FIGURE 22.4   **A Formal Report (continued)**

Conclusions

Repeat main points relevant to purpose and audience.

1. President's Choice Financial sales representatives should target all customers who want to take advantage of PC points for purchase, and no interest fees.

2. President's Choice Financial sales representatives should especially target students and young families.

3. In their sales presentation, sales representatives should emphasize the unique advantages of President's Choice Financial No Fee Daily Bank Account, including

   - No monthly fees
   - No account minimum balance
   - Free and unlimited withdrawals
   - Free and unlimited online and telephone transactions
   - Free personalized cheques
   - PC points for Loblaws Companies purchases

Recommendations: The Sales Presentation

Recommendations are actions readers should take: writer has written report for new sales reps, including herself.

1. Introduce President's Choice Financial No Fee Daily Bank Account to the household financial decision makers.

2. Target household decision makers in young families, and students.

3. During the sales presentation,

   - Demonstrate the competitive advantages and financial savings that the President's Choice Financial No Fee Daily Bank account offers.
   - Obtain a completed application form by the end of the meeting.
   - Arrange for a follow-up meeting within a week to review the details of the new account once the application has been processed (processing takes up to two days).
   - Provide new clients with contact information so that they can get in touch with questions or concerns before the next meeting.

4. After the sales presentation is complete, provide customers with information regarding other President's Choice Financial products and services, and arrange to meet with them in two weeks' time to review their additional financial needs.

11

FIGURE 22.4 **A Formal Report (continued)**

References

Art Branch Inc. (2008). *PC Financial*. Retrieved June 25, 2008, from
http://www.canadabanks.net/default.aspx?article=PC+Financial

Canadian Bankers Association. (2006). *Taking a closer look—technology and banking*. Retrieved June 24,
2008, from http://www.cba.ca/en/content/stats/fastfacts/Technology_and_Banking.pdf

Canadian Bankers Association. (2008). *CBA—our industry—banks and the environment*. Retrieved
June 24, 2008, from http://www.cba.ca/en/ViewDocument.asp?fl=2&sl=386&tl=&docid=836

Canadian Bankers Association. (2008). *Competition in the financial services sector*. Retrieved June 24,
2008, from http://www.cba.ca/en/content/stats/fastfacts/080604%20-%20Competition%20
FINAL%20EN.pdf

IE Staff. (2007). *President's Choice financial and TD Canada Trust rank highest in customer satisfaction
with retail banks: J. D. Power*. Retrieved June 25, 2008, from
http://www.investmentexecutive.com/client/en/News/DetailNews.asp?id=40805&IdSection
=147&cat=147

J. D. Power & Associates. (2006). *Canadian retail banking customer satisfaction survey*. Retrieved June 27,
2008, from http://www.jdpower.com/corporate/news/releases/pressrelease.aspx?ID=2006223

Leah Tse. (2008). *A comparison of Canadian chequing accounts*. Retrieved June 24, 2008, from
http://www.highinterestsavings.ca/canadian-chequing-accounts

Loblaw Companies Ltd. (2008). *President's Choice® celebrates 10 years of feeding Canadians with an
appetite for a better way to bank*. Retrieved June 27, 2008, from
http://www.tradingmarkets.com/.site/news/Stock%20News/1207196/

Michael Citrome. (April 16, 2005). *Get more bank for your buck*. Retrieved June 26, 2008, from
http://proquest.umi.com.domweb.sheridanc.on.ca:2048/pqdweb?did=823283891&sid=2&Fmt=
3&clientId=43106&RQT=309&VName=PQD

President's Choice Financial. (2008). *Helpful stuff—talk to us*. Retrieved June 25, 2008, from
http://www.banking.pcfinancial.ca/a/helpful/helpfulInfo.page?refId=topnav

President's Choice Financial. (2008). *Legal stuff*. Retrieved June 24, 2008, from
http://www.banking.pcfinancial.ca/a/legal/dailyBanking.page

Scotiabank. (2008). *Opening a day-to-day bank account*. Retrieved June 26, 2008, from
http://www.scotiabank.com/cda/content/0,1608,CID456_LIDen,00.html

Scotiabank. (2008). *Our history—the Scotiabank story*. Retrieved June 26, 2008, from
http://www.scotiabank.com/cda/content/0,1608,CID8399_LIDen,00.html

Statistics Canada. (2007). Study: *inequality in wealth*. Retrieved June 25, 2008, from
http://www.statcan.ca/Daily/English/061213/d061213c.htm

Statistics Canada. (2008). *Canadian demographics at a glance*. Retrieved June 25, 2008, from
http://www.statcan.ca/english/freepub/91-003-XIE/91-003-XIE2007001.pdf

12

Marginal notes:

List all sources cited in the report.

APA style does not list email messages or interviews.

No period after URL

How Should I Submit the Report?

Follow instructions carefully. If you don't know, ask.

Pay attention to the recipient's instructions whenever you transmit any documents. If you don't, your material may not get read. Many organizations, for example, accept only job applications and résumés sent electronically. Some government RFPs define not only the format, content, and organization of vendors' responses, but also the method, date, and cutoff time of submission. The RFP might specify that the vendors' pricing description must be submitted in a separate envelope from that containing the work proposal. Proposals that do not conform to the submission specifications, like those submitted after the designated time, are not accepted.

EXPANDING A CRITICAL SKILL

Choosing a Long Report Format and Style

Many types of long reports exist in the workplace. Their formats and style vary according to purpose, audience expectations, organization, and discourse community.

Corporate annual reports are typically printed on glossy stock, filled with colour photos, charts, and graphs, and focused on information, such as financial statistics, that is important to investors. These reports may have dozens of pages, and be "perfect-bound," like a magazine or book. Other organizations choose to use fewer colours and pages, and inexpensive binding. Still other organizations put their reports online, to save money and paper.

Reports on scientific and engineering projects, like soil contamination remediation, highway repair efforts, or technology research and development, are frequently text-heavy, including jargon, but relatively light on visuals, which may be only the most technical of diagrams. They may have hundreds of pages and be bound in three-ring binders. A government report on the bereavement industry, or tax law revisions might also be dense with text. Plain covers and paper stock closer to copy bond are typical.

Text in reports may be arranged in single or multiple columns, and feature a "drop cap"—an enlarged letter at the beginning of an opening paragraph—and "pull quotes"—portions of the body text repeated and set apart graphically from the rest. Online reports routinely include "hypertext"—links to other documents—for readers.

Long reports are written more formally. They

- Use the third person (*employees, waste management services, the retail sales team, finance graduates*).

- Are impersonal: long reports avoid *I* and *you* because the data are more important than the writer; the facts are supposedly objective; in a document to multiple, even global audiences, it is not clear who "you" is.
- Avoid contractions: *they will* instead of *they'll*; *it is* instead of *it's*.

With so many possibilities, how do you decide on the appropriate format and style? Use your resources:

- Start with PAIBOC analysis.
- Review organizational models. Many organizations have a databank of reports, and generic report templates. Writers customize these for their purposes and audiences.
- Many organizations publish reports online, and some public and postsecondary libraries keep copies of government and annual reports. Use your research techniques to find these.
- Look at the report templates online: Microsoft Office Online provides a variety of templates (www.bdc.ca/en/business_tools/business_plan/default.htm); BDC offers templates and user guides to help writers prepare a business plan.
- Consult texts on writing reports, experts in your organization, or professional writers and graphic designers.
- Test your drafts with colleagues, and, where possible, with audiences similar to ones that will read your report.

The more specialized the report, the more likely experienced employees will write it. However, many organizations expect novice writers to participate. Use this opportunity to begin to learn a valuable transferable skill.

Language FOCUS

RFP means **request for proposal**. Many organizations will ask for proposals from companies to complete necessary work, such as the construction or repair of city roads.

Your organizational culture may have very clearly defined specifications about how to send reports to internal and external audiences. If you are don't know the expectations of your discourse community, ask a colleague or your supervisor.

MODULE SUMMARY

- Long formal reports can include any of a Transmittal, Executive Summary, Table of Contents with List of Illustrations, the Body itself, and Conclusions and Recommendations.

- Writing a long report takes time and organization:
  - Create a timeline for parts of the report.
  - Write the report in sections, starting with the Body, where you present facts that prove your position.
  - Jot down potential headings, both for the whole report, and for the sections in the Body ("The Problem," "The Results," "The Solution," "The Benefits").
  - When you revise the report, reshape the headings into **talking heads**, to preview the subsequent content for the reader, and contribute to clarity and understanding.
  - As you research and analyze your information, prepare an appendix summarizing your sources: responses to questionnaires, your figures and tables, and a complete list of references.

- All reports should include an overview, to preview the report's contents for the reader. In a formal report, this overview is called a **Summary**, or **Executive Summary**. The Summary
  - Sums up the whole report, and includes conclusions and recommendations
  - Goes first, on a separate page

- Is about one-tenth the length of the whole report

- The **Introduction** of the report contains a statement of Purpose and Scope. The **Purpose** statement includes the situation the report addresses, the investigations it summarizes, and the rhetorical purposes (to explain, to describe, to recommend). The **Scope** statement identifies the topics the report covers. The Introduction may also include **Limitations**, factors or problems that limit the scope of the report, or the validity of the recommendations; **Assumptions**, statements whose truth you assume, and which you use to prove your ideas; and **Methods**, explaining how you gathered your data.

- A **Background** or **History** section is for audiences that may need to read the report years later.

- **Conclusions** summarize the main ideas you make in the report body. All reports offer Conclusions. **Recommendations** are action items that would solve, or partially solve the problem.

- Include any supporting material your reader will need in the appendix of the report. The report ends with your sources. Business uses APA, and academia uses MLA (Module 19).

- Your choice of report format, style, and method of submission are as important as your content. Pay attention to the rules and norms of your discourse community. If you are unsure, ask someone who knows.

ASSIGNMENTS FOR MODULE 22

Questions for Critical Thinking

22.1 How do you decide on the length and formality of a report?

22.2 How do you decide what headings to use in the body of the report?

22.3 How do you decide how much background information to provide in a report?

22.4 How much evidence do you need to provide for each recommendation you make?

Exercises and Problems

As your instructor directs,

Submit the following documents for Problems 22.5 through 22.8:

a. The approved proposal

b. Two copies of the report, including

- Cover
- Letter or Memo of Transmittal
- Title Page
- Table of Contents
- List of Illustrations
- Executive Summary
- Body (Introduction, all information). Your instructor may specify a minimum length, a minimum number or kind of sources, and a minimum number of visuals.
- Conclusions and Recommendations
- Appendices, if useful or relevant
- References or Works Cited

c. Your notes and rough drafts

22.5   Writing a Feasibility Study

Write an individual or group report evaluating the feasibility of a plan or idea. Explain your criteria clearly, evaluate each alternative, and recommend the best course of action. Possible topics include the following:

1. What is the feasibility of your business idea? Write a business plan evaluating the opportunity for the startup of an entrepreneurial business.
2. What is the feasibility of the electric car for common use in your province?
3. What is the feasibility of high-speed commuter trains in your province? If such trains already exist, what is the feasibility of increasing their use, so that they become the primary mode of transportation throughout your province?
4. What is the feasibility of starting a blog for students in your program, or for employees in your organization?
5. What is the feasibility of starting a mentorship affiliation in your organization, or in your college/university program? What businesses or nonprofits might you affiliate with? What benefits would the mentors enjoy?
6. With your instructor's permission, choose your own topic.

22.6   Writing a Research Report

Write an individual or group library research report. Possible topics include the value of Wikipedia, social networking, your province's healthcare policies, your city's strategies for providing homeless shelters, Canadian copyright or defamation legislation related to Internet material, your province's small business support resources, or your province's welfare strategies. Or, with your professor's permission, choose your own topic.

Start the project by finding the most current information available online and in print.

22.7   Writing a Recommendation Report

Write an individual or group recommendation report. Possible topics are the following:

1. *Recommending courses.* What skills are in demand in your community? What courses at what levels should the local college or university offer? What accreditation courses should graduates in your programs pursue to increase their marketability and salaries?
2. *Improving sales and profits.* Recommend ways a small business in your community can increase sales and profits. Focus on one or more of the following: the products or services it offers, its advertising, its decor, its location, its accounting methods, its cash management, or any other aspect that may be keeping the company from achieving its potential. Address your report to the owner of the business.
3. *Increasing student involvement.* How might an organization on campus persuade more of the students who are eligible to join or to become active in its programs? Do students know that it exists? Is it offering programs that interest students? Is it retaining current members? What changes should the organization make? Address your report to the officers of the organization.
4. *Evaluating a potential employer.* What training is available to new employees? How soon is the average entry-level person promoted? How much travel and weekend work are expected? Is there a "busy season," or is the workload consistent year-round? What fringe benefits are offered? What is the corporate culture? Is the climate open, friendly, and encouraging? Nondiscriminatory? How economically strong is the company? How is it affected by current economic, demographic, and political trends?

Address your report to your college or university placement office; recommend whether the placement office should encourage students to work at this company.

Or, with your professor's permission, choose your own topic. Start the project by finding the most current information available online and in print.

22.8 Writing Up a Survey

Survey two groups of people on a topic that interests you. (For help in creating your survey, go to http://ezinearticles.com/?20-Top-Tips-To-Writing-Effective-Surveys&id=2622.) Possible groups are men and women, people in business and in English programs, younger and older students, students and non-students. Non-random samples are acceptable.

As your instructor directs,

a. Survey 40 to 50 people.
b. Team up with your classmates. Survey 50 to 80 people if your group has two members, 75 to 120 people if it has three members, 100 to 150 people if it has four members, and 125 to 200 people if it has five members.
c. Keep a journal during your group meetings and submit it to your instructor.
d. Write a memo to your instructor. (See Module 15 on working and writing in groups.)

As you conduct your survey, make careful notes about what you do so that you can use this information when you write your report. If you work with a group, record who does what. Use a memo format. Your subject line should be clear. Omit unnecessary words such as "Survey of." Your first paragraph serves as an introduction, but it needs no heading. The rest of the body of your memo might be divided into four sections with the following headings: Purpose, Procedure, Results, and Discussion. Alternatively, make your survey report more interesting by using talking headings.

In your first paragraph, briefly summarize (not necessarily in this order) who conducted the experiment or survey, when it was conducted, where it was conducted, who the subjects were, what your purpose was, and what you found out.

In your **Purpose** section, explain why you conducted the survey. What were you trying to learn? Why did this subject seem interesting or important?

In your **Procedure** section, describe in detail exactly what you did.

In your **Results** section, first tell whether your results supported your hypothesis. Use both visuals and words to explain what your numbers show. (See Module 23 on how to design visuals.) Process your raw data in a way that will be useful to your reader.

In your **Discussion** section, evaluate your survey and discuss the implications of your results. Consider these questions:

1. Do you think a scientifically valid survey would have produced the same results? Why or why not?
2. Were there any sources of bias either in the way the questions were phrased or in the way the subjects were chosen? If you were running the survey again, what changes would you make to eliminate or reduce these sources of bias?
3. Do you think your subjects answered honestly and completely? What factors may have intruded? Is the fact that you did or didn't know them, or that they were or weren't of the same sex, relevant?
4. What causes the phenomenon your results reveal? If several causes together account for the phenomenon, or if it is impossible to be sure of the cause, admit this. Identify possible causes and assess the likelihood of each.
5. What action should the reader take?

The discussion section gives you the opportunity to analyze the significance of your survey. Its insight and originality lift the otherwise well-written memo from the ranks of the merely satisfactory to the ranks of the above average and the excellent.

22.9 Writing Summaries

Go to www.nrtee-trnee.com/eng/news-media/events/other/20th-anniversary/20th-anniversary-forum-guide-eng.pdf, to view the government report titled *Securing Canada's Future in a Climate-Changing World*.

After reading the Introduction, compose an Executive Summary for any one of the reports, *Securing Canada's Ecosystems* (pp. 9–12), *Securing Canada's Energy Economy* (pp. 13–16), or *Securing Canada's Arctic Environment* (pp. 17–19).

As your instructor directs,

1. Form a team with two other students.
2. Read and discuss your versions of the Executive Summary.
3. Together, rewrite and revise to create your team's version of the Executive Summary.
4. Hand in for grading.

POLISHING YOUR PROSE

Improving Paragraphs

Good paragraphs demonstrate unity, detail, and variety. The following paragraph from a sales letter illustrates these three qualities:

> The best reason to consider a Schroen Heat Pump is its low cost. Schroen Heat Pumps cost 25 percent less than the cheapest competitor's. Moreover, unlike the competition, the Schroen Heat Pump will pay for itself in less than a year in energy savings. That's just 12 months. All this value comes with a 10-year unlimited warranty—if anything goes wrong, we'll repair or replace the pump at no cost to you. That means no expensive repair bills and no dollars out of your pocket.

A paragraph is **unified** when all its sentences focus on a single central idea. As long as a paragraph is about just one idea, a topic sentence expressing that idea is not required. However, using a topic sentence makes it easier for the reader to skim the document. (Essays use a *thesis statement* for the central idea of the entire document.) Sentences throughout the paragraph should support the topic sentence or offer relevant examples.

Transitions connect ideas from one point to another. Common transitions are *and, also, first, second, third, in addition, likewise, similarly, for example* (e.g.), *for instance, indeed, to illustrate, namely, specifically, in contrast,* and *on the other hand.*

Detail makes your points clearer and more vivid. Good details express clearly and completely what you mean. Use concrete words, especially strong nouns, verbs, adjectives, and adverbs that paint a picture in the reader's mind and say what you mean. Avoid unnecessary repetition.

Variety is expressed first in sentence length and patterns and second in the number of sentences in each paragraph. Most sentences in business writing should be 14 to 20 words, but an occasional longer or very short sentence gives punch to your writing.

The basic pattern for sentences is subject+verb+object (SVO): *Our building supervisor sent the forms.* Vary the SVO pattern by changing the order, using transitions and clauses, and combining sentences.

Also vary paragraph length. First and last paragraphs can be quite short. Body paragraphs will be longer. Whenever a paragraph runs eight typed lines or more, think about dividing it into two paragraphs.

Exercises

Rewrite the following paragraphs to improve unity, detail, and variety.

1. I used to work for McCandless Realty as a receptionist. My many experiences in the accounting field make me an ideal candidate for a position as senior administrative assistant with Graham, Chang, and Associates. I answered phones at McCandless. I typed there. I worked at Dufresne Plastics as a secretary. At McCandless, I also handled payroll. There are a lot of reasons why I liked Dufresne. These included the opportunity for training in data entry and Microsoft Word. I learned to type 70 WPM with no mistakes.

2. Mr. Walter Pruitt visited our business communication class yesterday. He spoke about the importance of co-op placements. Mr. Pruitt works for Global Energy. Global Energy provides network and service management to companies around the world. Mr. Pruitt, who works for Global Energy, told us he got his first job because of a co-op. A co-op is an opportunity for students to work with a company for a period of time to get business experience. Mr. Pruitt went to university and worked at a co-op placement for Global Energy. At first, Global Energy only wanted him to work for 10 weeks. Mr. Pruitt did such a good job, they kept him on another 10 weeks and another. Mr. Pruitt was offered a job by Global Energy when he graduated.

Check your answers to the odd-numbered exercise on page 553.

Using Visuals

Learning Objectives

After reading and applying the information in Module 23, you'll be able to demonstrate

Knowledge of

- How visuals tell stories
- How to choose appropriate visuals

Skills to

- Choose visuals to tell a story
- Match the visual to your story
- Choose ethical visuals
- Use visuals in your documents and presentations

Employability Skills 2000+ Checklist

In this module, the key skills from the Conference Board of Canada's Employability Skills 2000+ are

Communicate

○ read and understand information presented in a variety of forms (e.g., words, graphs, charts, diagrams)

○ share information using a range of information and communications technologies (e.g., voice, email, computers)

○ use relevant scientific, technological, and mathematical knowledge and skills to explain or clarify ideas

Manage Information

○ locate, gather, and organize information using appropriate technology and information systems

○ access, analyze, and apply knowledge and skills from a variety of disciplines (e.g., the arts, languages, science, technology, mathematics, social sciences, and the humanities)

Think & Solve Problems

○ assess situations and identify problems

○ recognize the human, interpersonal, technical, scientific, and mathematical dimensions of a problem

○ readily use science, technology, and mathematics as ways to think, gain and share knowledge, solve problems, and make decisions

Participate in Projects & Tasks

○ plan, design, or carry out a project or task from start to finish with well-defined objectives and outcomes

○ work to agreed quality standards and specifications

○ adapt to changing requirements and information

Pictures tell stories: charts and graphs make numbers meaningful; mall maps tell us where we are; your graduation photos document a rite of passage. Using visuals and text together "as tools to increase understanding" can "get our message across with great efficiency."[1]

Why Use Visuals?

Appropriate, attractive visuals tell your story immediately: they are faster and easier to understand, and more memorable.

Visuals condense and clarify data; visuals are a reader-friendly way to communicate your points.

Formal visuals are divided into tables and figures. **Tables** are numbers or words arranged in rows and columns; **figures** are everything else. In a document, formal visuals have both numbers and titles, such as "Figure 1. The Falling Cost of Computer Memory, 2004–2010."

In an oral presentation, the title is usually used without the number: "The Falling Cost of Computer Memory, 2004–2010." The title puts the story in context, indicating what your audience should look for in the visual, and why it is important. Informal or spot visuals are inserted directly into the text; they do not have numbers or titles.

In your rough draft, use visuals

- *To see that ideas are presented completely.* A table, for example, can show you whether you've included all the items in a comparison.
- *To find relationships.* For example, charting sales on a map may show that the sales representatives who made their quotas all have territories on the west coast or in the Atlantic provinces. Is the product one that appeals to coastal lifestyles? Is advertising reaching the coasts but not the prairie provinces, Ontario, or Quebec? Even if you don't use the visual in your final document, creating the map may lead you to questions you wouldn't otherwise ask.

In the final presentation or document, use visuals

- *To make points vivid.* Readers skim memos and reports; a visual catches the eye. The brain processes visuals immediately. Understanding words—written or oral—takes more time.
- *To emphasize material* that might be skipped if it were buried in a paragraph.
- *To present material more compactly and with less repetition* than words alone can.

The number and type of visuals you need depend on your purposes, your information, and the audience. You'll use more visuals when you want to show relationships and to persuade, when the information is complex or contains extensive numerical data, and when the audience values visuals.

Your visual is only as good as the underlying data. Check to be sure that your data come from a reliable source (Module 18).

FIGURE 23.1   PAIBOC Questions for Analysis

P   What are your **purposes** in communicating with visuals? Why are you using illustrations? Your purposes come from you, your organization, and the information you intend to convey.

A   Who is your **audience**? Who will read your message? What do they need to know? How will they use your visuals? Will they use them to follow instructions? to understand directions? to assemble something? to understand how a machine, a department or a process works? to see the future if they act a certain way now? What graphics/illustrations would most appeal to your audience? Why? What visuals would maximize your audience's understanding? Why?

I   What **information** must your visual include? What visual will cause your readers to think or do as you want them to? What images could tell your story dramatically and immediately? What numerical or quantitative data are you representing? What visuals would best convey that information?

B   What reasons or reader **benefits** support your position? What visuals would emphasize those benefits?

O   What audience **objections** do you anticipate? How can you use visuals to deemphasize or overcome audience objections?

C   What **context** will affect reader response? Consider your relationship to your readers, organizational culture, the economy, recent organizational developments, current morale, and the time of year. When choosing your illustrations, consider also your audience demographic, cultural values, and norms.

Employability Skills

What Are Stories, and How Do I Find Them?

A story is something that is happening or will happen. Look for relationships, patterns, and changes.

Stories are made up of symbols—words, images, colours, and icons—that enable us to create and translate meaning. The garbage can icon by the words "Recycle Bin" translate the computer's binary code into a story about what happens when we hit Delete. An organization's brand tells the story of its purposes and values.

Every visual should tell a story that is meaningful to your audience. Use the title of the visual to give your story context and emphasis.

Not a story: Asian Exports, 2007–2010

Possible stories: China and India Rule Export Trade
                        Chinese Garlic Exports Flood Canadian Market

Stories that tell us what we already know are rarely interesting. Instead, good stories do at least one of several things:

- Support a hunch you have
- Surprise or challenge so-called common knowledge
- Show trends or changes you didn't know existed
- Have commercial, cultural, or social significance
- Provide information needed for action
- Have personal relevance to you and the audience

You can find stories in three ways:

1. *Focus on a topic* (starting salaries, alternative music choices, Twitter demographics).
2. *Simplify the data* on that topic and convert the numbers to simple, easy-to-understand units.
3. *Look for relationships and changes.* For example, compare two or more groups: Do men and women have the same attitudes? Look for changes over time. Look for items that can be seen as part of the same group. For example, to find stories about Internet ads, you might group ads in the same product category—ads for cars, for food, for beverages.

When you think you have a story, test it against all the data to be sure it's accurate.

Some stories are simple straight lines: "Average Workweek," as illustrated in Figure 23.2. But other stories are more complex, with exceptions or outlying cases. Such stories will need more vivid illustration to do them justice. And sometimes the best story arises from the juxtaposition of two or more stories. In Table 23.1, *Canadian Business* magazine uses a **matrix table** to make a graphical comparison. The matrix provides a snapshot of English-speaking Canadians' satisfaction with certain industries.

Your audience should be able to *see* what the visual *says*:

> Does the chart support the title, and does the title reinforce the chart? So if I say in my title "sales have increased significantly," I want to see a trend moving up at a sharp angle. If not, if the trend parallels the baseline, it's an instant clue that the chart needs more thinking.[2]

FIGURE 23.2   **Average Workweek**

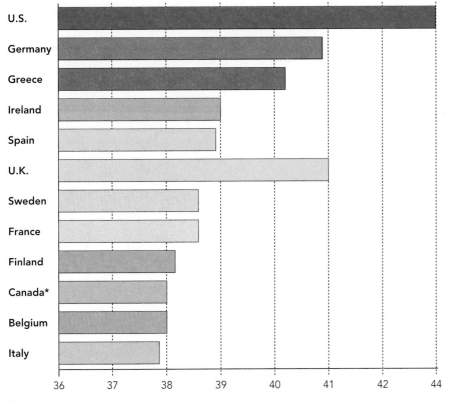

*Salaried employees.

France's lower house of parliament approved a government proposal to end the 35-hour workweek and boost employment and income.
Source: Eurostat, Statistics Canada, Bureau of Labor Statistics.

Checkpoint

The Six Components of Every Visual

1. A title that tells the story that the visual shows
2. A clear indication of what the data are
3. Clearly labelled units
4. Labels or legends identifying axes, colours, symbols, and so forth
5. The source of the data, if you created the visual from data someone else gathered and compiled
6. The source of the visual, if you reproduce a visual that someone else created

---

For optimum audience impact, use the "tell, show, tell" rule: first, *tell* your readers or listeners what they are about to see; next, *show* your audience what you promised to show them; finally, *tell* them the significance of the visual. And, of course, the visual must depict exactly what you said it would.

Almost every data set allows you to tell several stories. You must choose the story you want to tell. Dumps of uninterpreted data confuse and frustrate your audience; uninterpreted data undercut the credibility and goodwill you want to create.

TABLE 23.1   A Matrix Table Tells a Complete Story

Sector/Company	% Satisfied	% Just OK	% Unsatisfied
Customer Satisfaction Ratings			
Airlines	**32**	**30**	**38**
Air Canada	16	35	49
WestJet Airlines	89	9	1
Other	50	28	21
Banks	**46**	**30**	**25**
Bank of Montreal	38	36	26
Bank of Nova Scotia	42	37	21
Canadian Imperial Bank of Commerce	39	27	33
Credit unions	82	9	9
Royal Bank	41	35	25
TD Canada Trust	47	30	23
Other	54	21	24
Telephone companies	**53**	**31**	**16**
AT&T Canada	46	41	14
Bell Canada	54	30	16
TELUS	49	33	18
Other	60	28	13
Wireless providers	**51**	**30**	**19**
Bell Mobility	57	29	14
Fido	53	31	16
Rogers AT&T Wireless	45	31	23
TELUS Mobility	49	31	21
Other	60	18	21
Consultancies	**67**	**21**	**12**
Canada Customs and Revenue Agency	**37**	**35**	**28**
Performance over Last Year			
Airlines	19	33	48
Banks	23	50	27
Canada Customs and Revenue Agency	22	62	16
Consultancies	32	55	13
Telephone companies	25	62	13
Wireless providers	24	61	15
Will You Continue to Purchase?			
Airlines	57	26	17
Banks	57	23	20
Consultancies	60	28	12
Telephone companies	70	21	9
Wireless providers	62	23	15

Methodology: *Canadian Business* and General Content Corp. surveyed *Canadian Business*'s online readers last spring about their experiences with service providers in the banking, airline, telecom, consulting, and wireless industries. The survey received 926 valid responses, the overwhelming majority from English-speaking Canada. With a sample of this size, the results are considered accurate 19 times out of 20 within ±3.7 to ±4.5 percentage points, depending on the sector (except consultancies, which has an error margin of 8.9 points). Respondents tended to be executives or managers, with 80% of them working at businesses with fewer than 100 employees. And 74% of all respondents are involved in purchasing decisions.

Language FOCUS

The word **data** is the plural form of the Latin word *datum*, which is related to the verb "to give."

Does It Matter What Kind of Visual I Use?

Employability Skills

Yes! The visual must match the kind of story.

Visuals are not interchangeable. Use visuals that best present the data.

Whenever possible, create your own, original visuals. Use software to make charts, graphs, tables, and figures; use a digital camera to capture stories.

- Use **maps**, **diagrams**, and **graphics** to convey complex information (see Figure 23.3).
- Use images and **artwork** to reinforce themes.
- Use **tables** when the reader needs to be able to identify exact values (see Figure 23.4a).
- Use a chart or graph when you want the reader to focus on relationships.[3]
  - To compare a part to the whole, use a **pie graph** (see Figure 23.4b).
  - To compare one item to another item, or items over time, use a **bar graph** or a line graph (see Figures 23.4c and 23.4d).

Tables

Use tables only when you want the audience to focus on specific numbers.

- Round off to simplify the data (e.g., 35 percent rather than 35.27 percent; 34 000 rather than 33 942). Provide column and row totals or averages when they're relevant.
- Put the items you want readers to compare in columns rather than in rows to facilitate mental subtraction and division.
- When you have many rows, screen alternate entries or double-space after every five entries to help readers line up items accurately.

FIGURE 23.3   **A Visual That Tells the Story of Data Management**

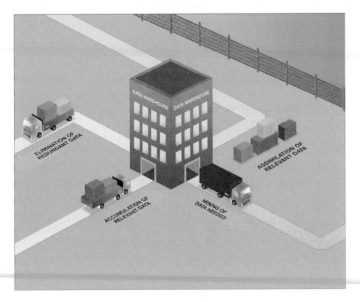

FIGURE 23.4 Choose the Visual to Fit the Story

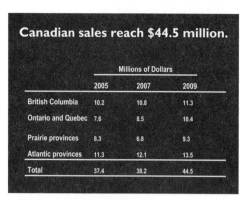

a. Tables show exact values.

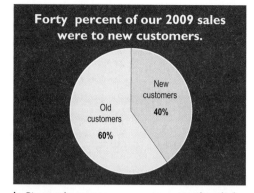

b. Pie graphs compare a component to the whole.

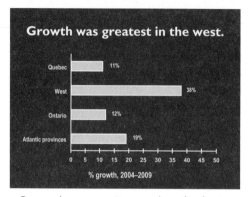

c. Bar graphs compare items or show distribution or correlation.

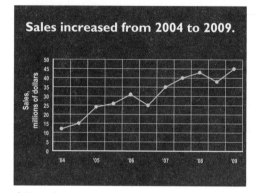

d. Line charts compare items over time or show distribution or correlation.

Pie Graphs

Graphs convey less specific information but are always more memorable.

Pie graphs force the audience to measure area. Research shows that people can judge position or length (which a bar graph uses) much more accurately than they can judge area. The data in any pie graph can be put in a bar graph.[4] Therefore, use a pie graph only when you are comparing one segment to the whole. When you are comparing one segment to another, use a bar graph, a line graph, or a map—even though the data may be expressed in percentages.

- Start at 12 o'clock with the largest percentage or the percentage you want to focus on. Go clockwise to each smaller percentage or to each percentage in some other logical order.
- Make the graph chart a perfect circle. Perspective circles distort the data.
- Limit the number of segments to five or seven. If your data have more divisions, combine the smallest or the least important into a single "miscellaneous" or "other" category.
- Label the segments outside the circle. Internal labels are hard to read.

Bar Graphs

Bar graphs are easy to interpret, because they ask people to compare distance along a common scale, which most people judge accurately. Bar graphs are useful in a variety of situations: to compare one item to another, to compare items over time, and to show correlations. Use horizontal bars when your labels are long; when the labels are short, either horizontal or vertical bars will work.

- Order the bars in a logical or chronological order.
- Put the bars close enough together to make comparisons easy.

- Label both horizontal and vertical axes.
- Put all labels inside the bars or outside them. When some labels are inside and some are outside, the labels carry the visual weight of longer bars, distorting the data.
- Make all the bars the same width.
- Use different colours for different bars only when their meanings are different: estimates as opposed to known numbers, negative as opposed to positive numbers.
- Avoid using perspective. Perspective makes the values harder to read and can make comparison difficult.

Several varieties of bar graphs exist. See Figure 23.4 for an example.

- **Grouped bar graphs** allow you to compare several aspects of each item or several items over time.
- **Segmented, subdivided, or stacked bars** sum the components of an item. It's hard to identify the values in specific segments; grouped bar charts are almost always easier to use.
- **Deviation bar graphs** identify positive and negative values, or winners and losers.
- **Paired bar graphs** show the correlation between two items.
- **Histograms or pictographs** use images to create the bars.

Line Graphs

Line graphs are also easy to interpret. Use line graphs to compare items over time, to show frequency or distribution, and to show correlations.

- Label both horizontal and vertical axes.
- When time is a variable, put it on the horizontal axis.

FIGURE 23.5   A Grouped Bar Graph Allows You to Compare Several Aspects over Time

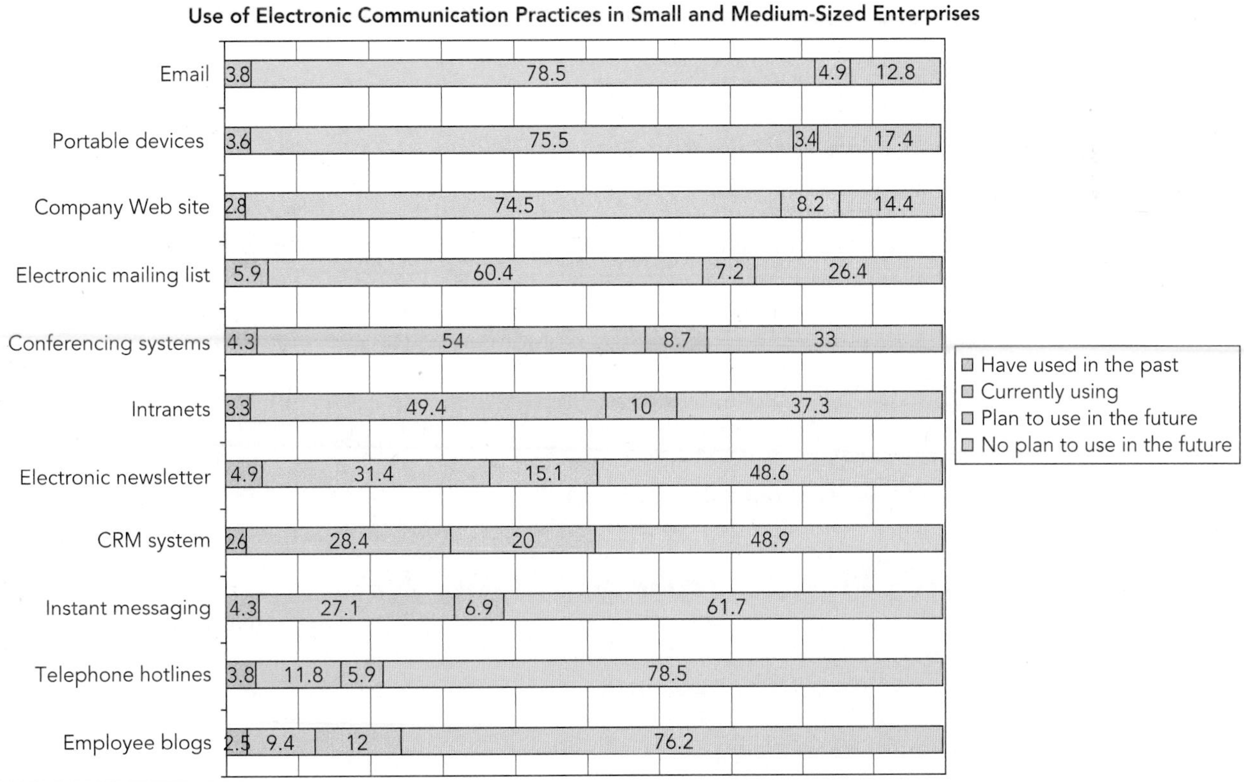

Use of Electronic Communication Practices in Small and Medium-Sized Enterprises

	Have used in the past	Currently using	Plan to use in the future	No plan to use in the future
Email	3.8	78.5	4.9	12.8
Portable devices	3.6	75.5	3.4	17.4
Company Web site	2.8	74.5	8.2	14.4
Electronic mailing list	5.9	60.4	7.2	26.4
Conferencing systems	4.3	54	8.7	33
Intranets	3.3	49.4	10	37.3
Electronic newsletter	4.9	31.4	15.1	48.6
CRM system	2.6	28.4	20	48.9
Instant messaging	4.3	27.1	6.9	61.7
Telephone hotlines	3.8	11.8	5.9	78.5
Employee blogs	2.5	9.4	12	76.2

Source: "Despite New Technology, Face-to-Face Conversations Are Still Top Form of Employee Communication in Small Businesses," IABC press release, May 22, 2008, http://news.iabc.com/index.php?s=43&item=144, retrieved September 21, 2009.

- Avoid using more than three different lines on one graph. Even three lines may be too many if they cross each other.
- Avoid using perspective. Perspective makes the values harder to read and can make comparison difficult.

Checkpoint

Tables are numbers or words arranged in rows and columns; **figures** are everything else. In a document, formal visuals have both numbers ("Figure 1") and titles. In an oral presentation, the title is usually used without the number.

What Design Conventions Should I Follow?

Tell your story effectively and ethically. Provide the context. Cite your sources.

Tell Your Story Effectively

Plan your visuals to achieve your purposes, and meet audience needs (Modules 5 and 17). The best visuals

- Use clear, simple, and relevant images
- Use metaphors and pictures that make connections and patterns obvious
- Put people in the picture: show people working well in teams; using the new software; driving further and cleaner in the hybrid
- Blend seamlessly and are balanced with the text[5]

Provide the Context

Every visual should

1. Give a title that tells the story the visual shows
2. Clearly indicate the data
3. Clearly label units
4. Provide labels or legends identifying axes, colours, symbols, and so forth
5. Give the source of the data, if you create the visual from data someone else gathered and compiled
6. Give the source of the visual, if you reproduce a visual that someone else created

Cite Your Sources   Like all intellectual property, visuals are protected by copyright. Whenever you use secondary sources, you must credit the author. Information on how to cite images correctly is available online, in style guide sites, and on your local and university and college library sites (Modules 18 and 19).

Can I Use Colour and Clip Art?

Use colour and clip art carefully.

Colour makes visuals more dramatic, but creates at least two problems. First, readers try to interpret colour, an interpretation that may not be appropriate. Second, meanings assigned to colours differ depending on the audience's culture and profession.

Connotations for colour vary from culture to culture and within cultures (Module 3). Blue suggests masculinity in North America, criminality in France, strength or fertility in Egypt, and villainy in Japan. Red is sometimes used to suggest danger or stop in North American culture; it means go in China and is associated with festivities. Yellow suggests caution or cowardice in North America, prosperity in Egypt, grace in Japan, and femininity in many parts of the world.[6]

Corporate, national, or professional associations may supersede these general cultural associations. Some people associate blue with IBM or Hewlett-Packard and red with Coca-Cola, communism, or Japan. People in specific professions learn other meanings for colours. Blue suggests *reliability* to financial managers, *water* or coldness to engineers, and *death* to healthcare professionals. Red means *losing money* to financial managers, *danger* to engineers, but *healthy* to healthcare professionals. Green usually means *safe* to engineers, but *infected* to healthcare professionals.[7]

These various associations suggest that colour is safest with a homogenous audience that you know well. In an increasingly multicultural workforce, colour may send signals you do not intend.

When you do use colour in visuals, experts suggest the following guidelines:[8]

- Use no more than five colours when colours have meanings.
- Use glossy paper to make colours more vivid.
- Be aware that colours always look brighter on a computer screen than on paper, because the screen sends out light.

In any visual, use as little shading and as few lines as are necessary for clarity. Don't clutter up the visual with extra marks. When you design black-and-white graphs, use shades of grey rather than stripes, wavy lines, and checks to indicate different segments or items.

EXPANDING A CRITICAL SKILL

Integrating Visuals into Your Text

Refer to every visual in your text. Normally give the table or figure number in the text but not the title. Put the visual as soon after your reference as space and page design permit. If the visual must go on another page, tell the reader where to find it:

As Figure 3 shows (p. 10), …

(See Table 2 on page 3.)

Summarize the main point of a visual before you present the visual itself. Then when readers get to it, they'll see it as confirmation of your point.

Weak: Listed below are the results.

Better: As Figure 4 shows, sales doubled in the last decade.

How much discussion a visual needs depends on the audience, the complexity of the visual, and the importance of the point it makes. If the material is new to the audience, you'll need a fuller explanation than if similar material is presented to this audience every week or month. Help the reader find key data points in complex visuals. If the point is important, discuss its implications in some detail.

In contrast, one sentence about a visual may be enough when the audience is already familiar with the topic and the data, when the visual is simple and well designed, and when the information in the visual is a minor part of your proof.

When you discuss visuals, spell out numbers that fall at the beginning of a sentence. If spelling out the number or year is cumbersome, revise the sentence so that it does not begin with a number.

Correct: Forty-five percent of the cost goes to pay wages and salaries.

Correct: The year 1992 marked the official beginning of the European Economic Community.

Clip Art

In memos and reports, resist the temptation to make your visual "artistic" by turning it into a picture or adding clip art. **Clip art** is predrawn images that you can import into your newsletter, sign, or graph. A small drawing of a car in the corner of a line graph showing the number of kilometres driven might be acceptable in an oral presentation or a newsletter, but it is out of place in a written report. Indeed, because of its blandness and ubiquity, clip art can diminish and trivialize content.

Statistician and visual design expert Edward Tufte uses the term **chartjunk** for visual details—"the encoded legends, the meaningless color[,] the logo-type branding"—that at best are irrelevant to the visual, and at worst mislead the reader.[9] Turning a line graph into a highway to show kilometres driven makes it harder to read: it's hard to separate the data line from lines that are merely decorative.

If you use clip art, do so ethically: make it relevant to your content; be sensitive to your audience's pluralistic interpretations; be sure that the images of people show a good mix of both sexes, various races and ages, and various physical conditions (Module 3).

What Else Do I Need to Check For?

Be sure that the visual is accurate and ethical.

Always double-check your visuals to be sure that the information is accurate. Be aware, however, that many visuals have accurate labels but misleading visual shapes. Visuals communicate quickly; audiences remember the shape, not the labels. If the reader has to study the labels to get the right picture, the visual is unethical even if the labels are accurate.

Figure 23.6 is distorted by chartjunk and dimensionality. In an effort to make the visual interesting, the artist used a picture of a young man (presumably an engineer) rather than simple bars. By using a photograph rather than a bar, the graph implies that all engineers are young, nerdy-looking white men. Women, people of colour, and men of other appearances are excluded. The photograph also makes it difficult to compare the numbers. The number represented by the tallest figure is not quite five times as great as the number represented by the shortest figure, yet the tallest figure takes up twelve times as much space and appears even bigger than that. Two-dimensional figures distort data by multiplying the apparent value by the width as well as by the height—four times for every doubling in value. Perspective graphs are especially hard for readers to interpret—avoid them.[10]

People manipulate images for a variety of reasons, some artistic, many commercial. Only the informed person qualifies for citizenship in the global marketplace. Be prepared to question the validity of all data; your personal and professional well-being depend on these critical thinking skills.

Even simple bar and line graphs may be misleading if part of the **scale** is missing, or **truncated**. Truncated graphs are most acceptable when the audience knows the basic data set well. For example, graphs of the stock market almost never start at zero; they are routinely truncated. This omission is acceptable for audiences who follow the market closely.

Data can also be distorted when the context is omitted. For example, a drop may be part of a regular cycle, a correction after an atypical increase, or a permanent drop to a new, lower plateau.

You can do several things to make your visuals more accurate:

- Differentiate between actual and estimated or projected values.
- When you must truncate a scale, do so clearly with a break in the bars or in the background.

FIGURE 23.6   **Chartjunk and Dimensions Distort Data**

How much is that engineer in the window?

Here's how much an employee in Silicon Valley was worth over the past year, determined by dividing the value of a sample acquisition by the number of employees acquired.

$5.6 million

$1.9 million

$1.3 million

Nov. 2000   **July 2001**   **Nov. 2001**

GETTY IMAGES (3)

- Avoid perspective and three-dimensional graphs.
- Avoid combining graphs with different scales.
- Use images of people carefully in histograms to avoid sexist, racist, or other exclusionary visual statements.

Can I Use the Same Visual in My Document and in My Presentation?

Employability Skills 2000+

Use it in both only if the table or graph is simple.

For presentations, simplify paper visuals. To simplify a complex table, cut some information, round off the data even more, or present the material in a chart rather than in a table.

Visuals for presentations should have titles but don't need figure numbers. Know where each visual is so that you can return to one if someone asks about it during the question period. Use clip art only if it's relevant, and does not obscure the story you're telling with the visual.

MODULE SUMMARY

- Appropriate, attractive visuals tell stories concisely and immediately: visuals are faster and easier to understand, and more memorable.

- In your rough draft, use visuals to see that ideas are presented completely, and to identify patterns and relationships. In your reports and presentations, use visuals to make points vivid, to emphasize material the audience might overlook, and to present material more efficiently and more compactly than words alone can do.

- Use more visuals when you want to show relationships, when the information is complex, or contains extensive numerical data, and when the audience values visuals.

- Pick data to tell a story, to make your point. To find stories, look for relationships and changes. Writers and illustrators create worthy stories through research: they
  - Follow up on hunches
  - Find data that challenge accepted wisdom, have commercial, cultural or social significance, or indicate new trends
  - Identify information that requires immediate action, or has personal relevance for them and their audiences

- When you think you have a story, test it against all the data to be sure it's accurate.

- Formal visuals are divided into tables and figures. Tables are numbers or words arranged in rows and columns; figures are everything else, including clip art and photographs.

- The best visual depends on the kind of data and the point you want to make with the data.

- Visuals represent a point of view; they are never neutral. And you are legally and ethically responsible for creating and using visuals that
  - Represent data accurately, both literally and by implication
  - Avoid chartjunk: decorations and details that are irrelevant or misleading
  - Give the source of the data

- Appropriate visuals are both accurate and ethical. They
  - Give a title that tells the story the visual shows
  - Clearly indicate the data
  - Clearly label units
  - Provide labels or legends identifying axes, colours, symbols, and so forth
  - Give the source of the data, if you created the visual from data someone else gathered and compiled
  - Give the source of the visual, if you reproduce a visual someone else created

ASSIGNMENTS FOR MODULE 23

Questions for Critical Thinking

23.1   Identify three specific types of reports that rely heavily on visuals.

23.2   Why and how does clip art trivialize a topic? Give a report and a presentation example.

23.3   How could you take a photograph to tell a story?

23.4   Is it ethical to use dramatic pictures and visual metaphors to motivate people to give to charity? Why or why not?

Exercises and Problems

23.5   Evaluating Text and Images

Evaluate the following student report excerpt using these criteria:

1. The visuals tell a story.
2. The writer has used the best visuals to convey the story.
3. The visuals use clear, simple, and relevant images.
4. The writer balances visuals and text.
5. The writer integrates visuals and text.
6. The visuals and text together communicate the message compactly.

The Career Centre's brochures and information sheets are helpful for students.

	Total		Male		Female	
	Number	Percentage	Number	Percentage	Number	Percentage
Agree strongly	25	25%	14	28%	11	22%
Agree somewhat	56	56%	27	54%	29	58%
Disagree somewhat	11	11%	5	10%	6	12%
Disagree strongly	8	8%	4	8%	4	8%
Total	100	100%	50	100%	50	100%

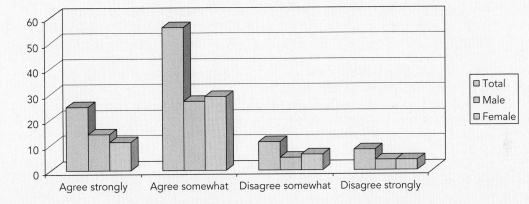

When asked to indicate if they felt that the Career Centre's brochures and information sheets are helpful for students, 56 percent of respondents indicated that they agreed somewhat with this statement; of these respondents 27 were male and 29 female. Twenty-five percent of respondents indicated that they agreed strongly that the Career Centre's brochures and information sheets are helpful for students; of these respondents 14 were male and 11 female. Eleven percent of respondents indicated that they somewhat disagreed that the Career Centre's brochures and information sheets are helpful for students; of these respondents 5 were male and 6 female. Eight percent of respondents indicated that they strongly disagreed that the Career Centre's brochures and information sheets are helpful for students; of these respondents 4 were male and 4 female. This data suggests that the large majority of respondents feel that the Career Centre's brochures and information sheets are helpful for students, and that the same number of males and of females feel this way.

How likely are you to use the Career Centre in the future?

	Total		Male		Female	
	Number	Percentage	Number	Percentage	Number	Percentage
Very likely	37	37%	18	36%	19	38%
Somewhat likely	55	55%	29	58%	26	52%
Not likely	8	8%	3	6%	5	10%
Total	100	100%	50	100%	50	100%

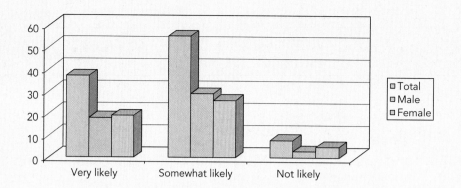

When asked to indicate how likely they are to use the Career Centre in the future, 55 percent of respondents indicated that they are somewhat likely to use the Career Centre in the future; of these respondents 29 were male and 26 female. Thirty-seven percent of respondents indicated that they will be very likely to use the Career Centre in the future; of these respondents 18 were male and 19 female. Eight percent of respondents indicated that they will not likely use the Career Centre in the future; of these respondents 3 were male and 5 female. This data suggests that most students are likely to use the Career Centre in the future, and that males and females are almost equally likely to use the Career Centre in the future.

23.6   Matching Visuals with Stories

What visual(s) would make it easiest to see each of the following stories?

1. Canada buys 35 percent of U.S. exports.
2. Undergraduate enrolment rises, but graduate enrolment declines.

3. Population growth will be greatest in southwestern Ontario, in Montreal and its suburbs, and in Mahone Bay, Nova Scotia.
4. Companies with fewer than 200 employees created a larger percentage of new jobs than did companies with more than 5000 employees.
5. Canada's population is aging.

23.7   Evaluating Visuals

Evaluate each of the following visuals using these questions:

- Is the visual's message clear?
- Is it the right visual for the story?
- Is the visual designed appropriately? Is colour, if any, used appropriately?
- Is the visual free from chartjunk?
- Does the visual distort data or mislead the reader in any way?

1. Corruption Perceptions Index

Consistently high corruption in low-income countries amounts to an "ongoing humanitarian disaster" against a backdrop of continued corporate scandal with wealthy countries backsliding too.

Source: Transparency International, "2008 Corruption Perceptions Index," 2008, http://www.transparency.org/news_room/in_focus/2008/cpi2008, retrieved January 24, 2009.

2.

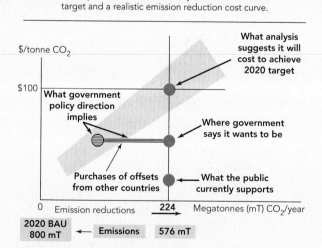

Governments consistently underestimate the cost of reducing GHG emissions, and Canadians have unrealistic ideas about how much they will have to pay for emission reductions. The result has been Canada's dismal failure to achieve any targets set to date.

Source: Rick Hyndman, "The Cost of Carbon," *Alternatives Journal* 35(1) (2009): 31.

3.

How My Time Will Be Used

17.95% or 7 hours

30.77% or 12 hours

12.82% or 5 hours

10.26% or 4 hours

15.38% or 6 hours

5.13% or 2 hours

7.69% or 3 hours

- ■ Gathering info
- ▨ Analyzing info
- ▨ Preparing progress report
- ☐ Organizing info
- ▨ Writing draft
- ■ Revising, editing draft
- ☐ Typing, editing report

4.

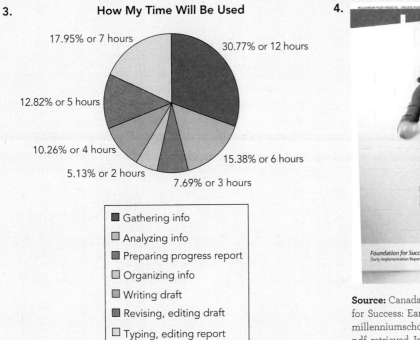

Source: Canada Millennium Scholarship Foundation, "Foundations for Success: Early Implementation Report," 2008, p. 1, http://www. millenniumscholarships.ca/images/Publications/090113_FFS_EIR. pdf, retrieved January 20, 2009.

5.

Median Earnings* and Employment for Full-Year, Full-Time Earners, All Occupations, Both Sexes, for Canada, Provinces, and Territories

	Median Earnings, Full-Year, Full-Time Earners**		Employment, Full-Year, Full-Time Earners		
Geographic Name	**2005**	**2000**	**% Change**	**2005**	**2000**
Canada	**$41,401**	**$40,443**	**2.4%**	**9,275,765**	**8,685,225**
Northwest Territories	$60,119	$56,122	7.1%	13,845	11,540
Nunavut	$58,088	$50,542	14.9%	6,520	5,085
Yukon Territory	$49,787	$47,611	4.6%	9,995	8,620
Ontario	$44,748	$44,440	0.7%	3,690,665	3,527,040
Alberta	$43,964	$40,782	7.8%	1,067,890	936,180
British Columbia	$42,230	$43,715	−3.4%	1,113,370	1,024,235
Quebec	$37,722	$37,836	−0.3%	2,136,700	1,997,110
Newfoundland and Labrador	$37,429	$36,079	3.7%	111,580	104,920
Nova Scotia	$36,917	$36,165	2.1%	255,050	234,950
Manitoba	$36,692	$35,425	3.6%	348,340	337,100
Saskatchewan	$35,948	$33,785	6.4%	286,895	276,415
New Brunswick	$35,288	$34,763	1.5%	198,770	187,875
Prince Edward Island	$34,140	$33,561	1.7%	36,135	34,135

*Medians are not available for counts less than 250.

**Earnings are in 2005 constant dollars.

Source: Statistics Canada, "Median Earnings and Employment for Full-Year, Full-Time Earners, All Occupations, Both Sexes, for Canada, Provinces and Territories—20% Sample Data" (table), 2008, Income and Earnings Highlight Tables, 2006 Census, Catalogue No. 97-563-XWE2006002 (Ottawa: Released May 1, 2008), http://www12.statcan.ca/english/census06/data/highlights/Earnings/Table801.cfm?Lang=E&T=801&GH= 4&SC=1&S=1&O=D, retrieved January 25, 2009.

23.8   Interpreting Data

As your instructor directs,

a. Identify at least four stories in one or more of the following data sets.

b. Create visuals for three of the stories.

c. Write a memo to your instructor explaining why you chose these stories and why you chose these visuals to display them.

d. Write a short report to some group that might be interested in your findings, presenting your visuals as part of the report. Possible groups include career counsellors, financial advisors, radio stations, advertising agencies, and local restaurants.

e. Brainstorm additional stories you could tell with additional data. Specify the kind of data you would need.

1.

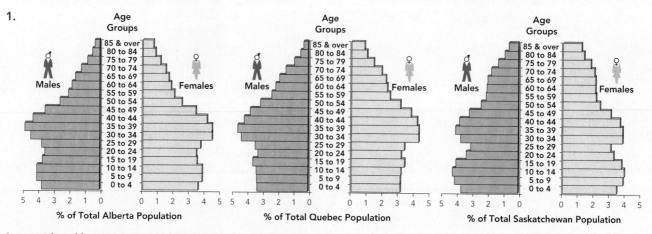

% of Total Alberta Population   % of Total Quebec Population   % of Total Saskatchewan Population

Source: Adapted from Statistics Canada website, 2001 Census of population pyramid by gender http://www12.statcan.ca/english/census01/products/analytic/companion/age/provpymds.cfm

2. **Labour Force Characteristics. Seasonally Adjusted, by Province (monthly) (Newfoundland and Labrador, Prince Edward Island, Nova Scotia, New Brunswick)**

	June 2009	July 2009	June 2009 to July 2009	July 2008 to July 2009	June 2009 to July 2009	July 2008 to July 2009
			(thousand)		(%)	
Canada						
Population	27,292.3	**27,326.0**	33.7	383.2	0.1	1.4
Labour force	18,416.7	**18,363.2**	–53.5	169.3	–0.3	0.9
Employment	16,824.8	**16,780.3**	–44.5	–302.1	–0.3	–1.8
Unemployment	1,591.9	**1,583.0**	–8.9	471.5	–0.6	42.4
Participation rate (%)	67.5	**67.2**	–0.3	–0.3	—	—
Unemployment rate (%)	8.6	**8.6**	0.0	2.5	—	—
Employment rate (%)	61.6	**61.4**	–0.2	–2.0	—	—
N.L.						
Population	428.5	**428.8**	0.3	2.6	0.1	0.6
Labour force	254.6	**256.0**	1.4	3.4	0.5	1.3
Employment	215.0	**212.2**	–2.8	–6.2	–1.3	–2.8
Unemployment	39.6	**43.8**	4.2	9.6	10.6	28.1
Participation rate (%)	59.4	**59.7**	0.3	0.4	—	—
Unemployment rate (%)	15.6	**17.1**	1.5	3.6	—	—
Employment rate (%)	50.2	**49.5**	–0.7	–1.7	—	—

P.E.I.

Population	116.0	**116.2**	0.2	1.6	0.2	1.4
Labour force	78.9	**78.9**	0.0	0.8	0.0	1.0
Employment	69.3	**69.2**	−0.1	−0.5	−0.1	−0.7
Unemployment	9.6	**9.7**	0.1	1.4	1.0	16.9
Participation rate (%)	68.0	**67.9**	−0.1	−0.3	—	—
Unemployment rate (%)	12.2	**12.3**	0.1	1.7	—	—
Employment rate (%)	59.7	**59.6**	−0.1	−1.2	—	—

N.S.

Population	772.2	**772.5**	0.3	3.6	0.0	0.5
Labour force	500.0	**496.4**	−3.6	7.8	−0.7	1.6
Employment	452.8	**450.9**	−1.9	−4.2	−0.4	−0.9
Unemployment	47.2	**45.5**	−1.7	11.9	−3.6	35.4
Participation rate (%)	64.8	**64.3**	−0.5	0.8	—	—
Unemployment rate (%)	9.4	**9.2**	−0.2	−2.3	—	—
Employment rate (%)	58.6	**58.4**	−0.2	−0.8	—	—

N.B.

Population	621.5	**621.7**	0.2	3.4	0.0	0.5
Labour force	404.0	**402.7**	−1.3	2.9	−0.3	0.7
Employment	366.9	**364.9**	−2.0	0.0	−0.5	0.0
Unemployment	37.0	**37.8**	0.8	2.9	2.2	8.3
Participation rate (%)	65.0	**64.8**	−0.2	0.1	—	—
Unemployment rate (%)	9.2	**9.4**	0.2	0.7	—	—
Employment rate (%)	59.0	**58.7**	−0.3	−0.3	—	—

Note: Population 15 and over.
Source: Statistics Canada, CANSIM, Table 282-0087 and Catalogue No. 71-001-XIE, http://www40.statcan.gc.ca/l01/cst01/lfss01a-eng.htm, retrieved August 7, 2009.

3. Distribution and Growth of Census Families, Canada, 2001 and 2006

Census Families	2001		2006		Percentage Growth 2001 to 2006
	Number	**Percentage**	**Number**	**Percentage**	
Total	8,371,020	100.0	8,896,840	100.0	6.3
Couple families	7,059,830	84.3	7,482,775	84.1	6.0
Married	5,901,420	70.5	6,105,910	68.6	3.5
Common-law	1,158,410	13.8	1,376,865	15.5	18.9
Lone-parent families	1,311,190	15.7	1,414,060	15.9	7.8
Female parent	1,065,360	12.7	1,132,290	12.7	6.3
Male parent	245,825	2.9	281,775	3.2	14.6

Source: Statistics Canada, censuses of population, 2001 and 2006, http://www12.statcan.ca/english/census06/analysis/famhouse/tables/table1.htm, retrieved August 7, 2009.

4. Total Amount of Need-Based Aid Received (selected periods)

	Nominal Dollars				Real 2007 Dollars			
	3-Year Average 1996–97 to 1998–99	3-Year Average 2001–02 to 2003–04	2-Year Average 2005–06 to 2006–07	Most Recent Year 2006–07	3-Year Average 1996–97 to 1998–99	3-Year Average 2001–02 to 2003–04	2-Year Average 2005–06 to 2006–07	Most Recent Year 2006–07
BC	$416,095,380	$593,727,633	$627,952,704	$626,417,234	$507,026,795	$644,820,024	$635,734,838	$626,417,234
AB	$263,918,201	$359,855,456	$365,989,155	$370,026,729	$321,630,109	$390,744,376	$370,463,831	$370,026,729
SK	$108,976,376	$144,512,363	$137,082,058	$128,222,955	$132,702,345	$157,067,067	$138,886,275	$128,222,955
MB	$62,592,971	$69,830,122	$76,623,394	$77,466,357	$76,270,455	$75,870,679	$77,560,240	$77,466,357
ON	$1,587,113,212	$1,199,287,285	$1,516,904,730	$1,547,470,490	$1,936,181,252	$1,302,334,986	$1,535,279,799	$1,547,470,490
QC	$762,150,489	$662,807,442	$884,066,330	$897,989,660	$930,246,408	$719,212,786	$894,823,593	$897,989,660
NB	$122,206,038	$133,866,672	$160,042,258	$158,268,662	$149,003,196	$145,359,259	$162,042,729	$158,268,662
NS	$124,354,148	$139,131,572	$163,711,942	$162,701,583	$151,457,611	$151,152,291	$165,748,343	$162,701,583
PE	$18,834,649	$26,085,027	$26,001,487	$26,288,597	$22,944,814	$28,336,450	$26,319,385	$26,288,597
NL	$150,810,181	$97,204,794	$87,193,874	$85,897,614	$183,833,749	$105,758,471	$88,287,846	$85,897,614
Canada	$3,617,051,646	$3,426,308,367	$4,045,567,931	$4,080,749,880	$4,411,296,734	$3,720,656,389	$4,095,146,879	$4,080,749,880

Number of Student Loan Recipients

	3-Year Average 1996–97 to 1998–99	3-Year Average 2001–02 to 2003–04	2-Year Average 2005–06 to 2006–07	Most Recent Year 2006–07
BC	54,256	65,889	56,661	56,306
AB	39,548	42,518	37,884	37,884
SK	14,186	16,128	14,442	13,828
MB	9,648	9,949	9,343	9,305
ON	188,892	151,055	182,016	182,016
QC	158,416	129,704	131,809	131,809
NB	14,766	15,652	15,987	15,683
NS	18,142	16,959	16,275	16,110
PE	2,528	3,319	3,239	3,239
NL	20,435	12,754	9,750	9,640
Canada	520,818	463,926	477,405	475,820

Source: Joseph Berger and Andrew Parkin, "Ten Things You Need to Know … About Financial Support for Post-Secondary Students in Canada," Millennium Research Note #7 (Montreal: Canada Millennium Scholarship Foundation, October 2008), pp. 5–6, http://www.millenniumscholarships. ca/images/Publications/081022_Ten_Things_EN.pdf, accessed September 24, 2009.

5. **Student Enrolment in Programs Offered at Private Career Colleges**

Programs	Response	Males	Females
Trades/technical training	**7.1%**	**20.9%**	**1.8%**
Construction/other trades	2.2%	7.4%	0.2%
Aviation	1.4%	3.5%	0.5%
Driver training	1.2%	3.9%	0.1%
Automotive service/business/retail	0.4%	1.1%	0.1%
Electronics/engineering/robotics	0.2%	0.7%	—
Civil engineering technology	0.1%	0.4%	—
Other traders/technical training	1.6%	3.9%	0.6%
Health	**38.1%**	**15.8%**	**46.8%**
Health care/health services	17.9%	10.8%	20.7%
Hairdressing	7.4%	1.6%	9.7%
Beauty/esthetics/cosmetology	7.1%	0.6%	9.7%
Dental care	1.9%	0.2%	2.6%
Alternative health care (acupressure)	1.3%	1.1%	1.3%
Other health	2.5%	1.5%	2.9%
Other service	**10.0%**	**9.5%**	**10.2%**
Law and security	3.3%	4.3%	3.0%
Child & youth worker/special ed./education assistant	2.1%	0.6%	2.7%
Child care	1.7%	0.1%	2.4%
Counselling	0.7%	0.5%	0.8%
Social services/community support	0.6%	0.2%	0.7%
Other service	1.5%	3.8%	0.6%
Media/information technology	**23.6%**	**28.6%**	**21.7%**
Office business administration	13.1%	8.1%	15.3%
Computers	4.8%	10.9%	2.3%
Radio/television/film/music	3.9%	6.1%	3.0%
Desktop publishing/multimedia	0.4%	0.9%	0.2%
Journalism/photography	0.3%	0.3%	0.2%
Other media/information technology	1.1%	2.4%	0.7%
Design	**4.4%**	**7.2%**	**3.3%**
Interior decorating/design	0.9%	0.4%	1.1%
Fashion/design/merchandising	0.4%	0.1%	0.5%
Other design	2.9%	6.5%	1.6%
Other	**16.8%**	**18.0%**	**16.3%**
Performing arts	4.5%	2.7%	5.3%
Bible/theological	3.8%	6.5%	2.9%
Hospitality/tourism/travel	3.6%	2.4%	4.0%
Culinary/cook/chef	1.8%	3.5%	1.2%
Animal care	0.7%	0.1%	1.0%
General upgrading	0.7%	1.2%	0.5%
Other	1.6%	1.9%	1.5%

Notes: Numbers may not add up to 100% due to rounding.

n = 13,721 (weighted data).

Source: R. A. Malatest & Associates Ltd., *Survey of Canadian Career College Students* (Ottawa and Montreal: Human Resources and Social Development Canada and Canada Millennium Scholarship Foundation, May 24, 2007), p. 26, http://www.millenniumscholarships. ca/images/Publications/080331_Phase_I_Institutional_Survey.pdf, retrieved September 24, 2009.

23.9 Graphing Data from the Web

Find data on the Web about a topic that interests you. Sites that provide data include

- http://www.canoe.ca
- http://www.statcan.ca
- http://www.findarticles.com
- Graphic, Visualization, & Usability Center's WWW surveys: http://www.cc.gatech.edu/gvu/user_surveys/

As your instructor directs,

a. Identify at least seven stories in the data.
b. Create visuals for three of the stories.
c. Write a memo to your instructor explaining why you chose these stories and why you chose these visuals to display them.
d. Write a short report to some group that might be interested in your findings, presenting your visuals as part of the short report.
e. Print out the data and include it with a copy of your memo or report.

POLISHING YOUR PROSE

Being Concise

Being concise in business writing means using only necessary words to make your point, without sacrificing politeness or clarity. Wordy sentences may confuse or slow readers:

Wordy: All of our employees at Haddenfield and Dunne should make themselves available for a seminar meeting on the 5th of August 2010, at 10 o'clock in the morning. Please make sure you come to the conference room on the 2nd Floor of the Main Complex.

Concise: Please plan to attend a seminar at 10 A.M., August 5, 2010, in the Main Complex 2nd Floor conference room.

Being concise does not mean eliminating necessary information. Sometimes you'll have to write longer sentences to be clear.

Nor does being concise mean using short, choppy sentences.

Choppy: We have a new copier. It is in the supply room. Use it during regular hours. After 5 P.M., it will be shut down.

Concise: A new copier is available in the supply room for use before 5 P.M.

Use concrete words. Instead of vague nouns and verbs with strings of modifiers, use specifics.

Vague: The person who drops off packages talked about the subject of how much to charge.

Concrete: The delivery person discussed fees.

Avoid vague or empty modifiers. Words like *very, some, many, few, much, kind of/sort of,* and so forth, usually can be cut.

Cut redundant words or phrases. Don't say the same thing twice. *Cease and desist, first and foremost, the newest and latest, official company policy, 24 storeys tall, said out loud,* and *return back* are all redundant.

Avoid unnecessarily complex constructions. Instead of *the bid that won the contract,* use *the winning bid.*

Stick to simple verb tenses. Standard edited English prefers them. Instead of "I *have been attending* Royal Roads University" use "I *attend* Royal Roads University." Instead of "By 2011, I *will have completed my degree*" use "I *will graduate* by 2011."

Exercises

Rewrite the following sentences to make them concise.

1. It would be in your best interest to return the order form to us as quickly as possible.
2. Our official records show that you are a very responsible person.
3. The automobile that is blue belongs to the woman in charge of legal affairs.
4. The mainframe computer is located in our subterranean basement.
5. Call us on the telephone if you want to confirm your order.
6. We faxed a reproduced copy of the application on the fax machine.
7. Enclosed along with the rest of this job application letter is a list of references who can talk about my job qualifications because I used to work for them.
8. I enjoyed the presentation very much.
9. To begin with, let me start by telling you some stories about our guest of honour.
10. The guy that runs our advertising department yelled loudly across the parking lot that a delivery truck had left its two headlights on.

Check your answers to the odd-numbered exercises on page 553.

CASES FOR COMMUNICATORS

Attracting Supporters

You work for HaberNat, a not-for-profit organization committed to environmental protection. HaberNat's mandate: to generate public and corporate support (opinion and revenue) to influence businesses and governments to act more quickly and firmly on environmental concerns.

HaberNat needs inexpensive ways to communicate its message, and recruit support. The organization wants to explore the feasibility of using community and social networking sites to (1) establish and expand its presence, (2) raise Canadians' awareness of environmental issues, and (3) influence people to act individually and collectively to agitate for change.

Your manager has asked you and your colleagues to research and report on the feasibility of the idea, recommending two free sites that would attract and build grassroots supporters.

Individual Activity

As you begin your research, consider your audience and purposes. Your manager may be the originator, and one of the readers of the report. Your findings, however, must identify and analyze two sites that will appeal to a widely diverse audience: the young demographic that frequents such sites; an older, affluent audience who may visit these sites; political and environmental activists; people who know little or nothing about the environment; HaberNat employees who would be comfortable using these sites to encourage public participation.

You need to know who uses community/social networking sites, when, how and why. What age? What gender? Where do they live? What are their occupations? What, if any, social role do they play in their communities? What sites would environmentally aware people visit?

Who doesn't use these sites? Why not? What have they in common? What would encourage them to frequent such sites?

How useful are these sites? How are they beneficial? How and to whom are they detrimental? How can a potential user assess their value? What criteria exist to evaluate a site's reliability, validity or benefit? And are such criteria necessary?

What municipal/provincial legislation currently shapes users' environmentally conscious attitudes and behaviours?

How would people benefit from laws passed to protect the environment? What objections would people have to such legislation?

Where will you get the most current data? Whom will you interview/survey to get the information you need?

Group Activity

Form a group with two or three colleagues. Draft a plan outlining your research, analysis, and writing. Create a timeline for your primary and secondary research, and for analyzing, composing, revising, and editing the report.

Before you draft your survey and interview questions, consider:

- Whom can we interview? Who are the experts?
- Who is the population for a survey?
- Is our sample random, convenience, or judgment?
- What types of questions should we ask—open, closed, probes?
- How does the sample type affect our ability to generalize our findings?

As you write your questions, ask yourself

- Are the questions clear and neutral?
- Do the questions cover the information we need to know to research, analyze, and identify two appropriate sites for HaberNat's purposes?
- What assumptions do my questions make? Are these appropriate assumptions?
- Are we using branching questions where appropriate?
- Are the questions sequenced so that easier ones precede more difficult ones?

Decide on subjects for your interview(s) and your survey, and on the questions you will use. Gather and analyze your results.

Conduct your secondary research. Find relevant information on the most popular sites. Who uses these? Why? When? How often? What benefits to these sites offer? What are the drawbacks? How might HaberNat use them?

Analyze and synthesize your findings. Draw conclusions from your data. Is the idea feasible? If so, recommend two sites. If not, explain why. Brainstorm the stories your data should tell, and create visuals that best tell those stories.

Write the report, with visuals.

Job Hunting

After graduation with a B.Comm. from St. Mary's University, Joe Voltan began to pursue his dream job: a career in financial analysis and forecasting. Joe's positive attitude and experiences enable him to job search with confidence. Having worked throughout his secondary and postsecondary schooling, Joe has became adept at the process, from exploring the hidden job market to preparing a proven interview strategy. Of course, his superb interpersonal skills have contributed both to the job search itself, and to his career successes.

Joe describes his job hunting practices as a combination of preparation, personal networking, and focused follow-up.

"When looking for a job, I check the Web—workopolis.com, jobbank.ca, government sites. However, I have never found a job that way. Every job I have found came from networking: meeting people, asking friends and colleagues what they know about work available in the field I want. Job hunting has changed: many companies recruit by encouraging their employees to refer candidates."

Presently Joe works for one of Canada's five major banks.

"Prior to obtaining my current position, I was a manager at a local company. One of my employees also worked for the bank. When I told him I was interested in getting into the financial industry, he referred me though an employee database. This referral led to my first interview."

What should prospective candidates know about interviews?

"The interview process is challenging; it's very thorough, with a combination of behavioural and situational questions ('Tell me about a time when you had a serious conflict with a team member. What did you do?' 'What would you do if you had a serious conflict with a team member? How would you handle it?') Interviewers are looking for specific examples of value. You need to be very prepared, and have a strategy. I follow the STAR method: in anticipating the questions, I identify the *situation*, my *task*, my *action*, and the *result*. Also, as you move up in the company, you can anticipate more people will be involved in asking questions in the interview.

"After the interview, I always call to arrange a meeting with, or a telephone call from one of the interviewers. I ask for feedback on my answers, for specifics on

how I could improve, and most important, for information on where my answers differed from what the interviewers were looking for. I'm always trying to improve for the next possibility."

Originally hired as a financial service representative, Joe now captains his own team of FSRs, a job he found through an internal posting. Joe attributes his positive work experiences to his focus and attitude, characteristics that got him the initial position: "In a time of e-managing, we tend to rely too much on technology to deliver the message. Managers need to know that face time is the most valuable for employees. Whether I am delivering good news or bad news, I always ask the employee for a meeting to explain the situation, to try to arrive at a mutual understanding, and to agree on an action plan."

PAIBOC ANALYSIS

1. In what three ways does Joe identify his audiences' needs?

2. How does Joe decide what information to prepare for the interview?

3. How does Joe get additional information, post-interview?

4. In what specifics does the STAR strategy reflect PAIBOC analysis?

Researching Jobs

Learning Objectives

After reading and applying the information in Module 24, you'll be able to demonstrate

Knowledge of

- Job search strategies
- Information interviews
- The hidden job market
- New job interview practices

Skills to

- Begin to realistically self-assess
- Find information about employers
- Use the Internet in your job search
- Find posted jobs and explore the hidden job market
- Present your non-traditional experience positively
- Prepare for job interviews

Employability Skills 2000+ Checklist

In this module, the key skills from the Conference Board of Canada's Employability Skills 2000+ are

Communicate

○ read and understand information presented in a variety of forms (e.g., words, graphs, charts, diagrams)

○ write and speak so others pay attention and understand

○ share information using a range of information and communications technologies (e.g., voice, email, computers)

○ use relevant scientific, technological, and mathematical knowledge and skills to explain or clarify ideas

Manage Information

○ locate, gather, and organize information using appropriate technology and information systems

○ access, analyze, and apply knowledge and skills from a variety of disciplines (e.g., the arts, languages, science, technology, mathematics, social sciences, and the humanities)

Think & Solve Problems

○ assess situations and identify problems

○ recognize the human, interpersonal, technical, scientific, and mathematical dimensions of a problem

○ readily use science, technology, and mathematics as ways to think, gain and share knowledge, solve problems, and make decisions

○ check to see if a solution works, and act on opportunities for improvement

Participate in Projects & Tasks

○ plan, design, or carry out a project or task from start to finish with well-defined objectives and outcomes

○ work to agreed quality standards and specifications

○ adapt to changing requirements and information

○ continuously monitor the success of a project or task and identify ways to improve

---

Perhaps you already have a job waiting for you; perhaps your skills are in such demand that employers will seek you out. If, however, you're not sure how to secure your ideal job, the modules in this unit will help you find your way.

The first step in any job search is to analyze and identify your own abilities and interests—for, as Richard Bolles explains in his classic job-hunter's guide *What Color Is Your Parachute?*, the most successful job hunting method hasn't changed:

> Do thorough homework on yourself. Know your best skills, in order of priority. Know the fields in which you want to use those skills. Talk to people who have those kinds of jobs. Find out whether they're happy, and how they found their jobs. Then choose the places where you want to work, rather than just those places that have advertised openings. Thoroughly research these organizations before approaching them. Seek out the person who actually has the power to hire you for the job that you want. Demonstrate to that person how you can help the company with its problems. Cut no corners; take no shortcuts. That method has an 86 percent success rate.[1]

What Do I Need to Know About Myself to Job-Hunt?

Your need to realistically self-assess: identify your knowledge, skills, abilities, interests, and values.

Each person could happily do several jobs. Personality and aptitude tests can tell you what your strengths are, but they won't say, "You should be X." In preparation for the job search, and for the interview, you need to answer specific questions like these:

- What achievements have given you the most satisfaction? Why did you enjoy them?
- Would you rather have firm deadlines or a flexible schedule? Do you prefer working alone or with other people? Do you prefer specific instructions and standards for evaluation or freedom and uncertainty? How comfortable are you with pressure? How do you manage multiple deadlines? How much challenge do you want?
- Are you willing to take work home? Are you prepared to travel? How important is recognition to you? How important is money compared to having time to spend with family and friends?
- Where do you want to live? What features in terms of weather, geography, and cultural and social life do you see as ideal?
- What do you want from your work? Do you work to achieve certain purposes or values, or is work "just a way to make a living"? How important are the organization's culture and ethical standards to you?

Once you have identified in writing what is most important to you, look at the job market to see where you can find what you want. For example, your greatest interest is athletics, but you aren't good enough for the pros. Your job market analysis might suggest several alternatives. You might

- Teach sports and physical fitness as a high school coach or a corporate fitness director
- Cover sports for a newspaper, a magazine, or a TV station
- Go into management or sales for a professional sports team, a health club, or a company that sells sports equipment
- Create or manage a sports Web page

What Do I Need to Know About Companies That Might Hire Me?

You need to know as much as you can.

Organizations always have room for people who demonstrate motivation, energy, and critical thinking. Preparation through research demonstrates all these skills. Moreover, to adapt your letter and résumé to a specific organization, and to shine at the interview, you need information both about the employer and about the job itself. You can find this information free through numerous resources (see Figure 24.1).

You'll need to know

- *The jobs available.* Start your research online, at the library or the college or university career centre. Libraries' research databases provide resources for every part of your job hunt: the best local and national companies to work for (www.canadastop100.com/fp10); postings on Workopolis, Monster.ca and Working.com; municipal, provincial and national labour market, apprenticeship, and skilled trades information—even salary averages and negotiation tips.

FIGURE 24.1 **Web Job Sites Covering the Job Search Process**

Archeus WorkSearch **www.garywill.com/worksearch**	The Rockport Institute **www.rockportinstitute.com**
Career Builder **www.careerbuilder.ca**	Spherion Career Centre **www.spherion.com**
Fast Company **www.fastcompany.com/career**	WetFeet.com **http://wetfeet.com**
The Five O'Clock Club **www.fiveoclockclub.com**	Workopolis **www.workopolis.com**
Job Hunter's Bible (Dick Bolles) **www.jobhuntersbible.com**	Vault **www.vault.com**
Monster **www.monster.ca**	

Notebooks at campus placement offices often have fuller job descriptions than appear in ads. Talk to friends who have graduated recently to learn what their jobs involve. Request information interviews to learn more about opportunities that interest you.

- *The name and address of the person who should receive your cover letter and résumé.* Check the ad or the organization's Web site, or call the company. An advantage of calling is that you can find out whether your contact prefers a courtesy title (*Mr., Ms.,* or *Mrs.*).
- *What the organization does, and at least four or five facts about it.* Knowing the organization's products and services enables you to describe how your specific work will make a contribution. Understanding the organization's values, goals, market, and competition allows you to define specifically how your skills outshine other candidates'.

Useful facts include the following:

- Market share
- Competitive position
- New products, services, or promotions
- Technology or manufacturing equipment applications
- Plans for growth or downsizing
- Challenges the organization faces
- The corporate culture (Module 2)

You can find these facts on the Internet, including information about corporate culture and even anonymous statements from employees. Check blogs, professional electronic mailing lists, and electronic bulletin boards. Employers sometimes post specialized jobs online; they're always a good way to get information about the industry you hope to enter.

Industry Canada's Canadian Company Capabilities (CCC, at www.ic.gc.ca/eic/site/ccc-rec.nsf/eng/home) free, searchable database provides full data, including contact names, for over 60 000 national businesses.[2]

Canadians such as Laura Archer see the world as their workplace. Laura, born and raised in Charlottetown, trained in nursing at the University of P.E.I. After working in California, Thailand, and India, Laura joined *Médecins sans frontiers*. She now works in Africa.

TABLE 24.1   **Where to Get Addresses and Facts About Companies**

General Directories	**Dun and Bradstreet**
Directory of Corporate Affiliations	Franchise Annual: Directory
Dun's Million Dollar Directory	Hoover's Handbook of American Business
Standard & Poor's Register of Corporations, Directors, and Executives	O'Dwyer's Directory of Public Relations Firms
Thomas Register of American Manufacturers	The Rand McNally Bankers' Directory
Specialized Directories and Resource Books	Scott's Business Directory
	Standard Directory of Advertisers ("Red Book")
Accounting Firms and Practitioners	Television Factbook
Directory of Hotel and Motel Systems	Traders

The directories listed in Table 24.1 provide information such as net worth, market share, principal products, and the names of officers and directors. Ask your librarian to identify additional directories. To get specific financial data (and to see how the organization presents itself to the public), get the company's annual report on the Web (www.orderannualreports. com/?cp_code=A628&mkt_code=a0109cabs&utm_source=_bjgi9bb7bhphyv&utm_ content=cbus1&utm_medium=email). (*Note:* Only companies whose stock is publicly traded are required to issue annual reports. In this day of mergers and buyouts, many companies are owned by other companies. The parent company may be the only one to issue an annual report.)

Many company Web sites provide information about training programs and career paths for new hires. To learn about new products, plans for growth, or solutions to industry challenges, read business newspapers such as *National Post*, *The Globe and Mail*, *The Wall Street Journal*, or *Financial Post*; business magazines such as *Report on Business*, *Canadian Business*, *Strategy Magazine*, *Fortune*, *Business Week*, and *Forbes*; and trade journals. Each of these has indices listing which companies are discussed in a specific issue. A few of the trade journals available are listed in Table 24.2.

TABLE 24.2   **Examples of Trade Journals and Magazines**

Advertising Age	Canadian Musician	Financial Analysts Journal
Business to Business Magazine	Computer Dealer News	Graphic Arts Monthly
CAmagazine	Computing Canada	HR Focus
Canada Employment Weekly	Direction Informatique	Information Highways
Canadian Auto World	Essense (Canadian Federation of Chefs & Cooks)	Medical Post
Canadian Business	Farm & Country (Ontario commercial farmer trade)	Northern Miner (mining news)
The Canadian Firefighter		The Western Producer (Saskatoon)

How Should I Use Social Networking Sites?

Consider your purpose and audiences: post a specific profile, on appropriate sites, keep it updated, and nurture your contacts.

Although social networking will not replace the power of face-to-face meetings, savvy job searchers use all the tools available to reach their target audiences. Such tools include social media communications—blogging and networking sites—that now attract a diverse demographic.[3] Recruiters and employers routinely search social networking sites for likely candidates.

Career coach professionals recommend using specific sites and strategies to attract recruiters' attention:[4]

- Network on those sites that would most likely attract people (and employers) in the industries you are most interested in.
- Join in the online discussions whenever you have an opportunity to share your knowledge.
- Network on those sites offering the most technological advantages, and use them for positive influence. For example, LinkedIn permits you to post relevant information and create presentations to showcase your skills.
- Use the Internet for instructions on how and why job searchers should use these sites (www.youtube.com/watch?v=IzT3JVUGUzM, http://learn.linkedin.com/what-is-linkedin, and www.askdavetaylor.com/how_do_i_use_linkedin_to_find_a_job.html).
- Be discreet. Many recruiters and potential employers check candidates' online presence:

  - Limit your digital networking to career-related sites.
  - Keep your profile updated.
  - Check your privacy box.

Remove any material that might demonstrate poor judgment.

Checkpoint

In an **information interview** you talk to someone who works in the area you hope to enter, to find out what the day-to-day work involves and how you can best prepare to enter that field.

What Is the Information Interview?

Information interviews are a sophisticated form of networking. They're crucial if you're not sure what you want to do.

Perhaps in reaction to the proliferation of social networking sites, or perhaps because it simply makes sense, more and more communications professionals argue for the value of face time over virtual connections.[5] Although you will want to use every medium possible to demonstrate your hire-ability, remember that people tend to hire people they know, and no technology can match the sense of knowing that meeting face-to-face brings.

Employability Skills

In an **information interview**, you talk face-to-face to someone who works in the area you hope to enter. The interview allows you to find out what the day-to-day work involves, and how you can best prepare to enter that field. However, when you're prepared, you can use the information interview to make a positive impression, and to self-recruit ("I want to work for you!").

An information interview can

- Help you decide whether you'd like the job
- Give you specific information that you can use to present yourself effectively in your résumé and application letter
- Establish a positive image of you in the mind of the interviewer, so that he or she thinks of you when openings arise

To set up an information interview, phone, or write a letter like the one in Figure 24.2. If you write, phone the following week to set up a specific time, and to begin to establish that all-important personal contact.

In an information interview, you might ask the following questions:

- What are you working on right now?
- How do you spend your typical day?
- How does what you do make or save the organization time or money?
- How have your duties changed since you first started working here?
- What do you like best about your job? What do you like least?
- What do you think the future holds for this kind of work?
- How did you get this job?
- What courses, activities, and/or jobs would you recommend to someone who wanted to do this kind of work?

Immediately after your interview, mail a handwritten note thanking the person for his or her time, and information. A graceful thank-you letter demonstrates your emotional and your social intelligence—critical interpersonal skills when employers are making hiring decisions.

FIGURE 24.2   Letter Requesting an Information Interview

774 Sherbrooke Street East
Montreal, PQ H8S 1H1

April 18, 2010

Kam Yuricich
Clary Communications
1420 Sherbrooke Street East
Montreal, PQ H3G 1K9

Dear Mr. Yuricich:

You-attitude focuses on the reader's importance.

Your talk to McGill's PRSSA Chapter last week about the differences between working for a PR firm and being a PR staff person within an organization really interested me. Your advice would be invaluable to me as I find my niche in the workforce.

Emotional appeal flatters the reader.

Information establishes the writer's credibility.

Last summer I enjoyed a co-op placement with Management Horizons. Although some of my assignments were gofer jobs, my supervisor, Jason Correila, gave me the chance to work on several brochures and to draft two speeches for managers. I enjoyed this variety and would like to learn more about the possibility of working in a PR firm. Could I schedule an information interview with you to learn more about how public relations consultants work with their clients?

The specific request makes a logical appeal.

Emphasizes the reader's expertise.

Perhaps we could discuss the courses you think would best prepare me for PR work. I have a year and a half left before graduation and would like to choose electives that would make me most employable.

Tells the reader the limits of the request.

When convenient for you, I would greatly appreciate 30 minutes of your time. I'll call you early next week to set up an appointment.

Makes it easy for the reader.

Sincerely,

Lee Tan

Lee Tan

Unadvertised jobs are called the **hidden job market**. Referral interviews, an organized method of networking, offer the most systematic way to tap into those jobs. Schedule **referral interviews** to learn about current job opportunities in your field.

What Is the "Hidden Job Market"? How Do I Tap into It?

The hidden market—jobs that are never advertised—is open to those who know how to use networking techniques. Referral interviews and prospecting letters can help you find it.

Most great jobs are never advertised—and the number rises the higher up the job ladder you go. More than 60 percent of all new jobs come not from responding to an ad but from networking with personal contacts.[6] Some of these jobs are created especially for a specific person. These unadvertised jobs are called the **hidden job market**; creating your own opportunities to meet and work with others informally—through volunteer community involvement, for example—is the optimum method of tapping into this market.

Referral interviews, an organized method of networking, offer another way to tap into these jobs. Schedule referral interviews to learn about current job opportunities in your field. Sometimes an interview that starts out as an information interview turns into a referral interview.

A referral interview gives you information about current opportunities available in the area you're interested in, refers you to other people who can tell you about job opportunities, and enables the interviewer to see that you could make a contribution to his or her organization. Therefore, the goal of a referral interview is to put you face-to-face with someone with the power to hire you: the owner of a small company, the division vice-president or branch manager of a big company, or the director of the local office of a provincial or federal agency.

Start by scheduling interviews with people you know who may know something about that field—professors, co-workers, neighbours, friends. Join your alumni association; network with alumni who now work where you would like to work. Your purpose in talking to them is to (1) get advice about improving your résumé and about general job-hunting strategies and (2) become a known commodity and thereby get referrals to other people. In fact, go into the interview with the names of people you'd like to talk to. If the interviewee doesn't suggest anyone, say, "Do you think it would be a good idea for me to talk to X?"

Then, armed with a referral from someone you know, call the former and say, "So-and-so suggested I talk with you about job-hunting strategy." If the person says, "We aren't hiring," you say, "Oh, I'm not asking you for a job. I'd just like some advice from a knowledgeable person about the opportunities in banking (or desktop publishing, technical services, etc.) in this city." If this person does not have the power to create a position, ask for more referrals at the end of this interview. (You can also polish your résumé, if you get good suggestions.)

Even when you talk to the person who could create a job for you, you do not ask for a job. To give you advice about your résumé, however, the person has to look at it. When a powerful person focuses on your skills, he or she will naturally think about the problems and needs in that organization. When there's a match between what you can do and what the organization needs, that person may be able to create a position for you.

Remember the two truisms of job hunting: *self-recruitment is still the number one way to get hired, and people hire people they know*. Although the idea of cold-calling may seem daunting, you'll find most people receptive. You are likely to get the interview when you mention a familiar name ("So-and-so suggested I talk with you") and sound enthusiastic. Prepare as carefully for these interviews as you would for a job interview. Think of good questions in advance; know something about the general field or industry; learn as much as you can about the specific company.

Always follow up information and referral interviews with personal thank-you letters. Use specifics to show that you paid attention during the interview, and enclose a copy of your revised résumé.

How Do I Present My Non-traditional Experiences?

Address the employer's potential concerns positively.

Many people bring a variety of non-traditional experiences to the job search. These experiences often build the transferable skills that employers search for. In a world where the ability to learn is recognized as the key to employability, your communication skills will determine whether you get the job.

This section gives advice on presenting your previous experience positively.

EXPANDING A CRITICAL SKILL

Selling Yourself in the New Work World

In the new world of work, non-traditional employment has replaced the cradle-to-grave job security of your grandparents. "Almost 40 per cent of Canadians are earning a living as temps, part-timers, contract workers or self-employed consultants, and their numbers are growing."

Although small and medium-sized businesses offer the best employment opportunities for today's job seekers, all employers, regardless of company size, seek people who are well prepared, can think on their feet, and demonstrate values that match those of the organization.

To better ensure that match, hiring processes are also evolving. Because the traditional employment interview has proven inadequate, employers are trying other methods, including multiple interviews, team interviews, behavioural interviews, and psychological testing. Aspiring candidates should prepare thoroughly to answer specifically the most important hiring question: What have you got to offer that will keep us competitive?

- Research the organization, the industry, and current challenges.
- Know the corporate culture, and be prepared to describe specifically how your skills and values fit that culture.

- Prepare to answer behavioural questions, such as "Describe a situation in which you diffused a potential conflict"; "Describe a situation in which you demonstrated leadership skills"; "Why did you apply for this job? [Give] an example of a difficult situation you were in with people and how you handled it."
- Prepare for expert recruiters who will dig for unrehearsed answers (and character insights) with such queries as "When is it okay to lie? How far would you go to close a deal? What does independence mean to you?"

Astute interviewees understand that even the deceptively simple, kickoff question, "Tell me about yourself," translates as "Tell me specifically why I should hire you." Savvy employment searchers come prepared with specific examples to answer that question.

Source: Wallace Immen, "Job Hunting 101," *The Globe and Mail*, February 18, 2009, p. C1; Ron McGowan, "Forget a Job: Grads Must Sell Selves to New World of Work," *The Globe and Mail*, May 4, 2004, p. C1; Wallace Immen, "Thinking on Your Feet Gets a Foot in the Door," *The Globe and Mail*, September 16, 2005, p. C3; Andy Holloway, "Recruit Right: A Guide to Finding the Best Fit," *Canadian Business*, October 10–23, 2005, p. 123; and Arlen H. Hirsch, "'Tell Me About Yourself' Response Is Trickier Than You Might Think," *The Globe and Mail*, November 10, 2004, p. C9.

"All My Experience Is in My Family's Business"

In your résumé, simply list the company you worked for. For a reference, instead of a family member, list a supervisor, client, or vendor who can talk about your work. Since the reader may wonder whether "Jim Clarke" is any relation to "Clarke Construction Company," be ready to answer interview questions about why you're looking at other companies. Prepare an answer that stresses the broader opportunities you seek but doesn't criticize your family, or the family business.

"I've Been out of the Job Market for a While"

You need to prove to a potential employer that you're up to date and motivated:

- Research changes in your field to identify prospective employers' priorities. When you can demonstrate that you can make an immediate contribution, you'll have a much easier sell. To do that, however, you need to know what the employer needs: What skills are employers looking for?
- Be active in professional organizations. Attend meetings; read magazines, newspapers, and trade journals.
- Learn the computer programs that professionals in your field use.
- Show how your at-home experience relates directly to the workplace. Multitasking, organizing food bank drives, managing projects, chairing PTA meetings, dealing with unpredictable situations, building consensus, listening, raising money, and making presentations are all transferable skills.
- Create a portfolio of your work—even if it's for imaginary clients—to demonstrate your expertise and transferable skills.[7] Most of Canada's provinces and territories offer prior learning assessment and recognition (PLAR) to adults with work experience. On the basis of a demonstration of the requisite knowledge and skills, you can get credit for postsecondary courses. Most high-level courses require that candidates prepare a proposal and a portfolio of academic and work projects to demonstrate subject knowledge and skills.

"I Want to Change Fields"

Learn about the skills needed in the job you want. Learn the language of the industry. Then you can identify a good reason (from the prospective employer's point of view) for choosing to explore a new field. "I want a change" or "I need to get out of a bad situation" will not convince an employer that you know what you're doing.

Think about how your experience relates to the job you want. Jack is an older-than-average student who wants to be a pharmaceutical sales representative. He has sold wood stoves, served subpoenas, and worked on an oil rig. A chronological résumé makes his work history look directionless. But a skills résumé (Module 25) could focus on persuasive ability (selling stoves), initiative and persistence (serving subpoenas), and technical knowledge (courses in biology and chemistry).[8]

"I Was Fired"

First, deal with the emotional baggage. You need to reduce negative feelings to a manageable level before you're ready to job-hunt.

Second, try to learn from the experience. You'll be a much more attractive job candidate if you can show that you've learned from the experience—whether your lesson is improved work habits or the need to choose a job where you can do work you're proud of.

Third, suggests Phil Elder, an interviewer for an insurance company, call the person who fired you and say something like this: "Look, I know you weren't pleased with the job I did at company X. I'm applying for a job at company Y now and the personnel director may call you to ask about me. Would you be willing to give me the chance to get this job, so that I can try to do things right this time?" All but the hardest of heart, says Elder, will give you one more chance. You won't get a glowing reference, but neither will the statement be so damning that no one will be willing to hire you.[9]

"I Don't Have Any Experience"

You can get experience in several ways:

- Take a fast-food job—and keep it. If you do well, you might be promoted to a supervisor within a year. Use every opportunity to learn about the management and financial aspects of the business.
- Volunteer. Coach a community little-league team, join the PTA, help out at your local food bank, canvass for charity. If you work hard, you'll quickly get an opportunity to do more: manage a budget, write fundraising materials, and supervise other volunteers.
- Freelance. Design brochures, create Web pages, do tax returns for small businesses. Use your skills—for free, if you have to at first.
- Write. Create a portfolio of ads, instructions, or whatever documents are relevant for the field you want to enter. Ask a professional—an instructor, a local businessperson, someone from a professional organization—to critique them. Volunteer your services to local fundraising organizations and small businesses.

Pick something in which you interact with other people, so you can show you work well in an organization.

If you're in the job market now, think carefully about what you've really done. Write sentences using the action verbs in Table 25.1 on page 462. Think about your experiences and skills development in courses, in volunteer work, in unpaid activities. Focus especially on your communications skills: problem solving, critical thinking, managing projects, working as part of a team, persuasive speaking, and writing. Solving a problem for a hypothetical firm in an accounting class, thinking critically about a report problem in business communication, working with a group in a marketing class, and communicating with people at the senior centre where you volunteer are all valuable experiences, even if no one paid you.

If you're not actually looking for a job but just need to create a résumé for this course, ask your instructor whether you may assume that you're graduating and add the things you hope to do between now and that time.

"I'm a Lot Older Than the Other Employees"

Mature workers remain in demand for their sophisticated interpersonal and communications abilities. Uninformed employers are concerned that older people won't be flexible, up to date, or willing to be supervised by someone younger. You can counter these fears:

- Keep up to date. Read trade journals; attend professional meetings.
- Learn the computer programs your field uses. Refer to technology in the résumé, job letter, and interview: "Yes, I saw the specifications for your new product on your Web site."
- Work with younger people, in classroom teams, in volunteer work, or on the job. Be able to cite specific cases where you've learned from young people and worked well with them.
- Use positive emphasis (Module 7). Talk about your ability to relate to mature customers, the valuable perspective you bring. Focus on fairly recent events, not ones from 20 years ago.
- Show energy and enthusiasm to counter the stereotype that older people are tired and ill.

Language FOCUS

The phrase **mature workers** is used to identify workers who are older, usually those between the ages of 50 and 65. Module 3, Communicating Across Cultures, discusses biased language. Using the word "mature" rather than "old" is an example of using bias-free language, as "mature" indicates someone with experience and knowledge, whereas "old" does not have the same positive connotations.

On a final note, the most successful job hunters are prepared: they seek opportunities to impress others positively and they understand that everyone they meet is both a potential employer and a potential customer.

MODULE SUMMARY

- Begin your job search by assessing your priorities, abilities, and interests. Do this assessment in writing, to make it real, and to note the information that might go on your résumé.

- Use directories, annual reports, recruiting literature, business periodicals, trade journals, and Web pages to get information about employers, and job search tips.

- The most effective way to find the job you want is to self-recruit. The second most effective way is through a referral. Both these methods depend on your ability to network.

- Information and referral interviews can help you tap into the **hidden job market**—jobs that are not advertised. Collect contact names by networking: talk to friends, relatives, salespeople, and suppliers; do volunteer and community work. Ask for an **information interview** to find out what the daily work involves, and how you can best prepare to enter the field. Or schedule brief **referral interviews** to learn about current job opportunities in your field.

- Prepare carefully for these interviews: these people know other people, and can offer suggestions and other referrals.

- Use social networking sites discreetly. Join business/industry-related sites, get involved in online discussions, update your profile frequently, and use the site's technology to showcase your skills.

ASSIGNMENTS FOR MODULE 24

Questions for Critical Thinking

24.1 What networking sites would be most relevant for a career in your field? Why?

24.2 Identify three community and/or volunteer activities that would expand your networking opportunities.

24.3 Suggest three reasons how knowing the corporate culture of a potential employer can make your job search much more successful.

Exercises and Problems

24.4 Beginning Your Self-Inventory

Initiate the job-hunting process on the nextSteps.org Job Search site (www.nextsteps.org/jobsearch) by completing the inventory questionnaire. Note the results as part of the process of knowing yourself.

24.5 Evaluating Career Web Sites*

Evaluate three or more Web sites for job hunters, considering the following questions:

- Is the site easy to navigate?

- Is it visually attractive?
- Are any ads unobtrusive?
- Does it contain good advice?
- Does it let job hunters specify who may not see their posted résumés (e.g., the current employer)?
- Does it have any features that you don't find in other career Web sites?

*Inspired by a problem written by Gary Kohut, University of North Carolina at Charlotte.

24.6   Networking

Write to a friend who is already in the workforce, asking about one or more of the following topics:

- Are any jobs in your field available in your friend's organization? If so, what?
- If a job is available, can your friend provide information, beyond the job listing, that will help you write a more detailed, persuasive letter? (Specify the kind of information you'd like to have.)
- Can your friend suggest people in other organizations who might be useful to you in your job search? (Specify any organizations in which you're especially interested.)

24.7   Gathering Information About an Industry

Use six recent issues of a trade journal to report on three to five trends, developments, or issues that are important in an industry.

As your instructor directs,

   a. Share your findings with a small group of students.
   b. Summarize your findings in a memo to your instructor.
   c. Present your findings orally to the class.
   d. Email your findings to the other members of the class.
   e. Form a group with two other students to write a blog summarizing the results of this research.

24.8   Gathering Information About a Specific Organization

Gather printed information about a specific organization, using several of the following methods:

- Use the most current edition of *The Career Directory*.
- Check the company's Web site.
- Read the company's annual report.
- Talk to someone who works there.

- Pick up relevant information at your local board of trade or chamber of commerce.
- Read articles in trade publications and online at *The Globe and Mail, National Post, The Wall Street Journal,* or *Financial Post* that mention the organization (check the indices).
- Get the names and addresses of its officers (from a directory or from the Web).
- Read recruiting literature provided by the company.

As your instructor directs,

   a. Share your findings with a small group of students.
   b. Summarize your findings in a memo to your instructor.
   c. Present your findings orally to the class.
   d. Email your findings to the other members of the class.
   e. Form a group with two other students to write a blog summarizing the results of this research.

24.9   Conducting an Information Interview

Interview someone working in a field you're interested in. Use the questions listed in the module or the shorter list here:

- How did you get started in this field?
- What do you like about your job?
- What do you dislike about your job?
- What three other people could give me additional information about this job?

As your instructor directs,

   a. Share the results of your interview with a small group of students.
   b. Write up your interview in a memo to your instructor.
   c. Present the results of your interview orally to the class.
   d. Email a summary of your interview to other members of your class.
   e. Write to the interviewee thanking him or her for taking the time to talk to you.

POLISHING YOUR PROSE

Using Details

Details are especially important in reader benefits (Module 8), reports, résumés, job application, and sales letters. Customers or potential employers look for specific details to help them make decisions, such as what makes your product better than the competition's or how your experience would help the reader. Here's an example:

> I can offer you more than ten years of advertising experience, including five years of broadcast sales in Ottawa, where I generated more than $19 million in revenue, as well as three years with J. Walter Thompson,

Toronto's leading advertising company. For the first four years of my career, I also wrote advertising copy, including hundreds of local and regional radio spots for such diverse products as cookies, cat food, fishing tackle, and children's toys. I also wrote print pieces, including the entire 15-month campaign for Vancouver-based "Uncle Bill's Electronic Bazaar," which increased sales by nearly 37 percent during that period.

Reader Benefits

What features or experiences make your product or service unique? useful? cost-effective?

Weak: With the Stereobooster, your car will sound great.

Better: The Stereobooster safely gives your car audio system a full 30 watts per channel of sheer sound excitement, double that of other systems on the market—all for under $50.

The Five Senses

Describe sight, sound, taste, touch, and smell. Some sensations are so powerful that they immediately conjure up thoughts or emotions—the smell of fresh coffee, the sound of ocean waves, the feeling of sunlight against the skin.

Concrete Nouns and Verbs

Concrete nouns and verbs are better than more general nouns and verbs combined with adjectives and adverbs. For instance, *manager* and *15 months* are more concrete than *the person in charge* or *a while*. Concrete words make meaning clear and vivid:

Weak: At my last job, I typed stuff.

Better: As a clerk typist II for Hughes and Associates, I typed hundreds of memos, letters, and reports.

Increase your vocabulary by reading a variety of materials. Keep a dictionary and thesaurus handy. Do crossword puzzles or computer word games to practise what you know.

Adjectives and Adverbs That Count

Omit or replace vague or overused adjectives and adverbs: *basically, some, very, many, a lot, kind/sort of, partly, eventually*. Increasingly, novice writers are using *so* as an adjective, as in "He was so happy about the promotion." Exactly how happy is this?

Conversational English, Not Jargon or Obscure Words

In general, choose the more conversational option over jargon or obscure words: *exit, typical,* or *second to last* rather than *egress, quintessential,* or *penultimate*.

Exercises

Add details to the following sentences.

1. I work for a company.
2. The person in charge of our department wants some files.
3. Sometime in the future I will get a job in my field.
4. It's been a while since I went there.
5. Our product will help you.
6. There are lots of reasons why you should hire me.
7. This product is so much better than its competitors.
8. We will have a meeting in the afternoon.
9. My experience makes me a good candidate for this job.
10. We plan to travel to a couple of provinces sometime next month.

Check your answers to the odd-numbered exercises on page 553.

Creating Persuasive Résumés

Learning Objectives

After reading and applying the information in Module 25, you'll be able to demonstrate

Knowledge of

- Current résumé-writing practices

Skills to

- Create the résumé that best showcases your qualifications
- Make your experience relevant to employers
- Increase the number of "hits" your résumé receives

Employability Skills 2000+ Checklist

In this module, the key skills from the Conference Board of Canada's Employability Skills 2000+ are

Communicate

- ◯ write and speak so others pay attention and understand

- ◯ share information using a range of information and communications technologies (e.g., voice, email, computers)

Manage Information

- ◯ locate, gather, and organize information using appropriate technology and information systems

Demonstrate Positive Attitudes & Behaviours

- ◯ feel good about yourself and be confident
- ◯ deal with people, problems, and situations with honesty, integrity, and personal ethics

- ◯ recognize your own and other people's good efforts

Learn Continuously

- ◯ be willing to continuously learn and grow
- ◯ assess personal strengths and areas for development

- ◯ identify and access learning sources and opportunities
- ◯ plan for and achieve your learning goals

A **résumé** summarizes your qualifications so persuasively that you get an interview. When you're in the job market, having a résumé prepares you for every opportunity. When you're employed, having a current résumé allows you to assess your skills improvement; this ongoing inventory makes it easier for you to take advantage of other job opportunities that come up.

Even if you're several years away from job hunting, preparing a résumé now will make you more conscious of what to do in the next two or three years to make yourself a more attractive candidate. Writing a résumé is also an ego-building experience: the person who looks so good on paper is *you!*

If your skills are in great demand, you might be able to ignore every résumé-writing guideline and still get a good job. In a tough labour market, however, and when you have to compete against many applicants, these guidelines can help you showcase your employability skills.

Tailor your job communications to your unique qualifications. Adopt the wording or layout of an example if it is relevant to your own situation, but don't be locked into the forms in this book: you have different strengths; your résumé will be different too.

How Can I Encourage the Employer to Pay Attention to My Résumé?

Show how your qualifications fit the job and the company.

Your résumé can be screened in two ways: electronically or by a person. If people do the reading, employers may skim the résumés quickly, putting them into two piles: "reject" and "maybe." In the first round, each résumé may get as little as 2.9 seconds of the reader's

Employability Skills

FIGURE 25.1 **PAIBOC Questions for Analysis**

P What are your **purposes** in creating a résumé? The résumé must display your knowledge, skills and analytical abilities: you are recording your interpersonal and vocational aptitudes, and shaping a persuasive story. Your ultimate purpose is to get the interview.

A Who is your **audience**? Who will scan/read your résumé? What does your audience value, and how do you know? How can you create a résumé that will attract and hold your audience's attention?

I What **information** should you include in your résumé? What information is the employer looking for? What do you know about the industry? the employer? What life/work experiences will make you stand out from other candidates? What keywords should you use to frame that information for immediate and maximum positive emphasis?

B What communication and technical skills can you offer to immediately **benefit** the potential employer?

O What audience **objections** do you anticipate? How can you create a résumé that stands out positively among all those others?

C What **context** will affect your reader's response? Consider your relationship to the reader, the reader's values and expectations, the economy, recent organizational developments, current morale, and the time of year.

attention. Then the reader goes through the "maybe" pile again, weeding out more documents. If there are a lot of résumés (and some companies get 2 000 a week), résumés may get only 10 to 30 seconds in this stage. After the initial pile has been culled to one-half or one-hundredth of the initial pile, the remaining documents will be read more carefully to choose the people invited for interviews.

Alternatively, your résumé may be electronically scanned into a job-applicant tracking system. Then a computer does the first set of cuts. The employer specifies the keywords from the job description, listing the knowledge, skills, and abilities that the ideal applicant would have. Sometimes personal characteristics (e.g., *hard worker, good writer, willing to travel*) are included. The employer receives the résumés that match the keywords, arranged with the most "hits" first. The employer then chooses the interviewees.

In the current job market, you need both a paper résumé that's attractive to the human eye and a scannable résumé that serves your purposes in a job-applicant tracking system. You can do several things to increase the chances that a human being will pay attention to your résumé:

- Quantify your skills and activities: "increased sales 10 percent"; "supervised five people"; "implemented a data entry system that saved the company $5 000."
- Emphasize achievements that
  - Are most relevant to the position for which you're applying
  - Demonstrate your superiority to other applicants
  - Are recent
- Use the keywords and technical terms of the industry and the organization; find these in the ad, in trade journals, and from job descriptions.
- Make your paper résumé attractive and readable: use picture-frame placement, plenty of white space, and a serif font (Times New Roman, for example); bold the major headings.
- Include transferable skills: the ability to write and speak well, to identify and solve problems, to think critically and creatively, to work well independently and with others, to speak other languages, and to use a variety of computer programs.
- Design one résumé to appeal to the human eye and the second to be easily processed by an electronic scanner.
- Revise and edit your résumé to ensure it's error-free: grammar and spelling mistakes will cost you the interview.

You may need to create several different résumés. But the more carefully you customize your résumé to a specific employer, the greater your chances for getting an interview.

What Kind of Résumé Should I Use?

Use the format that makes you look best.

Depending on their experience and the audience, people use one of three kinds of résumés: **chronological**, **functional** or **combination**, or **skills**.

Employability Skills

The chronological résumé summarizes what you have accomplished, starting with the most recent events and going backwards, that is, using **reverse chronology**. It emphasizes degrees, job titles, and dates. Figure 25.2 shows a chronological résumé. Use a chronological résumé when you have limited relevant work experience and your education and experience show

- A logical preparation for the position for which you're applying
- A steady progression leading to the present

EXPANDING A CRITICAL SKILL

Creating Attention-Getting Résumés

Keep your résumé simple and specific: you have only a few minutes to attract and hold recruiters' attention. Follow these strategies to create a résumé that gets you the job interview:

Play with Layout and Design

If submitting a hard copy

- Use a laser printer to print your résumé on high-quality letter-sized paper. White paper is standard for business résumés; cream, pale grey, and parchment colours are also acceptable.
- Make your résumé readable and attractive:
  ○ Use the same font throughout: Arial and Times New Roman are business standards.
  ○ Vary font size: use 12-point for headings, and 11-point type for the text to get more on a page.
  ○ Bold and italicize for emphasis; use bullets in lists.
  ○ Showcase your desktop publishing skills: try smaller margins; use lines or borders.
  ○ Use enough white space to make your résumé easy to read.
- Avoid résumé templates; they suggest lack of creativity and interest.

If emailing your résumé,

- Attach it as a Word or PDF document.
- Save the document with your name included in the filename so that the recruiter can easily retrieve it among others.

Consider the Content

Employers want to interview eligible candidates. Ensure your résumé emphasizes your eligibility.

- Highlight skills relevant to the position and the organization.
- Be specific: reframe experiences into skills; provide facts and numbers.
- Be clear: use short, concrete nouns, and active verbs to describe your skills.
- Be honest. Even if potential employers don't check—and increasingly they do—lies and exaggerations are often glaringly obvious.

Proofread

Employers assume that the résumé represents your best work. Proofread, and then have someone else proofread for you, to ensure the document is perfect. Especially check

- Spelling of your college, university, and your employers
- Parallelism (Module 11)
- Consistency: headings, bullets, abbreviations
- Dates
- Phone numbers, email addresses, and URLs

FIGURE 25.2   **A Chronological Résumé**

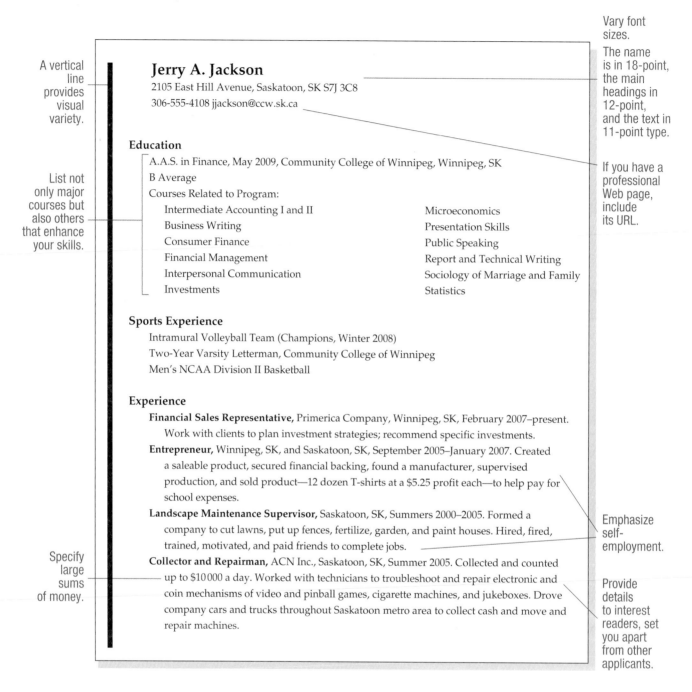

A vertical line provides visual variety.

List not only major courses but also others that enhance your skills.

Specify large sums of money.

Vary font sizes.

The name is in 18-point, the main headings in 12-point, and the text in 11-point type.

If you have a professional Web page, include its URL.

Emphasize self-employment.

Provide details to interest readers, set you apart from other applicants.

Jerry A. Jackson

2105 East Hill Avenue, Saskatoon, SK S7J 3C8

306-555-4108 jjackson@ccw.sk.ca

Education

A.A.S. in Finance, May 2009, Community College of Winnipeg, Winnipeg, SK

B Average

Courses Related to Program:

Intermediate Accounting I and II

Business Writing

Consumer Finance

Financial Management

Interpersonal Communication

Investments

Microeconomics

Presentation Skills

Public Speaking

Report and Technical Writing

Sociology of Marriage and Family

Statistics

Sports Experience

Intramural Volleyball Team (Champions, Winter 2008)

Two-Year Varsity Letterman, Community College of Winnipeg

Men's NCAA Division II Basketball

Experience

Financial Sales Representative, Primerica Company, Winnipeg, SK, February 2007–present. Work with clients to plan investment strategies; recommend specific investments.

Entrepreneur, Winnipeg, SK, and Saskatoon, SK, September 2005–January 2007. Created a saleable product, secured financial backing, found a manufacturer, supervised production, and sold product—12 dozen T-shirts at a $5.25 profit each—to help pay for school expenses.

Landscape Maintenance Supervisor, Saskatoon, SK, Summers 2000–2005. Formed a company to cut lawns, put up fences, fertilize, garden, and paint houses. Hired, fired, trained, motivated, and paid friends to complete jobs.

Collector and Repairman, ACN Inc., Saskatoon, SK, Summer 2005. Collected and counted up to $10 000 a day. Worked with technicians to troubleshoot and repair electronic and coin mechanisms of video and pinball games, cigarette machines, and jukeboxes. Drove company cars and trucks throughout Saskatoon metro area to collect cash and move and repair machines.

The **functional** or **combination résumé** emphasizes the applicant's most important (to the reader) job titles and responsibilities, or functions, regardless of chronology. Usually, the functional résumé reverts to the reverse chronology listing for information not related to paid employment, as reflected in Figure 25.3 on page 457. Use the functional/combination résumé if

- Your work experiences match the position responsibilities.
- Your skills and expertise match the position requirements.

- Your education and experience are not the usual route to the position for which you're applying.
- You want to deemphasize your formal education.

FIGURE 25.3 **A Functional or Combination Résumé**

Dennis Crawford
65 Dunnet Drive
Barrie, ON L4N 0J6
705.220.4807
dcrawford@sympatico.ca

Summary of Qualifications

- A highly skilled executive sales professional specializing in the CCTV/Video Surveillance marketplace
- Inducted into the company's President's Club four times for exceeding sales by 115% to 149%

Recognized for achievements in

- Regional & National Account Management
- Sales & Marketing Strategies
- Consultative Sales
- Product Management & Promotion
- Project Management
- Technical Sales Training
- Systems Design & Implementation
- Forecasting & Budgets

Professional Experience

Panasonic Canada Inc., Mississauga ON
A global leader in consumer and industrial electronics manufacturing and sales

National Account Manager, Professional Imaging & Display Solutions Group *(2008–2009)*
Identified and managed high-profile national re-seller accounts while developing new growth opportunities through strategic networking with large national end-user accounts within Canada

- Developed a new national sales and marketing strategy while managing the Panasonic sales activities of 3 high-profile national re-seller accounts with over 35 sales professionals between them
- Identified, engaged, and closed new business opportunities with national re-seller accounts for a projected increase in sales of $500K within year one
- Successfully presented B2B strategies to high-profile end-user accounts securing net new business in excess of $1.5 million for select re-seller accounts
- Consultant to professional engineers, architects, sales professionals, and end users for the design and implementation of complex video solutions that exceed customer expectations
- Key liaison and consultant to product manager for industry trade shows and national marketing initiatives, often collaborating on booth design, marketing concepts, and product presentations for large industry trade shows, national technical sales seminars, and new product launches

Regional Account Manager, Central Division
Professional Imaging & Display Solutions Group *(2001–2008)*
Identified and managed regional re-seller accounts while developing new growth opportunities through strategic networking with Ontario regional and national end user accounts

- Developed sales and marketing strategies that successfully managed the Panasonic sales activities of 14 regional re-seller accounts with over 80 sales professionals
- Increased sales and market share within a territory that represented 40% of the departments annual sales forecast and budget
- Presented B2B strategies to several high profile end user and regional accounts resulting in a P.O for over $1 million, setting a new record within the department
- Successfully organized, managed, and led an offsite national sales meeting on behalf of National Sales & Marketing Manager, opening channels of communication to a new level within the department. Still considered by my peers to be the most effective and constructive sales meeting of record for the department
- Created and led successful product and sales training seminars, presenting at industry trade shows and technical product launches across Canada. Educated over 100 sales personnel and several hundred end users and consultants on the benefits of technology and products offered by Panasonic Canada Inc.

FIGURE 25.3   A Functional or Combination Résumé (continued)

Dennis Crawford
65 Dunnet Drive
Barrie, ON L4N 0J6
705.220.4807
dcrawford@sympatico.ca

Product Manager, Professional Imaging & Display Solutions Group *(2000–2001)*
Technical product sales liaison among Panasonic factories, internal sales, service, and upper management representatives, external sales, and end user clientele

- Redesigned, developed, and deployed a struggling national product training program targeted at over 35 Panasonic re-sellers with sales representatives in excess of 150 people, several hundred end users, consultants, and engineers, and over a dozen internal sales, service, and management staff across Canada
- Developed and presented strategies to factory representatives based on competitive product and market data resulting in a more focused approach to product development for the North American market
- Managed product promotion and Regional Account Manager's involvement at industry trade shows both locally and nationally, aiding in the increase of product awareness and knowledge of our sales and customer base
- Successfully provided pre- and post-technical sales and system design support to over 35 re-sellers and three distribution accounts with a combined sales force of over 200 people, and over a dozen Panasonic internal sales, marketing, and technical service support people

KM Video & Security, Mississauga ON *1990–2000*
An industry leader in the design and implementation of complex video surveillance systems for medium and large businesses

Service Technician, CCTV Products *(1993–2000)*
Technical service representative responsible for maintaining complex video solutions for KM clientele

- Maintained a high level of customer service support by successfully diagnosing and repairing complex system/product faults, effectively reducing system downtime, and maintaining the integrity of security solution
- Facilitated open communication between sales and customer service departments resulting in more efficient customer service for our key clientele
- Designed, developed, and maintained weekly/monthly/yearly service contract schedule for key customers and successfully delegating work orders to service technicians for service contract clientele, increasing productivity by over 25% which positively contributed to sales

Installation Technician, CCTV Products *(1990–1993)*
Installed complex video surveillance solutions

- Team lead responsible for the installation and commissioning of complex video surveillance solutions
- Consultant to sales staff regarding installation estimates and project management ensuring efficient use of installer's time and meeting strict deadlines to ensure project profitability
- Trainer of end users, internal sales and service staff on the operation of complex video solutions

Education

York University, Schulich School of Business

Sheridan College, School of Applied Arts & Technology
Architectural Technician Diploma (1987–1990)

Panasonic Canada Inc.

Canadian Professional Sales Association

The **skills résumé** emphasizes the skills you've acquired through work experience. Figure 25.4 shows a skills résumé. Use a skills résumé when

- You want to combine experience from paid jobs, activities or volunteer work, and courses to show the extent of your experience in transferable and technical skills: administration, finance, speaking, and so on.
- Your education and experience are not the usual route to the position for which you're applying.
- You're changing fields.
- Your recent work history might create the wrong impression (e.g., it has gaps, shows a demotion, shows job-hopping, etc.).

FIGURE 25.4 **A Skills Résumé**

Mohammed Shaffer
210 Steeles Avenue (West), Brampton, Ontario L6Y 2K3
905-555-3828 mshaffer@sympatico.ca

Objective

To find a challenging information technology position where my communication and technical skills will make a valuable and valued contribution to the organization

Profile

- Motivated team player with good organizational, communication, and people skills
- Quick learner and good problem solver
- Detail-oriented and analytical
- Able to work independently and under pressure
- Meticulous and adept manager of time-critical projects
- Trained and experienced in superb customer service skills
- Unix, Linux, Windows XP, NT, and Vista, Mac Snow Leopard, VMS, VB6, Perl, Java, SQL, Novell Net Ware 5.0
- System Analysis, DataBase Design, Data Communication, and LAN
- Knowledge of quality control procedures and software testing
- Seismic Data processing on VAX/VMS platform

Education

- Systems Analyst Post-Diploma Program
  2008–2009   Sheridan College, Brampton ON

- Master of Science & Technology in Applied Geophysics
  2006–2009   Indian School of Mines, Dhanbad, India

- Bachelor of Science (Major in Physics)
  2002–2006   Calcutta University, India

Achievements

- A average in all Sheridan Institute courses
- First class with distinction at Masters level (OGPA 4.02/5)
- Class and Residence Prefect college and university levels

1 of 2

Annotations:
- Excellent philosophy
- Highlights communication and technical skills
- Concrete and specific details

The best résumés convey relevant details as concisely and attractively as possible. Most résumés use bullet points, omit *I*, and use sentence fragments that may be punctuated as complete sentences. Complete sentences are acceptable, as are *me* and *my*, if they are the briefest way to present information.

FIGURE 25.4   **A Skills Résumé (continued)**

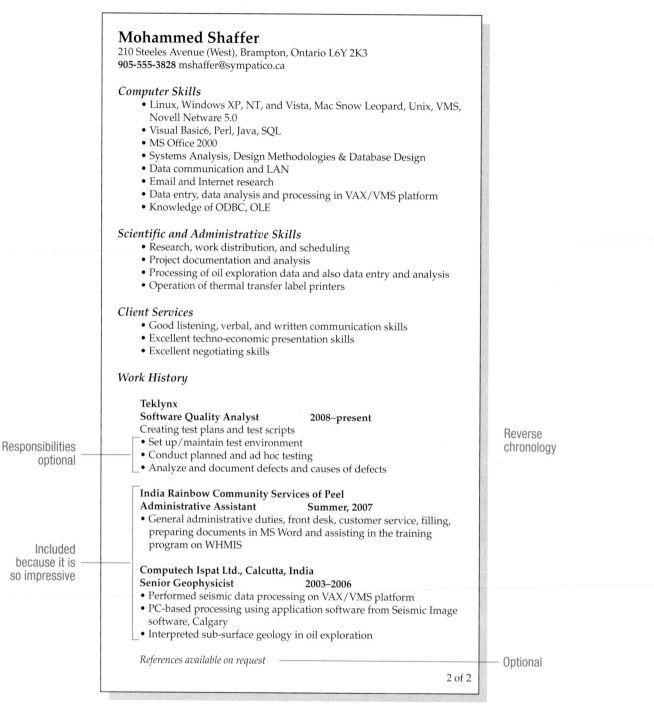

Responsibilities optional

Included because it is so impressive

Reverse chronology

Optional

Mohammed Shaffer
210 Steeles Avenue (West), Brampton, Ontario L6Y 2K3
905-555-3828 mshaffer@sympatico.ca

Computer Skills
- Linux, Windows XP, NT, and Vista, Mac Snow Leopard, Unix, VMS, Novell Netware 5.0
- Visual Basic6, Perl, Java, SQL
- MS Office 2000
- Systems Analysis, Design Methodologies & Database Design
- Data communication and LAN
- Email and Internet research
- Data entry, data analysis and processing in VAX/VMS platform
- Knowledge of ODBC, OLE

Scientific and Administrative Skills
- Research, work distribution, and scheduling
- Project documentation and analysis
- Processing of oil exploration data and also data entry and analysis
- Operation of thermal transfer label printers

Client Services
- Good listening, verbal, and written communication skills
- Excellent techno-economic presentation skills
- Excellent negotiating skills

Work History

Teklynx
Software Quality Analyst   2008–present
Creating test plans and test scripts
- Set up/maintain test environment
- Conduct planned and ad hoc testing
- Analyze and document defects and causes of defects

India Rainbow Community Services of Peel
Administrative Assistant   Summer, 2007
- General administrative duties, front desk, customer service, filling, preparing documents in MS Word and assisting in the training program on WHMIS

Computech Ispat Ltd., Calcutta, India
Senior Geophysicist   2003–2006
- Performed seismic data processing on VAX/VMS platform
- PC-based processing using application software from Seismic Image software, Calgary
- Interpreted sub-surface geology in oil exploration

References available on request

2 of 2

How Do Résumé Formats Differ?

They showcase you differently, depending on your experiences, your purpose (the job you're applying for), and your audience.

A chronological résumé, such as the one in Figure 25.2, focuses on when, then what, and emphasizes academic qualifications. Experience is organized by date, with the most recent job first. The functional or combination résumé (Figure 25.3) showcases the applicant's qualifications according to relevant job functions, or responsibilities. Extensive experience, not dates or academic degrees, is the focus. Seasoned and highly qualified applicants use this format.

A skills résumé, such as the one in Figure 25.4, summarizes experience and acquired skills needed for the job. Under each heading, the résumé lists, in order of importance, paid and unpaid work (in classes, activities, and community groups). An Employment History section lists job titles (or functions), employers, city, and province.

Chronological Résumés

In a chronological résumé, start with the Education heading. Under Work Experience or Employment History, include employment dates, position or job title, organization, city, province, and other details: seasonal, full- or part-time status, job duties, special responsibilities, and promotions with companies. Include unpaid jobs and self-employment if they provided relevant skills (e.g., supervising people, budgeting, planning, persuading). If you've held co-op or intern placements (very significant to employers), include these under a separate heading such as Co-operative Placement Experience.

Normally, go back as far as the summer after high school. Include earlier jobs if you started working someplace before graduating from high school but continued working there after graduation. However, give minimal detail about high school jobs. If you worked full-time after high school, make that clear.

If as an undergraduate you've earned a substantial portion of your college or university expenses, say so, either under Experience or in the Interpersonal or Skills Profile section with which you can begin the résumé. (Graduate students are expected to support themselves.)

> These jobs paid 40 percent of my university expenses.
>
> Paid for 65 percent of expenses with jobs, scholarships, and loans.

Omit information about low-level jobs, unless they illustrate experience important to your reader. Use details when they display your attitudes, abilities, or talents. Tell how many people you trained or supervised, how much money you budgeted or raised. Describe the aspects of the job you did.

Too vague:	2007–2009	Sales Manager, the *Daily Collegian*, Mount Royal College, AB. Supervised staff; promoted ad sales.
Good details:	2007–2009	Sales Manager, the *Daily Collegian*, Mount Royal College, AB. Supervised 22-member sales staff; helped recruit, interview, and select staff; assigned duties and scheduled work; recommended best performer for promotion. Motivated staff to increase paid ad sales 10 percent over previous year's sales.

Verbs or gerunds (the *-ing* form of verbs) always create a more dynamic image than do nouns, so use them on résumés that will be read by people rather than computers. (Rules for scannable résumés to be read by computers come later in this module.) In the revisions below, nouns, verbs, and gerunds are in bold type.

Nouns:	2007–2009	Chair, Income Tax Assistance Committee, Winnipeg, MB. Responsibilities: **recruitment** of volunteers; flyer **design**, **writing**, and **distribution** for **promotion** of program; **speeches** to various community groups and nursing homes to advertise the service.

Verbs:	2007–2009	Chair, Income Tax Assistance Committee, Winnipeg, MB. **Recruited** volunteers for the program. **Designed**, **wrote**, and **distributed** a flyer to promote the program; **made presentations** to various community groups and nursing homes to advertise the service.
Gerunds:	2007–2009	Chair, Income Tax Assistance Committee, Winnipeg, MB. Responsibilities included **recruiting** volunteers for the program; **designing**, **writing**, and **distributing** a flyer to promote the program; and **presenting** to various community groups and nursing homes to advertise the service.

Note that the items in the list must be in parallel structure. Table 25.1 lists action verbs that work well in résumés.

TABLE 25.1 Action Verbs for Résumés

accomplished	assessed	combined	cultivated	discharged
achieved	assigned	communicated	customized	discussed
acted	assisted	compiled	debugged	dispensed
adapted	assured	completed	decided	displayed
addressed	attended	composed	decreased	disseminated
acquired	audited	computed	dedicated	documented
activated	authorized	conceived	defined	drafted
adjusted	automated	conducted	delegated	earned
administered	began	concluded	delineated	edited
adopted	billed	condensed	delivered	educated
advised	budgeted	conferred	documented	elected
advanced	built	constructed	demonstrated	eliminated
aided	calculated	consulted	depicted	employed
allocated	calibrated	contracted	derived	engaged
altered	canvassed	contributed	described	engineered
analyzed	carried out	controlled	designed	ensured
announced	categorized	converted	detailed	entertained
answered	caused	cooperated	detected	equipped
appointed	changed	coordinated	determined	estimated
appraised	charted	corresponded	developed	evaluated
approved	clarified	corrected	devised	examined
arranged	classified	costed	diagnosed	exchanged
ascertained	collaborated	counselled	differentiated	expanded
assembled	collected	created	directed	expedited
experimented	inquired	officiated	recorded	studied
explained	inspected	operated	rectified	strengthened
explored	instituted	orchestrated	reduced	submitted
extracted	instructed	organized	referred	summarized
fabricated	insured	oversaw	refined	supervised
facilitated	integrated	packaged	regulated	supplied

TABLE 25.1   **Action Verbs for Résumés** (continued)

filed	interfaced	paid	related	supported
filled	interpreted	participated	released	surveyed
financed	interviewed	performed	removed	taught
finalized	introduced	persuaded	reorganized	tested
formed	invented	planned	repaired	theorized
forwarded	investigated	positioned	reported	timed
founded	justified	practised	represented	traced
furnished	labelled	precipitated	researched	trained
gathered	licensed	predicted	responded	transferred
generated	located	prepared	restored	transformed
graded	maintained	prescribed	retained	translated
graduated	managed	presented	retrieved	transmitted
granted	manipulated	preserved	reviewed	transported
guarded	manufactured	presided	revised	transposed
guided	mapped	prevented	sampled	treated
handled	marketed	priced	saved	tutored
helped	maximized	printed	scheduled	updated
identified	measured	produced	screened	upgraded
implemented	mechanized	programmed	searched	used
illustrated	mediated	projected	secured	utilized
imported	minimized	protected	selected	validated
improved	mobilized	provided	sold	valued
improvised	modelled	published	served	verified
incorporated	monitored	purchased	set	visited
induced	motivated	questioned	set up	worked
inducted	negotiated	qualified	settled	wrote
influenced	modified	rated	solicited	
informed	observed	received	started	
initiated	obtained	recommended	stimulated	

Good résumés provide accurate details about what you've done, rather than exaggerate.

Functional or Combination Résumés

The functional résumé focuses on the *what*; this format provides the flexibility to highlight relevant job responsibilities or functions, and to include a variety of experiences. Mature, highly skilled people with the right job credentials use the functional résumé to describe their extensive skills.

Begin with Career Achievements or Career Highlights, where you summarize your primary professional accomplishments. The Employment History is most important: describe your work responsibilities and subsequent skills as they relate to the position for which you are applying. Later in the résumé, identify conferences, clubs, and professional associations in reverse chronology to demonstrate your industry currency. Unless applying for a job for which your education credentials are paramount (like an academic position) and you have those credentials, place Education near the end of this format.

Skills Résumés

Skills résumés use the *skills* or *aspects* of the job you are applying for as headings, rather than the category title or the dates of the jobs you've held (as in a chronological résumé). For entries under each skill, combine experience from paid jobs, unpaid work, classes, activities, and community service.

Use headings that reflect the jargon of the job for which you're applying: *logistics* rather than *planning* for a technical job; *procurement* rather than *purchasing* for a civilian job with the military. Figure 25.5 shows a skills résumé for someone who is changing fields. Marcella suggests that she already knows a lot about the field she hopes to enter by using its jargon for the headings.

You need at least three headings related to the job in a skills résumé; to have six or seven is not uncommon. Give enough detail to convince the reader that you have developed the requisite skill sets through a variety of experience. Put the most important category—**from the reader's perspective**—first.

A job description can give you ideas for headings. Possible headings and subheadings for skills résumés include

Administration	**Communication**
Alternatives or subheadings:	Alternatives or subheadings:
Coordinating	Conducting Meetings
Evaluating	Editing
Implementing	Fundraising
Negotiating	Interviewing
Planning	Speaking
Keeping Records	Negotiating
Scheduling	Persuading
Solving Problems	Proposal Writing
Budgeting	Report Writing
Supervising	

Many jobs require a mix of skills. Include the skills that you know will be needed in the job you want.

In a skills résumé, list your paid jobs under Employment History near the end of the résumé (see Figure 25.4). List only job title, employer, city, province, and dates. Omit details about what you did, since you will have already used them under Experience.

FIGURE 25.5   **A Skills Résumé for Changing Job Fields**

On the first page of a skills résumé, put skills directly related to the job for which you're applying.

The centred format is eye-catching but it can be hard to read. Here, bold headings draw the reader's eye.

Marcella G. Cope

370 Mahon Avenue
Vancouver, BC V7M 3E1
250-555-1997
mcope@postbox.com

Objective

Put company's name in objective.

To help create high-quality CD-ROM products in Metatec's New Media Solutions Division

Editing and Proofreading Experience

- **Edited** a textbook published by Simon and Schuster, revising with attention to format, consistency, coherence, document integrity, and document design.
- **Proofed** training and instructor manuals, policy statements, student essays and research papers, internal documents, and promotional materials.
- **Worked with authors** in a variety of fields including English, communication, business, marketing, economics, education, history, sociology, biology, agriculture, computer science, law, and medicine to revise their prose and improve their writing skills by giving them oral and written feedback.

Writing Experience

- **Wrote** training and instructor manuals, professional papers, and letters, memos, and reports.
- **Co-authored** the foreword to a forthcoming textbook (Fall 2010) from NCTE press.
- **Contributed** to a textbook forthcoming (Fall 2010) from Bedford Books/St. Martin's Press.

Computer Experience

Computer experience is crucial for almost every job. Specify the software and hardware you've worked with.

- **Designed** a Web page using Microsoft Front Page (www.cohums.ohio-state.edu/english/People/Bracken.1/Sedgwick/)
- **Learned and used** a variety of programs on both Macintosh and PC platforms:
    Word processing and spreadsheets
    Microsoft Project
    FrontPage
    PageMaker
    Aspects (a form for online synchronous discussion)
    Storyspace (a hypertext writing environment)
    PowerPoint
    Email

Other Business and Management Experience

- **Developed** policies, procedures, and vision statements.
- **Supervised** new staff members in a mentoring program.
- **Coordinated** program and individual schedules, planned work and estimated costs, set goals, and evaluated progress and results.
- **Member of team that directed** the nation's largest first-year writing program.

Marcella G. Cope

Page 2

Employment History

- **Graduate Teaching Associate,** Department of English, the University of Victoria, September 2006–Present. Taught Intermediate and First-Year Composition.
- **Writing Consultant,** University Writing Centre, Simon Fraser University, January–April 2007
- **Program Administrator,** First-Year Writing Program, the University of Victoria, September 2006–January 2009

Honours

- **Phi Kappa Phi Honour Society,** inducted 2008. Membership based on performance in top 10 percent of graduate students nationwide.
- **Letters of Commendation,** 2003. Issued by the Director of Graduate Studies in recognition of outstanding achievement.
- **Dean's List**

Education

- **Master of Arts,** June 2008, the University of Victoria. Cumulative GPA: 4.0/4.0.
- **Bachelor of Arts,** June 2006, Simon Fraser University. Graduated with Honours.

Checkpoint

A **chronological résumé** summarizes what you did in a timeline, starting with the most recent events and going backward (**reverse chronology**). Use a chronological résumé when your education and experience

- Are a logical preparation for the position for which you're applying
- Show a steady progression leading to the present

Use a **functional** or **skills résumé** in these cases:

- Your education and experience are not the usual route to the position.
- You're changing fields.
- You want to combine experience from paid jobs, activities, volunteer work, and courses.
- Your recent work history might create the wrong impression.

What Parts of Résumé Formats Are the Same?

Increasingly all résumés begin with an attention-grabbing heading, such as Career Achievements, Career Highlights, Communication and Technical Skills, or Interpersonal Profile.

Every résumé should have an overview of your communication skills and an Education section. Career Objective, Honours and Awards, and References are optional.

Career Objective

Many job coaches and recruiters consider Career Objective statements irrelevant, and a waste of valuable space and placement.[1]

However, if you want to include a career objective statement, write it like the job description the employer might use in a job listing. Keep your statement brief—two or three lines at most. Tell what you want to do and what level of responsibility you want to hold.

Ineffective career objective:	To offer a company my excellent academic foundation in hospital technology and my outstanding skills in oral and written communication.
Better career objective:	Selling state-of-the-art Siemens medical equipment.

Including the employer's name in the objective is a nice touch.

As an alternative to writing a career objective statement, put the job title or field under your name:

Joan Larson Ooyen	Terence Garvey	David R. Lunde
Marketing	Technical Writer	Corporate Fitness Director

Interpersonal Profile/Communications Skills, Career Achievements

Highlight proficiency in foreign and computer languages, and identify your outstanding communication skills, in order of importance to the reader:

- Excellent researcher, writer, and editor
- Conversant in all software applications
- Multilingual: speak, read, and write Arabic, English, and Punjabi
- Proficient in Internet, intranet, and LAN

The functional or combination résumé uses career achievements to showcase measurable accomplishments:

- Started seasonal landscaping business Spring 2007; by Spring 2009 employed six full-time employees, generating revenues of $300 000.
- Generated revenue of $2.5 million over quota as Western Division Sales Manager.
- Implemented employee mentoring program resulting in a 40 percent increase in retention.
- Created new assembly procedure that cut production costs by 25 percent.
- Developed procedures manual now used in every national and international office.

Education

Education can be your first major category if you've just earned (or are about to earn) a degree, if you have a degree that is essential or desirable for the position you're seeking, or if you lack relevant work experience. Put Education later if you need all of page one to emphasize your skills and experience, or if you lack a degree that other applicants may have.

Include summer school if you took optional courses or extra electives to graduate early. Include study abroad, even if you didn't earn college credits. If you got a certificate for international study, give the name and explain the significance of the certificate.

Professional certifications can be listed under Education, under or after your name, or in a separate category.

Include your GPA only if it's good. Because grade point systems vary, specify what your GPA is based on: "3.4/4.0" means 3.4 on a 4.0 scale. If your GPA is under 3.0 on a 4.0 scale, use words rather than numbers: "B average." If your GPA isn't impressive, calculate your average in your major and your average for your last 60 hours. If these are higher than your overall GPA, consider using them.

List in reverse chronological order each degree earned; field of study; date; school, city, province, or state of any graduate work; short courses and professional certification courses; university, college, community college, or school from which you transferred.

B.S. in personnel management, June 2009, University of Waterloo, Waterloo, ON

A.S. in office management, June 2009, Georgian Community College, Barrie, ON

To fill a page, you can also list selected courses, using short descriptive titles rather than course numbers. Use a subhead such as "Courses Related to Major" or "Courses Related to Financial Management" that will allow you to list all the courses (including psychology, speech, and business communication) that will help you in the job for which you're applying.

Bachelor of Science in management, May 2009, University of Guelph, Guelph, ON
  GPA: 3.8/4.0
  Courses Related to Management:
  Personnel Administration   Business Decision-Making
     Finance   International Business
     Management I and II   Marketing
     Accounting I and II   Legal Environment of Business
     Business Report Writing   Business Speaking
Salutatorian, Eastview High School, June 2006, Toronto, ON

A third option is to list the number of hours in various subjects, especially if the combination of courses qualifies you for the position for which you're applying.

B.Sc. in marketing, May 2009, St. Francis Xavier University, Nova Scotia
  30 hours in Marketing
  15 hours in Spanish
  9 hours in Human Resources Management

Honours and Awards

The Honours and Awards heading creates a positive impression even when the reader skims the résumé. Include this category for all awards that reflect your drive for achievement and recognition.

Include the following kinds of entries in this category:

- Listings in recognition books (e.g., *Who's Who in Web Design*)
- Academic honour societies (Specify the nature of Greek-letter honour societies so the reader understands that these are more than social clubs.)

- Fellowships and scholarships
- Awards given by professional societies and community associations
- Major awards given by civic groups
- Music accreditation and awards; varsity letters; selection to provincial or national sports teams; finishes in provincial, national, or Olympic meets (These might also go under Activities but may look more impressive under Honours. Put them under one category or the other—not both.)

Omit honours such as "Miss Congeniality" that work against the professional image you want your résumé to create.

As a new graduate, you should try to put Honours on page one. In a skills and functional or combination résumé, place Honours and Awards on page two or three, depending on the space your Work Experience takes.

Build your praise portfolio: keep a file of letters, emails, thank-cards, and notes lauding your job performance.

References

Including references on a separate page anticipates the employer's needs and removes a potential barrier to your getting the job. You can, however, omit this category on your résumé, since prospective employers now take it for granted that applicants will supply references when required.

When you list references, use three to five. Include at least one professor and at least one employer or advisor—someone who can comment on your work habits and leadership skills.

Always ask the person's permission to list him or her as a reference. Don't say, "May I list you as a reference?" Instead, say, "Can you speak specifically and positively about my work?" Jog the person's mind by taking along copies of work you did for him or her and a copy of your current résumé. Tell your references what points you'd like them to stress in a letter.

Keep your list of references up to date. If it's been a year or more since you asked someone, ask again—and tell the person about your recent achievements.

References the reader knows are by far the most impressive. In a functional and skills résumé, choose people to recommend you who can testify to your abilities in the most important skills areas.

What Should I Do If the Standard Categories Don't Fit?

Create new ones.

Create headings that match your qualifications: Computer Skills, Military Experience, Foreign Languages, Summer and Part-Time Jobs, Marketing Experience, Publications, Exhibitions, Professional Associations.

Employability Skills

The items Education and Experience (if you use the latter term) always stand as separate categories, even if you have only one item under each head. Combine other headings so that you have at least two long or three short items under each heading. For example, if you're in one honour society, two social clubs, and on one athletic team, combine them all under Activities and Honours.

If you have more than seven items under a heading, consider using subheadings. For example, a student who had a great many activities might divide them into Student Government, Other Campus or Extracurricular Activities, and Community Service.

Put your strongest categories near the top and at the bottom of the first page. If you have impressive work experience, you might want to put that category first after your name, Education in the middle of the page, and your address at the bottom.

Should I Limit My Résumé Length?

Don't limit the length if you have lots of qualifications.

The average résumé is now two pages, unless you need more space to emphasize your qualifications. Executive search firm founder Michael Stern (Michael Stern Associates, Toronto) says readability always trumps conciseness: "someone with a lot of experience and expertise is better going to three pages than trying to fit everything on two pages of tiny, hard-to-read type."[2]

If you do use more than one page, the second page should have at least 10 to 12 lines. Use a second sheet and staple it to the first so that readers who skim see the staple and know that there's more. Leave less important information for the second page. Put your name and "Page 2" or "Cont." on the second page. If the pages get separated, you want the reader to know whom the qualifications belong to and that the second page is not your whole résumé.

How Do I Create a Scannable Résumé?

Take out all your formatting.

Employability Skills

Figure 25.6 shows an example of a scannable résumé. To increase the chances that the résumé is scanned correctly,

- Use a standard typeface: Helvetica, Futura, Optima, Times Roman, New Century Schoolbook, Courier, Univers, or Bookman.[3]
- Use 12- or 14-point type.
- Use the "ragged right" style—that is, do not use *justification* (which stretches each line out to the same length). Scanners can't always handle the extra spaces between words and letters that justification creates.
- Don't italicize or underline words—even for titles of books or newspapers that grammatically require such treatment.
- Put the text in bold to make sure letters don't touch each other. Then remove the bold.
- Don't use lines, boxes, script, leader dots, or borders.
- Don't use two-column formats or indented or centred text.
- Put each phone number on a separate line.
- Use plenty of white space.
- Don't fold or staple the pages.
- Don't write anything by hand on your résumé.

FIGURE 25.6   **A Scannable Résumé**

Jerry A. Jackson

Keywords: family financial management; financial planning; retirement planning; investment sales; computer modelling; competitive; self-starter; hard worker; responsible; self-managing; collegiate athletics; sales experience

Campus Address
St. Mary's Road
Winnipeg, SK R2H 1J2
(306) 555-5718
Email address: jjackson@ccw.sk.ca
Created a Web page on saving for life goals, such as a home, children's education, and retirement: http://hotmail.com/jackson.2495/home.htm

Permanent Address
2105 East Hill Avenue
Saskatoon, SK S7J 3C8
(306) 555-4108

Summary of Qualifications
High energy. Played sports during two years of college. Started two businesses.
Sales experience. Sold both clothing and investments successfully.
Presentation skills. In individual and group presentations, spoke to groups ranging from 2 to 75 people. Gave informative, persuasive, and inspirational talks.
Financial experience. Knowledgeable about stocks and bonds, especially energy and telecommunication companies.
Computer experience. Microsoft Word, Excel, SPSS, PowerPoint, and Dreamweaver.
Experience creating Web pages.

Education
A.A.S. in Finance, May 2009, Community College of Winnipeg, Winnipeg, SK
B Grade Point Average
Comprehensive courses related to program provide not only the basics of family financial management but also skills in communication, writing, speaking, small groups, and computer modelling
Intermediate Accounting I and II
Business Writing
Consumer Finance
Financial Management
Interpersonal Communication
Investments
Microeconomics
Presentation Skills
Public Speaking
Report and Technical Writing
Sociology of Marriage and Family
Statistics

Sports Experience
Intramural Hockey Team (Champions, Winter 2008)
Two-Year Varsity Letterman, Community College of Winnipeg
Men's NCAA Division II Basketball

Annotations (right margin):

Use 12- or 14-point type in a standard typeface. Here, Times Roman is used.

In keywords, use labels and terms that employers might include in job listing.

Give as much information as you like. The computer doesn't care how long the document is.

Don't use columns. Scanners can't handle them.

FIGURE 25.6   A Scannable Résumé (continued)

Experience

Financial Sales Representative, Primerica Company, Winnipeg, SK, February 2007–present. Work with clients to plan investment strategies; recommend specific investments, including stocks, bonds, mutual funds, and annuities.

Entrepreneur, Winnipeg, SK, and Saskatoon, SK, September 2005–January 2007. Created a saleable product, secured financial backing, found a manufacturer, supervised production, and sold product—12 dozen T-shirts at a $5.25 profit each—to help pay for school expenses.

Landscape Maintenance Supervisor, Saskatoon, SK, Summers 2000–2005. Formed a company to cut lawns, put up fences, fertilize, garden, and paint houses. Hired, fired, trained, motivated, and paid friends to complete jobs. Managerial experience.

Collector and Repairman, ACN Inc., Saskatoon, SK, Summer 2005. Collected and counted up to $10 000 a day. Worked with technicians to troubleshoot and repair electronic and coin mechanisms of video and pinball games, cigarette machines, and jukeboxes. Drove company cars and trucks throughout Saskatoon metro area to collect cash and move and repair machines.

Willing to relocate
Willing to travel
Canadian citizen

> Don't justify margins. Doing so creates extra spaces that confuse scanners.

- Send a laser copy. Stray marks defeat scanners.
- To increase the number of matches or "hits,"
  - Use a Keywords section under your name, address, and phone. In it, put
    - Degrees, job field or title, accomplishments
    - Interpersonal strengths and attitudes: *dependable, skill in time management, leadership, sense of responsibility*.[4]
- Use industry buzzwords and jargon, even if redundant. For example, "Web page design and HTML coding" will "match" either "Web" or "HTML" as a keyword.
  - Use nouns. Some systems don't handle verbs well.
  - Use common headings such as Summary of Qualifications, Strengths, Certifications, as well as Education, Experience, and so on.
- Use as many pages as necessary.
- Mention specific software programs (e.g., Adobe Dreamweaver, FrontPage) that you've used.
- Be specific and quantifiable. "Managed $2 million building materials account" will generate more hits than "manager" or "managerial experience." Listing Microsoft FrontPage as a skill won't help as much as "Used Microsoft FrontPage to design an interactive Web page for a national fashion retailer, with links to information about style trends, current store promotions, employment opportunities, and an online video fashion show."
- Join honour societies and professional and trade organizations, since they're often used as keywords.[5]
- Spell out Greek-letter societies (the scanner will mangle Greek characters, even if your computer has them): "Pi Sigma Alpha Honour Society." For English words, spell out the organization name; follow it with the abbreviation in parentheses: "College Newspaper Business and Advertising Managers Association (CNBAM)." That way, the résumé will be tagged whether the recruiter searches for the full name or the acronym.
- Put everything in the résumé, rather than "saving" some material for the cover letter. Although some applicant tracking systems can search for keywords in cover letters and other application materials, most only extract information from the résumé, even though they store the other papers. The length of the résumé doesn't matter.

How Should I Prepare an Online Résumé?

Follow these guidelines.

With the popularity of the Web, you may want to post your résumé online. If you don't know hypertext markup language (HTML), the programming that displays Web pages in your browser, you can save your résumé as HTML in Word or WordPerfect. However, if you're claiming the ability to code Web pages as one of your skills, use real HTML.

In your Web résumé,

- Include an email link at the top of the résumé under your name.
- Omit your street addresses and phone numbers. (A post office box is okay.) Employers who find your résumé on the Web will have the technology to email you.
- Consider having links under your name and email address to the various parts of your résumé. Use keywords and phrases that tell the viewer what you offer: *Marketing Experience.*
- Link to other pages that provide more information about you (a list of courses, a report you have written) but not to organizations (your university, and employer) that shift emphasis away from your credentials.
- Be businesslike: link to other pages only if they highlight or demonstrate your abilities, and convey the same professional image as your résumé.
- Put your strongest qualification immediately after your name and email address. If the first screen doesn't interest readers, they won't scroll through the rest of the résumé.
- Specify the job you want.
- Specify city and province for educational institutions and employers.
- Use lists, indentations, and white space to create visual variety.
- Proofread the résumé carefully.

MODULE SUMMARY

- Your résumé should fill at least one page. Use two or more pages if you have extensive experience and activities.
- Make the résumé attractive and readable: use plenty of white space, bold headings, and revise and edit to perfection.
- Emphasize your key points:
  - Put them in headings.
  - Use keywords.
  - List them vertically.
  - Provide details.
- Emphasize information that is
  - Relevant to the job you want
  - Expressed in industry- and ad-related language
  - Specific about how you can contribute to the job

- Résumés use sentence fragments. Make items concise and parallel. Emphasize action verbs and gerunds.
- The **chronological** résumé summarizes your experiences and activities in a timeline, starting with the most recent events and going backwards. It emphasizes degrees, dates, and job titles. Use a chronological résumé when your education and experience
  - Are a logical preparation for the position
  - Show a steady progression leading to the present
- **Functional** and **skills** résumés emphasize your experiences and applied skills. Use a skills résumé when
  - Your education and experience are not the usual route to the position for which you are applying.
  - You are changing fields.

○ You want to showcase the extent of your experience from a combination of paid jobs and community and volunteer work.

○ Your recent work history may create the wrong impression (has gaps, indicates a demotion, shows job-hopping, etc.).

• To create a scannable résumé, create a plain text using industry jargon, buzzwords, and acronyms.

• In a Web résumé, put your strongest qualification(s) first, and specify the position you want. Omit street addresses and phone numbers, consider having links to parts of the résumé, and proofread carefully.

ASSIGNMENTS FOR MODULE 25

Questions for Critical Thinking

25.1 Where can you find keywords to use in your résumé? What criteria would you use to choose those keywords?

25.2 What are the arguments for and against listing references on your résumé?

25.3 What information should you include in a career objective statement? Why?

Exercises and Problems

25.4   Analyzing Your Accomplishments

1. List the 10 accomplishments that give you the most personal satisfaction. These might be achievements that other people wouldn't notice. They can be accomplishments you've done recently, or things you did years ago.

   Use jot notes or clustering to answer the following questions for each accomplishment:

   a. What skills or knowledge did you use?
   b. What personal traits did you exhibit?
   c. What about this accomplishment makes it personally satisfying to you?

2. Find a print ad or Web post position in a company or industry that appeals to you.
3. Create achievement statements on each of your accomplishments:

   a. Use the language of the advertised position and the industry.
   b. Start with your accomplishments that appear most relevant to the position.
   c. Quantify your accomplishments when possible.

As your instructor directs,

   a. Share your answers with a small group of students.
   b. Summarize your answers in a memo to your instructor.
   c. List the most significant of these on your résumé.

25.5   Remembering What You've Done

Use the following list to jog your memory about what you've done. For each, give three or four details as well as a general statement.

Describe a time when you

1. Used facts and figures to gain agreement on an important point
2. Identified a problem faced by a group or organization and developed a plan for solving the problem
3. Made a presentation or a speech to a group
4. Responded to criticism
5. Interested other people in something that was important to you and persuaded them to take the actions you wanted
6. Helped a group deal constructively with conflict
7. Demonstrated creativity

As your instructor directs,

   a. Identify which job(s) each detail is relevant for.
   b. Identify which details would work well on a résumé.
   c. Identify which details, further developed, would work well in a job letter.

25.6   Evaluating Career Objective Statements

None of the following career objective statements is effective. What is wrong with each as it stands? Which might be revised to be satisfactory? Which should be dropped?

1. To use my acquired knowledge of accounting to eventually own my own business
2. A progressively responsible position as a MARKETING MANAGER where education and ability would have valuable application and lead to advancement

3. To work with people responsibly and creatively, helping them develop personal and professional skills
4. A position in international marketing that makes use of my specialization in marketing and my knowledge of foreign markets
5. To design and maintain Web pages

25.7 Writing a Paper Résumé

Write a résumé on paper that you could mail to an employer or hand to an interviewer at an interview.

As your instructor directs,

a. Write a résumé for the field in which you hope to find a job.
b. Write two different résumés for two different job paths you are interested in pursuing.
c. Adapt your résumé to a specific company you hope to work for.

25.8 Writing a Scannable Résumé

Take the résumé you like best from Problem 25.7 and create a scannable version of it. Post your résumé on three industry-specific Web sites.

POLISHING YOUR PROSE

Proofreading

Wait until the final draft is complete to edit and proofread. There is no point in proofreading words and passages that might change. (Some writers claim to proofread documents while they're composing; this practice is like trying to mow the lawn and trim the hedges at the same time.)

Editing includes checking for you-attitude and positive emphasis, fixing any sexist or biased language, and correcting grammatical errors.

Proofreading means making sure that the document is free from typos. Check each of the following aspects:

- **Spelling.** Scan for misspelled or misused words that spell checkers don't catch: *not* instead of *now*, *you* instead of *your*, *its* instead of *it's*, *their* instead of *there* or *they're*, *one* instead of *won*, and so forth.
- **Consistency.** Check abbreviations and special terms.
- **Names.** Double-check the reader's name.
- **Punctuation.** Make sure that parentheses and quotation marks come in pairs. Be on the lookout for missing or extra commas and periods.
- **Format.** Look for errors in spacing, margins, and document design, especially if you compose your document on one computer and print it out at another. Use the correct format for citations—MLA, APA, Chicago, and so on.
- **Numbers and dates.** Double-check all numbers to make sure they add up. Make sure page numbers appear where they should and are sequential. Do the same for tables of contents or appendices. Check dates.

Proofreading is as individual as writing style. Try these methods or invent your own:

- *Read the document from the last word to the first* to catch spelling errors.
- *Read the document in stages*—first page, second page, third page—with plenty of "rest" in between so you are fresh for each page.
- *Read pages out of sequence* so you can concentrate on the characters on the page rather than the meaning.
- *Read the document aloud*, listening for awkward or incorrect phrasing.
- *Ask a friend to read the document aloud*, voicing punctuation, while you follow along with the original.

Whatever your approach, build time into the composing process for proofreading. If possible, finish the document a day or two before it's due to allow enough time. (If the document is a 100-page report, allow even more time.) If you're in a hurry, use a spell checker, proof the document yourself, and ask a friend or colleague to proof it as well.

Exercises

Proofread the following passages:

1. Ours are a company worth doing business with. Your can count on our promiss to provide not only the best service but, also the finest in materials, fit, and, finish. All of are products our made to exacting specifications meaning that you received the best product for the best prices. If you aren't satisfied

for any reason, simply call the toll-free hotline at 1-800-555-1212 to get a promp refund. Or you can right us at: The John Doe Company, 123 Main Street Anytown Canada M6V 2B4. Remember; our moto is "the customers is always's right?

2. Resumee for Kathy Jones
332 West Long Strt.
Moncton, New Brunswick E4Z 1Z8
614-555-8188

Objection

A management position in fullfilament services where my skills, expereince can be best be used to help your company acheeve it's goals.

Relevent Experience:

2006 to Present Day: Ass. Manager for high-end sports equipment distributor. Responsible for checking new customers out.

1999–2005: Owned and Operated Jones, Inc., a telephone order proceing company for lady's apparel.

2000: Received a plague for Must Promising Executive of the Year" from *Monthly* Magazine.

2002: Delivery address to local high school seniors on why accuracy is important in business.

Special Skills

Type 7 or more words per minute
Studied English all my life. Fluent in French.
Shot at local gun club.

Check your answers to the odd-numbered exercises on page 553.

Creating Persuasive Application Letters

Learning Objectives

After reading and applying the information in Module 26, you'll be able to demonstrate

Knowledge of

- The two types of application letter formats

Skills to

- Organize the solicited application letter
- Organize the prospecting application letter
- Catch the reader's interest even when the company isn't planning to hire
- Show that you have the qualifications for the job
- Persuade the employer that you're in the very top group of applicants
- Use information about the company effectively in your letter

Employability Skills 2000+ Checklist

In this module, the key skills from the Conference Board of Canada's Employability Skills 2000+ are

Communicate

○ read and understand information presented in a variety of forms (e.g., words, graphs, charts, diagrams)
○ write and speak so others pay attention and understand

○ share information using a range of information and communications technologies (e.g., voice, email, computers)
○ use relevant scientific, technological, and mathematical knowledge and skills to explain or clarify ideas

Manage Information

○ locate, gather, and organize information using appropriate technology and information systems

○ access, analyze, and apply knowledge and skills from a variety of disciplines (e.g., the arts, languages, science, technology, mathematics, social sciences, and the humanities)

Think & Solve Problems

○ assess situations and identify problems
○ recognize the human, interpersonal, technical, scientific, and mathematical dimensions of a problem

○ readily use science, technology, and mathematics as ways to think, gain and share knowledge, solve problems, and make decisions
○ check to see if a solution works, and act on opportunities for improvement

Demonstrate Positive Attitudes & Behaviours

○ feel good about yourself and be confident

○ deal with people, problems, and situations with honesty, integrity, and personal ethics

Participate in Projects & Tasks

○ plan, design, or carry out a project or task from start to finish with well-defined objectives and outcomes

The purpose of a job application letter, and your résumé, is to impress the recruiter enough to want to interview you. If you get a job through interviews arranged by a campus placement office or through contacts, you may not need to write a letter. However, you will need a letter if you want to work for an organization that isn't interviewing on campus, or when you change jobs. A well-written application letter captures the recruiter's interest, ensuring he or she will read your résumé. The letter is also your first step in showing a specific company what you have to offer.

The best application letters are customized to their audiences. Use the cover letter to provide a brief preview of your résumé, focusing on

• Key requirements of the job for which you're applying, using the language in the job posting
• Skills and knowledge that differentiate you from other applicants

FIGURE 26.1 **PAIBOC Questions for Analysis**

P   What are your **purposes** in writing? As usual, you have several: to attract and hold attention; to stand out favourably from other candidates; to demonstrate you have researched the organization and the position; to preview your résumé.

A   Who is your **audience**? What audience characteristics are relevant to this particular message? What does your audience want to know? How much time will you audience give your message? What can you do to favourably influence your audience to continue reading?

I   What **information** must your message include?

   In a cover letter, highlight (1) the superiority of your skills and (2) the fit between the organization's needs and your qualifications.

B   What reasons or reader **benefits** can you use to support your position?

   Use the application letter to briefly summarize the qualifications you bring to the position, and the value to the organization.

O   What **objections** can you expect your readers to have? What elements of your message will your audience perceive as negative? How can you write to overcome audience objections, or deemphasize negative elements?

C   How will the **context** affect reader response? Consider your relationship to the reader, the reader's values and expectations, recent organizational history and current morale, the economy, the time of year, and any special circumstances surrounding the message exchange.

   Here is the overriding cultural context: recruiters want to interview only those prospects whose application letter and résumé demonstrate their value to the organization.

- Language and information that demonstrates your knowledge of the organization and the industry
- Experiences expressed in transferable, marketable skills

Note that the advice in this book applies to job-hunting in Canada. Conventions, expectations, and criteria differ from culture to culture: different norms apply in different countries. Even within Canada, different discourse communities (Module 2) may have different preferences. For example, letters applying for sales jobs might need to be more aggressive than the samples in this module. Whether you're seeking employment in your home province, nationally, or internationally, however, your PAIBOC analysis (see Figure 26.1) is vital to your success. Well-written job application letters are the most persuasive messages.

Every employer wants businesslike employees who understand professionalism. Follow these guidelines to make your application letter professional:

- Create your letter on a computer. Use a standard serif font (Times Roman) in 12-point type.
- Address your letter to a specific person. If the reader is a woman, call the office to find out whether she prefers a courtesy title (Module 9).
- Use the language of the organization and the industry.
- Use contact or employee names if the reader knows them and thinks well of them, if they think well of you and will say good things about you, and if you have permission to use their names.
- Always connect an experience (course work, co-op placement, community involvement) with a resultant skill that you know the prospective employer wants.
- Unless you're applying for a creative job, use business stationery and a conservative style: few contractions, no sentence fragments, clichés, or slang.
- Edit the letter carefully and proof it several times to make sure it's perfect.

What Kind of Letter Should I Use?

Customizing your application to your audience guarantees positive results: seven Canadians made the finalist roster for Australian Tourism Board's "best job in the world," based on their YouTube application videos. The job: living on Hamilton Island for six months, and blogging about it. The pay: $150 000. To view applicants' videos, go to www.islandreefjob.com.[1]

It depends on whether the company has asked for applications.

Two different hiring situations call for two different kinds of application letters. Write a **solicited letter** when you know that the company is hiring: you've seen an ad, you've been advised to apply by a professor or friend, or you've read online or in a trade publication that the company is expanding.

Sometimes, however, the advertised positions may not be what you want, or you may want to work for an organization that has not announced that it has openings in your area. Then the situation calls for an **unsolicited** or **prospecting letter**.

Prospecting letters help you tap into the hidden job market (Module 24). In some cases, your prospecting letter may arrive at a company that has decided to hire but has not yet announced the job. In other cases, companies create positions to get a good person who is on the market.

Language FOCUS

To **prospect** means to search or explore. In the 1800s in Canada and the United States, people joined gold rushes to prospect for gold. They hoped to become rich by finding an unexplored area full of gold. When you are writing a prospecting letter, imagine yourself as a gold miner looking for that hidden job. While the job may not make you rich, at least you may find one that no one else knew existed!

How Are the Two Letters Different?

They begin and end differently.

When you know the company is hiring, organize your letter in this way:

1. State that you're applying for the job (phrase the job title as your source phrased it). Tell where you learned about the job (Web, referral, ad). Briefly show that you have the major qualifications required by the ad: a degree, professional certification, job experience, and so forth. Summarize your other qualifications briefly in the same order in which you plan to discuss them in the letter. This **summary sentence** or **paragraph** then covers everything you will talk about, and serves as an organizing device for your letter.

> I have a good background in standard accounting principles and procedures and a working knowledge of some of the special accounting practices of the oil industry. This working knowledge is based on practical experience in the oil fields: I've pumped, tailed rods, and worked as a roustabout.
>
> Let me put my oil industry experience and accounting knowledge to work for Standard Oil.

2. Develop your major qualifications in detail. Be specific about what you've done; relate your achievements to the work you'd be doing in this new job. This is not the place for modesty!

3. Develop your other qualifications, even if the ad doesn't ask for them. (If the position description states numerous qualifications, pick the most important three or four.) Show what separates you from the other prospects who will also apply. Demonstrate your knowledge of the organization.

4. Ask for an interview; tell when you'll be available to be interviewed. End on a positive note.

Figures 26.2 and 26.3 are examples of a solicited letter.

FIGURE 26.2 **A Solicited Letter (1)**

880 Middlegate Road
Mississauga, ON L4Y 1M3

September 5, 2009

Mr. William Chen
Director
The Resources Corporation
2025 Sheppard Avenue East
Toronto, ON M2J 1V7

Dear Mr. William Chen:

Please consider my application for the position of **Auditor**, advertised in the *Toronto Star*, September 3, 2007. My education and auditing experience, and my organizational, analytical, and communication skills make me an ideal candidate for the position.

After graduating in Business Administration, Finance, I received my CA designation in November 2005. My Finance program focused on the Canadian regulatory/securites industry standards and by-laws. Indeed, in my third year at Centennial College, I completed an analytical report about the Canadian regulatory and security market. During my co-operative placement with Tort, Tort, and Tort, I also assisted CA's in their field examinations and in-office desk reviews of regulatory filings of association audit jurisdiction firms. Although we often worked under intense pressure, my organizational and communication skills helped me to graduate with an A+ average; furthermore, based on my performance with the firm, Tort, Tort, and Tort offered me a full-time position upon graduation.

Instead, I chose to work as a financial sales representative for Templeton Trust. As you know, financial selling is a highly competitive field, but I enjoy competing. While in high school, for example, I created a business, hired a staff, and recruited clients. My entrepreneurial experiences taught me the value of hard work, dedication, and accountability, requisite qualities for auditors.

In the last year, as financial sales representative for Templeton Trust, I've honed my analytical and communication skills while helping clients develop financial plans and investment products tailored to their needs. I welcome the opportunity to contribute my knowledge and skills to the continuing success and superb reputation of The Resources Corporation.

Can we meet to discuss this possibility? I can be reached at (416) 555-4415, to arrange an interview time and date at your convenience.

Sincerely,

Jerry Jackson

Jerry Jackson
Enclosure: Résumé

Annotations (left margin):
Addresses reader as ad indicates.

Begin as few sentences as possible with "I."

Shows self-motivation, sales and managerial skills; demonstrates active learner with transferable skills.

Annotations (right margin):
Block format is standard in business.

Paragraph 1 is thesis or controlling paragraph. It repeats language of the ad and identifies the specific qualifications the rest of the letter will demonstrate.

Provides specific auditing experience.

Details demonstrate applicant has excellent communication skills.

Ask for the interview.

FIGURE 26.3   **A Solicited Letter (2)**

Addresses reader as ad indicates

Repeats words of the ad

Specifics directly connect the experience with the resultant skill

Demonstrates research and industry awareness

638 Changery Court
Lethbridge, AB T1J 2A5
May 21, 2009

Shelley Aquina
Human Resources Manager
Home Outfitters
425 18 Avenue Northwest
Calgary AB T2N 2G6

Dear Shelley Aquina:
RE: File # 7664566-F

Please consider me for the position of sales manager, advertised in the *Calgary Sun*, Saturday, May 20. I possess the educational background, work experience, and exceptional organizational and communication skills for which you have advertised.

In June I will graduate with a business administration diploma from Mount Royal College, Calgary, Alberta. Throughout my college career I worked with peers on a variety of projects, including sales proposals, formal reports, and sales presentations. In my third year I was chosen team captain for our marketing project, a year-long analysis, and oral and written report of possible marketing initiatives for a Calgary client, MediaWaves. My responsibilities included identifying time lines, delegating tasks, negotiating conflicts among group members, reporting to the client and our Marketing professor, and revising and editing the final 30-page report. Our team project not only secured the top grade in the class, but the client also accepted our recommendations, resulting in an immediate 10 percent sales increase for MediaWaves.

Since Grade 11 I have worked part-time and summers at Canadian Tire in Lethbridge, Alberta. Starting as a stock clerk, I worked my way up to sales associate. My supervisor has commented on my excellent sales skills, particularly my product knowledge and ability to up-sell. During my employment with Canadian Tire—a high-energy, fast-paced environment—I learned to focus calmly on clients' concerns and to communicate confidently. As a result of my performance, I was promoted to assistant manager. While working part-time, attending school, and participating in varsity basketball, I learned to juggle multiple priorities, to manage my time, and to problem-solve.

Please see my résumé for further details.

The market for home decorations and furnishings has become increasingly competitive, and, with the entry of American big-box stores like Heritage Homes, it promises to become even more so. I would welcome an opportunity to apply my skills to increase your market share. Please call me at 403-555-4339 to arrange an interview time and date at your convenience.

Sincerely,

Carlos DeLeon
ENC: résumé

Quotes file number as ad requests

Thesis or controlling paragraph tells the reader what's going to be proven in the letter

Jargon of the marketing industry

Skills would have been identified in the ad as necessary for the position

Asks for the interview

Prospecting

When you don't have any evidence that the company is hiring, organize your letter this way:

1. Catch the reader's interest.
2. Create a **bridge** between the attention-getter and your qualifications. Focus on what you know and can do. Since the employer is not planning to hire, he or she won't be impressed with the fact that you're graduating. Summarize your qualifications briefly in the same order in which you plan to discuss them in the letter.

3. Develop your strong points in detail. Be specific. Relate what you've done in the past to what you could do for this company. Show that you know something about the company. Identify the niche you want to fill.

4. Ask for an interview and tell when you'll be available for interviews. (Don't tell when you can begin work.) End on a positive, forward-looking note.

Figure 26.4 presents this pattern visually. Figure 26.5 shows an example of a prospecting letter.

FIGURE 26.4

How to Organize a Prospecting Letter

Attention-Getter
Details
Details
Request for Action

FIGURE 26.5   **A Prospecting Letter**

Kristine Manalili
2 Inverary Court
Porters Lake, Nova Scotia B3E 1M8
902-555-6488 kmanalili@hotmail.com

2009-06-25

Mr. John Harrobin
HealthRhab Inc.
2653 Dublin Street
Halifax, NS B3K 3J7

Dear Mr. Harrobin:

Providing an athlete with physiotherapy can assist with a debilitating injury in the short term but may not provide the long-term product and therapy information necessary for complete recovery. It can be a real challenge finding employees who are conversant with the latest injury-management modalities, who are familiar with the most current injury-management support equipment, and who also work well with rehabilitating clients. However, you will see from my enclosed résumé that I have this useful combination of skills.

Rita Haralabidis tells me that HealthRhab needs people to identify injury-management therapy and equipment for your clients. My education and work experience have provided me with the injury evaluation and product knowledge that you require. While studying at Nunavut Arctic College's Sports Injury Management program, for example, I provided more than 200 hours of successful client care at the College clinic.

Moreover, I was able to apply the most current therapy modalities and to learn about sophisticated sports injury products and equipment while serving my four-month co-op term at Wu's Sports Clinic in Victoria, British Columbia. Wu's Clinic is renowned for its progressive therapy options. My co-op placement provided me with practical experience in injury prevention and treatment. Equally important, I learned about the latest equipment, products, and techniques available to maximize client rehabilitation and recovery.

My communication skills and product knowledge would enable me to adapt immediately to clients' specific needs and to develop programs for your clients. I am flexible, a quick study, and committed to proactive health care. I will call you next week to arrange a mutually convenient time when we can discuss putting my talents to work for HealthRhab.

Sincerely,

Kristine Manalili
Enclosed: Résumé

Annotations:

Kristine creates a boxed "letterhead"

In an unsolicited or prospecting letter, open with a sentence that ① Create reader interest ② Provides a natural bridge to talking about yourself

Refers to her enclosed résumé

Refers to mutual acquaintance

Shows knowledge of the company

Demonstrates knowledge and skills she promised in first paragraph

Relates what she's done to what she could do for this company

Promises action

The First Paragraph of a Solicited Letter

When you know that the firm is hiring, refer to the specific position in your first sentence. Your letter can then be routed to the appropriate person, thus speeding up consideration of your application. Identify where you learned about the job: "the position of junior accountant announced in Sunday's *Vancouver Sun*," "Kadji Kado, our placement director, told me that you are looking for...."

Note how the following paragraph picks up several of the characteristics of the ad:

Ad:	Business Education Instructor at University of New Brunswick. Candidate must possess a bachelor's degree in Business Education. Will be responsible for providing in-house training to business and government leaders.... Candidate should have at least six months' office experience. Prior teaching experience not required.
Letter:	Please consider me for the position of **Business Education Instructor**, advertised on Workopolis.com. My Business Education degree, knowledge of adult education principles, and previous office experience make me the ideal candidate for the position.

Good word choices can help set your letter apart from the hundreds of letters the company is likely to get in response to an ad. The following first paragraph of a letter in response to an ad by Allstate Insurance Company shows knowledge of the firm's advertising slogan and sets itself apart from the dozens of letters that start with "I would like to apply for...."

> The Allstate Insurance Company is famous for its "Good Hands Policy." I would like to lend a helping hand to many Canadians as a financial analyst for Allstate, as advertised in yesterday's *National Post*. I have an Accounting Co-op diploma from Georgian College and I have worked with figures, computers, and people.

Note that the last sentence forecasts the organization of the letter, preparing for paragraphs about the student's academic background and (in this order) experience with "figures, computers, and people."

First Paragraphs of Prospecting Letters

In a prospecting letter, asking for a job in the first paragraph is dangerous; unless the company plans to hire but has not yet announced openings, the reader is likely to throw the letter away. Instead, catch the reader's interest. Then in the second paragraph shift the focus to your skills and experience, showing how they can be useful to the employer.

Here is an effective first paragraph and the second paragraph of a letter applying to be a computer programmer for an insurance company:

> Computers alone aren't the answer to demands for higher productivity in the competitive insurance business. Merging a poorly written letter with a database of customers just sends out bad letters more quickly. But you know how hard it is to find people who can both program computers and write well.
>
> My education and training have given me this useful combination of skills. I'd like to put my degree in computer technology and my business writing experience to work in Sun Canada's service approach to insurance.

Last Paragraphs

In the last paragraph, indicate when you'd be available for an interview. If you're free any time, say so. But it's likely that you have responsibilities in class and work. If you'd have to go out of town, there may be only certain days of the week or certain weeks that you could leave town for several days. Use a sentence that fits your situation.

> I could come to Thunder Bay for an interview anytime between March 17 and 21.
>
> Please call me at 519-555-4229, for an interview time and date at your convenience.

Should you wait for the employer to call you, or should you call the employer to request an interview? In a solicited letter, you may want to wait to be contacted: you know the employer wants to hire someone, and if your letter and résumé show that you're one of the top applicants, you'll get an interview.

In a prospecting letter, definitely call the employer. Because the employer is not planning to hire, you'll get a higher percentage of interviews if you're assertive. When you do call, be polite to the person who answers the phone.

If you're writing a prospecting letter to a firm that's more than a few hours away by car, say that you'll be in the area the week of such-and-such and could stop by for an interview. Some companies pay for follow-up visits, but not for first interviews. A company may be reluctant to ask you to make an expensive trip when it isn't yet sure it wants to hire you.

End the letter on a positive note that suggests you look forward to the interview and that you see yourself as a person who has something to contribute, not as someone who just needs a job.

> On Wednesday, April 25, I will call you between 9:00 and 9:30 A.M. to schedule a time when we can discuss how my skills can contribute to RIM's continued growth.

What Parts of the Two Letters Are the Same?

The body paragraphs discussing your qualifications are the same.

In both solicited and prospecting letters you should follow these guidelines:

- Address the letter to a specific person.
- Indicate the specific position for which you're applying.
- Be specific about your qualifications.
- Show what separates you from other applicants.
- Demonstrate knowledge of the company and the position.
- Refer to your résumé (which you would enclose with the letter).
- Ask for an interview.

Showing a Knowledge of the Position and the Company

If you can substitute another inside address and salutation and send out the letter without any further changes, it isn't specific enough. Use your knowledge of the position and the company to choose relevant evidence from what you've done to support your claims that you could help the company. (See Figures 26.3 and 26.5.)

Employability Skills

One or two specific details are usually enough to demonstrate your knowledge. Be sure to use the knowledge, not just repeat it. Never present the information as though it will be news to the reader. After all, the reader works for the company and presumably knows much more about it than you do.

Employability Skills

Separating Yourself from Other Applicants

Your knowledge of the company separates you from other applicants. You can also use course work, an understanding of the field, and experience in jobs and extracurricular events to show that you're unique.

This student example uses summer jobs and course work to set herself apart from other applicants:

> A company as diverse as Monsanto requires extensive record keeping as well as numerous internal and external communications. Both my summer jobs and my course work have prepared me for these responsibilities. As office manager for Safety Express Limited, I was in charge of most of the bookkeeping and letter writing for the company. I kept accurate records for each workday, and I often entered more than 100 transactions in a single day. In business and technical writing courses I learned how to write persuasive letters and memos and how to present extensive data in clear and concise reports.

Checkpoint

When writing a **job letter**, you must

- Address the letter to a specific person
- Indicate the specific position for which you're applying
- Be specific about your qualifications
- Show what separates you from other applicants
- Show a knowledge of the company and the position
- Refer to your résumé (which you would enclose with the letter)
- Ask for an interview

How Long Should My Letter Be?

Highlight the fit between the position and your qualifications clearly and concisely.

Your cover letter and résumé may be one of hundreds under review. The more readable your application letter, the more likely you will attract the favourable attention of those responsible for deciding whom to interview. Keep your letter as concise and clear as possible. Write one page or less.

Without eliminating content, make each sentence concise to be sure that you're using space as efficiently as possible. If your letter is still slightly over a page, use smaller margins, a type size that's one point smaller, or justified proportional type to get more on the page.

If you need more than a page, use it. The extra space gives you room to be more specific about what you've done and to add details about your experience that separate you from other applicants. Employers don't want longer letters, but they will read them *if* the letter is well written and *if* you establish early in the letter that you have the credentials and skills the company needs.

How Do I Create the Right Tone?

Use you-attitude and positive emphasis.

You-attitude and positive emphasis help you sound assertive without being arrogant.

You-Attitude

Unsupported claims may sound overconfident, selfish, or arrogant. Create you-attitude (Module 6) by describing exactly what you have done and by showing how that relates to what you could do for this employer.

EXPANDING A CRITICAL SKILL

Targeting a Specific Company in Your Letter

If your combination of skills is in high demand, a one-size-fits-all letter may get you an interview. But when you must compete against dozens—perhaps hundreds or even thousands—of applicants for an interview slot, you need to target your letter to the specific company. Targeting a specific company also helps you prepare for the job interview.

The Web makes it easy to find information about a company. The example below shows how applicants could use information posted on the Sleeman Breweries Limited Web site, at www.sleeman.com.

Check for Facts About the Company

Like most corporate Web sites, Sleeman offers dozens of facts about the company. A computer network administrator might talk about helping to keep the 3 500 LANs working well. A Web weaver might talk about supporting a new investor relations site, or about developing even more interactive content for both national and international potential investors. Someone in corporate communications, advertising, marketing, or multimedia programs might write a prospecting letter about Sleeman's recent media campaign. An interviewee with experience in international business might pitch the company on the know-how necessary to do business in Boston, Germany, and South Africa. And someone in human resources management might talk about the electronic processing of HR data benefits for the thousands of employees joining this expanding company, or about current recruitment and retention strategies for the company that CIBC World Markets Inc. calls "a well-managed, creative company."

Check News Releases and Speeches

Recent press releases have covered everything from the company's national expansion—across the Maritimes, into Quebec, and western Canada—to its international partnerships with U.S., German, and South African breweries. Anyone in international business might talk about helping Sleeman expand its base into China—and beyond.

In May 2009, in recognition of its "commitment to the environment and its sustainable packaging practices," the company received "a *Certificate of Environmental Sustainability* from corrugated supplier Atlantic Packaging Products Ltd...." Students about to complete environmental studies, marketing, finance, and management programs might demonstrate how their course work and experience prepare them to expand this and similar community-focused programs; or students might offer technical or managerial expertise on the best way for Sleeman Breweries to adopt e-business strategies for its continuing growth.

Check the Corporate Culture

In his interviews, Chair and CEO John Sleeman emphasizes that his family-owned business produces a quality product based on his great-great-grandfather's recipe. The company's Web site material also refers to the family beer-making tradition and the site's design reinforces this commitment to traditional values. These promotional strategies appeal to the mature consumers who buy Sleeman beers. Yet Sleeman's partnership arrangements and media advertisements indicate the company's enthusiasm for creativity and flexibility. Prospective job applicants would do well to stress their creative abilities and their support of community arts activities.

Sources: Canadian Packaging staff, "Cheers to Sleeman," *Canadian Packaging*, June 12, 2009, retrieved August 12, 2009, http://www.canadian-manufacturing.com/canadianpackaging/news/sustainabilitynews/article.jsp?content=20090612_100716_6988; 2009 CBS Interactive Inc., "Sleeman Breweries Ltd.," *BNET Industries*, retrieved August 12, 2009, http://resources.bnet.com/topic/sleeman+breweries+ltd.html; Michael Van Aelst, quoted in Oliver Bertin, "Sleeman Brew Balance of Risk and Caution," *The Globe and Mail*, June 20, 2001, p. M1.

Lacks you-attitude: An inventive and improvising individual like me is a necessity in your business.

You-attitude: Building a summer house-painting business gave me the opportunity to find creative solutions to challenges.

Remember that the word *you* refers to your reader. Using *you* when you really mean yourself or "all people" can insult your reader by implying that he or she still has a lot to learn about business.

Since you're talking about yourself, you'll use *I* in your letter. Do so sparingly. Reduce the number of *I*'s by revising some sentences to use *me* or *my*.

> Under my presidency, the Agronomy Club …
>
> Courses in media and advertising management gave me a chance to …
>
> My responsibilities as a co-op student included …

In particular, avoid beginning every paragraph with *I*. Begin sentences with adverbs (*presently*, *currently*), prepositional phrases, or introductory clauses.

Positive Emphasis

Be positive. Don't plead ("Please give me a chance") or hedge ("I cannot promise that I am substantially different from everyone else").

Avoid word choices with negative connotations (Module 7). Note how the following revisions make the writer sound more confident.

Negative: I have learned an excessive amount about writing through courses in journalism and advertising.

Excessive suggests that you think the courses covered too much—hardly an opinion likely to endear you to an employer.

Positive: Courses in journalism and advertising have taught me to recognize and to write good copy. My profile of a professor was published in the campus newspaper; I earned an A on my direct mail campaign for the Canadian Dental Association to persuade young adults to see their dentist more often.

How Should I Write an Email Application?

Compose a document using a word-processing program. Then attach it to a courteous email message.

Employability Skills

When you submit an email letter (see Figure 26.6) with an attached résumé, you need to

- Use a plain, professional-sounding email address, such as your own name (Module 25).
- Tell in what word-processing program your scannable résumé is saved.
- Put the job number or title for which you're applying in your subject line and in the first paragraph.
- Prepare your letter in a word-processing program with a spell checker to make it easier to edit and proof the document.
- Don't send anything in all capital letters.

FIGURE 26.6   **An Email Application Letter**

Attach your scannable résumé.

Omit salutation.

Choose details that use words from job ad and interest reader.

Repeat name and email address at the end.

Put job number in the subject line and the first paragraph.

Tell what program it's in.

If you have a Web page, list it to show that you're technologically savvy. Keeping the "http://" in the URL creates a hotlink in many email programs.

To: r_h_catanga@ibm.com
From: Tracey McKenna <mckenna.74@rogers.ca>
Subject: Application for jof17747
Cc:
Bcc:
Attached: D:\Jobhunt\resume.scan;

Attached is a scannable résumé in WordPerfect for the accounting position announced on IBM's Web site (jof17747). I will receive a B.Sc. in accountancy from McMaster this August and plan to take the CPA exam in December.

As a result of my studies, I've learned to identify the best measures for fixed assets and property controls and to figure inter-company/intra-company and travel expenses. I can analyze expenditures and compare them to past statements to identify trends and recommend ways to reduce costs.

Furthermore, I can use Excel to create computer graphics to provide the clear, reliable accounting data that IBM needs to continue growing each year. Please visit my Web page to see the report I wrote on choosing the best method to accelerate depreciation.

My three years of experience at Allstate have given me the opportunity to take leadership and show responsibility. I developed a procedure for making out arbitration reports that saved so much time I was asked to teach it to the other employees in my department.

At your convenience, I could come to Toronto for an interview any Tuesday or Thursday afternoon.

Tracey McKenna
mckenna.74@rogers.ca
http://www.mcmaster/business/students/mckenna/report.htm

- Don't use smiley faces or other emoticons.
- Put your name and email address at the end of the message. Most email programs send along the "sender" information on the screen, but a few don't, and you want the employer to know whose letter this is!

MODULE SUMMARY

- When you know the company is hiring, send a solicited application letter. When self-recruiting, send a prospecting or unsolicited cover letter.
- Organize your solicited letter this way:
  - State that you are applying for the job, and tell where you learned about the job (ad, referral, etc). Briefly show that you have the major qualifications for the position. In your opening paragraph, summarize your qualifications in the order in which you discuss them in the letter.

  - Develop your major qualifications in detail.
  - Develop your other qualifications. Show what separates you from the other candidates who will apply. Demonstrate your knowledge of the organization.
  - Ask for an interview; say when you are available to be interviewed, and to begin work. End on a positive note.
- Organize your prospecting letter this way:
  - Catch the reader's interest.

- Create a bridge between the opening and your qualifications. Summarize your qualifications in the order in which you discuss them in the letter.
- Develop your strong points in detail. Relate what you've done in the past to what you could do for this company. Demonstrate your knowledge of the company. Identify the specific position you are interested in.
- Ask for an interview and state when you are available for interviews. End on a positive note.
- In both letters,
  - Address the letter to a specific person.
  - Indicate the specific position for which you are applying.

- Be specific about your qualifications.
- Show what separates you from the other applicants.
- Demonstrate your knowledge about the company and the position.
- Refer to your résumé (which you enclose or send with the letter).
- Ask for an interview.
- Use your knowledge of the company, your course work, your understanding of the field, and your experience in jobs and extracurricular activities to show that you're unique.
- Use you-attitude by providing specific details, and by relating what you have done with what the employer needs. Use positive emphasis to sound confident.

ASSIGNMENTS FOR MODULE 26

Questions for Critical Thinking

26.1 Identify four ways you can write a cover letter that differentiates you positively from other applicants.

26.2 What techniques can you use in the first paragraph to catch the reader's positive interest immediately?

26.3 Identify four methods you can use to create you-attitude throughout your letter.

26.4 When you submit your application letter and résumé by email, what should you write in the email itself?

Exercises and Problems

26.5   **Analyzing First Paragraphs of Prospecting Letters**

The following are first paragraphs in prospecting letters written by new graduates. Evaluate the paragraphs on these criteria:

- Is the paragraph likely to interest the reader and motivate him or her to read the rest of the letter?
- Does the paragraph have some content that the student can use to create a transition to talking about his or her qualifications?
- Does the paragraph avoid asking for a job?

1.   Ann Gibbs suggested that I contact you.

2.   Each year, the holiday shopping rush makes more work for everyone at Zellers, especially for the Credit Department. While working for Zellers Credit Department for three holiday seasons and summer vacations, I became aware of many credit situations.

3.   Whether to plate a five-centimetre eyebolt with cadmium for a tough, brilliant shine or with zinc for a rust-resistant, less expensive finish is a tough question. But similar questions must be answered daily by your salespeople. With my experience in the electroplating industry, I can contribute greatly to your customer growth.

4.   Prudential Insurance Company did much to help my university career, as the sponsor of my National Merit Scholarship. Now I think I can give something back to Prudential. I'd like to put my education, including a degree in finance from _____ University, to work in your investment department.

5.   Since the beginning of Delta Electric Construction Co. in 1997, the size and profits have grown steadily. My father, being a stockholder and vice-president, often discusses company dealings with me. Although the company has prospered, I understand there have been a few problems of mismanagement. I feel with my present and future qualifications, I could help ease these problems.

26.6 Improving You-Attitude and Positive Emphasis in Job Letters

Revise each of these sentences to improve you-attitude and positive emphasis. You may need to add information.

1. I understand that your company has had problems due to the mistranslation of documents during international ad campaigns.
2. Included in my résumé are the courses in finance that earned me a fairly attractive grade average.
3. I am looking for a position that gives me a chance to advance quickly.
4. Although short on experience, I am long on effort and enthusiasm.
5. I have been with the company from its beginning to its present unfortunate state of bankruptcy.

26.7 Writing a Solicited Letter

Write a letter of application in response to an announced opening for a full-time job that a new graduate could hold.

Turn in a copy of the listing. If you use option (a), (b), or (d) below, your listing will be a copy. If you choose option (c), you will write the listing and can design your ideal job.

a. Respond to an ad in a newspaper, in a professional journal, in the placement office, or on the Web. Use an ad that specifies the company, not a blind ad. Be sure that you are fully qualified for the job.
b. Find a job description and assume that it represents a current opening. Use a directory to get the name of the person to whom the letter should be addressed.
c. If you have already worked somewhere, assume that your employer is asking you to apply for full-time work after graduation. Be sure to write a fully persuasive letter.
d. Respond to one of the listings below. Use a directory or the Web to get the name and address of the person to whom you should write.

1. Cotts Beverages is hiring an **assistant auditor**. Minimum 12 hours of accounting experience. Work includes analysis and evaluation of operating and financial controls and requires contact with many levels of company management. Extensive travel (50 percent of job hours) required through the Canadian West, along with some international work. Effective written and oral communication skills a must, along with sound decision-making abilities. Locations: Edmonton, Toronto, Halifax, New York, Los Angeles, Dallas, Atlanta, Philadelphia, Denver, Chicago. Refer to job FA-2534.

2. Roxy Systems (Roxy.com) seeks **Internet marketing coordinators** to analyze online campaigns and put together detailed reports, covering ad impressions and click-through rates. Must have basic understanding of marketing; be organized, creative, and detail-oriented; know Microsoft Excel; have excellent communication skills; and be familiar with the Internet. Send letter and résumé to mike@roxy.com.

3. Bose Corporation seeks **public relations/communications administrative associate** (Job Code 117BD). Write, edit, and produce the in-house newsletter using desktop publishing software. Represent the company to external contacts (including the press). Provide administrative support to the manager of PR by scheduling meetings, preparing presentations, tabulating and analyzing surveys, and processing financial requests. Excellent organizational, interpersonal, and communication skills (both written and oral) required. Must be proficient in MS Office and FileMaker Pro.

4. The Gap is hiring **executive development program trainees**. After completing 10-week training programs, trainees will become assistant buyers. Prefer people with strong interest and experience in retailing. Apply directly to the store for which you want to work.

5. A local nonprofit seeks a **coordinator of volunteer services**. Responsibilities for this full-time position include coordinating volunteers' schedules, recruiting and training new volunteers, and evaluating existing programs. Excellent listening and communication skills required.

26.8 Writing a Prospecting Letter

1. Look in the business sections of your local and/or the national newspapers for stories that suggest an organization is expanding, and may be hiring for positions in various areas. Identify an area or department (accounting, finance, human resources, information technology, marketing, publicity and promotion, research and development, etc.) in which you would like to work.
2. Apply for a specific position. The position can be one that already exists, or one that you would create, if you could, to match your unique blend of talents. Be sure that you are fully qualified for the job.
3. Use the Web or directories to get the name and address of the person with the power to create a job for you.

POLISHING YOUR PROSE

Using *You* and *I*

You-attitude (Module 6) means that you'll use lots of *you*s in business messages. However, use *you* only when it refers to your reader. When you mean "people in general," use another term.

Incorrect:	When I visited your office, I learned that you need to find a way to manage your email.
Correct:	When I visited your office, I saw the importance of managing one's email.
Incorrect:	Older customers may not like it if you call them by their first names.
Correct:	Older customers may prefer being called by courtesy titles and their last names.

Omit *you* when it criticizes or attacks the reader.

Not you-attitude:	You didn't turn your expense report in by the deadline.
You-attitude:	Expense reports are due by the fifth of each month. We have no record of receiving your report.

When you talk about what you've done, use *I*.

Correct:	In the past month, I have completed three audits.

In general, keep *I*'s to a minimum. They make you sound less confident and more self-centred.

Weak:	I think that we would save money if we bought a copier instead of leasing it.
Better:	We would save money by buying a copier instead of leasing it.
Weak:	I want to be sure that I understand how I will be affected by this project.
Better:	How will this project affect our unit?

When you write a document that focuses on you (such as a progress report or a job application letter), vary sentence structure so that you don't begin every sentence with *I*.

Correct:	This job gave me the opportunity to …
Correct:	As an intern, I …
Correct:	Working with a team, I …

When you use a first-person pronoun as part of a compound subject or object, put the first-person pronoun last.

Correct:	She asked you and me to make the presentation.
Correct:	You, Mohammed, and I will have a chance to talk to members of the audience before the dinner.

Be sure to use the right case. For the above two examples, you might omit the other part(s) of the compound to see the case you should use, as follows:

She asked me.

I will have a chance.

These are grammatically correct, so you would use the same form when you restore the other words.

Exercises

Revise the following sentences to eliminate errors and improve the use of *you* and *I*.

1. I worked with a team to create a class Web page. I was responsible for much of the initial design and some of the HTML coding. I also tested the page with three people to see how easily they could navigate it. I and the other team members presented the page to a committee of local businesspeople.
2. I have taken a lot of time and trouble to get a copy of *Using Excel* for each of you.
3. If you offend someone in the team, you need to resolve the conflict you have created.
4. Please return the draft to me and Mehtap.
5. I think that it would be a good idea for us to distribute an agenda before the meeting.
6. I have asked each department head if he or she had information to announce at the meeting, collated the responses, and arranged the topics to cover in an agenda. I have indicated how much time each topic will take. I am herewith distributing the agenda for Friday's meeting.
7. You haven't made the Web page accessible to users with impaired vision.
8. My last job showed me that you have to be able to solve problems quickly.
9. I observed department meetings during my co-op. I also sat in on client meetings. I designed PowerPoint™ slides for client presentations. I participated in strategy sessions. Finally, I drafted brochures.
10. The client asked me and my supervisor to explain our strategy more fully.

Check your answers to the odd-numbered exercises on page 553.

Managing the Interview Process

Learning Objectives

After reading and applying the information in Module 27, you'll be able to demonstrate

Knowledge of

- Job interview best practices
- The attitudes and behaviours employers seek

Skills to

- Be your best self at a job interview
- Plan and practise for the interview
- Answer traditional interview questions
- Prepare for behavioural and situational interviews
- Participate in phone or video interviews
- Make a good impression in follow-up letters and emails

Employability Skills 2000+ Checklist

Communicate

○ read and understand information presented in a variety of forms (e.g., words, graphs, charts, diagrams)

○ write and speak so others pay attention and understand

○ share information using a range of information and communications technologies (e.g., voice, email, computers)

○ use relevant scientific, technological, and mathematical knowledge and skills to explain or clarify ideas

Manage Information

○ locate, gather, and organize information using appropriate technology and information systems

○ access, analyze, and apply knowledge and skills from various disciplines (e.g., the arts, languages, science, technology, mathematics, social sciences, and the humanities)

Think & Solve Problems

○ assess situations and identify problems

○ seek different points of view and evaluate them on the basis of facts

○ recognize the human, interpersonal, technical, scientific, and mathematical dimensions of a problem

○ readily use science, technology, and mathematics as ways to think, gain and share knowledge, solve problems, and make decisions

○ check to see if a solution works, and act on opportunities for improvement

Demonstrate Positive Attitudes & Behaviours

○ feel good about yourself and be confident

○ recognize your own and other people's good efforts

Be Adaptable

○ be innovative and resourceful: identify and suggest alternative ways to achieve goals and get the job done

○ learn from your mistakes and accept feedback

○ cope with uncertainty

Learn Continuously

○ be willing to continuously learn and grow

○ assess personal strengths and areas for development

○ identify and access learning sources and opportunities

Work with Others

○ accept and provide feedback in a constructive and considerate manner

Participate in Projects & Tasks

○ develop a plan, seek feedback, test, revise, and implement

Even when you've prepared thoroughly, job interviews are scary: you know what you want, but you don't feel in control of the situation. When you are prepared, however, you can harness the adrenaline to work for you so that you make the best possible impression to get the job you want.

Today many employers expect job candidates to

- Follow instructions to the letter. The owner of a delivery company tells candidates to phone at a precise hour. Failing to do so means that the person can't be trusted to deliver packages on time.[1]
- Participate in many interviews, including the panel or group interview. In these interview situations, several people in the organization are present throughout the interview. Each person is assigned a question to ask the candidate, and the whole team assesses the applicant's interview performance.
- Have one or more interviews by phone, computer, or video.
- Take one or more tests, including psychological/personality assessments, aptitude tests, computer simulations, and essay exams where you're asked to explain what you'd do in a specific situation.
- Be approved by the team you'll be joining. In companies with self-managed work teams, the team has a say in who is hired.
- Provide—at the interview or right after it—a sample of the work you're applying to do. You may be asked to write a memo or a proposal, calculate a budget on a spreadsheet, make a presentation, or do a mini-teach.

Successful job applicants prepare an interview strategy tailored to their audience.

What's the Best Interview Strategy?

Prepare so that you get what you want.

Develop an overall strategy based on your answers to these three questions:

1. *What do you want the interviewer to know about you?* Pick two to five points that represent your strengths for that particular job. These facts may be achievements, positive character traits (such as enthusiasm, attention to detail, creativity), and experiences that qualify you for the job, and separate you from other applicants.

   Identify and write down a specific action or accomplishment to support each strength (Module 25). For example, be ready to give an example to prove that you're "hardworking." Show how you have saved money, served customers better, or led the team in other organizations where you've worked. Then at the interview, listen to every question to see how you can make one of your key points part of your answer. If the questions don't allow you to make your points, bring them up at the end of the interview.

2. *What disadvantages or weaknesses do you need to minimize?* Expect to be asked to explain apparent weaknesses in your record: lack of experience, so-so grades, or gaps in your record.

3. *What do you need to know about the job and the organization to decide whether to accept this job if it is offered to you?* Research to ensure the organization is the right fit for you. Analyze the company Web site: its language, colours, and navigation can tell you plenty about organizational values. Read blogs, bulletins and associated industry journals.

In Nelvana's creative environment, employees are hired because they possess both the skills to do the job and the creativity to imagine original ideas. Applicants' portfolios are expected to contain evidence of both.

Network. Use information interviews (Module 24) as opportunities to scope out the reception area, the way visitors are greeted and treated, congruence between mission statement and morale. Talk to as many employees and friends of employees as you can.

Keep a list of topics you want to research further. Before the interview, prioritize these, and reframe them as questions to ask during the interview. (See page 502–503 for ideas.)

Checkpoint

Interview Strategy

Plan an interview strategy based on these three questions:

1. What two to five facts about yourself do you want the interviewer to know?
2. What disadvantages or weaknesses do you need to overcome or minimize?
3. What do you need to know about the job and the organization to decide whether you want to accept this job if it is offered to you?

What Details Should I Think About?

Decide what you'll wear, how to get there, and what you'll bring with you.

What to Wear

Your interview clothing should be at least as formal as the clothing of the person likely to interview you. When the interview is scheduled, ask the person who invites you whether the company has a dress policy. If the dress is "casual," wear a button-up shirt and a good-quality skirt or pants, not jeans.

If you're interviewing for a management or office job, wear a business suit in a conservative colour (black, grey, or navy) and a season-appropriate fabric. If you've got good taste and a good eye for colour, follow your instincts.

If fashion isn't your strong point, thumb through newspapers and magazines for ideas, or visit stores, noting details—the exact shade of blue in a suit, the number of buttons on the sleeve, the placement of pockets, the width of lapels. You can find quality clothes at bargain prices in second-hand and vintage clothing shops in your town or city.

If you're interviewing for a position that involves working, visiting, or supervising muddy or dirty sites, wear sturdy clothes that suggest you're willing to get dirty.[2] In this case, looking "good" is less important than looking businesslike.

Consider the corporate culture. A woman interviewing for a job at Gap wore a matching linen skirt and blouse that were similar to Gap clothing. Her clothing was evidence that she'd researched the job.[3]

Choose comfortable shoes. The last thing you want to be thinking about during an important interview is how much your feet hurt! You may also do a fair amount of walking during the office visit or plant trip.

Take care of all the details. Check your heels to make sure they aren't run-down; make sure your shoes are shined. Have your hair cut or styled conservatively. Keep jewellery and makeup understated. Personal hygiene must be impeccable. If you wear cologne or perfume, keep it to a minimum.

How to Get There

If you're going to a place you haven't been before, do a practice run at the same time of day your interview is scheduled for. Check out bus transfers or parking fees. On the day of the interview, leave early enough so that you'll get to the interview 15 minutes early.

Use the extra time to check your appearance in the restroom mirror and to look through the company publications in the waiting room. If an accident does delay you, call to say you'll be late.

What to Bring to the Interview

Bring extra copies of your résumé. If your campus placement office has already given the interviewer a data sheet, present the résumé at the beginning of the interview: "I thought you might like a little more information about me."

Bring something to write on, something to write with, and a typed list of the questions you want to ask.

Bring copies of your work or a portfolio: an engineering design, a copy of a report you wrote on a job or in a business writing class, an article you wrote for the campus paper. You don't need to present these unless the interview calls for them, but they can be very effective.

Bring the names, addresses, and phone numbers of your references if you haven't already provided them.

Bring complete details about your work history and education, including dates and street addresses, in case you're asked to fill out an application form.

If you can afford it, buy a briefcase to carry these items. An inexpensive briefcase is fine.

What Notes to Take

During or immediately after the interview, write down the details:

- The name of the interviewer, or all the people you talked to, if it's a group interview or an office visit (The easiest way to get the interviewer's name is to ask for his or her card.)
- The traits/facts the interviewer seemed to like best about you
- Any negative points or concerns that came up that you need to counter in your follow-up letter or phone calls
- Answers to your questions about the company
- The date you'll hear from the company
- Details you'll want to include in your follow-up thank-you letter

What Should I Practise Before the Interview?

Practise everything, and often; practice builds confidence.

Your interviewing skills will improve with practice. Rehearse everything you can: put on the clothes you'll wear and practise entering a room, shaking hands, sitting down, and answering questions. Ask a friend to interview you, and tape the interview. Saying answers out loud is surprisingly harder than saying them in your head.

If you don't have your own DVD camera, use your campus taping facilities so that you can watch your sample interview. Taping is more valuable if you can do it at least twice, so you can modify behaviour the second time and check to see whether the modification works.

How to Act

Should you "be yourself"? There's no point in assuming a radically different persona. If you do, you run the risk of getting into a job that you'll hate (though the persona you assumed might have loved it). On the other hand, we all have several selves: we can be lazy, insensitive, bored, slow-witted, and tongue-tied, but we can also be energetic, perceptive, interested, intelligent, and articulate. Be your best self at the interview.

To increase your confidence, review your positive personality traits and accomplishments—the things you're especially proud of having done—in writing (Module 25). You'll make a better impression if you have a firm sense of your own self-worth.

Every interviewer repeats the advice that parents often give: Sit up straight, don't mumble, look at people when you talk. It's good advice for interviews. Be aware that many people respond negatively to smoking.

 Cultural **FOCUS**

If you are from a culture in which smoking is acceptable (or if you are a smoker), try not to smoke at all before the interview. Tobacco smoke clings to fabric and a nonsmoker will be able to smell it. If you do need to smoke before the interview, try not to smoke at least 30 minutes before the interview. Never smoke as soon as you leave the interview. Wait until you are away from the property, as you never know who may be watching you leave.

Office visits that involve meals and semi-social occasions call for sensible choices. When you order, choose something that's easy and not messy to eat. Watch your table manners. Eat a light lunch, with no alcohol, so that you'll be alert during the afternoon. At dinner or an evening party, decline alcohol if you don't drink, or are underage. If you do drink, accept just one drink: you're still being evaluated. Be aware that some people respond negatively to applicants who drink hard liquor.

Parts of the Interview

Every interview has an opening, a body, and a close.

In the **opening** (two to five minutes), good interviewers will try to put you at ease. Some interviewers will open with easy questions about your major or interests. Others open by telling you about the job or the company. If this happens, listen so you can answer later questions to show that you can do the job, and contribute to the company that's being described.

The **body** of the interview (10 minutes to an hour) is an all-too-brief time for you to highlight your qualifications and find out what you need to know to decide if you want to accept a second interview. Expect questions that allow you to showcase your strong points, and questions that probe any weaknesses evident from your résumé. (You were neither in school nor working last fall. What were you doing?) Normally the interviewer will also try to sell you on the company, and give you an opportunity to ask questions.

Be aware of time so that you can make sure to get to your key points and questions: "We haven't covered it yet, but I want you to know that I...." "I'm aware that it's almost 10:30. I do have some more questions that I'd like to ask about the company."

In the **close** of the interview (two to five minutes), the interviewer will usually tell you what happens next: "We'll be bringing our top candidates to the office in February. You should hear from us in three weeks." One interviewer reports that he gives applicants his card and tells them to call him. "It's a test to see if they are committed, how long it takes for them to call, and whether they even call at all."[4]

Close with an assertive statement. Depending on the circumstances, you could say: "I've enjoyed learning more about ITracks; I'd really like to see the new system you talked about." "This job seems to be a good match with my qualifications and expertise."

How Should I Answer Traditional Interview Questions?

Choose answers that fit your qualifications and your interview strategy.

As Table 27.1 shows, successful applicants use different communication behaviours than do unsuccessful applicants. Successful applicants are more likely to

- Use the company name during the interview
- Support their claims with specific details
- Ask specific questions about the company and the industry

In addition to practising the content of questions, try to incorporate tactics recommended in column 3 of Table 27.1.

Checkpoint

Successful Interviewees

- Know what they want to do.
- Have researched the company in advance.
- Use the company name in the interview.
- Support skills and knowledge claims with specifics.
- Use industry language.
- Ask specific questions.
- Talk more of the time.

The following questions are frequently asked during interviews. Prepare on paper before the interview so that you'll be able to come up with answers that are responsive, honest, and paint a positive picture of you.

Choose answers that fit your qualifications and your interview strategy.

1. Tell me about yourself..

   Don't launch into an autobiography. Instead, talk about your achievements as they relate to the organization's culture and goals. Give specific examples to prove each of your strengths.

2. What makes you think you're qualified to work for this company? Or: I'm interviewing 120 people for two jobs. Why should I hire you?

   This question might feel like an attack. Use it as an opportunity to state your strong points: your qualifications for the job, the skills, knowledge, and character traits that separate you from other applicants.

TABLE 27.1   The Communication Behaviours of Successful Interviewees

Behaviour	Unsuccessful Interviewees	Successful Interviewees
Statements about the position	Had only vague ideas of what they wanted to do; changed "ideal job" up to six times during the interview.	Were specific and consistent about the position they wanted; were able to tell why they wanted the position.
Use of company name	Rarely used the company name.	Referred to the company by name four times as often as unsuccessful interviewees.
Knowledge about company and position	Made it clear that they were using the interview to learn about the company and what it offered.	Made it clear that they had researched the company; referred to specific brochures, journals, or people who had given them information.
Level of interest, enthusiasm	Responded neutrally to interviewer's statements: "OK," "I see." Indicated reservations about company or location.	Expressed approval of information verbally and nonverbally; explicitly indicated desire to work for this particular company.
Nonverbal behaviour	Made little eye contact; smiled infrequently.	Made eye contact often; smiled.
Picking up on interviewer's cues	Gave vague or negative even when a positive answer was clearly desired ("How are your math skills?").	Answered positively and confidently—and backed up the claim with a specific example of "problem solving" or "toughness."
Response to topic shift by interviewer	Resisted topic shift.	Accepted topic shift.
Use of industry terms and technical jargon	Used almost no technical jargon.	Used technical jargon: "point of purchase display," "NCR charge," "two-column approach," "direct mail," "big pharma."
Use of specifics in answers	Gave short answers—10 words or fewer, sometimes only one word; did not elaborate. Gave general responses: "fairly well."	Supported claims with specific personal experiences, comparisons, statistics, statements of teachers and employers.
Questions asked by interviewee	Asked a small number of general questions.	Asked specific questions based on knowledge of the industry and the company. Personalized questions: "What would my duties be?"
Control of time and topics	Interviewee talked 37 percent of the interview time; initiated 36 percent of the comments.	Interviewee talked 55 percent of the total time, initiated subjects 56 percent of the time.

Source: Based on research reported by Lois J. Einhorn, "An Inner View of the Job Interview: An Investigation of Successful Communicative Behaviors," *Communication Education* 30 (July 1981): 217–28; and Robert W. Elder and Michael M. Harris, eds., *The Employment Interview Handbook* (Thousand Oaks, CA: Sage, 1999), pp. 300, 303, 327–28.

3. What two or three accomplishments have given you the greatest satisfaction?

   Pick accomplishments that you're proud of, that create the image you want to project, and that enable you to share one of the things you want the interviewer to know about you (Module 25, Exercise 25.4). Focus not just on the end result, but also on the transferable skills—teamwork, problem solving, and critical thinking—that made the achievement possible.

4. Why do you want to work for us? What is your ideal job?

   Even if you're interviewing just for practice, make sure you have a good answer—preferably two or three reasons you'd like to work for that company. Do your homework; know everything possible about the company and the job. If you don't seem to be taking the interview seriously, the interviewer won't take you seriously, and you won't even get good practice.

5. What college or university courses did you like best and least? Why?

   This question may be an ice-breaker; it may be designed to discover the kind of applicant the organization is looking for. If your favourite class was something outside your program, prepare an answer that shows that you have qualities that can help you in the job you're applying for: "My favourite class was Canadian Literature. We got a chance to think on our own, rather than just regurgitate facts; we made presentations to the class every week. I found I really like sharing my ideas with other people and presenting reasons for my conclusions about something."

6. Why are your grades so low?

If possible, show that the cause of low grades has now been solved or isn't relevant to the job you're applying for: "My father almost died last year, and my schoolwork really suffered." "When I started, I didn't have any firm goals. Since I discovered the program that is right for me, my grades have all been B's or better." "I'm not good at multiple-choice tests. But you need someone who can work with people, not someone who can take tests."

7. What have you read recently? What movies have you seen recently?

These questions may be ice-breakers; they may be designed to probe your intellectual depth. Be prepared: read at least one book or magazine (regularly) and see at least one movie that you could discuss at an interview.

8. Show me some samples of your writing.

The year you're interviewing, go through your old papers and select the best ones, retyping them if necessary, so that you'll have samples if you're asked for them. Show interviewers essays, reports, or business documents, not poetry or song lyrics.

If you don't have samples at the interview, mail them to the interviewer immediately after the interview.

9. Where do you see yourself in five years?

Employers ask this question to find out whether you are a self-starter or if you passively respond to what happens. You may want to have several scenarios for five years from now to use in different kinds of interviews. Or you may want to say, "Well, my goals may change as opportunities arise. But right now, I want to...."

10. What are your interests outside work? What campus or community activities have you been involved in?

Although it's desirable to be well rounded, naming 10 interests might work against you: the interviewer might wonder when you'll have time to work. If you mention your fiancé(e), spouse, or children in response to this question ("Well, my fiancé and I like to go sailing"), it is perfectly legal for the interviewer to ask follow-up questions ("What would you do if your spouse got a job offer in another town?"), even though the same question would be illegal if the interviewer brought up the subject first.

11. What have you done to learn about this company?

An employer may ask this to see what you already know about the company (if you've read the recruiting literature, the interviewer doesn't need to repeat it). This question may also be used to see how active a role you're taking in the job search and how interested you are in this job.

12. What adjectives would you use to describe yourself?

Use only positive ones. Be ready to illustrate each with a specific example of something you've done.

13. What is your greatest strength?

Employers ask this question to give you a chance to sell yourself and to learn something about your values. Pick a strength related to work, school, or activities: "I'm good at working with people." "I can really sell things." "I'm good at solving problems." "I learn quickly." "I'm reliable. When I say I'll do something, I do it." Be ready to illustrate each with a specific example of something you've done.

14. What is your greatest weakness?

Employers ask this question to get a sense of your values and self-awareness. Use a work-related negative, and emphasize what you're doing about it. Interviewers won't let you get away with a "weakness" like being a workaholic or just not having any experience yet. Instead, use one of the following three strategies:

a. Discuss a weakness that is not related to the job you're being considered for, and that will not be needed even when you're promoted. End your answer with a positive related to the job:

> **For a creative job in advertising:** I don't like accounting. I know it's important, but I don't like it. I even hire someone to do my taxes. I'm much more interested in being creative and working with people, which is why I find this position interesting.
>
> **For a job in administration:** I don't like selling products. I hated selling cookies when I was a Girl Guide. I'd much rather work with ideas—and I really like selling the ideas that I believe in.

b. Discuss a weakness that you are working to improve:

> In the past, I wasn't a strong writer. But last term I took a course in business writing that taught me how to organize my ideas and how to revise. Now I'm a lot more confident that I can write effective reports and memos.

c. Discuss a work-related weakness:

> Sometimes I procrastinate. Fortunately, I work well under pressure, but a couple of times I've really put myself in a bind.

15. Why are you looking for another job?

> Stress what you're looking for in a new job, not why you want to get away from your old one.

If you were fired, say so. There are four acceptable ways to explain why you were fired:

a. You lost your job, along with many others, when the company downsized for economic reasons.
b. It wasn't a good match. Add what you now know you need in a job, and ask what the employer can offer in this area.
c. You and your supervisor had a personality conflict. Make sure you show that this was an isolated incident and that you normally get along well with people.
d. You made mistakes, but you've learned from them and are now ready to work well. Be ready to offer a specific anecdote proving that you have indeed changed.

16. What questions do you have?

This gives you a chance to cover things the interviewer hasn't brought up; it also gives the interviewer a sense of your priorities and values. Don't focus on salary or fringe benefits. Instead, prepare a typed list of specific questions such as,

- What would I be doing on a day-to-day basis?
- What kind of training programs do you have? If, as I'm rotating among departments, I find that I prefer one area, can I specialize in it when the training program is over?

- How do you evaluate employees? How often do you review them? Where would you expect a new trainee (banker, staff accountant, salesperson) to be three years from now?
- What happened to the last person who had this job?
- How are interest rates (a new product from competitors, imports, demographic trends, government regulation, etc.) affecting your company?
- How would you describe the company's culture?
- This sounds like a great job. What are the drawbacks?

Increasingly, candidates are asking about work–life balance and about the control they'll have over their own work:

- Do people who work for you have a life off the job?
- If my job requires too much travel, can I change jobs without doing serious damage to my career?
- Do you offer flextime?
- How much pressure do you have to achieve your projects? How much freedom is there to extend a deadline?[5]

You won't be able to anticipate every question you may get. (One interviewer asked applicants, "What vegetable would you like to be?" Another asked, "If you were a cookie, what kind of cookie would you be?")[6] Check with other people who have interviewed recently to find out what questions are being asked in your field.

How Can I Prepare for Behavioural and Situational Interviews?

Think about skills you've used that could transfer to other jobs. Learn as much as you can about the culture of the company you hope to join.

Many companies are now using behavioural or situational interviews. **Behavioural interviews** ask the applicant to describe actual behaviours, rather than plans or general principles. Thus, instead of asking, "How would you motivate people?" the interviewer might ask, "Tell me what happened the last time you wanted to get other people to do something." Follow-up questions might include, "What exactly did you do to handle the situation? How did you feel about the results? How did the other people feel? How did your superior feel about the results?"

In your answer,

- Describe the situation.
- Tell what you did.
- Describe the outcome.
- Show that you understand the implications of what you did, and suggest how you might modify your behaviour in other situations.

For example, if you did the extra work yourself when a team member didn't do his or her share, does that fact suggest that you do not handle conflict well, or prefer to work alone? You might go on to demonstrate that doing the extra work was appropriate in that situation, but that you could respond differently in other situations.

Since behavioural questions require applicants to tell what they actually did—rather than to say what ought to be done—interviewers feel they offer better insight into how someone will actually function as an employee. Figure 27.1 lists common behavioural questions.

FIGURE 27.1   **Behavioural Interview Questions**

Describe a situation in which you

1. Created an opportunity for yourself in a job or volunteer position.
2. Used writing to achieve your goal.
3. Went beyond the call of duty to get a job done.
4. Communicated successfully with someone you disliked.
5. Had to make a decision quickly.
6. Overcame a major obstacle.
7. Took a project from start to finish.
8. Were unable to complete a project on time.
9. Used good judgment and logic in solving a problem.
10. Worked under a tight deadline.
11. Worked with a tough boss.
12. Handled a difficult situation with a co-worker.
13. Made an unpopular decision.
14. Gave a presentation.
15. Worked with someone who wasn't doing his or her share of the work.

Situational interviews put you in a situation that allows the interviewer to see whether you have the qualities the company is seeking.

Situational interviews may also be conducted using traditional questions but evaluating behaviours other than the answers. For its customer assistance centre, Greyhound hired applicants who made eye contact with the interviewer and smiled at least five times during a 15-minute interview.[7]

Increasingly common is the situational interview that asks you to do—on the spot—the kind of thing the job would require. An interviewer for a sales job handed applicants a ballpoint pen and said, "Sell me this pen." (It's OK to ask who the target market is and whether this is a repeat or a new customer.)

Candidates who make it through the first two rounds of interviews for sales jobs at Dataflex are invited to participate in a week's worth of sales meetings, which start at 7 A.M. four times a week. The people who participate—not merely attend—are the people who get hired.[8] Other interview requests include asking applicants to participate in role-plays, to make presentations, or to lead meetings.

How Can I Prepare for Phone or Video Interviews?

Practise short answers. Retape until you look good.

Try to schedule phone interviews for home, not work, and for a time when things will be quiet. If a company wants to interview you on the spot, accept only if the timing is good. If it isn't, say so: "We just sat down to dinner. Could you call back in 30 minutes?" Then get your information about the company, ask your roommates to be quiet, and get your thoughts in order. And use a land line to ensure good reception.

Three strategies are important when preparing for a phone interview:

- Research the company information, and identify in writing how your qualifications can make a contribution.
- Tape yourself so you can make any adjustments in pronunciation and voice qualities.
- Practise short answers to questions. After giving a short answer in the interview, say, "Would you like more information?" Without a visual channel, you can't see the body language that tells you someone else wants to speak.

During the interview, listen closely to the questions; speak slowly; do the interview standing up: "an erect and confident poise will help you come across more confidently."[9]

Two kinds of video interviews exist. The first is a live interview using videoconferencing equipment. For this kind of interview, use the same guidelines as for a phone interview. In the second kind, the company sends a list of questions, asking the applicant to tape the responses.

If you're asked to prepare a videotape,

- Practise your answers.
- Tape the interview as many times as necessary to get a tape that presents you at your best.
- Be specific. Since the employer can't ask follow-up questions, you need to be detailed about how your credentials could help the employer.

For both kinds of interviews, smile when you talk to put more energy into your voice.

How Should I Follow Up the Interview?

Send a letter that reinforces positives and overcomes any negatives. Use PAIBOC analysis to clarify your message content.

Following up the interview is a multiple process. First, immediately after the interview, make notes on any questions and ideas that impressed you. These notes can help focus your first letter.

Then, on the basis of your PAIBOC analysis, send an email or hardcopy letter to reinforce positives from the first interview, to overcome any negatives, and to get information you can use to persuade the interviewer to hire you (see Figure 27.2).

Career coach Kate Weldon suggests asking the following questions in a follow-up phone call:

- "What additional information can I give you?"
- "I've been giving a lot of thought to your project and have some new ideas. Can we meet to go over them?"
- "Where do I stand? How does my work compare with the work others presented?"[10]

A letter (whether a hard copy or an email attachment) is a more formal follow-up message than an email. Base your decision on which to send on your audience analysis. A letter thanking your hosts is essential, however, when your interview includes an office visit or other forms of hospitality. A well-written letter can be the deciding factor that gets you the job.[11] In your letter be sure to do the following:

- Thank the interviewer for his or her time and hospitality.

Take notes during and immediately after the interview: they're the source of your follow-up letters.

FIGURE 27.2   PAIBOC Questions for Analysis

> **P** What are your **purposes** in writing? You have several: to demonstrate your emotional intelligence; to emphasize your interest in the job; to reinforce the fit between the organization and you; to influence the recruiter's opinion positively.
>
> **A** Who is your **audience**? What do they value? What do they need? How can you further demonstrate to your audiences that you have the qualifications and interpersonal skills they seek?
>
> **I** What **information** must your message include? What information—about the company and the position—did the interviewers emphasize? What further information can you provide to favourably impress your readers?
>
> **B** What reasons or reader **benefits** can you use to support your position?
>
> **O** What **objections** can you expect your readers to have? What negative elements of your message must you deemphasize or overcome?
>
> **C** How will the **context** affect the reader's response? Think about your relationship to the reader, the economy, the goals of the organization, the time of year, and any special circumstances.

- Reinforce the interviewer's positive impressions.
- Counter any negative impressions that may have come up at the interview.
- Use the language of the company, and refer to specific things you learned during your interview or saw during your visit.
- Be enthusiastic.
- Refer to the next step: whether you'll wait to hear from the employer or whether you want to call to learn about the status of your application.

Be sure that the letter is well written and error-free. One employer reports,

> I often interviewed people whom I liked, ... but their follow-up letters were filled with misspelled words and names and other inaccuracies. They blew their chance with the follow-up letter.[12]

Career coaches and recruiters concur. Sending poorly written emails, using shorthand language and/or emoticons, texting: all can reflect sloppy work habits and poor judgment.[13]

Figures 27.3 and 27.4 offer examples of follow-up messages.

As part of the process, some career coaches suggest writing additional letters developing a discussion, or answering a question that came up in the interview. These notes indicate your interest in the job, and keep you in the interviewers' minds.[14]

Checkpoint

Follow-Up Letters

A letter after an office visit should

- Remind the interviewer of what he or she liked about you
- Counter any negative impressions
- Use the jargon of the company and refer to specifics from the visit
- Be enthusiastic
- Refer to the next move

FIGURE 27.3 **A Follow-Up Email**

From: Ahmed Dhanray <adhanray@rogers.ca>
To: dland@wilson.ca
Sent: Monday, August 11, 2010, 5:45 PM
Subject: Thank you

Dear Delmarie Land:

Acknowledges hospitality and reinforces interest in the position —

Thank you for your hospitality during my interview last Thursday. After visiting Wilson International and speaking with you and your team, I am convinced that a career in logistics is the right choice for me.

Seeing Kelly, Gene, and Leah work together to coordinate an international client's shipment gave me a sense of the deadlines you have to meet and of the collaboration required for customer service success. As we discussed, I learned to meet deadlines and work collaboratively during my summer co-op placement with Crowley Logistics. As I mentioned during the interview, my team at Crowley suggested a computerized warehouse system that saved the company more than $30 000 in its first year of implementation. I welcome the opportunity to make a similar contribution at Wilson.

Reminds the reader of strengths

Follow-up makes it easy for the reader —

Please call me at 416-555-4567 if you have additional questions, or if I can provide you with more information.

Sincerely,
Ahmed Dhanray

FIGURE 27.4 **A Follow-Up Letter**

71 Autumn Ridge Road
Kitchener, ON N2P 2J6

March 23, 2010

Mr. Gino Focasio
Human Resources Department
Mueller Canada
8069 Lawson Road
Milton, ON L9T 5C4

Dear Mr. Focasio:

Thank you for interviewing me for the industrial engineering technician position, available in your Milton plant. I appreciate the time that Ms. Rossiter, Mr. Alverez, Mr. Storino, and you gave me.

Refers to important items he saw and heard during the interview

My expertise in jig and fixture design, and in AutoCAD software, would contribute to your commitment to continuous improvement, as described by Mr. Storino during the interview. Seeing your machining and assembly processes assured me that I would be able to apply my CNC programming experience to benefit the company.

Reminds interviewer of his strong points

Provides positive confirmation of interest in the position —

Again, thank you for your time and for the plant tour. I am very excited at the prospect of working with Mueller Canada. Please call me at 519-555-5912, or email me at zhang@hotmail.com if you have any additional questions.

Makes it easy for the reader to respond

Sincerely,

Zhang Huang
Zhang Huang

What If My First Offer Isn't for the Job I Most Want?

Phone your first-choice employer to find out where you are on that list.

Some employers offer jobs at the end of the office visit. In other cases, you may wait for weeks or even months to hear. Employers almost always offer jobs orally. You must say something in response immediately, so plan some strategies.

If your first offer is not from your first choice, express your pleasure at being offered the job, but do not accept it on the phone. "That's great! May I let you know?" Most firms will give you a week to decide.

Then call the other companies you're interested in. Explain, "I've just gotten a job offer, but I'd rather work for you. Can you tell me what the status of my application is?" Nobody will put that information in writing, but almost everyone will tell you over the phone. With this information, you're in a better position to decide whether to accept the original offer.

The skilled trades continue to be underemployed, despite their multiple attractions: excellent remuneration, numerous opportunities, and work flexibility. York Region's Apprenticeship project, supported by the Ontario Youth Apprenticeship Program, offers high school students a semester of technical apprenticeship, under the tutelage of skilled co-op teachers. Licensed skilled trades workers, including plumbers, electricians, and construction workers, can make over $100 000 annually. Yet a recent Manpower Inc. survey found that "66 percent of the 1000 Canadian firms surveyed were having difficulty filling positions, including those in the skilled construction trades."

Make your acceptance contingent on a written job offer confirming the terms. That letter should spell out not only salary but also fringe benefits and any special provisions you have negotiated. If something is missing, call the interviewer for clarification: "We agreed that I'd be reviewed for a promotion and higher salary in six months, but I don't see that in the letter." You have more power to resolve misunderstandings now than you will after six months or a year on the job.

When you've accepted one job, let the other places you visited know that you're no longer interested. Then they can go to their second choices. If you're second on someone else's list, you'll appreciate other candidates' removing themselves so the way is clear for you. Because the world is a small place, because everyone is the customer, and because you may someday want to work for the company you're currently turning down, follow the *KISS* formula: *Keep it short and simple.*

Dear Jackson Phillips:

Thank you for offering me the sales position in your electronics division.

Since Allied Signal enjoys an international reputation for innovative quality products, I'm pleased to be considered as part of the Allied team.

After a great deal of thought, however, I have decided to look for employment opportunities closer to home while investigating courses for an advanced degree. I must, therefore, decline your offer.

Again, thank you for your consideration.

Sincerely,

EXPANDING A CRITICAL SKILL

Projecting Professional Attitude

As more Canadians use clothing to reflect their personalities and/or ethnicities, organizations are adopting more flexible dress codes.

Even on dress-down or casual Fridays, however, organizations still expect employees to take care of business. Attention to detail, organization, accuracy, economy, and courtesy are the norm. According to Max Messruer, chairperson of Accountemps and author of the best-selling *Job Hunting for Dummies*® (IDG Books Worldwide), what you wear determines others' perceptions of you, and directly affects your career advancement.

On casual days, wear clothes in good condition that are one or two "notches" below what you'd wear on other days. If suits are the norm, choose blazers and slacks or skirts. If blazers and slacks or skirts are the norm, choose sweaters or knit sport shirts; khakis, simple skirts, or dressier jeans; or simple dresses. Wear good shoes and always be well groomed. Avoid anything that's ill-fitting or revealing.

Other symbols also convey professionalism. Your work area, for instance, says a lot about you. If your organization allows employees to personalize their desks or offices with photographs, knickknacks, and posters, don't display so much that you seem frivolous. And never display offensive photos or slogans, even in an attempt to be funny. The same caution goes for screen savers and radio stations. It isn't professional to play a morning "shock jock" who uses coarse language and offensive stereotypes.

If your organization allows employees to listen to music, keep the volume at a reasonable level. If your organization allows, consider wearing headphones.

Avoid playing computer games, surfing the Web inappropriately, or ordering personal items on company time.

These activities are fine on your own clock, but unethical, and in some cases illegal, on the organization's clock. You can be fired for browsing for inappropriate material online.

Keep your voicemail message succinct and professional—find out what co-workers say in theirs.

Keep your desk organized. File papers; keep stacks to a minimum. Throw away anything you don't need. Don't store food in your office. Clean periodically. Water your plants.

The volume of your voice can also disturb others. Although most people wouldn't shout across an office, many of us don't realize how loud our voices can be when we're excited or happy. Keep personal conversations to a minimum, in person and on the phone.

Learn the culture of your organization and fit into it as much as you can. When in doubt, model your dress and behaviour on someone the organization respects.

MODULE SUMMARY

- To be your own best self at the interview,
  - Develop an overall interview management strategy based on your answers to these three questions:
    1. What two to five personal or professional characteristics do you want the interviewer to know about you?
    2. What disadvantages or weaknesses do you want to overcome or minimize?
    3. What do you need to know about the organization and the job to decide whether or not you want to accept this job if it is offered to you?

  - Plan the interview logistics—what to wear, how to get there, what to bring—so that you can concentrate on rehearsing a confident interview session.
    1. Wear clothes appropriate for the position.
    2. Bring an extra copy of your résumé, something to write on and with, copies of your best work, and a list of typed questions you want to ask.
  - Rehearse: ask a friend to interview you; watch yourself on tape so that you can evaluate and modify your behaviour.

- During and immediately after the interview, note the name of the interviewer, positives and negatives, answers to your questions, and the date you will hear from the company.
- Successful applicants are prepared; they
  - Know what they want to do
  - Use the company name throughout the interview
  - Demonstrate that they have researched the company
  - Support claims with specific examples and stories
  - Use industry and company jargon
  - Ask specific questions
  - Talk more of the time
- In behavioural interviews, recruiters ask applicants to describe actual behaviours and outcomes.
  - To answer a behavioural question, describe the situation, tell what you did, describe the outcome, show that you understand the implications of your behaviour, and describe how you might modify your behaviour in other situations.

- Situational interviews put you in a situation that allows the interviewer to see whether you have the qualities the company is seeking.
- For a phone interview, ensure you have no distractions, do the interview standing up, and listen carefully to each question before giving concise answers.
- If you answer questions on videotape, retape to show your best self.
- Use follow-up phone calls to reinforce positives from the first interview, to overcome any negatives, and to get information you can use to persuade the interviewer to hire you.
- Use a follow-up letter to
  - Remind the reviewer of your qualities
  - Counter any negative impressions
  - Use the language of the industry and company to refer to specifics that came up in the interview, or that you saw in your visit
  - Be enthusiastic
  - Refer to next steps

ASSIGNMENTS FOR MODULE 27

Questions for Critical Thinking

27.1 How can you demonstrate your greatest strengths during an interview?

27.2 How can you deal with your weaknesses if they come up during an interview?

27.3 What are your options if you are asked what you believe is an illegal interview question? Which option seems best to you? Why?

27.4 Why is "mirroring" an interviewer's communication style a good interview tactic?

Exercises and Problems

27.5   Interviewing Job Hunters

Talk to students at your school who are interviewing for jobs this term. Possible questions to ask them include the following:

- What field are you in? How good is the job market in that field this year?
- What questions have you been asked at job interviews? Were you asked any stress or sexist questions? any really oddball questions?
- What answers seemed to go over well? What answers bombed?
- Were you asked to take any tests (skills, physical, drugs)?
- How long did you have to wait after a first interview to learn whether you were being invited for an office visit? How long after an office visit did it take to learn whether you were being offered a job? How much time did the company give you to decide?

- What advice would you have for someone who will be interviewing next term or next year?

As your instructor directs,

  a. Summarize your findings in a memo to your instructor.
  b. Report your findings orally to the class.
  c. Join a group of two or three other students to write a blog describing the results of your survey.

27.6   Interviewing an Interviewer

Talk to someone who regularly interviews candidates for entry-level jobs. Possible questions to ask are

- How long have you been interviewing for your organization? Does everyone on the management ladder at your company do some interviewing, or do people specialize in it?

- Do you follow a set structure for interviews? What are some of the standard questions you ask?
- What are you looking for? How important are (1) good grades, (2) leadership roles in extracurricular groups, or (3) relevant work experience? What advice would you give to someone who doesn't have one or more of these?
- What behaviours do students exhibit that create a poor impression? Think about the worst candidate you've interviewed. What did he or she do (or not do) to create such a negative impression?
- What behaviours make a good impression? Recall the best student you've ever interviewed. Why did he or she impress you so much?
- How does your employer evaluate and reward your success as an interviewer?
- What advice would you give to someone who still has a year or so before the job hunt begins?

As your instructor directs,

  a. Summarize your findings in a memo to your instructor.
  b. Report your findings orally to the class.
  c. Team up with a small group of students to write a group report describing the results of your survey.
  d. Write to the interviewer thanking him or her for taking the time to talk to you.

27.7   Preparing an Interview Strategy

On the basis of your analysis for Problems 27.5 and 27.6, prepare an interview strategy.

  1. List two to five things about yourself that you want the interviewer to know before you leave the interview.
  2. Identify any weaknesses or apparent weaknesses in your record and plan ways to explain them or minimize them.
  3. List the points you need to learn about an employer to decide whether to accept an office visit or plant trip.

As your instructor directs,

  a. Share your strategy with a small group of students.
  b. Describe your strategy in a memo to your instructor.
  c. Present your strategy orally to the class.

27.8   Preparing Answers to Behavioural Interview Questions

Tell about

  1. A conflict you have been part of and your role in resolving it

  2. A team you have worked in and the role you played
  3. A time you were asked to behave in a way you thought was unethical
  4. A time you were unable to complete a project by the due date
  5. A time you handled a difficult situation with a co-worker
  6. A time you overcame a major obstacle
  7. A time you adapted to a difficult situation

As your instructor directs,

  a. Share your answers with a small group of students.
  b. Present your answers in a memo to your instructor, and explain why you've chosen the examples you describe.
  c. Present your answers orally to the class.

27.9   Preparing Questions to Ask Employers

Prepare a list of questions to ask at job interviews.

  1. Prepare a list of three to five general questions that apply to most employers in your field.
  2. Prepare two to five specific questions for each of the three companies you are most interested in.

As your instructor directs,

  a. Share the questions with a small group of students.
  b. List the questions in a memo to your instructor.
  c. Present your questions orally to the class.

27.10   Writing a Follow-Up Letter After an Office Visit or Plant Trip

Write a follow-up email message or letter after an office visit or plant trip. Thank your hosts for their hospitality; relate your strong points to things you learned about the company during the visit; overcome any negatives that may remain; be enthusiastic about the company; and submit receipts for your expenses so you can be reimbursed.

27.11   Clarifying the Terms of a Job Offer

Last week, you got a job offer from your first-choice company, and you accepted it over the phone. Today, the written confirmation arrived. The letter specifies the starting salary and fringe benefits you had negotiated. However, during the office visit, you were promised a 5 percent raise after six months on the job. The job offer says nothing about the raise. You do want the job, but you want it on the terms you thought you had negotiated.

Write to your contact at the company, Damon Winters.

POLISHING YOUR PROSE

Matters on Which Experts Disagree

Any living language changes. New usages appear first in speaking. Here are five issues on which experts currently disagree:

1. Plural pronouns to refer to *everybody*, *everyone*, and *each*. Standard grammar says these words require singular pronouns: *his* or *her* rather than *their*.
2. **Split infinitives**. An infinitive is the form of a verb that contains *to*: to understand. An infinitive is "split" when another word separates the *to* from the rest of an infinitive: *to easily understand, to boldly go*. The most recent edition of the *Oxford English Dictionary* allows split infinitives. Purists disagree.
3. *Hopefully* to mean *I hope that*. *Hopefully* means "in a hopeful manner." However, a speaker who says "Hopefully, the rain will stop" is talking about the speaker's hope, not the rain's.
4. *Verbal* to mean *oral*. *Verbal* means "using words." Therefore, both writing and speaking are verbal communication. Nonverbal communication (e.g., body language) does not use words.
5. Comma before *and* (the serial or series comma). In a series of three or more items, some experts require a comma after the next to last item (the item before the *and*); others don't.

Ask your instructor and your boss whether they are willing to accept the less formal usage. When you write to someone you don't know, use standard grammar and usage.

Exercises

Each of the following sentences illustrate informal usage. (a) Which would your instructor or your boss accept? (b) Rewrite each of the sentences using standard grammar and usage.

1. Everyone should bring their laptops to the sales meeting.
2. The schedule includes new product information, role-plays with common selling situations and awards to the top salespeople.
3. To really take advantage of the meeting, you need to bring all of your new product info.
4. Prepare to make a brief verbal report on a challenging sales situation.
5. Think of a time when it was hard to even get in the door to see a potential customer.
6. Hopefully, we will have time to work through many of these situations in our role-plays.
7. Awards include best rookie sales representative, the most improved region, everyone who beat their quota and sales representative of the year.
8. We'll feature verbal quotes from customers in our radio ads.
9. Our Web page will let people listen to each customer summarizing verbally what they like best about our products.
10. Hopefully, the Web page will be live so that we can access it during the meeting.

Check your answers to the odd-numbered exercises on page 554.

CASES FOR COMMUNICATORS

Getting Résumé Recognition

The average online job applicant can be invisible to potential employers, hidden among the résumés crowding their databases and in-boxes.

Online job boards have greatly increased organizations' pool of potential applicants. However, technology has also resulted in an exponential increase in the number of résumés flooding human resources departments. In response, many companies now use special software programs that filter out all but those résumés containing specific keywords. Other companies now include questionnaires as part of the online application process; these questionnaires are designed to assess the "fit" of the candidate. Still other companies have stopped using the general job boards, and rely instead on niche job boards (like iHireNursing.com, Retailjobs.com, and Accountants.com) that focus on special skills or career areas.

Tailoring your résumé to match specific jobs is critical today, especially when applying for a position online. You need to research your potential position carefully so that you can include relevant details and keywords. General-purpose boards may provide an overview of employment opportunities, but you're more likely to find a job on niche boards and employment sites operated by organizations, colleges and universities, and professional organizations.

Indisputably, however, the best way to stand out among other applicants—and to learn about jobs in the hidden job market—is to know someone within the company. Networking continues to be the most effective job search strategy. And today's technology helps you to make and maintain those connections by taking advantage of social networking sites, blogs, personal Web sites, podcasting, and email.

Sources: Bob Tedeschi, "Listing Top Jobs but Charging Candidates to Seek Them, "*The New York Times*, June 4, 2007, retrieved August 22, 2009, from http://www.nytimes.com/2007/06/04/technology/04ecom.html; David Koeppel, "Web Can Help, but a Job Hunt Still Takes a Lot of Hard Work," *The New York Times*, retrieved August 22, 2009, from http://query.nytimes.com/gst/fullpage.html?res=9503E0D71530F931A2575AC0A9629C8B63& sec=&spon=&pagewanted=allT; Shawn Taylor, "With So Many Résumés on the Internet, Many End Up Cyber-Trashed," *Chicago Tribune*, January 30, 2002, retrieved August 16, 2002, from http://www.chicagotribune.com; Barbara Reinhold, "Why Networking?," Monster.ca, retrieved October 30, 2006, from http://content.monster.ca/6759_en-CA_p1.asp; Pamela La Gioia, "Techniques for Finding Telecommuting Employment," retrieved October 30, 2006, from http://www.ivc.ca/jobs/findingemployment.html; Workopolis. ca, retrieved October 7, 2009, from http://www.workopolis.com/work.aspx? action=Transfer&View=Content/Common/ResourceCentre/career911/ resumes/ResumeIntroView&lang=EN.

Individual Activity

Imagine you are a consultant at an employment services company. In this position, you offer job seekers advice and expertise on targeted job searches, résumés, cover letters, and interviewing.

The company has an extensive database of employment resources, but you and your colleagues constantly have to work to keep the information complete and accurate. In addition to your consulting schedule, you must identify one career path per week and do an exhaustive search of placement and informational resources in that field.

Your task is to identify a career in which your clients are interested, and create a list of resources that you could use to help clients find job leads, get information, and identify networking possibilities. Use all information options available to you, including the local library, school resources, and the Internet, among others.

Before you begin your search, consider the following questions:

- What general directories or resource books could I use?
- What specialized directories or resource books should I investigate?
- What trade journals could I explore?
- What general online search sites have I identified?
- What niche sites could I explore?
- Which social networking sites would offer information or resources?

- Which professional organizations would have information or resources?
- What major companies in the field should I investigate?
- What are their competitors?
- What additional career information could I find in my campus placement office?
- Do I know anyone who is already in the field?
- How can I access alumni networks or placement services?
- Have I reviewed local and national papers for job leads?
- What professional electronic mailing lists or electronic bulletin boards would be relevant?
- What other resources could I explore to find out more about opportunities in this field?

Group Activity

(*Note:* To prepare for this group activity, find at least three job postings that include detailed descriptions of the position, required skills, and hiring company. These types of postings are relatively easy to find on online job search engines such as Workopolis.com and Monster.ca. Copy these postings and distribute them to each member of the group.)

As a consultant at an employment services company, you meet regularly with your colleagues to review the quality of the company's offerings and to hone your skills through group training. Last week, in a discussion about client needs, you realized that, as a result of the upswing of employment opportunities in the area, your company has seen an increased number of clients who need help targeting their cover letters and résumés for specific positions.

Review the first job posting. As you read, consider the following:

- What are the keywords in this posting?
- What specific information, if any, does the posting highlight about the company, its industry, or its products or services?
- What are the specific skills required for the position?

As a group, discuss the advice that you might give to someone applying for this position. What advice could you give to this client on targeting a cover letter or résumé?

Answer the following questions:

- What are the keywords you would expect this employer to look for in a résumé?
- What active words should your client try to use in a résumé or cover letter?
- What skills or types of skills should your client emphasize?
- What details about the company could or should the client include in this solicited letter?

Review each job posting. How do you think this type of exercise might benefit you as you prepare your own résumé and cover letters, and begin to interview for positions?

Revising Sentences and Paragraphs

Writing *style* is the result of the conscious choices that writers make to convey meaning. Style elements include every symbol the writer uses, including

- Page layout and design
- Typeface and size
- White space, bullets, headings, and subheadings
- Format and organizational pattern
- Paragraph and sentence length
- Word choice

Style describes the way writers choose to use these elements.

Good business style creates messages that are easy for the audience to read and understand. Effective writers work on their individual style through revision and editing, consciously shaping their style to meet the needs of their audiences and to achieve their purposes.

What Is Good Business Writing Style?

Good business style is polite, friendly, and natural.

Good business writing sounds like one person talking to another. Although academic writing is traditionally more formal than business writing (see Table A.1), professors also like essays that are lively, engaging, and grammatically correct.

Most people have several styles of talking, which they vary *depending on their audience*. Good writers have several styles, too. A memo to your boss complaining about the delays from a supplier may be informal, perhaps, depending on your relationship, even chatty; a letter to the supplier demanding better service will be more formal.

Keep the following points in mind when you choose a level of formality for a specific document:

- Always err on the side of courtesy: use a friendly, informal style for someone you've talked with.
- Avoid contractions, slang, and even minor grammatical lapses in documents you write to people you don't know. Abbreviations are only acceptable in email messages if they're part of the group's culture.
- Avoid *business-speak* and clichés that obscure meaning and add clutter.
- Pay particular attention to your style when you have to write uncomfortable messages, such as when you write to people in power or when you must give bad news.

When people feel insecure or under stress, their writing style shows it: they rely on nouns rather than verbs; they use longer sentences and paragraphs, and they use more multisyllabic words.[1] Confident people are more direct. Revise and edit your writing so that you sound confident, whether or not you feel that way.

TABLE A.1   Different Types of Style

	Conversational Style	Good Business Style	Traditional Term-Paper Style
Formality	Highly informal	Conversational; sounds like a real person talking	More formal than conversation would be, but retains a human voice
Use of contractions	Many contractions	OK to use occasional contractions	Few contractions, if any
Pronouns	Uses *I*, first- and second-person pronouns	Uses *I*, first- and second-person pronouns	First- and second-person pronouns kept to a minimum
Level of friendliness	Friendly	Friendly	No effort to make style friendly
Personal	Personal; refers to specific circumstances of conversation	Personal; may refer to reader by name; refers to specific circumstances of readers	Impersonal; may generally refer to "readers" but does not name them or refer to their circumstances
Word choice	Short, simple words; slang	Short, simple words but avoids slang	Many abstract words; scholarly, technical terms
Sentence and paragraph length	Incomplete sentences; no paragraphs	Short sentences and paragraphs	Sentences and paragraphs usually long
Grammar	Can be ungrammatical	Uses standard edited English	Uses standard edited English
Visual impact	Not applicable	Attention to visual impact of document	No particular attention to visual impact

Good business style allows for individual variation. Your writing style contributes to your narrative voice (see Polishing Your Prose, Module 12, page 227) and expresses how you feel about both your audience and your topic.

What Rules Should I Follow?

In writing, as in design, less is more: keep it short and specific.

Some rules are grammatical conventions. For example, standard edited English requires that each sentence has a subject and verb and that they agree. Business writing normally demands standard grammar, but exceptions exist. Promotional materials such as brochures, advertisements, and sales and fundraising letters may use sentence fragments to mimic the effect of speech.

Other rules may be conventions adopted by an organization so that its documents are consistent. For example, a company might decide to capitalize job titles (e.g., Production Manager), although grammar doesn't require the capitals, or to use a comma before "and" in a series, though a sentence can be grammatical without the comma. A different company might make different choices.

Still other rules attempt to codify what sounds good. "Never use I," "Never start sentences with *and*, *but*, or *because*, and "Use big words" are examples. These rules must be applied selectively, if at all. Think about your audience, the discourse community, your purposes, and the situation (Module 2). If you want the effect produced by an impersonal style and big words, use them. But use them only when you want the distancing they produce.

In fact, readers rate writers who use clear, simple language and easy-to-read fonts as more intelligent than those who choose to express themselves in a more complicated style.[2]

You can do several things to create your own, readable style:

- Read and write every day. Reading not only expands your vocabulary; regular reading also improves syntax (the way you put words together to make sentences), and your grammar, punctuation, and usage. Furthermore, research proves that reading fiction makes you smarter. Psychology professor, novelist, and Toronto team leader Keith Oatley proved that reading fiction improved people's social intelligence.[3]
- Start with a clean page or screen, so that you aren't locked into old sentence structures.
- Try WIRMI: What I Really Mean Is.[4] Then revise accordingly.
- Try reading your draft aloud to someone sitting nearby. If the words sound stiff, they'll seem stiff to a reader, too.
- Ask someone else to read your draft out loud. Readers stumble if the words on the page aren't what they expect to see. Revise for clarity in the places readers stumble.

What Should I Look for When I Revise Sentences?

Try these six techniques to make your writing readable.

1. Use active verbs whenever possible.
2. Use strong action verbs to carry the weight of your sentences.
3. Make your writing concise.
4. Vary sentence length and sentence structure.
5. Use parallel structure.
6. Put your readers in your sentences.

1. Use Active Verbs Whenever Possible

"Who does what" sentences emphasize the action that creates clear and interesting writing.

A verb is **active** if the subject of the sentence does the action the verb describes. Business communication favours the use of active verbs. A verb is **passive** if the subject is acted on. Passives are usually made up of a form of the verb *to be* plus a past participle. Passive has nothing to do with the past tense. Passives can be past, present, or future:

> were received (passive past)
> is recommended (passive present)
> will be implemented (passive future)

To identify a passive verb, find the verb. If the verb describes something that the subject is doing, the verb is active. If the verb describes something that is being done to the subject, the verb is passive.

Active	**Passive**
The customer received 500 widgets.	Five hundred widgets were received by the customer.
I recommend this method.	This method is recommended by me.
The provincial agencies will implement the program.	The program will be implemented by the provincial agencies.

To change a passive verb to an active one, you must make the agent ("by _____" in < >) the new subject. If no agent is specified in the sentence, you must supply one to make the sentence active.

Passive	**Active**
The request was approved by the <plant manager>.	The plant manager approved the request.
A decision will be made next month. No agent in sentence.	The committee will decide next month.
A letter will be sent informing the customer of the change. No agent in sentence.	[You] Send the customer a letter informing her about the change.

If the active sentence does not have a direct object, no passive equivalent exists.

Active	**(No Passive Exists)**
I would like to go to the conference.	
The freight charge will be $1 400.	
The phone rang.	

Passive verbs have at least three disadvantages:

1. If all the information in the original sentence is retained, passive verbs make the sentence longer. Passives take more time to understand.[5]
2. If the agent is omitted, it's not clear who is responsible for doing the action.
3. When many passive verbs are used, or when passives are used in material with many big words, the writing can be boring and pompous.

However, passive verbs are desirable in some situations:

- Use passives to **emphasize** the object receiving the action, not the agent.

> Your order was shipped November 15.

The customer's order, not the shipping clerk, is important.

- Use passives to provide coherence within a paragraph. A sentence is easier to read if "old" information comes at the beginning of a sentence. When you have been discussing a topic, use the word again as your subject even if that requires a passive verb.

> The bank made several risky loans in 2006. These loans were written off as "uncollectable" in 2009.

Using loans as the subject of the second sentence provides a link between the two sentences, making the paragraph as a whole easier to read.

- Use passives to avoid assigning blame.

> The order was damaged during shipment.

An active verb would require the writer to specify who damaged the order. The passive here is more tactful.

2. Use Strong Action Verbs to Carry the Weight of Your Sentence

The verb is the most important word in an English sentence, and active words (*send, met, see, ask, reply, tell, start, end, fall, rise*) create word pictures for clarity that copula verbs (*is, are, was, were, seem, appear, become, became*) cannot. Since the verb is the most important word in any sentence, put the weight of your sentence in the verb. When the verb is a form of *to be*, revise the sentence to use a more forceful verb.

Weak: The financial advantage of owning this equipment instead of leasing it is 10 percent after taxes.

Better: Owning this equipment rather than leasing it will save us 10 percent after taxes.

Nouns ending in *-ment*, *-ion*, and *-al* often hide verbs.

make an adjustment	adjust
make a payment	pay
make a decision	decide
reach a conclusion	conclude
take into consideration	consider
make a referral	refer
provide assistance	assist

Use verbs to present the information more forcefully.

Weak: We will perform an investigation of the problem.

Better: We will investigate the problem.

Weak: Selection of a program should be based on the client's needs.

Better: Select the program that best fits the client's needs.

3. Make Your Writing Concise

Writing is **wordy** if the same idea can be expressed in fewer words. Unnecessary words bore your reader, and make your meaning more difficult to follow, since the reader has to keep all the extra words in mind while trying to understand your meaning.

Good writing is concise. Concise writing may be long because it is packed with ideas. In Modules 6 to 8, you saw that revisions to create positive influence and emphasis, and to develop reader benefits, were frequently longer than the originals, because the revision added information not given in the original.

Sometimes you may be able to look at a draft and see immediately how to tighten it. When wordiness isn't obvious, try the following strategies to make your writing more concise.

a. Eliminate words that say nothing.
b. Use gerunds (the *-ing* form of verbs) and infinitives to make sentences shorter and smoother.
c. Combine sentences to eliminate unnecessary words.
d. Put the meaning of your sentence into the subject and verb to use fewer words.

The purpose of eliminating unnecessary words is to save the reader time, not simply to see how few words you can use. You aren't writing a telegram, so keep the little words that make sentences complete. (Incomplete sentences are fine in lists where all the items are incomplete.)

The following examples show how to use these four techniques.

a. Eliminate Words That Say Nothing

Cut words that are already clear from other words in the sentence. Substitute single words for wordy phrases.

Wordy: Keep this information on file for future reference.

More Concise: Keep this information for reference.

                    File this information.

Wordy: Ideally, it would be best to put the billing ticket just below the screen and above the keyboard.

More Concise: If possible, put the billing ticket between the screen and the keyboard.

Phrases beginning with *of*, *which*, and *that* can often be shortened.

Wordy: the question of most importance

More Concise: the most important question

Wordy: the estimate that is enclosed

More Concise: the enclosed estimate

Sentences beginning with *There is/are* or *It is* delay important information and bore the reader. Tighten these sentences for readability.

Wordy:	There are three reasons for the success of the project.
More Concise:	Three reasons explain the project's success.
Wordy:	It is the case that college and university graduates make more money.
More Concise:	College and university graduates make more money.

Check your draft. If you find these phrases or any unnecessary words, eliminate them.

b. Use Gerunds and Infinitives to Make Sentences Shorter and Smoother

A **gerund** is the -*ing* form of a verb; grammatically, it is a verb used as a noun. In the sentence, "Running is my favourite activity," *running* is the subject of the sentence. An **infinitive** is the form of the verb that is preceded by *to*: *to run* is the infinitive.

In the revision below, a gerund (*purchasing*) and an infinitive (*to transmit*) tighten the sentence.

| **Wordy:** | A plant suggestion has been made where they would purchase a fax machine for the purpose of transmitting test reports between plants. |
| **More Concise:** | The plant suggests purchasing a fax machine to transmit test reports between plants. |

Even when gerunds and infinitives do not greatly affect length, they often make sentences smoother and more conversational.

c. Combine Sentences to Eliminate Unnecessary Words

In addition to saving words, combining sentences focuses the reader's attention on key points, makes your writing sound more sophisticated, and sharpens the relationship between ideas, thus making your writing more coherent.

| **Wordy:** | I conducted this survey by telephone on Sunday, March 22. I questioned two groups of third-year and fourth-year students—male and male—who, according to the Student Directory, were still living in the dorms. The purpose of this survey was to find out why some third-year and fourth-year students continue to live in the dorms even though they are no longer required by the university to do so. I also wanted to find out if there were any differences between male and female third-year and fourth-year students in their reasons for choosing to remain in the dorms. |
| **More Concise:** | On Sunday, March 22, I phoned male and female third-year and fourth-year students living in the dorms to find out (1) why they continue to live in the dorms even though they are no longer required to do so and (2) whether men and women had the same reasons for staying in the dorms. |

d. Put the Meaning of Your Sentence into the Subject and Verb to Use Fewer Words

Put the core of your meaning into the subject and verb of your main clause. Think about what you mean and try saying the same thing in several different ways. Some alternatives will be more concise than others. Choose the most concise one.

| **Wordy:** | The reason we are recommending the computerization of this process is because it will reduce the time required to obtain data and will give us more accurate data. |
| **Better:** | We are recommending the computerization of this process because it will save time and give us more accurate data. |

Concise: Computerizing the process will give us more accurate data faster.

Wordy: The purpose of this letter is to indicate that if we are unable to mutually benefit from our seller–buyer relationship, with satisfactory material and satisfactory payment, then we have no alternative other than to sever the relationship. In other words, unless the account is handled in 45 days, we will have to change our terms to a permanent COD basis.

Better: A good buyer–seller relationship depends on satisfactory material and satisfactory payment. You can continue to charge your purchases from us only if you clear your present balance within 45 days.

4. Vary Sentence Length and Sentence Structure

Readable prose mixes sentence lengths and varies sentence structure. Most sentences should be between 14 and 20 words. A really short sentence (fewer than 10 words) can add punch to your prose. Really long sentences (more than 30 words) are danger signs.

You can vary sentence patterns in several ways. First, you can mix simple, compound, and complex sentences. **Simple sentences** have one main clause:

> We will open a new store this month.

Compound sentences have two main clauses joined with *and, but, or,* or another conjunction. Compound sentences work best when the ideas in the two clauses are closely related.

> We have hired staff, and they will complete their training next week.
>
> We wanted to have a local radio station broadcast from the store during its grand opening, but the DJs were already booked.

Complex sentences have at least one main and one subordinate clause; they are good for showing logical relationships.

> When the stores open, we will have balloons and specials in every department.
>
> Because we already have a strong customer base in the north, we expect the new store to be just as successful as the store in the City Centre Mall.

Compound-complex sentences have two or more main clauses with one or more subordinate clauses; these sentences combine interdependent, complex ideas:

> Although we have a strong customer base in the north, we expect the new store to attract younger, urban professionals, and, therefore, we'll be focusing our promotional efforts on this particular demographic.

You can also vary sentences by changing the order of elements. Normally the subject comes first.

> We will survey customers later in the year to see whether demand warrants a third store on campus.

To create variety, begin some sentences with a phrase or a dependent clause.

> Later in the year, we will survey customers to see whether demand warrants a third store on campus.
>
> To see whether demand warrants a third store on campus, we will survey customers later in the year.

Use these guidelines for sentence length and structure:

- Always edit sentences for conciseness. Even a 15-word sentence can be wordy.
- When your subject matter is complicated or full of numbers, make a special effort to keep sentences short.
- Use longer sentences
  - To show how ideas are linked to each other
  - To avoid a series of short, choppy sentences
  - To reduce repetition
- Group the words in long and medium-length sentences into chunks that the reader can process quickly.[6]
- When you use a long sentence, keep the subject and verb close together.

Let's see how to apply the last three principles.

Try for an Average Sentence Length of 14 to 20 Words

The sentence below is hard to read not simply because it is long but also because it is shapeless. Just cutting it into a series of short, choppy sentences doesn't help. The best revision uses medium-length sentences (between 15 and 20 words) to show the relationship between ideas.

Too long: It should also be noted in the historical patterns presented in the summary that though there were delays in January and February, which we realized were occurring, we are now back where we were about a year ago, and although we are not off line in our collect receivables as compared to last year at this time, we do show a considerable over-budget figure because of an ultraconservative goal on the receivable investment.

Choppy: There were delays in January and February. We knew about them at the time. We are now back to where we were about a year ago. The summary shows this. Our present collect receivables are in line with last year's. However, they exceed the budget. The reason they exceed the budget is that our goal for receivable investment was very conservative.

Better: As the summary shows, we have now regained our position of a year ago, although there were delays in January and February (of which we were aware). Because our receivable investment goal was conservative, our present collectables exceed the budget, and are in line with last year's.

Group Words in Sentences into Chunks

The "better" revision above has seven chunks. In the list below, the chunks starting immediately after the numbers are main clauses. The indented chunks indicate subordinate clauses and parenthetical phrases.

1.   As the summary shows,
2. we have now regained our position of a year ago,
3.   although there were delays in January and February
4.   (of which we were aware).
5.   Because our receivable investment goal was very conservative,
6. our present collectables exceed the budget,
7. and are in line with last year's.

The first sentence has four chunks: (1) a subordinate clause, (2) the main clause of the first sentence, (3) another subordinate clause followed by (4) a parenthetical phrase. The second sentence begins with (5) a subordinate clause explaining the reason for the reversal. The sentence's (6) main clause, followed by the conjunction *and*, shows that a further explanation is coming. Another main clause (7) completes the sentence. At 27 and 20 words, respectively, these sentences aren't short, but they're readable because no chunk is longer than 10 words.

Any sentence pattern will become boring if it is repeated sentence after sentence. Use different sentence patterns—different kinds and lengths of chunks—to keep your prose interesting.

Keep the Subject and Verb Close Together

Often you can move the subject and verb closer together if you put the modifying material in a list at the end of the sentence. For maximum readability, present the list vertically.

Hard to read: Movements resulting from termination, layoffs and leaves, recalls and reinstates, transfers in, transfers out, promotions in, promotions out, and promotions within are presently documented through the Payroll Authorization Form.

Smoother: The following movements are documented on the Payroll Authorization Form: termination, layoffs and leaves, recalls and reinstates, transfers in and out, and promotions in, out, and within.

Still better: The following movements are documented on the Payroll Authorization Form:

- Termination
- Layoffs and leaves
- Recalls and reinstates
- Transfers in and out
- Promotions in, out, and within

Sometimes you will need to change the verb and revise the word order to put the modifying material at the end of the sentence.

Hard to read: The size sequence code, which is currently used for sorting the items in the NOSROP lists and the composite stock list, is not part of the online file.

Smoother: The online file does not contain the size sequence code, which is currently used for sorting the items in the composite stock lists and the NOSROP lists.

5. Use Parallel Structure

Words or ideas that share the same logical role in your sentence must also be in the same grammatical form. Whatever part of speech (noun or verb; verb recommended) you choose to begin your list must start every other part of the list; otherwise your reader has to work harder to understand your meaning.

Parallelism is a powerful device for making your writing smoother and more forceful. Note the **parallel structure** in the following examples:

Faulty: Errors can be checked by reviewing the daily exception report or note the number of errors you uncover when you match the lading copy with the file copy of the invoice.

FIGURE A.1   **Use Parallelism to Make Your Writing More Concise**

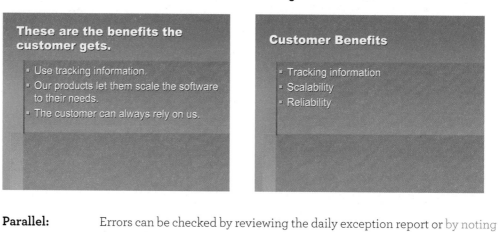

Parallel: Errors can be checked by reviewing the daily exception report or by noting the number of errors you uncover when you match the lading copy with the file copy of the invoice.

Also parallel: Check errors, by noting

1. The number of items on the daily exception report
2. The number of errors discovered when the lading copy and the file copy are matched

Note that a list in parallel structure has to fit grammatically into the umbrella sentence (or stem) that introduces the list. (See Figure A.1.)

6. Put Your Readers in Your Sentences

Use second-person pronouns (*you*) rather than third-person (*he, she, one*) to give your writing more impact. *You* is both singular and plural; it can refer to a single person or to every member of your organization.

Third person: Funds in a participating employee's account at the end of each six months will automatically be used to buy more stock unless a "Notice of Election Not to Exercise Purchase Rights" form is received from the employee.

Second person: Once you begin to participate, funds in your account at the end of each six months will automatically be used to buy more stock unless you submit a "Notice of Election Not to Exercise Purchase Rights" form.

Be careful to use *you* only when it refers to *your reader*.

Incorrect: My visit with the outside sales rep showed me that your schedule can change quickly.

Correct: My visit with the outside sales rep showed me that schedules can change quickly.

Checkpoint

Revise for Readability

- Use active verbs.
- Use action verbs.
- Use as few words as necessary.
- Vary sentence length and sentence structure.
- Use parallel structure.
- Put your readers in your sentences.

What Should I Look for When I Revise Paragraphs?

Check for topic sentences and transitions.

Paragraphs are visual and logical units. Use them to chunk your sentences.

1. Begin Most Paragraphs with Topic Sentences

A good paragraph has **unity**: it develops only one idea, or topic. The **topic sentence** states the main idea and provides a base on which to structure your document. Your writing will be easier to read if you make the topic sentence explicit and put it near the beginning of the paragraph.[7]

Hard to read (no topic sentence):	In fiscal 2008, the company filed claims for refund of federal income taxes of $3 199 000 and interest of $969 000 paid as a result of an examination of the company's federal income tax returns by the Canada Revenue Agency for the years 2005 through 2008. It is uncertain what amount, if any, may ultimately be recovered.
Better (paragraph starts with topic sentence):	The company and the Canada Revenue Agency disagree about whether the company is liable for back taxes. In fiscal 2009, the company filed claims for a refund of federal income taxes of $3 199 000 and interest of $969 000, paid as a result of an examination of the company's federal income tax returns by the Canada Revenue Agency for the years 2005 through 2008. It is uncertain what amount, if any, may ultimately be recovered.

A good topic sentence provides *reader redundancy*: it forecasts the structure and content of the paragraph.

> Plan B has economic advantages.

(Prepares the reader for a discussion of B's economic advantages.)

> We had several personnel changes in June.

(Prepares the reader for a list of the month's terminations and hires.)

> Employees have complained about one part of our new policy on parental leaves.

(Prepares the reader for a discussion of the problem.)

When the first sentence of a paragraph is not the topic sentence, readers who skim may miss the main point. Move the topic sentence to the beginning of the paragraph. If the paragraph does not have a topic sentence, you will need to write one. Without a single sentence that serves as an "umbrella" to cover every sentence, the paragraph lacks unity. To solve the problem, either split the paragraph into two, or eliminate the sentence that digresses from the main point.

2. Use Transitions to Link Ideas

Transition words and sentences signal connections between ideas.

Transitions tell whether the next sentence continues the previous thought or starts a new idea; they tell whether the idea that comes next is more or less important than the

TABLE A.2   Transition Words and Phrases

To Show Addition or Continuation of the Same Idea	To Introduce an Example	To Show That the Contrast Is More Important Than the Previous Idea	To Show Time
and	for example (e.g.)	but	after
also	for instance	however	as
first, second, third	indeed	nevertheless	before
in addition	to illustrate	on the contrary	
likewise	namely		**To Indicate Time Relations**
similarly	specifically	**To Show Cause and Effect**	next
		as a result	then
To Introduce the Last or Most Important Item	**To Contrast**	because	until
finally	in contrast	consequently	when
furthermore	on the other hand	for this reason	while
moreover	or	therefore	
			To Summarize or End
			in conclusion
			in summary
			finally

previous thought. Table A.2 lists some of the most common transition words and phrases.

How Does Corporate Culture Affect Style?

Different cultures may prefer different styles.

Different organizations and bosses may have different ideas about what constitutes good writing. If the style the company prefers seems reasonable, use it.

If the style doesn't seem reasonable—if you work for someone who likes flowery language or wordy paragraphs, for example—you have several choices.

- Use these proven techniques. Sometimes seeing good writing changes people's minds about the style they prefer.
- Help your organization learn about writing. Add up-to-date writing reference texts to the company library. (If your company doesn't already offer employees a reference library, start one online.)
- Recognize that a style serves many communication purposes. An abstract, hard-to read style may forge group identity or emphasize exclusivity. For example, government, medical, and legal writing reflect highly specialized knowledge accessible only to the initiated. When big words, jargon, and wordiness are central to a group's self-image, change will be difficult, since changing style will mean changing the corporate culture.
- Ask. Often the documents that end up in files aren't especially good. Later, other workers may find these documents and imitate them, thinking they represent a corporate standard. Bosses may prefer better writing.

Building your own writing style takes energy and effort, but it's well worth the work. Good style makes every document more effective; moreover, developing a good style builds confidence, critical thinking, and competence, and makes you, the writer, valuable to every organization.

REVISING EXERCISES AND PROBLEMS

A.1   Changing Verbs from Passive to Active

Identify the passive verbs in the following sentences and convert them to active verbs. In some cases, you may need to add information to do so. You may use different words as long as you retain the basic meaning of the sentence. Remember that imperative verbs are active, too.

1. The marketing plan was prepared by Needra Smith.
2. With the assistance of computers, inventory records are updated and invoices are automatically issued when an order is entered by one of our customers.
3. When the Web page is finalized, it is recommended that it be routed to all managers for final approval.
4. As stated in my résumé, Polish is a language I speak fluently.
5. All employees being budgeted should be listed by name and position. Any employee whose name does not appear on the "September Listing of Salaried Employees" must be explained. If this employee is a planned replacement, indicate who will be replaced and when. If it is an addition, the reason must be explained.

A.2   Using Strong Verbs

Revise each of the following sentences to use stronger verbs.

1. The advantage of using colour is that the document is more memorable.
2. Customers who make payments in cash will receive a 1 percent rebate on all purchases.
3. When you make an evaluation of media buys, take into consideration the demographics of the group seeing the ad.
4. We provide assistance to clients who are in the process of reaching a decision about the purchase of hardware and software.
5. We maintain the belief that Web ads are a good investment.

A.3   Reducing Wordiness

1. Eliminate words that say nothing. You may use different words.

    a. It is necessary that we reach a decision about whether or not it is desirable to make a request that the office be allowed the opportunity and option of hiring additional workers.
    b. The purchase of a new computer will allow us to produce form letters quickly. In addition, return on investment could be calculated for proposed

repairs. Another use is that the computer could check databases to make sure that claims are paid only once.

    c. There are many subjects that interest me.

2. Use gerunds and infinitives to make these sentences shorter and smoother.

    a. The completion of the project requires the collection and analysis of additional data.
    b. The purchase of laser printers will make possible the in-house production of the newsletter.
    c. The treasurer has the authority for the investment of assets for the gain of higher returns.

3. Combine sentences to show how ideas are related and to eliminate unnecessary words.

    a. Some buyers want low prices. Other buyers are willing to pay higher prices for convenience or service.
    b. We projected sales of $34 million in the third quarter. Our actual sales have fallen short of that figure by $2.5 million.
    c. We conducted this survey by handing out questionnaires on January 10, 11, and 12. Our office surveyed 100 customers. We wanted to see whether they would like to be able to leave voicemail messages for their representatives. We also wanted to find out whether our hours are convenient for them. Finally, we asked whether adequate parking was available.

A.4   Improving Parallel Structure

Revise each of the following sentences to create parallelism.

1. Training programs
    - Allow employees to build skills needed for current and future positions
    - Employees enjoy the break from routine work
    - Training programs are a "fringe benefit" that helps to attract and retain good employees
2. Newsletters enhance credibility, four times as many people read them as read standard ad formats, and allow soft-sell introduction to prospective customers.
3. When you leave a voicemail message, it gives the listener a poor impression when you start with a negative or an apology.
    - Summarize your main point in a sentence or two.
    - The name and phone number should be given slowly and distinctly.

- The speaker should give enough information so that the recipient can act on the message.
- Tell when you'll be available to receive the recipient's return call.

A.5 Editing Sentences to Improve Style

Revise these sentences to make them smoother, less wordy, and easier to read. Eliminate jargon and repetition. Keep the information; you may reword or reorganize it. If the original is not clear, you may need to add information to write a clear revision.

1. The table provided was unclear because of hard to-understand headings.
2. By working a co-op or intern position, you may have to be in school an additional year to complete the requirements for graduation, but this extra year is paid for by the income you make in the co-op or intern position.
3. There is a seasonality factor in the workload, with the heaviest being immediately prior to quarterly due dates for estimated tax payments.
4. Informational meetings will be held during next month at different dates and times. These meetings will explain the health insurance options. Meeting times are as follows:

   October 17, 12:00 P.M.–1:00 P.M.
   October 20, 4:00 P.M.–5:00 P.M.
   October 23, 2:00 P.M.–3:00 P.M.
5. Listed below are some benefits you get with OHIP:
   1. Routine doctors' visits will be free.
   2. No hassle about where to get your prescriptions filled.
   3. Hospitalization is covered 100 percent.

A.6 Putting Readers in Your Sentences

Revise each of the following sentences to put readers in them. As you revise, use active verbs and simple words.

1. Mutual funds can be purchased from banks, brokers, financial planners, or from the fund itself.
2. Every employee will receive a copy of the new policy within 60 days after the labour agreement is signed.
3. Another aspect of the university is campus life, with an assortment of activities and student groups to participate in and lectures and sports events to attend.

A.7 Using Topic Sentences

Make each of the following paragraphs more readable by opening each paragraph with a topic sentence. You may be able to find a topic sentence in the paragraph and move it to the beginning. In other cases, you'll need to write a new sentence.

1. At Disney World, a lunch put on an expense account is "on the mouse." McDonald's employees "have ketchup in their veins." Business slang flourishes at companies with rich corporate cultures. Memos at Procter & Gamble are called "reco's" because the model P&G memo begins with a recommendation.
2. The first item on the agenda is the hiring for the coming year. Nicky has also asked that we review the agency goals for the next fiscal year. We should cover this early in the meeting since it may affect our hiring preferences. Finally, we need to announce the deadlines for grant proposals, decide which grants to apply for, and set up a committee to draft each proposal.
3. Separate materials that can be recycled from your regular trash. Pass along old clothing, toys, or appliances to someone else who can use them. When you purchase products, choose those with minimal packaging. If you have a yard, put your yard waste and kitchen scraps (excluding meat and fat) in a compost pile. You can reduce the amount of solid waste your household produces in four ways

A.8 Writing Paragraphs

Write a paragraph on each of the following topics:

a. Discuss your current communication style. Include as evidence your use of e-devices, and your use of space.
b. Visit BMO Bank of Montreal's Business Coach podcasts for small business owners at www.bmo.com/business. Summarize one of the podcasts for your peers.
c. Explain how technology is affecting the field you plan to enter.
d. Explain why you have or have not decided to work while you attend college or university.
e. Write a profile of someone who is successful in the field you hope to enter.

As your instructor directs,

a. Label topic sentences, active verbs, and parallel structure.
b. Edit a classmate's paragraphs to make the writing more concise and smoother.
c. Post your revised and edited paragraph on your blog.

Editing for Grammar and Punctuation

With the possible exception of spelling, grammar is the one aspect of writing that writers seem to find most troublesome. Your document represents you and your organization; it's a permanent record of your capability. Documents and emails with mechanical errors interfere with readability, reflect poorly on the quality of your work, and, ultimately, cost time and money.

What Grammatical Errors Should I Focus On?

Focus these seven errors.

Good writers edit for subject–verb agreement and noun–pronoun agreement, to use the right pronoun case, to avoid dangling modifiers and misplaced modifiers, and to correct parallelism and predication errors.

Agreement

Singular subjects use singular verbs; plural subjects use plural verbs.

Incorrect: The accountants who conducted the audit was recommended highly.

Correct: The accountants who conducted the audit were recommended highly.

Subject-verb agreement errors often occur when other words come between the subject and the verb. Edit your draft by finding the subject and the verb of each sentence.

Canadian and American usage treats company names and the words *company* and *government* as singular nouns. British usage treats them as plural:

Correct (Canada): Clarica Insurance trains its agents well.

Correct (U.S.): Allstate Insurance trains its agents well.

Correct (U.K.): Lloyd's of London train their agents well.

Use a plural verb when two or more singular subjects are joined by *and*.

Correct: Larry McGreevy and I are planning to visit the client.

Use a singular verb when two or more singular subjects are joined by *or*, *nor*, or *but*.

Correct: Either the shipping clerk or the superintendent has to sign the order.

When the sentence begins with *Here* or *There*, make the verb agree with the subject that follows the verb.

Correct: Here is the booklet you asked for.

Correct: There are the blueprints I wanted.

Note that some words that end in *s* are considered singular and require singular verbs.

Correct: A series of meetings is planned.

When a situation doesn't seem to fit the rules, or when following a rule produces an awkward sentence, revise the sentence to avoid the problem.

Problematic: The plant manager, in addition to the sales representative, (was, were?) pleased with the new system.

Better: The plant manager and the sales representative were pleased with the new system.

Problematic: None of us (is, are?) perfect.

Better: All of us have faults.

Errors in *noun-pronoun agreement* occur if a pronoun is of a different number (singular or plural) or person than the word it refers to.

Incorrect: All drivers of leased automobiles are billed $100 if damages to his automobile are caused by a collision.

Correct: All drivers of leased automobiles are billed $100 if damages to their automobiles are caused by collisions.

Incorrect: A manager has only yourself to blame if things go wrong.

Correct: As a manager, you have only yourself to blame if things go wrong.

The following words require a singular pronoun:

anyone	each	everyone	nobody
everybody	either	neither	a person

Correct: Everyone should bring his or her copy of the manual to the next session on changes in the law.

Because pronoun pairs (*his or hers*), necessary to avoid sexism, may seem cumbersome, substitute words that take plural pronouns (*people, employees, persons*) or use second-person *you*.

Each pronoun must refer to a specific word. If a pronoun does not refer to a specific term, add a word to correct the error.

Incorrect: We will open three new stores in the suburbs. This will bring us closer to our customers.

Correct: We will open three new stores in the suburbs. This strategy will bring us closer to our customers.

Hint: Make sure *this* and *it* refer to a specific noun in the previous sentence. If either refers to an idea, add a noun ("this strategy") to make the sentence grammatically correct.

Use *who* and *whom* to refer to people and *which* to refer to objects. *That* can refer to anything: people, animals, organizations, and objects.

Correct: The new executive director, who moved here from St. John's, is already making friends.

Correct: The information that she wants will be available tomorrow.

Correct: This confirms the price that I quoted you this morning.

Case

Case refers to the grammatical role a noun or pronoun plays in a sentence. Table B.1 identifies the case of each personal pronoun.

Use **subjective** or **nominative** pronouns for the **subject** of a clause.

Correct: Shannon Weaver and I talked to the customer, who was interested in learning more about integrated software.

TABLE B.1 **The Case of the Personal Pronoun**

	Nominative (subject of clause)	Possessive	Objective	Reflexive/Intensive
Singular				
1st person	I	my, mine	me	myself
2nd person	you	your, yours	you	yourself
3rd person	he/she/it one/who	his/her(s)/its one's/whose	him/her/it one/whom	himself/herself/itself oneself
Plural				
1st person	we	our, ours	us	ourselves
2nd person	you	your, yours	you	yourselves
3rd person	they	their, theirs	them	themselves

Use **possessive** pronouns to show who or what something belongs to.

Correct: Microsoft Office 2007 will exactly meet her needs.

Use **objective pronouns** as **objects** of verbs or prepositions.

Correct: When you send in the quote, thank her for the courtesy she showed Shannon and me.

Hint: Use *whom* when *him* or *her* would fit grammatically in the same place in your sentence.

> I am writing this letter to (who, whom?) it may concern.
>
> I am writing this letter to him.

Whom is correct.

> Have we decided (who, whom?) will take notes?
>
> Have we decided she will take notes?

Who is correct.

Reflexive pronouns emphasize a noun or pronoun that has already appeared in the sentence.

I **myself** think the call was a very productive one.

Reflexive pronouns are used very infrequently in English Canadian business practice, since they emphasize the writer or speaker unnecessarily.

Do not use reflexive pronouns as subjects of clauses, or as objects of verbs or propositions.

Incorrect: Elaine and myself will follow up on this order.

Correct: Elaine and I will follow up on this order.

Incorrect: He gave the order to Dan and myself.

Correct: He gave the order to Dan and me.

Note that the first-person pronoun comes *after* names or pronouns that refer to other people.

Dangling Modifier (DM)

Modifiers are words or phrases that give more information about the subject, verb, or object in a clause. A modifier dangles when the word it modifies is not actually in the sentence. The solution is to reword the modifier so that it is grammatically correct.

Incorrect: Confirming our conversation, the truck will leave Monday. [The speaker is doing the confirming. But the speaker isn't in the sentence.]

Incorrect: At the age of eight, I began teaching my children about business. [This sentence says that the author was eight when he or she had children who could understand business.]

Correct a dangling modifier in one of these ways:

1. Recast the modifier as a subordinate clause.

Correct: As I told you, the truck will leave Monday.

Correct: When they were eight, I began teaching my children about business.

2. Revise the main clause so its subject or object can be modified by the now-dangling phrase.

Correct: Confirming our conversation, I have scheduled the truck to leave Monday.

Correct: At the age of eight, my children began learning about business.

Hint: Whenever you use a verb or adjective that ends in *-ing*, make sure it modifies the grammatical subject of your sentence. If it doesn't, reword the sentence.

Misplaced Modifier (MM)

A *misplaced modifier* is a word, phrase, or clause that appears beside a different element of the sentence than the writer intended, causing confusion or misinterpretation.

Incorrect: Customers who complain often alert us to changes we need to make. [Does the sentence mean that customers must complain frequently to teach us something? Or is the meaning that frequently we learn from complaints?]

Correct a misplaced modifier by moving it closer to the word it modifies or by adding punctuation to clarify your meaning. If a modifier modifies the whole sentence, use it as an introductory phrase or clause; follow it with a comma.

Correct: Often, customers who complain alert us to changes we need to make.

Parallelism

Items in a series or list must have the same grammatical structure.

Not parallel: In the second month of your internship, you will

1. Learn how to resolve customers' complaints
2. Supervision of desk staff
3. Interns will help plan store displays

Parallel: In the second month of your internship, you will

1. Learn how to resolve customers' complaints
2. Supervise desk staff
3. Plan store displays

Also parallel: Duties in the second month of your internship include resolving customers' complaints, supervising desk staff, and planning store displays.

Hint: When you have two or three items in a list (whether the list is horizontal or vertical), make sure the items are in the same grammatical form. Write lists vertically to make them easier to see.

Predication Errors

The predicate of a sentence must fit grammatically and logically with the subject to avoid **predication errors**. In sentences using *is* and other linking verbs, the complement must be a noun, an adjective, or a noun clause.

Incorrect: The reason for this change is because the OSC now requires fuller disclosure.

Correct: The reason for this change is that the OSC now requires fuller disclosure.

Make sure that the verb describes the action done by or done to the subject.

Incorrect: Our goals should begin immediately.

Correct: Implementing our goals should begin immediately.

How Can I Fix Sentence Errors?

Learn to recognize main clauses.

A **sentence** contains at least one main clause. A **main** or **independent clause** is a complete statement, with a subject and a verb. A **subordinate** or **dependent clause** contains both a subject and a verb, but is not a complete statement and cannot stand by itself; it depends on an independent clause (a sentence or complete thought) for meaning. A phrase is a group of words that does not contain a verb.

MAIN/INDEPENDENT CLAUSES

Your order will arrive Thursday.

He dreaded talking to his supplier.

I plan to enrol in summer-school classes.

SUBORDINATE/DEPENDENT CLAUSES

If you place your order by Monday

Because he was afraid the product would be out of stock

Since I want to graduate next spring

Although I was prepared for the test

PHRASES

With our current schedule

As a result

A clause with one of the following words will be subordinate:

after	if
although, though	since
because	when, whenever
before	until while, as

Using the correct punctuation will enable you to avoid three major sentence errors: comma splices, run-on sentences, and sentence fragments.

Comma Splices (CS)

A **comma splice** or **comma fault** occurs when writers join two main clauses with only a comma.

Incorrect: The contest will start in June, the date has not been set.

Correct a comma splice in one of the following four ways:

- If the ideas are closely related, use a semicolon rather than a comma.

Correct: The contest will start in June; the exact date has not been set.

- If they aren't closely related, start a new sentence.

Correct: The contest will start in June. We need to determine the exact date.

- Add a coordinating conjunction (*and, but, or, for, nor, yet*).

Correct: The contest will start in June, but the exact date has not been set.

- Subordinate one of the clauses.

Correct: Although the contest will start in June, the date has not been set.

Remember that you cannot use just a comma with the following transitional words when they begin an independent clause:

however	therefore	nevertheless	moreover

Instead, use a semicolon to separate the clauses, or start a new sentence.

Incorrect: Computerized grammar checkers do not catch every error, however, they may be useful as a first check before an editor reads the material.

Correct: Computerized grammar checkers do not catch every error; however, they may be useful as a first check before an editor reads the material.

Language FOCUS

Do not overgeneralize the rule about using a semicolon before **however.** If the word "however" begins a new thought, use a semicolon. If the word "however" is being used to add to a thought, as in "Julian thought that the movie was terrible. I, however, thought it was fantastic," use a comma.

Run-on Sentences (RO)

A **run-on sentence** strings together several main clauses using *and, but, or, so,* and *for.* Run-on sentences and comma splices are "mirror faults." A comma splice uses *only* the comma and omits the coordinating conjunction, while a run-on sentence uses *only* the conjunction and omits the comma. Correct a short run-on sentence by adding a comma. Separate a long run-on sentence into two or more sentences. Consider subordinating one or more of the clauses.

Incorrect: We will end up with a much smaller markup but they use a lot of this material so the volume would be high so try to sell them on fast delivery and tell them our quality is very high.

Correct: Although we will end up with a much smaller markup, volume will be high since they use a lot of this material. Try to sell them on fast delivery and high quality.

Sentence Fragments (Frag)

In a **sentence fragment**, a group of words that is not a complete sentence is punctuated as if it were a complete sentence. Sentence fragments often occur when a writer thinks of additional detail that the reader needs. Fragments are acceptable in résumés, advertising, and sales letters, but they're rarely acceptable in other business documents.

Incorrect: Observing these people, I have learned two things about the program. The time it takes. The rewards it brings.

To fix a sentence fragment, either add whatever parts of the sentence are missing or incorporate the fragment into the sentence before it or after it.

Correct: Observing these people, I have learned that the program is time-consuming but rewarding.

Remember that clauses with the following words are not complete sentences. Join them to a main clause.

after	if
although, though	since
because	when, whenever
before, until	while, as

Incorrect: We need to buy a new computer system. Because our current system is obsolete.

Correct: We need to buy a new computer system because our current system is obsolete.

When Should I Use Commas?

Use commas only to signal the reader.

Commas, like other punctuation marks, are road signs to help readers predict what comes next, thereby contributing to ease and speed of reading, or **readability**. The easier you make it for the reader to scan and understand the text, the more credible you appear, and the more likely it is that the reader will be persuaded to your point of view.

When you move from the subject to the verb, you're going in a straight line; no comma is needed. When you end an introductory phrase or clause, the comma tells readers the introduction is over and you're turning to the main clause. When words interrupt main clause, like this, commas tell the reader when to turn off the main clause for a short side route and when to return.

What Punctuation Should I Use Inside Sentences?

Use punctuation to clarify meaning for your reader.

A good writer knows how to use the following punctuation marks: apostrophes, colons, commas, dashes, hyphens, parentheses, periods, and semicolons.

Apostrophes

1. Use an apostrophe in a contraction to indicate that a letter has been omitted or to indicate a number has been omitted.

We're trying to renegotiate the contract.

The '90s were years of restructuring for our company.

2. To indicate possession, add an apostrophe and an *s* to the word.

> The corporation's home office is in Vancouver, British Columbia.

Apostrophes to indicate possession are especially important when one noun in a comparison is omitted.

> This year's sales will be higher than last year's.

When a word already ends in an *s*, you may add only an apostrophe to make it possessive.

> The meeting will be held at St. Johns' convention centre.

Adding an *s* and an apostrophe would not be incorrect, but doing that can make pronunciation difficult.

With many terms, the placement of the apostrophe indicates whether the noun is singular or plural.

Incorrect: The program should increase the participant's knowledge. [Implies that only one participant is in the program.]

Correct: The program should increase the participants' knowledge. [Many participants are in the program.]

Hint: Use *of* in the sentence to see where the apostrophe goes.

> The figures of last year = last year's figures
>
> The needs of our customers = our customers' needs

Possessive pronouns (e.g., *his*, *ours*) do not have apostrophes. The only exception is *one's*.

> The company needs the goodwill of its stockholders.
>
> His promotion was announced yesterday.
>
> One's greatest asset is the willingness to work hard.

TABLE B.2   What Punctuation Tells the Reader

Mark	Tells the Reader
Period	We're stopping.
Semicolon	What comes next is another complete thought, closely related to what I just said.
Colon	What comes next is an illustration, an example, or a qualification of what I just said.
Dash	What comes next is a dramatic example of or a shift from what I just said.
Comma	What comes next is a slight turn, but we're going in the same direction.

3. Use an apostrophe to make plurals that could be confused for other words. However, other plurals do not use apostrophes.

> I earned A's in all my business courses.

Colons

1. Use a colon to separate the main clause (sentence) from a list, explanation, or qualification that explains the last element in the clause. The items in the list are specific examples of the word that appears immediately before the colon.

> Please order the following supplies:
>
> printer ribbons
>
> computer paper (20-lb. white bond)
>
> bond paper (25-lb., white, 25% cotton)
>
> company letterhead
>
> company envelopes

Because English is a living language, grammar, punctuation, and usage rules evolve over time; however, current contemporary Canadian usage indicates a preference for lowercase after the colon. Some authorities suggest capitalizing the first letter after the colon only if a complete sentence follows.

> Please order the following supplies: printer ribbons, computer paper (20-lb. white bond), bond paper (25-lb., white, 25% cotton), company letterhead, and company envelopes.

Avoid using a colon when the list is grammatically part of the main clause.

Incorrect: The rooms will have coordinated decors in natural colours such as: eggplant, moss, and mushroom.

Correct: The rooms will have coordinated decors in natural colours such as eggplant, moss, and mushroom.

Correct: The rooms will have coordinated decors in a variety of natural colours: eggplant, moss, and mushroom.

Even if the list is presented vertically, there is no need to introduce the list with a colon if the words in the stem are not a complete sentence.

2. Use a colon to join two independent clauses when the second clause explains or restates the first clause.

> Selling is simple: give people the service they need, and they'll come back with more orders.

Language FOCUS

Only use a colon only if the sentence preceding it is a complete thought, such as in "I need the following supplies for camping: a tent, a sleeping bag, and a canteen." Do not use a colon if the list is part of the sentence, as in "I need a tent, a sleeping bag, and a canteen."

Commas

1. Use commas to separate the main clause from an introductory clause, the reader's name, or words that interrupt the main clause. Note that commas both precede and follow the interrupting information.

> J. Camaya, the new sales manager, comes to us from the Saskatoon office.

A **non-essential clause** gives extra information that is not needed to identify the noun it modifies. Because nonessential clauses give extra information, they need extra commas.

> Sue Decker, who wants to advance in the organization, has signed up for the company training program in sales techniques.

Do not use commas to set off information that restricts the meaning of a noun or pronoun. **Essential clauses** give essential, not extra, information.

> Anyone who wants to advance in the organization □ should take advantage of on-the-job training.

Do not use commas to separate the subject from the verb, even if you would take a breath after a long subject.

Incorrect: Laws regarding anyone collecting $5 000 or more on behalf of another person, apply to schools and private individuals as well to charitable groups and professional fundraisers.

Correct: Laws regarding anyone collecting $5 000 or more on behalf of another person □ apply to schools and private individuals as well to charitable groups and professional fundraisers.

2. Use a comma after the first clause in a compound sentence if the clauses are very long or if they have different subjects.

> This policy eliminates all sick leave credit of the employee at the time of retirement, and payment will be made only once to any individual.

Do not use commas to join independent clauses without a conjunction. Doing so produces comma splices.

3. Use commas to separate items in a series. Using a comma before the *and* or *or* is not required by some authorities, but using a comma always adds clarity. The comma is essential if any of the items in the series themselves contain the word *and*.

> The company contributes equally to full hospital coverage for eligible employees, spouses, and unmarried dependent children under age 21.

Language FOCUS

Many students are taught the pause rule for comma use. This rule states that if you were to pause when reading, add a comma. This is a broad overgeneralization and is not appropriate for this level of writing.

Dashes

Use dashes to emphasize an aside, or break in thought.

> Ryertex comes in 30 grades—each with a special use.

To type a dash, use two hyphens with no space before or after.

Hyphens

1. Use a hyphen to indicate that a word has been divided between two lines.

> Attach the original receipts for lodging, trans-
> portation, and registration fees.

Divide words at syllable breaks. If you aren't sure where the syllables divide, look up the word in a dictionary. When a word has several syllables, divide it after a vowel or between two consonants. Don't divide words of one syllable (e.g., *used*); don't divide a two-syllable word if one of the syllables is only one letter long (e.g., *acre*).

2. Use hyphens to join two or more words used as a single adjective.

> Order five 10- or 12-m lengths.
>
> It's a 10-year-old plan.
>
> The computer-prepared Income and Expense statements will be ready next Friday.

The hyphen clarifies meaning. In the first example, five lengths are needed, not lengths of 5, 10, or 12 metres. In the third example, without the hyphen, the reader might think that *computer* was the subject and *prepared* was the verb.

Parentheses

1. Use parentheses to set off words, phrases, or sentences explaining or commenting on the main idea.

> For the thinnest Ryertex (1 mm) only a single layer of the base material may be used, while the thickest (10 cm) may contain more than 600 greatly compressed layers of fabric or paper. By varying the fabric used (cotton, asbestos, glass, or nylon) or the type of paper, and by changing the kind of resin (phenolic, melamine, silicone, or epoxy), we can produce 30 different grades.

Any additional punctuation goes outside the second parenthesis when the punctuation applies to the whole sentence. It goes inside when it applies only to the words in the parentheses.

> Please check the invoice to see whether credit should be issued. (A copy of the invoice is attached.)

2. Use parentheses for the second of two numbers presented both in words and in digits.

> Construction must be completed within two (2) years of the date of the contract.

Periods

1. Use a period at the end of a sentence. Leave one space before the next sentence.
2. Use a period after some abbreviations. When a period replaces a person's name, leave one space after the period before the next word. In other abbreviations, no space is necessary.

> P. Chow has been named vice-president for marketing.
>
> The B.C. division plans to hire 10 new M.B.A.s in the next year.

The tendency today is to reduce the use of punctuation. It would also be correct to write

> The BC division plans to hire 10 new MBAs in the next year.

Language FOCUS

If you have been educated in a system which uses British English, you are probably familiar with the term **full stop**. Most North Americans refer to the full stop as a **period**.

Semicolons

1. Use semicolons to join two independent clauses when they are closely related.

> We'll do our best to fill your order promptly; however, we cannot guarantee a delivery date.

Using a semicolon suggests that the two ideas are very closely connected. Using a period and a new sentence is also correct but implies nothing about how closely related the two sentences are.

2. Use semicolons to separate items in a series when the items themselves contain commas.

> The final choices for the new plant are Edmonton, Alberta; Sydney, Nova Scotia; Mississauga, Ontario; Quebec City, Quebec; Winnipeg, Manitoba; Yellowknife, Northwest Territories; and Victoria, British Columbia.

Hospital benefits are also provided for certain specialized care services such as diagnostic admissions directed toward a definite disease or injury; normal maternity delivery, Caesarean-section delivery, or complications of pregnancy; and inpatient admissions for dental procedures necessary to safeguard the patient's life or health.

Hint: A semicolon could be replaced by a period and the next word capitalized. It has a sentence on both sides.

What Do I Use When I Quote Sources?

Use quotation marks, square brackets, and ellipses when quoting sources.

Quotation marks, square brackets, ellipses, and underlining are necessary when you quote material.

Quotation Marks

1. Use quotation marks around the names of brochures, pamphlets, and magazine articles.

   Enclosed are 30 copies of our pamphlet "Saving Energy."

   You'll find articles like "How to Improve Your Golf Game" and "Can You Keep Your Eye on the Ball?" in every issue.

In Canada and the United States, periods, and commas go inside quotation marks. Colons and semicolons go outside. Question marks go inside if they are part of the material being quoted.

2. Use quotation marks around words to indicate that you think the term is misleading.

   These "pro-business" policies actually increase corporate taxes.

3. Use quotation marks around words that you are discussing as words.

   Forty percent of the respondents answered "yes" to the first question.

   Use "Ms." as a courtesy title for a woman unless you know she prefers another title.

It is also acceptable to use underlining or to italicize words instead of using quotation marks. Choose one method and use it consistently.

4. Use quotation marks around words or sentences that you quote from someone else.

   "The Fog Index," says its inventor, Robert Gunning, is "an effective warning system against drifting into needless complexity."

Square Brackets

Use square brackets to add your own words to or make changes in quoted material.

MPP Smith's statement:	"These measures will increase the deficit."
Your use of Smith's statement:	According to MPP Smith, "These measures [in the new tax bill] will increase the deficit."

The square brackets show that Smith did not say these words; you add them only so that the quotation makes sense in your document.

Ellipses

Ellipses are made up of three spaced dots. In the days of typewriting, three spaced periods were used for an ellipsis; nowadays, if using a word processor, a true ellipsis (which is a single character) should be used.

When an ellipsis comes at the end of a sentence, use a period immediately after the last letter of the sentence. Then add the three spaced dots or true ellipsis. A space follows the last of the dots.

1. Use ellipses to indicate that one or more words have been omitted in the middle of quoted material. You do not need ellipses at the beginning or end of a quote.

> *The Wall Street Journal* notes that Japanese magazines and newspapers include advertisements for a "$2.1 million home in New York's posh Riverdale section ... 185 acres of farmland [and] ... luxury condos on Manhattan's Upper East Side."

2. In advertising and direct mail, use ellipses to imply the pace of spoken comments.

> If you've ever wanted to live on a tropical island ... cruise to the Bahamas ... or live in a castle in Spain ... you can make your dreams come true with Vacations Extraordinaire.

Italics Versus Underlining

1. Underlining causes the reader's eye to **fixate**, or stop unnecessarily, thereby interfering with both reading speed and retention. Unless you're typing or handwriting documents, it is preferable to use italics to indicate titles or emphasis:

> *Calgary Sun*
>
> *Maclean's*
>
> *Boom, Bust and Echo 2000*

Titles of brochures and pamphlets are put in quotation marks rather than in italics.

2. Italicize words to emphasize them.

> Here's a bulletin that gives you, in handy chart form, *workable data* on more than 50 different types of tubing and pipe.

Note: You may alternatively use bold to emphasize words.

How Should I Write Numbers and Dates?

Spell out numbers under 10 and those used at the beginning of sentences.

Spell out numbers from one to nine. Use digits for numbers 10 and over in most cases. Always use digits for amounts of money.

Numbers (e.g., *19 percent*) should not begin sentences. Spell out any number that appears at the beginning of a sentence. If spelling it out is impractical, revise the sentence so that it does not begin with a number.

> Fifty students filled out the survey.
>
> The year 1992 marked the official beginning of the European Economic Community.

When two numbers follow each other, use words for the smaller number and digits for the larger number.

In dates, use digits for the day and year. The month is normally spelled out. Be sure to spell out the month in international business communication. Canadian usage puts the year first: *09/01/10* means *January 10, 2009*. United States usage puts the month first, so *01/10/07* means *January 10, 2009*. European usage puts the day first, so *10/01/09* means *January 10, 2009*.

Modern punctuation uses a comma before the year only when you give both the month and the day of the month:

> May 1, 2007

but

> Summers 2005–07
>
> August 2010
>
> Fall 2008

No punctuation is needed in military or European usage, which puts the day of the month first: 13 July 2009. Do not use spaces before or after the slash used to separate parts of the date: 5/99–10/09.

Use a hyphen or short dash (en dash) to join inclusive dates.

> March-August 2009 (**or write out:** March to August 2009)
>
> '98-'03
>
> 1996–2010

Note: You do not need to repeat the century in the date that follows the hyphen or dash: 2000–10. But do give the century when it changes: 1999–2010.

How Do I Mark Errors I Find When Proofreading?

Use these standard proofreading symbols.

Use the proofreading symbols in Figure B.1 to make corrections when you don't have access to a computer. Figure B.2 shows how the symbols can be used to correct a typed text.

FIGURE B.1   **Proofreading Symbols**

✐	delete	[	move to left
ℛ	insert a letter	]	move to right
¶	start a new paragraph here	⌐	move up
(stet)	stet (leave as it was before the marked change)	�	move down
(tr) ∿	transpose (reverse)	#	leave a space
(lc)	lowercase (don't capitalize)	⌒	close up
≡	capitalize	‖	align vertically

FIGURE B.2   **Marked Text**

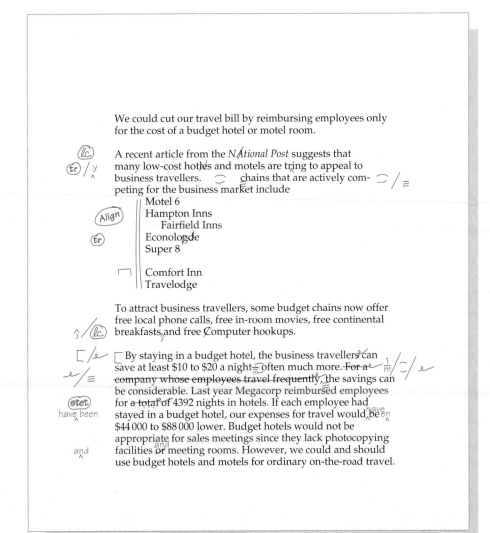

We could cut our travel bill by reimbursing employees only for the cost of a budget hotel or motel room.

A recent article from the *National Post* suggests that many low-cost hotles and motels are tring to appeal to business travellers. chains that are actively competing for the business market include

Motel 6
Hampton Inns
Fairfield Inns
Econologde
Super 8

Comfort Inn
Travelodge

To attract business travellers, some budget chains now offer free local phone calls, free in-room movies, free continental breakfasts, and free Computer hookups.

By staying in a budget hotel, the business travellers can save at least $10 to $20 a night—often much more. For a company whose employees travel frequently, the savings can be considerable. Last year Megacorp reimbursed employees for a total of 4392 nights in hotels. If each employee had stayed in a budget hotel, our expenses for travel would been $44 000 to $88 000 lower. Budget hotels would not be appropriate for sales meetings since they lack photocopying facilities or meeting rooms. However, we could and should use budget hotels and motels for ordinary on-the-road travel.

EDITING EXERCISES AND PROBLEMS

B.1   Making Subjects and Verbs Agree

Identify and correct the errors in the following sentences.

1. My education and training has prepared me to contribute to your company.
2. I know from my business experience that good communication among people and departments are essential in running a successful corporation.
3. A team of people from marketing, finance, and production are preparing the proposal.
4. The present solutions that has been suggested are not adequate.
5. There has also been suggestions for improving the airflow in the building.

B.2   Using the Right Pronoun

Identify and correct the errors in the following sentences.

1. A new employee should try to read verbal and nonverbal signals to see which aspects of your job are most important.
2. With people like yourself giving gifts, the Habitat for Humanity program will be able to grow.
3. If a group member doesn't complete their assigned work, it slows down the whole project.
4. Todd drew the graphs after him and I discussed the ideas for them.
5. Thank you for the help you gave Joanne Jackson and myself.

B.3   Fixing Dangling and Misplaced Modifiers

Identify and correct the errors in the following sentences.

1. As one of the students in a good program, our company is interested in interviewing you.
2. By making an early reservation, it will give us more time to coordinate our trucks to better serve your needs.
3. Children are referred to the Big Brother or Big Sister program by their school social workers, often from underprivileged homes.
4. At times while typing and editing, the text on your screen may not look correct.
5. All employees are asked to cut back on energy waste by the manager.

B.4   Creating Parallel Structure

Identify and correct the errors in the following sentences.

1. We help clients
   - Manage change
   - Marketing/promotion
   - Developing better billing systems
2. Volunteers need a better orientation to Planned Parenthood as a whole, to the overall clinic function, and to the staff there is also a need to clarify volunteer responsibilities.
3. The benefits of an online catalogue are
   1. We will be able to keep records up to date.
   2. Broad access to the catalogue system from any networked terminal on campus.
   3. The consolidation of the main catalogue and the catalogues in the departmental and branch libraries.
   4. Cost savings.
4. You can get a reduced rate on your life insurance if you have an annual medical exam. Another rebate is available to employees who do not use tobacco. Exercising for 30 minutes a day three times a week also entitles employees to an insurance rebate.
5. The ideal job candidate will be able to
   - Create and maintain Web pages.
   - The ability to create PowerPoint™ slides is expected.
   - It would be best if the candidate could speak a second language.

B.5   Correcting Sentence Errors

Identify and correct the errors in the following sentences.

1. Videoconferencing can be frustrating. Simply because little time is available for casual conversation.
2. Not everyone is promoted after six months some people might remain in the training program a year before being moved to a permanent assignment.
3. Pay yourself with the Automatic Savings Account, with this account any amount you choose will be transferred automatically from your chequing account to your savings account each month.
4. You can take advantage of several banking services. Such as automatic withdrawal of a house or car payment and direct deposit of your paycheque.
5. Our group met seven times outside class, we would have met even more if we could have found times when we could all get together.

B.6 Providing Punctuation Within Sentences

Provide the necessary punctuation in the following sentences. Note that not every box requires punctuation.

1. The system ☐ s ☐ user ☐ friendly design ☐ provides screen displays of work codes ☐ rates ☐ and client information.
2. Many other factors also shape the organization ☐ s ☐ image ☐ advertising ☐ brochures ☐ proposals ☐ stationery ☐ calling cards ☐ and so on.
3. Miss Manners ☐ author of ☐ Miss Manners ☐ Book of Modern Manners ☐ ☐ says ☐ ☐ Try to mention specifics of the conversation to fix the interview permanently in the interviewer ☐ s ☐ mind and be sure to mail the letter the same day ☐ before the hiring decision is made ☐ ☐
4. What are your room rates and charges for food service ☐
5. We will need accommodations for 150 people ☐ five meeting rooms ☐ one large room and four small ones ☐ ☐ coffee served during morning and afternoon breaks ☐ and lunches and dinners.
6. The Operational Readiness Inspection ☐ which occurs once every three years ☐ is a realistic exercise ☐ that evaluates the ☐ Royal Canadian Air Cadet ☐ s ☐ ability to mobilize ☐ deploy ☐ and fight.
7. Most computer packages will calculate three different sets of percentages ☐ row percentages ☐ column percentages ☐ and table percentages ☐
8. In today ☐ s ☐ economy ☐ it ☐ s almost impossible for a firm to extend credit beyond it ☐ s ☐ regular terms.
9. The Ministry of Transportation does not have statutory authority to grant easements ☐ however ☐ we do have authority to lease unused areas of highway right ☐ of ☐ way.
10. The program has two goals ☐ to identify employees with promise ☐ and to see that they get the training they need to advance.

B.7 Providing Punctuation

Provide the necessary punctuation in the following sentences. Note that not every box requires punctuation.

1. To reduce executive assistants ☐ overtime hours ☐ the office should hire part ☐ time secretaries to work from 5:00 to 9:00 P.M.
2. Since memberships can begin at any time during the year ☐ all member ☐ s ☐ dues are recognized on a cash basis ☐ when they are received.
3. I would be interested in working on the committee ☐ however ☐ I have decided to do less community work ☐ so that I have more time to spend with my family.
4. One of the insurance companies ☐ Allstate Insurance ☐ ☐ Fredericton ☐ ☐ NB ☐ said it hopes to persuade the provincial government to reconsider the rule.
5. The city already has five ☐ two ☐ hundred ☐ bed hospitals.
6. Students ☐ run the whole organization ☐ and are advised by a board of directors from the community.
7. I suggest putting a bulletin board in the rear hallway with all the interviewer ☐ s ☐ pictures on it.
8. ☐ Most small businesses just get enough money to open the doors ☐ ☐ says Mr. Quinn ☐ adding ☐ that the $10 000 or so of savings he used to start up simply wasn ☐ t enough ☐ ☐
9. Otis Conward Jr ☐ ☐ ☐ who grew up in this area ☐ now heads the Council for Economic Development.
10. Volunteers also participate in a one ☐ on ☐ one pal program.

B.8 Fixing Errors in Grammar and Punctuation

Identify and correct the errors in the following passages.

a. Company's are finding it to their advantage to cultivate their suppliers. Partnerships between a company and its suppliers can yield hefty payoffs for both company and supplier. One example is Bombardier, a Montreal headquartered company. Bombardier makes airplanes, subway cars and control systems. They treat suppliers almost like departments of their own company. When a Bombardier employee passes a laser scanner over a bins bar code the supplier is instantly alerted to send more parts.
b. Entrepreneur Trip Hawkins appears in Japanese ads for the video game system his company designed. "It plugs into the future! he says in one ad, in a cameo spliced into shots of U.S kids playing the games. Hawkins is one of several U.S. celebrities and business people whom plug products on Japanese TV.
c. Between 1989 and 2009 the number of self-employed grew by more than 40 percent to 2.4 million; but this growth includes a huge increase of one person operations. "The self-employed sector now accounts for more than 16 percent of all workers; an increase from 13 percent in 1989. According to bizSmarts report Self-Employment in Canada, Trend's and Prospect's, over the next ten years, self-employment will become even more dominant in the Canadian labour market

B.9   Identifying Audience Concerns About Grammar

Most readers care passionately about only a few points of grammar. Survey one or more readers (including your boss, if you have a job) to find out which kinds of errors concern them. Use a separate copy of this survey for each reader.

Directions: Each of the following sentences contains an error. Please circle Y if the error bothers you a good bit; S if the error bothers you slightly; and N if you would not be bothered by the error (or perhaps even notice it).

Y S N   1.   She brung her secretary with her.

Y S N   2.   Him and Richard were the last ones hired.

Y S N   3.   Wanted to tell you that the meeting will be November 10.

Y S N   4.   Each representative should bring a list of their clients to the meeting.

Y S N   5.   A team of people from administration, human services, and animal control are preparing the proposal.

Y S N   6.   We cannot predict, how high the number of clients may rise.

Y S N   7.   He treats his clients bad.

Y S N   8.   She asked Eva and I to give a presentation.

Y S N   9.   Update the directory by reviewing each record in the database and note any discrepancies.

Y S N   10. He has went to a lot of trouble to meet our needs.

Y S N   11. She gave the report to Davlic and myself.

Y S N   12. I was unable to complete the report. Because I had a very busy week.

Y S N   13. The benefits of an online directory are
   a.   We will be able to keep records up-to-date.
   b.   Access to the directory from any terminal with a modem in the county.
   c.   Cost savings.

Y S N   14. By making an early reservation, it will give us more time to plan the session to meet your needs.

Y S N   15. She doesn't have no idea how to use the computer.

Y S N   16. The change will not effect our service to customers.

Y S N   17. Confirming our conversation, the truck will leave Monday.

Y S N   18. The sessions will begin January 4 we will pass around a sign-up sheet early in December.

Y S N   19. I will be unable to attend the meeting, however I will send someone else from my office.

Y S N   20. Its too soon to tell how many proposals we will receive.

Compare your responses with those of a small group of students.

- Which errors were most annoying to the largest number of readers?
- How much variation do you find in a single workplace? in a single type of business?

As your instructor directs,

   a.   Present your findings to the class in a short group report.
   b.   Present your findings to the class in an oral presentation.

Credits

PASSIM

Employability Skills text and icons: *Employability Skills 2000+ Brochure 2000 E/F* (Ottawa: The Conference Board of Canada, 2000). Reprinted with permission.

FIGURES AND TABLES

Table 2.2, page 30: Based on Isabel Briggs Myers, "Effects of Each Preference in Work Situations," *Introduction to Type* (Palo Alto, CA: Consulting Psychologists Press, 1962, 1980).

Table 3.1, page 48: Adapted from David A. Victor, *International Business Communication* (New York: HarperCollins, 1992), Table 5.1, p. 148. Reprinted by permission of Addison-Wesley Educational Publishers Inc.

Figure 3.1, page 48: Adapted from Farid Elashmawi and Philip R. Harris, *Multicultural Management 2000: Essential Cultural Insights for Global Business Success* (Houston: Gulf, 1998), p. 169.

Table 3.2, page 49: Reproduced by permission. From *Multicultural Management 2000.* © 1998, Gulf Publishing Company, Houston, TX, 800-231-6275. All rights reserved.

Table 3.3, page 54: Adapted from Farid Elashmawi and Philip R. Harris, *Multicultural Management 2000: Essential Cultural Insights for Global Business Success* (Houston: Gulf, 1998), p. 113.

Table 3.4, page 56: Adapted from Farid Elashmawi and Philip R. Harris, Multicultural Management 2000: *Essential Cultural Insights for Global Business Success* (Houston: Gulf, 1998), p. 139.

Figure 4.2, page 73: Private communication, Joe Taleroski to Steve Kaczmarek, August 9, 2005.

Figure 5.1, pages 87–88: Adapted from Elk and Deer Inventory Certificates with permission of Alberta Agriculture and Rural Development.

Figure 6.1, page 108: Courtesy of The Salvation Army, Ontario Central Division. Reprinted with permission.

Table 8.3, page 141: Wallace Immen, "Easing Gas Pains, Fueling Loyalty," Globe Careers, *The Globe and Mail*, May 28, 2008, p. C1.

Figure 13.5, page 239: Graphic design: Imagine Creative Communications Inc. © 2008 *The Art of Marketing*.

Figure 15.1, page 283: Paul Benjamin Lowry, Aaron Curtis, and Michelle Rene Lowry, "Building a Taxonomy and Nomenclature of Collaborative Writing to Improve Interdisciplinary Research and Practice," *Journal of Business Communications* 2004 41: 66. Reprinted by permission of Sage Publications.

Table 18.1, page 323: OPL: Online Databases, http://www.opl.on.ca/research/databases.

Table 21.1, page 370: Adapted from Richard C. Freed, Shervin Freed, and Joseph D. Romano, *Writing Winning Proposals: Your Guide to Landing the Client, Making the Sale, Persuading the Boss* (New York: McGraw-Hill, 1995), p. 21.

Figure 21.4, page 374: Courtesy BFR Inc.

Figure 23.2, page 417: Eurostat, Statistics Canada, Bureau of Labor Statistics.

Figure 23.3, page 419: Brian O'Mara-Croft, "Every Picture Tells a Story," *Communication World*, September/October 2008, p. 25.

Figure 23.6, page 425: Getty Images.

Figure 23.8, page 427: Reprinted by permission of Lindsay Hopton, Sheridan Graduate and Silver Medallist, Business Administration Finance.

Figure 23.9, page 428: Reprinted by permission of Lindsay Hopton, Sheridan Graduate and Silver Medallist, Business Administration Finance.

Figure 23.10, page 428: Transparency International.

Figure 23.11, page 428: Rick Hyndman, "The Cost of Carbon," *Alternatives* 35 (2009): 1, http://www.alternativesjournal.ca.

Figure 23.13, page 429: The Canada Millennium Scholarship Foundation.

Two tables, page 427: Reprinted by permission of Lindsay Hopton, Sheridan Graduate and Silver Medallist, Business Administration Finance.

Tables, page 432–433: The Canada Millennium Scholarship Foundation.

Table, page 433: R. A. Malatest & Associates, *Survey of Canada Career College Students, Phase 2: In School Student Survey* (Montreal: Canada Millennium Scholarship Foundation, 2008).

Figure 25.3, page 457: Courtesy Spike Anderson.

PHOTOS AND CARTOONS

Page 1: Mike Marsland/Yale University.

Page 5, two people at computers: © Digital Vision.

Page 5, two oil workers: Royalty Free/Corbis.

Page 9: © PhotoDisc.

Page 12: Jessica Lander.

Page 25: Courtesy of Lee Scott, WoW Company.

Page 31, hockey players and fans: © The Canadian Press (Darryl Dyck).

Page 31, Palestinian students: © The Canadian Press/Associated Press (Anja Niedringhaus).

Page 32: © Jason Halstead, Sun Media.

Page 35, Best Buy: © Nicky Beecham.

Page 35, Future Shop: © Nicky Beecham.

Page 45: © Dick Hemingway.

Page 46: © Dick Hemingway.

Page 47: © The Canadian Press (Image Source).

Page 50: © Rhiana Sneyd.

Page 52: © Digital Vision.

Page 71: © absolut_100/istockphoto.

Page 74: Comstock/PictureQuest.

Page 98: Diane Burns and S. Venit, "What's Wrong with This Paper?," *PC Magazine* 17 (October 13, 1987): 174–75.

TEXT

Polishing Your Prose: Answer Key

Here are possible solutions to the odd-numbered Polishing Your Prose exercises. Check with your instructor on any other solutions you propose.

Module 1: Sentence Fragments

1. Because people are constantly fiddling with their BlackBerrys, even during meetings and training sessions, we need to establish some ground rules about electronic etiquette. People also surf the Web on their laptops, and leave meetings to look at email and listen to voicemail messages. I am not convinced that our preoccupation with technology is really saving us time and money, or contributing to productivity.

Module 2: Comma Splices

1. The conference call came at 1 P.M., and we took it immediately.
3. After Janelle drafted her problem-solving report, she sent a copy to each committee member for review.
5. Katy called the hotel in Montreal for a reservation; the desk staff booked a room for her immediately.
7. I'll have Tina call the main office, and you ask Polsun to set up an appointment for the four of us tomorrow.
9. I like to make oral presentations; they're fun.

Module 3: Making Subjects and Verbs Agree

1. Each of us is entitled to company healthcare benefits.
3. The price of our stocks is increasing.
5. We order a dozen new toner cartridges each month.
7. Marina Schiff and her assistant are attending the conference in Halifax.
9. Professor Beauparlant, Mr. Kincaid, and Ms. Carolla are on the guest list and plan to sit at the same table.

Module 4: Commas in Lists

1. Please send me the "fruit of the month" in April, May, June, and July. (Last comma is optional.)
3. The special parts division is opening offices in Brampton, Ontario; Fredericton, New Brunswick; and Big Salmon, Yukon.
5. I need to telephone Mary, Frank, and Paul, to finish my report, and mail copies of it to Ted, Sam, and Latanya. (While semicolons might be used after *Paul* and *report*, commas are acceptable because the groupings of listed items are understandable with commas.)
7. The weather affects our offices in Montreal, New York City, and Philadelphia.
9. Elizabeth, Tyrone, Mark, and Sara presented the team's recommendations.

Module 5: Active and Passive Voice

1. Unless the context of the sentence is negative, change to active voice: The vice-president of finance signed the contract.
3. The visitors' arrival is more important than who is expecting them. Therefore, use passive voice.
5. Changing this sentence to active voice would cast blame. Therefore, use passive voice.
7. The human resources administrator returned phone calls.
9. Return phone calls within 24 hours.

Module 6: Using the Apostrophe for Contractions and *It's/Its*

1. It's too bad that the team hasn't finished its presentation.
3. It's going to require overtime because the data centre needs its reports quickly.
5. The company will announce its new name at a press conference.
7. It's a good idea to keep your travel receipts in a separate file.
9. The Saskatoon office will share its findings with the other branch offices.

Module 7: Using the Apostrophe to Show Possession

1. Research indicates most Canadians feel responsible for the world's global warming.
3. Canadians' views of the economy reflect their confidence in the stock market.
5. We meet the local, provincial, and federal governments' standards for quality control.
7. The committee's duties will be completed after it announces its decision.
9. We'll decide whether to have more computer training sessions on the basis of employees' feedback.

Module 8: Plurals and Possessives

1. Canadian companies are competing effectively in the global market.
3. Managers' ability to listen is more important than their technical knowledge.
5. The community social workers tell clients about services available in their neighbourhoods.
7. Information about the new community makes the family's move easier.
9. Memos are internal documents, sent to other workers in the same organization. Letters are for external readers.

Module 9: Making Pronouns Agree with Their Nouns

1. An administrative assistant should help his/her boss work efficiently. *Or:* Administrative assistants should help their bosses work efficiently.
3. The company announces its quarterly profits today.
5. A CEO's pay is often based on the performance of his/her company. *Or:* CEOs' pay is often based on the performance of their companies.
7. In my first month of work, I learned to check my email at least three times a day.
9. The team will present its recommendations to the Executive Committee. (Correct.)

Module 10: Correcting Dangling Modifiers

1. After working here a year, you are covered by dental insurance.
3. I bought my daughter her first share of stock when she was 10.
5. By calling ahead of time, you can make reservations efficiently.
7. Posting risqué material on Facebook shows poor judgment, because potential employers can access this material even years later.
9. If you share files with our legal department, our attorneys can work better with you.

Module 11: Applying Parallel Structure

1. Last week, Alain and Rochelle flew to Toronto, Montreal, Quebec City, and Lansing.
3. To ship a package:
   1. Fill out an address form.
   2. Specify on the form how the package should be sent.
   3. Have your supervisor initial the appropriate box on the address form if you want the package shipped by overnight mail.
5. Appointments can be scheduled in 5-minute, 10-minute, 15-minute, or 20-minute intervals.
7. This report discusses Why We Should Upgrade Capital Equipment, Why We Should Increase Staff by 25 Percent, Why We Should Decrease Employee Turnover, and Why We Should Identify New Product Markets.
9. Use the telephone to answer customer questions, email to send order confirmations, and our Web page to take orders.

Module 12: Finding Your Narrative Voice

1. This voice sounds authoritative, perhaps even threatening due to the constant use of *will* commands and all caps in *NO EXCEPTION.*
3. Appropriate.
5. Wordiness and obsolete language ("It has been brought to our attention") make this voice seem contrived.
7. Obsolete and redundant language make this voice unintelligible.
9. Writer's emphasis on his/her time, choice of language and use of caps create rude, aggressive voice.

11. Numerous negatives reflect a domineering, negative voice.

Module 13: Correcting Run-On Sentences

1. The marketing department ordered new, four-colour brochures. They are very nice.
3. Let's schedule a meeting next week. We'll talk about your promotion so you can transition easily into the new job.
5. Employees may request benefits changes during the annual enrolment period. Supervisors should pass out the required forms, and employees should have them completed by the deadline on the form.
7. Mohammed should make sure he specifies 20-lb. rather than 15-lb. paper stock, Jenna should call the print shop and ask whether the employees need anything, and Bruce should tell Ms. Winans we appreciate her letting us know we originally ordered the wrong stock.
9. A few customers are concerned about the shipping date, but the mailroom is sure we can ship overnight. I think there's no reason to be concerned.

Module 14: Using Colons and Semicolons

1. That file on the Richman proposal: can you send me a copy by tomorrow, please?
3. Watch out: some people think there's a certain "ick" factor to social networking.
5. Strange: I thought I already signed up for another six months.
7. Remember: when we turn on the break room lights, everyone is to yell, "Happy Birthday, Susharita."
9. The best gig he ever had was his ten-month posting in Amsterdam. The night life is spectacular; everything's open: museums, pubs, shops. He was sad to come home.

Module 15: Delivering Criticism

1. We need to make this report meet our company's standards.
3. This assignment must have library resources.
5. The information in this brochure is terrific. Let's work on making the design match the content.
7. Our instructor said that we have to use at least five sources.
9. Would you help me to better understand this proposal?

Module 16: Using Hyphens and Dashes

1. Our biggest competitors—including those in the Asian and European markets—introduced more product models during the fourth quarter.
3. Please pick up three 2-by-4 posts at the lumberyard.
5. Painters from the building services department plan to give Tarik's office two coats of paint.
7. The latest weather reports suggest that travel over South and Latin America may be interrupted by storms.
9. You can email the results to my office in the early morning.

Module 17: Choosing Levels of Formality

1. On Monday, I inspected our inventory.
3. Though the representative was firm, we eventually negotiated a settlement.
5. The manager postponed making a decision.

7. In my last job, I worked as a gofer for the marketing manager.
9. This report has problems.

Module 18: Combining Sentences

1. To get promoted quickly at our company, be organized, be on time, and meet deadlines.
3. Changing the toner cartridge on the photocopier is simple. To begin, open the front panel. Find the green tabs and depress them with your thumbs. Next, pull the black toner cartridge out and put it in the recycling box. Slide a new toner cartridge into the compartment until the green tabs snap back into place. Finally, close the panel.
5. The tornado plan for our building has five parts: first, listen for the tornado alert siren; second, go to your designated shelter area in the basement of the building; third, be sure to take the stairs and not the elevator; fourth, sit down on the floor; fifth, cover your head with your arms.

Module 19: Using APA and MLA Style

APA format:

1. Nikiforuk, A. (2008, November 6). Slip sliding away. *Alternatives, 34*(6), 14–15.
3. Cox, M. (2004). Business courtesy declining, many executives say. *Human Resources Professionals Association of Ontario.* Retrieved [date retrieved] from http://www.gdhrpa.ca/HRPA/HRResourceCentre/KnowledgeCentre/newscluster2/Business+Courtesy+Declining.htm
5. Do not list in References. Identify telephone calls in text as personal communication. Give name of caller and date.

MLA format:

1. Nikiforuk, Andrew. "Slip Sliding Away." *Alternatives* 34.6 (2008): 14–15. Print.
3. Loomis, John. Telephone interview. 20 June 2009.
5. Cox, Mark. "Business Courtesy Declining, Many Executives Say." *Human Resources Professionals Association of Ontario.* Web. 30 August 2006.

Module 20: *Who/Whom* and *I/Me*

1. Karen and I visited Shawnee Community College last week.
3. Dr. Jacobsen, who serves on the Board of Directors, is retiring.
5. Who is the most experienced person on your staff?
7. Between you and me, my supervisor told me the committee will decide who gets the promotion.
9. Three people at the firm who can speak a second language are Van, Chang, and I.

Module 21: Writing Subject Lines and Headings

1. An Introduction from the New Customer Service Department Supervisor. (Better with actual name.)
3. Your donation of blood on Tuesday can save a life.
5. Insurance Rates Will Increase July 31.

7. Research; Logistics; Profit
9. Clemente Research Group's Five-Year Goals; Clemente Research Group's Ten-Year Goals; Clemente Research Group's Fifteen-Year Goals

Module 22: Improving Paragraphs

1. My experience in the secretarial field makes me an ideal candidate for a position as senior administrative assistant with Graham, Chang, and Associates. As a receptionist at McCandless Realty, I typed, answered phones, and handled payroll. Then, as a secretary at Dufresne Plastics, I took training courses in data entry and Microsoft Word and learned to type 70 WPM with no mistakes.

Module 23: Being Concise

1. Please return the order form ASAP.
3. The blue car is the legal affairs director's.
5. Call to confirm your order.
7. The enclosed references can discuss my job qualifications further.
9. Let me start by sharing stories about our guest of honour.

Module 24: Using Details

1. I am the Webmaster for the Jessica London Company.
3. In June, I plan to graduate from Seneca Community College and start my career in respiratory therapy at St. Ann's Hospital.
5. Fortified with antioxidants and Vitamins D and K, EnVigorate Power Drink will make you feel healthy and energetic all day long.
7. The new Mark VII pool filter is 33 percent more energy-efficient than competitors' filters and features a 10-year warranty, the best on the market.
9. More than 17 years of experience and $7.9 million in real estate sales make me the ideal candidate for district sales manager.

Module 25: Proofreading

1. Ours is a company worth doing business with. You can count on our promise to provide not only the best service but also the finest in materials, fit, and finish. All of our products are made to exacting specifications, meaning that you receive the best product for the best prices. If you aren't satisfied for any reason, simply call the toll-free hotline at 1-800-555-1212 to get a prompt refund. Or you can write us at The John Doe Company, 123 Main Street, Anytown, Canada M6V 2B4. Remember, our motto is "The customer is always right."

Module 26: Using *You* and *I*

1. Our team created a class Web page. I was responsible for much of the initial design and some of the HTML coding. Four of us tested the page to see how easily we could navigate it. We presented the page to a committee of local businesspeople.
3. Team members should resolve any conflicts they have created with other team members.

5. Please distribute an agenda before the meeting.
7. Make the Web page accessible to users with impaired vision.
9. During my co-op placement, I observed department meetings, sat in on client meetings, designed PowerPoint™ slides for client presentations, participated in strategy sessions, and drafted brochures.

Module 27: Matters on Which Experts Disagree

1. Everyone should bring his or her laptop to the sales meeting.
3. To take advantage of the meeting fully, you need to bring all of your new product information.

5. Think of a time when it was hard even to get in the door to see a potential customer.
7. Awards include best rookie sales representative, the most improved region, everyone who beat his or her sales quota, and sales representative of the year.
9. Our Web page will let people listen to each customer summarizing orally what he or she likes best about our products.

Notes

Unit One Opener

Katz Helena, "Word Power," *Homemakers*, Summer 2003, p. 110; Heather Andrews Miller, "Kahnawake Teen Knows How to Get the Job Done," *Windspeaker*, 2003, retrieved November 5, 2005, from http://www.ammsa.com/windspeaker/topnews-Feb-2003.html#anchor374139; Ed Kromer, "MBAs Help Plan Kahnawake Library," *McGillReporter* 35(15) (May 8, 2003), retrieved November 5, 2005, from http://www.mcgill.ca/reporter/35/15/kahnawake; "Student Profile: Skawenniio Barnes '10," *Yale Tomorrow*, May 13, 2008, retrieved March 23, 2009, from http://yaletomorrow.yale.edu/news/barnes.html.

Module 1

1. "Technical Training Ain't All It's Cracked Up to Be," *The Training Report*, January/February, 2000, p. 8.
2. Daniel H. Pink, "Revenge of the Right Brain," *Wired* 13(2) (February 2005), retrieved April 5, 2008, from http://www.wired.com/wired/archive/13.02/brain.html.
3. Ann Kerr, "Hard Lessons in Soft Skills," *The Globe and Mail*, February 21, 2003, p. C1.
4. Workopolis.com, 2009, retrieved April 10, 2009, from http://campusen.workopolis.com/work.aspx?action=Transfer&View=Content/JobSeeker/JobSearchView&lang=EN; Job Bank, 2009, retrieved April 10, from http://www.jobbank.gc.ca/dispjb_eng.aspx?OrderNum=4224237&Source=JobPosting&ProvId=99&OfferpPage=50&Student=No; CareerBuilder.ca., 2009, retrieved April 10, 2009, from http://www.careerbuilder.ca/CA/JobSeeker/Jobs/JobDetails.aspx?IPath=CAHPCS%3fSC_CMP2%3dJS_CA_HP_JS1000++CUSTOMER+SERVICE+JOBSKV&APath=2.21.0.0.0&job_did=J3I83L6ZHYDM7WBX3QB.
5. Elaine Vets, "Voice Mail Converts Boss into a Secretary," *The Columbus Dispatch*, August 10, 1995, p. 3E; Rochelle Sharpe, "Work Week," *The Wall Street Journal*, September 26, 1995, p. A1.
6. Heather Sokoloff, "Engineers Forced to Learn How to Write," *National Post*, May 28, 2003, p. A6.
7. "International Adult Literacy and Skills Survey: Building on Our Competencies," *The Daily*, November 30, 2005, retrieved April 10, 2009, from http://www.statcan.gc.ca/daily-quotidien/051130/dq051130b-eng.htm.
8. Terrence Belford, "Engineers Need 'Soft' Skills," *The Globe and Mail*, January 13, 2003, p. B10.
9. 'What Should I Charge for My Work' or 'How Much Do I Pay a Writer?,' PWAC site, retrieved April 6, 2008, from http://www.writers.ca/whattopay.htm.
10. Workopolis.com, http://search3.workopolis.com/jobshome/db/work.job_posting?pi_job_id=7630586&pi_search_id=616018147&pi_sort=POST_DATE&pi_curjob=12&pi_maxjob=500.

11. H. Wilkie, "Communicate Well and Prosper," *The Globe and Mail*, February 27, 2004.
12. Elizabeth Allen, "Excellence in Public Relations & Communication Management," IABC/Dayton Awards Banquet, Dayton, OH, July 12, 1990.
13. Watson Wyatt Worldwide, "Effective Communication: A Leading Indicator of Financial Performance," 2005/2006 Communication ROI Study™, retrieved April 10, 2009, from http://www.watsonwyatt.com/research/resrender.asp?id=w-868&page=1.

Module 2

1. Audiences 1, 3, and 4 are based on J. C. Mathes and Dwight Stevenson, *Designing Technical Reports*: *Writing for Audiences in Organizations*, 2nd ed. (New York: Macmillan, 1991), p. 40. The fifth audience is suggested by Vincent J. Brown, "Facing Multiple Audiences in Engineering and R&D Writing: The Social Context of a Technical Report," *Journal of Technical Writing and Communication* 24(1) (1994): 67–75.
2. "2006 Census: Labour Market Activities, Industry, Occupation, Education, Language of Work, Place of Work and Mode of Transportation," *The Daily*, March 4, 2008, http://www.statcan.ca/Daily/English/080304/d080304a.htm; "Canada's Changing Labour Force, 2006 Census: The Provinces and Territories—The Aging Workforce—Baby Boomers Edging Closer to Retirement," http://www12.statcan.ca/english/census06/analysis/labour/ov-cclf-23.cfm; and "Canada's Changing Labour Force, 2006 Census: The Provinces and Territories—Immigrants in the Workforce—Majority of Recent Immigrants Went to Ontario's Labour Market," http://www12.statcan.ca/english/census06/analysis/labour/ov-cclf-28.cfm.
3. Peter Urs Bender, "Identifying Your Personality Type," retrieved November 16, 2009, from http://www.peterursbender.com/quiz/index.html, retrieved July 26, 2006.
4. Isabel Briggs Myers, *Introduction to Type* (Palo Alto, CA: Consulting Psychologists Press, 1980).
5. Isabel Briggs Myers and Mary H. McCaulley, *Manual: A Guide to the Development and Use of the Myers-Briggs Type Indicator* (Palo Alta, CA: Consulting Psychologists Press, 1985), pp. 251, 248, respectively.
6. Keith McArthur, *The Globe and Mail*, June 6, 2005, retrieved July 26, 2006, from http://www.theglobeandmail.com/servlet/story/RTGAM.20050606.wxrbrand06/BNStory/Business.
7. Aldo Santin, "Canadian Tire's Catalogue Is History," *The Gazette*, March 26, 2008, retrieved April 13, 2009, from http://www2.canada.com/montrealgazette/news/business/story.html?id=c7febd59-933e-4ef7-ba59-8a2972ed88c5.

8. Erin Anderssen, "They Know When You Are Sleeping, They Know When You're Awake and Whether You Like Sushi," Globe Focus, *The Globe and Mail*, December 18, 2004, pp. F1 and F8, retrieved July 26, 2006, from http://www.theglobeandmail.com/servlet/story/RTGAM.20041220.gtcover20/BNStory/einsider/?pageRequested=all; http://www.tetrad.com/pricing/can/prizmce.html, retrieved July 26, 2006.

9. Craig Silverman, "The Traditional Job Interview: That's So Yesterday," *The Globe and Mail*, April 7, 2008, retrieved November 11, 2009, from http://www.theglobeandmail.com/servlet/story/RTGAM.20080407.wlintvu07/BNStory/lifeWork/home.

10. TD-Canada Trust Web site, http://www.tdcanadatrust.com, and Royal Bank Web site, http://www.royalbank.com, both retrieved August 25, 2006.

11. Matt Siegel, "The Perils of Culture Conflict," *Fortune*, November 9, 1998, p. 258.

12. "Top 10 Reasons to Work at Google," Google Jobs, 2009, retrieved April 13, 2009, from http://www.google.com/intl/en/jobs/lifeatgoogle/toptenreasons.html and http://www.google.com/intl/en/jobs/lifeatgoogle/toptenreasons.html.

13. Linda Driskill, "Negotiating Differences Among Readers and Writers," Conference on College Composition and Communication, San Diego, CA, March 31–April 3, 1993.

Module 3

1. H. A. Falasi, "Just Say 'Thank You': A Study of Compliment Responses," *The Linguistics Journal* 2(2): 2, retrieved May 1, 2008, from http://www.linguistics-journal.com/April_2007_haf.php.

2. Ibid., 8, retrieved May 1, 2008, from http://www.linguistics-journal.com/April_2007_haf.php.

3. "Teamwork Differs for Men and Women," *University of Toronto Magazine*, Autumn 2005, p. 10.

4. "More Than 200 Different Ethnic Origins Reported," *The Daily*, April 28, 2008, retrieved April 15, 2009, from http://www.statcan.gc.ca/daily-quotidien/080402/dq080402a-eng.htm.

5. Statistics Canada, "Canada's Ethnocultural Mosaic, 2006 Census: National Picture," p. 1, retrieved April 15, 2009, from http://www12.statcan.ca/english/census06/analysis/ethnicorigin/more.cfm; Canadian Heritage site, retrieved April 15, 2009, from http://www.pch.gc.ca/progs/multi/respect_e.cfm.

6. "Canadian Cities & Provinces of the Future 2005/06," *FDI Magazine*, June 7, 2005, retrieved November 11, 2009, from http://www.fdimagazine.com/news/fullstory.php/aid/1250/CANADIAN_CITIES_PROVINCES_OF_THE_FUTURE_2005_06.html.

7. Statistics Canada, "Some Facts About the Demographic and Ethnocultural Composition of the Population," retrieved April 28, 2008, from http://www.statcan.gc.ca/pub/91-003-x/2007001/4129904-eng.htm#2.

8. Erin Anderssen, "People Deficit Gives Workers Upper Hand," *The Globe and Mail*, January 22, 2003, p. A6.

9. Ibid.

10. Statistics Canada, "Some Facts About the Demographic and Ethnocultural Composition of the Population," pp. 2–3, retrieved April 28, 2008, from http://www.statcan.ca/english/freepub/91-003-XIE/2007001/few-en.htm.

11. Ibid.

12. "CARP Announces 'It's the Zoomers, Stupid' Press Conference," CNW Group site, retrieved April 17, 2009, from http://www.newswire.ca/en/releases/archive/September2008/15/c4428.html.

13. Richard Sweeney, "Millennial Behaviors & Demographics," December 22, 2006, retrieved April 17, 2009, from http://74.125.95.132/search?q=cache:ZBXEFHEBypYJ:library1.njit.edu/staff-folders/sweeney/Millennials/Article-Millennial-Behaviors.doc+millennials+%2B+behaviours&cd=1&hl=en&ct=clnk&client=firefox-a.

14. Rob McMahon, "Millennials in the Workplace," *straight.com*, January 31, 2008 (Vancouver Free Press, 2009), retrieved April 18, 2009, from http://www.straight.com/article-130265/millennials-in-the-workplace.

15. "Multiculturalism," *Vive le Canada*, November 26, 2005, retrieved July 26, 2006, from Canadian Heritage site, http://www.pch.gc.ca/progs/multi/respect_e.cfm.

16. David A. Victor, *International Business Communication* (New York: HarperCollins, 1992), pp. 148–60.

17. John Webb and Michael Keene, "The Impact of Discourse Communities on International Professional Communication," in Carl R. Lovitt with Dixie Coswami, eds., *Exploring the Rhetoric of International Professional Communication: An Agenda for Teachers and Researchers* (Amityville, NY: Baywood, 1999), pp. 81–109.

18. "Student Won't Be Expelled over Facebook Study Group," CBC.ca, March 18, 2008, retrieved May 1, 2008, from http://www.cbc.ca/canada/toronto/story/2008/03/18/facebook-avenir.html.

19. Christina Haas and Jeffrey L. Funk, "'Shared Information:' Some Observations of Communication in Japanese Technical Settings," *Technical Communication* 36(4) (November 1989): 365.

20. Laray M. Barna, "Stumbling Blocks in Intercultural Communication," in Larry A. Samovar and Richard E. Porter, eds., *Intercultural Communication* (Belmont, CA: Wadsworth, 1985), p. 331.

21. Marjorie Fink Vargas, *Louder Than Words* (Ames: Iowa State University Press, 1986), p. 47.

22. Michael Argyle, *Bodily Communication* (New York: International University Press, 1975), p. 89.

23. Jerrold J. Merchant, "Korean Interpersonal Patterns: Implications for Korean/American Intercultural Communication," *Communication* 9 (October 1980): 65.

24. Ray L. Birdwhistell, *Kinesics and Context: Essays on Body Motion Communication* (Philadelphia: University of Philadelphia Press, 1970), p. 81.

25. Paul Ekman, Wallace V. Friesen, and John Bear, "The International Language of Gestures," *Psychology Today* 18(5) (May 1984): 64.

26. Brenda Major, "Gender Patterns in Touching Behavior," in Clara Mayo and Nancy M. Henley, eds., *Gender and Nonverbal Behavior* (New York: Springer-Verlag, 1981), pp. 26, 28.

27. "Minor Memos," *The Wall Street Journal*, February 12, 1988, p. 1.

28. "Doing Business in India: 20 Cultural Norms You Need to Know," *Business Intelligence Lowdown*, March 6, 2007, p. 1, retrieved May 1, 2008, from http://www.businessintelligencelowdown.com/2007/03/doing_business_.html.

29. Natalie Porter and Florence Gies, "Women and Nonverbal Leadership Cues: When Seeing Is Not Believing," in *Gender and Nonverbal Behavior*, ed. Clara Mayo and Nancy M. Henley (New York: Springer-Verlag, 1981), pp. 48–49.

30. Lawrence B. Nadler, Marjorie Keeshan Nadler, and Benjamin J. Broome, "Culture and the Management of Conflict Situations," in William B. Gudykunst, Lea P. Stewart, and Stella Ting-Toomey, eds., *Communication, Culture, and Organizational Processes* (Beverly Hills, CA: Sage, 1985), p. 103.

31. Argyle, *Bodily Communication*, p. 90.

32. Mary Ritchie Key, *Paralanguage and Kinesics* (Metuchen, NJ: Scarecrow, 1975), p. 23.

33. Fred Hitzhusen, conversation with Kitty Locker, January 31, 1998.

34. Lisa Davis, "The Height Report: A Look at Stature and Status," New York Times Special Features, *Columbus Dispatch*, January 19, 1988, p. E1.

35. Deborah Tannen, *That's Not What I Meant!* (New York: William Morrow, 1986).

36. Karen Ritchie, "Marketing to Generation X," *American Demographics*, April 1995, pp. 34–36.

37. Marina Jimenez, "The Linguistic Divide," *The Globe and Mail*, April 17, 2009, p. L1.

38. Daniel N. Maltz and Ruth A. Borker, "A Cultural Approach to Male–Female Miscommunication," in John J. Gumperz, ed., *Language and Social Identity* (Cambridge: Cambridge University Press, 1982), p. 202.

39. Vincent O'Neill, "Training the Multi-Cultural Manager," Sixth Annual EMU Conference on Languages and Communication for World Business and the Professions, Ann Arbor, MI, May 7–9, 1987.

40. Akihisa Kumayama, comment during discussion, Sixth Annual EMU Conference on Languages and Communication for World Business and the Professions, Ann Arbor, MI, May 7–9, 1987.

41. Brenda Arbeláez, statement to Kitty Locker, December 12, 1996.

42. "Participation and Activity Limitation Survey," *The Daily*, December 3, 2007, retrieved May 9, 2008, from http://www.statcan.ca/Daily/English/071203/d071203a.htm.

Module 4

1. Leslie Butler, personal communication, November 26, 2005.

2. See especially Linda Flower and John R. Hayes, "The Cognition of Discovery: Defining a Rhetorical Problem," *College Composition and Communication* 31 (February 1980): 21–32; and the essays in two collections: Charles R. Cooper and Lee Odell, *Research on Composing: Points of Departure* (Urbana, IL: National Council of Teachers of English, 1978), and Mike Rose, ed., *When a Writer Can't Write: Studies in Writer's Block and Other Composing-Process Problems* (New York: Guilford Press, 1985).

3. Rebecca E. Burnett, "Content and Commas: How Attitudes Shape a Communication-Across-the-Curriculum Program," Association for Business Communication Convention, Orlando, FL, November 1–4, 1995.

4. Peter Elbow, *Writing with Power: Techniques for Mastering the Writing Process* (New York: Oxford University Press, 1981), pp. 15–20.

5. See Gabriela Lusser Rico, *Writing the Natural Way* (Los Angeles: J. P. Tarcher, 1983), p. 10.

6. Rachel Spilka, "Orality and Literacy in the Workplace: Process- and Text-Based Strategies for Multiple Audience Adaptation," *Journal of Business and Technical Communication* 4(1) (January 1990): 44–67.

7. Fred Reynolds, "What Adult Work-World Writers Have Taught Me About Adult Work-World Writing," *Professional Writing in Context: Lessons from Teaching and Consulting in Worlds of Work* (Hillsdale, NJ: Lawrence Erlbaum Associates, 1995), pp. 18–21.

8. Raymond W. Beswick, "Communicating in the Automated Office," American Business Communication Association International Convention, New Orleans, LA, October 20, 1982.

9. This three-step process is modelled on the one suggested by Barbara L. Shwom and Penny L. Hirsch, "Managing the Drafting Process: Creating a New Model for the Workplace," *Bulletin of the Association for Business Communication* 57(2) (June 1994): 10.

10. Glenn J. Broadhead and Richard C. Freed, "The Variables of Composition: Process and Product in a Business Setting," *Conference on College Composition and Communication Studies in Writing and Rhetoric* (Carbondale, IL: Southern Illinois University Press, 1986), p. 57.

11. Robert Boice, "Writing Blocks and Tacit Knowledge," *Journal of Higher Education* 64(1) (January/February 1993): 41–43.

Module 5

1. Linda Reynolds, "The Legibility of Printed Scientific and Technical Information," in Ronald Easterby and Harm Zwaga, ed., *Information Design* (New York: Wiley, 1984), pp. 187–208.

2. Joseph Kimble, "Writing for Dollars, Writing to Please," *The Scribes Journal of Legal Writing* 6 (1996–1997): 14–15.

3. Once we know how to read English, the brain first looks to see whether an array of letters follows the rules of spelling. If it does, the brain then treats the array as a word (even if it isn't one, such as *tweal*). The shape is processed in individual letters only when the shape is not enough to suggest meaning. Jerry E. Bishop, "Word Processing: Research on Stroke Victims Yields Clues to the Brain's Capacity to Create Language," *The Wall Street Journal*, October 12, 1993, p. A6.

4. Jakob Neilsen, "Top Ten Mistakes in Web Design," May 1996, retrieved October 24, 2006, from http://www.useit.com/alertbox/9605.html.

5. Nicholas Keung, "Wanted: Minorities," *Toronto Star*, March 18, 2006, pp. B1 and B3.

Module 6

1. Lima Paul, "An On-line Concierge Service's Ticket to Success," Technology, Small & Medium Business, *The Globe and Mail*, July 14, 2005, p. B8, and Eservus Online Concierge Services, retrieved June 13, 2008, from http://toronto.eservus.com.

2. Artwork produced in the Enrichment Program at The Salvation Army's Broadview Village, an adult residential program. Residents attend school, a day program, or work placement training in the Toronto area.

Module 7

1. Charles E. McCabe, edited and updated by Ryan P. Allis, "Motivating and Retaining Employees," 2004, retrieved August 8, 2006, from http://www.zeromillion.com/business/employeemotivate.html.

2. Jill Lambert, "The Economics of Happiness," *Canadian Business*, Summer 2005, pp. 184–187.

3. Mayo Clinic, "Mayo Clinic Study Finds Optimistic People Live Longer," February 8, 2000, retrieved August 8, 2006, from http://www.mayoclinic.org/news2000-rst/603.html.

4. The Business Link, "The Makeup of a Successful Entrepreneur," 2005, retrieved August 8, 2006, from http://www.cbsc.org/alberta/newsletter/February2005_1.html.

5. Jim Sutherland, "Cold Warrior," Report on (Small) Business, *The Globe and Mail*, October 6, 2005, retrieved August 8, 2006, from http://www.theglobeandmail.com/servlet/ArticleNews/TPStory/LAC/20051006/SB10SHAN//?query=royal+bank.

6. Annette N. Shelby and N. Lamar Reinsch, Jr., "Positive Emphasis and You-Attitude: An Empirical Study," *Journal of Business Communication* 32(4) (October 1995): 303–327.

7. Mark A. Sherman, "Adjectival Negation and the Comprehension of Multiply Negated Sentences," *Journal of Verbal Learning and Verbal Behavior* 15 (1976): 143–57.

8. Margaret Baker Graham and Carol David, "Power and Politeness: Administrative Writing in an 'Organized Anarchy,'" *Journal of Business and Technical Communication* 10(1) (January 1996): 5–27.

9. John Hagge and Charles Kostelnick, "Linguistic Politeness in Professional Prose: A Discourse Analysis of Auditors' Suggestion Letters, with Implications for Business Communication Pedagogy," *Written Communication* 6(3) (July 1989): 312–39.

Module 8

1. Wray Herbert, "A Recipe for Motivation: Easy to Read, Easy to Do," *Scientific American*, February 2009, retrieved May 2, 2009, from http://www.scientificamerican.com/article.cfm?id=a-recipe-for-motivation.

2. See Tove Helland Hammer and H. Peter Dachler, "A Test of Some Assumptions Underlying the Path–Goal Model of Supervision: Some Suggested Conceptual Modifications," *Organizational Behavior and Human Performance* 14 (1975): 73.

3. Edward E. Lawler, III, *Motivation in Work Organizations* (Monterey, CA: Brooks/Cole, 1973), p. 59. Lawler also notes

a third obstacle: people may settle for performance and rewards that are just OK. Offering reader benefits, however, does nothing to affect this obstacle.

4. Abraham H. Maslow, *Motivation and Personality* (New York: Harper & Row, 1954).

5. Stephen J. Stine, "Managing the Millennials: Part 1," *HRHero.com*, April 4, 2008, retrieved May 2, 2009, from http://www.hrhero.com/hl/040408-lead-millennials.html; Claire Raines, "Managing Millennials," 2002, retrieved January 1, 2010, from http://generationsatwork.com/articles_millenials.php.

6. John J. Weger reports Herzberg's research in *Motivating Supervisors* (New York: American Management Association, 1971), pp. 53–54.

7. Diane L. Coutu, "Human Resources: The Wages of Stress," *Harvard Business Review*, November–December 1998, pp. 21–24; and Charles Fishman, "Sanity, Inc.," *Fast Company*, January 1999, pp. 85–99.

8. Susan Greco, "Hire the Best," *Inc.*, June 1999, pp. 32–52.

9. Kevin Leo, "Effective Copy and Graphics," DADM/DMEF Direct Marketing Institute for Professors, Northbrook, IL, May 31–June 3, 1983.

Module 10

1. Sinclair Stewart and Richard Bloom, "BlackBerry Battle Chills Bay St. Gossips," July 7, 2005, retrieved August 8, 2006, from http://www.theglobeandmail.com/servlet/ArticleNews/TPStory/LAC/20050107/BLACKBERRY07/TPNational/TopStories; Javad Heydary, "Is Your Boss Monitoring Your BlackBerry?," *E-Commerce Times*, May 26, 2005, retrieved August 8, 2006, from http://www.ecommercetimes.com/story/43376.html; Jaikumar Vijayan Boston, "Lawsuit Reveals an Open BlackBerry," *Computerworld*, January 18, 2005, retrieved May 6, 2009, from http://computerworld.co.nz/news.nsf/0/A0DF45190F24C05BCC256F8C00018087?OpenDocument&pub=Computerworld.

2. H. Lotherington, and Yejun Xu, "How to Chat in English and Chinese: Emerging Digital Language Conventions," *ReCALL* 16(2): 308–329, retrieved August 8, 2006, from http://www.yorku.ca/foe/People/Faculty/ProfilesFac/file_Lothering_Xu_2004.pdf; Heather Lotherington, "NetSpeak Changes Offline Communication," G4TechTV.ca, retrieved November 16, 2009, from http://techtvcanada.ca/callforhelp/guests/0148A.shtml.

3. Sara Kiesler, Jane Siegel, and Timothy W. McGuire, "Social Psychological Aspects of Computer-Mediated Communication," *American Psychologist* 39(10) (October 1984): 1129. People still find it easier to be negative in email than on paper or person; see John Affleck, "You've Got Bad News," *Associated Press*, June 19, 1999.

4. Bettina A. Blair, "Teaching Technology," email to Kitty Locker, October 22, 1999.

5. Stephen Baker and Heather Green, "Blogs Will Change Your Business," BusinessWeek, May 2, 2005, retrieved January 1, 2010 from www.businessweek.com/magazine/content/05_18/b3931001_mz001.htm

6. Jeff Wuorio, "Blogging for Business: 7 Tips for Getting Started," Microsoft.com, retrieved May 6, 2009,

from http://www.microsoft.com/smallbusiness/resources/marketing/online-marketing/blogging-for-business-7-tips-for-getting-started.aspx#Bloggingforbusinesstipsforgettingstarted.

Module 11

1. Richard C. Whitely, *The Customer-Driven Company* (Reading, MA: Addison-Wesley, 1991), pp. 39–40.
2. In a study of 483 subject lines written by managers and M.B.A. students, Priscilla S. Rogers found that the average subject line was five words; only 10 percent of the subject lines used 10 or more words; see Rogers, "A Taxonomy for Memorandum Subject Lines," *Journal of Business and Technical Communication* 4(2) (September 1990): 28–29.
3. An earlier version of this problem, the sample solutions, and the discussion appeared in Francis W. Weeks and Kitty O. Locker, *Business Writing Cases and Problems*, 1984 ed. (Champaign, IL: Stipes, 1984), pp. 64–68.

Module 12

1. Jack W. Brehm, *A Theory of Psychological Reactance* (New York: Academic Press, 1966).
2. John D. Pettit, "An Analysis of the Effects of Various Message Presentations on Communicatee Responses," Ph.D. dissertation, Louisiana State University, 1969; and Jack D. Eure, "Applicability of American Written Business Communication Principles Across Cultural Boundaries in Mexico," *Journal of Business Communication* 14 (1976): 51–63.
3. Lillian H. Chaney and Jeanette S. Martin, *Intercultural Business Communication* (Englewood Cliffs, NJ: Prentice Hall Career and Technology, 1995), p. 185; and Larry A. Samovar and Richard E. Porter, *Communication Between Cultures* (Belmont, CA: Wadsworth Publishing, 1990), pp. 234–44.
4. Gabriella Stern, "Companies Discover That Some Firings Backfire into Costly Defamation Suits," *The Wall Street Journal*, May 5, 1993, B1.
5. An earlier version of this problem, the sample solutions, and the discussion appeared in Francis W. Weeks and Kitty O. Locker, *Business Writing Cases and Problems* (Champaign, IL: Stipes, 1980), pp. 40–44.

Module 13

1. "How Maple Leaf Foods Is Handling the Listeria Outbreak," CBC News, August 28, 2008, retrieved May 10, 2009, from http://www.cbc.ca/money/story/2008/08/27/f-crisisresponse.html, and Doug Powell, August 24, 2008, "McCain Apologizes for Maple Leaf Listeria; Excellent Risk Communication, Will the Management of the Risk Stand Scrutiny?," Barfblog, retrieved May 10, 2009, from http://barfblog.foodsafety.ksu.edu/2008/08/articles/food-safety-communication/mccain-apologizes-for-maple-leaf-listeria-excellent-risk-communication-will-the-management-of-the-risk-stand-scrutiny; and Jeff Sharom, "McCain Takes Aim at Listeria Oversight," *Science Canada*, April 21, 2009, retrieved November 11, 2009, from http://sciencecanada.blogspot.com/2009/04/mccain-takes-aim-at-listeria-oversight.html.
2. For a discussion of sales and fundraising letters, see Kitty O. Locker, *Business and Administrative Communication*, 5th ed. (Burr Ridge: Irwin/McGraw-Hill, 2000), pp. 276–301.
3. J. C. Mathes and Dwight W. Stevenson, *Designing Technical Reports: Writing for Audiences in Organizations* (Indianapolis: Bobbs-Merrill, 1979), pp. 18–19.
4. Karen Lowry Miller and David Woodruff, "The Man Who's Selling Japan on Jeeps," *Business Week*, July 19, 1993, pp. 56–57.
5. Daniel J. O'Keefe, *Persuasion* (Newbury Park, CA: Sage, 1990), p. 168; Joanne Martin and Melanie E. Powers, "Truth or Corporate Propaganda," in Louis R. Pondy, Thomas C. Dandridge, Gareth Morgan, and Peter J. Frost, eds., *Organizational Symbolism* (Greenwich, CT: JAI Press 1983), pp. 97–107; and Dean C. Kazoleas, "A Comparison of the Persuasive Effectiveness of Qualitative Versus Quantitative Evidence: A Test of Explanatory Hypotheses," *Communication Quarterly* 41(1) (Winter 1993): 40–50.
6. "Phoning Slow Payers Pays Off," *Inc.*, July 1996, p. 95.
7. An earlier draft of this problem and analysis appeared in Francis W. Weeks and Kitty O. Locker, *Business Writing Problems and Cases* (Champaign, IL: Stipes, 1980), pp. 78–81.
8. Kimberly White, "The Wiki Business Plan," *The Globe and Mail*, May 26, 2008, p. B1.

Module 14

1. "Listening," retrieved October 18, 2008, from http://accel-team.com/communications/busComms_02.html. © 2008 Accel-Team.
2. Rich Whittle, "Improve Your Listening Skills," Dane Carlson's Business Opportunities Weblog, July 2, 2008, retrieved October 26, 2008, from http://www.business-opportunities.biz/2008/07/02/improve-your-listening-skills.
3. Kara Aaserud, "The 7 New Truths About Your Customers and Why You Need to Know Them," *Profit*, March 2009, pp. 34–40, retrieved November 11, 2009, from http://www.canadianbusiness.com/entrepreneur/sales_marketing/article.jsp?content=20090201_30010_30010.
4. Ibid.
5. Ibid.
6. Adapted from "Communicating Across Cultures," Building Collaborative Solutions Inc. site, 2004, retrieved August 14, 2006, from http://www.bcsolutions.org/olccommacrosscultures.html; and Chadwick Fleck, "Understanding Cheating in Nepal," *Electronic Magazine of Multicultural Education* 2(1) (1999), retrieved August 14, 2006, from http://www.eastern.edu/publications/emme/2000spring/fleck.html.
7. "Listen Up and Sell," *Selling Power*, July/August 1999, p. 34.

Module 15

1. D. M. Zinni, Barry Wright, and Mark Julien, "Research Forum: Want to Retain Employees? Try a Networking Group," *HRProfessional*, July/August 2005, retrieved August 14, 2006, from http://www.yorku.ca/hrresall/frm2005~08.htm; and Olivia Li, "Top 90 Employers," *The Toronto Star*, October 17, 2009, pp. U1–6.

2. Bonita Summers, "Workplace Without Borders: Why Companies Are Using Social Networking as a Team Building Tool," *Your Workplace* 11(2) (March/April 2009): 32, 34.

3. For a fuller listing of roles in groups, see David W. Johnson and Frank P. Johnson, *Joining Together: Group Theory and Group Skills* (Englewood Cliffs, NJ: Prentice Hall, 1975), pp. 26–27.

4. Beatrice Schultz, "Argumentativeness: Its Effects in Group Decision-Making and Its Role in Leadership Perception," *Communication Quarterly* 30(4) (Fall 1982): 374–75; Dennis S. Gouran and B. Aubrey Fisher, "The Functions of Human Communication in the Formation, Maintenance, and Performance of Small Groups," in Carroll C. Arnold and John Waite Bowers, eds., *Handbook of Rhetorical and Communication Theory* (Boston: Allyn and Bacon, 1984), p. 640; and Curt Bechler and Scott D. Johnson, "Leadership and Listening: A Study of Member Perceptions," *Small Group Research* 26(1) (February 1995): 77–85.

5. Nance L. Harper and Lawrence R. Askling, "Group Communication and Quality of Task Solution in a Media Production Organization," *Communication Monographs* 47(2) (June 1980): 77–100.

6. Rebecca E. Burnett, "Conflict in Collaborative Decision-Making," in Nancy Roundy Blyler and Charlotte Thralls, eds., *Professional Communication: The Social Perspective* (Newbury Park, CA: Sage, 1993), pp. 144–62.

7. Kimberly A. Freeman, "Attitudes Toward Work in Project Groups as Predictors of Academic Performance," *Small Group Research* 27(2) (May 1996): 265–82.

8. Nancy Schullery and Beth Hoger, "Business Advocacy for Students in Small Groups," Association for Business Communication Annual Convention, San Antonio, TX, November 9–11, 1998.

9. Jim Camp, *Start with No* (New York: Crown Business, 2002), pp. 151–154.

10. Paul Benjamin Lowry, Aaron Curtis, Michelle René Lowry, "Building a Taxonomy and Nomenclature of Collaborative Writing to Improve Interdisciplinary Research and Practice," *Journal of Business Communication* 41(2004): 66, 67, DOI: 10.1177/0021943603259363, retrieved June 19, 2009, from http://job.sagepub.com/cgi/reprint/41/1/66.pdf.

11. Rebecca Burnett, "Characterizing Conflict in Collaborative Relationships: The Nature of Decision-Making During Coauthoring," Ph.D. dissertation, Carnegie-Mellon University, Pittsburgh, PA, 1991.

12. Kitty O. Locker, "What Makes a Collaborative Writing Team Successful? A Case Study of Lawyers and Social Service Workers in a State Agency," in Janis Forman, ed., *New Visions in Collaborative Writing* (Portsmouth, NJ: Boynton, 1991), pp. 37–52.

13. Lisa Ede and Andrea Lunsford, *Singular Texts/Plural Authors: Perspectives on Collaborative Writing* (Carbondale, IL: Southern Illinois Press, 1990), p. 66.

14. Paul Benjamin Lowry, Aaron Curtis, Michelle René Lowry, "Building a Taxonomy and Nomenclature of Collaborative Writing to Improve Interdisciplinary Research and Practice," *Journal of Business Communication* 41(2004): 66–97, DOI: 10.1177/0021943603259363, retrieved June 19, 2009, from http://job.sagepub.com/cgi/reprint/41/1/66.pdf.

15. Meg Morgan, Nancy Allen, Teresa Moore, Dianne Atkinson, and Craig Snow, "Collaborative Writing in the Classroom," *Bulletin of the Association for Business Communication* 50(3) (September 1987): 22.

Module 16

1. "Scientific Study Finds Meetings at Work Decrease Employee Well-Being, But Not for Everyone," *ScienceDaily*, February 2006, retrieved August 24, 2006, from http://www.sciencedaily.com/releases/2006/02/060224192947.htm.

2. Kevin Voight, "Don't Mind Your Own Business at Work," *The Globe and Mail*, January 26, 2005, p. C10.

3. Michael Schrage, "Meetings Don't Have to Be Dull," *The Wall Street Journal*, April 29, 1996, p. A12.

4. Eric Matson and William R. Daniels, "The Seven Deadly Sins of Meetings," *Fast Company Handbook of the Business Revolution*, 1997, p. 29.

5. Ibid., p. 30.

6. Rich Young, "Social Media: How New Forms of Communications Are Changing Job Search and Career Management," *IABC Communicator*, January/February 2009, p. 3.

7. H. Lloyd Goodall, Jr., *Small Group Communications in Organizations* (Dubuque, IA: William C. Brown, 1985), pp. 39–40.

8. Roger K. Mosvick and Robert B. Nelson, *We've Got to Start Meeting Like This: A Guide to Successful Meeting Management*, rev. ed. (Indianapolis: Park Avenue, 1996), p. 177.

9. Gina Imperator, "You Have to Start Meeting Like This," *Fast Company*, December 19, 2007, retrieved June 24, 2009, from http://www.fastcompany.com/magazine/23/begeman.

10. Boris Koechlin, "Video: Putting a Face on Government," NetworkedGovernment site, retrieved June 23, 2009, from http://www.netgov.ca/cp.asp?pid=70.

11. Salvador Apud and Talis Apud-Martinez, "Global Teams: Communicating Across Time, Space and, Most Important, Cultures," *CW Bulletin*, 2006, retrieved June 23, 2009, from http://www.iabc.com/cwb/archive/2006/0306/apud.htm.

12. Ibid.

Module 17

1. Carol Hymowitz, "When You Tell the Boss, Plain Talk Counts," *The Wall Street Journal*, June 16, 1989, p. B1.

2. Linda Driskill, "How the Language of Presentations Can Encourage or Discourage Audience Participation," paper presented at the Conference on College Composition and Communication, Cincinnati, OH, March 18–21, 1992.

3. Some studies have shown that previews and reviews increase comprehension; other studies have found no effect. For a summary of the research see Kenneth D. Frandsen and Donald R. Clement, "The Functions of Human Communication in Informing: Communicating and Processing Information," in Carroll C. Arnold and John Waite Bowers, eds., *Handbook of Rhetorical and Communication Theory* (Boston: Allyn and Bacon, 1984), pp. 340–41.

4. Ray Alexander, *Power Speech: Why It's Vital to You* (New York: AMACOM, 1986), p. 156; Wharton Applied

Research Center, "A Study of the Effects of the Use of Overhead Transparencies on Business Meetings," reported in Martha Jewett and Rita Margolies, eds., *How to Run Better Business Meetings: A Reference Guide for Managers* (New York: McGraw-Hill, 1987), pp. 109–110, 115.

5. Robert S. Mills, conversation with Kitty O. Locker, March 10, 1988.

6. Phil Thiebert, "Speechwriters of the World, Get Lost!," *The Wall Street Journal*, August 2, 1993, A10.

7. Edward Tufte, "PowerPoint Is Evil," *Wired*, September 2003, retrieved June 22, 2009, from http://www.wired.com/wired/archive/11.09/ppt2.html; Virginia Galt, "Glazed Eyes a Major Peril of Using PowerPoint," *The Globe and Mail*, June 4, 2005, p. B10; and Dave Paradi, "Slide Makeover Video Podcast," retrieved June 22, 2009, from http://www.youtube.com/watch?v=jArg6s4KARo&feature=related.

8. Brian Mara-Croft, "Every Picture Tells a Story," *IABC Communication World, Visual Appeal* 25(5) (September/October 2008): 22–25.

9. Stephen E. Lucas, *The Art of Public Speaking*, 2nd ed. (New York: Random House, 1986), p. 248.

10. John Case, "A Company of Businesspeople," *Inc.*, April 1993, p. 90.

11. Edward J. Hegarty, *Humor and Eloquence in Public Speaking* (West Nyack, NY: Packer, 1976), p. 204.

12. Carmine Gallo, "Manage Your Fear of Public Speaking," *BusinessWeek*, December 30, 2008, retrieved June 22, 2009, from http://www.businessweek.com/smallbiz/content/dec2008/sb20081230_141498.htm; and Daniel J. DeNoon, "Fear of Public Speaking Hardwired," *WebMD*, April 20, 2006, retrieved June 22, 2009, from http://www.webmd.com/anxiety-panic/guide/20061101/fear-public-speaking.

13. S. A. Beebe, "Eye Contact: A Nonverbal Determinant of Speaker Credibility," *Speech Teacher* 23 (1974): 21–25, cited in Marjorie Fink Vargas, *Louder Than Words* (Ames, IA: Iowa State University Press, 1986), pp. 61–62.

14. J. Wills, "An Empirical Study of the Behavioral Characteristics of Sincere and Insincere Speakers," Ph.D. dissertation, University of Southern California, 1961, cited in Marjorie Fink Vargas, *Louder Than Words* (Ames, IA: Iowa State University Press, 1986), p. 62.

Module 18

1. "Welcome to Knowledge Ontario," Knowledge Ontario site, 2008, retrieved January 28, 2008, from http://www.knowledgeontario.ca.

2. J. Fear, Reference Librarian, personal communication, January 27, 2008.

3. Sharine Mansour, Professor, Journalism New Media, personal communication, July 8, 2009.

4. "RSS Feeds—A Tutorial," PRESSfeed, 2009, retrieved July 9, 2009, from http://www.press-feed.com/howitworks/rss_tutorial.php#whatarewebfeeds.

5. Cynthia Crossen, "Margin of Error: Studies Galore Support Products and Positions, but Are They Reliable?," *The Wall Street Journal*, November 14, 1991, pp. A1, A7.

6. Tracie Rozhon, "Networks Criticize Report on Male Viewers," *The New York Times*, November 26, 2003,

retrieved from Business & Company Resource Center, http://galenet.galegroup.com; and "Neilson Explains Male TV Ratings," *Adweek*, December 1, 2003, retrieved from Business & Company Resource Center, http://galenet.galegroup.com.

7. "Whirlpool: How to Listen to Consumers," *Fortune*, January 11, 1993, p. 77.

8. Mansour, ibid., and email, July 10, 2009.

Module 19

Notes are given in the module, in the illustrations of APA and MLA bibliographies referring to in-text citations.

Module 20

1. Telephone interview with Lee-Anne E. Bell, B.Sc., Associate ENVIRON EC (Canada) Inc., June 30, 2009, and Franco Agar, B.A. Honours, KPMG Support, Global Applications, July 6, 2009.

2. Agar, ibid.

3. Christine Peterson Barabas, *Technical Writing in a Corporate Culture: A Study of the Nature of Information* (Norwood, NJ: Ablex Publishing, 1990), p. 327.

Module 21

1. Peter Pook, Vice-President, Research and Development, Fisher Price Toys, personal communication with author, July 15, 2009.

2. Meryl K. Evans, "Writing an RFP (Request for Proposal)," *Ezine @rticles*, retrieved June 27, 2009, from http://ezinearticles.com/?Writing-an-RFP-(Request-for-Proposal)&id=1795; and "Writing a Request for a Proposal (RFP)," *meryl.net*, 2009, retrieved July 30, 2009, from http://www.meryl.net/tag/rfp.

3. Janice Redish, *Letting Go of the Words: Writing Web Content That Works* (San Francisco: Morgan Kaufmann Publishers, 2007); Jakob Nielsen, "Writing Style for Print vs. Web," *Jakob Nielsen's Alertbox*, June 9, 2008, retrieved June 28, 2009, from http://www.useit.com/alertbox/print-vs-online-content.html; and Mindy McAdams, "Tips for Writing for the Web," November 19, 2006, retrieved June 28, 2009, from http://www.macloo.com/webwriting/index.htm.

Module 22

1. Natalie Canavor and Claire Meirowitz, "Summaries: A Good Way to Make Life Easier for Your Readers," *CW Bulletin*, pp. 1–4, retrieved January 17, 2009, from http://www.iabc.com/cwb/archive/2009/0109/WorkingWords.htm.

Module 23

1. Brian O'Mara-Croft, "Every Picture tells a story," *Communication World*, September–October 2008. IABC. pp. 23–24.

2. Gene Zelazny, *Say It with Charts: The Executive's Guide to Successful Presentations*, 2nd ed. (Burr Ridge, IL: IPRO, 1981), p. 52.

3. Most of these guidelines are given in Zelazny, *Say It with Charts: The Executive's Guide to Successful Presentations*.

4. W. S. Cleveland and R. McGill, "Graphical Perception: Theory, Experiments, and Application to the Development of Graphic Methods," *Journal of the American Statistical Association* 79(3 & 7) (1984): 531–53, cited in Jeffry K. Cochran, Sheri A. Albrecht, and Yvonne A. Greene, "Guidelines for Evaluating Graphical Designs: A Framework Based on Human Perception Skills," *Technical Communication* 36(1) (February 1989): 27.

5. Brian O'Mara-Croft, pp. 22–25.

6. L. G. Thorell and W. J. Smith, *Using Computer Color Effectively: An Illustrated Reference* (Englewood Cliffs, NJ: Prentice Hall, 1990), pp. 12–13; William Horton, "The Almost Universal Language: Graphics for International Documents," *Technical Communication* 40(4) (1993): 687; and Thyra Rauch, "IBM Visual Interface Design," *STC Usability PIC Newsletter*, January 1996, p. 3.

7. Thorell and Smith, p. 13.

8. Ibid., pp. 49–51, 214–15.

9. Edward Tufte, "PowerPoint Is Evil," *WIRED*, Issue 11.09 | September 2003, retrieved August 23, 2009 from http://www.wired.com/wired/archive/11.09/ppt2.html.

10. Ibid.

11. Thophilus Addo, "The Effects of Dimensionality in Computer Graphics," *Journal of Business Communication* 31, no. 4 (October 1994): 253–65.

Module 24

1. Richard Bolle, "Here's How to Pack Your Parachute," *Fast Company*, September 1999, p. 242.

2. Industry Canada, "Canadian Company Capabilities," January 2, 2008, retrieved March 3, 2009, from http://www.ic.gc.ca/eic/site/ccc-rec.nsf/eng/home.

3. Rich Young, "Social Media: How New Forms of Communications Are Changing Job Search and Career Management," *IABC Toronto, Communicator*, January/February 2009, pp. 1, 3; Omar El Akkad, "The Medium Is No Longer the Message," *The Globe and Mail*, March 10, 2009, p. A3; Wallace Immen, "Job Hunting 101 … A Guide for the New Realities of These Tougher Times," *The Globe and Mail*, February 18, 2009, p. C1; Heather Havenstein, "One in Five Employers Uses Social Networks in Hiring Process," *ComputerWorld*, September 12, 2008, retrieved August 8, 2009, from http://www.computerworld.com/s/article/9114560/One_in_five_employers_uses_social_networks_in_hiring_process; Joan Vinall Cox, personal communication, June 8, 2009; Kathy Voltan, personal communication, March 14, 2008.

4. Ibid., all sources.

5. Lydia Nacawa, "The Information Meeting," Centre de Recherche D'Emploi, Cote Des Neiges Job Search Centre site, retrieved March 9, 2009, from http://www.crecdn.com/en/the-information-meeting; John Izzo, "In Your Face—Far More Effective," *The Globe and Mail*, August 15, 2008, p. C1; and "The Informational Interview: A Key Networking Event," Bayt.com, 2009, retrieved August 15, 2009, from http://www.bayt.com/job/career-article-842.

6. Heather Huhman, "Networking as a Job Search Tool (Part 5): Find a Mentor," *examiner.com*, September 10, 2009, retrieved August 15, 2009, from http://www.examiner.com/x-828-Entry-Level-Careers-Examiner~y2008m9d10-Networking-as-a-job-search-tool-part-5-Find-a-mentor.

7. Carl Quintanilla, "Coming Back," *The Wall Street Journal*, February 22, 1996, p. R10; and Megan Malugani, "How to Re-enter the Health-Care Job Market," *Columbus Dispatch*, March 22, 2000, p. 13.

8. LeAne Rutherford, "Five Fatal Résumé Mistakes," *Business Week's Guide to Careers* 4(3) (Spring/Summer 1986): 60–62.

9. Phil Elder, "The Trade Secrets of Employment Interviews," Association for Business Communication Midwest Convention, Kansas City, MO, May 2, 1987.

Module 25

1. Allison Green, "7 Things to Leave Off Your Resume," *US News & World Report*, March 2, 2009, retrieved March 6, 2009, from http://www.usnews.com/blogs/outside-voices-careers/2009/03/02/7-things-to-leave-off-your-resume.html; and Kimberly Lankford, "A New Resume for a New Year," Your Money, *Kiplinger's Personal Finance Magazine* 59(1) (January 2005): 87, retrieved March 7, 2009, from http://find.galegroup.com/itx/infomark.do?contentSet=IAC-Documents&docType=IAC&type=retrieve&tabID=T003&prodId=AONE&docId=A126207190&userGroupName=sols_oakvillerpa&version=1.0&searchType=BasicSearchForm&source=gale.

2. Wallace Immen, "How Did You Get to the Top with That Résumé?," *The Globe and Mail*, October 12, 2005, p. C3.

3. Beverly H. Nelson, William P. Gallé, and Donna W. Luse, "Electronic Job Search and Placement," Association for Business Communication Convention, Orlando FL, November 1–4, 1995.

4. Rebecca Smith, *Electronic Résumés & Online Networking: How to Use the Internet to Do a Better Job Search, Including a Complete, Up-to-Date Resource Guide* (Franklin Lakes, NJ: Career Press, 1999), pp. 191–96.

5. Taunee Besson, *The Wall Street Journal National Employment Business Weekly: Résumés* (New York: John Wiley and Sons, 1994), p. 245.

Module 26

1. Omar El Akkad, "Have YouTube, Will Travel: Australia's Experiment in Social Media," *The Globe and Mail*, March 4, 2009, p. A10.

Module 27

1. Thomas Petzinger, Jr., "Lewis Roland's Knack for Finding Truckers Keeps Firm Rolling," *The Wall Street Journal*, December 1, 1995, p. B1.

2. Judith A. Swartley to Kitty Locker, March 20, 1989.

3. Sherri Eng, "Company Culture Dictates Attire for Interviews," *Columbus Dispatch*, August 25, 1996, p. 33J.

4. The Catalyst Staff, *Marketing Yourself* (New York: G. P. Putnam's Sons, 1980), p. 179.

5. Sue Shellenbarger, "New Job Hunters Ask Recruiters, 'Is There Life After Work?,'" *The Wall Street Journal*, January 29, 1996, p. B1; and Sue Shellenbarger, "What Job

Candidates Really Want to Know: Will I Have a Life?," *The Wall Street Journal*, November 17, 1999, p. B1.

6. Donna Stine Kienzler, letter to Ann Granacki, April 6, 1988.

7. Christopher Conte, "Labor Letter," *The Wall Street Journal*, October 19, 1993, p. A1.

8. Richard C. Rose and Echo Montgomery Garrett, "Guerrilla Interviewing," *Inc.*, December 1992, pp. 145–47.

9. "Job Application and Interview Advice," Job-Application-and-Interview-Advice.com, 2007–2009, retrieved November 16, 2009, from http://www.job-application-and-interview-advice.com/job-interview-article.html.

10. Kate Weldon, *Through the Brick Wall: How to Job-Hunt in a Tight Market* (New York: Villard Books, 1992), p. 244.

11. Carol A. Hacker, *Job Hunting in the 21st Century: Exploding the Myths, Exploring the Realities* (Boca Raton: St. Lucie Press, 1999), p. 154.

12. Ray Robinson, quoted in Dick Friedman, "The Interview as Mating Ritual," *Working Woman*, April 1987, p. 107.

13. Sarah E. Needleman, Thx 4 Cing me, Wud Luv a Job!," *The Globe and Mail*, August 15, 2008, p. C3; G. L. Hoffman, "How to Write the Perfect Thank-You Note After the Interview," *U.S.ANEWS*, February 10, 2009, retrieved March 15, 2009, from http://www.usnews.com/blogs/outside-voices-careers/2009/2/10/the-perfect-thank-you-note-after-the-interview.html; Katharine Hansen, Ph.D., "FAQs About Thank You Letters," QuintCareers.com, retrieved August 25, 2009, from http://www.quintcareers.com/thank_you_letters.html; and Jeramy Colvin, "How to Send a Thank You Note After a Job Interview," eHow.com, retrieved November 16, 2009, from http://www.ehow.com/how_4729287_thank-note-after-job-interview.html.

14. Wallace Immen, "Job Hunting 101: A Guide for the New Realities of These Tougher Times," *The Globe and Mail*, February 18, 2009, p. C1; Kathryn Lee Bazan, "The Art of the Follow Up After Job Interviews," QuintCareers.com, retrieved November 16, 2009, from http://www.quintcareers.com/job_interview_follow-up.html; David Nassief, "How to Follow Up After an Interview," About.com, retrieved August 25, 2009, from http://jobsearch.about.com/od/interviewsnetworking/a/intfollowup.htm; and Yana Parker, "Guide to Follow-Up Letters," The DamnGoodResume site, retrieved August 25, 2009, from http://www.damngood.com/ready/exmpl/follow-up.html.

Revising Sentences and Paragraphs

1. Robert L. Brown, Jr., and Carl G. Herndl, "An Ethnographic Study of Corporal Writing: Job Status as Reflected in Written Text," *Functional Approaches to Writing: A Research Perspective*, ed. Barbara Couture (Norwood, NJ: Ablex, 1986), pp. 16–19, 22–23.

2. "The Secret of Impressive Writing? Keep It Plain and Simple," *ScienceDaily*, November 1, 2005, retrieved August 19, 2009, from http://www.sciencedaily.com/releases/2005/10/051031075447.htm.

3. Sam Kornell, "Read Novels, Be Smarter," TheStar.com, retrieved August 16, 2008, from http://www.thestar.com/article/475516.

4. Linda Flower, *Problem-Solving Strategies for Writing* (New York: Harcourt Brace Jovanovich, 1981), p. 39.

5. Harris B. Savin and Ellen Perchonock, "Grammatical Structure and the Immediate Recall of English Sentences," *Journal of Verbal Learning and Verbal Behavior* 4 (1965): 348–53; Pamela Layton and Adrian J. Simpson, "Deep Structure in Sentence Comprehension," *Journal of Verbal Learning and Verbal Behavior* 14 (1975): 658–64.

6. Arn Tibbetts, "Ten Rules for Writing Readably," *Journal of Business Communication* 18(4) (Fall 1981): 55–59.

7. Thomas N. Huckin, "A Cognitive Approach to Readability," *New Essays in Technical and Scientific Communication: Research, Theory, Practice*, ed. Paul V. Anderson, R. John Brockmann, and Carolyn R. Miller (Farmingdale, NY: Baywood, 1983), pp. 93–98.

Index